Psychology, Law, and Criminal Justice

A Publication of the European
Association of Psychology and Law

Psychology, Law, and Criminal Justice

International Developments in Research and Practice

Edited by
Graham Davies
Sally Lloyd-Bostock
Mary McMurran
Clare Wilson

W DE G

Walter de Gruyter · Berlin · New York 1996

Prof. *Graham M. Davies*, Department of Psychology, Leicester University, England
Sally Lloyd-Bostock, Research Fellow, Centre for Socio-Legal Studies, Oxford University, England
Mary McMurran, Consultant Clinical Psychologist, Rampton Hospital, Honorary Research Fellow, University of Birmingham, England
Clare Wilson, Lecturer, Department of Psychology, Leicester University, England

♾ Printed on acid-free paper which falls within the guidelines of the ANSI to ensure permanence and durability.

Library of Congress Cataloging-in-Publication Data

Psychology, law, and criminal justice : international developments in research and practice / edited by Graham Davies ... [et al.].
p. cm.
Collection of papers from the Third European Conference of Law and Psychology, held in Oxford, Sept. 1992.
Includes bibliographical references and index.
ISBN 3-11-013858-1
1. Psychology, Forensic. 2. Evidence, Expert. 3. Children as witnesses. I. Davies, Graham, 1943– . II. European Conference of Law and Psychology (3rd : 1992 : Oxford, England)
K5462.P75 1995
345',067–dc20
[342.567] 95-22785
CIP

Die Deutsche Bibliothek – Cataloging-in-Publication Data

Psychology, law, and criminal justice : international developments in research and practice / ed. by Graham Davies ... – Berlin ; New York : de Gruyter, 1995
ISBN 3-11-013858-1
NE: Davies, Graham [Hrsg.]

Printing: WB-Druck GmbH, Rieden am Forggensee. – Binding: Dieter Mikolai, Berlin. – Cover Design: Johannes Rother, Berlin. – Printed in Germany.

Preface

In September 1992, over 250 delegates from 15 different countries met in Oxford for the Third European Conference of Law and Psychology. This collection of papers gives an indication of the range and variety of issues discussed during the four days at Wadham and Keble Colleges. The organising Committee of Ray Bull, Graham Davies (Chair), David Farrington, Sally Lloyd-Bostock, Mary McMurran, Joanna Shapland, John Spencer and Geoffrey Stephenson owe a debt of gratitude to the many people and organisations who ensured the event was a success and that the papers presented would be read by an even wider audience.

Essential financial guarantees were generously provided by the Centre for Socio-Legal Studies, the University of Oxford. Together with the Department of Psychology, the University of Leicester, they also underwrote some incidental costs and provided the necessary secretarial and administrative support. We are most grateful to Rita Benford, Jenny Dix and Jeannette Price for their time, energy and commitment, both to the Conference and the preparation of this book.

The Economic and Social Research Council provided the necessary financial assistance to ensure that a number of delegates from Eastern Europe could present their work. The ESRC also provided a subsidy toward the typesetting costs of preparing the proceedings.

The Committee of the European Association of Psychology and Law and especially its acting President, Friedrich Lösel, offered continuing encouragement and advice. We are also grateful to Sir Stephen Brown, President of the Family Division of the Royal Courts of Justice for agreeing to open the Conference and to our invited speakers, Dan Olweus, Ronald Roesch and Willem Wagenaar, all of whom have contributed to this volume.

Clare Wilson joined the original editorial team for the production of this book and has taken on many of the tedious but essential editorial tasks. Jean Wright at Oxford has been responsible for the excellent liaison we have enjoyed with Bianka Ralle and her colleagues at Walter de Gruyter during the complex process of production.

The Editors

Contents

Part VIII: Prison Psychology

Part IX: European Perspectives on Law and Psychology

Introduction

Graham Davies, Sally Lloyd-Bostock, Mary McMurran and Clare Wilson.

While European research on psychology and law has a long and honourable history, cross-European collaboration and contact is a relatively recent development. Historians of psychology may well identify a meeting hosted by the late Arne Trankell in Stockholm in 1981 as the first deliberate attempt to bring together researchers from the Anglo-American tradition of legal research with their European counterparts (Trankell, 1982). It was Trankell's wish that some European organisation embracing lawyers and psychologists should emerge from this meeting. While informal collaboration continued, for instance at the Swansea Conference on Law and Psychology (Muller, Blackman & Chapman, 1984), a formal organisation was still some 10 years away.

The first of the current series of European Law and Psychology Conferences was instigated by Hans Crombag in Maastricht, Holland, in 1988 (van Koppen, Hessing & van den Heuvel, 1988). This was followed by a second Conference organised by Friedrich Losel and his colleagues in Nurnberg, Germany, in 1990 (Losel, Bender & Bliesener, 1992). The third Conference, from which these edited papers are derived, was held at Wadham and Keble Colleges of the University of Oxford, England, in September 1992. The Oxford Conference saw the formal inauguration of the European Association of Psychology and Law dedicated to encouraging the cooperation of lawyers, psychologists and other social scientists on matters of common concern and overseeing future Conferences.

The choice of Oxford was particularly apposite for this Conference in that its Centre for Socio-Legal Studies has played a leading role in stimulating the study of legal problems by psychologists. With the support of the United Kingdom Social Science Research Council (later the Economic and Social Research Council), Sally Lloyd-Bostock organised a series of ground-breaking conferences, many of which were attended by psychologists and lawyers from other European countries as well as Britain and the United States. This resulted in a series of edited volumes published over a five year period from 1979 which identified many of the themes which figure in the current volume (Farrington, Hawkins & Lloyd-Bostock, 1979; Lloyd-Bostock, 1981a, 1981b; Lloyd-Bostock and Clifford, 1983; Lloyd-Bostock, 1984). These included such traditional concerns of European research as eyewitness testimony, delinquency, judicial decision making and the role of the court expert, but also new themes, many derived from civil law: accident compensation, family law and children's law. This series of Conferences began in 1977, the year which saw the formation of the first British organisation devoted to law and psychology: the Division of Criminological and Legal Psychology of the British Psychological Society.

Some 140 papers were presented at the Third European Conference of Law and Psychology. The papers submitted and selected for publication have been grouped around nine themes. No attempt is made in this overview to summarise or mention all the published papers. Rather, common concerns and general issues illuminated by these contributions will be identified.

The first theme, *Eyewitness Testimony* represents one of the oldest and best established strands of research in psychology and law. The current set of papers illustrates the range of methodologies which have been employed to explore this contentious issue. These span orthodox laboratory techniques with a high degree of control but little pretentions to forensic realism, through the recall of films and events staged in front of unsuspecting audiences to studies of witnesses and persons involved in actual court cases. Clearly, each of these various methodologies represents a different compromise between realism and control. There is no one methodology which embodies all virtues, rather solid findings emerge by identifying common findings from disparate procedures: what Ellsworth (1991) terms 'convergent validity'.

The second theme, *Interviewing* represents a more recent direction for forensic psychologists. Researchers have been accused at times of being overly 'defense oriented' and showing too much concern for wrong convictions and not enough for effective law enforcement (Yuille, 1986). One answer to this charge has been the recent attempts described in these papers to examine how police interview suspects and victims of crime and to develop more effective methods of eliciting information from both groups (Gudjonsson, 1992). Foremost among these methods is the Cognitive Interview developed by Fisher and Geiselman (1992) which aims to harness the findings of laboratory research on memory to the more practical concerns of serving police officers charged with interviewing and interrogation duties.

Children in the Legal System reflects the concerns in many parts of Europe and North America over the way both Criminal and Civil law treat children who must come before the courts. Much of this concern has been fuelled by the realisation in many developed countries of the widespread prevalence of child sexual and physical abuse. This has led to large numbers of children being called upon to give evidence in the courts and has raised issues concerning the competency of children relative to adults as witnesses and whether special measures need to be introduced into the courts to facilitate the reception of children's statements (Dent and Flin, 1992). The increasing trend toward divorce has also created major problems for children involved in family breakdowns and these issues too are explored in this section.

Legal Decision Making continues to be a popular area of research as attested by the number of papers grouped under this heading. Many concern themselves with decision making in juries which are a key feature of the adversarial judicial system practised in Britain and the United States (Hastie, Penrod & Pennington, 1983). In the adversarial system, judges play no direct part in the determination of guilt. Rather, their role is largely that of a referee: to ensure the trial is fairly conducted by the prosecuting and defence barristers and to sum up the evidence prior to the jury's deliberations. In the inquisitorial system practised in continental Europe on the other hand, judges play a key role both in interrogating witnesses and determining the guilt or otherwise of the accused. Given their pivotal role, it is not surprising that psychologists have now turned their attention to the decision making processes of such judges (Wagenaar, van Koppen and Crombag, 1993).

Perceptions and Reactions to Criminality covers the emerging area of public perception of and reactions to, crime. Research on how victims of crime come to terms with their experience and the influences this has on their cognitive perspective is another area of growth which contradicts the view that legal psychology is purely defense-centred. The pronouncements of victims and the way the media chooses to report crime can have a powerful influence on the legislative climate in which new laws and sentencing procedures are developed. The fluctuating public perception of crime and criminals represent a linked area of great potential interest in psycho-legal research.

Correlates of Offending deals with the study of the determinants of anti-social and criminal behaviour. Knowledge of risk and protective factors provides a basis for the development of programmes aimed at prevention and modification of offending behaviour (Monahan & Steadman, 1994). Longitudinal studies assist in identifying individuals who are most likely to offend in future and help to target prevention programmes on those most at risk. Such research and theory serve to extend and clarify the public debate on the 'causes of crime'.

Prevention and Treatment of Offending is an allied topic of major concern to criminological psychologists. Recent years has seen an increase in the importance of early intervention and this is reflected in papers on school-based programmes. The oft-expressed view that 'nothing works' in prevention and treatment programmes has been the subject of increasing challenge, focusing on the promising results of cognitive-behavioural interventions which are described in several contributions. The extension of such programmes to existing offenders also provides some hope of curtailing rises in the European prison population.

Prison Psychology embraces the comparative study of penal regimes in different parts of Europe. Contributors to this section underline the differences as well as similarities in approach to the incarceration of criminals. There appears to be much to be gained by the exchange of information and ideas, though the problems of successfully grafting an isolated feature from one system onto another with a very different history and penal philosophy should not be underestimated.

The final theme, *European Perspectives on Law and Psychology* looks at different legal systems in Europe from the perspective of the psychologist. New democratic regimes such as those in Spain and Poland have sought to place psychology and psychologists in a central position in the criminal justice system. Spanish forensic psychologists form one of the largest and most active groups in Europe and it is fitting, therefore, that the next European Conference of Law and Psychology should take place in Barcelona in April 1994. No doubt many of the themes explored in Oxford will be extended and developed and will form yet another milestone in the development of Psychology and Law as an international discipline.

References

Dent, H., & Flin, R. (1992). *Children as witnesses*. Chichester, England: Wiley.

Ellsworth, P. C. (1991). To tell what we know or wait for Godot? *Law and Human Behavior*, *15*, 77-90.

Farrington, D. P., Hawkins, K., & Lloyd-Bostock, S. E. (1979). *Psychology, law and legal processes*. London: Macmillan.

Fisher, R., & Geiselman, R. E. (1992). *Memory enhancing techniques for investigative interviewing: The cognitive interview*. Springfield, IL: C. C. Thomas.

Gudjonsson, G. H. (1992). *The psychology of interrogation, confessions and testimony*. Chichester. England: Wiley.

Hastie, R., Penrod, S., & Pennington, N. (1983). *Inside the jury*. Cambridge, MA: Harvard University Press.

Lloyd-Bostock, S. (1981a). *Psychology in legal contexts: Applications and limitations*. London: Macmillan.

Lloyd-Bostock, S. (1981b). *Law and Psychology: Papers presented at SSRC law and psychology conferences, 1979-1980*. Oxford: Centre for Socio-Legal Studies.

Lloyd-Bostock, S. (1984). *Children and the law*. Oxford: Centre for Socio-Legal Studies.

Lloyd-Bostock, S., & Clifford, B. R. (1983). *Evaluating witness evidence: Recent psychological research and new perspectives*. Chichester, England: Wiley.

Losel, F., Bender, D., & Bliesener, T. (1992). *Psychology and law: International perspectives*. Berlin: de Gruyter.

Monahan, J., & Steadman, J. (1994). *Violence and mental disorder*. Chicago: University of Chicago Press.

Muller, D. J., Blackman, D. E., & Chapman, A. J. (1984). *Psychology and law*. Chichester, England: Wiley.

Trankell, A. (1982). *Reconstructing the past: The role of psychologists in criminal trials*. Stockholm: Norstedts.

van Koppen, P. J., Hessing, D. J., & van den Heuval, G. (1988). *Lawyers on psychology and psychologists on law*. Lisse, The Netherlands: Swets & Zeitlinger.

Wagenaar, W. A., van Koppen, P. J., & Crombag, H. F. M. (1993). *Anchored narratives*. Hemel Hempstead, England: Harvester Wheatsheaf.

Yuille, J. C. (1986). Meaningful research in the police context. In J. C. Yuille (Ed.), *Police selection and training* (pp. 225-246). Dordrecht, The Netherlands: Nijhoff.

Contributors

Peter B. Ainsworth, Dept of Social Policy & Social Work, University of Manchester, Manchester M13 9PL, UK

Marisa L. Alonso-Quecuty, Faculty of Psychology, University of La Laguna, Tenerife, Spain

M. Teresa Anguera, Centre d'Estudis Juridics, Generalitat de Catalunya, C/Roger de Flor 196, 08013-Barcelona, Spain

Ramon Arce, Dpto de Psicologia Social, Facultad de Psicologia, Universidad de Santiago De Compostela, Spain

Jordi Bajet i Royo, Centre de'Estudis Juridics de la Generalitat de Catalunya, Barcelona, Spain

Doris Bender, Institut für Psychologie, Universität Erlangen-Nürnberg, Bismarckstrasse 1, D-91054 Erlangen, Germany

Ian Berg, Department of Psychiatry, University of Leeds, 15 Hyde Terrace, Leeds 2, UK

Thomas Bliesener, Institut für Psychologie, Universität Erlangen-Nürnberg, Bismarckstrasse 1, D-91054 Erlangen, Germany

Julian C. W. Boon, Department of Psychology, University of Leicester, Leicester LE1 7RH, UK

Janos Boros, Hungarian National Prison Administration, Ministry of Justice, 1055 Budapest, Szalay U. 16, Hungary

Serge Brochu, School of Criminology, University of Montreal, PO Box 6128 Station A, Montreal, Quebec, Canada H3C 3J7

Ray Bull, Dept of Psychology, Portsmouth University, King Charles Street, Portsmouth PO1 2ER, UK

Brian T. R. Clifford, Dept of Psychology, University of East London, The Green, Stratford, London E15 4LZ, UK

Herbert L. Collier, Southwest Psychological Services, 4227 N. 32nd St., Phoenix, Arizona, USA

David J. Cooke, Clinical Psychologist, Glasgow Caledonian University and The Douglas Inch Centre, 2 Woodside Terrace, Glasgow G3 7UY, UK

Órla Cronin, Department of Psychology, University of Southampton, Southampton SO9 5NH, UK

Brian L. Cutler, Department of Psychology, Florida International University, North Miami, Florida 33181, USA

Alicja Czerederecka, Institute of Forensic Research, ul Westerplatte 9, 31-033 Krakow, Poland

Katharina Dahmen-Zimmer, Institute of Psychology, University of Regensburg, D-93040, Regensburg, Germany

Graham M. Davies, Department of Psychology, University of Leicester, Leicester LE1 7RH, UK

Adriaan J. M. Denkers, Vakgroep Sociale Psychologie, Vrije Universiteit, de boelelaan 1081, 1081 HV, Amsterdam, The Netherlands

Margarita Diges, Facultad De Psicologia, Universidad autonoma de Madrid, Campus De Canto, Blanco, Madrid 28049, Spain

Paul Donnelly, University of Westminster, Division of Psychology, 309 Regent Street, London W1R 8AL, UK

Regine Drewniak, Kriminologisches Forschungsinstitut Niedersachsen e.V , Leisewitzstrasse 41, D-30175 Hannover, Germany

Richard Eaves, Department of Psychology, University of Southampton, Southampton SO9 5NH, UK

Thomas Fabian, Institute of Psychology and Cognition Research, University of Bremen, PO Box 330440, D-28334 Bremen, Germany

Francisca Fariña, Dpto de Psicologia Social, Facultad de Psicologia, Universidad de Santiago De Compostela, Spain

David P. Farrington, Institute of Criminology, 7 West Road, Cambridge, UK

Ronald P. Fisher, Department of Psychology, Florida International University, North Miami Campus, North Miami, Florida 33181, USA

Catherine Fitzmaurice, Cranfield School of Management, Cranfield University, Cranfield, Bedfordshire MK43 0AL, UK
Jaume Funes, Centre d'Estudis Juridics, Generalitat de Catalunya, C/Roger de Flor 196, 08013-Barcelona, Spain
Vicente Garrido Genoves, Faculty of Psychology and Education, University of Valencia, 46010 Valencia, Spain
Richard C. George, City of London Police, 26 Old Jewry, London EC2, UK
Marja Hatunen, Prison Psychologist, Keravan Nuorisovankila, PL133, 04201 Kerava, Finland
Clive R. Hollin, School of Psychology, University of Birmingham, Edgbaston, Birmingham B15 2TT, UK
Gareth V. Hughes, District Psychologist, Correctional Service of Canada, District Parole Office, 920 Princess Street, Kingston, Ontario K7L 1H1, Canada
Vicente J. Ibanez-Valverde, Villagarcia No. 4, 5th floor, Madrid 280011, Spain
John Jackson, Faculty of Law, University of Sheffield, Sheffield S10 1FL, UK
Iwona Jakubowska, Institute of Applied Social Sciences, Warsaw University, Podchorazych 20, Poland
Teresa Jaskiewicz-Obydzinska, Instytut Ekspertyz Sadowych, ul. Westerplatte 9, 31-033 Krakow, Poland
Richard Kemp, University of Westminster, Division of Psychology, 309 Regent Street, London W1R 8AL, UK
Gerhard Kette, Psychology Department, University of Linz, A-4040 Universität Linz, Austria
Vladimir J. Konečni, University of California, San Diego, La Jolla, California 92093, USA
Sally Lloyd-Bostock, Centre for Socio-Legal Studies, Wolfson College, Oxford OX2 6UD, UK
Sandra Loohs, Institute of Psychology, University of Regensburg, D-93040, Regensburg, Germany
Friedrich Lösel, Institut für Psychologie, Universität Erlangen-Nürnberg, Bismarckstrasse 1, D-91054 Erlangen, Germany
Pilar de Luis-Cabarga, Villagarcia No. 4, 5th floor, Madrid 280011, Spain
Eulalia Luque, Centre d'Estudis Juridics, Generalitat de Catalunya, C/Roger de Flor 196, 08013-Barcelona, Spain
David J. Main, Department of Psychology, University of Dundee, Dundee DD1 4HN, UK
Antonio L. Manzanero, Department of Basic Psychology, University Autonoma of Madrid, Cantoblanco, 28049 Madrid, Spain
Harry McAllister, Department of Psychology, Aberdeen University, Kings College, Old Aberdeen AB9 2UB, UK
Michelle R. McCauley, Department of Psychology, Florida International University, North Miami Campus, North Miami, Florida 33181, USA
Hilary McCormack, Crown Attorney's Office, 161 Elgin Street, Ottawa, Canada K2P 2K1
Cynthia McDougall, Prison Service Psychology, Room 415, Cleland House, Page Street, London SW1P 4LN, UK
Mary McMurran, Clinical Psychology Department, Rampton Hospital, Retford, Notts DN22 OPD, UK
Sandra B. McPherson, Clinical & Forensic Psychology, 12434 Cedar Road, Suite 15, Cleveland Heights, Ohio 44106, USA
Amina Memon, Department of Psychology, Southampton University, Highfield, Southampton, UK
David Milner, , University of Westminster, Division of Psychology, 309 Regent Street, London W1R 8AL, UK
Stephen Moston, School of Psychology, University of New South Wales, Sydney 2052, Australia
Ann Van Neygen, Universiteit Gent, Faculteit Psychologie, H. Dunantlaan 2, B-9000 Gent, Belgium
Beth G. Nielsen, Department of Criminal Science, Institute of Law, University of Aarhus, Denmark
Dan Olweus, Dept of Psychosocial Science, University of Bergen, Oisteinsgate 3, N-5007 Bergen, Norway
Margit Oswald, Technische Universität Chemnitz-Zwickau, Philosophische Fakultät, Sozialpsychologie, Postfach 964, D-09009 Chemnitz, Germany

Pilar de Paul Velasco, Social Psychology Department, Universidad Complutense de Madrid, Spain
Carol Pearson, University of Westminster, Division of Psychology, 309 Regent Street, London W1R 8AL, UK
Candida C. Peterson, Department of Psychology, The University of Queensland, McElwain Psychology Building, St Lucia, Queensland 4072, Australia
Margaret-Ellen Pipe, Department of Psychology, University of Otago, PO Box 56, Dunedin, New Zealand
Santiago Redondo, Generalitat de Catalunya, Centre d'Estudis Juridics i Formacio Especialitzada, Roger de Flor 196, 08013-Barcelona, Spain
Julian V. Roberts, Associate Professor, Faculty of Social Sciences, University of Ottawa, 1 Stewart, Ottawa, Ontario, Canada K1N 6N5
Ronald Roesch, Department of Psychology, Simon Fraser University, Burnaby, BC, Canada V5A 1S6
Donald Rogers, Dept. of Psychology, Keele University, Staff. ST5 5BG, UK
Franco Scarpa, Director, Judicial Psychiatric Hospital, Montelupo Fiorentino, Italy
Jorge Sobral, Dpto de Psicologia Social, Facultad de Psicologia, Universidad de Santiago De Compostela, Spain
Siegfried L. Sporer, Department of Psychology, University of Aberdeen, King's College, Old Aberdeen AB9 2UB, UK
Michael A. Stadler, Institut für Psychologie, Universität Bremen, Postfach 330440, D-28334 Bremen, Germany
Paula Stanley, Cranfield School of Management, Cranfield University, Cranfield, Bedfordshire MK43 0AL, UK
Max Steller, Institut für Forensische Psychiatrie, Freie Universität Berlin, Limonenstr. 27, D-12203 Berlin, Germany
Nichola Towell, University of Westminster, Division of Psychology, 309 Regent Street, London W1R 8AL UK
Renate Volbert, Institut für Forensische Psychiatrie, Freie Universität Berlin, Limonenstr. 27, D-12203 Berlin, Germany
Aldert Vrij, Dept of Psychology, University of Portsmouth, Portsmouth PO1 2ER, UK
Willem A. Wagenaar, PO Box 9555, 2300 RB Leiden, The Netherlands
Brit Weisath, Directorate of Health, Postbox 8128 Dep, 0032 Oslo 1, Norway
Petra Wellershaus, Institut fur Forensische Psychiatrie, Freie Universitat Berlin, Limonenstr. 27, D-12203 Berlin, Germany
Peter Wetzels, Kriminologisches Forschungsinstitut Niedersachsen e.V., Leisewitzstrasse 41, D-30175 Hannover, Germany
J. Clare Wilson, Psychology Department, University of Leicester, Leicester LE1 7RH, UK
Frans W. Winkel, Dept of Social Psychology, Free University, De Boelelaan 1081, 1081 HV Amsterdam, The Netherlands
Simone de Winter, Department of Social Psychology, de Boelelaan 1081, 1081 HV Amsterdam, The Netherlands
Jozef Wójcikiewicz, Forensic Science Dept, Jagellonian University & Institute of Forensic Research, 31-007 Cracow, Poland
Justine Woods, University of Westminster, Division of Psychology, 309 Regent Street, London W1R 8AL, UK
Daniel B. Wright, Psychology Department, City University, Northampton Square, London EC1V 0HB, UK
Donna Wright, University of Westminster, Division of Psychology, 309 Regent Street, London W1R 8AL, UK
Rianne can der Zanden, University of Westminster, Division of Psychology, 309 Regent Street, London W1R 8AL, UK

Part I
Eyewitness Testimony

The Perceived Credibility of Rape Victims During a Police Interview: An Experiment among Victim Assistance Workers

Frans W. Winkel and Simone de Winter

Introduction

Disclosure of the criminal incident by the victim to others sometimes constitutes a stress inducing experience in itself. Victims are at risk of secondary victimization, of psychological harm that results from inappropriate responses from potential helping resources, such as friends, relatives, victim assistance workers, police officers, or criminal justice personnel. Due to these responses victims are re-victimized or wounded again. In many victimological analyses of secondary victimization a social - psychological perspective is clearly missing. For example Winkel and Koppelaar (1991) and Winkel (1991) argued that inadequate responding to crime victims might also be the result of biases in the process of forming impressions of victims, and biases in the process of making judgements about their statements. They report empirical evidence suggesting that all sorts of irrelevant (victim-, offender-, crime situation- or observer-related) features may, inadvertently, have a negative impact on the perceived credibility of victims. In the present experiment the relation between the perceived credibility of a rape victim and two victim-related features - the victim's skin colour and her ethnically determined nonverbal behaviour during an interview - and various observer - related features, will be considered in more detail.

Theoretical Perspective

Victim's skin color The idea that a victim's different skin color may result in more negative credibility assessments of her statement by an observer/interviewer is related to the saliency effect or figure-ground phenomenon, reported in the information processing literature (Chapman, 1967; Hamilton, 1981). Basically this effect implies that salient stimuli are processed and interpreted in a different way than non-salient stimuli. Observers automatically tend to experience salient stimuli as more beautiful or uglier than non-distinctive stimuli (=background). To be colored in a predominantly white society makes for a salient stimulus (Surinamers). Duncan (1976) for example revealed that an ambiguous shove is considered to be more violent, if committed by a black instead of a white person. Winkel (1990) moreover reports that native Dutch subjects, who were exposed to news headlines, referring with equal frequency to Surinamer and Dutch perpetrators, tend to over-estimate the number of headlines referring to Surinamers. A similar perspective is visible in Tajfel's (1978) theorising, suggesting that members of ingroups tend to evaluate members of outgroups more negatively.

Victim's nonverbal behavior Biased perceptions of the credibility of a rape victim may also be considered from the perspective of nonverbal communication errors. Generally, interactions between parties - for example a police officer or victim assistance worker interviewing a (potential) rape victim - do not consist of a mere verbal exchange of information. These interactions also involve nonverbal communication, that is an exchange of information on the basis of the nonverbal behavior displayed by the parties. There is strong empirical evidence suggesting that both the patterning and the meaning attributed to these nonverbal behaviors are also ethnically determined (Bochner, 1982; Vrij, 1991). Vrij and Winkel (1991) report differences between black (Surinamers) and white Dutch citizens in the rate at which various nonverbal behaviours occur, for example regarding hand and arm movements, gaze behaviour, preferred interpersonal distances; other studies (Winkel & Vrij, 1990; Winkel 1991a; Vrij & Winkel, 1992) reveal cultural differences in the interpretations of these nonverbal components. Together, these studies provide empirical support for a more or less characteristic "black" and "white" style of nonverbal interaction, to which differential meanings are attributed, in the sense that black styles generally leave less favourable impressions in white observers. As a consequence we hypothesize that a victim's black nonverbal style of communicating tends to undermine the credibility of her statements. This hypothesis also resembles the saliency effect, assuming that black nonverbal behaviors are simply more distinctive ("figure") to white observers, who are basically "expecting" ("ground") white styles of interaction.

Observer characteristics There is an extensive body of research on mock jury decisionmaking that consistently shows that verdicts are determined by individual differences between jurors. Observer characteristics form part of the set of extra-legal factors which, legally, should have no bearing on the verdict (Weir & Wrightsman, 1990). The more general literature on rape also demonstrates that various observer characteristics shape differential social perceptions and attributions of responsibility to rape victims (Krahé, 1988, 1991). In an attempt to further enhance the available research we included the following observer characteristics in the analysis: empathy for the victim, estimated number of false reports, conditional acceptance of forced sex, cultural conceptions and Surinamer culture orientedness.

Mehrabian and Epstein (1972, p. 525) note that in the role-taking approach an empathic person is defined as an individual "who can imaginatively take the role of another and can understand and predict that person's thoughts, feelings and actions". In this perspective empathy is mainly viewed as a quality aiding accurate judgments and stimulating more precise social insights. Empirically, Deitz, Blackwell, Daley, and Bentley (1982), Sulzer and Burglas (1968), Deitz, Littman, and Bentley (1984) and Kanekar, Pinto, and Mazumdar (1985) report that empathy toward rape victims will result in attributing less responsibility to the victim, a higher responsibility to the perpetrator, in less lenient verdicts, and a stronger sensitivity for situational attributions in explaining the event. Parallel to this we assume that empathy for the victim will be positively associated with perceptions of credibility.

Cognitive processing of rape-related information will also be influenced by the observer's pre-existing ideas about the likelihood of false rape reports in general

(Krahé, 1991; De Winter & Mutsaers, 1990). Observers estimating this likelihood to be high will also be more likely to consider a given rape scenario as false and will probably form less favourable impressions of a woman, reporting a given incident to the police.

An important dimension emerging in "rape myth acceptance" or "rape attitude" scales concerns the conditional acceptance of forced sex (Barnett & Field, 1977; Burt, 1980; Schwartz, Williams, & Pepitone-Rockwell, 1981). Various items in these scales reflect the idea that forced sex is acceptable under certain conditions: certain female behaviours are construed as creating legitimate opportunities to utilize force or violence. Observers acknowledging a high number of such conditions will probably perceive rape victims as less credible. Sometimes these conditions are related to the rape victim's cultural origin. Huijbrechts (1990), Deug (1990) and Wostman (1990) for example note that both victim assistance workers and police officers sometimes assume that hitting wives or beating females is a normal and accepted response in Surinamer, or other foreign cultures. Observers characterized by such cultural conceptions will probably consider an actual incident as unimportant or inconsequential, a rape report to the police as trivial, or will judge the victim as less credible.

Research related to the "contact hypothesis" (Amir, 1969; Amir & Ben Ari, 1989; Galper 1973; Horwitz & Rabbie, 1989; Lavrakas, Buri, & Mayzner, 1976; Vrij & Winkel, 1989) suggests that inter-group or inter-ethnic contact may enhance positive perceptions of outgroups. We may thus assume that observers having frequent direct contacts with Surinamers, and those who have Surinamer friends and aquintances, or more generally, observers who are Surinamer culture oriented will probably engage in more favourable perceptions of the credibility of Surinamer victims. A related observer characteristic concerns the degree in which the observer has an open and flexible attitude towards interviews with victims of a different ethnic origin. A more flexible attitude here means that the observer is aware of the fact that for example establishing rapport with a Surinamer victim may simply take more time and energy, and may call upon special skills of the interviewer. Their counterparts will more strongly adhere to "closed minded" slogans, like "now that these foreigners are here, they have to adapt to our own customs", or foreigners do not need a privileged treatment in this regard. We assume that this flexibility will be positively associated also with more favourable impressions formed of Surinamer victims.

In concluding this section we note that the following general hypotheses were formulated: (1) a victim's black skin colour; and (2) a victim's black nonverbal style of communication will result in more negative impressions of that victim. A negative impression here encompasses, that: the victim will be considered less credible, and more responsibility for the incident will be attributed to her. The available juridical evidence will be considered as less convincing, while the psychological damage emanating from the incident will be perceived as less serious. Finally, the event will be attributed more strongly to the victim's behaviour or character, and less strongly to situational circumstances. The third hypothesis states that the observer characteristics specified will either enhance or thwart the credibility of the victim.

Method

Sample Subjects constitute a random sample of 286 victim assistance workers, of which 19% were male and 81% female. Their mean age was 46 years. As to educational level, 4% form part of the low, 42% of the intermediate, and 54% of the high level.

Procedure All subjects were exposed to a video of a vice squad officer inter-viewing a victim. The video starts with pictures of a woman approaching a police station. A commentator (not visible) announces, that the woman had come to the police station that very morning in order to file charges of a rape; she had been given some opportunity to tell her own story. A summary of her story emerges on screen (see Box 1), while pictures are shown of an officer interviewing the woman.

Box 1:
Margreet (Rinia) tells that she went to a party of her girlfriend Carla. Carla lives about 30 km further.
She went to the party by bus and intended to return with the latest bus.
However, later in the evening it is really getting pleasant.
Her girlfriend Carla suggests her to stay.
She can't sleep at Carla's place.
She can sleep though at Peter's place, a friend of Carla.
She goes home with Peter.
She decides to sleep on the floor, but she is getting sick and has to vomit.
After returning from the bathroom, she is not able to fall asleep.
She takes her sleeping bag and lies down next to Peter at a two-person bed.
She tells that Peter raped her afterwards.
The next morning she took the first bus home.
That very morning she came here to file charges of a rape, without having discussed this with anybody.

The commentator then continues with the following text:
The vice squad officer has taken ample time for Margreet (Rinia) to tell her own story. He did everything possible to establish rapport. In the meantime he has also informed her about the procedural aspects of filing charges. She has agreed that the officer will write her report down on paper. In order to do so as detailed as possible he goes through her story again, while asking her several questions.

In a few moments you will see fragments from this interview. While watching this video, please try to imagine yourself in the position of the interviewing officer. After this video it is your task to decide whether or not this incident actually constituted a rape. Be attentive to all the information this video is presenting, such as the appearance of the woman, and the way she behaves. In order to make a first impression of the woman possible in an easy way the sound of the picture is faded away.

The interviewing officer asked a total of four questions, emerging on screen as subtitles. These questions were: (1) what happened when you both arrived at his home?; (2) did you tell Peter that you only joined him to sleep at his place; (3) why didn't you leave the bed immediately, and; (4) did you make it clear to him that you did not want it. The questions posed took 10 seconds each; the vicitm's answers took about 20 seconds. The victim thus spoke for 80 seconds in total, while listening for 40 seconds. After viewing the video, subjects were handed out a questionnaire.

Independent variables The independent variables were incorporated in the videos. The role of victim in all experimental conditions was enacted by one and the same actress, who had a round, white face, full lips, and black eyes. In the black skin colour condition she was given a Surinamer appearance through changing her skin colour and hair style. A professional make-up man was used to accomplish this. In the white nonverbal style condition the victim three times gazed away from the interviewer for five seconds while speaking, and once for 1.5 seconds during listening. Moreover she made five gestures and one body movement while speaking. In the black nonverbal style condition the victim five times gazed away for five seconds while speaking; during listening she once gazed away for six seconds. Moreover, this latter victim made two body movements, eight gestures, and two self-touches. These frequencies were based on previous studies (Vrij, 1991; Vrugt & Kerkhof, 1982; Hall, 1984; Hall & Halberstadt, 1986).

Measures The Perceived Credibility Scale (PCS) was used to measure the major dependent variable. PCS consists of several subscales, namely: perceived credibility of the victim (α=.87 in the present sample); attribution of responsibility (α=.90); perceived seriousness of the consequences resulting from the incident (α=.90); the convincingness of the available evidence (α=.80), and the use of behaviour (α=.91), character (α=.82) and situational attributions (α=.75).

The questionnaire also entailed measures of the relevant observer variables. In the present questionnaire a total of six such variables were included: empathy for the victim, expected number of false reports, conditional acceptance of forced sex, cultural conceptions, flexibility in interviewing victims of a different ethnic origin and Surinamer culture orientedness. For a more detailed description of these observer variables we refer to De Winter and Winkel (1992).

Results

To examine hypothesis 3, the six observer variables were regressed on a composite of the dependent variables, representing a general positive or negative evaluation of the victim ('s statements). Almost all predictive variables significantly affect this overall evaluation: conditional acceptance of forced sex (ß= .43; t=8.53, p<.001); estimated number of false reports (ß=.25; t=5.48, p<.001); Surinamer culture orientedness (ß=.14; t=3.22, p<.01); cultural conceptions (ß=.17; t=3.40, p<.001); flexibility (ß=.01; t=1.84, p<.03) and empathy (ß=.08; t=.28, ns). Together these variables explain about 50% of the variance in the composite. Conditional acceptance and number of false reports are clearly the strongest predictors, together explaining 43% of the variance. Additional stepwise regression analyses on each dependent variable separately revealed a similar picture: in all separate equations conditional acceptance and number of false reports emerge as important predictor variables. In all cases the direction of the associations confirms the expectations formulated. In view of these outcomes it was decided to further examine these particular variables. Mean splits were conducted to dichotomize these variables.

Table 1: Mean scores (m) and F-statistics regarding the skin colour and the ethnically based non-verbal behaviour

	skin colour			**non-verbal behaviour**		
	white	**black**		**white**	**black**	
	m	**m**	**F**	**m**	**m**	**F**
credibility	2.98	3.30	7.69**	3.21	3.09	0.01
responsibility	3.12	3.61	7.61**	3.53	3.24	1.14
seriousness consequences	2.88	3.33	8.76**	3.26	2.99	1.44
evidence convincing	3.84	4.10	3.27*	4.21	3.78	4.48*
behaviour attribution	3.66	4.10	5.80**	4.07	3.74	3.47
character attribution	2.26	2.63	5.53**	2.47	2.43	0.15
situational attribution	3.74	3.49	0.26	3.40	3.37	0.03

Higher scores represent negative judgements of the woman (less credible, more responsible, consequences less serious, evidence less convincing, stronger behaviour - and character attributions and less to the situation.
* p < 0.05
** p < 0.01

Data were further analyzed on the basis of a 2 (black/white skin colour) x 2 (black/white nonverbal style) x 2 (high/low conditional acceptance) x 2 (high/ low number of false reports expected) design. A multivariate analysis of variance revealed three significant main effects, namely for skin colour ($F(7,264)=1.99$, $p<.05$), for conditional acceptance of forced sex ($F(7,264)=10.66$, $p<.001$) and for number of false reports ($F(7,264)=5.60$, $p<.001$).

The pattern of means pertaining to skin colour clearly confirm hypothesis 1: white victims are generally evaluated more positively than black victims. Univariate analyses of variance revealed six (out of a possible seven) significant differences. Black victims were perceived as less credible ($F(1,270)=7.69$, $p<.01$) and as more responsible for the event ($F(1,270)=7.61$, $p<.01$) than white victims. For black victims the consequences of the event were considered to be less serious ($F(1,270)=8.76$, $p<.01$), while the available evidence was seen as less convincing for these victims ($F(1,270)=3.27$, $p<.05$). Moreover the occurrence of the event was significantly more strongly attibuted to the black victim's behaviour ($F(1,270)=5.80$, $p<.01$) and to her character ($F(1,270)=5.53$, $p<.01$). Situational attributions were the only variable not significantly affected by skin colour. Together these results strongly confirm hypothesis 1.

Contrary to hypothesis 2 no significant main effects emerged for nonverbal behaviour. Table 1 appears to reveal a rather systematic trend, albeit marginal, for black nonverbal behaviour to be considered more favorably. However, only on the perceived strength of the juridical evidence a significant difference, following this trend, arised ($F(1,270)=4.48$, $p<.05$). None of the other differences reached significance. Thus, hypothesis 2 is clearly not supported.

Table 2: Mean scores (m) and F-statistics regarding 'estimated percentage of false reports' and 'conditional acceptance of sexual violence'.

	percentage false reports			conditional acceptance		
	low	high		low	high	
	m	m	F	m	m	F
credibility	2.80	3.75	17.0***	2.86	3.55	3.75*
responsibility	2.99	4.04	14.5***	2.79	4.20	29.34***
seriousness consequences	2.84	3.60	9.61**	2.79	3.58	5.34*
evidence convincing	3.66	4.53	12.5***	3.55	4.59	17.12***
behaviour attribution	3.41	4.10	31.9***	3.21	4.86	48.11***
character attribution	2.26	4.73	6.12*	2.097	2.99	18.94***
situational attribution	3.31	3.52	0.07	2.91	4.08	26.74***

Higher scores represent negative judgements of the woman (less credible, more responsible, consequences less serious, evidence less convincing, stronger behaviour - and character attributions and less to the situation.
* p < 0.05
** p < 0.01
*** p < 0.001

Victim assistance workers generally expecting a high number of false reports consistently supply more unfavourable impressions of the victim. Univariate analyses revealed significant differences on almost all separate dependent variables. Subjects expecting high numbers of false reports perceived the woman as less credible ($F(1,270)=17.00$, $p<.001$), attributed more responsibility to her ($F(1,270)=14.47$, $p<.0001$), considered the consequences emanating from the event as less serious ($F(1,270)=9.60$, $p<.01$), the evidence less convincing ($F(1,270)=12.55$, $p<.001$), and more strongly engaged in behaviour ($F(1,270)=31.87$, $p<.001$) and character attributions ($F(1,270)=6.12$, $p<.05$). Again, situational attributions were not significantly affected ($F(1,270)=.075$; ns). A similar configuration emerged with regard to conditional acceptance of forced sex. Significant differences were found on all dependents. Victim assistance workers seeing conditions under which forced sex is acceptable invariably express less favourable impressions: perceived credibility ($F(1,270)=3.75$, $p<.05$); attribution of responsibility ($F(1,270)=29.34$, $p<.001$); seriousness of consequences ($F(1,270)=5.34$, $p<.05$); convincingness evidence ($F(1,270)=17.12$, $p<.001$); behaviour attributions ($F(1,270)=48.11$, $p<.001$); character attributions ($F(1,270)=18.94$, $p<.001$), and situational attributions ($F(1,270)=26.74$, $p<.001$).

At a multivariate level only one significant interaction emerged, namely a skin colour by nonverbal behaviour interaction ($F(7,264)=2.39$, $p<.05$). Significant univariate differences were found on perceived credibility ($F(1,270)=4.62$, $p<.05$) and seriousness of consequences ($F(1,270)=6.30$, $p<.05$). The analyses revealed that black or white nonverbal behaviour do not make a difference when the victim is white, neither with regard to perceived credibility, nor regarding the seriousness of consequences. However, if the victim is black, black nonverbal behaviour tends to have a positive impact.

Discussion

Countering secondary victimization is an important objective of the European and North-American victim assistance movements. Proposed measures aimed at reducing this phenomenon typically focus on individuals and groups, which are active outside the direct realm of victim assistance work. Important targets in this respect are mental health professionals, social workers, police officers, criminal justice personnel, general practitioners, etc. The present findings suggest that such a focus is at least narrow-minded. Secondary victimization may also occur within the very movement itself. From this perspective, we appreciate the opportunity given by the Dutch Association for Victim Assistance to perform this study, and to discuss its results with their members.

More generally the present findings suggest that both victim characteristics and observer characteristics may bias credibility assessments. As to victims, our data revealed that black victims reporting a given scenario to the police make a less favourable impression than white victims. In particular, black victims are perceived as less credible, and as more responsible for the occurrence of the event. Black victims more strongly appear to encounter internal attributions: in explaining the event observers are inclined to blame the black victim's behaviour prior to the event, and they appear to make more references to the character of the victim. The psychological damage emanating from the event is considered to be less serious for black victims. Finally, the black victim's position in the criminal justice framework appears to be more delicate: the evidence available in her narrative is evaluated as less convincing. As to observer characteristics, our findings support the notion that various pre-conceived ideas about rape in general have an impact also on the evaluation of a specific scenario. Observers, inter alia expecting a high number of false reports, or conditionally accepting the use of force in sexual relations, form less favorable impressions of victims.

Unexpectedly, the nonverbal behaviour of the victim during the interview did not result in significant differences. These null-effects need further examination. In our view it is to early to conclude that black or white styles of nonverbal behaviour are irrelevant factors in explaining credibility assessments. The present findings are in obvious contrast with previous studies relating to possible perpetrators: these studies consistently reveal that black nonverbal behaviours are considered more suspect. White observers tend to interpret these black patterns as indicators of stress and tension. In a perpetrator context, these indicators appear to serve as an alarm signal that the actor is concealing the truth. However, in a victim context, these signs of stress and tension, may also indicate that the actor actually experienced something negative. Such an interpretation is particularly likely in victim assistance workers, whose basic training strongly focuses on taking all victim statements seriously. Police officers, on the other hand, may be much more familiar with questioning the veracity of a victim's account. Further studies should thus focus on police officers in order to find out whether or not the negative connotations of black nonverbal styles emerging in perpetrator contexts, will also arise in victimization contexts. In other words, the negative connotation of black nonverbal behaviours might actually reflect an interaction with specific observer characteristics, that were not examined in this study, for example the observer's ideas about the main goals (offering comfort vs. a focus on truthfulness) of the interview of victims.

References

Amir, Y. (1969). Contact hypothesis in ethnic relations. *Psychological Bulletin, 71*, 319-342.

Amir, Y., & Ben Ari, R. (1989, June). *Psychologists trying to make changes in intergroup relations: When to do and when not to do.* Paper presented at the 2nd Regional Conference of the International Association for Crosscultural Psychology, Free University, Amsterdam.

Barnett, N. J., & Feild, H. S. (1977). Sex differences in university students' attitudes toward rape. *Journal of College Student Personnel, 18*, 93-96.

Bochner, S. (1982). The social psychology of crosscultural relations. In S. Bochner (Ed.), *Cultures in contact: Studies in crosscultural interaction.* Oxford: Pergamon.

Burt, M. R. (1980). Cultural myths and support for rape. *Journal of Personality and Social Psychology, 38*, 217-230.

Chapman, L. J. (1967). Illusory correlation in observational report. *Journal of Verbal Learning and Verbal Behavior, 6*, 115-155.

Deitz, S. R., Blackwell, K. T., Daley, P. C., & Bentley, B. J. (1982). Measurement of empathy toward rape victims and rapists. *Journal of Personality and Social Psychology, 43*, 372-384.

Deitz, S. R., Littman, M., & Bentley, B. J. (1984). Attribution of responsibility for rape: The influence of observer empathy, victim resistance and victim attractiveness. *Sex Roles, 10*, 261-280.

Deug, F. (1990). *En dan ben je pas echt ver van huis: Turkse en Marokkaanse vrouwen en meisjes over sexueel geweld en de hulpverlening.* Utrecht: Stichting tegen Sexueel Geweld.

Duncan, B. L. (1976). Differential social perception and attibution of intergroup violence: Testing the lower limits of stereotyping blacks. *Journal of Personality and Social Psychology, 34*, 590-598.

Galper, R. E. (1973). Functional race membership and recognition of faces. *Perceptual and Motor Skills, 37*, 455-462.

Hall, J. A. (1984). *Nonverbal sex differences: Communication accuracy and expressive style.* Baltimore, MD: Johns Hopkins University.

Hall, J. A., & Halberstadt, A. G. (1986). Smiling and gazing. In J. S. Hyde & M. C. Linn (Eds.), *The psychology of gender: Advances through meta-analysis.* Baltimore, MD: John Hopkins University Press.

Hamilton, D. L. (1981). Illusory correlation as a bias for stereotyping. In D. L. Hamilton (Ed.), *Cognitive processes in stereotyping and intergroup behavior.* New Jersey: Erlbaum.

Horwitz, M., & Rabbie, J. M. (1989). Stereotypes of groups, group members, and individuals in categories: A differential analysis. In D. Bar-Tal, C.F. Graumann, A. W. Kruglanski, & W. Stroebe (Eds.), *Stereotyping and prejudice: Changing conceptions.* New York: Springer Verlag.

Huijbrechts, V. (1990). *Hulpverlening aan allochtone vrouwen: Verslag van een literatuurstudie (1980-1990) naar de hulpverlening aan Turkse, Marokkaanse, Surinaamse en Antilliaanse vrouwen met psychisch en psycho-sociale problemen.* Utrecht: Nederlands Centrum Buitenlanders.

Kanekar, S., Pinto, N., & Mazumdar, D. (1985). Causal and moral responsibility of victims of rape and robbery. *Journal of Applied Social Psychology, 15*, 622-637.

Krahé, B. (1988). Victim and observer characteristics as determinants of responsibility attributions to victims of rape. *Journal of Applied Social Psychology, 18*, 50-58.

Krahé, B. (1991). Police officers' definitions of rape: A prototype study. *Journal of Community and Applied Social Psychology, 1*, 223-244.

Lavrakas, P. J., Buri, J. R., & Mayzner, M. S. (1976). A perspective on the recognition of other race faces. *Perception and Psychophysics*, *20*, 475-481.

Mehrabian, A., & Epstein, N. (1972). A measure of emotional empathy. *Journal of Personality*, *40*, 525-543.

Sulzer, J. L., & Burglass, R. K. (1968). Responsibiliy attribution, empathy, and punitiveness. *Journal of Personality*, *36*, 272-282.

Schwartz, J., Williams, H., & Pepitone-Rockwell, F. (1981). Construction of a Rape Awareness Scale. *Victimology*, *6*, 110-119.

Tajfel, H. (1978). Social categorisation, social identity and social comparison. In H. Tajfel (Ed.), *Differentiation between social groups: Studies in the social psychology of intergroup relations*. London: Academic Press.

Vrij, A. (1991). *Misverstanden tussen politie en allochtonen: Sociaal-psychologische aspecten van verdacht zijn*. Amsterdam: VU-Uitgeverij.

Vrij, A., & Winkel, F. W. (1989). Recognition of own and other-race faces: The effect of quality versus quantity of crosscultural interaction. *Journal of Police and Criminal Psychology*, *5*, 24-30.

Vrij, A., & Winkel, F. W. (1991). Cultural patterns in Dutch and Surinamer nonverbal behavior: An analysis of a simulated police/citizen encounter. *Journal of Nonverbal Behavior*, *15*(3), 10-18.

Vrij, A., & Winkel, F. W. (1992). Crosscultural police-citizen interactions: The influence of race, beliefs and nonverbal communication on impression formation. *Journal of Applied Social Psychology*, *22*, 1546-1559.

Vrugt, A., & Kerkstra, A. (1982). Verschillen tussen mannen en vrouwen in nonverbaal gedrag. *Nederlands Tijdschrift voor de Psychologie*, *37*, 393-429.

Weir, J. A., & Wrightsman, L. S. (1990). The determinants of mock jurors' verdicts in a rape case. *Journal of Applied Social Psychology*, *20*, 901-919.

Winkel, F. W. (1990). Crime reporting in newspapers: An exploratory study of the effects of ethnic references in crime news. *Social Behaviour*, *5*, 87-101.

Winkel, F. W. (1991). Conclusions and recommendations of the Task Force on Victims' rights and the justice system. In E. C. Viano (Ed.), *International perspectives: Onati proceedings series: Vol. 9. Victims' rights and legal reforms* (pp. 340-347). Onati: IISL.

Winkel, F. W. (1991a). Interaction between the police and minority group members: Victimization through the incorrect interpretation of nonverbal behavior. *International Review of Victimology*, *2*, 15-28.

Winkel, F. W., & Vrij, A. (1990). Interaction and impression formation in a crosscultural dyad: Frequency and meaning of culturally determined gaze behaviour in a police interview setting. *Social Behaviour*, *5*, 335-350.

Winkel, F. W., & Koppelaar, L. (1991). Rape victims' style of self-presentation and secondary victimisation by the environment: An experiment. *Journal of Interpersonal Violence*, *6*, 29-41.

Winter, S. M. de, & Mutsaers, P. A. M. (1990). *Vooraf-informatie en oordeelsvorming: Wat is bij zedenverhoren de invloed van voorafinformatie op de beoordeling van een vrouw die aangifte van verkrachting doet?* Unpublished manuscript, Vrije Universiteit, vgr. Sociale Psychologie, Amsterdam.

Winter, S. M. de, & Winkel, F. W. (1992). *De gepercipieerde geloofwaardigheid van slachtoffers van verkrachting tijdens het verhoor: Een experiment onder hulpverleners*. Amsterdam: Vrije Universiteit, vgr. Sociale Psychologie.

Wöstman, M. (1990). Discriminatie en onverschilligheid: Over verschillende manieren van rekening houden met de cultuur. *Tijdschrift voor Criminologie*, *3*, 179-189.

The Perceived Truthfulness of Children's and Adults' Testimony: the Oath versus the Competency Test

Candida C. Peterson

Courtrooms throughout the English-speaking world have traditionally taken a rather dim view of child witnesses, doubting their capacity, at least until the age of 14, to comprehend either the difference between truth and falsehood or the need for truthfulness in court. For this reason, in the wake of the 1779 case. *R. v. Brasier* (168 ER 202) children were typically precluded from taking the oath (a precondition for testifying) until after they passed a "competency test" which probed their religious beliefs, their ability to supply a satisfactory lexical definition of lying, their fears of punishment for perjury, and so on. In recent years, the practice of selectively testing children's competency has come into question, and law reforms relating to the qualification of child witnesses have been implemented in many common law jurisdictions (see Spencer & Flin, 1990, for a recent review). However, despite the court's concerns, there is presently little empirical evidence about how competency testing, or the oath, may shape jurors' perceptions of child (or adult) witnesses and their testimony. The primary purpose of the present study was to explore these issues.

A secondary purpose was to help clarify existing empirical uncertainty over whether jurors are biased in favour of, or against, the testimony of child witnesses. Goodman et al.'s (1984) initial study of undergraduate and community-resident mock jurors' ratings of either written summaries or videotapes of testimony by a bystander witness aged six-, ten-, or 30-years suggested a bias against the six-year-old, who was judged as significantly less credible than the 30-year-old. This finding was subsequently replicated by Leippe and Romanczyk (1989, Study 2). However in a further experiment (Study 4) in the same series Leippe and Romanczyk discovered that when mock jurors were given actual transcripts of the witnesses' testimony instead of paraphrased summaries, an opposite result emerged. The six-year-old was judged as significantly more credible than the 30-year-old. Similarly, Ross, Miller and Moran (1987) found that an eight-year-old witness was viewed as more truthful than a 21-year-old by undergraduate mock jurors, while Nigro et al. (1989) likewise observed higher credibility ratings of child than adult prosecution witnesses and, unlike most previous research, a greater inclination to convict the defendant when an eight-year-old testified in a powerful speech style than when the key witness was an adult. To complicate the picture still further, some studies (e.g. Johnson & Grisso, 1986; Luus & Wells, 1992) have revealed no significant differences in perceived credibility between child and adult witnesses. However, some evidence of a pro-child bias did emerge in Luus and Wells' study in the form of jurors' selective insensitivity to inaccuracies in the eight-year-old's testimony, rating it as credible as an adult's when, in fact, under cross examination it contained more errors.

These striking variations among the results of studies all testing the same age-bias hypothesis using similar experimental paradigms highlights the need for further investigation of mock jurors' evaluations of the truthfulness of child versus adult witnesses. To this end, the age variable was incorporated, along with the hitherto relatively neglected variable of witness gender, into the present design. In addition, we used actual transcripts in place of paraphrased summaries of the witnesses' testimony as a further test of the hypothesis emerging from Leippe and Romanczyk's (1989) study suggesting that when verbatim details of children's testimony are provided, the bias against the young witness may be overcome or even reversed.

Method

Subjects The participants who took the role of mock jurors in this study were 102 Australian university students from introductory psychology courses. They ranged in age from 18 through 22 years, and 67% were female. None were parents, law students or former jurors, but 14% had been inside an Australian courtroom at least once, either as a witness, a plaintiff, a defendant or an observer.

Design A between-subjects design was used, with eight separate groups of mock jurors responding to one of eight different experimental conditions. In two of these the chief witness was a boy aged seven, in two a girl aged seven, in two a man of 20 and in the remaining two a 20-year-old woman. Each of the four witnesses appeared in two different conditions. In one of these, he or she qualified to testify by taking the oath and, in the other, by means of a competency test. Numbers of subjects exposed to each condition were 12, 10, 15, 14, 12, 15, 12 and 12, respectively.

Materials The stimuli and response measures were presented in printed booklets. The cover page included a consent form, a description of the procedures used to preserve subjects' anonymity, and a brief summary of the role and responsibilities of a juror in a real trial, followed by a query as to whether the subject felt capable of imagining him/herself in the role of juror. (All subjects replied affirmatively to this question.) The second page sought demographic particulars, and the third presented the following case summary. The case was based closely upon Leippe and Romanczyk's (1989, Study 4, p. 129), though modified for consistency with its stated setting in Australia. It read as follows:

> This is a murder case. A man was held up at knifepoint on a deserted inner-suburban street in Brisbane. The sole eye-witness to the event was seven-year-old [20-year-old] Kim Smith, who watched the event from the second-floor bedroom window of his/her [grandmother's apartment/rented flat]. The apartment overlooks the street where the stabbing took place. Before the trial Kim identified the defendant from a police line-up that included him along with five other similar-looking men. The case has now come to trial.

The fourth page contained what was described as "a verbatim transcript of the witness's testimony". Depending upon the experimental condition, it began either with a competency test (see below) or with the witness placing his [her] hand on the Bible and repeating, in full, the standard courtroom oath, namely: "I swear to tell the truth, the whole truth and nothing but the truth, so help me God". The competency test for the child witness was modified slightly from one used in the 1977 Australian case *R. v. Brown* (Qd.R.220). It read as follows:

Kim Smith, aged seven-years, was taken to the witness stand near the judge's bench. When she [he] was comfortably seated, the judge began:
Judge: Now, Kim, do you know what it means to tell the truth?
Kim: Yes.
Judge: Tell the court what it means.
Kim: It means to tell everything exactly as it is.
Judge: Do you know what it means to promise?
Kim: Yes.
Judge: Do you promise to tell the truth in court today?
Kim: Yes.
Judge: Will you stick to that?
Kim: Yes.
Judge: You won't tell lies?
Kim: No.
Judge: Do you know what would happen if you told a lie in court today?
Kim: I'd get into big trouble and I might go to jail.

The adult competency test was identical except that the phrase "to be factually inaccurate" was appended to the witness's definition of telling the truth, and the reply: "I'd be liable for perjury and might go to jail" was substituted for the final line, for greater authenticity.

The testimony itself was also a modified version of Leippe and Romanczyk's (1989, p. 129). It was in two parts, beginning with a response to counsel's query about the perpetrator's appearance, followed by event descriptions in reply to the question: "What happened next?". As in Leippe and Romanczyk's study, the wording of child and adult versions of the testimony was varied slightly, based on piloting in which individuals of the same age as the hypothetical witnesses had been asked to paraphrase the story in their own words.

The response measures, adapted from previous research (e.g. Goodman et al., 1984; Ross et al., 1987) required subjects to rate the witness and the defendant's guilt on seven-point scales. Positions of positive and negative response alternatives were counterbalanced. The dependent measures were:

(a) How often did this witness tell lies? (never = 7; very often = 1)
(b) How intelligent was this witness? (very = 7; not at all = 1)
(c) How truthful was this witness? (extremely = 7; not at all = 1)
(d) How accurate was the testimony given by this witness? (extremely = 7; not at all = 1)
(e) Did this witness tell the whole truth? (always = 7; never = 1)
(f) Was the defendant guilty or innocent? (definitely guilty = 7; definitely innocent = 1).

Procedure Subjects arrived at the laboratory in groups of three to eight and completed the task independently under the supervision of a female experimenter in a single session lasting approximately 35 minutes.

Results

Table 1: Mean ratings by mock jurors of male and female child and adult witnesses who qualified to testify by means of the oath or the competency yest

	Qualification Method: Competency Test				Oath			
Witness	*Boy*	*Girl*	*Man*	*Woman*	*Boy*	*Girl*	*Man*	*Woman*
Number of mock jurors	(n=10)	(n=14)	(n=15)	(n=12)	(n=12)	(n=15)	(n=12)	(n=12)
Response Dimension								
Told no lies	6.70	6.86	6.13	6.58	6.50	6.47	5.67	6.25
Was truthful	6.00	6.07	5.20	5.17	5.67	5.40	4.75	5.42
Told whole truth	6.20	5.79	4.87	4.83	6.58	5.53	4.25	5.42
Gave accurate testimony	5.00	5.29	4.67	4.08	5.33	4.60	4.25	3.83
Witness intelligence	4.60	3.93	4.33	3.67	4.33	4.20	3.83	3.83
Defendant guilt	4.60	4.86	4.53	5.00	5.50	4.53	4.42	4.33

Table 1 shows mock juror's mean ratings of each of the four witnesses under the two qualification conditions on each dependent variable. Using a 2 (qualification method) x 2 (witness age) x 2 (witness sex) design, six separate ANOVAs were computed to examine differences in the dependent variables as a function of the eight experimental conditions. The results indicated that qualification method exerted a significant effect on ratings of the truthfulness of the witness, $F(1,94) = 4.03$, $p<.0.5$. There was also a statistically significant main effect of the witness's age, $F(1,94) = 16.36$, $p<.001$. But there was no effect of witness gender, $F<1$, and no significant two-way or three-way interactions (all p's>.10). In other words, witnesses of each age and gender who qualified to testify by passing a competency test were perceived as more truthful ($M = 5.59$) than children or adults who took the oath ($M = 5.05$). In addition, child witnesses were rated as more truthful overall than adult witnesses.

Similarly, the mock jurors rated the witnesses who had passed the competency test as telling lies less often than the same witnesses under oath, $F(1,94) = 4.94$, $p<.05$. Child witnesses were also rated as lying less often than adult witnesses, $F(1,94) = 8.53$, $p<.01$, but no other main effects or interactions were statistically significant (all p's>.10).

The significant effect of qualification method upon the witness's perceived truthfulness and lying provides empirical support for the suggestion that a juror's confidence in the honesty of a child witness is boosted when the child is required to take a competency test. Interestingly, however, the same honesty-enhancing effect applied equally to adult witnesses. Thus jurors' belief that the child was too immature to testify truthfully would not seem to explain this positive effect due to competency testing.

The main effect of age accords with some previous research (e.g. Leippe & Romanczyk, 1989, Study 4; Ross, Miller & Moran, 1987) in revealing a bias in favour of the truthfulness of child witnesses. Since the transcripts of testimony used in this study were similar to those used in a study by Leippe and Romanczyk's (1989, Study 4) where a similar result emerged, these results reinforce the hypothesis that provision of actual verbatim transcripts of the child witness's testimony selectively enhances the child's perceived credibility.

We separately explored juror's evaluations of whether the witness told "the whole truth". The rationale for this analysis was that since the oath explicitly defines courtroom truthfulness in this way, a witness under oath might be perceived as adhering more closely to this criterion than a competency-tested witness who has simply promised to tell the truth. A statistically significant main effect of witness age emerged, $F(1,94) = 16.28$, $p<.001$, along with an interaction between witness age and gender, $F(1,94) = 5.26$, $p<.05$. But there were no other significant main effects or interactions (all F's <1). In other words, the type of qualification method did not influence jurors' belief that the witness testimony embodied "the whole truth". But the two child witnesses were perceived as adhering more closely to this stringent criterion for truthfulness than were the adults, with the sharpest contrast being between the boy witness ($M = 6.41$) and the man ($M = 4.59$).

The stereotype that children remember less about witnessed events than adults, but are correspondingly less motivated to invent deliberate falsehoods, predicted a contrast between mock jurors' perceptions of witness honesty and witness accuracy, with children scoring higher on the former dimension and adults higher on the latter. However, the present results revealed no such effect. Instead, the testimony provided by the child witness was viewed as significantly more accurate than the adults', $F(1,94) = 15.41$, $p<.001$, with no significant effects due to gender, $F(1,94) = 3.08$, $p>.05$; qualification method $F(1,94) = 1.87$, $p>.10$; two-way interactions, (all Fs <1) or the three-way interaction, $F(1,94) = 2.20$, $p>.10$.

We included a question about perceived intelligence of the witness as a possible mediator of the effect of qualification upon credibility. Since the competency test provides mock jurors with more information about the witness's mental ability than does the simple repetition of the oath, it seemed conceivable that the positive relationship we observed between succeeding on a competency test and perceived honesty could be an indirect effect of an apparently brighter witness. But this hypothesis was disconfirmed. The type of qualification method did not exert any statistically significant main effect upon the witness's perceived intelligence, $F<1$. Nor were any of the two-way or three-way interactions involving intelligence statistically significant (all ps>.10). However, there were significant main effects due to witness age, $F(1,94) = 4.04$, $p<.05$, and witness gender, $F(1,94) = 5.00$, $p<.05$. The two child witnesses ($M=4.24$) were seen as more intelligent than the two adult witnesses ($M=3.94$), and the two male witnesses ($M=4.27$) as brighter than the two female witnesses ($M=3.92$).

There were no significant main effects of qualification method upon subjects' ratings of the defendant's guilt, $F<1$. Nor did the main effects due to witness age, $F(1,94) = 2.30$, $p>.10$; or witness gender, $F<1$, achieve significance. However, the two-way interaction between qualification method and witness gender did significantly influence guilt ratings, $F(1,94) = 4.69$, $p<.05$. Comparison between means revealed that female child and adult witnesses were more persuasive in yielding a guilty verdict when they qualified by means of the competency test ($M=4.92$) than by means of the oath ($M=4.44$) whereas the reverse was true of male witnesses ($M=4.56$

and 4.96, respectively). No other interaction involving guild was statistically significant (all ps >.10).

Discussion

These results indicate that success on a competency test enhances a witness's perceived honesty. Compared to identical witnesses giving identical testimony under oath, children and adults who qualified to testify by passing the type of competency test traditionally reserved for children in English-speaking courtrooms were rated as more truthful and less prone to tell lies. The absence of differences due to the witness's age suggests that mock jurors do not share the law's selective mistrust of children's honesty. Instead, jurors were persuaded to credit testimony following a successful competency test equally, regardless of whether the witness was a child or an adult, suggesting that it was the information about the witness contained in the test itself, rather than a stereotype about children's inability to give truthful evidence, that explained the positive effect. Similarly, the finding that qualification method did not influence jurors' ratings of the witness's intelligence or accuracy indicated that the enhancement of perceived honesty could not be explained away as a global "halo" effect around competency-tested witnesses. Nor was there any evidence to suggest that the extra information about intelligence that success on the competency test supplied was responsible for the boosting of the competent witness's perceived truthfulness above that of an identical witness under oath. Instead, the effects of competency testing were direct, specific to honesty, and uncomplicated by interactions with the witness's age or gender. Therefore, the competency test appears to effectively serve the purpose for which it was originally designed by the courts, namely: to demonstrate to triers-of-fact that the witness is capable both of comprehending, and of abiding by, the special obligations of truthfulness in the courtroom over and above the equivalent in everyday life. Indeed, in contrast to the law's preference for evidence on oath from any witness deemed as capable of comprehending religious or secular penalties for perjury, these data suggest that competency testing may serve this purpose more effectively for witnesses of all ages than simple repetition of the oath.

In addition, the present findings align themselves with the growing body of empirical evidence (e.g. Ross et al,. 1989) showing that mock jurors accord greater credibility to testimony by a child witness than to comparable testimony by an adult. It would seem that the failure of most recent studies to replicate the early suggestion (e.g. Goodman et al., 1984; Leippe & Romanczyk, 1987, Study 2) that mock jurors are biased *against* testimony by child witnesses may reflect methodological refinements. In particular these data reinforce Leippe and Romanczyk's suggestion that the use of paraphrased summaries in some of the early studies, rather than the actual transcripts testimony in the witnesses' own words (as in the present case) may help to account for an apparent anti-child bias. As Luus and Wells (1992) explained "being asked to respond to an age category ... is a condition that is more likely to allow stereotypes to surface in human judgment than when an individual vivid member of that category is shown in detail" (p. 85).

From a practical standpoint, these results have direct relevance to the growing concern across most historically common law jurisdictions (Spencer & Flin, 1990) about what role competency testing should play in trials involving child witnesses. Persuasive arguments favouring the elimination of competency testing have been made on at least two grounds. First, the competency test imposes added stress upon the witness of tender years who is already likely to find the court appearance more stressful than an adult witness. Second, the competency test may sometimes be applied inappropriately by judges who lack formal training on how to interview children. These arguments are in no way challenged by the present study's results.

On the other hand, the present findings do suggest a need to closely examine the possible consequences of law reforms relating to the competency-testing of child witnesses upon jurors' reception of the child's evidence. When the option of not submitting a very young witness to a competency test is exercised by the court, the effect may be detrimental to the witness's perceived honesty and credibility. As Spencer (1990) has noted, the child's competency to distinguish truth from falsehood should ideally affect the court's assessment of the "weight of his evidence but not its admissibility" (p. 1751). The present results suggest that jurors may give greater weight to evidence supplied by witnesses passing competency tests than by those taking the oath because it is seen as more truthful. By extension, one might hypothesize that jurors would be persuaded more by sworn evidence from a child under oath than by unsworn evidence from a child who takes neither the oath or a competency test (we are currently testing this hypothesis in ongoing research). However, pending these new data and replication of the significant effects observed in the present study, one might cautiously conclude that the issue of consistency in the qualification procedures applied to different age groups and across various legal jurisdictions is an important one. In view of their varying effects on the perceptions of witness honesty, some uniformity in the methods of qualification applied to witnesses of various ages may need to be addressed before equal justice in cases involving children can finally be achieved.

References

Goodman, G. S., Golding, J. M., & Haith, M. M. (1984). Jurors' reactions to child witnesses. *Journal of Social Issues*, *40*, 139-156.

Johnson, M. K., & Grisso, T. J. (1986, August). *On the credibility of child eyewitnesses: The jury is still out*. Paper presented at American Psychological Association Conference.

Leippe, M. R., & Romanczyk, A. (1989). Reactions to child (versus adult) eyewitnesses. *Law and Human Behavior*, *13*, 103-132.

Luus, E., & Wells, G. L. (1992). The perceived credibility of child eyewitnesses. In H. Dent & R. Flin (Eds.), *Children as witnesses*. Chichester: Wiley.

Nigro, G. N., Buckley, M. A., Hill, D. E., & Nelson, J. (1989). When juries "hear" children testify: The effects of eyewitness age and speech style on jurors' perceptions of testimony. In S. J. Ceci, D. F. Ross, & M. P. Toglia (Eds.), *Perspectives on children's testimony*. New York: Springer-Verlag.

Ross, D. L., Miller, B. S., & Moran, P. (1987). The child in the eyes of the jury. In S. J. Ceci, D. F. Ross, & M. P. Toglia (Eds.), *Perspectives on children's testimony*. New York: Springer-Verlag.

Spencer, J. (1990). Children's evidence and the Criminal Justice Bill. *New Law Journal*, *140*, 1750-1751.

Spencer, J., & Flin, R. (1990). *The evidence of children: The law and the psychology*. London: Blackstone.

Cases cited

R. v. *Brasier* (1779) 168 ER 202.

R. v. *Brown* (1977) Qd.R.220.

The Relation between Consistency and Accuracy of Eyewitness Testimony

Ronald P. Fisher & Brian L. Cutler

In a typical criminal investigation, victims and bystander eyewitnesses are interviewed repeatedly. By the time a case appears in court, an eyewitness may have been interviewed ten or more times: by a uniformed police officer, a detective, one or more attorneys representing the prosecution, and other attorneys representing the defendant. These interviews are conducted by different people, at different times, under different conditions, and for radically different purposes.

Given the variety of conditions under which the interviews are conducted, it is not unusual for eyewitnesses to generate inconsistent accounts of the crime details. When interviewed in a friendly manner by the prosecuting attorney, the witness may confidently recall that the perpetrator had a mustache, but when badgered by the defense attorney, the witness claims that the perpetrator was clean-shaven. What do such inconsistencies of recollection indicate about the accuracy of the witness's testimony? Should jurors assign lower credibility to witnesses who give inconsistent reports? How diagnostic is consistency of recollection for accuracy?

Our informal survey of judges and lawyers indicates that they strongly believe inconsistency to reflect inaccurate testimony. Their general view is that witnesses who contradict themselves should be assigned lower credibility. A recent job analysis shows that public defenders rate as very important (mean rating = 6.1 on a 1-7 scale) the task of listening to information to find inconsistencies in the witness's statements (Prager, Moran, & Sanchez, 1992). Noted defense strategists (e.g. Bailey & Rothblatt, 1971) suggest trying to elicit inconsistent recollections from witnesses. Bailey and Rothblatt state explicitly: "Capitalize on these conflicts. This is the *most effective way of discrediting [the witness's] entire testimony*" (p. 177; emphasis ours). To ensure that inconsistent recollections are duly noted, Ginger (1977) recommends techniques to instruct jurors of the value of such recollections for the purpose of impeaching witnesses. Indeed, this folk knowledge has made its way formally into the legal system. In evaluating a witness's testimony, jurors are instructed to consider, "Did the witness at some other time make a statement that is inconsistent with the testimony he gave in court" (Florida Standard Jury Instructions in Criminal Cases, 1987, #2.04, sub-para 8).

Despite the legal community's general belief in the maxim, that inconsistency of testimony is diagnostic of inaccuracy, we have been unable to find any empirical research to support (or refute) the claim. Most psychological studies of memory employ a single-test paradigm. As a consequence, information about consistency of responding is generally unavailable. Several isolated studies using the multiple-test procedure have been reported; however, these studies were conducted for other theoretical purposes and do not even report the data on consistency of recollection (e.g. Briggs, 1957; McDaniel & Masson, 1985; Tulving, 1968). Recently a study by Poole and White (1991) shed some light on the matter by conducting a multiple-test procedure and scoring the responses for consistency. Unfortunately, their subjects produced very few inconsistent statements (proportion of inconsistent statements across age groups varied from .00 to .007) so that the data base is minimal. Furthermore, the authors did not compare the accuracy of consistent and inconsistent statements. In sum, there are practically no directly relevant empirical studies on the consistency-accuracy relation. The common belief about the relation, although firmly entrenched, may be just a belief.

We therefore examined empirically the relation between consistency and accuracy of recollection in a controlled setting where we could objectively measure the accuracy of a witness's testimony. In fact, are witnesses who make inconsistent statements any less accurate than those who make consistent statements?

A simplistic model served as a conceptual guideline to explore the relationship between consistency of reporting and accuracy of identification (see Figure 1). This model suggests that the relationship between consistency of reporting and accuracy of identification is mediated by accuracy of the witness's report. That is, witnesses who provide consistent reports (descriptions) are more accurate in their descriptions of the perpetrator than are witnesses who provide inconsistent descriptions. Further, witnesses who provide accurate descriptions of the perpetrator better identify the perpetrator than witnesses who provide inaccurate descriptions. We therefore expected strong positive correlations (a) between consistency of reporting and accuracy of reporting, (b) between accuracy of reporting and accuracy of identification, and (c) between consistency of reporting and accuracy of identification.

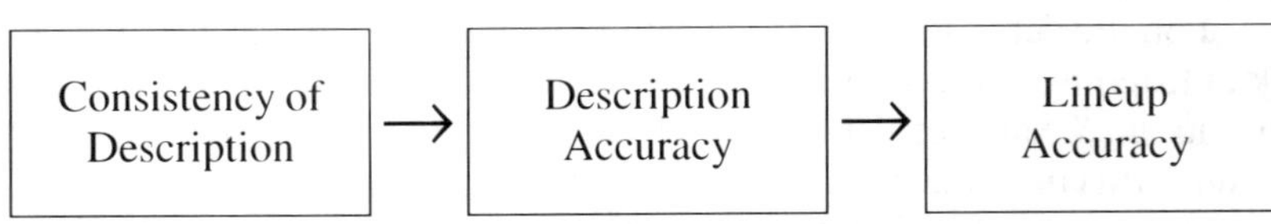

Figure 1: Relationship between Consistency of Description and Lineup Accuracy

Method

A common procedure was employed in all four experiments. One or more confederate intruders interrupted an ongoing university class and apparently stole an object of value (either a professor's wallet, a wristwatch, or some video equipment). The intruders were in view for approximately 30-150 seconds. Shortly thereafter, the student-witnesses (undergraduates from Florida International University) were informed that the intrusion was staged and was conducted for research purposes. Within the next few hours or days, the witnesses described the intruder(s). These initial descriptions were given either in answer to a pre-printed questionnaire (Experiments 1 and 2) or in an interactive interview format (Experiments 3 and 4). Several days later, the witnesses again described the intruder(s). Immediately after this second description, the witnesses were shown one or more videotaped lineups or photoarrays and attempted to identify the intruders. For half of the witnesses, the intruder appeared as one of the members of the lineup (photoarray) and for half, the intruder was absent. The witnesses indicated either the number of the intruder in the lineup (photoarray) or that the intruder was not in the lineup.

Experiment one. Thirty-three students observed the "thief" as he took a wallet from the front of the room. Forty minutes later, the witnesses completed a 16-item questionnaire about the thief's physical appearance (e.g. "What color was the thief's hair?"). The witnesses answered the identical questionnaire five days later. Immediately after, the witnesses observed a five-person lineup and tried to identify the thief.

Experiment two. Twenty-seven students observed as two "thieves" (one male and one female) took some video equipment from the front of the classroom. Twenty minutes later, the witnesses completed the same 16-item questionnaire as in Experiment 1. Two days later the witnesses answered the same questionnaire, and again attempted to identify the thieves from five-person photoarrays. Each witness attempted two photoarray identifications, one of the male thief and one of the female thief. In one of these tests, the target was present and in the other the target was absent.

Experiment three. A total of 135 students observed as two "thieves" (one male and one female) took some video equipment from the front of the classroom. Either later that day or up to three days later, the witnesses participated in a face-to-face, interactive interview with a trained interviewer. During the interviews, the witnesses described the actions that occurred and the physical appearances of the two thieves. The interviews typically lasted approximately 5-15 minutes and were tape recorded for later scoring. Approximately half of the witnesses were interviewed in a fashion that simulated a standard police interview and half were interviewed with the Cognitive Interview. The police interview entailed a sequence of preplanned short-answer questions and was generally hurried (see Fisher, Geiselman, & Raymond, 1987, and George & Clifford, 1992, for descriptions); the Cognitive Interview was conducted at a slower pace and used more open-ended questions and other techniques to invoke the principles of context reinstatement, focused retrieval, guided imagery. and witness-compatible questioning (see Fisher & Geiselman, 1992 for a complete description). Two weeks later, the witnesses participated in a second interview (either standard police or Cognitive). Approximately one quarter of the witnesses participated in each of the four combinations of first and second interviews (Standard/Standard, Standard/Cognitive, Cognitive/Standard, and Cognitive/Cognitive). Immediately after the second interview, all witnesses attempted to identify the two thieves in two five-person photoarray tests (one test for the male thief and one for the female thief).

Experiment four. Eighty-five students observed as two "thieves" took a wristwatch from the front of the classroom. Approximately 15 minutes later another person (the victim) entered the classroom to retrieve his wristwatch that he had accidentally left in the room. He was told that it had been taken earlier. The witnesses were thus exposed to three separate people: two thieves and one victim. Either later that day or up to two days later, the witnesses participated in a face-to-face, interactive interview. One week later, they participated in a second interview. As in Experiment 3, type of first interview (Standard or Cognitive) and type of second interview (Cognitive or Standard) were manipulated, with approximately one quarter of the witnesses participating in each of the four combinations of first interview x second interview. Immediately after the second interview, all witnesses attempted to identify the two thieves and the victim in three five-person photoarray tests (one for the male thief, one for the female thief, and one for the victim).

Results

The descriptive statements were scored for accuracy and for consistency. Accuracy was evaluated by comparing the witness's response to the actual thieves or the victim. Only positive statements were scored. That is, a response was scored as correct or incorrect only if the witness assigned an attribute to the dimension probed (e.g. "he had blond hair"). If a witness failed to respond to a question or said "I don't know", the response was not scored. For each bit of information (e.g. hair color), all of the responses (across all of the witnesses) were assembled. The resulting catalogue of responses was then scored for accuracy independently by several research assistants who finally reached consensus about the accuracy of each response.

Consistency was evaluated by comparing a witness's statement across the two interviews. Only those instances in which the witness produced a positive response on both interviews were scored. If the witness failed to respond to a question or said "I don't know" on either the first of the second interview (or both), the question was not scored for consistency. Thus, an inconsistent response reflects a contradiction, describing the person/object one way on one interview and differently on the other interview. As with the accuracy measure, pairs of responses were evaluated by a team of research assistants until consensus was reached about the inconsistency of a pair of statements.

Identification was scored by assigning a value of 1 for a correct response (either a Hit or a Correct Rejection) and a value of 0 for any incorrect response (either a Miss or a False Identification).

For each witness, the proportion of correct statements, the proportion of consistent statements, and the accuracy of his/her identification were calculated. Note here that, because questions that were not given positive responses were not scored, "proportion of correct statements" refers to the proportion of all statements made (not necessarily number of questions asked) that were answered correctly. Thus, if a witness responded to five of the 10 questions and was correct on 4 and incorrect on 1, he/she would receive a "proportion correct" score of .8 (4 of 5). Similarly, "proportion of consistent statements" refers to the proportion of all scorable pairs of statements (positive answer on both interviews) that were consistent. Proportions were used instead of number of correct (or inconsistent) statements to equate witnesses for the total number of statements made, which varied considerably across witnesses.

Correlation coefficients were calculated (a) between proportion of consistent statements and proportion of correct statements, (b) between proportion of correct statements and identification accuracy, and (c) proportion of consistent statements and identification accuracy. These scores are presented in Table 1, separately for each target person (one target in Experiment 1; two targets in Experiments 2 and 3; three targets in Experiment 4). Thus, for example, the line corresponding to Study 4a refers only to the identification of and the consistency and accuracy of statements about one particular target, the male thief in Experiment 4. Table 1 shows that all of the correlations are rather low. The range of correlation coefficients for the proportion consistent/proportion correct metric was from .01 to .37 (weighted mean = .24); the range for proportion correct/identification accuracy was from -.16 to .27 (weighted mean = .16); the range for proportion consistent/identification accuracy was from -.06 to .23 (weighted mean = .10).

Table 1: Correlations between Consistency and Accuracy of Eyewitness Reports

Exp.	(N)	Consistency/ Description Accuracy	Description Accuracy ID Accuracy	Consistency/ ID Accuracy
1	(33)	.08	–.16	–.04
2a	(27)	.01	.24	–.02
2b	(27)	.09	.17	–.06
3a	(135)	.26*	.15	.15
3b	(135)	.37*	.13	.23*
4a	(85)	.10	.11	–.04
4b	(85)	.24*	.26*	.20*
4c	(85)	.33*	.27*	.02
Weighted Means		.24*	.16*	.10

* = $p < .05$
Total N = 612

These low correlations seem not to reflect a restricted range of scores, as the proportions of consistent statements and the proportions of accurate statements varied substantially in all of the experiments. There are potentially greater measurement problems for the identification accuracy metric, as identification performance was based on only one dichotomous score per witness. Nevertheless, there is not even a hint of a strong correlation, as all of the correlations hover around zero. Furthermore, the correlations were no stronger when the identification accuracy rates were closest to .5, the area with greatest sensitivity (Experiments 2b, 3a, 3b, 4a), than when they were at the extremes, either close to 0 (Experiments 1, 4b, 4c) or close to 1.0 (Experiment 2a). Instead, the correlations were universally low.

One possible explanation for the failure to obtain strong correlations between proportion consistent statements and either of the other measures of accuracy is that consistency is not a psychologically meaningful dimension. That is, perhaps inconsistency simply reflects noise in the data and is not related to anything meaningful. We therefore altered our research question somewhat and asked, not whether inconsistency of description predicts another outcome measure, but instead, whether other variables predict consistency of description. Specifically, we examined whether the similarity between the interviewing conditions at the first and second interviews might affect the proportion of consistent statements.

We reexamined the proportion-of-consistent-statements data from Experiments 3 and 4, in which the type of first and second interviews (Standard or Cognitive) were varied orthogonally. The pattern was almost identical in the two experiments. There was no main effect of either type of first interview or type of second interview, all Fs < 1. However, there was a significant interaction between the two interviews, $F = (1, 131) = 3.69$, $.05 < p < .10$ for Experiment 3, and $F = 11.18\ (1, 81)$, $p < .05$ for Experiment 4. The proportion of consistent statements was higher when the two types of interview were similar (either Standard/Standard or Cognitive/Cognitive) than when the two were different (Standard/Cognitive or Cognitive Standard). The mean proportion of consistent statements (averaged across Experiments 3 and 4) for the four combinations were: Standard/Standard = .79; Cognitive/Cognitive = .79; Standard/Cognitive = .73; Cognitive/Standard = .73.

Discussion

Across the four experiments reported here, the overriding theme is that inconsistency of description is not highly predictive of inaccuracy of recollection. Inconsistency of description was neither strongly related to the accuracy of the description nor to the accuracy of identification.

Technically, four of the eight correlations between consistency of description and accuracy of description were significant, and there was one (of eight) significant correlation between consistency of description and identification accuracy. From a practical perspective, however, these significant correlations are not terribly important, as the magnitude of the correlations was low (the highest being .37). Thus even though the correlation may have been significant, little of the variance in accuracy can be explained by inconsistency.

One should always be sceptical of findings demonstrating either null effects or effects of small magnitude, as sometimes these can be explained by uninteresting artifacts, specifically, insensitive data. At least in the present study, insensitivity seems not to be the explanation, as inconsistency was related to other variables (similarity of the two interviews).

Although we did not find in our experiments that inconsistency was strongly related to inaccuracy, we do not wish to rule out the possibility that under some conditions the two may be strongly correlated. In fact, we have found at least one instance (recollection of passages read earlier) in which consistency and accuracy are strongly correlated (Fisher, Cutler, McCauley, Brock, & Hecht, in preparation). Furthermore, at some level, consistency and accuracy must be related, as logically, an inconsistent response guarantees that at least one response must be incorrect. Our argument is not so much that inconsistency and accuracy are not related, but that the relationship may be considerably weaker, more complex, or less ubiquitous than most people believe. As such, we caution legal decision-makers against reflexively interpreting inconsistency as an indicator of inaccuracy. In the words of the poet Emerson, "Foolish consistency is the hobgoblin of small minds". For those who are more swayed by the sciences, there was no empirical evidence before the current study to support the claim that inconsistency is necessarily diagnostic of inaccuracy. Four experiments later there remains no empirical support.

If the accepted view of the consistency-accuracy relation is incorrect and witnesses are impeached after making inconsistent statements, there are severe consequences for the legal system. The primary concern is that potentially valuable witness information is being withheld from the court for inappropriate reasons. Since the ability to make a correct decision presumably depends on the quality of evidence provided, any diminution of relevant information will lead to less accurate decisions. This is particularly problematic in criminal cases, where the majority of eyewitness evidence is provided by one side, the State. In such cases, the loss of eyewitness evidence not only leads to more errors in general, but almost always biases the case in one direction, against the State.

Although we have argued that our results refute the claim that inconsistency is necessarily diagnostic of inaccuracy, we urge caution in generalizing these results to actual legal cases. As far as we know, these are the only experiments that bear on the issue, so the collective corpus of data (four experiments, 612 witnesses) is not very large. More important, the conditions of our experiments do not necessarily replicate the critical components of legal cases. For example, the witnesses in our experiments had no motivation to fabricate, as their testimony was not going to promote or prevent a real person's incarceration. By comparison, in many criminal cases witnesses are motivated to fabricate. Our results may not generalize to these cases. The reader no doubt can think of many other important dimensions on which our experiments differ from real-life legal cases. We do not wish to argue, therefore, that inconsistency does not indicate inaccuracy and that jurors should never attend to inconsistencies in a witness's testimony. Rather, we wish to offer a more cautious approach, that jurors should not assume that inconsistency *necessarily* indicates inaccuracy.

Assuming that there are some conditions in which inconsistency is predictive of inaccuracy, our goal should be to develop guidelines for witnesses to discriminate between those instances in which inconsistency and inaccuracy are related and those in which they are not related. Toward that goal, we encourage others to pursue the underlying relation.

References

Bailey, F. L., & Rothblatt, H. B. (1971). *Successful techniques for criminal trials*. Rochester: The Lawyers Co-operative Publishing Co. & Bancroft-Whitney Co.

Briggs, G. E. (1957). Retroactive inhibition as a function of the degree of original and interpolated learning. *Journal of Experimental Psychology, 53*, 60-67.

Fisher, R. P., Cutler, B. L, McCauley, M. R., Brock, P., & Hecht, S. (In preparation). *The relation between consistency and accuracy of eyewitness testimony*.

Fisher, R. P., & Geiselman, R. E. (1992). *Memory-enhancing techniques for investigative interviewing: The cognitive interview*. Springfield: Charles C. Thomas.

Fisher, R. P., Geiselman, R. E., & Raymond, D. S. (1978). Critical analysis of police interviewing techniques. *Journal of Police Science and Administration, 15*, 177-185.

Florida Standard Jury Instructions in Criminal Cases (1981).

George, R., & Clifford, B. (1992). Making the most of witnesses. *Policing, 8*, 185-198.

Ginger, A. F. (1975). *Jury selection in criminal trials*. Triburon, CA: Lawpress.

McDaniel, M. A., & Masson, M. E. J. (1985). Altering memory representations through retrieval. *Journal of Experimental Psychology: Learning, Memory and Cognition, 11*, 371-385.

Poole, D. A., & White, L. T. (1991). Effects of question repetition on the eyewitness testimony of children and adults. *Developmental Psychology, 27*, 975-986.

Prager, I. R., Moran, G., & Sanchez, J. (1992). *Assistant public defenders: Job analysis project.* Unpublished manuscript. Florida International University, Miami.

Tulving, E. (1968). Theoretical issues in free recall. In T. R. Dixon & D. L. Horton (Eds.), *Verbal behavior and general behavior theory*. Englewood Cliffs: Prentice-Hall Inc.

The "Authenticity Error" in Real Lineup Procedures. Effects of Suspect-Status and Corresponding Psychological Dissimilarities between Target Person and Distractors: An Experimental Study

Thomas Fabian, Michael Stadler and Peter Wetzels

Introduction

Lineups are sometimes the only way for the police to establish the identity of an offender. However, the results of a lineup procedure can only be used as evidence in court if the witness recognizes the suspect exclusively because of the similarity between the person identified in the lineup and the mnemonic representation of the person seen before in the situation of the criminal act (Köhnken, 1984). In order to meet this requirement the suspect may not differ substantially from the persons used as distractors in the lineup in any particular way.

Psychological research has detected many possible errors that can be made in lineup procedures (Loftus, 1979; Gniech & Stadler, 1981, 1984; Malpass & Devine, 1983; Köhnken, 1990; Stadler, Schindler, & Fabian, 1992), which affect the validity of its results. If all possible errors identified in the literature are taken into consideration and a theoretically "perfect" lineup procedure is carried out, in which non-suspects are used as distractors, it may still be possible to identify the suspect without having been a witness of the criminal act in question. Such an identification without a mnemonic representation of the perpetrator may be possible because of the specific psychological situation of the suspect in a real lineup.

Even if the suspect does not differ physically from the other persons used as distractors in the lineup, he nevertheless differs in his psychological state. As Altavilla has already pointed out in the early fifties, it is very important not to underestimate the emotional impact of being a suspect (Altavilla, 1955, p. 253).

Whether or not the suspect is the offender, he—in contrast to the persons employed as distractors—may be frightened and will experience the lineup procedure as a threatening situation. Furthermore the suspect may suffer loss of control because he is forced to take part in the lineup procedure and his future situation depends on the reaction of the witness over whom he has no influence. In Germany, the persons used as distractors in lineups are usually policemen who do not have to fear any consequences when identified by a witness. These psychological differences between the suspect and the distractors may also be revealed by nonverbal cues.

The following two hypotheses were derived from our assumptions:

Hypothesis 1: Suspects differ in their psychological states from non-suspects used as distractors in real lineup procedures.

Hypothesis 2: Suspects' behaviour in a real lineup is perceived as more authentic than the behaviour of those used as distractors.

If empirical data support hypotheses 1 and 2, the following hypothesis 3 can be deduced:

Hypothesis 3: It is possible for non-witnesses to identify a suspect in a lineup procedure although they have never seen him before because of his different psychological state and his greater behavioural authenticity revealed by non-verbal cues.

From an ethical point of view it would seem impossible to induce the aforementioned feelings, which are characteristic for suspects in a laboratory experiment in order to test these three hypotheses. Therefore, we were fortunate that the second author was called as an expert witness in a criminal court case and was given a video documentation of a real lineup procedure. Two studies using this video-tape were conducted.

Study 1

In study I the first hypothesis—suspects differ in their psychological states from non-suspects used as distractors in real lineup procedures—and the second hypothesis—the suspects' behaviour is more authentic than the behaviour of non-suspects used as distractors—were tested.

Method

Two different trials of a real lineup were filmed on the aforementioned video-tape supplied by a penal court. We copied the sequences during which the six persons in the lineup were observed by the witness. The first of these two sequences lasted 17 seconds, and the second lasted 31 seconds. The lineup consisted of six persons, the suspect (target person) and five policemen (distractors). Each person in the lineup carried a number on his chest. In the second sequence of the lineup procedure all persons carried different numbers and they were standing in a different order than in the first sequence. The following numbers were carried in the order: 3, 5, 10, 1, 12, 8, and 12, 4, 8, 5, 3, 2; the suspect carried number 12 in the first sequence and number 4 in the second sequence.

The video-tape with both sequences was shown six times to each of 26 undergraduate psychology students individually. At each showing the subjects were instructed to observe only one of the six persons in the lineup specified by the two different numbers they carried. Instructions were different for each subject regarding the order of the persons specified. Subjects were given a questionnaire every time they had observed one person. The questionnaire consisted of a list of 15 adjectives with bipolar ("very ..." to "not at all ...") seven-point rating scales. Among the adjectives seven were related to symptoms of stress and another seven related to loss of control in the sense of feeling helpless. An extra adjective was included concerning the authenticity of the behaviour. Subjects were instructed to rate the degree of how much each adjective could be applied to each person observed on the video-tape.

Results

Table 1 shows that the mean ranks of the six persons in the lineup differ significantly concerning almost all adjectives. While the distractor No. 8/5 was rated as the one showing most signs of stress, the target person was rated as the most insecure, least confident, most apathetic, helpless, introverted, anxious and dejected. The target person was also rated as the most authentic, while the distractor No. 8/5 who was rated as the one showing most signs of stress was rated as the second least authentic.

Table 1: Mean rank ratings of psychological state and authenticity of suspect and distractors

	3/12 MR	5/8 MR	10/3 MR	1/2 MR	**12/4** MR	8/5 MR	*p*
Stress							
excited	3.83	3.35	4.56	3.29	3.73	**2.25**	***
strained	4.19	3.69	4.48	2.96	3.06	**2.62**	***
quiet	3.23	3.48	2.15	3.69	3.81	**4.63**	***
calm	2.98	3.33	2.15	3.94	3.98	**4.62**	***
hectic	4.06	3.13	4.23	3.23	3.73	**2.62**	**
tense	3.58	3.73	4.44	3.17	3.06	**3.02**	*
relaxed	3.12	2.94	2.46	4.08	4.13	**4.27**	***
Loss of control							
insecure	3.34	3.68	4.60	3.68	**2.72**	2.98	**
confident	3.77	3.13	2.15	3.98	**4.52**	3.44	***
apathetic	2.65	4.06	4.27	2.73	**2.40**	4.88	***
helpless	3.17	3.60	4.35	3.37	**3.10**	3.42	n.s.
introverted	3.00	4.10	4.52	2.40	**2.06**	4.92	***
anxious	3.69	3.38	4.38	3.79	**2.83**	2.92	*
dejected	3.46	3.73	4.19	3.17	**2.71**	3.73	n.s.
Authenticity							
authentic	3.37	4.21	3.69	3.63	**2.00**	4.10	***

Friedman Test: * $p \leq .05$ ** $p \leq .01$ *** $p \leq .001$
seven-point rating scale (1 = "very ..." to 7 = "not at all"); target person = No. 12/4
N = 26 raters

A two-dimensional data matrix with the six persons in the lineup as objects and the 26 independent ratings of the authenticity of behaviour of these persons as variables was transmitted to a hierarchical cluster analysis. As the dendrogram in Figure 1 shows, two clusters can be identified.

While the distractors are found in cluster 1, the target person is the only element of cluster 2. The distance of the target person to cluster 1 reaches the maximum of the standardized distance measure. This result shows that the target person was not only rated as the most authentic, but that the non-suspects are more similar to each other than to the target person regarding their authenticity of behaviour. Therefore, the target person can be distinguished from the other persons with respect to the authenticity perceived by observers who never saw any of the persons in the lineup before. The results of study I support hypotheses 1 and 2.

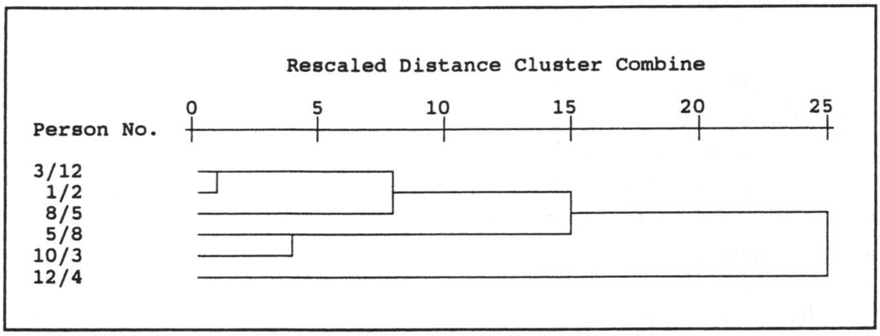

Variables: Authenticity-ratings of 26 independent raters: Squared euclidean distance measure: Agglomeration method: Ward; target person = No. 12/4

Figure 1: Hierarchical Cluster Analysis of persons in the real lineup regarding their authenticity.

Study 2

In study II the third hypothesis—that it is possible for non-witnesses to identify a suspect in lineup procedure although they have never seen him before because of his different psychological state revealed by non-verbal cues—was tested. In this experimental study, two additional hypotheses were tested:

Hypothesis 4: Subjects who are merely asked whether or not there is a suspect in the lineup (open-ended question) will more often answer "I don't know" than those who are told there is a suspect in the lineup (forced choice).

Hypothesis 5: Subjects who are told there is a suspect in the lineup (forced choice) will more often choose the target person than subjects who are only asked whether or not there is a suspect in the lineup (open-ended question).

Previous experimental research with subjects who had been witnesses has shown that the rate of false alarms increases following biased instruction when no suspect is present (Malpass & Devine, 1981; Köhnken & Maass, 1988). Instead of being witnesses, in this study subjects will be—according to hypothesis 3—non-witnesses. Hypothesis 4 is simply based on the phenomenon well-known from social psychology that forced choice instruction—that does not produce reactance—increases the tendency to come to a decision. Hypothesis 5 is based on the assumption that there is an interaction between the increase of the tendency to come to a decision and the existence of non-verbal cues resulting in a higher rate of correct identifications of the suspect.

Method

In study II the same video-tape as in study I was used as stimulus material. The video-tape was shown in group experiments. The total sample (N = 330) of subjects consisted of 60 psychology students (1st and 2nd year), 208 law students (1st to 3rd year), 32 administration employees and 30 middle-aged adults without higher education.

Answering sheets with two different instructions were randomly distributed among the subjects. The first instruction (forced choice condition) reads as follows:

In the following film you will see six persons in two separate lineup procedures. These persons carry different numbers in each sequence. Among these persons there is one person accused of a criminal offence. Please mark the number of the person you think is the accused in the following two diagrams for both trials.

In the second instruction (open-ended question), the beginning of the third sentence "Among these persons there is one person accused of ..." was substituted by "Among these persons there may be one person accused of ...". On both answering sheets were two rows of boxes with the numbers carried by the persons in both sequences of the lineup. Subjects were asked to mark one of the numbers in each of the two rows of boxes, if they thought this number was carried by a suspect. On the reverse side of the answering sheet subjects were asked to state the reasons why they thought the person they chose was the suspect.

Results

Table 2 shows the distribution of judgements in the first trial.

Table 2: Frequency of judgements made by Ss in the first trial

	numbers carried by the persons in the lineup						
I don't know	3	5	10	1	**12**	8	Σ
57	38	34	48	42	72	21	255

expected value: 42.5; expected %: 16.7%; observed: 28.2%; $Chi^2 = 34.26$; $p < .001$
target person = No. 12
N = 330; missing cases = 18

Eighteen subjects made no judgement in the first trial (which only lasted 17 seconds) and 57 subjects answered "I don't know". Of the remaining 255 judgements, 42.5 judgements (16.7%) would have been expected for each person in the lineup if randomly selected by the subjects. In contrast, the observed number of judgements regarding the target person was 28.2%. Such distribution has the statistically highly significant random probability of p < .001. While 72 subjects chose the target person as the suspect, the other persons in the lineup were chosen by only 21 up to 48 subjects. This result is even clearer in the second trial (Table 3).

Table 3: Frequency of judgements made by Ss in the second trial

	numbers carried by the persons in the lineup						
I don't know	12	**4**	8	5	3	2	Σ
30	19	97	44	41	42	57	300

expected value: 50; expected %: 16.7%; observed: 32.3%; $Chi^2 = 68.00$; $p < .001$
target person = No. 4
N = 330; missing cases = 0

In the second trial, 30 subjects answered "I don't know" and 300 subjects made a judgement. Ninety-seven subjects (32.3%) chose the target person, while 50 judgements (16.7%) would have been expected if judgements were randomly distributed. These results support hypothesis 3.

As some subjects chose different persons in the two trials, we also looked at the distribution of judgements among the group of subjects (n = 97) who made consistent judgements.

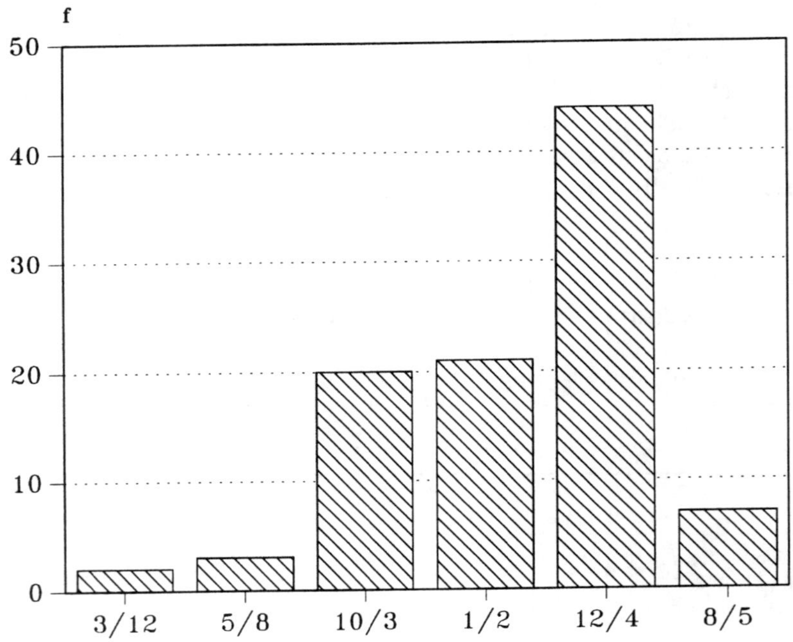

target person = No. 12/4

Figure 2: Distribution of consistent judgements in both trials.

As Figure 2 shows, 44 (45%) of those subjects with consistent judgements chose the target person carrying numbers 12 and 4, two other persons received 20 (No. 10/3) and 21 (No. 1/2) judgements. The remaining three persons were altogether chosen by only 12 subjects making consistent judgements.

What were the reasons for choosing the target person? Those subjects who made consistent choices of the target person gave the following answers:

- target person behaved in an authentic way;
- target person was least play acting;
- target person tried to hide his face;
- target person appeared apathetic;
- target person seemed to be uninvolved;
- target person was indifferent;
- target person seemed to suffer more than the others.

These answers correspond to the results of study I, where the target person was rated by another group of subjects as the person who showed most signs of loss of control and as being the most authentic.

In order to test hypotheses 4 and 5, the sample was split in two groups according to the type of instruction received. The first group consisted of subjects who had a forced choice instruction, and the second group consisted of subjects who were given an open-ended question.

Table 4: Comparison "Forced Choice" vs. Open-ended question"

	forced choice	open-ended	*p*
1st trial	$n = 56$	$n = 156$	
"I don't know"	20 (12.8%)	37 (23.7%)	$Chi^2 = 6.20$; $p < .01$
target person	40 (29.4%)	32 (26.9%)	$Chi^2 = 0.20$; n.s.
2nd trial	$n = 160$	$n = 170$	
"I don't know"	10 (6.3%)	20 (11.8%)	$Chi^2 = 3.03$; $p < .05$
target person	60 (40.0%)	37 (24.7%)	$Chi^2 = 8.10$; $p < .01$

A comparison of these two groups (Table 4) shows that 20 subjects with the forced choice instruction answered "I don't know" in the first trial, whereas 37 subjects with the open-ended question gave the same answer. While there were altogether less "I don't know" answers in the second trial, there were still twice as many among the group with the open-ended instruction. These results support hypothesis 4.

Table 4 shows furthermore that there is no significant difference between the two groups regarding the number of correct judgements, i.e. choosing the target person in the first trial, while there is a significantly higher number of correct judgements among the group with the forced choice instruction in the second trial. These results do not support hypothesis 5 clearly. While the results of the first trial are not in accordance with our hypothesis, the results of the second trial support hypothesis 5.

Discussion

The results of the analysis of a real lineup procedure in study I support our first hypothesis that suspects differ in their psychological states from non-suspects used as distractors in real lineup procedures. The results revealed significant differences on the dimension loss of control with the suspect being perceived as showing more signs of loss of control than the persons employed as distractors. Differences were also found concerning the stress related items, but on this dimension it was not the target person but a distractor who was perceived as showing more signs of stress than the other five persons in the lineup. This may be due to the fact that the videotaped lineup stemmed from a rather spectacular criminal court case. The police officers employed as distractors were themselves strongly interested in the solving of the case as well as highly aware of public control and attention. They were therefore—although for other reasons than the suspect—also tense and under stress. One can also not rule out the possibility that the police officers, assuming that the suspect experienced stress, may have tried to imitate the experience of stress. The police officers might therefore well have appeared to give off stress signals, while, on the other hand, giving the overall impression of lower authenticity. As there were clear differences in ratings on authenticity between the suspect and the non-suspects, this interpretation as well as our hypothesis 2 are supported by our data.

Both results taken together point to the conclusion that a further systematic error can occur in lineup procedures carried out in the usual setting with one person knowing himself to be a suspect and other persons knowing that they are not suspects. We will call this systematic error the "authenticity error".

The source of this "authenticity error" lies in the correspondence between the objective status (a) of a person (suspect vs. non-suspect) and related differences in psychological state (b). This psychological state reveals itself by non-verbal cues which are to a large extent not subject to deliberate control. Therefore, differences in (b) can be identified. Due to the correspondence between (a) and (b), these differences then make possible a deduction concerning differences in (a), and thus may lead to an accurate identification of a suspect without the existence of a matching mnemonic picture.

In this study only one real lineup procedure could be analyzed. This suffices to prove the existence of the described "authenticity error". However, we cannot say how often this error actually occurs in the practice of lineup procedures. The probability of the occurrence of this error will be influenced for example by the quality of the mnemonic picture conserved by the witness as well as by other marginal conditions of the lineup. Concluding from our study, it can be said that in lineup procedures including non-suspects as distractors it is not possible to rule out the possibility that witnesses might base their decision on non-verbal cues which point to differences in the psychological state of the persons in the lineup. They might choose a person without being able to match this person to their menmonic picture, or choose that person who stands out from the others in order to complement a hazy menmonic picture.

In study II, the consequences of the "authenticity error" could be shown with the real-life material. Subjects who had never before seen the target person were nonetheless able to identify the suspect in the lineup more often than would be expected in a random choice. It is worth pointing out that the two distractors who were rated as being the least authentic in study I were among the three persons who got the fewest consistent judgements in study II. The reasons for their judgements as reported by the subjects in study II concern their perception of differences in psychological state and authenticity, thus corresponding to the results in our first study.

In this context, the differences between forced-choice vs. open-ended questions are of further importance. While hypothesis 4 was supported by our results in both trials—subjects answered more often "I don't know" when given the open-ended question—hypothesis 5 was only supported by the results of the second trial, which may be due to the fact that the presentation in the first trial lasted only 17 seconds. However, the differences between the groups with forced choice instruction and open-ended question indicate that the forced choice instruction intensifies the effect of the non-verbal cues revealed by the target person.

In real-life lineups, the effects of the "authenticity error" might therefore well be especially strong, if there is a forced choice situation as well as a hazy mnemonic picture. To put it differently, there exists an interaction between the already known systematic error of biased instruction and the "authenticity error".

Regarding further research in legal psychology the results of our studies point to the conclusion that there exists a systematic error variable—i.e. the psychological state of a person actually accused in a criminal court case—which cannot be reproduced and manipulated easily outside of real court cases in an experimental laboratory with subjects who are not actual suspects. One way to overcome these restrictions is the method used here, i.e. to use stimulus material recording real life situations. This specific version of a "Wirklichkeitsexperiment" (reality experiment) (cf. Stern, 1902) requires, however, a more intensive cooperation between science and legal practice. This could probably add to a further refinement of recording techniques in this area. Better recordings and extended possibilities to interview witnesses after lineup procedures would be of great value for experimental replication studies to analyse the systematic error described here, and possible marginal conditions influencing its effects. As Malpass and Devine (1984) have pointed out, realism is an important aspect of psychological research on witness testimony.

Note Study 1 was carried out with the support of Regina Munzel.

References

Altavilla, E. (1955). *Forensische Psychologie II.* Graz: Styria.

Gniech, G., & Stadler, M. (1981). Die Wahlgegenüberstellung - methodische Probleme des kriminalistischen Wiedererkennungsexperiments. *Strafverteidiger*, *1*, 565-570.

Gniech, G., & Stadler, M. (1984). Methodische Probleme beim kriminalistischen Gegenüberstellungsexperiment. *Zeitschrift für Sozialpsychologie*, *15*, 194-198.

Köhnken, G. (1984). Zum Beweiswert von Identifizierungen durch Augenzeugen: Eine methodologische Analyse. *Forensia*, *5*, 1-21.

Köhnken, G. (1990). Fehlerquellen im Gegenüberstellungsverfahren. In G. Köhnken & S. L. Sporer (Eds.), *Identifizierung von Tatverdächtigen durch Augenzeugen* (pp. 157-177). Stuttgart: Verlag für Angewandte Psychologie.

Köhnken, G., & Maass, A. (1988). Eyewitness testimony: False alarms or biased instructions? *Journal of Applied Psychology*, *73*, 363-370.

Loftus, E. F. (1979). *Eyewitness testimony.* Cambridge, MA: Harvard University Press.

Malpass, R. S., & Devine, P. G. (1981). Guided memory in eyewitness identification. *Journal of Applied Psychology*, *66*, 343-350.

Malpass, R. S. & Devine, P. G. (1983). Measuring the fairness of eyewitness identification lineups. In S. Lloyd-Bostock & B. R. Clifford (Eds.), *Evaluating Witness Evidence* (pp. 81-102). Chichester: John Wiley & Sons.

Malpass, R. S., & Devine, P. G. (1984). Research on suggestion in lineups and photospreads. In G. L. Wells & E. F. Loftus (Eds.), *Eyewitness Testimony* (pp. 64-91). Cambridge: Cambridge University Press.

Stadler, M., Schindler, H. & Fabian, T. (1992). The influence of eyewitness observation and photographic presentation on the identification of persons in lineups. In F. Lösel, D. Bender, & T. Bliesener (Eds.), *Psychology and Law* (pp. 286-291). Berlin: de Gruyter.

Stern, W. (1902). Zur Psychologie der Aussage. *Zeitschrift für die gesamte Strafrechtswissenschaft*, *22*, 315-370.

Misinformation Methodologies: Explaining the Effects of Errant Information[1]

Daniel B. Wright

A prevalent line of research in eyewitness testimony concerns the susceptibility of eyewitness reports to misleading postevent information, or *misinformation*. Beginning with Loftus' pioneering work in the seventies (cf. 1979), several psychology experiments have demonstrated that subjects who have errant postevent information suggested to them often report remembering this as opposed to the information originally shown. Psychologists, however, are divided about the explanations of this effect. According to Loftus, the misinformation damages the original memory trace, leaving a *blended* representation. McCloskey and Zaragoza (1985), however, have argued that other explanations are plausible. Two alternative explanations are that many subjects fail to encode the original information (the *vacant slot* explanation) or that both pieces of information may coexist in separate memory traces. In this paper I review these explanations, describe some of the methodologies that have been used to differentiate between them and discuss the implications of the findings both for theories of cognitive psychology and for judicial matters.

In United States courtrooms it has long been accepted that to be permissible expert testimony "must be sufficiently established to have gained general acceptance" (*Frye v. US*, 1923, p. 1014).[2] Because of the disagreement among psychologists on why the misinformation effect occurs, it is at present questionable whether testimony on the subject should be admissible. According to Egeth and McCloskey "it is no means clear that expert psychological testimony would improve jurors' ability to evaluate eyewitness testimony [and it may have] detrimental effects" (Egeth & McCloskey, 1984, p. 301). Even among those who feel expert testimony should be permissible, it is agreed "the issue is controversial" (Wells, 1984, p. 313).

Although there has been a movement away from strict adherence to the Frye criterion towards accepting evidence if it is scientifically valid and reliable (Giannelli, 1981), the Frye criterion still serves as a guideline (see Kassin, Ellsworth, & Smith, 1989). This is due to difficulties within the judicial system for assessing the validity and reliability of scientific research. The judicial system is composed of, according to Moenssens, Inbau, and Starrs (1986), "lawyers [who] as a group evidence an appalling degree of scientific illiteracy ... [and] many judges [who] simply do not understand evidence based on scientific principles" (p. 7).

The permissibility of expert testimony on the subject has been argued at great length (see discussions in *American Psychologist*, 1983, v. 38 and *American Psychologist*, 1984, v. 39). Here, I explore the reasons why there is no general agreement among psychologists. The central issue is that the experimental findings are open to different interpretations. Each time a particular methodology has been used which apparently falsifies one or other of the explanations, counter arguments are put forward which successfully defend the explanation under attack.

Explanations for the Misinformation Effect

To make this discussion more comprehensible, I will refer to a typical experimental scenario in which misled subjects view a COKE can in the original presentation of a slide sequence but in a postevent narrative have 7-Up suggested. Three main explanations, the vacant slot, blend and coexistence explanations, each produce a different prediction for what cognitive representations the misled subjects would have in their minds after they had just been presented with the two incompatible stimuli. Figure 1 illustrates these.

The vacant slot explanation proposes that the misinformation effect can be attributed to a proportion of the subjects failing to encode the original information. Because these subjects have not encoded the original information, COKE in our example, when they read the misinformation about 7-Up, it does not contradict any existing beliefs and therefore is easily accepted.

According to the blend explanation, subjects encode the misinformation within the same cognitive structure as the original information, resulting in a composite representation. There are conceptual difficulties determining what this blend might be (though see Metcalfe, 1990), but essentially it is some combination of the two.[3] The blend depicted in Figure 1 is not intended to make claims about its form, only to represent the combination. The critical factor of this explanation is that the original trace is damaged. Given a forced choice recognition test between the original and the postevent stimulus subjects will reply with whichever one is most similar to the resulting blend.

The third explanation states that the original and misinformation coexist and are stored separately. A variety of factors may lead to subjects choosing the misinformation at testing. These include social desirability, where subjects answer what they believe the experiment wants to hear; source misattribution, where subjects recall both stimuli but forget from where they remember each; memory salience, where regardless of other factors subjects respond with the most salient of the two traces; and the notion that the original trace may exist but is not accessible at testing (see Morton, Hammersley, & Bekerian, 1985).

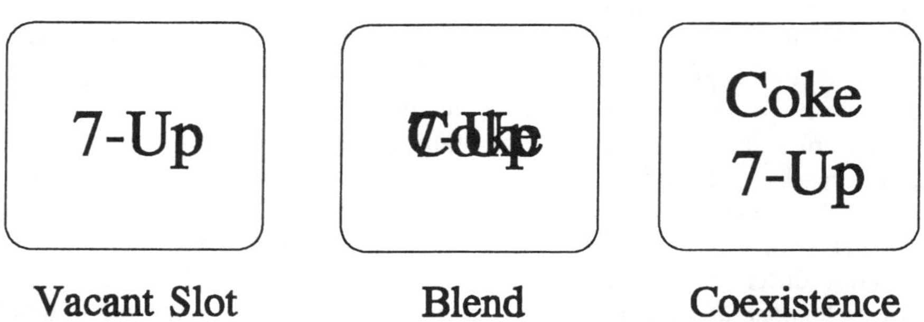

Figure 1: What the different explanations predict will be in misled subjects' memory after being presented with errent postevent information.

In comparing these three explanations it is important to recognize that they are proposed as a means of accounting for a particular effect, they are not statements about what necessarily always occurs; they all may contribute to the effect. Research has attempted to show which of the explanations accounts for most of the observed effect.

Past Research Techniques

The basic framework for misinformation experiments involves the presentation of original information, followed by some misinformation and then a testing procedure to determine which of the stimuli, if either, is remembered. In this section some of the main techniques used to discriminate between the blend and the coexistence explanations are described. Several of these methodologies have been previously discussed (Fruzzetti, Toland, Teller, & Loftus, 1992; Zaragoza & McCloskey, 1989) and therefore will be only briefly summarized.

The most influential testing procedure is what has been referred to as the standard set-up. In a typical experiment, all the subjects view a slide sequence. Half of them then read a postevent narrative which includes an errant detail; the misinformation. At testing subjects are given a forced choice recognition test between the original and the misinformation. The result is that more of the misled subjects choose the misinformation than control subjects who were not misled.

McCloskey and Zaragoza (1985) modified this testing procedure in an attempt to demonstrate that the original memory trace is not damaged by the misinformation. After a similar presentation sequence, they gave subjects a forced choice recognition test between the original information and a previously unseen foil. In six experiments using this procedure, they found control and misled subjects performed at approximately the same level. While these studies appear to show that the misinformation does not damage the original memory trace, Loftus, Schooler and Wagenaar (1985) note that this procedure is not sensitive to memory blends In particular, it is likely that the original stimulus will be more similar to a blend of the original and misinformation than an unseen foil (although see note 2). Therefore, subjects with a blend representation in their memory are likely to choose the original information in a forced two choice recognition test than some previously unseen foil.

Other testing procedures have also been used. These include asking YES/NO questions (Tversky & Tuchin, 1989; Belli, 1989), measuring response time and confidence (Loftus, Donders, Hoffman, & Schooler, 1989), probing subjects after testing (Zaragoza & Koshmider, 1989) and allowing second guesses (Loftus, 1979). The problem is trying to make the procedure sensitive enough to differentiate these explanations because each yields similar predictions.

Another set of experimental techniques which have been used are warning subjects that the information in the postevent narrative may not be correct. These can be distinguished by two factors: whether the warning is presented before or after the narrative and whether it is a specific or a vague warning. Clearly a specific warning before the presentation, of the form: "you are about to read a paragraph in which a 7-Up can is described, in the slide sequence it was not a 7-Up", will alter the way in which people encode the information. More interestingly, a vague warning prior to presentation, which attributes the narrative to a naïve source, also limits interference (Smith & Ellsworth, 1987). Presenting the warning before the misinformation, however, dramatically alters the task demands, in particular, the encoding of the misinformation.

Presenting warnings after the misinformation has been encoded yields more interesting predictions of what subjects' cognitive representations should be like at testing. Greene, Flynn and Loftus (1982) conducted one of the first warning studies in which they compared a warning given before the misinformation was presented with one presented afterwards. Warning subjects before the presentation of misinformation limited interference but warning them afterwards did not. Christiaansen and Ochalek (1983) also used a warning after an errant narrative was read. They found that warned subjects were able to edit out errant details. The warnings used in both these studies were, however, vague. The more specific of these, Christiaansen and Ochalek's (1983) warning, read "a few [of the narrative's statements] are incorrect" (p. 469). This is not specific enough to assume that the misled subjects would be aware that the misinformation was indeed false.

Cognitive Surgery: Unveiling the Remnants

In order to know if the original memory trace has been damaged, it is necessary to gently, but precisely, extract the misinformation from the misled subject, revealing whatever remnants of the original memory trace exist. The tool for this *cognitive surgery* is a highly specific warning. Lindsay (1990) and Wright (1993) have each used specific warnings presented after the errant postevent narrative. Before describing their results it is worth showing the predictions of three explanations when a specific warning is used after the misinformation.

The predictions are depicted in Figure 2. According to the vacant slot explanation, warned subjects who otherwise would have replied with the misinformation will correctly respond only at chance levels because they would not have encoded the original information. The blend explanation predicts that what remains will be a damaged memory trace. (As with Figure 1, the illustration in Figure 2 is not making a statement about the exact form this trace will take, but is meant to convey that the damaged trace may still bear some resemblance to the original stimuli.) In a forced choice recognition test, subjects should reply with the original information rather than the unseen foils, but to a lesser extent than if the original memory trace not been damaged. According to the coexistence explanation removing the misinformation trace will leave the subjects in the same mental state as they would have been if no misinformation had been previous presented. Their recognition accuracy on subsequent tests should be similar to groups who had no misinformation presented. Details of these predictions and how they can be estimated are given in the appendix of Wright (1993).

Lindsay's (1990) warning was given two days after subjects read the postevent narrative. It read "there is no question on this test for which the correct answer was mentioned in the story [i.e. the postevent narrative]" (p. 1080). With this two day lag he concluded that the misinformation did interfere with the original information.

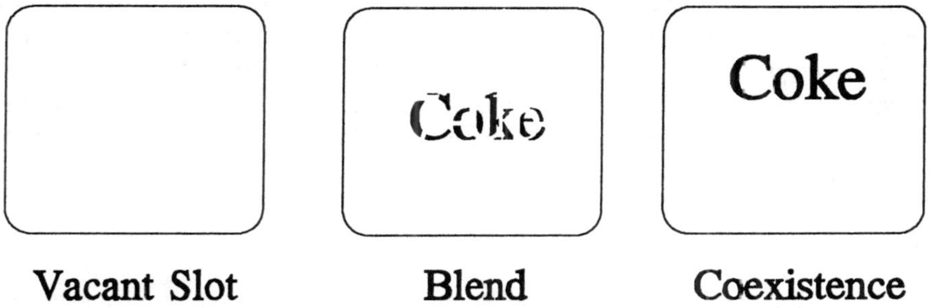

Figure 2: What the different explanations predict will be in misled subjects' memory after being given a specific warning.

Wright (1993) also used a specific warning but his warning was presented immediately after subjects read the postevent narrative. His results suggested that the coexistence explanation worked better than the blend explanation.

The critical difference between these two studies was that Lindsay's addressed distant interference and Wright's addressed recent interference. It appears that in the short term, contradictory traces may coexist but as time elapses they combine. This makes intuitive sense if we consider the memory for both the original and the misinformation to be composed of a content element and a source element. Even where the content elements are different, if their sources are also different, then they will not be contradictory. The problem occurs when the source elements decay, which research in social psychology indicates should happen first (Pratkanis, Greenwald, Lieppe, & Baumgardner, 1988). At this point the content elements will contradict and a blend representation may result in order to resolve the discrepancy. The notion that individual episodic traces exist in the short term but are incorporated into more generic structures as time passes has received support from several areas in cognition. This is described by Brewer (1986) as the partial reconstructivist view.

In short duration experiments, where the source element has not decayed, misled subjects may still report the misinformation either because they have errantly confused the two sources (source misattribution) or they simply do not attempt to remember which source element is linked with which content element. Because accessing the source would not be helpful for long term remembering, which is the more common activity, it presumably would not be a strategy used naturally. Therefore, even though identifying the sources of the content elements is a strategy which subjects could use effectively (see Zaragoza & Koshmider, 1989), subjects would not naturally attempt to do so. It follows that if a witness is being questioned soon after an event, asking her/him to say from where s/he remembers the information may be a useful strategy to suggest, but after a longer delay it may not be as helpful.

Several points are worth summarizing. First, past research has failed to disentangle the explanatory cause of the misinformation effect, principally because the predictions for each, in terms of experimental data, are too similar. Second, using a specific warning presented immediately after the misinformation does, theoretically, allows these explanations to be disentangled. Two studies, Lindsay (1990) and Wright

(1993), which used specific warnings have been discussed. Though their findings differed, together they suggest that in the short term multiple traces may coexist, but as time passes a blend is formed. Though further laboratory and field research is necessary, because of the improved methodological techniques, it can be hoped that in the near future there will be ample agreement in psychological quarters to allow expert courtroom testimony on the topic.

References

Belli, B. F. (1989). Influences of misleading postevent information: Misinformation interference and acceptance. *Journal of Experimental Psychology: General, 118*, 72-85.

Brewer, W. F. (1986). What is autobiographical memory? In D. C. Rubin (Ed.), *Autobiographical memory* (pp. 25-49). New York: Cambridge University Press.

Christiaansen, R. E., & Ochalek, K. (1983). Editing misleading information from memory: Evidence for the coexistence of original and post-event information. *Memory & Cognition, 11*, 467-475.

Egeth, H. E., & McCloskey, M. (1984). Expert testimony about eyewitness behavior: Is it safe and effective? In G. L. Wells & E. F. Loftus (Eds.), *Eyewitness testimony: Psychological perspectives* (pp. 283-303). London: Cambridge University Press.

Fruzzetti, A. E., Toland, K., Teller, S. A., & Loftus, E. F. (1992). Memory and eyewitness testimony. In M. Gruneberg & P. Morris (Eds.), *Aspects of memory: Vol. 1. The practical aspects* (pp. 18-50). London: Routledge.

Gianelli, P. C. (1981). General acceptance of scientific tests - Frye and beyond. In E. J. Imwinkelried (Ed.), *Scientific and expert testimony*, (pp. 11-32). New York: Practising Law Institute.

Greene, E., Flynn, M. S., & Loftus, E. F. (1982). Inducing resistance to misleading information. *Journal of Verbal Learning and Verbal Behavior, 21*, 207-219.

Kassin, S. M., Ellsworth, P. C., & Smith, V. L. (1989). The "General Acceptance" of psychological research on eyewitness testimony: A survey of the experts. *American Psychologist, 44*, 1089-1098.

Lindsay, D. S. (1990). Misleading suggestions can impair eyewitnesses' ability to remember event details. *Journal of Experimental Psychology: Learning, Memory and Cognition, 16*, 1077-1083.

Loftus, E. F. (1979). *Eyewitness testimony*. Cambridge, MA: Harvard University Press.

Loftus, E. F., Donders, K., Hoffman, H. G., & Schooler, J. W. (1989). Creating new memories that are quickly accessed and confidently held. *Memory & Cognition, 17*, 607-616.

Loftus, E. F., Schooler, J. W., & Wagenaar, W. A. (1985). The fate of memory: Comment on McCloskey and Zaragoza. *Journal of Experimental Psychology: General, 114*, 375-380.

McCloskey, M., & Zaragoza, M. (1985). Misleading postevent information and memory for events: Arguments and evidence against memory impairment hypotheses. *Journal of Experimental Psychology: General, 114*, 1-16.

Metcalfe, J. (1990). Composite holographic associative recall model (CHARM) and blended memories in eyewitness testimony. *Journal of Experimental Psychology: General, 89*, 609-626.

Moenssens, A. A., Inbau, F. E., & Starrs, J. E. (1986). *Scientific evidence in criminal cases* (3rd Ed.). New York: Foundation Press.

Morton, J., Hammersley, R. H., & Bekerian, D. A. (1985). Headed records: A model for memory and its failures. *Cognition, 20*, 1-23.

Pratkanis, A. R., Greenwald, A. G., Lieppe, M. R., & Baumgardner, M. H. (1988). In search of reliable persuasion effects: III. The sleeper effect is dead. Long live the sleeper effect. *Journal of Personality and Social Psychology, 54*, 203-218.

Smith, V. L., & Ellsworth, P. C. (1987). The social psychology of eyewitness accuracy: Misleading questions and communicator expertise. *Journal of Applied Psychology*, *72*, 294-300.

Tversky, B., & Tuchin, M. (1989). A reconciliation of the evidence on eyewitness testimony: Comments on McCloskey and Zaragoza (1985). *Journal of Experimental Psychology: General*, *118*, 86-91.

Wells, G. L. (1984). A reanalysis of the expert testimony issue. In G. L. Wells & E. F. Loftus (Eds.), *Eyewitness testimony: Psychological perspectives* (pp. 304-314). London: Cambridge University Press.

Wright, D. B. (1993). Misinformation and warnings in eyewitness testimony: A new testing procedure to differentiate explanations. *Memory*, *1*, 153-166.

Zaragoza, M. S., & Koshmider, J. W. (1989). Misled subjects may know more than their performance implies. *Journal of Experimental Psychology: Learning, Memory and Cognition*, *15*, 246-255.

Zaragoza, M. S., & McCloskey, M. (1989). Misleading postevent information and the memory impairment hypothesis: Comment on Belli and reply to Tversky and Tuchin. *Journal of Experimental Psychology: General*, *118*, 92-99.

[1] This research was prepared as part of the author's doctoral dissertation and as such was financially supported by a LSE studentship and an ORS scholarship. Further financial support came from a grant from the University of London's Central Research Fund, awarded to the author to investigate misinformation and eyewitness testimony. Helpful comments came from many including Julie Dockrell, George Gaskell and Rachel Wright.

[2] Frye vs. United States, 291 F. 1013 (D.C. Cir. 1923).

[3] More specific predictions about the form of the resultant blend are obviously welcomed. It is this imprecision, not the notion that memories combine, which McCloskey and Zaragoza (1985, pp. 15-16) are most adamantly against.

Previous Knowledge and Delay in the Recall of Filmed Events[1]

Margarita Diges

Introduction

Modern research, on the role that knowledge structures stored in memory play on a variety of processing functions like perception, categorization, encoding, retrieval, and comprehension, has made us familiar with notions such as natural categories, frames, scripts, schemata or mental models. In every case, the aim of the research has been to show that organized knowledge structures of particular stimuli and events present in the environment: (a) provide for more efficient processing of these stimuli and events; (b) influence the particular interpretation of an ambiguous stimulus event; and (c) can lead to falsely remembered congruent details because of inferences made at encoding, retention or retrieval of information. In contrast, the absence, or the inadequate selection, of a knowledge structure results in poorer or null processing of data (see Alba & Hasher, 1983, for a critical review).

Support for the view that a previous knowledge structure has important consequences for the processing of related incoming information in social or everyday domains comes from two different lines of research. The first is centred on the findings of Bargh and his colleagues (Bargh, 1984; Bargh & Pietromonaco, 1982). They showed that priming trait concepts (even without awareness that trait concepts have actually been primed) do influence the later judgment of a target person in terms of the primed trait. The frequent use of a construct or category appears to result in a chronic likelihood of using the category to process social inputs (Higgins & Bargh, 1987). Individual differences emerge in the content of these frequently activated or "chronically accessible" categories (Higgins, King, & Mavin, 1982), so that, for a given domain, subjects could be classified as "chronics" or "nonchronics", depending on their possession or not of a "chronically accessible" category relevant for the domain (Bargh, 1988).

There are some processing advantages for "chronic" subjects when relevant information to the "chronically accessible" category is present in the environment. There are automatic paths associated with information relevant to the category, and the stimuli relevant to the category are processed automatically. In comparison to "nonchronics", "chronic" subjects need less attentional resources to process information related to the category, when the focus of automatic and attentional processes is the same (Bargh, 1984, 1988; Higgins & Bargh, 1987).

On the other hand, Conway and Bekerian (1987) found that knowledge of everyday contexts can facilitate the processing of highly associated information (i.e. faster recognition of an emotive word after the prior presentation of a context-related sentence). For Bekerian and Conway (1988) "everyday context" knowledge includes not only information about those general classes of situations that people ordinarily experience, but also about those situations that most people never, or seldom have, encountered in their lives. Everyday context includes information about rules governing social behaviour, actors, actions and reactions. Bekerian and Conway also recognised that, although some of everyday context knowledge is accessible to conscious awareness, its operations are not exclusively conscious.

The influence of attitudes on eyewitness memory also spread to qualitative aspects of recall. Boon and Davies (1988, Exp. 3) found a clear relationship between the subjects' previous attitude (toward or against the 1985 miners' strike in UK) and their selection of a line drawing, depicting an ambiguous picture, seen in a former part of the experiment. Six line drawings, which were based on the original picture were shown. They varied in the degree in which a police officer appeared threatening. Subjects who had supportive opinions of the strike showed a strong tendency to select the more threatening drawing, while those subjects opposing the strike exclusively selected the less threatening drawing. This finding gives support to the claim that previous beliefs bias the interpretation of ambiguous information seen before.

There is less empirical support for the contention that false recall might be induced from semantic knowledge structures. In fact, there is still some debate concerning the finding of the "passive intrusions in episodic memory" (Alba & Hasher, 1983; Higgins & Bargh, 1987). Several reasons can account for the difficulties to reach significant results. First, short retention intervals between encoding and retrieval of information, and simple verbal materials as stimuli, may promote both an accurate (i.e. verbatim) recall and an easy discrimination between the originally presented information and its interpretation. In this way experimental conditions and materials may put difficulties to the finding of intrusion errors.

Secondly, while recall performance vary with prior knowledge (i.e. the activation of a schema or its content), recognition varies minimally (Alba & Hasher, 1983), so it may also be differences in the sensitivity of retrieval measures to "catch" intrusions from prior knowledge or beliefs.

Thirdly, some " passive intrusions" are not commission errors as they are right inferences from semantic knowledge. Despite their internal origin, they are "hints" in a memory test becoming indistinguishable from real hints. Recent analyses on qualitative aspects of recall has shown interesting differences between descriptions of externally (perceived) and internally (imagined or suggested) generated memories (Johnson & Raye, 1981; Schooler, Gerhard, & Loftus, 1986; Schooler, Clark, & Loftus, 1988), and differences between the recollective experience which accompanies episodic and semantic retrieval (Tulving, 1985).

The work of Loftus and her colleagues on "suggested" memories has shown that a distortion (or false recall) can be induced in memory through the use of postevent suggestions (Loftus, 1979). Based on the postulated differences between perceived and imagined memories (Johnson & Raye, 1981), descriptions of true and distorted memories have been found to differ in several aspects. Descriptions of true memories contain more sensorial and contextual details and less of the subject's cognitive processes than do descriptions of false memories. Moreover, false memory descriptions mention more often the object's function, the pronoun "I" and verbal hedges, and sometimes are longer than descriptions of true memories (Schooler et al., 1986, 1988).

On the other hand, although the false recall produced by misleading questions is externally induced, the resulting description is founded on general or semantic knowledge. So, it is likely that these aspects of recollective experience (not explicitly requested) reflect to some degree the origin of the memory. Moreover, when explicitly asked, subjects seem to be capable of differentiating the recollective experience which accompanies a memory mainly based on episodic system from the recollective experience of a memory mainly based on semantic system (Tulving, 1985). Tulving claims that when "ecphoric" information, the amalgam of episodic and semantic information available to retrieval, is more heavily weighted towards the episodic side (i.e. it is mainly based on the episodic trace), the recollective experience is one of "remembering". When ecphoric information is mostly semantic, the subject' s experience is of "knowing" that an item has been presented before.

Some experimental findings suggest that subjects are capable of discriminating between rich and poor episodic traces. When the episodic trace of an event is impoverished, whether because of its more automatic encoding (a word read vs. generated, Gardiner, 1988, Exp. 2; divided attention vs. full attention at encoding, Gardiner & Parkin, 1990), or whether because of a long retention interval, (Tulving, 1985, Exp. 2), subjects continue to retrieve information via the semantic system. But they feel that their experience is not of "remembering", but of "knowing".

At this point it is worth noting that delay between encoding and misinformation, peripheral detail (probably not attended), and plausibility (automatic encoding) are variables which have been shown to increase the likelihood of accepting misleading information (Hall, Loftus, & Tousignant, 1984), resulting in suggested memories.

In summary, it seems that people may differentiate between distinct experiences, associated to the relative involvement of semantic system on their episodic memory performance, if asked implicitly (like in descriptions of suggested memories) or explicitly (like in "known" and "remembered" judgments).

Taken together findings and theoretical notions, we can advance some predictions on the recall and recollective experience of a belief-related event by subjects who strongly maintain this belief. In a situation in which we could activate an affective knowledge structure in the memories of subjects (a "chronic category", in the terminology of Higgins & Bargh, 1987), related to the event to-be-remembered, we could expect better encoding and retrieval of perceptual information, and more distortions, both as consequences of the semantic structure involvement. As false recall or inventions are sometimes correct because they correspond to plausible inferences from the semantic knowledge structure used, they may not appear as distortions, but instead they are "imagined" details or actions. So, we could expect that some characteristics of internally generated memories, such as more mention of cognitive processes and dubitative expressions, may appear. It seems quite possible that some of the above expectations would be more apparent when the recall test is delayed because of the fading of episodic traces.

To examine the accuracy of these predictions we selected a short filmed event, depicting a traffic accident. A car is seen while going along an avenue until it arrives at an intersection, where it is intercepted by another car, resulting in a collision of the two cars. The first car was seriously damaged in the collision. However the drivers were not recognizable.

Following the claims established by Bargh (1984) about processing advantages for a "chronic" category, when activated by relevant information present in the environment, an adequate category and its relevant stimulus were needed. A belief related to people as drivers consists of assumed differences between men and women, that is, driver stereotypes with regard to sex. When differences are favourably biased towards men as drivers, it could say that the stereotype is a "masculine" one. On the contrary, differences positively weighted towards women as drivers indicate a "feminine" stereotype. For both, the so-called "masculine" and "feminine" stereotypes, we assume that the underlying knowledge structure is a frequently and affectively loaded category, what has been called a "chronically accessible" category (Higgins & Bargh, 1987), or "everyday context" knowledge (Bekerian & Conway, 1988).

We can also assume that the relevant stimulus to the chronic category, or everyday context, is different in each case. For those who maintain a "masculine" stereotype, the relevant stimulus could be a male driver. For people who maintain a "feminine" stereotype, the relevant stimulus should be a woman as driver and protagonist of the event. If we prime this aspect of the everyday context (the belief about the actor), and direct the subject's attention to it, it may provoke a decrease in the amount of resources required to deal with the event. As a consequence, the subject will have a resource "surplus" in encoding the related information. By priming semantic knowledge which would lead us to use it as a framework, both for encoding and retrieval of information about the event, we can advance some specific hypotheses about quantity and quality of recall.

(1) At the stage of encoding, 'chronic' subjects primed with their relevant stimulus will be able to automatically process it, and devote more attentional resources on other aspects of the witnessed event. So, this better encoding will result in an increased retention and recall of sensorial and contextual information about the event.

(2) Distortions or alterations of the original memory might occur, whether as a consequence of biased interpretations or wrong guesses. Nevertheless, it should be kept in mind that the intrusion may sometimes coincide with the real occurrence, and it may be possible that free recall tests are not be very sensitive measures of stored information, at least when short retention intervals are employed. So, a larger amount of clear distortions should be expected to occur more often at a long rather than a short delay.

(3) Instead of clear intrusions or distortions, we suggest that the inferred details, or "self-suggestions", based on generic knowledge, would resemble internally generated memories, such as the "unreal" memories based on misleading information (Schooler et al., 1986). For both inferences and suggestions to be discriminated from real memories, the principles of reality monitoring (Johnson & Raye, 1981) could be applied. If "self-suggested" memories, resulting from the automatic activation of a chronic category by a relevant stimulus, are different from the more "real" memories, mostly based on episodic information, free recall narratives would exhibit some of the reality monitoring cues. Therefore, we hypothesized that, compared to free recall

narratives of non-activated chronic categories, narratives from self-suggested memories would contain more information about the subject's cognitive processes, more dubitative expressions (Intraub & Hoffman, 1992), and they would be described with a larger number of words.

The present study was planned to obtain empirical support for these hypotheses.

Method

Subjects Subjects were selected for the experiment based on their responses to a questionnaire administered to 380 undergraduate students of psychology four months before. The questionnaire consisted of 15 characteristics related to driving, each of which students rated on a 10 point scale for its degree of male-descriptiveness and female-descriptiveness as drivers. The subject's task was to locate the male driver at any point on the scale for each trait (for example, driving speed, powerful car, resources in situations, safety consciousness, speed of reflex, etc.), and then repeat the task for a female driver.

It was considered that the subject would hold a strong stereotype depending on the resulting gap between male and female drivers for each trait and the final total. Thus, the scores ranged in a continuum from zero (males and females the same in all traits) to 135 (the maximum possible difference between the two sexes in all traits).

Two groups of 35 subjects each were initially selected on the basis of their scores. "Masculine" stereotype subjects were those who had the highest scores (about 10% superior of the total of subjects), because in all cases male drivers came out favourably in these evaluations. "Feminine" stereotype subjects were those who scored lowest (about 10% inferior of the total), that is, those who systematically tried to equate males and females as drivers. Some of these subjects (13) failed to come to the lab for the first time, and still some others were not available or were discarded for the second time to preserve a minimal balance in the "feminine" stereotype group, so the final sample was composed of 41 subjects. The "masculine" stereotype group included ten males and 11 females, and the "feminine" stereotype group was composed of seven men and 13 women.

Material Subjects were presented with a video film of a traffic accident (27 secs. duration). Half of each stereotype or "chronic" group (M and F groups) was randomly allocated to a condition in which they were told in advance that the protagonist driver was a man (MM and FM groups), while the remaining subjects were warned that the driver was a woman (MW and FW groups).

Design and procedure Subjects were shown the film in groups ranging from four to 12 people. They were told that, in the film a woman (a male, depending on experimental condition) was going to suffer a traffic accident, and they were asked to pay close attention to the film.

After viewing the video film subjects went to another room and they engaged during 15 minutes in a filler task (they were given a personality test unrelated to the experiment). After that subjects were asked to write their free recall taking as much time as they needed. Five or six weeks later, subjects were unexpectedly asked to return to the lab and to write again their free recall. As before, there were no time constraints. The experimental design is a factorial 2 ("masculine" vs. "feminine" stereotype) x 2 (male vs. female driver) x 2 (immediate vs. delayed recall), being the former two between-subject factors, and the later a within-subject factor. While it was not expected significant main effects of stereotypes nor driver sex on qualitative and quantitative measures of recall (described below), it was hypothesized a main effect of delay and significant effects of the interaction stereotype x driver sex, (primed chronic category by its relevant stimulus) on these variables, and that delay could make more apparent the interaction effects.

Results

Quantitative and qualitative characteristics of recall were measured separately, as we were interested not only on the amount of details recalled, but also on the recollective experience related to the act of remembering. Free recall narratives were first evaluated for accuracy and distortions.

Recall accuracy was measured by counting the number of micropropositions correctly remembered, following a procedure used in Diges, Rubio, and Rodríguez (1992) for scoring the recall of this film. Since micropropositions include sensorial and contextual details about objects, actions and agents, it was taken as a suitable measure for the perceptive attributes of memories.

Errors in sensorial and contextual reported details, as well as intrusions, additions or misinterpretations of actions were scored as *distortions*.

Accuracy An Analysis of Variance was computed on accuracy scores. No significant main effects of Stereotype, Driver Sex or Delay were found. But the Stereotype x Driver Sex interaction effect was significant for the total accuracy, $F(1,37) = 5.20$, $p < .03$, as expected. Primed groups scored higher than non-primed groups on immediate (MM = 17.18 vs MW = 16.20, and FW = 19.10 vs FM = 13.90) and delayed recall (MM = 17.82 vs MW = 14.30) and FW = 17.50 vs FM = 13.90).

Distortions The ANOVA, calculated on the distortion scores, revealed no main effects, but some interaction effects reached significance levels. First, there was a Stereotype x Delay interaction effect, $F(1, 37) = 5.07$, $p = .030$, showing that on immediate recall, "feminine" stereotype groups made more distortions than "masculine" groups, but the inverse was true on delayed recall. The triple interaction Stereotype x Driver Sex x Delay was also significant, $F(1, 37) = 4.45$, $p = .042$. In order to obtain a more precise interpretation of this interaction, separate ANOVAs for Immediate and Delayed scores were calculated. A significant Stereotype x Driver Sex interaction effect appeared on Delayed Distortion scores, $F(1, 37) = 7.52$, $p < .01$. Primed groups made more distortions than non-primed groups when Delayed recall (MM = 5.36 vs MW = 2.90 and FW = 3.90 vs FM = 2.80), but not on Immediate recall, indicating that the predicted result of intrusions from semantic memory would be more likely to appear at long retention delays.

Qualitative characteristics As we have advanced that "self-suggested" memories are based on inferences from generic structures, free recall narratives were assessed by two independent judges with regard to mention of cognitive operations and dubitative expressions (characteristics attributed to internally generated memories). Also, the length of the narratives in number of written words and order changes were measured. In cases in which the two judges differed in their ratings, agreement on ratings was attempted. If it was not possible to reach an agreement, these data were discarded.

Low scores on these qualitative measures were rearranged according to a new variable, which was intended to apprehend the aspects of interest to our hypothesis. In this way, mentions of cognitive operations and dubitative expressions were seen as indicating the cognitive (recollective) experience that accompanied the recall of the subject and the new "Cognitive Experience" score was obtained for each subject by summing his or her previous mentioning of cognitive processes and dubitative expressions. Results of the analyses of variance performed on each of these dependent measures are separately examined.

No significant main effects were found on "Cognitive Experience", but the effect of the Stereotypes x Driver Sex interaction was significant, F (1,37) = 4.80, p = .035, showing that the appearance of internal origin of memory were more often present on the narratives of primed groups on immediate recall (MM = 2.36 vs MW = 1.00, and FW = 2.70 vs FM = 1.10) and on delayed recall (MM = 2.18 vs MW = .70, and FW = 2.10 vs FM = 1.60).

The only significant effect on "Length of the Narrative" was again the Stereotype x Driver Sex interaction, F (1,37) = 7.42, p = .01. Subjects primed with their relevant stimulus seemed need more words to express their recall than non-primed subjects, on immediate recall (MM = 120.9 vs MW = 106.7, and FW = 136.6 vs FM = 94.20 and on delayed recall (MM = 116.55 vs MW = 88.60, and FW = 125.90 vs FM = 84.10).

The ANOVA computed on "Order Changes" revealed a main effect of Stereotypes, F (1,37) = 4.87, p = .034. "Masculine" stereotype groups changed more often the canonical order corresponding to the event development than "feminine" groups did, and this was true for immediate (MM = .54 and MW = .60 vs FW = .40 and FM = .40) and delayed recall (MM = .82 and MW = 1.20 vs FW = .20 and FM = .20). No other main effect nor interaction was significant.

Discussion

The results support the contention that encouraging prejudiced subjects to use their chronic categories in the processing of the event produces some differences on their later recalls. Compared with "masculine" and "feminine" subjects, non-primed, "masculine" subjects who were told that the protagonist of the accident was a man and "feminine" subjects who were said that the driver was a woman remembered the event in a different manner. As far as they include more sensorial and contextual details, "self-suggested" memories of these later subjects were more complete, but also included more errors or distortions. More interestingly, "self-suggested" memories revealed some of the characteristics ordinarily attributed to internally generated memories (Johnson & Raye, 1981), such as a greater mention of cognitive processes. Also, in agreement to some findings on characteristics of unreal memories (Schooler et al., 1986), self-suggested memories seemed to need a greater number of words to be expressed.

The dependent variable which showed unexpected results was "Changes of Order", that is, when subjects did not follow a canonical ordering of the episodes in the recall of the event (introduction, complication, and resolution). Because these changes could be seen as "unstructured production", an indicator of the truth of statements in child sexual abuse (Steller, 1989), it was expected these changes could be negatively related to self-suggested memories. Instead, results showed that deviations of the canonical order were more frequent for subjects who maintained "masculine" stereotypes. To my knowledge, there is no logical explanation for this result, and perhaps it needs a replication before an ad hoc explanation is attempted.

Concerning delay, it can be said that the passage of time did not have an uniform effect. Accuracy scores and length of the narratives were lower on delayed recall, but not enough to show a significant effect. In agreement with the advanced hypothesis, delay emphasized the increase of distortions as a consequence of the primed use of semantic knowledge at encoding, although this effect was accompanied with the delay x stereotype interaction. This is unexpected in that it showed that during immediate recall, "feminine" subjects committed more errors than "masculine" subjects, but the trend did not remain in delayed recall.

So, it is clear that prior knowledge, when especially primed to be applied to the suitable event, has some empirical effects on retrieval. First, results showed a better recall as a consequence of priming the use of a chronic category. In agreement with other results (Bargh & Pietromonaco, 1982) it seems that subjects in this situation can benefit from an increase in the automatization of the encoding process and the corresponding savings in the attentional resources, which will serve to "catch" more information about the event.

Second, identifiable distortions when chronic categories were primed did occur in a delayed recall test, implying that with longer retention intervals, expectancy-driven intrusions were evident. As Tulving (1985) stated, across the time the episodic trace become poorer and the ecphoric information at retrieval is more weighted towards the prior knowledge of the subject about the event. In this way, the greater involvement of the schematic structures makes more likely the use of prototypical expectations associated with them for filling in gaps, so creating false "self-suggestions".

Third, clear distortions are not the unique "self-suggestions". The present results showed that some not false but anyway inferred information was present in the free recall of subjects primed to use their chronic categories about the event. Indeed, the free narratives of these subjects contained more of the traits ordinarily attributed to imagined or unreal memories than the narratives of their non-primed counterparts. From this point of view, the term "self-suggested" memory seems suitable because it applies to a memory which is both suggested from the subject's prior knowledge, and distinct of a more real or perceptive memory.

Another interesting implication of the data is that "self-suggested" memories represent a case of discrimination failure, because the subject believes that they are externally generated. A similar discrimination failure may result from a misleading question when it induces an unreal memory in the work of Loftus and her colleagues.

Three aspects are shared by suggested and "self-suggested" memories. First, as above pointed out, it seems to be easier to induce an unreal memory when its referent is out of the attentional focus. So, a high degree of automatic processing is present in suggested and "self-suggested" memories, and automaticity has been linked to the component of 'familiarity" in recognition (Mandler, 1980).

Second, records of intentional constructive processes constitute a significant cue for deciding that the origin of a memory is internal (Johnson, Foley, Suengas, & Raye, 1988; Intraub & Hoffman, 1992), and the absence of such record provoked by automaticity may suggest to the subject that the memory has an external origin.

Third, the present data showed that "self-suggested" memories contain a great amount of sensorial and contextual details. Also, suggested memories do not differ from real memories in terms of geographical (contextual) details (Schooler et al., 1986).

Thus, the final result (for suggested and "self-suggested" memories) is an internal memory uncharacteristic of its class: it "sounds" familiar, has sensorial and contextual detail, and it lacks a record of intentional processes. On these bases, the subject would wrongly attribute the memory to a perception.

In summary, we found that prior knowledge increase the completeness of recall, but this is not obtained without a cost in form of an increase of distortions, more evident when recall is delayed. This problem has practical implications for eyewitnesses' recall in real settings. When faced with delinquency cases, people seldom have a "neutral " position. For example, stereotypes that put together delinquents and drug addiction could become a "chronically" accessible category, ready to be used when its relevant stimulus is present in the scene of a real aggression, or when some other person attract the attention to it by means of the stereotype' s label. As a consequence, later recall could be contaminated with distortions and misinterpretations of actions from the stereotype generic information and, most important, its increased completeness might render it to appear more credible.

References

Alba, J. W., & Hasher, L. (1983). Is memory schematic? *Psychological Bulletin, 93*, 203-231.

Bargh, J. (1984). Automatic and conscious processing of social information. In R. Wyer & T. Srull (Eds.), *Handbook of social cognition: Vol. III* (pp. 1-42). Hillsdale, NJ: L.E.A.

Bargh, J. (1988). Automatic information processing: Implications for communication and affect. In L. Donohew, H. Sypher & E.Higgins (Eds.), *Communication, social cognition and affect* (pp. 9-32). Hillsdale, NJ: L.E.A.

Bargh, J. & Pietromonaco, P. (1982). Automatic information processing and social perception: The influence of trait information presented outside of conscious awareness on impression formation. *Journal of Personality and Social Psychology, 43*, 437-449.

Bekerian, D. A., & Conway, M. A. (1988). Everyday contexts. In G. M. Davies & D. M. Thomson (Eds.), *Memory in context: Context in memory* (pp. 305-318). Chichester: John Wiley & Sons Ltd.

Boon, J. C. W., & Davies, G. (1988). Attitudinal influences on witness memory: Fact and fiction. In M. Gruneberg, P. Morris, & R. Sykes (Eds.), *Practical aspects of memory: Vol. I* (pp. 53-58). Chichester: John Wiley & Sons.

Conway, M. A., & Bekerian, D. A. (1987). Situational knowledge and emotions. *Cognition and Emotion, 1*, 145-191.

Diges, M., Rubio, M.E., & Rodríguez, C. (1992). Eyewitness memory and time of day. In F. Lösel, D. Bender, & T. Bliesener (Eds.), *Psychology and law. International perspectives* (pp. 317-320). Berlin: Walter de Gruyter.

Gardiner, J. M. (1988). Functional aspects of recollective experience. *Memory and Cognition, 16*, 309-313.

Gardiner, J. M., & Parkin, A. J. (1990). Attention and recollective experience in recognition memory. *Memory and Cognition, 18*, 579-583.

Hall, D. F., Loftus, E., & Tousignant, J. P. (1984). Postevent information and changes in recollection for a natural event. In G. L. Wells & E. F. Loftus (Eds.), *Eyewitness testimony. Psychological perspectives* (pp. 124-141). Cambridge: Cambridge University Press.

Higgins, E. T., & Bargh, J. (1987). Social cognition and social perception. *Annual Review of Psychology, 38*, 369-425.

Higgins, E. T., King, G. A., & Mavin, G. H. (1982). Individual construct accessibility and subjective impressions and recall. *Journal of Personality and Social Psychology, 43*, 35-47.

Intraub, H., & Hoffman, J. E. (1992). Reading and visual memory: Remembering scenes that were never seen. *American Journal of Psychology, 105*, 101-114.

Johnson, M. K., Foley, M. A., Suengas, A., & Raye, C. L. (1988). Phenomenal characteristics of memories for perceived and imagined autobiographical events. *Journal of Experimental Psychology: General, 117*, 371-376.

Johnson, M. K., & Raye, C. L. (1981). Reality monitoring. *Psychological Review, 88*, 67-85.

Loftus, E. F. (1979). *Eyewitness Testimony*. Cambridge, MA: Harvard University Press.

Loftus, E. F. (1982). Remembering recent experiences. In L. S. Cermak (Ed.), *Human memory and amnesia* (pp. 239-255). Hillsdale, NJ: L.E.A.

Loftus, E. F., Korf, N. L., & Schooler, J. W. (1989). Misguided memories: Sincere distortions of reality. In J. C. Yuille (Ed.), *Credibility assessment* (pp. 155-173). Dordrecht: Kluwer Academic Publishers.

Mandler, G. (1980). Recognizing: The judgment of previous occurrence. *Psychological Review, 87*, 252-271.

Schooler, J. W., Clark, C., & Loftus, E. F. (1988). Knowing when memory is real. In M. Gruneberg, P. Morris, & R. Sykes (Eds.), *Practical aspects of memory: Vol. 1* (pp. 83-88). Chichester: John Wiley & Sons.

Schooler, J. W., Gerhard, D., & Loftus, E. F. (1986). Qualities of the unreal. *Journal of Experimental Psychology: Learning, Memory, and Cognition, 12*, 171-181.

Steller, M. (1989). Recent developments in statement analysis. In J. C. Yuille (Ed.), *Credibility assessment* (pp. 135-154). Dordrecht: Kluwer Academic Publishers.

Tulving, E. (1985). Memory and consciousness. *Canadian Psychology, 25*, 1-12.

[1] This research was supported by the grant PB89-0170 from the DGCICYT.

Effects of Preparation on Internal and External Memories[1]

Antonio L. Manzanero and Margarita Diges

Johnson and Raye (1981) proposed a model based on the distinctive qualities of representations of internal and external memories and on the reasoning process which occurs in reality monitoring. According to this model, the information about memory representations are coded neither automatically nor directly in the precise moment when they are formed. They postulated the existence of four types of essential features through which people might differentiate between internal and external representations. External memories hold more contextual and sensorial features and more semantic details, while self-generated memories exhibit more information about cognitive operations. This Johnson and Raye (1981) theory has been supported by more recent studies (e.g. Johnson et al., 1984, 1988; Suengas & Johnson, 1988) which have also manipulated variables such as delay. The process which people use to discriminate the two kinds of memories depends on several factors. Johnson and Raye (1981) emphasise that it does not always follow the same pattern and that it will vary according to the memory information, the conditions at encoding and the costs of error.

Several experiments suggest the existence of characteristic features for different types of memory. For example, there are studies which have found differential features for external memories in comparison to self-generated events such as dreams (Johnson, Kahan, & Raye, 1984) or imagery (e.g. Johnson, 1988; Johnson, Foley, Suengas, & Raye, 1988; Johnson, Raye, Wang, & Taylor, 1979; Suengas & Johnson, 1988).

In this way, Johnson and Raye (1981) distinguished three categories of self-generated information: (a) re-representations of perceptual experience or memories about something previously experienced; (b) co-temporal thinkings, elaborative and associative processes which connect or enhance the on-going perceptual experience but which are not necessarily part of the original representation; (c) fantasies, which combine new information with imagined events. We could add three more categories of self-generated information: (1) that generated by misleading information; (2) self-suggested information on the basis of previous knowledge; and (3) lies.

The above-mentioned studies can be considered as an attempt to examine the *discrimination processes* between internal and external memories; their main aim has been to study the process that people follow to differentiate between their own memories. On the other hand, there are studies which have tried to examine the characteristic features of several types of memory information (Schooler et al., 1986, 1988; Alonso-Quecuty, 1992). These studies have used the differential features proposed by Johnson et al. in their model, and their main aim has been to examine how different types of memory information are affected by different variables. The aims are not the only thing in which these studies differ. Johnson et al. (1984, 1988) used daily live material, autobiographic memories from dreams and imaginings with the analysis based mainly on asking for the evaluation of the subject's own recall and application of discrimination rules. Schooler et al. (1986, 1988) analyzed the descriptions made by subjects about a single object. And Diges (1992) as well as Alonso-Quecuty (1992) studied each individual statement as a whole.

Schooler, Gerhard and Loftus (1986) used the Reality Monitoring Model to try to establish the characteristic features of really perceived objects and of the descriptions of not perceived but suggested objects. In their study, slides were shown to people depicting a traffic accident in a crossroad where there was a yield sign. A misled group saw the same series of slides but with a yield sign substituted for a stop sign. Afterwards, the misled group read questions which implied that the stop sign was a yield sign. The descriptions made by the misled subjects who admitted the suggested information as real were compared with the descriptions given by the real-information subjects. Schooler et al. (1986) identified a series of features which differentiated the two: descriptions of suggested memories were significantly longer and had more verbal hedges, more references to cognitive operations and less sensorial details than reality-originated descriptions.

Later, Schooler, Clark and Loftus (1988) carried out a second study which changed the material (three stolen objects replaced the yield sign) and the modality of recall (oral instead of written recall). The results showed that the suggested memories had more references to cognitive processes, more self-references (the pronoun "I" appeared more frequently) and more verbal hedges, whereas in the real memories there were more allusions to perceptive processes and more sensorial details. However, there were no differences in the length of descriptions of internally generated narratives compared to external memories.

Alonso-Quecuty (1992) has tried to differentiate between real memory and lies using the features proposed by Johnson and Raye (1981). For this purpose, she used as material a film of an incident. After the film, half of the subjects were asked to report the event lying in such a way that the aggressor was exculpated and later they had to report what really happened. The other half of the subjects were first asked for the real story and secondly for the false one. She also manipulated a second variable: time to prepare their reports (immediate or delayed). The descriptions of the lies contained more internal characteristics than the descriptions of the true stories, but only when subjects were asked to recall or lie immediately. Delayed true statements contained more internally generated, while delayed false statements contained more external characteristics, except for idiosyncratic information (what the subjects thought and felt during the event). In this latter case, the false statements contained less idiosyncratic information than the true statements.

Finally, Diges (1992) has studied the effect of previous knowledge or belief about typical events on the coding and retrieval of information about a witnessed event. In this study, subjects holding extreme masculine or feminine sex driver stereotypes were told that the driver in a filmed traffic accident was a man or a woman, and afterwards were asked to recall the event. Results showed that priming an extreme category or schema can improve immediate free recall, but any advantage disappeared with a delay of six weeks. Further, the delay increased the number of distortions or incorrect details reported consistent with the driver stereotypes. Memories based on extreme schemata showed the attributes of internally originated memories (Johnson & Raye, 1981) or suggested memories (Schooler et al., 1986) on immediate but not on delayed recall.

As can be seen, researchers have explored how several factors may influence attributes and discrimination processes in both internal and external memories. It has been observed that several variables have opposing effects on characteristic attributes for each of the two memory types, for example a lie and a real memory (Alonso-Quecuty, 1992).

Suengas (1991) points out five variables which influence reality monitoring processes: age, subject matter, delay, thinking or talking about memory contents, perceptive resemblance and the reduction in cognitive mechanisms.

Delay and, of course, thinking or talking about eyewitnessed events are major factors. As described by Alonso-Quecuty (1992), delay caused internal memories (those obtained by lies) to be intermingled, reducing differentiation from external memories, because subjects generate a very rich representation which could lead to reality characteristics appearing more often in lies.

Suengas and Johnson (1988) found that the most durable aspect of memory representations were contextual information; while the most degradable was idiosyncratic information. On the basis of these results, Suengas (1991) argued that the only source of errors between perceived and imagined events is idiosyncratic information: if we do not influence the process, delay produced better discriminations about the memory sources (Suengas, 1991). That could seem to be in disagreement with Alonso-Quecuty's results (1992). However, we must take into consideration the other variable mentioned by Suengas: thinking and talking about the events. Suengas (1991) affirmed that delay is useful because time exaggerates the differential characteristics of internally and externally originated information. She also argued that thinking about an event affects real and imagined memories in very different ways. If the event has emotive connotations, then thinking and talking about it will increase internal characteristics of the events. Because of that, discrimination will be more difficult. The emotive characteristics are among the most important aspects of a witnessed event. Thus, thinking and/or talking about an event reduce reality characteristics. To keep eyewitnesses from talking or thinking about an experienced event is very difficult, if not impossible.

In summary, the reality monitoring process involves discriminating among several memory sources. There are two general memory sources: perception and self-generation. Both types of descriptions of memory information have been found to differ in terms of the length of the narrative, the amount of sensorial and contextual details, the mentioning of cognitive processes and in general idiosyncratic information. Several studies have showed that these characteristics vary over time.

Therefore, it could be interesting to explore the effect of preparation on the characteristics of "internal" (imagined) and "external" (real) memories. Following recent research (Alonso-Quecuty, 1992; Suengas & Johnson, 1988) it was hypothesized that real memories of subjects in the preparation condition would contain more sensorial and contextual details and more internal characteristics - in terms of the Johnson and Raye (1981) reality monitoring - than subjects in the spontaneous condition. Also, statements of subjects asked to prepare a report of an imagined event should contain more external characteristics than the imagined memories of subjects who do not receive instructions about preparing their statements.

Method

Design and subjects

Two variables were of interest, the origin of the memory (perceived vs. imagined) and the preparation of reports (prepared vs. spontaneous), both manipulated as between-subjects factors. The subjects were 64 male and female undergraduate students from the University Autónoma of Madrid. Subjects were assigned at random to the four groups. Accuracy measures (sensorial and contextual details, distortions, impossible information and inventions), and qualitative variables associated with internal characteristics (explanations, length of the narrative, changes in the narrative order, mentioning of cognitive processes and hesitant expressions) were drawn from the free recall descriptions.

Materials and procedure

Half of the subjects were asked to remember a filmed traffic accident (27 seconds duration) shown on a video screen. The rest of the subjects were presented with an oral description of the accident and were asked to imagine it. Then half of each group were asked to recall immediately what they had seen or imagined, and the remainder were asked to prepare written reports.

Following a procedure used in previous work (Diges, 1988, Diges et al., 1992) the statements were typed and analyzed by two independent trained judges in terms of the presence or absence of the quantitative and qualitative variables. Later, they evaluated the whole statements. Final scores were assigned by agreement.

Results and Discussion

The analyses (ANOVA) showed that imagined declarations, compared with reality declarations, exhibited more sensorial and contextual details, $F(1,60)=164.782$, $p<.0001$; more distortions, $F(1,60)=4.034$, $p<.05$; more "impossible information", $F(1,60)=4.369$, $p<.05$, and were longer, $F(1,60)=20.233$, $p<.001$. Also, they had less explanations, $F(1,60)=4.722$, $p<.05$ and less hesitant expressions $F(1,60)=6.691$, $p<.01$. In other words, the imagined statements unexpectedly showed more external characteristics than the reality statements.

Spontaneous compared with prepared reports exhibit less sensorial and contextual details $F(1,60)=5.36$, $p<.05$; and less hesitant expressions $F(1,60)=5.874$, $p<.01$. The interaction effects of origin of memory x preparation of reports on hesitant expressions was also significant, $F(1,60)=5{,}874$, $p<.01$.

Because of these results are partially in disagreement with our predictions and with previous results, we explored further. Imagined reports had more sensorial and contextual details, associated to external memories. A check of the procedure showed that these results were due to the "imagine" instructions. It produced that the imagined narratives had more details than normal. Subjects under the reality condition had few opportunities to perceive all the details showed in the film. In the reality condition, events occurred quickly and, furthermore, subjects had to process several details simultaneously. Meanwhile, the "imagine" subjects were provided with a sequential description of the event, so they had more opportunities to process details.

Because of this, we considered it interesting to analyze separately the preparation effect on internal memories and on external ones. Moreover, by taking into consideration the results of other authors (Alonso-Quecuty, 1992; Suengas & Johnson, 1988) we hypothesized that preparation would produce an internalisation of the reality memories and an externalisation of imagined memories. Thus, each variable was analyzed independently in the internal and external groups. Results are presented first for the external memories and then for internal ones.

External memories

A t-test was computed on accuracy and qualitative scores. The effect of preparation on sensorial and contextual details ($t(28)=1.618$; $p< .05$) and on hesitant expressions ($t(28)=2.687$; $p< .01$) was significant in both cases. Thus, external prepared declarations had more hesitant expressions ($M=1.2$) than external spontaneous declarations ($M=0.267$).

We also observed that with preparation there were more sensorial and contextual details ($M=12.8$; $M=10.8$ respectively). These results could be due to the preparation process which consists not only in information organisation, but also in a higher effort to recall, both of which could lead to greater remembering.

These results are in accordance with the findings of Alonso-Quecuty (1992) who found that delayed narratives had more sensorial and contextual information and more idiosyncratic features. Also, our results coincide with the ones by Suengas and Johnson (1988) who found that delay produced that real narratives had the same amount of contextual information but modified idiosyncratic characteristics. They observed that thinking and talking about the stored information produced higher idiosyncratic scores when subjective and affective connotations were the main characteristics.

In summary, when previously experienced information is prepared, recall will exhibit more internal characteristics (idiosyncratic information) and greater amounts of detail than in the spontaneous conditions. In other words, preparation causes external declarations to become more internal.

Internal memories

A t-test was computed on accuracy and qualitative scores. The effect of preparation on sensorial and contextual details ($t(32)=1.867$; $p<.05$) and explanations ($t(32)=1.680$; $p<.05$) was significant.

Prepared imagined narratives had less idiosyncratic information, in the sense that there were less explanations (*M*=1.118) than in the spontaneous descriptions (*M*=2.294). Thus, the imagined memories lost their internal characteristics. And also, subjects under the prepared conditions recalled more details (*M*=31.588) than in the spontaneous condition (*M*=27.235), as happened in the real memory case, and because of the same reasons.

These results fit those of Alonso-Quecuty's (1992). She too found that delayed false declarations had less idiosyncratic information and more sensorial and contextual details than immediates. Thus, preparation causes internal narratives to become more external.

General Discussion

The Reality Monitoring Model (Johnson & Raye, 1981) was applied to the study of the effects of preparation on internal and external memories. Statements accuracy and idiosyncratic variables were assessed, given that their theory identifies these as the main variables to discriminate between internal and external memories.

The results showed that in the preparation condition, when subjects were asked to prepare their narratives about something previously experienced, the statements contained more internal characteristics than when subjects spoke spontaneously. On the other hand, the statements were more external when subjects were asked to prepare their declarations about an event previously imagined.

How could we explain this preparation effect on internal and external memories? It seems that in the reality condition, subjects perceive, code and store selected information about the events. When subjects were asked to prepare their memory statements, they recalled the memory traces and rebuilt the information. When it is time to talk about the event, they speak not about the perceived event but about the interpreted, coded reorganised, stored, recalled and rebuilt event. This is recall about a memory "trace" (perhaps, defined as a re-representation in terms of Johnson and Raye, 1981).

In the case of imagined events the process was very similar. Here the recall concerns an internally experienced event. When the imagined memory statement is tested in the preparation condition we have recall based upon a memory trace.

Every time we recall an event, internally or externally experienced, memory traces become more and more labile. Moreover, if during this time we prepare, talk or/and think about the event, these internal and external characteristics will be more and more affected. External memories become more internal, and internal memories become more external. When real memory statements are prepared there is a greater involvement of cognitive processes, which produces internalisation of the traces. In the case of imagination, preparation mainly produces an enrichment of the scene; in other words, more sensorial and contextual details and more coherence, and softer idiosyncratic characteristics which produce recall with more external characteristics than with immediate recall.

As the real or the imagined trace is more temporally distanced from the original it becomes more difficult to differentiate the source, because of trace impairment.

Subjects must reconstruct the scene and integrate all the suggested and self-suggested information (misleading information, lies, self-suggestions from previous knowledge, or imagination).

Our results lead us to think that the characteristic features proposed by the reality monitoring model (Johnson & Raye, 1981) might not be invariably applied to Statements Reality Analysis. For example, the statements of witnesses about an incident are analyzed after a considerable delay and victims and eyewitnesses report the events on many occasions. Both aspects imply that the reality characteristics would diminish. Moreover, some techniques of reality analysis (e.g. Steller, 1988) propose as a good method to guide the witnesses' recall the cognitive interview (Geiselman, 1988; Memon et al., 1990, 1991). This procedure produces more and more preparation of the statements, and because of that, it could provoke greater amounts of information but with fewer reality characteristics. Because of this risk, the main task should be to ensure that eyewitnesses' statements are analyzed as soon as possible. Delay is not the only difficulty for the analysis, additional time spent on report preparation could make the analysis impossible.

Finally, the increase of hesitant expressions in the real descriptions have an important implication about credibility. Although confidence do not correlate with accuracy (Wells & Murray, 1984), jurors base their credibility evaluations on the eyewitness confidence (Wells, Lindsay, & Ferguson, 1979). The greater amounts of doubt probably affect the eyewitness credibility.

In summary, preparation affects in a very important way the statements' accuracy in the case of eyewitnesses. It causes more detailed reports for both internal and external memories, but also it reduces statements' qualities. The first effect was already known, and we should also take note of the second.

References

Alonso-Quecuty, M. L. (1992). Deception detection and reality monitoring: A new answer to an old question? In F. Lösel, D. Bender, & T. Bliesener (Eds.), *Psychology and law. International perspectives* (pp. 328-332). Berlin: W. de Gruyter.

Diges, M. (1988, July). *The accuracy/credibility relationship is free recall of a filmed traffic accident.* Poster presented at NATO Advanced Institute on Credibility Assessment, Maratea, Italy.

Diges, M. (1992, September). *Previous knowledge and delay in the recall of filmed events.* Paper presented at the Third European Conference on Law and Psychology, Oxford, England.

Diges, M., Rubio, M. E., & Rodriguez, C. (1992). Eyewitness memory and time of day. In F. Lösel, D. Bender, & T. Bliesener (Eds.), *Psychology and law. International perspectives* (pp. 317-320). Berlin: W. de Gruyter.

Geiselman, R. E. (1988). Improving eyewitness memory through mental reinstatement of context. In G. M. Davies & D. M. Thomson (Eds.). *Memory in context: Context in memory.* New York: Wiley & Sons.

Johnson, M. K. (1988). Reality monitoring: An experimental phenomenological approach. *Journal of Experimental Psychology: General, 117*(4), 390-394.

Johnson, M. K., Foley, M. A, Suengas, A. G., & Raye, C. L. (1988). Phenomenal characteristics of memories for perceived and imagined autobiographical events. *Journal of Experimental Psychology: General, 117*(4), 371-376.

Johnson, M. K., Kahan, T. L., & Raye, C. L. (1984). Dreams and reality monitoring. *Journal of Experimental Psychology: General, 113*(3), 329-344.

Johnson, M. K, & Raye, C. L. (1981). Reality monitoring. *Psychological Review, 88*(1), 67-85.

Johnson, M. K., Raye, C. L., Wang, A. Y., & Taylor, T. H. (1979). Fact and fantasy: The roles of accuracy and variability in confusing imaginations with perceptual experiences. *Journal of Experimental Psychology: Human, Learning and Memory, 5*(3), 229-240.

Memon, A., & Bull, R. (1990, September). *The cognitive interview: Its origins, empirical support, evaluation and practical implication*. Paper presented at Second European Conference on Law and Psychology, Nürnberg, Germany.

Memon, A., & Bull, R. (1991, June). *La entrevista cognitiva: Cómo y por qué puede mejorar la memoria de un testigo*. I Encuentro Hispano-Británico de Psicología Jurídica, Pamplona.

Schooler, J. W., Clark, L. A., & Loftus, E. F. (1988). Knowing when memory is real. In M. M. Gruneberg, P. E. Morris, & R. N. Sykes (Eds.), *Practical aspects of memory: Current research and issues*. New York: Wiley.

Schooler, J. W., Gerhard, D., & Loftus, E. F. (1986). Qualities of the unreal. *Journal of Experimental Psychology: Learning, Memory, and Cognition, 12*(2), 171-181.

Steller, M. (1988). Recent developments in statement analysis. In J. C. Yuille (Ed.), *Credibility assessment*. The Netherlands: Kluwer Academic Publishers.

Suengas, A. G. (1991). El origen de los recuerdos. In J.M. Ruiz-Vargas (Ed.), *Psicología de la memoria*. Madrid: Alianza.

Suengas, A. G., & Johnson, M. K. (1988). Qualitative effects of rehearsal on memories for perceived and imagined complex events. *Journal of Experimental Psychology: General, 117*(4), 377-389.

Wells, G. L, Lindsay, R. C. L., & Ferguson, T. J. (1979). Accuracy, confidence, and juror perceptions in eyewitness identification. *Journal of Applied Psychology, 64*(4), 440-448.

Wells, G. L. & Murray, D. N. (1984). Eyewitness confidence. In G. L. Wells & E. Loftus (Eds.), *Eyewitness testimony. Psychological perspectives*. New York: Cambridge University Press.

[1] We are grateful to the pupils of Facultad de Psicología in Universidad Autónoma de Madrid. We are also grateful to Carmen Gentil for her help with the statement analysis, and to Clare Wilson and Miguel Muñoz for their help with the translation. This research was supported by grants from the Comunidad Autónoma of Madrid FPI nº C242/91 to A. L. Manzanero, and from DGICYT PB89-0170 to M. Diges.

Experimentally Induced Person Mix-ups Through Media Exposure and Ways to Avoid Them[1]

Siegfried Ludwig Sporer

Introduction

It has often been noted that reports of an event experienced in the past are not fully accurate but may be distorted by a variety of sources of errors. Expectations prior to observing an event may misguide our perceptions. Errors may also arise from information following the original observation. Distortions in recollections have best been documented as a function of misleading post-event information (misinformation effect). While these errors have practical implications in many aspects of life, e.g., in accounts of historical events or in news reporting, the most serious consequences may result when such errors occur in eyewitnesses' accounts in criminal or civil proceedings (for review, see Sporer, Malpass, & Köhnken, in press). For example, there have been several reports of mistaken identifications when a person seen at a different place at a different time is mistakenly identified by a witness as the culprit. This phenomenon has been referred to as unconscious transference (Loftus, 1976).

Loftus (1976) has shown experimentally that innocent bystanders observed earlier in a film of a bank robbery may later be mistaken for the culprit in a photospread. Although there has been some recent debate in the literature about the frequency of occurrence of mistaken identifications as a function of unconscious transference under ecologically more valid conditions (Read, Tollestrup, Hammersley, McFadzen, & Christensen, 1990; Ross, Toglia, Hopkins, Hanson, & Devenport, 1992), this serious source of error must be reckoned with as a possibility in criminal and civil proceedings.

The focus of this paper is on a related but not identical phenomenon: the misidentification of a person who has not been *personally* observed at a different place at a different time but one whose *appearance* has been suggested to the witness by misleading post-event information. This post-event information contains information that directs a witness to a specific person in a lineup who possesses a particular quality or a particular feature. As a consequence, the witness identifies the person suggested by this feature in the lineup although he (or she) may not be the actual culprit. We will call this more general phenomenon a "*mix-up*".

Verbal and Visual Post Event Information

Several experimental studies have demonstrated that a witness's memory for the appearance of a person can be contaminated by misleading post-event information. For example, Loftus and Greene (1980) have shown that memory for the face of a person seen may be distorted by reading a misleading verbal description (e.g., suggesting that the person had a moustache or curly hair when in fact he had not). This misleading information may either be "incorporated" in the witness's own description or even lead to a mistaken identification of a person possessing the particular feature.

In this paradigm, misleading post-event information is presented in *verbal* form. Jenkins and Davies (1985) and Davies and Jenkins (1985) extended this paradigm by introducing misleading post-event information *visually* by showing subjects a misleading composite that suggested some features not observed with the target. Under certain conditions (e.g., a short vs. a long exposure of the target in the film), *composite interference effects* were demonstrated both for verbal recall measures and for identifications (mix-ups).

Table 1 summarizes studies that have manipulated post-event information either verbally or visually and measured its effects on person descriptions, composite productions or person identifications. About half of the studies tested the memory for the target person verbally, having subject-witnesses recall the appearance of the target or describe the target on an adjective checklist. Some studies included a recognition test in form of a photospread with the target embedded among some foils (target-present lineup). Loftus and Greene (1980, Exp. 2) first presented to their subjects a target-absent lineup containing a foil that matched the misleading description, and later with a second photospread with both the target present and the misleading foil. Subjects who had picked the suggested person were likely to pick the misleading foil again the second time around, thus demonstrating a commitment effect to their erroneous choice.

Table 1: Verbal and Visual Postevent Information and its Influence on Person Descriptions and Identifications

Postevent Information	**Memory Test**	
	Reproduction (verbal)	**Recognition (visual)**
Verbal misleading Description		
Loftus & Greene (1980, Exp. 1)	Free description	
Loftus & Greene (1980, Exp. 2)		Photospread (first TA; then TP)
Visual Misleading Composite		
Jenkins & Davies (1985, Exp. 1)	Adjective Checklist	
Jenkins & Davies (1985, Exp. 2)		Photospread (TP)
Davies & Jenkins (1985, Exp. 1)	Adjective Checklist	
Davies & Jenkins (1985, Exp. 2)	Adjective Checklist	Photospread (TP)
Gibling & Davies (1988)		Photospread (TP)

Note: TP = Target Present; TA = Target Absent.

However, without this latter exception, the studies involving person identifications reported so far did not include target-absent lineups in the identification test, rendering the results somewhat equivocal (cf., Malpass & Devine, 1984, on the importance of *target-absent* lineups). In the studies to be reported below, we have included both target-present (TP) and target-absent (TA) lineups to remedy this deficit. We also wanted to explore whether the detrimental effect of misleading post-event information could be reduced or even counteracted by some specific interrogation techniques.

Countermeasures to Misleading Post Event Information

In Davies and Jenkins' (1985) second experiment, a recall task including the critical feature after as opposed to prior to the misleading information reduced the number of errors made (see also Yuille, 1984). One way to look at these results is to view the prior recall task as a method of *reinstatement of context* that should help witnesses in the memory task. Relatedly, Cutler, Penrod, and Martens (1987) had observed improved recognition performance under specific boundary conditions when subjects were allowed to reread their own prior descriptions before attempting an identification. Our goal was to follow up on these promising leads to test the efficacy of reinstatement of context procedures to counteract the misinformation effect.

Study 1

In our first experiment, we combined these two lines of research by: (1) manipulating post-event information by presenting either a good composite of the target, a misleading composite, or no composite (control condition); and by (2) providing half of the subjects the opportunity to reread their own prior description of the target before attempting a lineup identification.

In addition, we manipulated target presence at the lineup (TP vs. TA). Sex of subject was controlled for by distributing subjects of either sex equally across the cells of the experimental design. Dependent variables were proportions of correct identification decisions and the number of mix-ups. In addition, we assessed subjects' confidence after their lineup decision and the time with which they arrived at their decision. Correlational analyses with post-decision confidence and decision-time should also clarify whether these variables can be used for the post-hoc assessment of identification accuracy (see Sporer, 1992, 1993).

Method of Experiment 1 To test these notions, we focused exclusively on the visual mode at all three stages: in the presentation of the original information, the misleading post-event information and in the testing procedure. First, subject-witnesses watched a film of a staged theft in an optometrist's store that they were supposedly to judge for its artistic quality. After viewing the film, subjects answered some questions about it, including a questionnaire on descriptive details of the thief's face (the Aberdeen Face Rating Schedule; Ellis, 1986). After a one week delay, subjects were exposed to a newspaper article that contained either a good computer-generated facial composite, a misleading composite resembling one of the foils or no composite of the target. After a short filler activity, recognition of the target was tested either with target-present or target-absent photospreads. Subjects were instructed that the target could either be present or absent. Before making a recognition judgment, half the subjects were allowed to reread the description of the thief that they had given immediately after seeing the film, the other half was not given this opportunity. In Experiment 1, 154 subjects (75 male, 79 female) participated in the study for a monetary reward.

Major Findings of Experiment 1 Space limitations prevent a full account of the results of our experiments. We will not go into details of statistical analyses but restrict our report to major findings. All effects reported as reliable were significant with p < .05, unless otherwise noted.

In Experiment 1, few but significantly more mix-ups occurred as a function of the misleading composite (14%) as compared to the condition with the good composite (2%) or the no composite control (2%). Rereading of subjects' own prior description of the thief did not reduce this tendency. There were also a great number of foil identifications of other members in the lineup - which some authors consider legally irrelevant. The number of correct identification decisions overall was not affected by the composite manipulation nor did rereading the description that was supposed to reinstate context improve recognition performance.

Correct identification decisions were made with slightly more confidence than incorrect decisions (confidence-accuracy correlation in the total sample: $r(147)=.26$, $p < .01$). Choosing had not the expected moderator effect, with correlations being about equally high with choosers, $r(90)=.23$, $p < .05$, and non-choosers, $r(55)=.25$, $p < .10$. Decision-times that were collected for 149 subjects showed no relationship to identification accuracy ($r(147)=.03$, *ns*). Breaking down the sample into choosers and non-choosers did not alter this conclusion ($r(90)= -.02$ for choosers, and $r(55)=.06$ for non-choosers, both *ns*).

This study demonstrated that subject-witnesses can be misled by a composite when it resembles the general appearance of one of the foils in the photospread. However, the effect was not as large as one might have expected from other studies on the misinformation effect. Also, the effect could not be ameliorated by the reinstatement of context technique employed (rereading one's own description). This reinstatement procedure might have been ineffective because subjects might not have spent too much effort on the description task that was embedded among a variety of other questions about the film, and rereading a checklist may not be as useful as reading a description in one's own words. We also wondered about the overall poor recognition performance, in particular the high number of foil identifications both in target-absent and target-present lineups. Hence, we planned a follow-up study to explore some of these issues further.

Study 2

One of the reasons for the difficulties subjects had with the identification task was the highly homogeneous lineup which probably made it very difficult for them to pick the right person, even in target-present lineups. Consequently, we attempted to replicate this experiment, varying systematically lineup *similarity* by using a *homogeneous* and a *heterogeneous* lineup. In addition, we wanted to explore whether a modified reinstatement of context procedure, based on a visualization of the crime scene, including the target, just prior to attempting an identification would serve as a counter-measure to the misleading information (cf., Bekerian, Dennett, Hill, & Hitchcock, 1992). Two different *visualization techniques* were explored: one in which the vividness of each individual image of the events to be visualized had to be rated separately, and one in which the vividness of the total image was only to be rated once. A control group was not given any visualization instructions. Subject gender was again controlled by distributing male and female participants equally across the experimental cells.

In Experiment 2, 178 subjects (101 male, 77 female) participated, again for a monetary reward. They saw the same film but this time subjects were told to watch the film attentively (from the perspective of a customer) as they would later be asked details about the film.

Mix-ups and identification accuracy In Experiment 2, false identifications of the misleading foil (27%) were substantially higher than in the first study. This was particularly true with the target-absent photospread (40%) as revealed by a significant target-presence by post-event information interaction effect (see Figure 1). Visualization of the target before the identification task did not improve performance nor counteract the misinformation effect. In fact, with target-absent lineups, visualization led even to an increased number of mix-ups under the two visualization conditions. This finding contradicts the results of Gibling and Davies (1988) who had observed a beneficial effect of the cognitive interview technique: errors were reduced when context was reinstated through the cognitive interview. However, Gibling and Davies had used target-present lineups only. It is not clear whether the beneficial effect of the cognitive interview technique is restricted to situations when the target is actually present (like in Malpass & Devine's, 1981, study on the guided memory technique) or whether the visualization technique which we considered as the major element of the cognitive interview technique matters at all in person recognition.

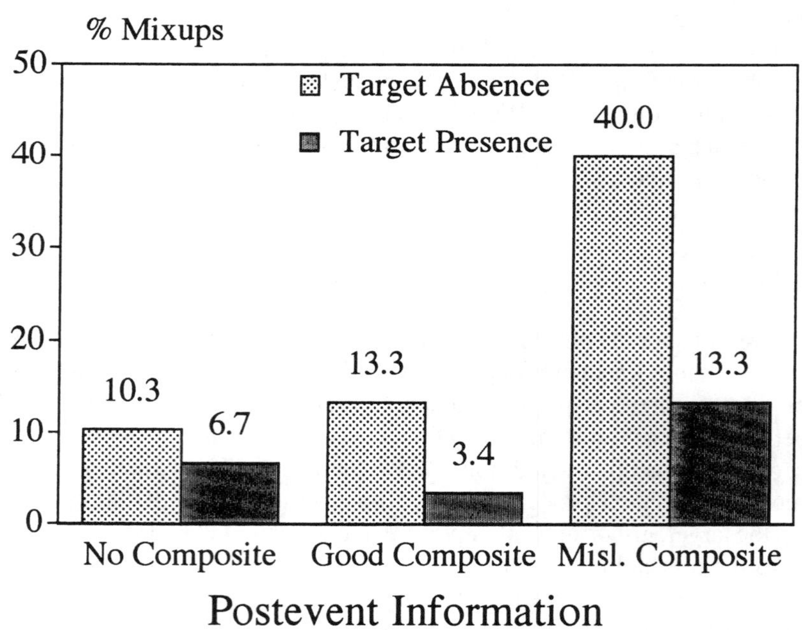

Figure 1: Mixups as a function of target presence and lineup similarity in Experiment 2

On a more positive side, in our study, testing with a homogeneous lineup led to significantly fewer mix-ups (14.9% false identifications of the misleading foil) than a low similarity lineup (28.6%) in target-absent lineups. In target-present lineups, mix-ups were not affected (10.4% vs. 4.9%, respectively). This pattern of results was reflected in a significant interaction between target-presence and lineup similarity.

To understand this effect more fully, we inspected the distribution of errors across lineup members separately for heterogeneous and homogeneous TA lineups. As is evident from Figures 2 and 3, in heterogeneous lineups false identifications are primarily of the person suggested by the misleading composite while in a homogeneous, more fair photospread errors are distributed about equally across all lineup members. Assuming that identifications of non-suspect foils are "known errors" to the police, they can be discounted. Hence the high similarity lineup may lead to a reduced number of mix-ups without sacrificing the power to detect the culprit in target-present lineups.

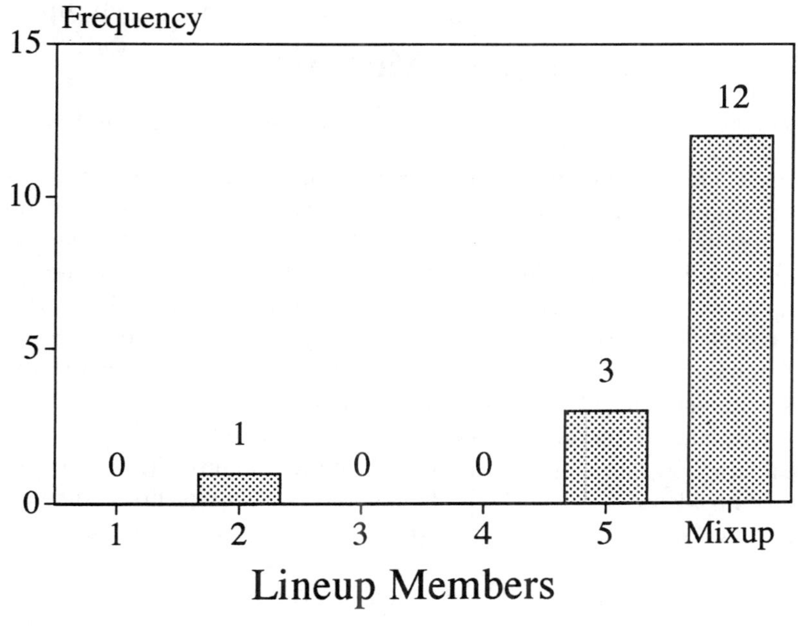

Figure 2: Distribution of false identifications in heterogeneous target-absent lineups

Interestingly, neither the number of correct identifications nor the overall number of false identifications (all false identifications, i.e., both of lineup members other than the misleading foil plus mix-ups) were affected by lineup similarity. Thus, using high similarity lineups does not necessarily imply that it would no longer be possible to detect the culprit when he is present. Conversely, they protect innocent people when the culprit is absent.

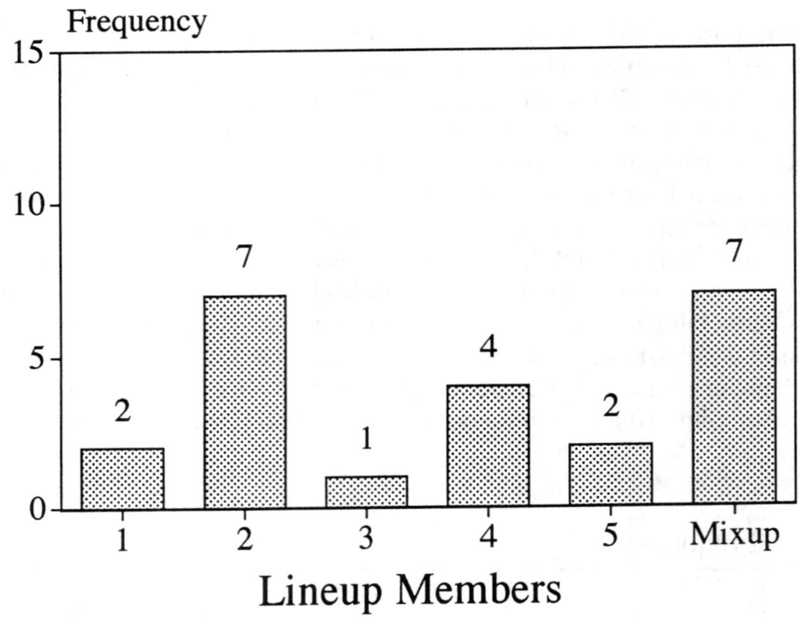

Figure 2: Distribution of false identifications in heterogeneous target-absent lineups

Confidence and decision times Post-decision confidence was significantly related to identification accuracy in the total sample, $r(163)=.19$, $p < .05$. This relationship was slightly stronger among choosers, $r(92)=.18$, $p < .10$, than non-choosers, $r(69)=.13$, $p > .25$). Decision-times tended to be negatively related to accuracy in the total sample ($N=165$) for which response latencies had been measured, ($r(163)= -.15$, but this correlation was only marginally significant ($p<.10$). For choosers, the observed relationship was reliably negative ($r(92)= -.25$, $p<.05$) while for non-choosers a non-significant positive relationship was observed ($r(69)=.09$, *ns*). In analysis of variance terms, this result corresponds to a significant choice by decision outcome interaction, i.e., subject-witnesses who correctly chose the thief did so faster than people misidentifying somebody. In contrast, correct rejections tended to take longer than incorrect rejections although this difference was not reliable.

General Discussion and Practical Implications

This study provides further support for the observation made by other researchers that people can be misled through misleading post-event information. While most previous studies have demonstrated the misinformation effect with rather minor details of the observed event our experiments have shown that the misinformation effect may involve nothing less than the identity of the protagonist. When a misleading composite of a person appears in the news mix-ups may occur as a function of media exposure. This danger is more likely when the observed target is not among the people from which the witness is supposed to recognize the person, i.e., in criminal-absent lineups. Notwithstanding the potential beneficial effects of composites - for example, helping to draw the readers' attention to a newspaper article - it appears that face composites may be "dangerous" to innocent suspects who resemble the composite.

Good composites, at least to the degree that they could be constructed by our operator - who was not too experienced - did not improve recognition of the target. In other words, good composites may not facilitate recognition in a sense that they could serve as contextual cues to improve recognition.

In practical terms, this would imply that even reasonably well constructed composites would not be likely to lead to the apprehension of the culprit. If witnesses themselves cannot profit from the composite how could it help other people to recognize the person at large who have nothing but the composite to go by (see also Davies, 1983)?

Countermeasures based on the reinstatement of context notion that we had hoped would remedy the detrimental effects of the misleading composite were not effective. In Experiment 1, subjects' rereading of their own description of the thief's face did neither help them in recognizing the target when he was in the lineup nor did it prevent subject-witnesses to choose the foil suggested to them by the misleading composite. This could be due to the fact that subjects did not take the original task of describing the thief's face with the Aberdeen Face Rating Schedule too seriously. It could also mean that the verbal feedback witnesses get from the face ratings do not provide them with the type of information needed for identifying the culprit - which at heart is a visual task (cf., Davies, 1983; Shepherd & Ellis, in press; Sporer, 1989, 1992).

Visualization of the face of the target as a measure to reinstate context prior to the identification task did also not help subject-witnesses in their overall performance nor in their ability to reject the foil suggested in the misleading composite condition. We had hoped that visualization would be one, perhaps the major component of the cognitive interview that should have increased witnesses' performance. Whatever the "active ingredient" of the cognitive interview technique is that has made this technique so successful with recall measures (see Fisher & Geiselman, 1992; Köhnken, 1992) the success of the cognitive interview with identification (recognition) procedures is still questionable (cf., Smith & Vela, 1992). Further research into the components of the cognitive interview and their relative effectiveness with different type of recall and recognition measures seems necessary (cf., Memon, Cronin, Eaves, & Bull, this volume).

On a more positive side the use homogeneous lineups did turn out as a useful countermeasure that led to a reduction of mix-ups. It should also be noted that this positive effect was not denigrated by a reduction of correct identifications as one might fear when the lineup task becomes too difficult when the lineup members are too similar to each other to allow good discrimination. Although the number of false identifications, counting all positive identifications except correct identifications, was high these choices followed an even distribution across lineup members. Insofar as identifications of foils other than the suspect may be regarded as "known errors" homogeneous lineups would seem preferable. This conclusion runs counter to recent recommendations put forth by Luus and Wells (1991) who have argued that lineup similarity may not be as crucial as long as the alternative members in the lineup resemble the description of the criminal. Although we agree with Luus and Wells' point that description similarity should be a prerequisite for the construction of lineups based on our data we would add that at least a moderate amount of similarity of lineup members - no "clones", of course - could help to prevent inadvertent errors that otherwise might go undetected. Thus, we conclude that homogenous lineups provide a procedural safeguard that may help to prevent miscarriages of justice at least in some cases.

Finally, we want to address the role confidence and decision-times can play in post-dicting eyewitness accuracy. Post-decision confidence showed a small but reliable relationship to identification accuracy in both studies. Only in Experiment 2, and here exclusively for *choosers*, were decision times for correct decisions made faster than for incorrect decisions. This pattern of results that is expressed in a significant choice by accuracy interaction corresponds to findings reported in several of our other studies (Sporer, 1992, 1993; for review, see Sporer, 1994). This distinction between choosers and non-choosers may play an important moderator role in the accuracy-confidence relationship as well although the difference between the respective correlations in the two sub-samples of the two studies reported here was not reliable like in our previous research (Sporer, 1992, 1993). We believe that decision-times and post-decision confidence may turn out to be more reliable assessment variables for retroactively gauging the accuracy of a positive eyewitness decision than has previously been thought.

References

Bekerian, D. A., Dennett, J. L., Hill, K., & Hitchcock, R. (1990). Effects of detailed imagery on simulated witness recall. In F. Lösel, D. Bender, & T. Bliesener (Eds.), *Psychology and law: international perspectives*. Berlin: De Gruyter.

Cutler, B. L., Penrod, S. D., & Martens, T. K. (1987). Improving the reliability of eyewitness identification: Putting context into context. *Journal of Applied Psychology*, *2*, 629-637.

Davies, G. M. (1983). Forensic face recall: The role of visual and verbal information. In S. M. A. Lloyd-Bostock & B. R. Clifford (Eds.), *Evaluating witness evidence: Recent psychological evidence and new perspectives* (pp. 103-123). Chichester: Wiley.

Davies, G. M., & Jenkins, F. (1985). Witnesses can be misled by police composite pictures: How and when. In F. L. Denmark (Ed.), *Social/ecological psychology and the psychology of women* (pp. 103-115). Amsterdam/New York/Oxford: Elsevier Publishers.

Ellis, H. (1986). Face recall: A psychological perspective. *Human Learning*, *5*, 189-196.

Fisher, R. P, & Geiselman, R. E. (1992). *The cognitive interview*. Chicago: Thomas Blackwell.

Gibling, F., & Davies, G. M. (1988). Reinstatement of context following exposure to post-event information. *British Journal of Psychology*, *79*, 129-141.

Jenkins, F., & Davies, G. (1985). Contamination of facial memory through exposure to misleading composite pictures. *Journal of Applied Psychology*, *70*, 164-176.

Köhnken, G. (1992, September). *The cognitive interview: A meta-analysis*. Paper presented at the Third European Law and Psychology Conference, Oxford, England.

Loftus, E. F. (1976). Unconscious transference in eyewitness identification. *Law and Psychology Review*, *2*, 93-98.

Loftus, E. F., & Greene, E. (1980). Warning: Even memory for faces may be contagious. *Law and Human Behavior*, *4*, 323-334.

Malpass, R. S., & Devine, P. G. (1981). Guided memory in eyewitness identification. *Journal of Applied Psychology*, *66*, 343-350.

Malpass, R. S., & Devine, P. G. (1984). Research on suggestion in lineups and photospreads. In G. L. Wells & E. F. Loftus (Eds.), *Eyewitness testimony: Psychological perspectives* (pp. 64-91). New York: Cambridge University Press.

Memon, A., Cronin, O., Eaves, R., & Bull, R. (1992, September). An empirical test of the "mnemonic components" of the CI: Can they explain the apparent memory enhancing effects of CI? Paper presented at the Third European Law and Psychology Conference, Oxford, England.

Read, J. D., Hammersley, R. H., Tollestrup, P., McFadzen, E., & Christensen, A. (1990). The unconscious transference effect: Are innocent bystanders ever misidentified? *Applied Cognitive Psychology*, *4*, 3-31.

Ross, D. F., Toglia, M. P., Hopkins, S., Hanson, E., & Devenport, J. (1992). *Lineup identification and mistaken identity: Evidence for a memory blending approach to unconscious transference*. Poster presented at the meeting of the American Psychology and Law Society, San Diego, CA.

Shepherd, J. W., & Ellis, H. D. (in press). Face recall - methods and problems. In S. L. Sporer, R. S. Malpass, & G. Köhnken (Eds.), *Psychological issues in eyewitness identification*. Hillsdale, NJ: Erlbaum.

Smith, S. M., & Vela, E. (1992). Environmental context-dependent eyewitness recognition. *Applied Cognitive Psychology*, *6*, 125-139.

Sporer, S. L. (1989). Verbal and visual processes in person identification. In H. Wegener, F. Lösel, & J. Haisch (Eds.), *Criminal behavior and the justice system: Psychological perspectives* (pp. 303-324). New York: Springer.

Sporer, S. L. (1992). Post-dicting eyewitness accuracy: Confidence, decision-times and person descriptions of choosers and non-choosers. *European Journal of Social Psychology*, *22*, 157-180.

Sporer, S. L. (1993). Eyewitness identification accuracy, confidence and decision times in simultaneous and sequential lineups. *Journal of Applied Psychology*, *78*, 22-33.

Sporer, S. L. (1994). Decision-times and eyewitness identification accuracy in simultaneous and sequential line-ups. In D. F. Ross, J. D. Read & M. P. Toglia (Eds.), *Adult eyewitness testimony: Current trends and developments* (pp. 300-327). New York: Cambridge University Press.

Sporer, S. L., Malpass, R. S., & Köhnken, G. (in press). *Psychological issues in eyewitness identification*. Hillsdale, NJ: Lawrence Erlbaum.

Yuille, J. C. (1984). Research and teaching with police: A Canadian example. *International Review of Applied Psychology*, *33*, 5-23.

[1] This research was supported by a grant from the Deutsche Forschungsgemeinschaft (German Science Foundation) to D. Meurer (Me 262/2/2). I would like to acknowledge the continuous help of Silke Franzen throughout this research, and of Angela aus dem Kahmen, who together with Ms Franzen created the stimulus materials for the film used in these studies and collected the data for Experiment 1. Data for Experiment 2 were collected by Silke Franzen and Gerd Mager to whom I am also grateful.

Detecting Fact from Fallacy in Child and Adult Witness Accounts[1]

María L. Alonso-Quecuty

Introduction

The Spanish press has recently reported the ratification by the High Court of a sentence for the kidnapping and abuse of a minor. The only witness for the accusation was a very young child: the victim. Nevertheless, the sentence read as follows:

> The child who has been the object of aggression does not relate or report the event in language neither elaborate nor dependent on a mental process of previous rationalization, but rather transmits the facts in a linear fashion... .

In spite of having accepted their testimony, the High Court continued to perceive the child witnesses as cognitively inept.

The doubts which have been presented concerning the capability of children as witnesses have historically been centred on two arguments; the limited nature of their memory and their incapacity to distinguish fact from fantasy. As far as the first argument is concerned, it is claimed that the quantity of exact details that children include in their statements is significantly inferior to that included by adults (error of omission). Where their incapacity for differentiating reality and imagination is concerned, the latter would result in their statements being contaminated by allusions to facts which did not actually occur (error of commission). In the same way it is claimed that the children are more suggestible than the adults (see Ceci, Toglia, & Ross, 1987 for a review).

In relation to the first argument, numerous research projects undertaken in recent years have demonstrated that, indeed, children spontaneously give less exact information than adults (see Hedderman, 1987). However, there has not been much research to analyse to what extent both children and adults are exact when elaborating false accounts of an event. The *first objective* of this work was to study the exact quantity of information that witnesses provide (children and adults) in both types of situations: when they are telling the truth and when they are lying about the same event. Likewise, we attempted to study what quantity of non-real information (confabulation) was given spontaneously by children as well as adults in both types of statements. Thus, we delve into the study of the second type of error, the error of commission.

The studies carried out in developmental psychology present children as being more likely to confuse reality and fantasy than adults and, therefore, children are thought to be more susceptible to errors of commission (Flavell, Flavell & Green, 1983). On the other hand, the results obtained in the field of mental pictures indicate that children think in terms of images more frequently than do adults (Kosslyn,

Margolis, Barrett, Goldknopf, & Daly, 1990), their imagination being more similar to an obvious action (for a review see Kosslyn, 1980). If this is so, this great similarity might induce children to confuse reality and fantasy when remembering an event. If they have a more vivid image of their fantasies than adults these fantasies are more "real" and more similar to a real event.

The process of discrimination between memories derived from external experiences (reality) and memories generated internally (fantasy) has been named reality-monitoring by Johnson and Raye (1981). According to these authors there are qualitative differences between both types of memories. Those generated externally contain more contextual information, more sensorial details and more semantic information about the event. On the other hand, those memories generated internally, possess more information about cognitive operations. Developmental research in this field shows children to be as competent as adults in the process of reality-monitoring with two exceptions: (a) when they are asked to discriminate between something carried out and something which they have only imagined having done (Johnson & Foley, 1984); and (b) when they must decide if they have said something or if they have only imagined having said it (Foley, Johnson, & Raye, 1983). In these tasks, children are less efficient than adults. The cause of these differences might be that the imagination of children is richer in perceptual (Foley et al., 1983) and semantic details (Foley, Santini, & Sopasakis, 1989). In both cases, discrimination would be rendered more difficult.

In my previous research, a connection had been established between reality-monitoring and true vs. false statements (Alonso-Quecuty, 1990, 1992, 1993). Indeed, true statements contained more contextual and sensorial information, the criteria predicted by the hypothesis of reality-monitoring for externally generated memories, and the false statements more internal information, the criteria predicted for internally generated memories.

The *second objective* was to study the possible application of the criteria for reality-monitoring to the study of the true and false statements of child and adult witnesses after having observed the simulation of an offence.

In addition in these previous studies conducted with adults, I had observed how the type of context (real vs. laboratory) affected the statements of the witnesses (Alonso-Quecuty, 1990, 1992). When the research was undertaken in a real context (e.g.: a young man who interrupted a class and assaulted the teacher verbally) we obtained significant differences of the variable Truth Value in the statement (Alonso-Quecuty, 1990). But when the research was undertaken in the laboratory (Alonso-Quecuty, 1992) using a video sequence of undramatic story (e.g.: a dispute) these differences were non significant. Only on one occasion did we obtain significant effects in the context of the laboratory and we achieved them by using a video sequence of extremely dramatic pictures (e.g. a rape) (Alonso-Quecuty, 1993).

In spite of what these results suggest, the different stimuli used in some of these studies have not enabled us to evaluate exactly to what extent the context of the study affected the witnesses' statements. On this occasion, we took the precaution of having a video camera, hidden behind the witnesses, which filmed everything that happened during the simulation of a criminal act.

Our *third objective* was to evaluate the effect that both types of experimental context (simulation of real facts vs laboratory) has on the witnesses statements (children and adults).

Starting from the results obtained from the developmental research of reality-monitoring and also from our own results from previous investigations, we formulated the following hypotheses.

Hypothesis 1 The true statements of adults will contain more accurate information than those of children. Besides, according to developmental psychology research, it is to be expected that children are more susceptible to errors of commision (confabulations) in their true statements.

Hypothesis 2 The true statements of the adult witnesses will be differentiated from the false ones. The true statements will be more similar to the memories of external origin and the false ones will be more similar to the memories of internal origin according to the criteria of differentiation for both types of memories of the reality-monitoring hypothesis (Alonso-Quecuty, 1990, 1992, 1993).

Hypothesis 3 The differences in content of the true vs. false statements will be affected by the age of the witnesses (Foley et al., 1983; 1989). The false statements given by children will contain more contextual and/or sensorial attributes than those given by adults.

Hypothesis 4 The differences in content of the true vs. false statements will be affected by the information content (Suengas, 1991). The statements (true v. false) given in the real context will be more similar to both types of memories (externally v. internally generated) than those given in the laboratory context.

Method

Subjects The sample was composed of 45 individuals: 25 boys and girls (from eight to ten years, with an average age of nine years) and 20 adults males and females (from 18 to 21 years, with an average age of 20 years).

Procedure The sample was divided in to two experimental groups. The number of adults and children in both groups was controlled. The subjects of Group 1 were in the parking area of the campus of the University of La Laguna waiting for a supposed psycholinguistic study. Once there, they were caught up in what, at first, appeared to be a criminal act. A teacher parked her car in the parking area of the campus in front of the subjects. One of the windows was left half open. Minutes later, two male youths approached the car, looked through the windows, opened the car through the half-opened window and took out a box which had been left on the back seat. An adult witness, who was actually a confederate, questioned their right to carry off the box and, after a short argument, the situation was cleared up when the youths identified themselves as students of the car owner who, in turn, had asked them to take the box to the laboratory. Subsequently, the subjects were taken to the laboratory where, in a second phase of the experiment, they gave two verbal versions of what had happenened (true vs. false). These verbal testimonies were recorded with an audio tape cassette.

The subjects in Group 2 (once again children and adults) watched the video recording together. Following that, they continued in the second phase of the experiment, identical to that of the Group 1, in which they were called upon to give two statements, one true and one false, of what they had seen.

Design There were three independent variables: the age of the witnesses (children vs. adults); the truth value of their statements (true vs. false); and the type of experimental context (real vs. laboratory).

The dependent variables were: (a) the accuracy of the statements; (b) the confabulation that they contained; and (c) the differentiating dimensions of memories generated externally/internally according to the hypothesis of reality-monitoring: contextual information, semantic information, sensorial details and internal information.

With the purpose of being able to carry out a correct evaluation of the criteria of accuracy and confabulation, a script was drawn up of how the event actually appeared in the video recording. Sixteen elements of the action were distinguished. Accurate information (in both true and false statements) was considered to be that given by the individual and that which corresponded to the 16 elements in the script. All other information which did not appear in the script either in the recording and which was total fabrication was understood to be confabulation. After carrying out the transcription of the statements, two judges scored each statement that coincided with one of the criteria of reality-monitoring.

Results

A series of ANOVAS were carried out. In all the variables (with the exception of the criterion internal information of reality-monitoring) significant interactions of the variables 2 (age) x 2 (truth value) x 3 (type of context) were obtained from the statements.

Accuracy A significant main effect of type of context was found. The statements were more accurate ($F(1,44)= 3.75$; $p<.05$) in the context of the laboratory. In the Group 1 (real context), the true statements of the adults contained more accurate information than the children's, but in the false statements the effect was reversed. The children demonstrated greater accuracy as far as the facts were concerned and as to how they really occurred. In the Group 2 (laboratory context) no significant difference was found.

Confabulations An interaction between the type of context and the truth value in the declarations was obtained ($F(1,44)= 4.06$; $p<.05$). While the true statements were not sensitive to context, the false statements made in the context of the laboratory contained more than double the confabulation obtained in a real context. In Group 1, the false statements of the children showed more confabulated information than the adults', but in the true statements the opposite was found. The adults contaminated their statements to a certain extent, which hardly occurred with the children ($F(1,24)= 11.02$;$p<.01$). Again in Group 2 no significant difference was found.

Contextual information A triple interaction, age x truth value x type of context, was obtained ($F(1,44)= 7.30$; $p<.01$). For Group 1, in the true statements of adults, there was more contextual information than in the false statements. In children, the effect was reversed. For Group 2 the similarity between the two statements of the children was very high.

Semantic information Another triple interaction, age x truth value x type of context, was obtained ($F(1,44) = 6.48$; $p < .01$). For Group 1, in the true statements of the adults, there was more semantic information than in the false ones. In children the effect was reversed. Again for Group 2 no significant difference was found.

Internal information A triple interaction, age x truth value x type of context, was obtained ($F(1,44)= 4.24$; $p< 05$). For Group 1 the statements of the adults presented more internal information than those of the children. For Group 2 no significant difference was found.

Sensorial details In this variable no interaction age x truth value x type of context was obtained. Only an interaction age x truth value was found in the Group 1 ($F1,24)= 4.03$; $p<.05$). For this group the true statements of the children presented more sensorial details than the false ones.

The results obtained in the real context confirm the first part of our first hypothesis has been confirmed. In the true statements, the children made errors of omission to a greater extent than the adults, but the latter made errors of commission more frequently than did the children. In the false statements, the adults were more conservative in their confabulations than the children.

The second hypothesis was partially confirmed. The true statements followed the model predicted for memories generated externally but only for adults. The false statements did not follow the model for memories generated internally.

The third hypothesis was confirmed in the real context only. The true and false statements were affected by the age of the witnesses. The false statements of the children were richer in contextual and semantic information (Foley et al., 1983, 1989).

In relation with the fourth hypothesis, it was discovered that the context of the study may generate very different patterns of results according to whether it is carried out in a real environment or within the walls of the laboratory.

These results are supported theoretically by previous research in which the existence of a series of factors that may affect reality-monitoring has been observed (Suengas, 1991). Among these the reduction of cognitive operations stands out. This term refers to processes such as reasoning, search, decision-making and also the creation of images which take place at the moment the memory is established. The results of several studies (e.g. Durso & Johnson, 1980) demonstrate that any image elicited after great reflection, effort or invention, should be easier to distinguish from something perceived than if the images are elicited without difficulty. According to Kosslyn (Kosslyn et al., 1990) children should have less difficulty than adults in generating very vivid fantasies. This lesser effort would contribute to a worse discrimination.

A second factor that, according to Suengas, would affect reality-monitoring is the *information content* (Suengas, 1991). This factor is closely related to the degree of self-reference contained in the information which is being remembered. That is to say, the degree of personal involvement of the individual with the information on which reality-monitoring is carried out. This personal involvement makes the reality monitoring process easier.

Our results demonstrate that the similarity between both types of statements (true vs. false) and both types of memories (real vs. imagined) is greater when the context is real (high degree of personal involvement), while telling the truth or lying where a video sequence (low degree of personal involvement) is concerned minimizes the difference between the statements and both types of memories. These results confirm those found in previous works (Alonso-Quecuty, 1990, 1992, 1993).

Johnson and Foley (1987) point out two limitations presented by reality-monitoring research when it comes to extrapolating its results to the psychology of testimony: (a) the artificial nature of the materials and the procedure; and (b) the instructions for the invention of an event given to subjects and which could generate fantasies which are very different to those which take place spontaneously, and which would produce richer and more vivid pictures.

The purpose of this research has not been the study of reality monitoring per se. Nevertheless the similarity found between both types of statements (true vs. false) and both types of memories (real vs. imagined) suggests that it is worth the trouble to study both truth and lies from the reality monitoring perspective.

References

Alonso-Quecuty, M. L. (1990). Recuerdo de la realidad percibida vs. imaginada. *Boletín de Psicología, 29*, 73-86.

Alonso-Quecuty, M. L. (1992). Deception detection and reality-monitoring: A new answer for an old question? In F. Lösel, D. Bender, & T. Bliesener (Eds.), *Psychology and law: International perspectives* (pp. 328-334). Berlin: Walter de Gruyter.

Alonso-Quecuty, M. L. (1993). *When truth and lies meet each other: The effects of the delay on lies.* Manuscript in preparation.

Durso, F. T., & Johnson, M. K. (1980). The effects of orienting tasks on recognition, recall, and modality confusion of pictures and words. *Journal of Verbal Learning and Verbal Behavior, 19*, 416-429.

Flavell, J. H., Flavell, E. R. & Green, F. L. (1983). Development in the appearance-reality distinction. *Cognitive Psychology, 15*, 95-120.

Feldman, R. S., Jenkins, L., & Popoola, O. (1979). Detection of deception in adults and children via facial expressions. *Child Development, 50*(2), 350-355.

Flavell, J. H., Flavell, E. R., & Green, F. L. (1983). Development of the appearance-reality distinction. *Cognitive Psychology, 15*, 95-120.

Foley, M. A., Johnson, M. K., & Raye, C. L. (1983). Age-related changes in confusion between memories for thoughts and memories for speech. *Child Development, 54*(2), 51-60.

Foley, M. A., Santini, C., & Sopasakis, M. (1989). Discriminating between memories: Evidence for children's spontaneous elaborations. *Journal of Experimental Child Psychology, 48*, 146-169.

Hedderman, C. (1987). *Children's evidence: The need for corroboration.* Research and Planning Unit Paper 41. London: Home Office.

Johnson, M. K., & Foley, M. A. (1984). Differentiating fact from fantasy: The reliability of children's memory. *Journal of Social Issues, 40*, 33-50.

Johnson, M. K. & Raye, C. L. (1981). Reality-monitoring. *Psychological Review, 88*, 67-85.

Kosslyn, S. M. (1980). *Image and mind.* Cambridge, MA: Harvard University Press.

Kosslyn, S. M., Margolis, J. A., Barrett, A. M., Goldknopf, E. J., & Daly, P. F. (1990). Age differences in imagery abilities. *Child Development*, *61*, 995-1010.

Lindsay, D. S., & Johnson, M. K. (1987). Reality monitoring and suggestionability: Children's ability to discriminate among memories from different sources. In S. J. Ceci, M. P. Toglia, & D. F. Ross (Eds.), *Children's eyewitness memory* (pp. 92-121). New York: Springer-Verlag.

Mandler, J. M. (1983). Representation. In J. H. Flavell & E. M. Markman (Eds.), *Handbook of child psychology: Vol. 3* (pp. 420-494). New York: Wiley.

Suengas, A. (1991). El origen de los recuerdos. In J. M. Ruiz-Vargas (Ed.), *Psicología de la memoria* (pp. 409-427). Madrid: Alianza.

[1] This investigation was supported by the Dirección General de Investigación Científica y Técnica (DGICYT) Grant nº PB 89-0170-C03-01

Is There Truth in the Eye of the Beholder? Causal Illusions in Children and Adults

Katharina Dahmen-Zimmer and Sandra Loohs

Introduction

During the last years, the growing interest in child witnesses has stimulated a lot of studies on child memory and comparisons of childrens' and adult's ability in recalling a witnessed event (for overviews see Cole & Loftus, 1987, or Davies, 1991). But, as for instance Dent (1992) points out, these studies are not directly comparable because they differ in many aspects (e.g. the age of the subjects; the presentation of real events, films, or pictures; the delay prior to recall, and the interview methodologies etc.). However, there is considerable agreement that adults and older children produce more complete records in recall than younger children, but younger ones do not necessarily produce more errors (Goodman et al., 1986). Children have been found to be as reliable in "cued recall" conditions as adults (Ceci et al., 1987), but perhaps less resistant against suggestive questions, especially if those concern peripheral details (Goodman et al., 1987). There are reasons to assume that this is not necessarily due to defects in childrens' memory or to suggestibility, but at least to some point it might be due to an interaction with other factors, for instance, the level of interest (Goodman et al., 1987), the nature of the task (Zaragoza, 1987), and the context in which it occurs (Melton & Thompson, 1987).

The present study investigated how the suggestibility of children and adults might be influenced by the demand characteristics of the task and the interview methodology. It deals with the question whether and how children and adults differ in perceiving physical causation correctly, especially in an ambiguous situation, and how assumptions about the causation influence other parts of their reports.

In everyday life we are usually well capable of perceiving causal connections; even children as young as three years have been shown to correctly perceive and report such connections (Shultz et al., 1986; Smith, 1979). But we can be mistaken in situations that are unfamiliar and/or provide only impoverished information, as demonstrated by the experiments on "phenomenal causality" by Michotte (1963). It has also been shown that reports of adult witnesses can be influenced by their observation of an apparent causal relation, which actually does not exist but which is perceived compellingly (Dahmen-Zimmer & Kraus, 1992). Other specific situations where organisms can be fooled about the reality of causal relations are for instance "superstitious behavior", which occurs in animals (Skinner, 1948) as well as in humans (Catania & Cutts, 1963); and "autoshaped behavior", also demonstrated in animals (Brown & Jenkins, 1968) and humans (Dahmen, 1988). In the social domain, cultural expectations, prejudices, and personal expectations about the behavior of other people may effect perception of causation (e.g. Allport & Postman, 1947; Hastorf & Cantril, 1954).

The following experiment deals with reports about an accident. It is investigated whether subjects are able to give veridical evidence about the cause of the perceived accident, even if the situation is ambiguous; how their assumptions about the causation influence other details of their reports; and whether and how childrens' verbal reports fit with their replaying the scene with toys.

Method

Subjects Sixty-seven subjects took part in the experiment; 36 students, 11 male and 25 female, mean age 22,9 years, range 19 to 36 years, and 31 children, 12 male and 19 female, mean age 9,7, range 7 to 11 years.

Stimulus material The stimulus material shown to the subjects consists of a video depicting a cyclist going down a road towards an intersection where a second cyclist drives up from the right. The first cyclist slows down. When the two cyclists meet, the second cyclist falls down dramatically. The video then shows the first cyclist again, stopping, putting down his bicycle, and going to the other man, who lies on the ground and clutches his left leg. He helps him to get up and supports him while they both leave the scene.

There were three versions of the accident, which differed in the depiction of the accident: (i) the two cyclists actually collided; (ii) the two cyclists passed each other and did not touch; (iii) the two cyclists passed each other but it was impossible to see, whether they touched each other or not. Each video lasted one minute.

The techniques of interviewing Both adults and children were first asked to report the content of the film, afterwards to describe the persons and the bicycles, and then to estimate the duration of the film. The most important items for this investigation dealt with the fall of one cyclist when the two bicycles passed each other. The subjects were asked why the second cyclist had fallen down, whether the two cyclists had collided, and whether one of the two cyclists was responsible for causing the fall. The adults put their answers down in writing, the children were interrogated orally, supported by a replay of the event with two toy bicycles.

Experimental design Two independent factors were manipulated for the assessment of their influence on the perception of the accident: (i) the age of the subjects, and (ii) the kind or the precision of information provided about the event.

Adults and children respectively were divided into three groups at random, each group viewed one version of the videotaped accident (see Table 1 for an overview of the experimental design).

Table 1: Experimental Design

Group	Number of Ss	Age	Information about the accident
1	12		collision
2	12	adults	no collision
3	12		ambiguous
4	11		collision
5	10	children	no collision
6	10		ambiguous

Procedure The entire experiment lasted approximately 15 minutes for the children and about one hour for the adults. It was introduced as an experiment on perception. The interview took place immediately after the video, mostly individually (entirely for the children), in some cases groups of two or maximally three adults saw the film together. It was pointed out to the children that they should not feel obliged to answer questions about topics they could not remember.

Scoring of the data The transcripts of the interviews were scored for the number of correct and incorrect points of information concerning the different topics. Items concerning the accident were categorized as a function of age and condition.

Results

Completeness and accuracy of the reports In response to free recall, the adult groups gave significantly more complete reports than the children (t=5.06; $p<0.01$), but did not differ in regard to accuracy. Furthermore, the adults' descriptions of the persons were more complete than childrens' descriptions, however again not differing in accuracy. In describing the bicycles, adults and children were comparable in the completeness of their reports, but the adults made significantly more errors than the children (t=2,39; $p<0.05$).

Children were significantly more exact in estimating the duration of the videos (*M*: 104.0 sec., *SD*: 73.4) than adults (*M*: 147.3 sec., *SD*: 62.3) (χ^2=12.93; df=2; $p<0.01$). The duration of the video was strongly overestimated by most adults; more children than adults assessed the duration correctly, and some children even underestimated the duration of the film (see Table 2).

Table 2: Estimation of the duration of the videos (percentage of Ss)

Age	Exact	Overestimation	Underestimation
Adults	13.9	86.1	–
Children	31.8	48.5	19.7

Reported causes of the accident In free recall, all the adults and nearly all the children (90%) who had seen the "actual collision" of the two bicycles described the accident correctly. 58.3% of the adults, and 30% of the children, who had seen "no collision", described the accident correctly, the verbal (written) descriptions of 41.6% of the adults, and of 70% of the children were incorrect. In contrast to their verbal reports, 70% of the children were correct when acting out the scene with two toy bicycles. In the "ambiguous" scene, where it was not possible to see, whether the two bicycles touch, the verbal (written) reports of 66.6% of the adults, and of 30% of the children were correct, while 33.3% of the adults, and 70% of the children were incorrect, but 90% of the children were correct when acting out the scene with the toy bicycles (see Table 3).

Table 3: Descriptions (play) of the accident (percentage of Ss)

Age	Information about the accident	Correctly described yes	Correctly described no	Correctly played yes	Correctly played no
	collision	100	–		
adults	no collision	58.3	41.6		
	ambiguous	66.6	33.3		
	collision	90	10	100	–
children	no collision	30	70	70	30
	ambiguous	30	70	90	10

When asked, "Why did the second cyclist fall down?" all the adults, who saw the "actual collision" of the two bicycles, and also all the children, reported that the other cyclist caused the fall. The adults, who saw "no collision" of the two bicycles, did not blame the other cyclist directly for causing the fall, but most of them supposed that indirectly a combination of his behavior and other circumstances (e.g. potholes) caused the fall; in contrast 50% of the children, who saw the same scene, blamed the other cyclist directly for causing the fall, and another 20% of them blamed the cyclist himself. In this condition the difference between adults and children was significant (χ^2=14.15; df=5; p=0.01).

In the "ambiguous" scene (where it was not recognizable whether the two bicycles touch), 75% of the adults blamed the other cyclist for indirectly causing the fall, and 16.7% blamed him for directly causing the fall; in the respective group of children the proportions were nearly opposite: here 70% of the children blamed cyclist one for directly causing the fall of cyclist two, the other 30% reported that he caused the fall indirectly. The difference between the two groups was significant (χ^2=4.40; df=1; p=0.03). In general, the childrens' answers contained significantly less multiple causal attributions than the adults' (χ^2=11.22; df=1; $p<0.01$). Usually the children named just one cause of the fall (see Table 4).

Table 4: Reported causes for the fall (percentage of Ss)

Age	Information about the accident	Reported causes of the fall cyclist 1	cyclist 1 indirectly	cyclist 1+ bad road	other circumst.	cyclist 2	no answer
	collision	100	–	–	–	–	–
adults	no collision	–	16.7	41.6	16.7	–	25
	ambiguous	16.7	75	–	–	–	8.3
	collision	100	–	–	–	–	–
children	no collision	50	10	10	10	20	–
	ambiguous	70	30	–	–	–	–

When the question suggested, the other cyclist was to blame: "Is the other cyclist particularly to blame for the fall?" nearly all the adults (91.7%), and nearly all the children (90.9%), who saw the actual collision, blamed cyclist one, the other subjects (8.3% of the adults and 9.1% of the children) blamed both cyclists. 33.3% of the adults, and 70% of the children, who actually saw no collision, nevertheless blamed cyclist one. In the condition with the ambiguous scene even 66.6% of the adults, and 80% of the children still blamed cyclist one (see Table 5).

Table 5: Answers to the question: "Is particularly the other cyclist to blame for the fall?" (percentage of Ss)

Age	Information about the accident	yes	no	both cyclists	no answer
	collision	91.7	–	8.3	–
adults	no collision	33.3	33.3	–	33.3
	ambiguous	66.6	33.3	–	–
	collision	90.9	–	9.1	–
children	no collision	70	20	10	–
	ambiguous	80	20	–	–

Other details of the reports Additionally, checks were made as to whether the subjects, who perceived the relation between the fall of one cyclist and the behavior of the other cyclist as causal gave reports which differed in other details from those who did not.

The question, whether one or both of the cyclists slowed down before the fall (as cyclist one actually did), is answered in the negative by significantly more children and adults, who mostly supposed that the two bicycles collided, than by the groups who rather supposed that no collision had occurred (χ^2=23.45; df=1; p<0.01) (see Table 6).

Table 6: Summarized answers to the question: "Did one (or both) of the cyclists slow down?" (percentage of Ss)

Predominate assumption	cyclist 1 slowed down	cyclist one did not slow down
collision	28	72
no collision	82.1	17.9

Discussion

Completeness and accuracy of the reports The general results concerning completeness and accuracy of the reports fit well into the literature on adult and child witnesses, that is, adults gave more complete reports than children, but they didn't differ in accuracy. This was also true for the descriptions of persons, but surprisingly, children were significantly better in describing the bicycles, probably because this was more in their field of interest and attention.

As has been frequently observed before, the duration of the video was overestimated by most adults, but it turned out that more children than adults reported the exact duration of the video, and in contrast to the adults some children even underestimated the duration. That is, the childrens' estimations were more exact but also more heterogeneous than the adults' reports.

Reported causes of the accident In their answers to the questions concerning the cause of the fall, children and adults, who saw the actual collision, correctly blamed the other cyclist for causing it. But even if no physical contact had been shown, about one in three adults, and two in three childrens' verbal/written answers blamed the other cyclist contrary to the facts. If only ambiguous information was available, the tendency to blame cyclist one was even stronger: two out of three adults and four out of five children attributed the responsibility for the fall to this cyclist. Children as well as adults fell into the trap of interpreting the meeting of the two cyclists as causal for the fall. As in other situations, where humans and other animals can be fooled about the reality of causal relation, the effect was stronger the more ambiguous the scene. There is of course a huge ecological advantage in the fast perception of causal relations. It is more important for humans and other animals to perceive causal relations immediately than to rule out possible causal illusions (Dahmen-Zimmer & Kraus, 1982).

The results show that both children and adults incorrectly reported a causal relationship that actually did not exist. When interrogated, significantly more children than adults were mistaken, but the children were significantly more correct if they acted out the scene, than if they gave verbal reports (χ^2=7.70; df=1; p<0.01). There was no significant difference between adults and children in falsely perceiving this causation, if childrens' nonverbal acting out of the scene was compared to adults' written reports. The information given by the childrens' replay of the scene was even more correct than the adults' written reports. That is, childrens' deficiencies in giving evidence might be due at least partially to their lack of verbal abilities, and not to their perception or memory.

Obviously childrens' mistakes when interrogated cannot be attributed to childrens' lack of attention or interest in the film. They did not differ significantly from the adults in their free recall - that is enacting the scene - and they were as correct as the adults in describing the persons, and significantly better in describing the bicycles.

Other details of the reports Subjects, who perceived the relation between the fall of one cyclist and the behavior of the other cyclist as causal (correctly or mistakenly) gave reports which differed in also another detail from those who did not. Adults as well as children who supposed that a collision actually took place, mostly denied that cyclist one slowed down; in contrast subjects, who supposed that there was no collision, mostly answered in the affirmative. This corresponds with studies on how subjects' implicit "schemata" or "scripts" influence their reports (Bartlett, 1932; Goodman, 1980).

Summary

In summary: adults and children can be mistaken in reporting a causal relationship which actually does not exist, and thereby falsely blame a participant of an accident. The more ambiguous the given information, the stronger the illusion.

When interrogated, significantly more children than adults fall into this trap, but in non-verbal free recall there is no significant difference in the correctness of the written information given by adults, and the nonverbal information given by the children when they act out the scene with toys. That is, childrens' deficiencies in giving evidence might at least in part be due to their lack of verbal abilities, and not to their perception or memory. Subjects' assumptions about the causes of the accident (correct as well as incorrect) also influenced those other details in the report which were associated with the "schema" or "script" of this event.

References

Bartlett, F. C. (1932). *Remembering*. Cambridge: Cambridge University Press.

Ceci, S., Ross, D. F. & Toglia, M. P. (1987). Suggestibility of childrens' memory: Psycholegal implications. *Journal of Experimental Psychology: General, 116*, 38-49.

Cole, C. B., & Loftus, E. F. (1987). The memory of children. In S. J. Ceci, M. P. Toglia, & D. F. Ross (Eds.), *Childrens' eyewitness memory*. New York: Springer Verlag.

Dahmen, K. (1988). Von der Wahrnehmung zum Handeln. Verhaltenskontrolle durch "affordances". *Gestalt Theory, 1O*, 35-45.

Dahmen-Zimmer, K., & Kraus, M. (1992). "Phenomenal causality" in eyewitness report. In F. Lösel, D. Bender, & T. Bliesener (Eds.), *Psychology and law*. Berlin: de Gruyter.

Davies, G. (1991). Research on childrens' testimony: Implications for interviewing practice. In C.R. Hollin & K. Howells, K. (Eds.), *Clinical approaches to sex offenders and their victims* (pp. 93-115). Chichester: Wiley.

Dent, H. (1992). The effects of age and intelligence on eyewitnessing ability. In H. Dent & R. Flin (Eds.), *Children as witnesses*. Chichester: J. Wiley

Goodman, G. S. (198O). Picture memory: How the action schema affects retention. *Cognitive Psychology*, 12, 473-495.

Goodman, G. S., & Reed, R. S. (1986). Age differences in eyewitness testimony. *Law and Human Behavior, 10*, 317-332.

Goodman, G. S., Aman, C., & Hirschman, J. (1987). Child sexual and physical abuse. In S. J. Ceci, M. P. Toglia, & D. F. Ross (Eds.), *Childrens' eyewitness memory*. New York: Springer Verlag.

Melton, G. B., & Thompson, R. A. (1987). Getting out of a rut: Detours to a less travelled path in child-witness research. In S. J. Ceci, M. P. Toglia, & D. F. Ross (Eds.) *Childrens' eyewitness memory*. New York: Springer Verlag.

Shultz, T. R., Fischer G.W., Pratt, C. C., & Rulf, S. (1986). Selection of causal rules. *Child Development*, *57*, 143-152.

Smith, C. L. (1979). Childrens' understanding of natural language hierarchies. *Journal of Experimental Child Psychology*, *27*, 437-458.

Zaragoza, M. S. (1987). Memory, suggestibility, and eyewitness testimony in children and adults. In S. J. Ceci, M. P. Toglia, & D. F. Ross (Eds.) *Childrens' eyewitness memory*. New York: Springer Verlag.

Part II
Interviewing

From Denial to Admission in Police Questioning of Suspects

Stephen Moston

False Confessions

Psychological research on police interviewing procedures has, until relatively recently, focused almost exclusively on techniques for the questioning of witnesses. Interviews with suspects is an area that has seldom been researched. This is somewhat surprising as public and legal concern over police interviewing procedures almost exclusively centres on interviews with suspects and in particular, with the possibility that they may result in false confessions.

The possibility that police questioning may result in false confessions has been addressed in a series of papers by Gudjonsson (e.g., Gudjonsson & MacKeith, 1988; Gudjonsson & LeBegue, 1989; Gudjonsson, 1992). Gudjonsson and MacKeith (1988) propose that there are three principal types of false confession.

1. The voluntary confession This is offered in the absence of any form of external pressure. That is, a person volunteers an unsolicited confession to a police officer, even though that person has not committed any offence.

2. The coerced-compliant confession This form of admission is seen as resulting from coercion (real or imagined) during the questioning of a suspect. An individual may make a false confession during questioning because they perceive that this will bring some immediate instrumental gain. Perceived gains may include the cessation of questioning, or the possibility of being released.

3. The coerced-internalized confession There are occasions when through fatigue, pressure or suggestions, an innocent suspect actually comes to believe that they have committed an offence. The suspect will accept that they did commit an offence, typically because they do not trust their own memory and begin to accept the suggestions (at least temporarily) made by the interviewing officers (e.g., Gudjonsson & LeBegue, 1989).

Gudjonsson and Mackeith suggest that coerced-compliant confessions are most likely to result from aggressive interviewing techniques, whilst internalised confessions are produced by more gentle and subtle forms of questioning. Internalized confessions are most likely to result with individuals who have a tendency to become easily confused, lack confidence in their memory and show a marked susceptibility to suggestion. Both voluntary and coerced-internalised confessions are seen as relatively rare, coerced-compliant false confessions being believed to be the most prevalent.

Why Do Suspects Confess?

Regardless of an individual's actual involvement in an offence of which he or she is accused, Moston, Stephenson and Williamson (1992) propose there are three main sets of factors that may determine the suspect's initial response to an allegation: the background characteristics of the suspect (e.g., age, sex, criminal history) and offence (e.g., type of offence, offence severity); the contextual characteristics of the case (e.g., strength of evidence, legal advice); and the interviewer's questioning techniques. Interviewing techniques are in turn influenced by the interviewer's beliefs and attitudes which in their turn are largely determined by the background and contextual characteristics of the case. The suspect's subsequent and final responses during questioning will be determined by the suspect's calculation of the relative advantages of response change brought about by the interviewer's reaction to the suspect's initial response. That is, an initial denial might be changed to an admission.

Moston et al. analyzed over 1000 cases in which suspects were interviewed by police officers in England. In addition to collecting detailed records of the cases through a questionnaire attached to custody records they also analyzed over 500 taped records of interviews. This research found clear links between three case characteristics (strength of evidence, offence severity and legal advice) and the outcome of interviews.

Moston et al. (1992) suggested that police interviewing techniques played a relatively minor role in influencing confessions. There were two reasons for this conclusion. first, most admissions were freely volunteered at the outset of interviews and those suspects who denied an accusation at the outset of an interview typically maintained this denial throughout, even in the face of seemingly incontrovertible proof of their guilt.

The second and perhaps most surprising observation was that police interviewing skills were almost non-existent and only a limited range of questioning techniques were being employed. Interviewers often appeared to be more nervous than the suspects they were questioning. Many officers concluded interviews at the first sign of resistance from suspects whilst others doggedly continued with one technique or approach, resulting in pantomime-like sequences of "Oh, yes you did", "Oh no I didn't". Such repetitions rarely resulted in the alteration of a response.

Such findings run contrary to the popular mythology concerning police interviews with suspects. It is probably the case that most people believe that a typical interrogation begins with an initial denial from the suspect and it is only through skilled questioning by the interviewer that the inconsistencies of that person's statement become evident. Finally, when faced with the obvious contradictions between their earlier statement and the evidence, the suspect recants their denial and makes a full confession.

Police officers typically start interviews with the presumption that the suspect is guilty (Moston & Engelberg, 1994). Far from exonerating a suspect, denials are seen as attempted deceptions, thereby *reducing* the credibility of the suspect. Suspects are seemingly in a no win situation, if they protest their innocence the interviewer merely takes this as confirmation of guilt. If they say nothing, perhaps using their right to silence, this too is taken as confirmation of guilt (Moston, Stephenson & Williamson, 1993).

Following a denial the interviewer will try to persuade the suspect to confess, since the outcome of the interview, a denial, is seen as undesirable, possibly even as a failure on their part. Officers tend to work on the premise that a good outcome of an interrogation is a confession, interviewing competence often being defined by the numbers of confessions elicited. This approach sets the scene for the possibility of false confessions, in that officers may adopt questioning techniques that coerce the suspect into retracting their earlier statement, with any eventual admission seen as vindicating the necessity for such an approach.

In explaining this change of statement a great deal of emphasis is placed on the role played by police questioning techniques, specifically the psychological ploys adopted to manipulate the suspect's decision making. For example, as discussed earlier, police questioning techniques are thought to be largely responsible for eliciting both false coerced-compliant and coerced-internalised false confessions. This view has not been helped by the limited literature on police interviews with suspects (e.g., Inbau, Reid & Buckley, 1986; Royal & Schutt, 1976) which tends to concentrate on how to overcome denials and elicit confessions.

The Current Range of Persuasive Questioning Strategies

Although there is a relatively substantial literature describing police questioning techniques (e.g., Royal & Schutt, 1976; Inbau, Reid & Buckley, 1986; Leo, 1992), this is almost entirely confined to describing the procedures used by officers in the USA, where the legal restrictions on questioning show a marked difference to those set out in PACE. The following sections concentrate on describing the persuasive strategies used by police interviewers when questioning suspects who have made an initial denial. The term "feedback" is used to describe the subsequent strategies adopted by the police officers (Gudjonsson, 1984). Two broad categories of feedback are described, feedback in the absence of evidence and the use of evidence.

Feedback in the Absence of Evidence

This section describes some of the most commonly used persuasive strategies that are independent of the evidence in a case. Such strategies can be employed in almost any type of investigation. These strategies are often included in police training courses as examples of "psychological" ploys.

Simple repetition The simplest form of critical feedback that an interviewer can give is to repeat a question. This immediately tells the suspect that their previous answer was either incorrect or simply unacceptable. Studies of suggestibility in eyewitnesses have shown how repeated questioning can alter a child's responses (e.g., Moston, 1987). However, little is known about how repetition of questions affects suspects, although this form of feedback is incorporated into the Gudjonsson Suggestibility Scale (Gudjonsson, 1984).

Moston and Engelberg (1994) describe how, when interviewing suspects who use their right of silence, many interviewers try to elicit more concrete responses by repeating questions over and over again. On occasions this dogged "persistence" may be counterproductive, since the interviewer's credibility usually diminishes in line with the number of repetitions. As questions are repeated, the suspect is likely to repeat the same answer. In order to reinforce the significance of the question some interviewers repeat it in a more louder or more aggressive manner. Repeated questioning of this sort rarely seems to elicit changed replies and is probably most commonly used by unsophisticated interviewers who can think of no other questions, rather than for any intimidatory reason.

Commenting on body language Even though the detection of deception through observations of non-verbal cues is an almost entirely unreliable process (Kohnken, 1987; Moston, 1992), it is still a popular belief amongst police interviewers that the ability to spot deception is an essential aspect of interviewing competency (Oxford, 1991). Just as this misconception holds sway with police officers, it is probably fair to say that it is just as popular with suspects. That is, suspects may believe that interviewers possess such skills. This gives rise to the following strategy. The suspect may be told "I can tell you're lying, your body language gives you away", or that "it is obvious that you are lying, it's written on your face". In some interviews the interviewer can try to take on the role of a mind-reader ("I can tell that you're nervous") revealing the suspect's "hidden fears". Timing of the strategy can be crucial in influencing the behaviour of the suspect. If used at the outset of questioning, the interviewer's claims are likely to be dismissed as an obvious bluff, however later on in questioning the suspect may be more ready to accept that their deceit has been "uncovered".

Although this is a popular technique, the ethical foundations of this ploy need careful consideration. If the suspect is innocent, being told that their body language gives away their deceit may be an unnerving experience if the suspect believes in the interviewer's diagnostic powers. In many of the documented cases involving false confessions (e.g., Gudjonsson & Lebegue, 1989), the initial uncertainty of a suspect concerning an incident was replaced with a false belief that they had committed an offence. In many of these cases the polygraph was instrumental in convincing the suspect that their "lies" had been detected and thus revealing their guilt. Telling a suspect that his lies have been uncovered by "trained observations" may be similarly "effective" in eliciting false statements.

Sympathy for the victim In a study of why suspects made admissions during police questioning, Gudjonsson and Petursson (1991) report that sympathy for the victim was a factor that contributed towards the making of an admission. That is, when there was already one motive to confess, the secondary factor of sympathy for the victim, was sometimes cited as an additional incentive or reason for confessing. Many officers try to induce feelings of guilt from suspects by pointing out that the suspect might be able to make life easier for the victim, perhaps by sparing them the need for testifying in court, or officers may suggest that helping to recover stolen goods might simply be appreciated by the victim.

The Use of Evidence

The availability of evidence against the suspect is probably the most important aspect of persuasive questioning. Research has demonstrated that the more evidence there is against a suspect, the more likely that person is to make an admission (e.g., Softley et al., 1980; Moston et al., 1993). Although overall amount of evidence per se may predict admissions, it is also the case that different types of evidence are more or less likely to be associated with confessions. The following sections comment specifically on how evidence from victims/witnesses and other suspects is used in persuasive questioning.

Victim/independent witness evidence When confronted with strong evidence from an independent witness or victim, it is seemingly difficult for a suspect to make a denial. Nevertheless, this is often exactly what does happen, usually contrary to the interviewer's expectations. Victim/witness evidence is probably one of the most misused forms of evidence available to interviewers, particularly when used as a form of critical feedback.

After eliciting a suspect's version of events, the next logical step for the interviewer is to concentrate subsequent questioning on how it differs from the evidence in the case. The obvious temptation for the interviewer is to directly point out to the suspect that their story must be false, since it contradicts the evidence from the witness. When confronted by witness evidence, the almost inevitable consequence is that the suspect will disagree with this testimony. The following sequence then invariably follows: the interviewer asks "Is the witness lying?" and the suspect replies, "Well, I'm not saying that". This ambiguous response almost certainly undermines the perceived credibility of the suspect (Moston & Moston, 1991). Nevertheless, this form of evidence appears remarkably ineffective in persuading suspects to alter their statements.

In cases in which a victim/witness has provided a description of an offender, officers try to convince the suspect of the validity and importance of that testimony by asking the suspect to describe their clothing or appearance. Alternatively, the interviewer may be the one to describe the suspect's clothing or appearance. In each case the aim of questioning is to point out the distinctive appearance of the suspect. This is intended to convey the impression that the witness has made a detailed identification directly identifying the suspect. Unfortunately, the level of detail in most witness descriptions is inadequate for this purpose. The following example shows how this strategy is used.

Interviewer	Would you describe yourself to me? How tall are you?
Suspect	5ft 10, but you know that already, yeah.
Interviewer	What colour's your hair?
Suspect	My hair?
Interviewer	Hm mm.
Suspect	Mouse colour.
Interviewer	Fairish. What were you wearing last night, the same as you're wearing now?
Suspect	Yeah.
Interviewer	So, you've got a pair of blue jeans.

Suspect	Hm mmm.
Interviewer	A sports-type shirt.
Suspect	Yeah.
Interviewer	And this jacket.
Suspect	The jacket.
Interviewer	It's a green jacket, yes?
Suspect	Yes.
Interviewer	Which is very ... It's got quite a large motif on the back of it.
Suspect	A heart, yeah.
Interviewer	You were wearing this last night?
Suspect	Yeah.
Interviewer	A woman who lives nearby in the shop that had the window broken last night saw you and your friend trying to smash the window. Can you account for that?
Suspect	No. I was sitting there on the bench.

In this example the eyewitness description, as relayed by the interviewer, would appear to match that of the suspect. The witness had described (or at least this is implied) that the suspect had a green jacket with a large motif on it. The remainder of the description is rather ambiguous ("fair hair", "sports-type shirt" and "jeans"). In this case the appearance of the suspect was relatively distinctive, however, in most cases it is not. If the green jacket reference is removed the description could apply to almost anyone. Nevertheless, the interviewer will still make a connection between the eyewitness description, no matter how vague, and the person they are currently questioning.

Generally, police officers have a tendency to "iron out" any ambiguities in eyewitness statements, turning vague descriptions in into positive identifications of the suspect. For example, in the above transcript, note how the suspect's description of his hair colour ("mouse") is reinterpreted by the interviewer ("fairish"). It is unlikely that this occurs because of a deliberate attempt to deceive the suspect, but rather from the general belief that the suspect being interviewed is in fact guilty and that the witness was, therefore, undoubtedly describing that person. Further, for this strategy to have any credibility the suspect's self description must be seen to match that of the witness, hence the need to adjust any "erroneous" statements made by the suspect.

Accomplice evidence In many interviews, strong evidence against the suspect will have been provided by another suspect, possibly an accomplice. Although this is seemingly powerful testimony, it is often a source of problems in a manner similar to that with other forms of victim/witness evidence. For example, the following sequence often occurs.

Interviewer	Your friend says that you were the one who took the money.
Suspect	No.
Interviewer	So is this person lying?
Suspect	Well, no, I'm not saying that.
Interviewer	Is he lying or telling the truth?
Suspect	I suppose he must be lying.

The suspect's initial response to the testimony of their friend is to simply contradict the evidence. The suspect tries to avoid being tied down to accusing the friend of lying, but later, through necessity, tries to discredit that person. This eventually leaves the interviewer with two suspects each accusing the other. This sequence of questioning almost always keeps to the same basic script. The interviewer cites the evidence of the accomplice, the suspect eventually tries to shift the blame onto this other person, thereby hoping to discredit and invalidate their testimony (Moston & Moston, 1991).

With the introduction of tape recording, the suspect no longer has to take the interviewer's word concerning their colleague's statement. The taped accusation can be played to the suspect. When playing extracts of tapes to suspects, many interviewers tend to focus solely on statements that are clearly accusatory, that is, statements that implicate the suspect. While this can be an effective ploy, interviewer's also make allowances for the possible importance of less obviously evidential information, such as personal comments. Such comments can often evoke more of a response than direct accusations. For example, in one case a man was accused of theft from his firm by his manager. In the manager's statement the employee was described as being "always unreliable" and as missing numerous workdays because he was "forever ill". Although it is difficult to make a direct association between these statements and the suspect's subsequent behaviour, it seemed apparent that this personal criticism was a greater determinant of the resulting admission and series of accusations against the manager, than the evidential part of the manager's statement.

In some cases the interviewer might try an interesting variation on the theme of accomplice evidence. For example, in one interview concerning an allegation of theft from a carpark, the police officer said "I've had the benefit of speaking to your friend. I know the reason you were down there". This statement is worth further consideration. The interviewer does not directly state that the suspect's accomplice has actually made an incriminating statement, even though this is inferred. The claim could thus be a bluff. Essentially, the interviewer is trying to play on the mutual distrust that might exist between two suspects. In doing so the interviewer does not actually lie to the suspect, although the intention might be construed as misleading.

The Role of Interviewing Strategies in Eliciting Confessions

This paper has described some of the most commonly used strategies adopted by police officers for persuading suspects to retract initial denials. Whilst there are undoubtedly occasions when such strategies may be effective in persuading a suspect to make an admission, such cases seem to be the exception rather than the norm. The key question that remains is why do suspects choose to make admissions? Moston et al. (1992) described how admissions tended to be made at the outset of interviews, occasionally in response to the very first question in the interview. Given the apparent lack of interviewing skills displayed by police officers it might be tempting to assume that officers are not affecting the decision making of suspects. However, such a conclusion might be misleading. Whilst there is little evidence that police officers are manipulating the decision making of suspects during taped interviews, this does not preclude the possibility that statements made to the suspect away from recording equipment are important.

Research by Irving (e.g., Irving, 1980; Irving & McKenzie, 1988; Irving & McKenzie, 1989) has shown how the use of some interviewing ploys has apparently declined since the introduction of PACE, although numbers of admissions do not appear to have declined (see Moston & Stephenson, 1993 b). It may be that with the introduction of tape recording that officers are now influencing the behaviour of suspects prior to the switching on of the tape recorder inside the interviewing room. There is certainly a great deal of scope for any such discussions, either at the time of arrest, on the way to the station, inside the custody area, in the cells, or even in the interviewing room itself, in the moments before the tape recorder is switched on.

The current picture of police interviewing procedures might therefore be misleading. The range of strategies illustrated in this paper seem unlikely to elicit false confessions, given that they rarely ever elicit confessions even when the suspect is undoubtedly guilty and there is substantial evidence to convict them. This conclusion appears to contradict the research on false confessions by Gudjonsson (e.g., 1992) which suggests that police interviewing strategies are a key determinant of false confessions. However, the discrepancy may be explained by the fact that the current research was carried out on a representative sample of cases, with varying degrees of severity. These cases also involved taped interviews. Research by Gudjonsson has largely featured serious cases, many of which were conducted prior to the introduction of tape recording. Although it is still possible to find instances of coercion on taped interviews, only a minority of interviewers might be expected to be so foolish as to coerce a statement in the presence of recording equipment. The area of debate over the use of persuasive questioning techniques has consequently shifted away from the confines of the interview room to other, less easily observed venues.

References

Gudjonsson, G. H. (1984). A new scale of interrogative suggestibility. *Personality and Individual Differences*, *5*, 303-314.

Gudjonsson, G. H. (1992). *The Psychology of interrogations, confessions and testimony.* Chichester: Wiley.

Gudjonsson, G. H. and Lebegue, B. (1989). Psychological and psychiatric aspects of a coerced-internalized false confession. *Journal of the Forensic Science Society*, *29*, 261-269.

Gudjonsson, G. H., & MacKeith, J. A. C. (1988). Retracted confessions: Legal, psychological and psychiatric aspects. *Medicine, Science and the Law*, *28*, 187-194.

Gudjonsson, G., & Petursson, H. (1991). Custodial interrogation: why do suspects confess and how does it relate to their crime, attitude and personality? *Personality and Individual Differences*, *12*, 295-306.

Inbau, F. E., & Reid, J. E. (1967). *Criminal interrogations and confessions* (2nd ed.). Baltimore: Williams and Wilkins.

Irving, B. (1980). *Police interrogation: A case study of current practice. Royal Commission on Criminal Procedure Research Study No. 2*. London: HMSO.

Irving, B. L., & McKenzie, I. K. (1988). *Regulating custodial interviews: The effects of the Police and Criminal Evidence Act 1984: Vol. I.* London: The Police Foundation.

Irving, B. L., & McKenzie, I. K. (1989). *Regulating custodial interviews: The effects of the Police and Criminal Evidence Act 1984: Vol. II.* London: The Police Foundation.

Kohnken, G. (1987). Training police officers to detect deceptive eyewitness statements: Does it work? *Social Behaviour*, *2*, 1-17.

Leo, R. A. (1992). From coercion to deception: The changing nature of police interrogation in America. *Crime, Law and Social Change*, *18*, 35-59.

Moston, S. (1987). The suggestibility of children in interview studies. *first Language*, *7*, 67-78.

Moston, S. (1992). Can police officers distinguish between truthful and deceptive statements? *Policing*, *8*, 26-39.

Moston, S., & Engelberg, T. (in press). Police questioning techniques in tape recorded interviews with criminal suspects. *Policing and Society*.

Moston, S. & Moston, T. (1991). Challenging the obvious?: Suspect behaviour during police questioning. Paper presented at British Psychological Society Annual Conference, International Centre, Bournemouth.

Moston, S., & Stephenson, G. M. (1993). The changing face of police interrogation. *Community and Applied Social Psychology*, *3* 101-115.

Moston, S., Stephenson, G. M., & Williamson, T. (1992). The effects of case characteristics on suspect behaviour during police questioning. *British Journal of Criminology*, *32*, 23-40.

Moston, S., Stephenson, G. M., & Williamson, T. (1993). The incidence, antecedents and consequences of the use of the right to silence during police questioning. *Criminal Behaviour and Mental Health*, *3*, 30-47.

Oxford, T. (1991). Spotting a liar. *Police Review*, *15* February, 328-329.

Police and Criminal Evidence Act 1984 (1991). *Codes of practice (s.66)* (2nd ed.). London: HMSO.

Royal, R. F., & Schutt, S. R. (1976). *The gentle art of interviewing and interrogation*. New Jersey: Prentice-Hall.

Good Practice for Video Recorded Interviews with Child Witnesses for Use in Criminal Proceedings

Ray Bull

Introduction

In their excellent 1990 book entitled *The evidence of children* Spencer and Flin noted that an English lawyer Heydon in 1984 provided a summary of reasons adduced to justify the then legal suspicion concerning children's testimony. It may not surprise you to learn that little of what Heydon claimed is now supported by scientific research. Heydon stated that

> First, a child's powers of observation and memory are less reliable than an adult's. Secondly, children are prone to live in a make-believe world, so that they magnify incidents which happen to them or invent them completely. Thirdly, they are also very egocentric, so that details seemingly unrelated to their own world are quickly forgotten by them. Fourthly, because of their immaturity they are very suggestible and can easily be influenced by adults and other children. One lying child may influence others to lie; anxious parents may take a child through a story again and again so that it becomes drilled in untruths. Most dangerously, a policeman taking a statement from a child may without ill will use leading questions so that the child tends to confuse what actually happened with the answer suggested implicitly by the question. A fifth danger is that children often have little notion of the duty to speak the truth, and they may fail to realise how important their evidence is in a case and how important it is for it to be accurate. Finally, children sometimes behave in a way evil beyond their years. They may consent to sexual offences against themselves and then deny consent. They may completely invent sexual offences. Some children know that the adult world regards such matters in a serious and peculiar way, and they enjoy investigating this mystery or revenging themselves by making false accusations. (Heydon 1984, p. 84).

Since 1984, when Heydon made such claims, psychologists' scientific research has produced replicated results which are contrary to such views. On the basis of this research, laws and procedures relating to child witnesses in various countries have recently been changed or are being changed (e.g. Law Reform Commission of Western Australia, 1991).

In addition, very recent and much ongoing research by psychologists has been directed towards helping the interviewers of child witnesses to increase their interviewing skills and knowledge.

In October 1992 a report was published on behalf of the Secretary of State for Scotland by Lord Clyde concerning his inquiry into the removal of children from their homes in Orkney in 1991 (Clyde, 1992). In this report the skills of those who interviewed the alleged child victims of ritual sexual abuse were described as inadequate and deficient. In The Independent newspaper (Oct. 28, 1992) it was stated that "A Scottish Office spokesman said it was widely accepted that this was a difficult area. 'What we *don't* know about interviewing children would fill books' he said".

Among the recommendations in Lord Clyde's report were several concerning the interviewing of children.

In many countries new facilities include provision for the video recording of interviews. The *1991 Criminal Justice Act* (England and Wales) permits (from October, 1992) video recorded interviews with child witnesses to be shown in criminal trials. The objectives of this paper will be (i) to give an account of recent legislative changes in England and Wales relevant to child witnesses, (ii) to describe the consultative procedures adopted by the Home Office (the relevant government department) to produce the Memorandum of Good Practice, and (iii) to present information regarding the psychological research which underpins some of the contents of the Memorandum.

In England and Wales in 1988 legislation was introduced permitting children to testify in criminal trials via the "live video link" from another room in the court building. Also the statutory ban on convicting on the uncorroborated evidence of unsworn children was abolished, and with it the duty to warn the jury of the danger of accepting the evidence of a child.

Also in 1988 the Home Office set up a committee chaired by Judge Pigot. The committee's report proposed a number of innovations, one of these being that the evidence of children in criminal cases routinely be taken in advance of trial and recorded on videotape (Bull & Spencer, 1992). The 1991 Criminal Justice Act permits this for evidence-in-chief, but cross-examination must occur live at trial (the child witness probably testifying via a "live video link" from another room in the court building). The 1991 Act gives the judge discretion to exclude part (or all) of the video recording of an interview which she or he considers to have been conducted inappropriately.

In the House of Commons in 1991 the Home Office minister announced that his government department would be producing a code of practice for such video recorded interviews. The Home Office asked a psychologist (the author) and a lawyer (Professor Di Birch from the University of Nottingham) to produce a first working draft of the code by the summer of 1991. (This paper is based, in part, on that draft.) In the relatively few months available to me I had (i) to travel around England and Wales consulting with child witness interview practitioners (e.g. police officers, social workers), (ii) to consult with experts world wide, and (iii) to make sure that I was familiar with all the relevant (and upcoming) literature. The Home Office set up a policy steering group which consisted of a senior representative from each of a number of relevant bodies (e.g. the Criminal Bar Association, the Law Society, the Association of Chief Police Officers, the National Society for the Prevention of Cruelty to Children, the Association of Directors of Social Services, Childline, the Royal College of Psychiatrists, the National Children's Bureau, the British Psychological Society). The Home Office's revised version of our original working draft for the code was then sent for comment to each member of this group (who consulted their colleagues). The group then met (with the author and Professor Birch present) to discuss a "First Revise" and to make suggestions for its improvement. A "Second Revise" was produced by the Home Office which went through a similar procedure, as did a "Third Revise". A "Fourth Revise" was produced in January 1992 and this was distributed widely, with the Home Office inviting comments. A "Fifth Revise" was then produced and the finalised version was published in August 1992, its title being amended to "Memorandum of Good Practice".

The Memorandum of Good Practice covers a very wide range of issues. Advice on the legal conditions about which a criminal court may wish to be satisfied before admitting a video recording are included, as is guidance on the legal rules to be observed in producing an evidential recording acceptable to criminal courts (see also Birch, 1992). It gives guidance on what to do prior to an interview, including when and where to conduct a video recording. Guidance is also offered on the equipment to use. An essential component gives advice on conducting the interviews so that children can give as full an account as possible without undue influence taking place. The Memorandum also provides recommendations about post interview issues such as the storage, custody and disposal of such video recordings.

This paper will focus on the actual conducting of interviews, especially questioning techniques. The views expressed here are based upon research literature, professional publications and other information kindly made available to the author by many helpful people in various countries; they do not necessarily represent the views of any organisation.

Psychologists' research in the last ten years has confirmed that children (even very young ones) are usually able to give a worthwhile report of what happened to them if they are interviewed appropriately (see Bull, 1988; Davies, Stevenson-Robb, & Flin, 1986; Faller, 1990; Fivush & Hudson, 1990; Hedderman, 1987; Myers, 1987; Murray & Gough, 1991; Saywitz, Goodman, & Myers, 1990; Spencer & Flin, 1990; Vizard, 1991), However, inappropriate interviewing, especially that with a suggestive (Baxter, 1990; Ceci, De Simone, Putnick, & Nightingale, 1992; Doris, 1991; King & Yuille, 1989; Toglia, Ross, & Ceci, 1992), pressurising or leading style, can bias the child's report (White 1990).

Research has been conducted in which children witness complex events either live or via a video recording. This has found that, when asked simply to describe what happened in their own words, children most often produce reliable accounts. That is, the vast majority of what most of them say in these (often ingenious) studies (e.g. Price & Goodman, 1990) is an accurate account of what happened, but rarely is a full account given by anyone (Ceci, Toglia, & Ross, 1987; Dent & Flin, 1992; Irish Law Reform Commission, 1990; McGough, 1992; Oates, 1990; Perry & Wrightsman, 1991; Spencer, Nicholson, Flin, & Bull, 1990). However, young children usually report less than do older children or adults (Flin, Boon, Knox, & Bull, 1992; List, 1986). Therefore, especially with younger children, some form of questioning is often needed. However, such questioning should not affect the child's own account which should be requested before any questioning occurs.

In 1990 Sue White argued that "Until relatively recently, suspected victims of child sexual abuse did not receive much special consideration with reference to how they should be interviewed". She suggested that "Techniques for interviewing these young children have been based on practical experiences and are only now beginning to receive any research attention". She pointed out that "While a number of authors have made detailed suggestions of how best to interact with a child suspected of being a victim of sexual abuse ... interviewers have been forced to discover clinical techniques which work best in their particular situation". She believes that "The first goal in investigatory interviewing must be the gathering of data which are as true as possible a representation of the child's experiences and which are not subject to charges of being contaminated".

In the Introduction to their excellent 1990 edited book *Knowing and remembering in young children* Judith Hudson and Robyn Fivush made the important point that "younger children have not yet learned the conventional framework for recounting the past, and therefore depend more on the adult's questions to guide their recall than do older children". Thus the skill of questioning is a key issue in effective interviews with children (Garbarino & Stott, 1991; Toglia et al., 1992). Research has demonstrated that inappropriate questioning can bias the replies of adults as well as of children. Questions vary in the extent to which they can influence replies to them.

The main purpose of the Home Office Memorandum of Good Practice on video recorded interviews with child witnesses for criminal proceedings (produced in consultation with the Department of Health) is to help those making video recordings of interviews with child witnesses where it is intended that the result should be acceptable in criminal proceedings. Following the Memorandum is voluntary, but it may become widely accepted to do so. In Court questions are likely to be asked about whether an interview followed the Memorandum.

The *Criminal Justice Act 1991* gives criminal courts the power to decide that some, or all, of a video recorded interview with a child is not to be admitted as evidence. Thus, appropriate interviewing is essential if it is decided that a video recording of the interview should replace the child giving evidence-in-chief "live" on the day of the trial, probably many months after the alleged incident(s).

Relevant Aspects of the 1991 Criminal Justice Act

In order to be able to conduct video recorded interviews with child witnesses in a manner acceptable to criminal courts the interviewer will need to be familiar with the requirements and procedures of such courts.

The *Criminal Justice Act 1991* allows the judge to order that the child not be examined-in-chief on any matter, which in the opinion of the court has been adequately dealt with in the video recorded interview. In this way the recording can take the place of the child's evidence-in-chief if the interview is deemed worthwhile by the court. Cross examination (and any re-examination) will be conducted live.

Until recently the English criminal courts' requirement that witnesses be competent was interpreted as making it impossible to hear evidence from a child under six years of age. However, in 1991, the Court of Appeal ruled (R. v. Z., [1990] 3 W.L.R. 113) that a child of any age could give evidence provided that the judge deemed her or him sufficiently able to recount what happened and to understand the duty of speaking the truth (Spencer & Flin, 1993). The 1991 Criminal Justice Act attempts to abolish the competency requirement altogether, save as it applies to all witnesses, but clearly the interview with the child must be conducted in such a way as to permit the court to conclude that the child has sufficiently recalled what happened.

Planning the Interview

Interviews should not be conducted without adequate planning. The needs of each child, of each interview and of the interviewer may differ from one interview to another. No simple recipes/prescriptions are available which can be relevant to all interviews. What follows in this paper is guidance that may be appropriate to most interviews.

The child's level of development

As they grow older the vast majority of children become better at describing in their own words what happened to them. Their ability to answer questions reliably also improves as does their ability to resist suggestive or leading questions. However, individual children develop at different rates and so a child's chronological age can only be a very approximate guide to his or her level of development. Therefore, prior to interviewing a child witness, as much information as possible should be sought about her linguistic, cognitive and communicative development, as well as his or her degree of social, physical and sexual maturity (Goodman & Schwartz-Kenney, 1992). Such information should have an influence on the planning decisions about the probable pace of the interview, how to commence the interview, and its probable duration.

Timing

Most criminal trials involving child witnesses take place several months after the alleged incident(s) (Flin & Bull, 1990; Flin, Bull, Boon, & Knox, 1992). Psychologists' research has found that during such a delay period many witnesses forget aspects of what did happen, which they initially could remember. This has been found especially with younger children (Flin, Boon, Knox, & Bull, 1992; Pipe, 1992; Poole, 1992). In Australia, Alison Tucker and her colleagues concluded from their study that "more information may be recalled, and with greater accuracy, the sooner a child eyewitness is interviewed following a crime" (Tucker, Martin, & Luszez, 1990). A video recording of an interview with a child witness conducted as soon as possible can preserve his or her account, which might otherwise suffer from the passage of time. Thus, one of the reasons why the Home Office sought provision for children's video recorded evidence to be shown in criminal trials was to preserve the child's initial account. The video recorded interview should therefore be made as soon as there is reason to believe the child has something to say. Delay may lead the child to forget things he or she earlier could have remembered. However, interviews with child witnesses should not be rushed into.

Adequate planning should always take place which could involve any background information available, inter-agency discussion (e.g. between the police and social services), consideration of the child's needs, age and probable development. In this way the question of how best to conduct the interview can always be addressed. If the interview is well planned and well conducted this should reduce the need for repeated interviewing. However, for very young children, those with special needs, and those who are reticent, the interview might be *planned* to consume a smaller amount of time on a number of successive days. It may well be the case that some children may not recount all they can remember within a single interviewing session.

Conducting the Interview

The purpose of a video recorded interview with a child witness is to obtain as full and reliable an account as possible. Current and past criticisms of some interviews with child witnesses (e.g. Irish Law Reform Commission, 1989, 1990) have focused on the questioning techniques employed (Flin, Bull, Boon, & Knox, 1992, 1993). These criticisms have been concerned with the possibility that interviewers have (probably unwittingly) contaminated the child's account by virtue of the use of suggestive, leading, biasing or pressurising questions (Loftus & Davies, 1984).

In 1988 a well respected British child psychiatrist experienced at interviewing children who may have been abused (David Jones) made the sensible recommendation (Jones & McQuistion, 1988) of dividing interviews with such children into four phases which can be described as:

(i) rapport;
(ii) free narrative;
(iii) questioning;
(iv) closure.

In 1991 another very experienced psychiatrist (Eileen Vizard) made a similar recommendation, as did Aaron Hoorwitz in his fine (1992) book on interviewing children who may have been sexually abused. In the first working draft of the Memorandum which the author produced for the Home Office such a phased approach was adopted. However, within the questioning phase the draft and, the published Memorandum was much more specific about the various types of questioning and the most appropriate order in which these various forms of questions should be put within the questioning phase (following Saywitz, 1990).

The Memorandum recommends that normally the interviewing of child witnesses should be planned to pass through a number of phases (Jones, 1990; Jones, 1991) which firstly provide the child with the opportunity to describe in her own words what happened, and then proceed from general and open questions to specific and closed types of questions.

John Yuille (1988) has similarly recommended that in order to obtain as full a statement as possible from the child that is uncontaminated by the interviewer, a "step-wise" procedure be adopted. This "step-wise" procedure was developed in Germany over a number of decades (see Undeutsch 1982; Steller & Köhnken, 1989) by psychologists with substantial experience of interviewing children, who may have been sexually abused. It was developed in order to obtain an appropriate statement from the child which could then be analysed (that is, the statement) to determine whether it demonstrated the criteria thought to be associated with genuinely experienced events (see Köhnken, 1990; Steller & Boychuk, 1992).

In July 1992 John Yuille presented at a seminar held in London some preliminary findings from his Canadian field study designed to evaluate the effects of training interviewers in the "step-wise" approach. In British Columbia a joint training programme for police, social workers and prosecutors was set up. All the participants received several days' training in "step-wise" interviewing. With the permission of the "real life" witnesses interviewed before and after these interviewers had received the training, the tape recordings of nearly two hundred interviews were passed to researchers for evaluation. The research team developed a rating technique concerning the effectiveness of the interviews. Interviews were classified as "useless" firstly if no conclusion could be drawn about whether the child had been abused, and secondly if the interviewer conducted a poor interview. John Yuille reported that whereas 35% of the pre-training interviews were classified as "useless" (and this is a large percentage), only 14% of the post-training interviews were classified as "useless". This is an important finding. In addition, of the 156 people who received the interview training only one made a negative remark about it. Most described it as easy to follow.

Phase one: rapport

The essential first phase of an interview with a child witness is the establishing of rapport between the child and the interviewer (Boggs & Eyberg, 1990; Myers, 1987). Questioning of the child about the alleged incident(s) should never occur without adequate rapport firstly having been established. The child should be helped to relax and to feel as comfortable as possible. Children, especially young ones, may not be used to speaking to strangers. Indeed, many are taught not to do so.

The child could be asked to give an account of one or more "neutral" events in her life, and/or something which interests her (e.g. a hobby of hers, what her last holiday was like). With younger children, the rapport phase may need to involve play with toys or drawing to assist the child to relax and interact with the interviewer. (The Home Office Memorandum of Good Practice notes that "Such play should not be used during this phase to gather information relevant to the alleged offence"). In this way further information can be gathered to supplement what the interviewer knows about the child's social and communicative development. This information is essential in helping the interviewer decide upon the most suitable length and type of questions to ask the child later in the interview. The number of words used per sentence by the child in this rapport phase should guide the length of the interviewer's questions (to be asked later).

Towards the end of the rapport phase effort should be made to explain to the child what the interview will consist of, without undermining the integrity of the evidence. Providing the child with an appropriate explanation will assist the child to understand what to expect and to give an account of events, even the very young ones. Some children may assume that because they are being interviewed *they* must have done something wrong. Also some children may feel guilty about being involved in abusive acts (even as recipients). Therefore, great care must be taken when trying to explain to the child the need to speak the truth.

Phase two: free narrative account

If it is deemed appropriate, having established rapport, to continue with the interview then the child should be asked to provide *in her own words* an account of the relevant event(s). (Note that the purpose of the interview has been explained to the child during the rapport phase.) Only the most general, open-ended questions should be asked in this phase and only as guidance to the child concerning the general area of life experience relevant to the investigation (e.g. "Do you know why we are here today?" "Is there anything that you would like to tell me?"). This type of question is one that inquires in a non-specific manner. If the child responds in a positive way to such questions then the interviewer can encourage the child to give a free narrative account of events. During this phase the interviewer's role is to act as a facilitator, not an interrogator. Research findings consistently implicate the questioning strategies often used with children as greater sources of distortion to their testimony than memory deficits (Toglia et al., 1992). Therefore it is essential to avoid using inappropriate questions in the early parts of an interview. Every effort must be made to obtain information from the child which is spontaneous and uncontaminated by the interview (Lawrence, 1988).

With young children it should be communicated to them that the interviewer genuinely has no idea what has happened to them. Carole Menig-Peterson (1975) found that young children's communicative behaviour was influenced by their belief concerning adult interviewers' knowledge or naivety about the event the children were describing. In addition Fielding and Conroy (1992) and McGurk and Glachan (1988) have noted that younger children often are reluctant to believe that they know anything useful that adults do not already know. Young children often assume that because one adult knows what has happened to them (e.g. a perpetrator), other adults may somehow be privy to this knowledge (Toglia et al., 1992). In addition, in the interview they may feel that they are in a situation in which their usual rules of conversation with adults, in which adults already know the answers, are *reversed* or altered. Similarly interviewers must be aware that expecting a witness to speak in a frank way about personal/sexual matters reverses the usual convention of normal conversation in which many people talk about such matters only in an allusive way (Wattam - personal communication).

The interviewer should resist the temptation to speak as soon as the child appears to stop doing so. In his review of the role of "wait time" Tobin (1987) reported that teachers obtained fuller replies from pupils if they were able (which they found difficult) to wait longer than three seconds before speaking once pupils appeared to stop speaking. The interviewer must be patient and tolerant of pauses (including long ones) and silences. Additionally, the interviewer must be tolerant of what may appear to be accounts of irrelevant information from the child. The interviewer's desire to determine whether a child has witnessed abuse must not result in an over eager approach. "Active listening" could be used which involves letting the child know that what she has said has been heard by the interviewer reflecting this back in the child's *own* words.

An additional benefit of obtaining from the child an uncontaminated free narrative account may be (as Roger Shuy, 1986 suggests) that jurors may be more impressed by a free narrative account than "the more courtroom style of highly controlled, brief answer, fragmented testimony" which is occasioned by questioning. Research on interviewing adults has found that police officers often interrupt co-operative witnesses while they are speaking, even on relevant matters (Fisher, Geiselman, & Raymond, 1987).

Phase three: questioning

Open-ended questions In deciding whether or not to proceed on to a subsequent phase of the interview the needs of the child (and those of criminal justice) must be considered. If the child seems distressed the interviewer should make a judgement as to whether this is caused by the child giving her account or by the interviewing. If the latter, then pressing ahead with more interviewing is inappropriate. In asking any questions the interviewer must take account of the child's stage of development (which should have been noted during the rapport and free narrative phases as well as from pre-interview information).

When the child has finished the free narrative account (the length of which may vary as a function of a host of factors including the child's age) questions can be asked. However, it is most important that interviewers appreciate that there are *different types* of questions, some of which will be less likely to bias the child's account than others.

Open-ended questions ask the child to provide more information but in a way that does not lead nor pressurise the child. As Stephen Moston (1990) has argued, like all questions used in the interview they must be phrased in a manner which implies that an inability to remember is acceptable. Indeed, it should be made clear to the child during this phase that to reply "I can't remember" or "I don't know" can be an appropriate response.

For a child who provided little relevant information in the free narrative phase a focused yet open-ended question could be of the form "Is anything worrying you?" or "Are there some things you are not happy about?". Only one question should be asked per utterance. The language used in any questions must be appropriate for the child being interviewed. Rarely, if ever, would adult language be appropriate. Sentences should be simple and unambiguous, avoiding double negatives, embedded clauses and other confusing constructions.

For children whose free narrative account provided rather more relevant information the questions asked could be more focused yet still open-ended. For example, "Could you please tell me more about the man by the railway bridge?" (given that the child has mentioned a man by the bridge). If the witness becomes distressed even when questioned in this gentle way the interviewer should seriously consider moving away for a while from this topic and reverting to an earlier phase of the interview (e.g. re-building rapport). Such shifting away from and then back to a difficult topic for the child may need to re-occur several times in an interview.

Some questions employing the word "why" may be interpreted by children as attributing blame/guilt to them. Such questions should be avoided. Also to be avoided is the repeating of a question soon after a child has answered it since this can be interpreted by children as a criticism of their original response. Close repetition of a question may cause the child to change her answer to one she then thinks the interviewer wants to hear (Siegal, Waters, & Dinwiddy 1988). Poole and White (1991) reported (as did Moston in 1987) that when a question is repeated children tend to assume that their original answer must have been incorrect, and so they may therefore change their answer when the question is posed again.

Specific yet non-leading questions Before moving on to this phase the interviewer should again consider whether it is in the interests of the child to do so. This phase allows for extension and clarification of previously provided information both from the free narrative and subsequent phase. It also provides an opportunity for the child who has said very little in connection with the purpose of the interview to be reminded of what the focus of the interview is without the child being asked leading questions.

Adults sometimes falsely assume that children, even young ones, must know what is relevant. Understanding what is relevant assists a witness to focus his or her account and specific yet non-leading questions allow the interviewer to guide the witness in an evidentially sound manner. Questions must not be leading in the sense that the question implies the answer (even though in some cases it may be inevitable that questions will refer to disputed facts). The interviewer should be aware that most people, and especially young children, may give a reply to a question merely to meet the perceived needs of the interviewer (Gudjonsson, 1992). During this phase questions which require a "yes" or "no" answer, or ones which allow only one of two possible responses, should never be asked (Choi, 1991).

For a child who has already provided information that a man by the railway bridge hurt her and that he was wearing a jacket, a specific yet non-leading question could be "What colour was the man's jacket?".

If the child's account so far has mentioned repeated abuse, but has not described in any or sufficient detail separate incidents, this may now be the time to try to establish this. Young children find it more difficult to remember events if adult-appropriate language is used in the questioning (Saywitz, 1990). For example, calendar dates or days of the week may be inappropriate. It may be better to use life events meaningful to the child, say, before or after Christmas, a birthday or a holiday; on a school day or non school day. Regarding time of day, mentioning meal times, television programmes, bedtime and the like could be useful. Interviewers should try to establish the "labels" the child uses for various events and then use these in the questioning.

Closed questions If specific yet non-leading questions have not been sufficiently productive, then closed questions could be asked. Closed questions are ones that give the interviewee a limited number of alternative responses, but preferably more than two. For example, "Was the man's jacket you mentioned, green or red or blue or another colour. Or can't you remember?" Such a question would not normally be deemed a leading question. If a closed question permits only one of two responses then the response of both children and adults may not necessarily be a good indication of what is in their memory, especially if they are unwilling to give a "don't know" response and/or the interview setting has not emphasised this as an acceptable reply. Such a limited closed question may not be leading, but one has to consider how truly informative a reply to it is (Choi, 1991).

If after the end of this phase the interviewer is appropriately of the opinion that further questioning is still necessary then it could be decided to move into a phase of leading questions. However, there must be a *clear* appreciation that a leading style of questioning may have limited evidential value in criminal procedings.

Leading questions A leading question is one which implies the answer. Such questions would usually not be permitted as part of the child witness' live evidence-in-chief in a criminal trial. (In court counsel can object to the use of a leading question before a witness giving evidence-in-chief responds to it.) The greatest care must be taken when questioning the witness about central matters which are likely to be disputed in court. Leading questions, especially about such matters, are best left to the very final questioning phase, especially since the definition of a leading question depends in part on what the respondent has already said.

Both adult and child interviewees' responses to leading questions can be more the result of the questioning than of valid remembering. Some witnesses, and in particular young children, may be more willing to respond to "yes/no" questions with a "yes" response (Stone & Lemanek, 1990). If leading questions permitting only a "yes/no" response are asked, then it is imperative that these should be phrased so that questions on the same issue sometimes produce a "yes" response and sometimes a "no" response.

Responses to leading questions which relate to central facts which have not yet been described by the child in an earlier phase of the interview will probably be of limited evidential value in criminal trials. The video recording of these may well be deemed inadmissible in court (as may the remainder of the interview). Since when asking a leading question one cannot know whether the answer will provide more information than that suggested by the question, leading questions should only be asked about evidentially relevant matters when all the above phases have been passed through.

If a leading question is used because the child seems to need to be led, and it produces an evidentially relevant response (particularly one which contains relevant information not led by the question), then the interviewer should *immediately* refrain from asking further leading questions but revert to one of the non-leading phases described above. In this way the interview should avoid being one composed largely of leading questions. The potential for harm to the child should she not give an account could guide the decision as to whether to use leading questions.

The use of dolls and other props

There are a number of quite different purposes which dolls and other props may serve (Everson & Boat, 1990; Goodman & Aman, 1990; Vizard, 1991). One is to establish just what the words already used by the child refer to. Another use is for the child to demonstrate actions when the child has no appropriate vocabulary for this. Interviewers must be trained in the appropriate use of dolls and props. The Memorandum states that their use should not form a major part of the evidence presented to a criminal court, especially where interpretation of the child's use of such dolls is required (for example, when the child has not described in her own words what the dolls are doing). Once a verbal child has used a prop the interviewer should attempt to revert to an earlier phase of the interview (mentioned above) in order to obtain evidentially more robust information.

New interviewing procedures

Mel Pipe's on-going research in New Zealand and recent work in Germany by Dahmen-Zimmer and Loohs (1992) suggest that props/toys may assist children to give valid accounts in an evidentially sound way. This contrasts with the recent claim by Raskin and Esplin (1991) that "puppets, drawings, good touch/bad touch games, and toys are generally unnecessary and should be avoided whenever possible". Clearly such procedures can be used inappropriately, but much more research is necessary to develop adequate procedures. Raskin and Esplin have claimed that "They frequently distract the child from the task of providing complete and accurate descriptions, and they can be suggestive, provoke fantasy and lack a scientific basis". What researchers need to do is to develop scientifically based recommendations for the use of props and toys based on proper research. This is an urgent need.

Recently there has been an increase, from a very low base, in developing practice and in research on new methods for assisting children's recollection. These were not included in the Memorandum of Good Practice. One major reason for this was that there did not exist enough research-based information regarding their use in interviews relevant to criminal proceedings to determine the effectiveness of such procedures (e.g. the use of (i) play materials to prompt a child who has as yet said nothing about abuse, or (ii) "reconstructive" techniques in which the child is given scale models of houses, settings, people, or (iii) context reinstatement, for example as in the cognitive interview (Memon, Cronin, Eaves, & Bull, 1992; Memon & Bull, 1991), or (iv) preparatory interviewing procedures (e.g. Warren, Hulse-Trotter, & Tubbs, 1991; Saywitz, Moan, & Lamphear, 1991; Saywitz, Snyder, & Lamphear, 1990)).

Phase four: closing the interview

Recapitulation During this aspect of closing the interview the interviewer should check with the child that the interviewer has correctly understood the evidentially important parts (if any) of the child's account. This should be done using the child's own language not a summary provided by the interviewer in adult language (which could be mistaken but with which the child may nevertheless agree). If the child has described acts of sexual or physical abuse the interviewer could ask (in a skilful manner) if the child has seen films, videos, magazines or books of this nature.

Yuille (1988) suggests that a "suggestibility check" be conducted on the child, though many would argue against this unless there is very good reason to do so. (Raskin and Esplin (1991) make some good points on this issue.)

Closure The interviewer should always try to ensure that the interview ends appropriately. Every interview must have a closing phase conducted in the interest of the child. In this phase it may be a useful idea to discuss again some of the "neutral" topics mentioned by the child in the rapport phase.

In this phase, regardless of the outcome of the interview, every effort should be made to ensure that the child is not distressed but is in a positive frame of mind. Even if the appropriate, professional decision has been to terminate the interview before sufficient information has been gathered from the witness for criminal proceedings, the child must not be made to feel that she has failed. The child should be thanked for her time and effort and asked if there is anything more she wishes to say. It is now becoming a wider practice to give to the child (or accompanying person) a contact name and telephone number in case the child later decides that she has further matters she wishes to discuss with the interviewer.

Interviewing Children with Particular Needs

The sections above will have made it plain that a high level of skill is required to interview children for evidential purposes. It is most unlikely that such a level of skill will be demonstrated unless the interviewer is appropriately qualified, has been properly trained and is sufficiently experienced. This is even more so concerning the inter-viewing of very young children and those with particular or "special" needs which may include those with learning difficulty, or deafness/hearing difficulty, or blindness/seeing difficulty, or a speech impediment, or emotional disturbance (or some combination of these). Interviewing such children in a manner appropriate to them which is evidentially sound may prove the greatest challenge to interviewers, particularly since some of these children may find it difficult to produce a free narrative account and may need the assistance of specific or closed questions.

Recently in England the term "mental handicap or mental retardation" has been replaced by "learning difficulty or learning disability". In 1991 Ann Craft pointed out that people who work with those who have learning disability are becoming increasingly aware of their lack of expertise in assisting such people give accounts of what has happened to them. Some authors have persuasively argued (e.g. Turk & Brown, 1992; Westcott, 1991) that children with learning difficulty may well be those most at risk of sexual abuse, yet those most denied access to the justice system.

In 1992 Helen Westcott noted in her survey of teams from the National Society for the Prevention of Cruelty to Children (NSPCC) who worked with disabled children that "several workers specifically referred to feeling unsure of how to respond to the child, and how to work with him or her. For example, workers mentioned being unable to gauge how much the child had actually understood, and described their initial 'panic' reaction on working with a child with disabilities. This 'deskilling' effect needs to be recognised, and acted upon, to prevent it becoming a barrier to effective communication". To assist interviewers Bull and Cullen (1992) recently produced (at the request of the Crown Office in Scotland) a booklet to help prosecutors interview "witnesses who may have mental handicaps".

Walter Coles (1990), who is a member of the Royal Canadian Mounted Police, has reported that "Investigating cases of sexual abuse of persons with disabilities is extremely difficult" yet "Disabled persons have the right to be protected, and they have the right to live a life free of sexual abuse".

The recently published Home Office Memorandum of Good Practice stated that, where the child has a disability of any kind, particular care should be taken to "develop effective strategies for the interview to minimise the effect of such disabilities". However, Helen Westcott (1992) has pointed out that in the Memorandum "The real problems facing children with disabilities are not acknowledged". I agree with this. The Memorandum says very little on the extra procedures and skills which might assist children with special needs to give an account because so little is known on this topic, particularly in terms of procedures whose effectiveness has been *researched* and *evaluated*. Westcott, among others, has emphasised how rarely evidence from children with special needs has been used in court, even though they may well be at greater risk of abuse. She made the point that "Existing child protection services need to be revised to become accessible to all children (irrespective of disability) who may need to use them. Special training is essential for all professionals involved". But what should this "special training" consist of? There is so little good research on this topic (see Bull, 1994)

The Training of Interviewers

If interviewers receive suitable training (Aldridge, 1992) their video recorded interviews should be done well and appear so to any expert who watches the video recording of the interview. Appropriate training will not only focus on the issues addressed in this paper but should be extensive, wide ranging and well thought out. Such training will require extensive resources which are not yet being provided in all regions. Interviewers of child witnesses *are keen* to improve their skills and understanding of relevant issues. This laudable desire can only serve to reduce the frequency with which criminal courts will deem to be inappropriate part or all of a video recorded interview. *Adequate* training, plus the Memorandum of Good Practice, will assist the criminal justice system to give to children what they deserve, and will demonstrate the weaknesses within Heydon's quotation with which this chapter began.

References

Aldridge, J. (1992). The further training of professionals dealing with child witnesses. In H. Dent & R. Flin (Eds.), *Children as witnesses*. Chichester: Wiley.

Baxter, J. S. (1990). The suggestibility of child witnesses: A review. *Applied Cognitive Psychology*, *4*, 393-407.

Birch, D. (1992). Children's evidence. *Criminal Law Review*, 262-276.

Boggs, S., & Eyberg, S. (1990). Interview techniques and establishing rapport. In A. La Greca (Ed.), *Through the eyes of the child: Obtaining self-reports from children and adolescents*. Boston: Allyn and Bacon.

Bull, R. (1988). Children as witnesses. *Policing, 4*, 130-143.

Bull, R. (1994). Innovative techniques for the questioning of child witnesses especially those who are young and those with learning disability. In M. Zaragoza (Ed.), *Memory, suggestibility and eyewitness testimony in children and adults*. New York: Hemisphere.

Bull, R., & Spencer, J. (1992). Recent English changes in child witness laws, procedures, and a new Memorandum of Good Practice for Interviews. *Violence Update, 5*, 5.

Ceci, S., Ross, D., & Toglia, M. (1989). *Perspectives on children's testimony*. New York: Springer-Verlag.

Ceci, S. J., DeSimone, M., Putnick, M. E., & Nightingale, N. N. (1992). The suggestibility of children's recollections. In D. Cicchetti, & S. Toth (Eds.), *Child abuse, child development, and social policy*. Norwood, NJ: Ablex.

Ceci, S., Toglia, M., & Ross, D. (1987). *Children's eyewitness memory*. New York: Springer-Verlag.

Ceci, S., Leichtman, M., & Putnick, M. (1992). *Cognitive and social factors in early deception*. Hillsdale, NJ: Erlbaum.

Choi, S. (1991). Children's answers to yes-no questions: A developmental study in English, French, and Korean. *Developmental Psychology, 27*, 407420.

Clyde, J. (1992). *The Report of the Inquiry into the Removal of Children from Orkney in February 1991*. Edinburgh: HMSO.

Coles, W. (1990). Sexual abuse of persons with disabilities: A law enforcement perspective. *Developmental Disabilities Bulletin, 18*, 35-43.

Craft, A. (1991). NAPSAC in context. *Newsletter of the National Association for the Protection from Sexual Abuse of Adults and Children with Learning Disabilities*. Nottingham.

Dahmen-Zimmer, K., & Loohs, S. (1992, September). *Is there truth in the eye of the beholder?* Paper presented at the Third European Law and Psychology Conference, Oxford.

Davies, G., Stevenson-Robb, Y., & Flin, R. (1986). The reliability of children's testimony. *International Legal Practitioner, 11*, 95-103.

Dent, H., & Flin, R. (1992). *Children as witnesses*. Chichester: Wiley.

Doris, J. (1991). *The suggestibility of children's recollections: Implications for eyewitness testimony*. Washington, DC: American Psychological Association.

Everson, M. D., & Boat, B. W. (1990). Are anatomical dolls too suggestive? *The Advisor: American Professional Society on the Abuse of Children, 3*, 6-14.

Faller, K. C. (1990). Types of questions for children alleged to have been sexually abused. *The Advisor: American Professional Society on the Abuse of Children, 3*, 3-5.

Fielding, N., & Conroy, S. (1992). Interviewing child victims: Police and social work investigations of child sexual abuse. *Sociology, 26*, 103-124.

Fisher, R., Geiselman, R., & Raymond, D. (1987). Critical analysis of police interviewing techniques. *Journal of Police Science and Administration, 15*, 177-185.

Fivush, R., & Hudson, J. (1990). *Knowing and remembering in young children*. New York: Cambridge University Press.

Flin, R., Boon, J., Knox, A., & Bull, R. (1992). The effect of a five month delay on children's and adult's eyewitness memory. *British Journal of Psychology, 83*, 323-336.

Flin, R., & Bull, R. (1990). Child witnesses in Scottish criminal proceedings. In J. Spencer, G. Nicholson, R. Flin, & R. Bull (Eds.), *Children's evidence in legal proceedings: An international perspective*. Cambridge: Faculty of Law.

Flin, R., Bull, R., Boon, J., & Knox, A. (1992). Children in the witness box. In H. Dent & R. Flin (Eds.), *Children as witnesses*. Chichester: Wiley.

Flin, R., Bull, R., Boon, J., & Knox, A. (1994). Child witnesses in Scottish criminal trials. *International Review of Victimology*, *2*, 309-329.

Garbarino, J., & Stott, F. (1991). *What children can tell us: Eliciting, interpreting and evaluating information from children*. San Francisco: Jossey-Bass.

Goodman, G. S., & Aman, C. (1990). Children's use of anatomically detailed dolls to recount an event. *Child Development*, *61*, 1859-1871.

Goodman, G., & Schwartz-Kenney, B. (1992). Why knowing a child's age is not enough: Influences of cognitive, social and emotional factors on children's testimony. In H. Dent & R. Flin (Eds.), *Children as witnesses*. Chichester: Wiley.

Gudjonsson, G. (1992). *The psychology of interrogations, confessions and testimony*. Chichester: Wiley.

Hedderman, C. (1987). *Children's evidence: The need for corroboration*. Research and Planning Unit, *Paper 41*. London: Home Office.

Heydon, J. (1984). *Evidence, cases and materials*. London: Butterworths.

Hoorwitz, A. (1992). *The clinical detective*. New York: Norton.

Hudson, J., & Fivush, R. (1990). Introduction: What young children remember and why. In R. Fivush & J. Hudson (Eds.), *Knowing and remembering in young children*. New York: Cambridge University Press.

Irish Law Reform Commission. (1990). *Report on child sexual abuse*. Dublin: Law Reform Commission.

Irish Law Reform Commission. (1989). *Consultation paper on child sexual abuse*. Dublin: Law Reform Commission.

Jones, D. P. H. (1991). Interviewing children. In K. Murray & D. A. Gough (Eds.), *Intervening in child sexual abuse*. Edinburgh: Scottish Academic Press.

Jones, D. P. H. (1990). Talking with children. In R. K. Oates (Ed.), *Understanding and managing child sexual abuse*. London: Balliere Tindall.

Jones, D. P. H., & McQuiston, M. G. (1988). *Interviewing the sexually abused child*. London: Gaskell.

King, M. A., & Yuille, J. C. (1989). Suggestibility and the child witness. In S. Ceci, D. Ross, & M. Toglia (Eds.), *Child witnesses*. New York: Springer-Verlag.

Köhnken, G. (1990). The evaluation of statement credibility: Social judgement and expert diagnostic approaches. In J. Spencer, G. Nicholson, R. Flin & R. Bull (Eds.), *Children's evidence in legal proceedings: An international perspective*. Cambridge: Faculty of Law.

Law Reform Commission of Western Australia. (1991). *Report on evidence of children and other vulnerable witnesses*. Perth: LRCWA.

Lawrence, K. (1988). Let the child be heard. *Police Review*, *20* May, 1074-1075.

List, J. (1986). Age and schematic differences in the reliability of eyewitness testimony. *Developmental Psychology*, *22*, 5057

Loftus, E. F., & Davies, G. M. (1984). Distortions in the memory of children. *Journal of Social Issues*, *40*, 51-67.

McGough, L. (1992). *Fragile voices: Child witnesses in the American legal system*. New Haven, CT: Yale University Press.

McGurk, H., & Glachan, M. (1988). Children's conversation with adults. *Children and Society*, *2*, 20-34.

Memon, A., Cronin, O., Eaves, R., & Bull, R. (1992). *The cognitive interview and child witnesses*. Paper presented at the British Psychological Society Division of Criminological and Legal Psychology Annual Conference.

Memon, A., & Bull, R. (1991). The cognitive interview: Its origins, empirical support, evaluation and practical implications. *Journal of Community and Applied Social Psychology*, *1*, 291-307.

Menig-Peterson, C. (1975). The modification of communicative behaviour in preschool-aged children as a function of the listener's perspective. *Child Development*, *46*, 1015-1018.

Moston, S. (1987). The suggestibility of children in interview studies. *First Language*, *7*, 67-78.

Moston, S. (1990). How children interpret and respond to questions: Situational sources of suggestibility in eyewitness interviews. *Social Behaviour*, *5*, 155-167.

Murray, K., & Gough, D. (Eds.) (1991). *Intervening in child sexual abuse*. Edinburgh: Scottish Academic Press.

Myers, J. (1987). *Child witness law and practice*. New York: Wiley.

Oates, R. K. (1990). Children as witnesses. *The Australian Law Journal*, *64*, 129-134.

Perry, N., & Wrightsman, L. (1991). *The child witness: Legal issues and dilemmas*. Newbury Park, CA: Sage.

Peters, D. (1991). The influence of stress and arousal on the child witness. In J. Doris (Ed.), *The suggestibility of children's recollections: Implications for eyewitness testimony*. Washington, DC: American Psychological Association.

Pipe, M-E. (1992, May). *Recalling events one and two years later: Cues, props and reminiscence*. Paper presented at NATO Advanced Studies Institute, *The child witness in context*, Italy.

Poole, D. (1992, May). *Impact of a long delay on the eyewitness testimony of children and adults*. Paper presented at the NATO Advanced Studies Institute, *The child witness in context*, Italy.

Poole, D., & White, L. (1991). Effects of question repetition on the eyewitness testimony of children and adults. *Developmental Psychology*, *27*, 975-986.

Price, D. W. W., & Goodman, G. S. (1990). Visiting the wizard: Children's memory for a recurring event. *Child Development*, 61, 664680.

Raskin, D., & Esplin, P. (1991). Statement validity assessment: Interview procedures and context analysis of children's statements of sexual abuse. *Behavioural Assessment*, *13*, 265-291.

Saywitz, K., Moan, S., & Lamphear, V. (1991). *The effect of preparation on children's resistance to misleading questions*. Paper presented at the Annual Conference of the American Psychological Association on Child Development, San Francisco.

Saywitz, K. (1990). The child witness: Experimental and clinical considerations. In A. La Greca (Ed.), *Through the eyes of a child: Obtaining self-reports from children and adolescents*. Boston: Allyn and Bacon.

Saywitz, K. J., Goodman, G. S., & Myers, J. (1990). Can children provide accurate eyewitness reports? *Violence Update*, *September*, 3-11.

Saywitz, K., Snyder, L., & Lamphear, V. (1990). *Preparing child witnesses: The efficiency of memory training strategy*. Paper presented at the Annual Convention of the American Psychological Association, Boston.

Shuy, R. (1986). Language and the law. *Annual Review of Applied Linguistics*, *7*, 50-63.

Siegal, M., Waters, L., & Dinwiddy, L. S. (1988). Misleading children: Causal attributions for inconsistency under repeated questioning. *Journal of Experimental Child Psychology*, *45*, 438456.

Spencer, J., & Flin, R. (1990). *The evidence of children: The law and the psychology*. London: Blackstone.

Spencer, J., & Flin, R. (1993). *The evidence of children: The law and the psychology (2nd Ed.)*. London: Blackstone.

Spencer, J., Nicholson, G., Flin, R., & Bull, R. (1990). *Children's evidence in legal proceedings: An international perspective*. Cambridge: Faculty of Law.

Steller, M., & Boychuk, T. (1992). Children as witnesses in sexual abuse cases. In H. Dent & R. Flin (Eds.), *Children as witnesses*. Chichester: Wiley.

Steller, M., & Köhnken, G. (1989). Criteria-based statement analysis. In D. Raskin (Ed.), *Psychological methods in criminal investigation and evidence*. New York: Springer.

Stone, W., & Lemanek, K. (1990). Developmental issues in children's self-reports. In A. La Greca (Ed.), *Through the eyes of the child: Obtaining self-reports from children and adolescents*. Boston: Allyn and Bacon.

Tobin, K. (1987). The role of wait time in higher cognitive level learning. *Review of Educational Research*, *57*, 69-95.

Toglia, M., Ross, D., & Ceci, S. (1992). The suggestibility of children's memory. In M. Howe, C. Brainerd, & V. Reyna (Eds.), *The development of long-term retention*. New York: Springer-Verlag.

Tucker, A., Mertin, P., & Luszcz, M. (1990). The effect of a repeated interview on young children's eyewitness memory. *Australian and New Zealand Journal of Criminology*, *23*, 117-124.

Undeutsch, V. (1982). Statement reality analysis. In A. Trankell (Ed.), *Reconstructing the past*. Deventer, The Netherlands: Kluwer.

Vizard, E. (1991). Interviewing children suspected of being sexually abused: A review of theory and practice. In C. R. Hollin & K. Howells (Eds.), *Clinical approaches to sex offenders and their victims*. Chichester: Wiley.

Warren, A., Hulse-Trotter, K., & Tubbs, E. (1991). Inducing resistance to suggestibility in children. *Law and Human Behavior*, *15*, 273-285.

Westcott, H. (1992, May). The disabled child witness. Paper presented at the NATO Advanced Studies Institute, *The child witness in context*, Italy.

White, S. (1990). The investigatory interview with suspected victims of child sexual abuse. In A. La Greca (Ed.), *Through the eyes of a child*. Boston: Allyn and Bacon.

Yuille, J. C. (1988). The systematic assessment of children's testimony. *Canadian Psychology*, 29, 247-262.

Information Enhancement and Credibility Assessment of Child Statements: The Impact of the Cognitive Interview Technique on Criteria-Based Content Analysis

Max Steller and Petra Wellershaus

Introduction

Criteria-Based Content Analysis (CBCA) is the core component of Statement Validity Assessment, a structured approach to assess the veracity of accounts of child sexual abuse (Steller & Koehnken, 1989; Steller & Boychuk, 1992). CBCA was founded by the pioneering work of the German professor Udo Undeutsch (Undeutsch, 1967, 1982, 1989). It has since been used extensively in German juridical practice by expert witnesses (i.e. psychologists) to assess the veracity of children's accounts about sexual abuse.

CBCA consists of a set of defined criteria that describe specific content features of a statement. The more content criteria are fulfilled in a given statement the more likely it is that the statement is based on an experience of the reporting person, i.e. presence of content criteria is considered as indicator of truthfulness.

Table 1: Content Criteria for Statement Analysis[a]

General characteristics
1. Logical structure
2. Unstructured production
3. Quantity of details
Specific contents
4. Contextual embedding
5. Descriptions of interactions
6. Reproduction of conversation
7. Unexpected complications during the incident
Peculiarities of content
8. Unusual details
9. Superfluous details
10. Accurately reported details misunderstood
11. Related external associations
12. Accounts of subjective mental state
13. Attribution of perpetrator's mental state
Motivation-related contents
14. Spontaneous corrections
15. Admitting lack of memory
16. Raising doubts about one's own testimony
17. Self-deprecation
18. Pardoning the perpetrator
Offence-specific elements
19. Details characteristic of the offence

[a] Adapted from Steller & Koehnken (1989)

The theoretical basis (the so-called Undeutsch-hypothesis) of CBCA consists in the assumption that reality-based accounts (i.e. reports about experienced events) differ in content quality from fictitious accounts (i.e. invented stories, phantasy products). The content quality of a statement is operationalized by the amount of content criteria present in the given statement. Those criteria therefore are called reality criteria. Recently it has been corroborated by empirical research - simulation as well as field research (for a research review see Steller & Boychuk, 1992) - that the hypothesized qualitative difference between fictitious and truthful accounts does exist.

Unfortunately, in some recent publications CBCA has been misrepresented as a type of test for truthfulness. CBCA has been associated with the "lie detector" test (Whitcomb, 1992, p. 115). These misrepresentations neglect previous emphasis of authors about CBCA on the fact that CBCA is a semi-structured clinical approach that has to take into account cognitive capability and individual experience of the reporting child witness when applying content analysis and that at present there exists no basis for quantifying cut-off-scores for the content quality analysis (Steller, 1989). It has also been pointed out in previous publications about CBCA that the presence of reality criteria indicates truthfulness but that a lack of reality criteria may have several different reasons and must not be unequivocally interpretated as indicator of untruthfulness (Steller, 1989; Undeutsch, 1989).

CBCA historically originated in a climate of general distrust towards children as witnesses. Undeutsch (1967) pointed out that in practice, especially in child sexual abuse cases a general distrust about the credibility of child statements is not justified. By means of reality criteria many (or most) child statements about sexual abuse can be corroborated as truthful. (This argument is valid for the situation where a child has given a description of abuse - it does not address the baseline in cases of suspected abuse based upon interpretation of behavior signals, drawings or doll play.)

CBCA can be summarized as a complex methodology for "truth corroborating", it is not a lie detection method. This paper addresses the question whether the truth corroborating power of CBCA may be negatively influenced by a specific interview technique known as the Cognitive Interview.

The Cognitive Interview (CI) was developed to enhance the completeness and accuracy of eyewitness reports (Geiselman & Fisher, 1989).

Table 2: The Cognitive Interview Technique[a]

Four general memory enhancement techniques

1. Reconstruct the circumstances
2. Be complete
3. Recall in different orders
4. Change perspectives

Specific mnemonics

1. Physical appearance
2. Names
3. Numbers
4. Speech characteristics
5. Conversation

[a] Adapted from Geiselman & Fisher (1989)

The technique is based on general principles of memory and findings from laboratory investigations of memory. It consists of four general retrieval mnemonics presented to the witness prior to the narrative report phase of an interview. The witness is first asked to mentally recreate the environment of the incident, such as the place, weather, people, and other details. Since some people hold back information because they think it is too commonplace or unimportant, the witness is also instructed to report all information that is remembered. Another technique of the CI is to ask the witness to recall the events in different orders. Witnesses usually report the events in order from the beginning to the end of the incident. However, trying to recall backwards or beginning in the middle can lead to additional recall. Finally, the witness is asked to change perspectives by reporting the incident from the points of view of the various participants or observers. In order to elicit additional specific items of information, five additional retrieval mnemonics can be employed after the narrative phase of the interview. Witnesses are asked to recall numbers, names, conversations, speech-characteristics, and physical appearances of involved persons.

Several experiments showed that the CI elicited more correct information than standard interrogation procedures. Geiselman and Padilla (1988) demonstrated that recall performance can also be improved with children by means of the CI, although the change-perspective mnemonic may elicit some confabulations.

CBCA and the CI seem to be two valuable and scientifically based tools in dealing with children as witnesses. The following study addresses the question whether the two methods are compatible with each other or - to be more specific - how credibility assessment by means of CBCA (especially in sexual abuse cases) might be negatively influenced by the prior use of the CI.

Already, theoretical considerations suggest that the CI should not be used on a regular basis with child victim-witnesses in cases of alleged sexual abuse. In cases of alleged sexual abuse, the main forensic question to be resolved is whether the alleged incident took place or not. Use of the CI may interfere with the assessment of the credibility of a statement by means of CBCA. Since the memory enhancement techniques in the CI may affect content and structure of a statement, they may invalidate the use of content criteria for credibility assessment.

Asking the witness to mentally reconstruct the circumstances of the event has been shown to enhance the amount of details provided by witnesses who were motivated to produce correct information but had difficulties in doing so. The instruction to mentally reconstruct the circumstances of an event will probably affect the statement of a lying person, also. It can be assumed that such an instruction would lead to increased production of details and also increase the likelihood of descriptions that include "contextual embedding" (i.e. the "circumstances") of the alleged event. The request to remember the surroundings of the incident and the witness' thoughts and feelings can produce many details that a lying witness normally would not have reported. It is possible that the instructions by themselves give a (lying) witness the idea to report thoughts and feelings such as anxiety and disgust. Inducing the witness to provide details of the above-described qualities is incompatible with the use of the corresponding content criteria of statement analysis to assess the truthfulness of the account, as these contents were not reported spontaneously.

Instructing the witness to report everything that can be remembered not only may increase the quantity of reported details, but it also encourages talking about incidents of marginal importance to the alleged accusation. That would induce accounts of superfluous details, a further content criterion used for validity assessment. The instruction to recall the event in different orders obviously corresponds to the criterion of unstructured production. If a witness is instructed to recall the event not only from the beginning to the end, but also in reverse order or from a memorable point, the criterion "unstructured production" quite obviously is affected and rendered useless as an indicator of credibility.

The fourth technique of the CI instructs the witness to change perspectives. This may produce an account of the alleged perpetrator's mental state only because the witness was instructed to assume the role of a prominent character in the incident. Inducing this possibility by instruction makes it impossible to use the appearance of such accounts as a sign of the credibility of a report.

Experiment

In a simulation study with children it was examined whether the above hypothesized negative impact of the CI on CBCA actually occurs.

Methodology

The children's accounts came from a study conducted by Steller, Wellershaus and Wolf (1992; see also Steller, 1989, and Steller & Boychuk, 1992). The original aim of that study was to assess the validity of the Undeutsch-hypothesis. Children from first and fourth grades were asked to produce two stories in the context of a story-telling competition: one story was to be about an actually experienced event, the second story was to be fictitious. Events with personal involvement like "undergoing a medical treatment" or "being attacked by an animal or another child" were used as instructions for the accounts based on personal experience as well as instructions for the fictitious stories. The topics were chosen in order to secure ecological validity with respect to child sexual abuse: they imply variables like personal involvement, negative emotional tone and loss of control.

The children were interviewed by two psychology graduate students. Each interview included two parts.

In the first part a semi-structured interview designed to obtain as much information as possible in free narrative style was conducted. This interview format is usually used within the scope of credibility assessments by CBCA (Steller & Boychuk, 1992). In this experiment it was called "Standard Interview" (SI). (The elaborated statement analysis interview technique used as SI in this study is probably not comparable to the SI-procedures used in the CI-studies.)

In the second part three instructions according to the CI were presented to the child. The child was asked to mentally recreate the environment of the incident and to remember his/her subjective mental state as well as conversation(s). After that the child was asked to change perspective by reporting the incident from the point of view of the other participant of the interaction. This second part of the child's interview was called "Cognitive Interview", although it contained only parts of the suggested CI-instructions.

The total interviews (both parts, SI and CI) were recorded on tape and then transcribed. Out of 176 interviews (88 true, 88 fictitious) of the original study, a sample of only 10 interviews (five stories about an actually experienced event, five fictitious stories) were examined in the presented study. These ten stories had the same topic; namely "having had an accident with subsequent need of medical treatment". Subjects were only fourth-graders. Other possible moderating factors (for example children's verbal skills and time passed since the experience of the event) were also held constant.

Thirty-four undergraduate psychology students were trained as CBCA-raters. Being blind according to the truthfulness of the ten above-mentioned stories the raters applied the list of content criteria from Steller and Koehnken (1989) to the verbatim transcripts. All raters used a three-point scale ranging from 0 (= criterion non present) to 2 (= criterion strongly present). Half of the raters (n = 17) analyzed the interviews in whole length (i.e. both parts, SI and CI); they are called the CI-group. The other 17 raters only analyzed the first part of the interviews (SI); they are called the SI-group. Repetitions in a child's account had to be noted and did not raise the content-quality rating. Finally the students rated the truthfulness of each story as true or fictitious.

Data analysis

Two hypotheses were examined. The first hypothesis was that instructions to reconstruct the circumstances of the event and to recall verbal expressions and emotions as well as the instruction to report from the perspective of the main interaction partner would affect the statement of a lying person. Such instructions would lead to increased production of descriptions that fulfill the content criteria "Reproduction of conversation", "Accounts of subjective mental state" and "Attribution of perpetrator's mental state". Therefore, the extent of these three reality criteria would be rated higher in fictitious stories including the second interview part (= CI-instructions) compared to fictious stories without this part.

In order to test this hypothesis the fictitious stories from both rater-groups were compared on the above-mentioned reality criteria. The differences between the mean scores for each criterion over the five fictitious stories and over all 17 CI-raters versus all 17 SI-raters were calculated (the possible range of mean scores per criterion was from 0 to 2). t-tests for independent samples were calculated between the mean scores per criterion. (A nonparametric test for two independent samples (Mann-Whitney's U-Test) led to nearly the same results.)

Table 3: Means and Standard Deviations for the Criteria in Fictitious Accounts Based on a Standard Interview (M_{SI}, SD_{SI}) Respectively on Instructions Following the Cognitive Interview (M_{CI}, SD_{CI})

Content criteria	M_{SI}	SD_{SI}	M_{CI}	SD_{CI}	t_{emp}	p
General characteristics						
1. Logical structure	1.65	0.48	1.88	0.32	3.74	.00
2. Unstruct. production	1.39	0.49	1.47	0.50	1.08	.28
3. Details	1.39	0.49	1.41	0.50	0.31	.76
Specific contents						
4. Embedding	0.94	0.82	0.93	0.74	-0.09	.93
5. Interactions	0.75	0.71	0.80	0.74	0.43	.67
6. Conversation	0.64	0.61	1.01	0.48	4.47	.00
7. Complications	0.58	0.71	0.53	0.73	-0.42	.67
Peculiarities of the content						
8. Unusual details	0.86	0.83	0.80	0.87	-0.45	.65
9. Superfluous details	0.95	0.78	1.07	0.72	1.03	.31
10. Misunderstood	0.62	0.77	0.66	0.73	0.31	.76
11. Associations	0.09	0.33	0.24	0.50	2.16	.03
12. Subject's feelings	1.21	0.56	1.49	0.50	3.53	.00
13. Perpetrator's feelings	0.94	0.78	1.02	0.79	0.69	.49
Motivation-related contents						
14. Corrections	0.64	0.67	0.61	0.73	-0.29	.77
15. Lack of memory	0.59	0.66	0.82	0.73	2.17	.03
16. Doubts	0.22	0.50	0.14	0.41	-1.18	.24
17. Self-deprecation	0.53	0.83	0.64	0.90	0.80	.42
18. Pardoning	0.49	0.77	0.55	0.81	0.49	.63
Offence-specific elements						
19. Characteristic details	Does not qualify for type of stories told.					

Note: The data are based upon ratings on a three-point scale from 0 (absent) to 2 (strongly present).

The results show that the instruction to mentally recreate the environment of the incident and to remember one's own subjective mental state as well as conversation(s) led to increased production of descriptions that fulfill the content criteria "Reproduction of conversation" and "Accounts of subjective mental state" ($p < .001$). The extent of these two criteria were significantly higher in fictitious stories which included the second interview-part (= CI) than in the SI-condition. The instruction to change perspective by reporting the incident from the point of view of the partner led to slightly increased production of descriptions that fulfill the reality criterion "Attribution of perpetrator's mental state", but the difference was not significant ($p < .492$). For interpretating this result it has to be considered that many children in our study had difficulties complying with the change-perspective-task.

Additionally, the data suggested, that CI-instructions did not only interfere with reality criteria that were directly mentioned, but also with a majority of reality criteria. In the CI-group several criteria showed higher mean scores than in the SI-group. Significant results were found for the criteria "Logical structure", "Related external associations" and "Admitting lack of memory".

A second hypothesis concerned the performance of raters who analyzed both interview-parts of the stories (= CI-group). It was predicted that these raters would tend to rate more frequently a fictitious story as true than raters who only analyzed the first interview-part (= SI-group). Therefore, by rating the truthfulness of fictitious stories, raters from the CI-group would reach a higher number of false positives compared to the SI-group.

Table 4: Number and Percentage (%) of Hits (++, −−) and Misses (+−, −+) for True and Fictitious Stories for CI-group and SI-group

Actual state	Judged state (credibility assessment) (+)	(−)
(+)	True positives (++)	False negatives (−+)
SI-group	65 (38.24%)	20 (11.76%)
CI-group	72 (42.35%)	13 (7.65%)
(−)	False positives (+−)	True negatives (−−)
SI-group	48 (28.24%)	37 (21.76%)
CI-group	59 (34.71%)	26 (15.29%)

Note: The numbers are based upon the assessments of 17 students rating 5 true and 5 fictitious accounts based on a standard interview (SI-group) respectively 17 students rating 5 true and 5 fictitious accounts based on instructions following the cognitive interview (CI-group).

In order to test the second hypothesis the CI-group and the SI-group were compared with regard to the number of stories they had rated as true. A chi-square test confirmed that the CI-group rated significantly more stories as true than did the raters in the SI-group ($\chi^2 = 4.70$, df = 1, $p < .05$). The raters of both groups were also compared on the number of fictitious stories, which were rated as true (i.e. their number of false positives). A chi-square test suggested a higher frequency of false positives in the CI-group compared to the SI-group ($\chi^2 = 3.05$, df = 1, $p < .10$).

Discussion

The presented results show that the Cognitive Interview Technique has undesirable effects on Criteria-Based Content Analysis. Fictitious accounts that are collected by using instructions following the CI develop a content quality similar to true reports. CI reduces the discriminative power of CBCA.

Which practical implications do the presented results have? We assume that in about 90 percent of credibility assessments in criminal cases of alleged sexual abuse these allegations are based on experienced events. Accordingly expert witnesses have less experience in identifying fictitious allegations than in corroborating truthful accounts. Therefore, credibility assessment in sexual abuse cases can be considered as a signal detection task, in which an observer has to look out for an event with low frequency of occurence. It becomes clear, that any production of (disturbing, distracting) "noise" should be avoided. CI-instructions with lying witnesses have been shown by our study to produce "noise" in the meaning that the presence of reality criteria in false reports is enhanced by their use. In practice, this would make the detection task of false statements more difficult - as shown by the data of this study.

On the other hand, the corresponding danger of weakening the persuasive power of CBCA for the truthfully reporting child witnesses must not be overlooked. This unwelcome impact of the CI on the use of CBCA has to be taken very seriously in current practice of CBCA because the main function of CBCA in forensic practice is to corroborate truthful accounts.

Koehnken and Schimmossek (1991) and Koehnken, Finger, and Nitschke (1991) have presented findings on the relationship of the CI and CBCA. They argue that a previous CI will not jeopardize the discriminative power of a subsequent CBCA. Considering the practical forensic implications their arguments that cannot be reported here in any detail do not seem to us to be convincing.

It has to be kept in mind that the CI and CBCA have different goals. The CI was developed for increasing the amount and accuracy of information provided by a witness whose credibility is not in question, whereas statement analysis is designed to assess the credibility of a statement. For purposes of credibility assessment, it is most compelling when a statement with a high content quality has been obtained with little or no prompting or suggestive clues.

This reasoning can also be discussed in terms of experimental methodology: In an experiment an alternative hypothesis is more convincingly supported if the experiment is set up in a manner to favour the null-hypothesis. In a criminal sexual abuse case the null-hypothesis is that the alleging child is not telling the truth. In accordance with legal standards this null-hypothesis is considered as valid as long as it is not disproved, i.e. the alternative hypothesis (the child does tell the truth) has found no corroboration.

CBCA is a method to corroborate the alternative hypothesis in child sexual cases, i.e. the assumption that the child does tell the truth about the event. Therefore, we believe that in the interest of child victim-witnesses, the use of the CI should be avoided as long as the credibility of the child's statement may be questioned during the investigative and judicial processes. Its premature use would interfere with credibility assessment by CBCA and thereby weaken the position of the majority of child witnesses in sexual abuse cases. Only after it has legally been established that a child is telling the truth the CI could possibly be helpful in enhancing the amount of information, if this seems necessary for the legal proceedings.

In addition, ethical limitations for the use of the CI with potential victims of child (sexual) abuse should be considered. A kind of reinstatement of the context very often occurs with truthfully reporting victims in forensic interviews without according preceeding instruction. The accompanying emotional reactions can be indicators of truthfulness and therefore might be useful for the purpose of credibility assessment. On the other hand diagnostic goals and diagnostic procedures have their limitations where undue stress is exercised with child witnesses. Both of the authors of the study have many years of experience in forensic interviews with child victims of sexual abuse. On the basis of their experience they are more than reluctant to induce or enhance the reinstatement of context (of the original experience) with those victims.

References

Geiselman, R. E., & Padilla, J. (1988). Interviewing child witnesses with the cognitive interview. *Journal of Police Science and Administration, 16*, 236-242.

Geiselman, R. E., & Fisher, R. P. (1989). The cognitive interview technique. In D. C. Raskin (Ed.), *Psychological methods in criminal investigation and evidence* (pp. 191-215). New York: Springer.

Koehnken, G., Finger, M., & Nitschke, N. (1991). *Does a cognitive interview interfere with a subsequent criteria-based content analysis of a statement?* Unpublished manuscript.

Koehnken, G., & Schimmossek, E. (1991, July). *Criteria-based content analysis and the cognitive interview*. Paper presented at the International Conference on Memory, Lancaster, U. K.

Steller, M. (1989). Recent developments in statement analysis. In J. C. Yuille (Ed.), *Credibility assessment* (pp. 135-154). Dordrecht: Kluwer Academic Publishers.

Steller, M., & Koehnken, G. (1989). Criteria-based statement analysis. In D. C. Raskin (Ed.), *Psychological methods in criminal investigation and evidence* (pp. 217-245). New York: Springer.

Steller, M., Wellershaus, P., & Wolf, T. (1992). Realkennzeichen in Kinderaussagen: Empirische Grundlagen der Kriterienorientierten Aussageanalyse. *Zeitschrift fuer experimentelle und angewandte Psychologie, 39*, 151-170.

Steller, M., & Boychuk, T. (1992). Children as witnesses in sexual abuse cases: Investigative interview and assessment techniques. In H. Dent & R. Flin (Eds.), *Children as witnesses* (pp. 47-71). Chichester: Wiley.

Undeutsch, U. (1967). Beurteilung der Glaubhaftigkeit von Aussagen. In U. Undeutsch (Hrsg.), *Handbuch der Psychologie, Bd. 11: Forensische Psychologie* (S. 26-181). Goettingen: Hogrefe.

Undeutsch, U. (1982). Statement reality analysis. In A. Trankell (Ed.), *Reconstructing the past: The role of psychologists in criminal trials* (pp. 27.56). Stockholm: Norstedt & Soeners.

Undeutsch, U. (1989). The development of statement reality analysis. In J. C. Yuille (Ed.), *Credibility assessment* (pp. 101-119). Dordrecht: Kluwer Academic Publishers.

Whitcomb, D. (1992). *When the victim is a child*. National Institute of Justice, U.S. Department of Justice.

Enhancing Children's Eyewitness Testimony with the Cognitive Interview

Michelle R. McCauley and Ronald P. Fisher

Eyewitness or victim reports are often the only basis for initially investigating a crime. This is particularly true when the alleged crime consists of physical or sexual abuse. In such a circumstance it is often the alleged victim's description of what actions took place that initiates the investigation. Unfortunately, the incomplete and unreliable nature of eyewitness memory has been demonstrated repeatedly (see Ceci, Ross & Toglia, 1987; Loftus & Davies, 1984; Loftus 1979). Nevertheless, neither the necessity of using eyewitness memory nor the implications of faulty recall can be ignored.

Developmental differences in cognitive skills and communication abilities compound this problem when the eyewitness, or victim, is a child. The magnitude of the problem is great: it is estimated that every year there are 200,000 new cases of child sexual abuse in the United States (Finkelhor, 1984). Additionally, children are often witnesses to other types of crimes.

According to Goodman, Golding, and Haith, (1984) much of the controversy as to whether children are capable of being credible eyewitnesses is based on the public's intuitive beliefs about children's memory, not about the empirical research. In a survey done by Leippe, Brigham, Cousins and Romanczyk (1989) 96% of defense and 57% of prosecuting attorneys reported that, compared to adults, children are less or much less likely to recall information. When asked to predict jurors' perceptions of children's ability, 68% of defense and 77% of prosecuting attorneys said that jurors believe that 5 to 9-year-olds' ability to remember events is inferior to adults. Ross, Dunning, Toglia, and Ceci (1989) found that mock jurors believe that young witnesses (age six and eight) are less accurate than 21-year-old witnesses. Thus there appears to be a common perception that children's memories are inferior to adults.

There is substantial evidence that children's memory is different than adults'. Whereas an adult can store around seven items in short term memory a 5-year-old can only store five items (Ault, 1977). It is problematic to examine the difference between adult and children's long term memory because it is difficult to hold encoding constant. Qualitatively, there are strategies that adults use at encoding that children do not. For example, children do not spontaneously rehearse until after age seven (Flavell, Beach & Chinsky, 1966).

Evidence suggests that children can be as accurate as adults if they are asked appropriate questions. Goodman and Reed (1986) found little difference between adults' and 6-year-olds' memory when the subjects were questioned objectively. They compared 3-year-olds, 6-year-olds and adults' memories for a series of arm movements that the subjects performed with an experimenter. Four to five days later the subjects were asked to describe the event, the experimenter, and to identify the experimenter from a photo lineup. Leading, misleading, and objective (non-leading) questions were presented to the subjects. Goodman and Reed found no difference between 6-year-olds and adults' ability to accurately answer the objective questions. They found that, in general, children were more likely to be misled by incorrect suggestive questioning than were adults. However, when the misleading information was suggested about central actions that the experimenter performed there was not a significant age effect (cf. Parker, Haverfield & Thomas, 1986).

Several studies have evaluated child eyewitness memory solely for identification purposes. Chance and Goldstein (1984), Cohen and Harnick (1980) and Parker et al. (1986) all concentrated on the child's ability to identify a suspect from a photo line up. However, in addition to making an accurate identification children are often asked to describe the interaction that occurred between the child and the suspect. The focus of this interaction is often the actions and touches that occurred. This is especially true in sexual assault cases in which the child often has repeated interactions or knows the perpetrator and therefore identification is not the problem. It is for this reason that we set out to find a way to facilitate children's memory for actions as well identification.

The Cognitive Interview

Geiselman and Fisher have done extensive research on improving eyewitness memory in adults. Their research has focused on developing improved retrieval techniques, which they labeled the Cognitive Interview (Geiselman, Fisher, Firstenberg, Hutton, Sullivan, Avetissian & Prosk, 1984). The original Cognitive Interview (CI) was based on two main principles of memory: encoding specificity and varied retrieval. Encoding specificity states that the effectiveness of a retrieval cue depends on the amount of overlap between the cue and the encoded event (Flexser & Tulving, 1978; Tulving & Thompson, 1973). To increase the overlap between the cue and the encoded event, the eyewitness is encouraged to mentally reinstate the context of the event. This may require the subject to concentrate on the external factors surrounding the event as well as emotional factors and cognitive factors. Varied retrieval states that there may be several paths to the encoded event (Tulving, 1974). Thus the eyewitness may be encouraged to take another person's perspective of the event (e.g., "What would the clerk have seen?") or to report the event in different temporal orders (forward and backward).

Geiselman, Fisher, MacKinnon and Holland (1985) conducted the first empirical test of the CI using 17 experienced law enforcement agents as interviewers and college students as "witnesses". Compared to standard police interviewing techniques the CI produced 35% more accurate facts without a significant increase in inaccurate responses. To examine the generalizability of the above finding Geiselman, Fisher, MacKinnon and Holland (1986) replicated the study using non-student adult witnesses instead of college students as subjects. The results of the second study mirrored those of the first experiment: the CI resulted in 15% more accurate information than the standard police interview without an increase in inaccurate information.

Because of the original CI's success in enhancing adult eyewitness recall Geiselman and Padilla (1988) adapted it for use with children. Fifteen children between the ages of seven and 12 viewed a video taped robbery. The children were interviewed about the events in the video after three days. Compared to the standard interview, the CI produced 21% more accurate items reported without an increase in errors.

In a second test of the original CI with children (Geiselman, Saywitz & Bornstein, 1990) 38 children between seven and 11 years old played games involving actions and touching with an experimenter. After two days the children were given either a standard interview or a CI. In comparison to the standard interview, the CI increased the number of correct facts by 26% across both age groups without increasing the amount of incorrect information reported. This study also found that some children had difficulty taking another person's perspective or reporting events in different orders.

Revised CI

In light of the success of the CI in laboratory studies Fisher, Geiselman, Raymond, Jurkevich & Warhaftig (1987) revised it for use in field settings. They incorporated several communication principles as well as cognitive principles. The revised CI relies primarily on the following methods to assist recall and facilitate optimal communication. Two of the principles in the original version, encoding specificity and varied retrieval, were retained in the revised CI. In addition, three additional principles were incorporated: focused retrieval, extensive retrieval and witness-compatible questioning. Focused retrieval relies on the premise that there is only a finite amount of mental resources and that any disruptions or distractions will lower performance (Kahneman, 1973). Therefore it is important to help the witness keep focused by providing an environment conducive to retrieval (e.g., few interruptions). Extensive retrieval is grounded in the research that more retrieval attempts lead to better recall (Roediger & Payne, 1982). Subjects should be encouraged to try as many times as possible to search through their memory to recall the event. Witness-compatible questioning involves compatibility between the interviewer's choice of words and line of questioning and the eyewitness's vocabulary and train of thought. For example, if the witness is in the process of retrieving information about the target's hair color the next question asked should be about the hair, not about the escape vehicle (cf. Kintsch & Van Dijk, 1978). A more complete description of the revised CI is provided by Fisher and Geiselman (1992).

The first empirical test of the revised CI was conducted in the laboratory using college students as witnesses (Fisher, Geiselman, Raymond, Jurkevich, & Warhaftig, 1987b). The witnesses observed a video of a crime and were interviewed two days later either with the original version of the CI or the revised version. The interviewers were high school and college students trained to conduct both versions of the CI. The revised CI elicited 45% more accurate information than the original version without an increase in the amount of inaccurate information.

The revised CI was next assessed in a field setting with actual witnesses and victims of crimes (Fisher, Geiselman & Amador, 1989). Detectives from the Metro-Dade Police Department recorded several interviews with victims and witnesses. The detectives were then trained to use the CI. The detectives elicited 63% more information with the revised CI than did untrained detectives, and they elicited 48% more information from witnesses after they had been trained in the use of the revised CI than before training. Comparable findings with British police using the CI are reported by George (1991).

In light of the revised CI's success in facilitating adult recall we modified it for use with children. The modifications of the interview emerged from children's communication and cognitive limitations. First, because Geiselman et al. (1990) found that some children had difficulty taking another person's perspective and reporting events in different orders we deleted this from the interview. Second, children tend to provide short responses when speaking with adults unfamiliar to them; therefore we attempted to prime the children into providing elaborate detailed responses. This priming was achieved by asking children at the beginning of the interview to describe something they were all very familiar with - how they brush their teeth. We expected that this mode of detailed description that was elicited in the preliminary task would carry over into the actual interview. Third, in light of Ratner and Hill's (1991) finding that performing actions facilitated memory, the children were encouraged to demonstrate the actions in addition to providing a verbal description. Fourth, the interviewers used age-appropriate language. For example, instead of "I want you to close your eyes and mentally reinstate the context of the room" we instructed them to "Close your eyes and draw a picture in your head, like a video, of what the room looked like". Children had no difficulty relating to a video tape machine.

Method

Subjects The subjects in this study were 18 second graders from a private school in South Florida. Written consent was obtained from the parent or guardian of each subject. Consent was also obtained from each subject prior to participation in the experiment. All of the children whose parents gave consent agreed to participate.

Interviewers The interviewers were two students from Florida International University. The interviewers were trained in both the standard and revised CI.

Procedure The subjects were removed from class in groups of two and taken into a room where an adult experimenter unfamiliar to them was waiting. The subjects were asked first to sign a consent form which informed them that they did not have to participate and that they were free to quit any time they wished. The children were then randomly assigned either to watch or participate in an action/play session beginning with a Simon-says game led by the experimenter. The game consisted of 32 actions such as "Simon-says touch your toes" and "Simon-says close your eyes". Subsequent to the Simon-says game the subjects recited a nursery rhyme with the experimenter and then were photographed. Finally the children were escorted back to their classroom. The entire action/play session took approximately 10 minutes and was video taped.

Two weeks following the Simon-says game different researchers went back to the school and interviewed the subjects about the action/play session. Each subject was interviewed individually in a room other than where the action/play session had occurred. All the interviews were audio and video taped for later scoring.

The interviewers were informed that the subjects had been removed from class two weeks earlier to play a game with an adult. The subjects were interviewed using either the revised CI or standard interviewing procedures. Both the CI and standard interview began with rapport-building (e.g., "What is your favorite class at school?") to reduce the subjects' anxiety. Following rapport-building all subjects received instructions adapted from Geiselman et al. (1990) to reduce fabrication and encourage complete responses. These instructions directed the subjects: (a) "not to worry if you can not remember something", (b) "don't make anything up" and (c) "tell me everything you remember even if it does not seem important". Subjects in the standard interviewing condition were asked to give a free narrative of what they remembered about the action/play event. Next, the interviewers asked questions about any areas of the narrative in which elaboration was deemed necessary. This was accomplished by probing the subjects about any statements that were vague (e.g., "You said you played a game. Can you tell me more about it?").

Following rapport-building and the instructions to discourage fabrication and encourage complete responses the subjects receiving the revised CI were asked to describe how they brush their teeth. This was done so the interviewer could demonstrate to the child the completeness of responses they were expected to provide. At this point the interviewer overtly probed for details such as "What do you do before you put the tooth brush in your mouth?" "What do you do right after that?". Direct questions were included in this portion of the interview to convey to the child the necessity of reporting every detail.

The subjects were then asked to provide a free narrative of the action/play session. Following the free narrative the interviewer used guided mental imagery to assist the subject in mentally reinstating the context of the room in which the action/play session occurred. The subjects were asked to close their eyes and picture what the room looked like, everything that was in it, what it smelled like, who else was in the room, what the feeling of the room was and every detail about the room that they could remember. After the subjects indicated to the interviewer that they had a good mental image of the room they were asked to verbally describe it in as much detail as possible. After the subjects described the room, the interviewer asked them to mentally visualize all the actions that they did during the action play session. The subjects were instructed to visualize everything they did from the beginning of the action play session to the end when they went back to their classroom. The interviewers paused to give the subjects 45 seconds to form a clear mental image and to mentally go through all the actions that took place during the action/play session from beginning to end.

The interviewer then asked the subjects to verbally describe every action they did during the action/play session in as much detail as when they described brushing their teeth. After the subjects' free recall, the interviewer probed any areas in which the subjects were vague. For example, if a subject reported playing a game the interviewer waited until after the subject finished describing on his or her own and then probed about what type of game the subject played. The subjects were encouraged to demonstrate an action if they could not verbalize it.

Subsequent to describing the action/play session in both the CI and standard conditions subjects were asked if there was anything else they could remember. The interviewer repeated this question until a "no" response was obtained. After the subjects indicated that they could not recall anything else, they attempted to identify the original experimenter (the person with whom they played Simon-says) from a photo lineup. The lineup consisted of five color photos. The subjects viewed either a target-present lineup (i.e., the experimenter's photo was in the lineup) or a target-absent lineup (i.e., the experimenter's photo was removed from the lineup and replaced with a similar looking photo). The lineup was presented sequentially. Five "blank" cards were placed at the back of the stack of photos to reduce the possibility of subjects guessing how many photos were in the lineup. The subjects were told that the target may or may not be in the lineup and that an answer of "I don't know" was acceptable. They viewed each photo individually for as long as they wished prior to stating whether the photo was the target. The subjects were not allowed to go back and reexamine a photo after they had made a decision.

Results

Only the recalled facts about the Simon-says actions and the experimenter's appearance were assessed. Each fact recalled was compared to the video tape of the event to determine accuracy. The subjects in the revised CI condition recalled almost twice as many accurate facts as those in the standard interview condition (15.56 vs. 8.44 $t(16) = 2.98$ $p<.01$). There was not a significant difference in the number of inaccurate facts recalled, which was low for both groups. (0.77 vs. 0.33 $t(16) = 0.95$ $p>$ $.05$). Identification accuracy was at ceiling level in both the CI (100%) and standard groups (89%) thereby precluding meaningful comparison.

Discussion

This research set out to compare children's memory for actions and target identification across standard and cognitive interviewing conditions. The results of this study replicate previous findings with adults, that the revised CI elicits more accurate facts than a standard interviewing procedure. In addition the CI does not increase the number of inaccurate facts. It is noteworthy that the children's error rate was very low (4%). This was rather surprising given that almost all of the other studies we have conducted with adult eyewitnesses have generated between 15%-20% errors (Koehnken, 1992). These findings are consistent with the literature on free recall which shows that children and adults differ primarily in terms of amount of information reported not accuracy (Marin, Holmes, Guth, & Kovac, 1979).

The fact that the revised CI did not significantly affect identification scores is not interpretable because of the ceiling level performance. Note, however, that other studies with greater sensitivity failed to demonstrate a beneficial effect of the CI over standard interviews in tests of identification accuracy (Fisher, McCauley, & Geiselman, 1994).

It is conceivable that what we considered a "standard" interview may not reflect what is actually done by professional interviewers (our standard interview was based the procedure used by Geiselman and Padilla, 1988). To evaluate this possibility a second study, currently being analyzed, asked professional interviewers to design the "standard" interview for us (i.e., to reproduce their interview format in the context of the experimental actions). A preliminary analysis of this study indicates that our standard interview is not significantly different from what professional interviewers conduct.

A second caveat of the current research is that the subjects were asked to recall an innocuous event which is very different than the highly arousing event that is experienced by a child victim of a crime or sexual abuse. Although it is possible that high stress may influence the effectiveness of the CI with children, it should be reiterated that the CI was effective in two field studies with adults who were actual witness and victims of crimes (Fisher et al., 1989; George, 1991). Nevertheless, further research needs to address this issue by assessing the impact of different interviewing styles with children who are actual witnesses and victims.

In conclusion, we are confident that the revised CI can be used to facilitate children's recall. The data warrant continuing research in refining the revised CI for use with actual child victims and witnesses as well as with children in non-legal settings. We believe that many of the techniques used in the revised CI could be beneficial to health professionals, teachers, and other adults wishing to obtain information from children (Westcott, 1992).

References

Ault, R. (1977). *Children's cognitive development*. New York: Oxford University Press.

Ceci, S. J., Ross, D. F., & Toglia, M. P. (1987). Suggestibility of children's memory: Psycholegal implications. *Journal of Experimental Psychology: General, 116*, 38-49.

Chance, J. E., & Goldstein, A. G. (1984). Face-recognition memory implications for children's eyewitness testimony. *Journal of Social Issues, 40*, 69-85.

Cohen, R. L., & Harnick, M. A. (1980). The susceptibility of child witnesses to suggestion. *Law and Human Behavior, 4*, 201-212.

Flavell, J. H., Beach, D. R., & Chinsky, J. M. (1966). Spontaneous verbal rehearsal in a memory task as a function of age. *Child Development, 37*, 283-299.

Finkelhor D. (1984). *Child sexual abuse: New theory and research*. New York: Free Press.

Fisher, R. P., & Geiselman, R. E. (1992). *Memory-enhancing techniques for investigative interviewing: The cognitive interview*. Springfield Il.: Charles Thomas.

Fisher, R. P., Geiselman, R. E., & Amador, M. (1989). Field test of the cognitive interview: Enhancing the recollection of actual victims and witnesses of crime. *Journal of Applied Psychology, 74*(5), 1-6.

Fisher, R. P., Geiselman, R. E., Raymond, D. S., Jurkervich, L. M., & Warhaftig, M. L. (1987). Enhancing enhanced eyewitness memory: Refining the cognitive interview. *Journal of Police Science and Administration, 15*, 291-297.

Fisher, R. P., McCauley, M. R., & Geiselman, R. E. (1994). Improving eyewitness memory with the cognitive interview. To appear in D. Ross, J. Read, & M. Toglia (Eds.), *Eyewitness memory: Current trends and developments*. New York: Springer-Verlag.

Flexser, A. J., & Tulving, E. (1978). Retrieval independence in recognition and recall. *Psychological Review, 85*, 153-172.

Geiselman, R. E., Fisher, R. P., Firstenberg, I., Hutton, L. A., Sullivan, S. J., Avetissian, I. V., & Prosk, A. L. (1984). Enhancement of eyewitness memory: an empirical evaluation of the cognitive interview. *Journal of Police Science and Administration, 12*, 74-80.

Geiselman, R. E., Fisher, R. P., MacKinnon, D. P., & Holland, H. L. (1986). Enhancement of eyewitness memory with the cognitive interview. *American Journal Psychology, 99*, 385-401.

Geiselman, R. E., Fisher, R. P., MacKinnon, D. P., & Holland, H. L. (1985). Eyewitness memory enhancement in the police interview: Cognitive retrieval mnemonics versus hypnosis. *Journal of Applied Psychology, 70*, 401-412.

Geiselman, R. E., & Padilla, J. (1988). Interviewing child witnesses with the cognitive interview. *Journal of Police Science and Administration, 16*, 236-242.

Geiselman, R. E., Saywitz, K. J., & Bornstein, G. K. (1990). *Cognitive questioning techniques for child victims and witnesses of crime*. Unpublished manuscript.

George, R. (1991). *A field and experimental evaluation of three methods of interviewing witnesses/victims of crime*. Unpublished manuscript. London: Polytechnic of East London.

Goodman, G. S., Golding, J. M., & Haith, M. M. (1984). Juror's reactions to child witnesses. *Journal of Social Issues, 40*(2), 139-156.

Goodman, G. S., & Reed, R. S. (1986). Age difference in eyewitness testimony. *Law and Human Behavior, 10*, 317-332.

Kahneman, D. (1973). *Attention and effort*. Engelwood Cliffs, NJ: Prentice-Hall.

Kintsch, W., & van Dijk, T. A. (1978). Toward a model of text comprehension and production. *Psychological Review, 85*, 363-394.

Koehnken, G. (1992, September). *A meta-analysis on the effects of the cognitive interview*. Paper presented at the Third European Conference on Law and Psychology, Oxford, England.

Leippe, M. R., Brigham, J. C., Cousins, C., & Romanczyk, A. (1989). The opinions and practices of criminal attorneys regarding child eyewitnesses: A survey. In S. J. Ceci, D. F. Ross, & M. P. Toglia (Eds.), *Perspectives on children's testimony*. New York: Springer-Verlag.

Leippe, M. R., & Romanczyk, A. (1989). Reactions to child (versus adult) eyewitnesses. *Law and Human Behavior, 13*, 103-132.

Loftus, E. F. (1979). *Eyewitness testimony*. Cambridge, Mass.: Harvard University Press.

Loftus, E. F. & Davies, P. G. (1984). Distortions in the memory of children. *Journal of Social Issues, 40*, 51-67.

Marin, V., Holmes, D. L., Guth, M., & Kovac, P. (1979). The potential of children as eyewitnesses. *Law and Human Behavior, 3*, 295-305.

Parker, J. F., Haverfield, E., & Thomas, S. B. (1986). Eyewitness testimony of children. *Journal of Applied Social Psychology, 16*, 287-302.

Ratner, H. H., & Hill, L. (1991). The development of children's action memory: When do actions speak louder than words? *Psychological Research, 53*, 195-202.

Roediger, H. L. 3rd, & Payne, D. G., (1982). Hypermnesia: The role of repeated testing. *Journal of Experimental Psychology: Learning, Memory and Cognition, 8*, 66-72.

Ross, D. F., Dunning, D., Toglia, M. P., & Ceci, S. J. (1989). Age stereotypes, communication, modality and mock jurors' perceptions of the child witness. In S. J. Ceci, D. F. Ross, & M. P. Toglia (Eds.), *Perspectives on Children's Testimony*. New York: Springer-Verlag.

Tulving, E. (1974). Cue-dependent forgetting. *American Scientist, 62*, 74-82.

Tulving, E., & Thomson, D. M. (1971). Encoding specificity and retrieval processes in episodic memory. *Psychological Review, 80*, 352-373.

Westcott, H. L. (1992). The cognitive interview: a useful tool for social workers? *British Journal of Social Work, 22*, 519-533.

An Empirical Test of the Mnemonic Components of the Cognitive Interview[1]

Amina Memon, Órla Cronin, Richard Eaves, and Ray Bull

Introduction

Experimental studies of human memory have clearly demonstrated its limited capacity to store information, its reconstructive nature and its deterioration over time (e.g. Kail, 1979). It is also well established that the recall of information from memory is influenced by the strategies used to gain access to that information (Ornstein, Medlin, Stone, & Naus, 1985). This knowledge has in recent years, been applied to the practical problem of remembering in the context of eyewitness memory. The cognitive interview (CI) was developed by Geiselman and Fisher as a procedure for increasing the amount of correct information recalled by a witness (Geiselman, Fisher, MacKinnon, & Holland, 1985). CI was presented in the form of four "mnemonic" strategies and was derived from pooling research on retrieval pathways, encoding specificity, and schema related recall. The success of the CI relative to a standard police interview has been attributed to the cognitive, memory enhancing components of the procedure (e.g. Geiselman, 1988). In the "enhanced" CI (Fisher & Geiselman, 1992) a further increase in recall is attributed to other, more "social" aspects of the interview setting and procedure.

The aim of this paper is to evaluate experimentally the effectiveness of the cognitive components of the CI procedure using adult and child witnesses to staged events. Empirical support for the technique was generated by several studies of eyewitness memory performed by Fisher, Geiselman and colleagues which have been replicated by researchers in Germany. (See Memon & Koehnken, 1992 for a recent review.)

This paper reports some preliminary research in which the various mnemonic components of the CI were isolated and compared with a control group and in which we attempt to control for possible motivational elements induced by the CI (e.g to try harder). This paper also examines age differences in recall of event information and the effectiveness of CI instructions with child witnesses. This follows an earlier study with six year olds where the full CI was no more effective than a good standard interview (Memon, Cronin, Eaves, & Bull, 1992).

The Cognitive Interview

The original CI procedure (e.g. Geiselman et al., 1985; 1986) comprises four "cognitive" (mnemonic) techniques. The CI-trained interviewer encourages the interviewees/witnesses to use these techniques to help them remember.

The CI techniques are derived from two principles regarding the structure of memory. Firstly, according to Tulving (1974), multiple retrieval pathways exist to a given encoded memory of an event and so a variety of retrieval cues or strategies are needed to maximise the chances of a complete recall. Two such strategies are the "change order" and "change perspective" instructions which encourage interviewees to recount events in a variety of orders, and from a variety of perspectives, respectively. These techniques have been shown to be effective in eliciting extra details (Loftus & Fathi, 1985; Anderson & Pichert, 1978) and may work in part by reducing the extent to which prior knowledge, expectations and schema influence and/or limit recall (Norman and Bobrow, 1978).

The second principle adopted in the CI is Tulving and Thomson's Encoding Specificity theory (1973). A memory trace is made up of several features; to maximise recall, an effective retrieval cue needs to comprise as many of these features as possible. Context provides cues which increase feature overlap between initial witnessing and subsequent retrieval contexts (cf. Flexser & Tulving, 1978). Context reinstatement involves emotional elements ("How were you feeling at the time?"), which may work via state-dependent effects, perceptual features ("Put yourself back at the scene of the crime and picture the room, how did it smell, what could you hear?"), and sequencing elements ("What were you doing at the time?").

The perspective, order and context instructions are directly related to memory theory. The status of the fourth - an instruction to the witness to report every detail irrespective of perceived importance or triviality - as a mnemonic technique is not as clear. In practice, this instruction is given in conjunction with the instructions that precede each free recall by the witness, and is a means of enhancing the communication by the witness of the information elicited by whichever of the other techniques is being used at the time. Thus, use of this instruction recognises that, from a forensic point of view, even seemingly trivial facts can be important. For the purposes of this study, the "report every detail" instruction will not be considered as a separately assessable mnemonic technique, primarily because alone it does not instruct the witness to make a recall attempt, but instead is given as a supplementary instruction to those that do (Eaves, 1992).

The CI was developed, tested and refined in a series of studies employing trained interviewers (police and students), simulated incidents and police training films (e.g. Geiselman et al., 1985), and, more recently, in field studies using a small sample of detectives and witnesses to real events in Florida (Fisher, Geiselman, & Amador, 1989) and in the U.K. (George & Clifford, 1991). Later studies of the CI have largely used the "enhanced" version which includes some general principles for improving communication and facilitating the effective use of context reinstatement.

Acquisition of Mnemonic Competency

A review of the effects of rehearsal on memory retrieval across various groups shows that older children are more likely to engage in active rehearsal than younger ones and are more efficient in the implementation of mnemonic strategies (e.g. Ornstein et al., 1985). However, there is also evidence to suggest that if children are directed to relevant cues and sufficiently prompted to use cues, ages differences in recall performance are eliminated (Kobasigawa, 1974, Pipe, Gee, & Wilson, 1993).

This evidence suggests the cognitive interview, if appropriately applied, may facilitate recall in child witnesses. The CI has been modified in recent years and tested using children as witnesses to staged events. Memon and Koehnken (1992) review the recent research, a sample of which will be outlined here. Studies by Geiselman and colleagues (Geiselman & Padilla, 1988; Saywitz, Geiselman, & Bornstein, 1992) suggest that CI (the original procedure) is as effective with children as it is with adults, particularly if children are familiarised with the CI before being questioned. However, Koehnken, Finger, Nitschke, and Hofer (1992) report a substantial increase in confabulated details when the enhanced version of CI was used with children.

In an earlier study, we compared the original CI with an interview that was identical to it in all respects apart from the mnemonic techniques (this latter interview being called the standard interview or SI). We found no significant differences between CI and SI in a between subject or within subject comparison (Memon et al., 1992). There were qualitative differences in the interview transcripts which suggested that not all the child interviewees understood and could use the CI techniques (cf. Cronin, Memon, Eaves, Küpper & Bull, 1992). Interviewers showed some individual differences in their application of the various CI instructions. This was also noted in the Saywitz et al. (1992) study, where an overall positive effect of CI was recorded. On the basis of this earlier research we refined some of the CI instructions and incorporated a practice session in our design to encourage the children in this study to actively use the CI techniques. Before presenting the research, the methodological issues pertaining to the cognitive interview literature will be summarised.

Previous Research on CI: Methodological Problems

In earlier studies of CI (e.g. Geiselman et al., 1985) the experimenters set out to evaluate the effectiveness of the CI by comparing it with a "Standard Interview" (SI). Usually these SI's were modelled upon the police investigative interviewing practices used by officers untrained in CI techniques. Some of the officers had never received interview training of any description. The success of the CI over the SI has often been attributed to its mnemonic components. However, in the absence of a suitable control group (that is, interviews identical to the CI save for its special techniques) it is not possible to say why the CI is more effective.

The scoring procedure (particularly the definition of a "correct detail" and an "incorrect" and "confabulated" detail) has not been fully discussed in any of the previous publications. Some studies report an increase in confabulations when CI is used. Koehnken and Brockmann (1988) report an increase in confabulations with CI, but it is not clear what constitutes a confabulated detail.

Finally, recent research suggests the CI technique results in substantial increases in correct information recalled with nine to ten year olds (Koehnken et al., 1992). However, in the same study there was a corresponding increase in confabulated details. In this particular study, the CI interviewers asked twice as many questions as the SI interviewers and errors fell largely into the person and action description category. This work suggests it is important to monitor the type of errors that may occur when CI techniques are applied.

The Justification for Including a "Try Harder" Control Group

The observed success of the CI may be due to relatively more recall attempts than are generated by the SI (cf. Scrivner & Safer, 1988). In addition, motivation may be higher in the CI groups merely because of the complex instructions they receive. A "try harder" control group was therefore used in the studies presented below.

The Pilot Study

The pilot study (Eaves, 1992) examined the recall-enhancing properties of each of the mnemonic components of the original CI by studying them individually, comparing each one with the other two and the control group. The data from this study suggested that when the mnemonic techniques of the cognitive interview are isolated and tested individually, their so called mnemonic effects are no more apparent than the motivating effects of the "try harder" instruction. The design employed in the pilot study was retained in subsequent studies of CI in order to examine the effectiveness of the individual CI instructions (the change context, change perspective and change order) compared with a try harder control using larger samples of college students (experiment 1) and children of different ages (experiment 2). In each study interviewer differences were minimised by use of a fixed interview protocol in each condition.

Experiment 1: The Taunton College Study

There were 68 participants in this study: all were biology students (aged 17 and 18 years) attending a local sixth form college. The participants were randomly distributed across conditions: try harder (N=14), context reinstatement (N=18), change perspective (N=17) and change order (N=19).

The staged event involved a postgraduate student from the university (a stranger to the class) who interrupted a lesson in order to request the students' help in completing a questionnaire. Interviews took place 10-14 days after the event. Each of three interviewers followed a clear interview protocol for each condition. This comprised an initial free recall in which subjects were specifically asked to give as much information as possible about the person and event, followed by one of the four instruction conditions: (i) Try harder; (ii) Change Perspective (iii) Reinstate Context; (iv) Change Order. Full details of the instructions are available from the first author. In each condition, the first recall consisted of a narrative account of the event. If, on completion, the participants had neglected to make any reference to a description of the man, of what he did, of what he said, or of what happened to him, they were prompted once for each of these elements. This ensured that neglecting to mention an element would not be misidentified as inability to recall anything about it.

Coding and scoring of data There were three coders and scorers. Each coder went through a sample of transcripts and assigned information to various categories. At this point accuracy of details was not assessed. Inter-coder discrepancies were discussed by working through all the codes given for each transcript and coding rules were modified once a consensus had been reached.

The coding scheme that was used was determined to some extent by the details of the to-be-remembered event. For example, the central feature of the event was the "questionnaire" that participants were asked to complete. Thus we had a category where information about the questionnaire was placed. The other categories were: person descriptions, person action, location of persons and objects, temporal information and subjective information (information that was uncheckable including impressions of the event and person). Errors were coded as incorrect details (e.g. a blue shirt reported when the shirt was green) or confabulations (e.g. jacket reported when there was no jacket). Errors were coded and scored in the same way as correct details. For example, "he wore a green shirt and carried a black briefcase" was coded as a person descriptor with correct details assigned the following scores: one point for green and one point for shirt and errors scored as follows: one error score for black and one for briefcase.

Results A one way ANOVA showed no significant differences across conditions in free recall of correct or incorrect details (all F's<2). The number of errors in the free recall accounts were small (mean error rate 6%). All but two accounts were free from confabulations. A series of one way ANOVAs were then performed on the pooled accuracy data (i.e free recall score combined with additional details elicited following instructions). There were no significant differences between conditions across any of the comparisons (all Fs<1). As indicated in Table 1, the means tended to favour the "try harder" control group with the context reinstatement condition producing the least amount of overall correct information. An examination of types of information elicited under each condition showed some interesting trends. The amount of location information differed across conditions $F(3, 64)=7.71$, $p<.01$, with more details about locations in the try harder as compared to context conditions (Fisher PLSD=.589, $p<.05$). Furthermore, there were more details in the change perspective conditions as compared to the change context conditions (Fisher PLSD =.559, $P<.05$). The change order condition elicited more temporal details as compared to the change perspective condition (Fisher PLSD= .552, $p<.05$). These trends will be discussed in the conclusion section of the paper.

Table 1: Experiment one: mean number of "items of information" recalled in each condition

	Condition			
Dependent variables	**context try harder**	**change reinstatement**	**perspective**	**change order**
Total correct	31.43	25.72	30.76	29.63
Error rate	2.86	2.22	2.64	2.05
Confab.	0.21	0.17	0.06	0.05
Action	8.29	8.22	9.35	9.84
Description	7.14	6.17	6.41	7.12
Location	1.00	0.28	1.41	0.32
Object	8.21	4.16	5.35	4.89
Temporal	1.79	2.17	2.23	3.79
Other	5.00	4.72	5.94	3.68

There were no significant interviewer differences in total information, total correct information or errors (all *F*s<1). The main conclusion drawn from this study was that the CI instructions have no general effect over and above the motivational element to try harder. Since the interviewers correctly followed the interview protocols each time, such a finding cannot be attributed to the failure to instruct interviewees in the use of the technique. It may be the case however, that the interviewees were not following the instructions. When participants were asked informally at the end of the study which techniques they had used the only one mentioned was context re-instatement. It may be the case that our interviewees had not understood the instructions sufficiently. In the next study we included a "practice session" to give interviewees an opportunity to try out the techniques. As discussed above, there is some evidence to suggest that a practice session may maximise any beneficial effects of the CI (Saywitz et al., 1992).

Experiment 2: The Bevois Study

The participants were 68 children aged five to nine years divided on the basis of school year group. The youngest year group were five to six years (N=17), the intermediate group were six to seven years (N=19), and the oldest age group were eight to nine years (N=31). There was an approximately equal number of children in each of the four conditions.

The event took the form of two strangers taking part in a school assembly by reading and acting out a poem. The event lasted about 10 minutes and memory was tested approximately a week later. As in the previous study there were three interviewers (all were female) and an interview protocol was strictly adhered to by each interviewer. Each interview began with a practice session in which children were asked to describe what they did when they brushed their teeth in the morning. In most cases the children gave a brief account without any prompting. The interviewer then asked them to give a second account but this time it was preceded by the specific instruction to try harder, to change perspective, to change context or to change order. The younger children (five to six year olds) required more prompting in the last three conditions as they did not readily understand the instructions. Our observations during the practice session suggested that with guidance and prompting children became familiar and felt comfortable with the techniques. However, it was not possible to conclude from this that the children understood and could apply the techniques when asked to describe the event (this point is taken up in discussion).

The categories into which recall data could be placed were determined by the nature of the event (see Table 2 for a list of categories) and we followed the procedure for coding and scoring outlined earlier.

A three (age) by four (condition) analysis of variance on total correct information (free recall and cued recall data pooled[2]) showed a significant main effect of age $F(2,55)= 5.19$, $P<.01$ with the eight year olds producing significantly more correct information than the five year olds (Scheffé's $S= 6.23$, $P<.01$). The intermediate age group (six and seven years) did not differ significantly from either of the other two groups (cf. Davies, Tarrant, & Flin, 1989). There were no significant differences in errors or accuracy (number of items correctly recalled as a proportion of total number of items) as a function of age or condition (all *F*s <1). It is interesting to note that the younger children recalled less information but were no less accurate (cf. Poole & White, 1992, Saywitz et al., 1992).

An examination of age differences in total correct information as a function of information type showed significant effects for descriptive details $F\ (2, 55)=3.57$, $p<.05$. with the eight years olds producing more information within this category than the five year olds (Scheffé's S=4.55, P<.05). There was also a significant age effect on subjective information $F\ (2,55)=4.43$, $p<.05$ with the eight year olds producing more information in this category than the five year olds (Scheffé's S= 1.42, p<.05). Given the small frequency of errors within each category, the analysis of error type has to be interpreted with caution.

Table 2: Experiment two: mean number of "items of information" recalled in each condition (across all age groups)

Dependent variables	Condition: try harder	context reinstatement	change perspective	change order
Total correct	19.00	16.05	12.50	19.06
Error rate	5.33	4.31	3.37	6.83
Confab.	0.67	0.00	0.68	0.22
Action	1.73	1.37	1.12	0.89
Description	13.6	11.63	9.00	13.78
Location	0.07	0.21	0.12	0.11
Object	1.80	1.63	1.12	1.33
Temporal	0.67	0.21	0.00	0.33
Other	1.00	1.00	1.00	1.61

There was no significant main effect of condition on total correct information $F(3,55)=2.20$, $P>.05$ or errors. There were significant differences between conditions in total information (total correct plus errors $F\ (3, 64)=2.85$, $P<.05$) with the try harder and change order conditions producing more information than the change perspective instruction (Fisher PLSD= 7.78 and 7.43 respectively, p<.05). However, more errors occurred in these conditions, although as indicated earlier there was no significant main effect of condition on error means ($F(3,64)=2.33$, $p=.08$). There were no significant interactions between age and condition on any of the measures (all *F*s <1).

To summarise the data from experiment 2, there were no significant differences between the try harder control and mnemonic instruction conditions in total correct or incorrect information elicited. The results showed the youngest age group produced less correct information than the two older age groups but did not produce more errors and were no less accurate. In the absence of significant interactions between age and condition it is not possible to comment on age differences in performance under each condition. There are however, some notable trends in the means which warrant attention in further studies: (1) inspection of the means for total correct information suggest the youngest age group perform less well under the context conditions as compared to the eight year olds, which is consistent with the recent findings of Pipe et al., (1993); and (2) the youngest age group perform less well under the perspective conditions (cf. Saywitz, et al., 1992) and we argue below that this may be due in part to the difficulty the children have understanding this instruction.

In the three studies there were no significant between group differences in the effects of CI instructions as compared to a try harder control group. This leads to the conclusion that the memory enhancing effects of CI reported in earlier studies may be due to increased interviewer and interviewee motivation to work harder. We are undertaking further research to explore this hypothesis in more depth. One factor relating to use of the CI that has been overlooked in earlier research is that it relies upon the co-operation of the interviewer and witness. The way in which the CI instructions are communicated and the extent to which the witness understands them is therefore critical in determining the success or failure of the procedure. For example, with respect to the change perspective instruction we found that interviewees were more likely to understand what we meant if we asked them to adopt a different location perspective rather than a different person perspective (cf. Saywitz et al., 1992).

The necessity to prompt with specific questions poses an additional problem in interpreting the effects of CI on recall performance: namely, that any increases in information obtained with CI instructions may be an artefact of the language that has to be used to fulfil the instructions given, and not a product of memory improvement. For example, in one study (Memon et al., 1992) we found the CI increased the reporting of details about the location of various people and objects (cf. Smith, 1979) as compared to a similar interview where the special CI instructions were not applied. It was also noted in one of the studies reported in the present paper (experiment 2) that the "change order" instruction tended to produce more information about the timing of events. Such details may of course be relevant in some cases (cf. Fisher & Geiselman, 1992).

The difficulty in communicating the CI instructions to the witness is one problem. Another is that it is not clear to what extent the success of CI resides in the motivation of the CI interviewer to produce a better interview and more information. The CI clearly takes more time and effort to perform than what has been described as a standard interview (George, 1992, Saywitz et al., 1992). The major way in which the CI components may differ from the "try again" instruction is in the "novel" way they request the interviewee to recall further information. Although more recent studies of CI (e.g. Koehnken et al., 1992) have tried to ensure their control groups received equivalent levels of training to cognitive interviewers the motivational element has, prior to our studies, not been sufficiently addressed in earlier studies of CI. Future studies of CI need to include a try harder group as an additional control group and compare this group's performance with that of the so called standard interview group.

Physical context cues and props may have powerful effects on recall (see Gee & Pipe, 1993 for a recent review). Yet, in the present studies we found no effects of context. Gee and Pipe argue that young children (six year olds) are less likely to use spontaneously generated cues such as imagery, and the re-enactment of an event using cues and props makes communication easier than merely reinstating the environmental context. They also show that the types of cues used and the method of presenting them are important determinants of the amount and accuracy of information reported. This reinforces the point that was made earlier about the communication of CI techniques.

Because of its potential application in the field of police interviewing, it is essential to scrutinise very carefully the experimental data related to CI. An ESRC funded study is currently underway to look more closely at the ways in which differences in interviewer style, interviewer non-verbal behaviour and witness motivation may influence the potency of any effects obtained with the CI.

References

Anderson, R. C., & Pichert, J. W. (1978). Recall of previously unrecallable information following a shift in perspective. *Journal of Verbal Learning and Verbal Behaviour*, *17*, 1-12.

Cronin, Ó., Eaves, R., Küpper, B., Memon, A., & Bull, R. (1992, May). *The cognitive interview: A child centred approach?* Poster presented at the NATO Advanced Study Institute, The child witness in context: Cognitive, social and legal perspectives, La Lucca, Italy.

Cutler, B., & Penrod, S. D. (1988). Context reinstatement and eyewitness identification. In G. M. Davies & D. M.Thomson (Eds.), *Memory in context: Context in memory*. Chichester: Wiley.

Davies, G., Tarrant, A., & Flin, R. (1989). Close encounters of the witness kind: Children's memory for a simulated health inspection. *British Journal of Psychology*, *80*, 415-429.

Davies, G. M., & Thomson, D. M. (Eds.) (1988). *Memory in context: Context in memory*. Chichester: Wiley.

Eaves, R. (1992). *An evaluation of the efficacy of the mnemonic components of the cognitive interview*. Unpublished undergraduate dissertation, Psychology Department, University of Middlesex, UK.

Fisher, R. P., Geiselman, R. E., & Amador, M. (1989). Field test of the cognitive interview: Enhancing the recollection of actual victims and witnesses of crime. *Journal of Applied Psychology*, *74*, 722-727.

Fisher, R. P., & Geiselman, R. E. (1992). Memory-enhancing techniques for investigative interviewing: The cognitive interview. Illinois: Thomas.

Fisher, R. P., McCauley, M. R., & Geiselman, R. E. (1992). Improving eyewitness testimony with the cognitive interview. In D. Ross, J. D. Read, & M. Toglia (Eds.), *Adult eyewitness testimony: Current trends and developments*. New York: Cambridge University Press.

Flexser, A., & Tulving, E. (1978). Retrieval independence in recognition and recall. *Psychological Review*, *85*, 153-171.

Gee, S., & Pipe, M. (1993). *Helping children to remember: The influence of object cues on children's accounts of a real event*. Manuscript submitted for publication.

Geiselman, R. E. (1988). Improving memory through mental reinstatement of context. In G. M. Davies & D. M. Thomson (Eds.), *Memory in context: Context in memory*. Chichester: Wiley.

Geiselman, R. E., & Padilla, J. (1988). Interviewing child witnesses with the cognitive interview. *Journal of Police Science and Administration*, *16*, 236-242.

Geiselman, R. E., Fisher, R. P., MacKinnon, D. P., & Holland, H. L (1986). Eyewitness memory enhancement in the cognitive interview. *American Journal of Psychology*, *99*, 386-401.

Geiselman, R. E., Fisher, R. P., MacKinnon, D. P., & Holland, H. L (1985). Eyewitness memory enhancement in the police interview: Cognitive retrieval mnemonics versus hypnosis. *Journal of Applied Psychology*, *70*, 401-412.

George, R., & Clifford, B. (1991, April). *A field comparison of the cognitive interview and conversation management*. Paper presented at the British Psychological Society Annual Conference, Bournemouth, UK.

George, R. C. (1992). *A field evaluation of the cognitive interview.* Unpublished Master's Thesis, Polytechnic of East London.

Kail, R. (1979). *The development of memory in children.* New York: Freeman.

Kobasigawa, A. (1974). Utilisation of retrieval cues by children in recall. *Child Development, 45,* 127-134.

Koehnken, G., & Brockmann, C. (1988). Das kognitive interview: Eine neue explorationstechnik (nicht nur) fur die forensische aussagepsychologie. *Zeitschrift fur Differentielle und Diagnostische Psychologie, 9,* 257-265.

Koehnken, G., Finger, M., Nitschke, N. & Hfer, E. (1992). *Does a cognitive interview interfere with a subsequent Statement Validity Analysis?* Paper presented at the American Psychology and Law Society Meeting, San Diego.

Loftus, E. F., & Fathi, D. C. (1985). Retrieving multiple autobiographical memories. *Social Cognition, 3,* 280-295.

Mantwill, A., Aschermann, E., & Koehnken, G. (1992). *Kognitives interview und schemageleitete erinnerung.* Final Report, Grant No. Ko 882/3-1, Deutsche Forschungsgemeinschaft.

Memon, A., & Bruce, V. (1985). Context effects in episodic studies of verbal and facial memory: A review. *Current Psychological Research and Reviews, 4,* 349-369.

Memon, A., & Bull, R (1991). The cognitive interview: Its origins, empirical support, evaluation and practical implications. *Journal of Community and Applied Social Psychology, 1,* 291-307.

Memon, A., Cronin, O., Eaves, R., & Bull, R. (1992). The cognitive interview and child witnesses. In British Psychological Society Division of Criminological and Legal Psychology, *Children, evidence and procedure,* Occasional Paper No. 19.

Memon, A., & Koehnken, G. (1992). Helping witnesses to remember more: The cognitive interview. *Expert Evidence, 1,* 39-48.

Norman, D., & Bobrow, D. (1978). Descriptions: An intermediate stage in memory retrieval. *Cognitive Psychology, 11,* 107-123.

Orne, M. T. (1972). On the social psychology of the psychological experiment: With particular reference to demand characteristics and their implications. *American Psychologist, 17,* 776-783.

Ornstein, P. A., Medlin, R. G., Stone, B. P., & Naus, M. J. (1985). Retrieving for rehearsal: An analysis of active rehearsal in children's memory. *Developmental Psychology, 2,* 633-641.

Pipe, M .E., Gee, S., & Wilson, J. C. (1993). Cues, props and context: Do they facilitate children's event reports? In G. S. Goodman & B. Bottoms (Eds.), *Child victims, child witnesses: Understanding and improving testimony* (pp. 25-46). New York: Guilford.

Poole, D. A., & White, L. T. (1992, May). *Impact of a long delay on the eyewitness testimony of children and adults.* Poster presented at the NATO Advanced Study Institute, The child witness in context: Cognitive, social and legal Perspectives, La Lucca, Italy.

Saywitz, K., Geiseleman, R. E., & Bornstein, G. K. (1992). Effects of cognitive interviewing and practice on children's recall performance. *Journal of Applied Psychology, 77,* 744-756.

Scrivner, E., & Safer, M. A. (1988). Eyewitnesses show hypermnesia for details about a violent event. *Journal of Applied Psychology, 73,* 371-377.

Smith, S. M. (1979). Remembering in and out of context. *Journal of Experimental Psychology: Human Learning and Memory, 5,* 460-471.

Smith, S. M., & Vela, E. (1992). Environmental context-dependent eyewitness recognition. *Applied Cognitive Psychology, 6,* 125-140.

Tulving, E. (1974). Cue-dependent forgetting. *American Scientist, 62,* 74-82.

Tulving, E., & Thomson, D. M. (1973). Encoding specificity and retrieval processes in episodic memory. *Psychological Review, 80,* 353-370.

Weiss, L. (1969). Effects of subject, experimenter and task variables on compliance with the experimenter's expectation. *Journal of Projective Techniques, 33,* 247-255.

[1] We are grateful to the staff and pupils of Taunton College and Bevois Town School in Hampshire for their participation in this research. We are also grateful to Trudy Wright for her help with data collection and to Sigi Sporer for his comments on an earlier draft of the paper.

[2] Separate analysis of the free recall data was not possible given the small number of details (correct and incorrect) elicited by each participant. Many of the five to six year olds did not respond in free recall conditions unless the interviewer used a couple of prompts and this would also have made comparison of free recall across age groups difficult to interpret.

The Cognitive Interview - Does it Work?

Richard C. George and Brian R. Clifford

Introduction

The criminal investigative process relies heavily on gathering information. This information can come from various sources including the account given by any eyewitness or victim ("witness"). Information from the witness is considered the most important source of all by New York detectives (Sanders, 1986) and in the UK it is the stage with the greatest emphasis placed upon it by the Association of Chief Police Officers (ACPO)/Home Office National Investigative Interviewing Project Team (George and Bennett, 1992). Despite this police have, until recently, provided very little or no training in interviewing either witnesses or suspects (Cahill and Mingay, 1986) and have relied instead on "on the job" training (Shepherd, 1988). There is sparse knowledge of how police who have never received training interview witnesses, and indeed whether any commonality exists between these practitioners. One (secondary) aim of this study, therefore, was to identify and define any such commonality.

The Cognitive Interview (CI) was developed by Fisher and Geiselman in the mid 1980s to address this lack of training (e.g. Geiselman, Fisher, Firstenberg, Hutton, Sullivan, Avetissian and Prosk, 1984). The CI attempted to aid the interviewing officers by equipping them with mnemonic devices to assist the witness to recall his/her experiences in greater quantity and with better reliability. It thus began life as four retrieval mnemonics emanating from two principles of cognition (see Geiselman et al., 1984) and was later enhanced by adding further cognitive aspects and principles of communication taken from social psychology (Fisher and Geiselman, 1992).

Various assessments of the CI have been made in laboratory settings (e.g. Fisher, Geiselman, Raymond, Jurkevich, and Warhaftig, 1987; Koenken, Thuerer and Zoberbier, 1991; Boon and Noon, in press), but only one has been carried out in a field setting (Fisher, Geiselman and Amador, 1989), and most studies to date have tested the original CI. The major aim of this study was to further test the ecological validity of the enhanced CI, in an independent, UK and real life setting.

A second major aim was to improve the method employed to assess any extra information gained in different interview conditions. The paradigm employed in CI studies so far has relied upon raters (psychology students) judging the relevance of any piece of information given by the witness and using the total amount as the dependent variable. This is a subjective and difficult rating for psychology students to make for two reasons: firstly, they have little or no investigative experience; and secondly, any assessment of relevance before all facts are known is difficult, even for experienced investigators. The current study attempted to address this issue.

A third issue investigated in the current study was the comparison of CI with another form of interview training, one which has been growing in popularity among police forces: Conversation Management (CM). CM purports to teach officers to interview witnesses and suspects, relying almost entirely on aspects of social psychology. A typical CM course is longer than the CI training (five days against two days for CI) and deals with such issues as the mechanics of conversation, channels of communication, listening skills, planning the interview, self-presentation, introductions, conversational styles, question types, interviewing style and resistance. The fundamental difference between CI and CM is therefore the cognitive components of the CI; several of the social aspects are common to each.

Method

Design A 2x2x2 mixed Anova design was employed with the between subject factors being CI training (present or not), and CM (present or not); and training effect (before or after) as the within-subject factor. Seven different police officers served in each of the four cells created by the crossing of CI and CM. The four cells were labelled: "Control", "CI", "CI+CM" and "CM".

Police officers in the four different cells received the following training: control cell received no CI or CM training; CI cell received CI but no CM; CI+CM cell received CI and CM training and the CM cell received CM but no CI training.

Before any officer received any training he/she provided an audio tape recording of a real interview he/she had carried out with a real witness/victim of a crime. After receiving the training appropriate to their allotted condition the officers provided a second recording of a further real interview with a further, different, real witness. Officers in the control cell provided a tape of a second interview after a time delay equivalent to the time spent training in the other cells. These two sets of taped interviews served as the before and after materials upon which analyses were carried out.

Subjects (police interviewers) Twenty eight officers from Hertfordshire Constabulary were as far as possible randomly selected from 160 volunteers who were of the rank of Constable, had a minimum of five years experience as a police officer, had received no previous interview training, and whose current duties included the interviewing of witnesses/victims of crime. Officers were allocated to one of the four cells on a random but restricted basis to ensure as equal a distribution as possible of females, detectives and traffic officers to the four conditions. Allocation was otherwise random.

Procedure Following allocation to cells, but prior to training, officers provided an audio tape of an interview they had carried out with a witness. They were instructed to select an interview where the witness had witnessed an incident preferably involving the viewing of a suspect, and was not merely reporting a crime or other incident, e.g., a burglary.

Following the obtaining of all "before training" tapes, the training phase began. Police officers in the CI cell received two full days training of the enhanced CI by the first author (a recognised CI trainer in the City of London Police). The training was closely related to the model used by Fisher as learned by the first author on two visits to Florida International University, USA, and included lecturing, viewing video tapes of example interviews, and providing feedback on each participants' practice interviews.

Training of officers in the CM cell was carried out by a police officer who had successfully graduated from Shepherd's three-week workshop on learning, and learning to instruct, CM. Training in this condition lasted seven days, and included two extra days concentrating on witness issues to eliminate any bias towards suspect interviewing which may occur during the normal five-day training. As with the CI training, the officers were taught concepts and techniques and participated in practice interviews on which feedback was provided.

Officers in the CI+CM cell received two days CI training identical to the CI cell described above; this was followed by the standard five-day CM training. Finally in this cell the officers and instructors spent two hours discussing the integration of the CI with CM.

Control cell officers received no training.

Coding and scoring[1] Each interview tape was fully transcribed by a qualified audio typist and then timed from the opening case-relevant question to the closing case-relevant question. Administrative or rapport building sections within the case-relevant sections were excluded from the measured time of each interview.

Working from the typed transcripts each question asked was coded as one of, or a combination of, 16 types of probe (e.g. "leading"; "open and extension clarification"; "closed and request to image") and consecutively numbered. The classification included mnemonic aids and questions that requested a description of a suspect.

Resultant information from the witness/victim was scored alongside each coded question: firstly one mark was scored for each piece of new emergent information and placed into a grammatical category (who, what(verb), what(object), where, when, how, or why). This strict grammatical approach necessitated the extraction of the essence of what was said by the witness in certain cases to allow scoring.

Suppositions made and verbalizations recounted by the witness were coded.

The following example of an exchange between interviewer and interviewee and an explanation of how it would have been scored in this study is provided to clarify the scoring.

Interviewer: "What exactly happened when he walked into the room?"

Interviewee: "He pulled out a gun from a plastic bag, pointed it at me and told me to give him all the money. The gun was black. I was scared stiff but managed to press the alarm under the counter; he then ran out as if his life depended on it".

The question would have been coded as an "extension/clarification" question (being based on a previous reference in the interview), and as an "open" question (McKay, 1980). It would have been consecutively numbered (e.g. the tenth question asked), and placed alongside it would be the first layer of the coding of the answer (the grammatical categorisation). The grammatical categorisation (in the example) follows each segment in parenthesis :

He (who) pulled out (what-verb) a gun (what-object) from (where) a plastic (what-object) bag (what-object) pointed (what-verb) it (what-object) at me (where) and told me to give him all the money (what-verb). The gun (no new information) was black (what-object). I (who) was scared stiff (who) but managed to press the alarm (what-verb - counting "to sound the alarm" as one action) under the counter (where). He (who) then ran out (what-verb - counting "to run out" as one action) as if his life depended on it (how).

Thus, the total score for this reply is broken down into: 4xwho; 5xwhat-object; 5xwhat-verb (one of which was coded as a verbalisation); 3xwhere and 1xhow. The total score for information given by the interviewee on this question is therefore 18.

Results

The method of coding and scoring utilised in this study provided an enormous amount of data. (A second layer of coding was made to examine more closely the investigative value of information. This has not been described in this article.) Results presented here relate to the aims of the study as specified above, other results relating to subsidiary aims will be described elsewhere.

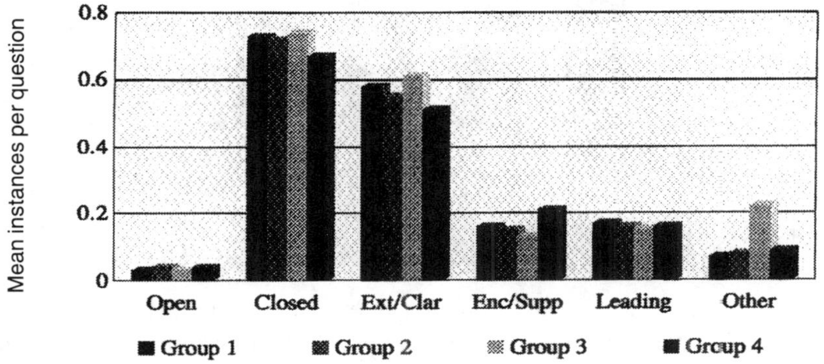

Figure 1: Mean Instance per Question Before Training

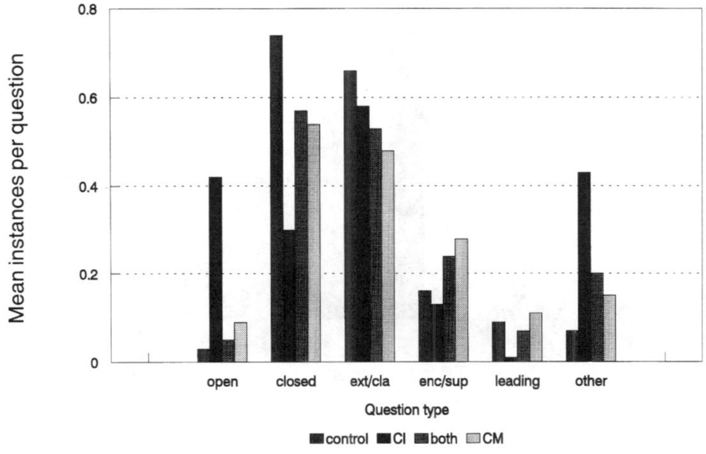

Figure 2: Mean Instance per Question After Training

Figure 1 shows clearly that officers who are not trained to interview nevertheless employ the same questioning strategies. The predominant type of questions asked are closed (between 6.74 and 7.99 per every 10 asked) and extension/clarification (between 5.08 and 6.76 per every 10 asked). Since each extension\clarification question will necessarily be either open or closed, and very few open questions were asked, it is probable that they occur together most of the time, making the most common question "extension\clarification - closed".

Figure 2 is the same breakdown after training. The CI cell is the only cell to have significantly changed, increasing in "open" questions and "other" questions (i.e. mnemonic aids) and decreasing in closed and leading questions.

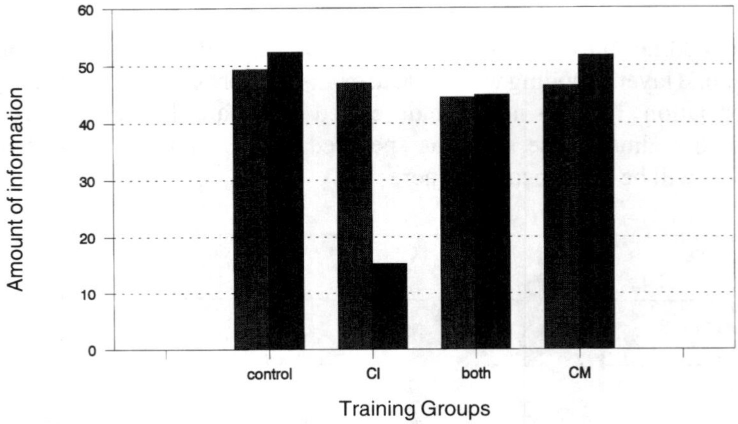

Figure 3: Question Rate as a Function of Training

A three-way Anova revealed a significant interaction between CI and Training ($F(1,48) = 8.4$, $p < .05$). A post hoc Newman-Keuls test showed that the interaction was explained by the drop in rate of questions asked by the CI cell (see Figure 3).

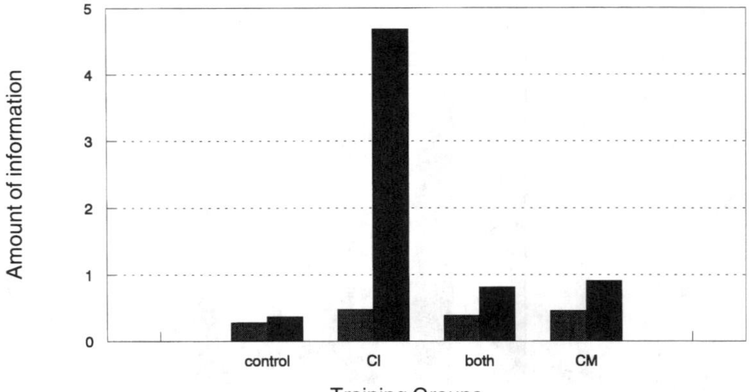

Figure 4: Open Questions per 10 Questions Asked

A three-way Anova showed a significant interaction between CI, CM and Training ($F(1,48) = 29.4$, $p < .001$). It is clear that this interaction is due to the massive increase the amount of open questions asked by the CI cell after training (Figure 4).

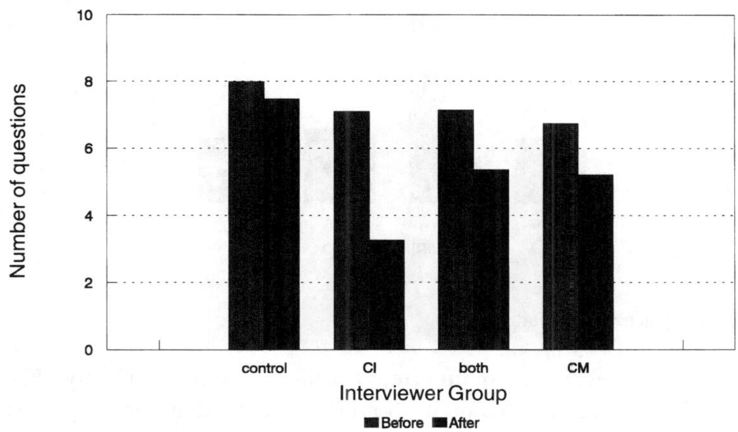

Figure 5: Closed Questions per 10 Questions Asked

Again a three-way Anova showed a significant interaction between all three factors ($F(1,48) = 6.05$, $p < .05$). Although there is some decrease in each of the trained cells the largest drop in the number of closed questions asked is in the CI trained cell, and this accounts for the effects (Figure 5).

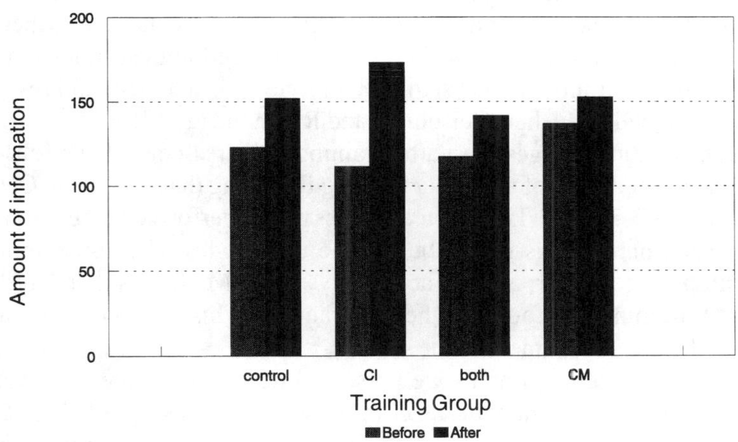

Figure 6: Gross Information per Question

Here, in the first measure of information elicited, a three-way Anova reveals an interaction of all three factors ($F(1,48) = 11.38$, $p < .01$) obviously caused by the large increase in information gained by officers in the CI cell after training (Figure 6).

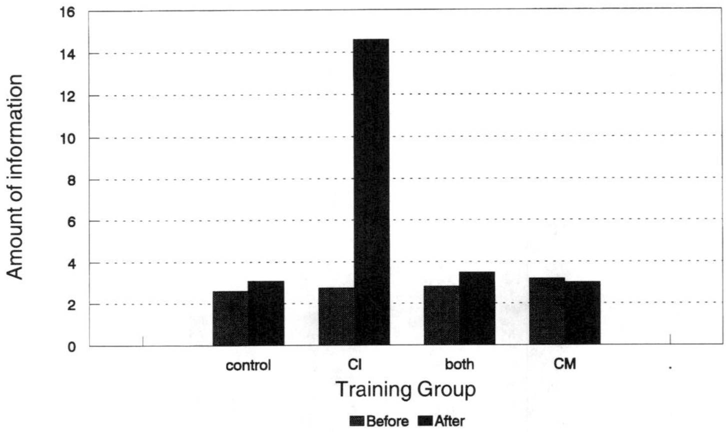

Figure 7: Gross Information per Time Unit

A three-way Anova revealed a main effect for the factor training only ($F(1,48) = 6.59$, $p < .05$). While non-significant it should be noted that the CI trained cell produced by far the greatest increase of pieces of information per 10 minutes of interview time (Figure 7).

Discussion

Interviewer behaviour The commonality in the interviews of the untrained officers provide baseline behaviour against which to assess the effects of training; it also, for the first time, defines the hitherto elusive "Standard Police Interview". It appears that police officers who have no common training nevertheless share the same schema for acquiring information from witnesses. In terms of the predominant question types used by officers before training, this "standard interview" is deficient and resembles the interviews critiqued by Fisher, Geiselman and Raymond (1987).

Interviewer behaviour changes most after training officers in the CI. The change is dramatic and far exceeds that of any other training including that of CI with CM. It is not clear why the officers trained in both techniques under-performed in relation to the "CI only" officers, but there is no doubt that the two modes of training somehow worked to confound each other; or more accurately since CM officers failed to change much, the CM training confounded the CI training. This was contrary to our expectations at the commencement of the study.

Three specific dependent variables are presented here to illustrate the change in interviewer behaviour. The dramatic drop in closed questions asked (Fig. 5) and increase in open questions (Fig. 4) by the CI cell are entirely commensurate with their large decrease in question rate (Fig. 3) and reflect improved listening skills and successful handing over of control of the flow of information to the witness.

Interviewee behaviour Not only does the interviewer change his/her questioning technique after CI training, the result is more information from the witness (Fig. 6). The amount of information he\she collects per question increases more than fivefold, no other cell even doubles, and officers trained in CM actually get slightly less. It is interesting that, in line with the untrained commonality in questioning, commonality in terms of the quantity of resultant information can now be seen, with less than 0.6 of a piece of information separating the untrained cells.

Figure 7 shows the amount of information elicited per time unit (ten minutes). Although the only significant effect is for training, the trend is very much in line with other results in the study, namely the CI trained cell outperforming all others. This is reflected in the increase made in that cell being more than three times larger than that made in any other cell.

Conclusions

In line with the previous field study carried out by Fisher et al. (1989) CI training has been shown to be effective. Officers trained in CI only emphatically altered the way they interviewed witnesses, and the real-life witnesses they interviewed gave more information as a result.

The coding system employed in this study did not rely on a subjective measurement of relevant information. The full benefit of the system will become apparent in future analyses when the information will be examined qualitatively and the effectiveness of component parts of the CI compared.

Officers trained in CM changed only marginally as, disappointingly, did those trained in both modes. CI training, despite being under half the length of CM training, was the most effective. The value of CM training for teaching suspect interviewing was not assessed in this study but its ability to change the behaviour of those interviewing witnesses must be in doubt. Different interview training packages clearly cannot be taken "off the shelf" and bolted together; CM training appears to confound the effects of the CI training.

The standard police interview, hitherto discussed without ever being defined, is now able to be described.

References

Boon, J. & Noon, E. (in press). The cognitive interview. *Psychology, Crime and the Law.*

Cahill, D., & Mingay, D. J. (1986). Leading questions and the police interview. *Policing*, 212-224.

Fisher, R. P., & Geiselman, R. E. (1992). *Memory-enhancing techniques for investigative interviewing: The cognitive interview*. Springfield, Ill.: Charles C. Thomas.

Fisher, R. P., Geiselman, R. E., & Amador, M. (1989). Field tests of the cognitive interview: Enhancing the recollection of actual victims and witnesses of crime. *Journal of Applied Psychology*, *74*, 722-727.

Fisher, R. P., Geiselman R. E., & Raymond, D. S. (1987). Critical analysis of police interview techniques. *Journal of Police Science and Administration*, *15*, 177-185.

Fisher, R. P., Geiselman, R. E., Raymond, D. S., Jurkevich, L. M., & Wharftig, M. L. (1987). Enhancing enhanced eyewitness memory: Refining the cognitive interview. *Journal of Police Science and Administration*, *15*, 291-297.

Geiselman, R. E., Fisher,R. P., Firstenberg, I., Hutton, L. A., Sullivan, S. J., Avetissian, I. V., & Prosk, A. L. (1984). Enhancement of eyewitness memory: An empirical evaluation of the cognitive interview. *Journal of Police Science and Administration*, *12*, 74-80.

George, R. C., & Bennett, P. (1992, September). *Making the most of it*. Paper presented at the Third European Conference on Psychology and Law, Oxford.

Kohnken, G., Thuerer, C., & Zoberbier, D. (1991). *The cognitive interview: Are the interviewers memories enhanced too?* Unpublished manuscript, University of Kiel, Germany.

MacKay, I (1980). *A guide to asking questions*. London: Bacie.

Sanders, G. S. (1986). *The usefulness of eyewitness research from the perspective of police investigators*. Unpublished manuscript, State University of New York at Albany.

Shepherd, E. (1988). Developing interview skills. In P. Southgate (Ed.) *New directions in police training*. London: Her Majesty's Stationary Office.

[1] The authors acknowledge the considerable contribution made by Dr Eric Shepherd who helped us design this coding and scoring system, and who initially encouraged us to address the problematical issue of relevance.

[2] No distinction was made in this study between those closed questions which were constructive and those which were destructive. A closed question may at any point in the interview be the most appropriate question to ask. The important point according to CI training is that closed questions are not asked in such a manner or at such a stage in the interview that the witness forms the expectation that closed questions will form the pattern of the entire interview, and consequently not applying all his\her mental resources.

Part III
Children in the Legal System

The Development of Children's Understanding of Legal Principles

Iwona Jakubowska

The aim of my work was to describe the mechanisms responsible for the formation of beliefs and moral and legal values in the development of an individual. I was inspired by the work of Piaget (Piaget, 1977). My study was conducted in 1980; it used a stratified random sample of children of Warsaw elementary and grammar schools.

The sample was made up of 477 children aged 9-10 years (*n* = 129), 14-15 years (*n* + 175), and 17-19 years (*n* = 173). Selection of the two younger groups was based on Piaget's theory. No criteria could be found in theories of moral development for selecting the third group but it seemed necessary to include that group as a contrast to the other two.

A second major influence on theory of moral development is the work of June Tapp and Laurence Kohlberg (Tapp & Kohlberg, 1971). In their research concerning the development of legal thinking, Tapp and Kohlberg focused on four problems: 1) How much are regulations and laws worth?; 2) What is the function of regulations and laws?; 3) What is the dynamics of submission to regulations?; and 4) What is the mutability of regulations and laws?

They asked four questions, treating them as indicators for research: 1) What would happen if regulations and laws did not exist?; 2) What is law?; 3) Why should people respect legal rules and regulations?; 4) Are there situations when it is possible not to respect legal rules and regulations?

On the basis of the results obtained, they classified people into one of the six stages characterizing the development of legal thinking.

In my research, I used four of Tapp and Kohlberg's questions. They were open and did not suggest any specific answer. Based on the results, I classified people into one of the six stages. My classification of answers may be inaccurate to some extent. The indicators used were inferred from the descriptions of characteristic answers from Tapp and Kohlberg's work.

According to Tapp and Kohlberg, each level and stage of the development of legal orientation is characterized by a different view on the essence of law and justification of the reasons why law should be observed.

Due to lack of space, all the answers obtained in my study cannot be quoted here. This is why the present paper will be limited to discussion of the answers that appeared most frequently in the separate age groups, and of my conclusions, not documented here with relevant data.

When asked, "What would happen if regulations and laws did not exist", respondents of all ages most frequently state that absence of the law would result in disorder, confusion, and chaos, the proportions being 42%, 35%, and 31% for the youngest, middle, and oldest group respectively. In the youngest group, the second most frequent answer specified the types of bad behaviour likely to emerge in the absence of laws (18%), and the third most frequent stressed the role of law as restraint to the bad inclinations of man (17%).

In the middle and oldest group, the second most frequent answer defined the role of law as restraint to the bad inclinations of man (28% and 18% respectively). The oldest children only (15%) mentioned law's functions of protecting the functioning of society, regulating social life, and protecting social order.

To recapitulate the above answers, it can be stated that the respondents' opinions evolve with age from perception of the functions of legal rules through their power of protection against evil to perception of those functions as creative for the existence of society.

The next question was, "Why should people observe legal rules and regulations?". Most respondents in all age groups stated that law protects against disorder and ensures peace and safety - 45%, 42% and 28% of answers respectively.

In the youngest age group, the second most frequent answer was that law prevents people from doing wrong things (12%) and ensures the existence of good (11% of answers).

In the middle and oldest age groups, the second most frequent answer stressed the function of law as a regulator of interpersonal relations - 10% and 25% of answers respectively.

Generally, a tendency can be noticed that is intensified with the age of transition from observance of law for fear of punishment to a perception of the functions of law in society.

When asked, "What is law?", the youngest children usually define law as a collection of principles to be observed (25%), and a collection of rules telling what is allowed and what is prohibited (19%); the answers of children aged 14-15 show a similar trend - 29% and 15% respectively. Respondents aged 17-18 usually define law as a collection of principles and norms of social life (25%), and through its function of regulating social coexistence (19%).

The above data suggest a transition with age from seeing law as nothing but obligatory to perceiving it as a regulator of coexistence in a social group.

The last question to be discussed here was whether legal rules and regulations should always be observed or do not have to be observed in specific situations. The answers suggest a decrease with age of the tendency to perceive legal rules and regulations as obligatory on account of the authority attributed to them and, instead, a growth with age of the tendency to treat them as functional for individuals. Also diminishing with age is the tendency to recognize unqualified rightness of legal rules and principles, and to renounce the validity of such rules and principles irrespective of their pertinence.

Generally, the results of my study corroborate the pattern described by Tapp and Kohlberg as typical of the development of legal thinking. With age, the tendency to perceive law and legal rules from the perspective of their functionality and value for the individual and society shows an explicit growth.

References

Piaget, J. (1977). *The moral judgement of the child.* Harmondsworth: Penguin.

Kohlberg, L. (1981). *Essays on moral development: Vol 1. The philosophy of moral development.* San Fransisco: Harper & Row.

Tapp J., & Kohlberg, L. (1971). Developing senses of law and legal justice. *Journal of Social Issues, 27*(2), 65-91.

Psychological Evaluation of Changes in Testimony Given by Sexually Abused Juveniles

Teresa Jaskiewicz-Obydzinska and Alicja Czerederecka

Introduction

Testimony made by juvenile victims in sexual crime cases constitutes essential evidence in a trial as the children are usually the only witnesses of the crime. At the same time they are only very young minors. In view of this, the evaluation of reliability of the testimony is of paramount importance.

In court practice it has long been an established fact that the stability of testimony i.e. its unchangeability in successive interrogations of a witness is the basic feature of reliability. However, the results of studies carried out in the field of psychology of testimony do not provide a basis for such an absolute evaluation. They show that the assumption that stability of testimony is indicative of reliability and the lack of stability suggests its unreliability might be an oversimplification. Although the authors who dealt with establishing criteria of testimony reliability suggested stability as one of them, they point out that it depends on the kind of stability, as in some conditions lack of stability may also be a convincing feature of reliability (Arntzen, 1989).

The stability of testimony, similar to other features of statements becomes the actual criterion of reliability only when it has been projected to certain psychological features of a witness.

The Subject and the Method of the Examination

The present work has been based on the results of examinations of 60 juvenile witness-victims of sexual abuse (including 13 boys and 47 girls). The psychological examination of these witnesses were carried out at the Institute of Forensic Research in connection with formulating an expertise concerning reliability of their testimony demanded by the courts and the Prosecutor Office.

The aim of the work was to establish:

(1) the relation between the quantity and the character of changes introduced by witnesses in their testimony and their personality;

(2) the relation of these factors to the evaluation of testimony reliability of the juveniles.

All children under examination were interrogated two to four times in each case. At least one of the interrogations took place in the presence of a psychologist, who, in turn, examined the witness and formulated an opinion. The occurrence of changes in testimony was found in 30 persons - half of the examined cases. The changes have been analyzed and classified according to the following categories:

(1) Completions: (a) of details essential to the event; (b) of interpretation of behaviour; (c) of explanation of incongruity in the testimony and the lack of consequence in people's behaviour.

(2) Omission of significant details.

(3) Transformations: (a) of details; (b) of interpretation of behaviour.

Assuming that the character of the changes introduced by witnesses into their testimony is closely related to their personality, psychological criteria have been established according to which psychological features have been classified, which, according to experts, had a crucial influence on the changes made by people under examination.

The criteria were the following:

(1) Development properties

(2) Individual properties

(3) Situational reactions.

Within these three groups of variables the following factors were considered:

(a) cognitive development (among which: intellectual level, ability of perception, memory, attention, vocabulary content).

(b) emotional development such as: reactivity, emotional dependence, fear reaction behaviour, defensive mechanisms, emotional involvement into the case.

(c) social development (attitude towards the surroundings characterized by openness, suspiciousness, striving for cooperation, susceptibility to the influence of the surroundings expressed by fear of social evaluation, fear of punishment, striving for being accepted by others).

(d) forming a self-image - such as self-criticism and a level of aspiration.

The rise in occurrence of the above-mentioned features was evaluated in a three-degree scale.

The influence of a situation on changes made in the testimony was accepted in cases where not due to permanent properties of an examined person, but were the result of a certain situation of the person being interrogated.

Taking into consideration the aim of the examination the following hypotheses have been put forward:

- changes occurring in testimony do not have decisive influence on the evaluation of their reliability. There is, however, a relationship between the categories of changes and testimony reliability.

- psychological factors are decisive for changes in testimony and affect its reliability. Among these, the most important are factors resulting from the social development of witnesses. Psychological data have been used: psychological interviews with parents, intelligence scale results, project method tests, data collected during observation of juveniles while being interrogated and examined, and data for case files. In each case the testimony made by witnesses has been analyzed. On such a basis, psychological factors underlying testimony and introduced changes were determined. Furthermore psychological evaluation of testimony reliability was carried out.

Characteristics of the Examined Group

All those examined were witnesses-victims of crimes of a sexual nature. Eighty percent of them encompassed all actions leading to taking sexual advantage of the examined, but only in 20% of the cases actual sexual intercourse took place. The participants were all aged between 5-15 years with the majority (60%) being between 11-15.

In 93% of the cases, the examination has been ordered by the Prosecution Office in the course of preliminary proceedings, in the remaining 7% in connection with the court case in progress.

The first interrogation of the examined took place within 30 days of the event (65% of the cases); the rest within six months from the event (32%) and only 3% later. The time lapse between successive interrogations varied from two days to several months but the majority of interrogations took place in the period from seven days to six months; only 3% of the witnesses were interrogated for the second time after six months.

Eighty five percent of the examined were interrogated twice; the rest three or four times. The perpetrators were persons unknown to the examined in 56% of the cases, known in 38% and members of the family in 6% of the cases. In 72% of the cases the testimony of the examined concerned one event which was the subject of the case; the remaining 28% dealt with events which occurred twice or more.

The behaviour of the juveniles during the actual event was most frequently passive - submissive to the perpetrators' orders (53%). The cooperation with the perpetrator took place in 20% of the examined, the remaining 27% of the juveniles showed an active resistance or other forms of defense (e.g. escape, effective crying for help, etc.).

In the evaluation of the experts the testimony of 86% of the examined were found to be reliable (including 63% highly reliable). In the remaining 14% of the cases they were evaluated as less reliable.

The Results of the Examination

The changes in testimony occurred in half of the number of the examined (Table 1). The most frequent category of change was the completion of the statements; in most cases they were completions providing essential details. The completions concerning the interpretation of the victim's behaviour and that of the perpetrator, as well as the explanations of the lack of incongruity in the testimony and the lack of consequence in the behaviour were rather rare. Changes in the form, also rare, concerned less essential details and the interpretations of the victim's behaviour and that of the perpetrator (Table 2).

Table 1: The changes and the reliability of testimonies

	Stable		Unstable		Total	
	N	%	N	%	N	%
Highly r.	22	36	16	27	38	63
Reliable	3	5	11	18	14	23
Less r.	5	9	3	5	8	14
Total	30	50	30	50	60	100

$r_p = 0.43$ average relationship power

Table 2: The character of the changes and the testimony reliability

	Completions			Transformations	
	1.1	1.2	1.3	3.1	3.2
Highly r.	14	1	1	4	1
Reliable	11	2	1	5	2
Less r.	2	–	–	1	–
Total	27	3	2	10	3

$r_p = 0.14$ low relationship power

Completions:
1.1 - of essential details
1.2 - of interpretation of behaviour
1.3 - of explanation of incongruity in the testimonies

Transformations:
3.1 - of details
3.2 - of interpretation

In the analyzed testimonies no changes were found belonging to the category of omitting essential details which had already been stated. There are two possible explanations. First, in the group under examination there were no cases of withdrawing an accusation which would have led to those details being deliberately concealed in successive interrogations. Second, the average lapse of time between consecutive testimonies was relatively short which might have been the reason for the lack of suppression processes (well known in the psychology of testimony) of these parts of the testimony which are painful for the examined and felt as a burden (e.g. the cooperation in the crime).

A certain relationship was found between the behaviour of the examined during the event and the introduction of changes into the testimony. The changes occurred predominantly in the group of the examined who, in the course of the event reacted passively and in the successive interrogations completed the description of the event with essential details (Table 3). There was a strong correlation between the occurrence of changes belonging to more than one category and the evaluation of the reliability. However, if the changes belonged to only one category there was no such correlation (Table 4).

Table 3: Comportment of the victims and the kind of changes in their testimonies

Category of changes	Comportment of victims Submission	Cooperation	Active defence	Total
Completions	11	3	3	17
Transformations	1	–	–	1
Multiple.cat.	4	5	3	12
Total	16	8	6	30

r_p = 0.41 average relationship power

Table 4: Number of categories of changes in the testimony and the reliability

	One		Multiple		Total	
	N	%	N	%	N	%
Highly r.	12	40	4	13	16	53
Reliable	4	13	7	23	11	36
Less r.	2	7	1	4	3	11
Total	18	60	12	40	30	100

r_p = 0.50 high relationship power

The analysis of psychological factors which, in the opinion of the experts were decisive for the introduction of changes, or the lack of them, gave interesting results. In general, the reasons for the lack of changes resulted probably from individual features of the witnesses. On the other hand, in the reliable testimony in which the changes did occur, the reasons for them could be ascribed both to the individual features and to simultaneous situational reactions. In both cases a high relationship power was found (Tables 5a and 5b).

Table 5a: Psychological reasons for changes in the testimony reliability, stable testimonies

	Criteria B		B+C		C		Total
	N	%	N	%	N	%	N
Highly r.	18	60	4	13	–	–	22
Reliable	1	3	1	3	1	3	3
Less r.	1	3	4	13	–	–	5
Total	20	66	9	29	1	3	30

r_p = 0.74 very high relationship power

B - individual features
C - situational reaction

Table 5b: Psychological reasons for changes in the testimony reliability, unstable testimonies

	Criteria						Total
	B		B+C		C		
	N	%	N	%	N	%	N
Highly r.	5	16	10	33	1	3	16
Reliable	2	6	8	27	1	3	11
Less r.	3	10	–	–	–	–	3
Total	10	32	18	60	2	6	30

$r_p = 0.53$ high relationship power

The analysis of the influence of the factors connected with the cognitive development on the changes in the testimony showed, first of all, a strong relationship between the general intellectual level of the examined and the occurrence of changes or the lack of them. A low intellectual level of the examined was often the reason for the changes in the testimony, whereas the high level of intellect secured their stability (Table 6).

Table 6: Victim's intellectual level as a reason of the changes in their testimonies

	Low		Average		High		Total
	N	%	N	%	N	%	N
Stable test.	5	16	4	13	8	27	17
Unst. test.	9	31	3	10	1	3	13
Total	14	47	7	23	9	30	30

$r_p = 0.50$ high relationship power

A high relationship was found between the intellectual level of the examined and the category of changes. An intellectual level below standard was most frequently the reason for the completion of the testimony, especially the completion providing essential details (Table 7). This fact has a practical value for establishing the mode of interrogation of such witnesses. Further analysis showed a strong interdependence between a high ability of perception and giving a uniform testimony. Such a property was predominantly found in the group whose testimony was evaluated as highly reliable. Surprisingly no relation was found between the memory and the introduction of changes in the testimony. It seems that this is connected with the fact that successive interrogations of witnesses were made with a short lapse of time between them and the memory was not important. A similar lack of correlation was found in connection with the ability of attention concentration. It is understandable if we take into consideration the crime situation and the subject of the testimony of the witnesses. There is a considerable difference between the situation of a witness describing the event in which he/she has actively participated and even cooperated with the perpetrator and the situation in which he has only been a passive observer. That is why the concentration of attention is not important.

Table 7: Victim's intellectual level and a kind of completions in the testimonies

Kind of changes	Intellectual level Low	Average	High	Total
Essential details	9	3	1	13
Interpretation of behaviour	–	–	–	0
Explanation of incongruity	–	1	1	2
Total	9	4	2	15

$r_p = 0.74$ very high relationship power

Emotional factors, as the reason for changes in the testimony in the group under examination, can be overlooked. An average correlation was found between the occurrence of fear reactions, reactivity and emotional dependence as the reasons for the introduction of changes and the evaluation of the reliability of the testimony. One should point out, however, the fact that these factors, as the reasons for changes, appeared exclusively in the testimony described as reliable, and they were not too intensive. The absence of acute fear relations in the examined group leads, to a conclusion that the sexual crime, unless it is drastic, is not such a traumatic event for a juvenile as it is commonly supposed. The trauma can however be deeper during the course of the proceedings.

The greatest number of correlations was found for the factors connected with social development of the subjects. Especially factors concerned with susceptibility to the influence of the social surroundings. As so, very much accentuated fear of social evaluation was a very important factor in introducing the changes in the testimony. Such a relation was clearly visible in the cases of the subjects whose testimony was described as highly reliable, so, if such a tendency could be found among the witnesses as the reason for introducing the changes in the testimony it can be assumed to be an important criterion of reliability. The need for acceptance turned out to be an equally important factor. The lack of symptoms of striving for acceptance during the testimony was very prominent in the group of the examined whose testimony was very stable and was, at the same time described as highly reliable (Tables 8, 9).

Table 8: Victim's fear of social disapproval and the testimony reliability

	Intensity of fear High	Average	Total
Highly reliable	6	–	6
Reliable	4	4	8
Less reliable	–	–	–
Total	10	4	14

$r_p = 0.64$ very high relationship power

Table 9: The need for acceptance and the testimony reliability

	Intensity of symptoms High	Average	Lack	Total
Highly reliable	–	1	14	15
Reliable	–	–	2	2
Less reliable	1	–	–	1
Total	1	1	16	18

$r_p = 0.88$ very high relationship power

This property, resistance to suggestions, is also an essential criterion of reliability. In the range of factors characterizing the attitude towards the social surrounding, striving for cooperation turned out to be very important. Symptoms of such behaviour of the witnesses do not however exert considerable influence on introducing the changes in the testimony: they were, however, found exclusively among the witnesses whose testimony was described as highly reliable Tables 10, 11).

Table 10: Striving for cooperation and the changes in the testimonies

	Intensity of symptoms High	Average	Lack	Total
Stable testimony	8	12	1	21
Unstable testimony	2	9	3	14
Total	10	21	4	35

$r_p = 0.38$ average relationship power

Table 11: Striving for cooperation and the testimonies reliability

	Intensity of symptoms High	Average	Lack	Total
Highly reliable	10	18	–	28
Reliable	–	3	3	6
Less reliable	–	–	1	1
Total	10	21	4	35

$r_p = 0.75$ very high relationship power

Some degree of importance can also be attached to the level of openness in communication with the surroundings. A small intensity of this property was advantageous to the testimony.

Among the factors connected with the formation of self-evaluation it was found that the level of self-criticism of the examined had a lot of influence, both on the introduction of changes into the testimony and its evaluation. The low level of self-criticism was responsible for introducing changes in the testimonies described as less reliable, whereas the high level of self-criticism was responsible for the changes in the testimony which was evaluated as highly reliable. In both cases a high relationship power was found (Table 12).

Table 12: The level of self-criticism and the changes in the testimonies

	Level of self-criticism			
	High	Average	Low	Total
Stable test.	–	3	1	4
Unstable testimonies	2	2	7	11
Total	2	5	8	15

$r_p = 0.57$ high relationship power

The level of aspiration, adequate to the ability of the subjects was found to be the reason for the absence of changes in the testimonies evaluated as highly reliable (Table 13).

Table 13: The level of self-criticism and the testimonies reliability

	Level of self-criticism			
	High	Average	Low	Total
Highly reliable	2	5	1	8
Reliable	–	–	4	4
Less reliable	–	–	3	3
Total	2	5	8	15

$r_p = 0.80$ very high relationship power

Development properties were not regarded as significant for the introduction of changes in testimony. Therefore they were not dealt with separately in this paper.

Summary and Conclusions

In summary the fact itself of the introduction of changes does not play a decisive role in the evaluation of the reliability of the testimony. On the other hand the quantitative and the qualitative analysis of the changes made by witnesses is quite important. The introduction of changes belonging to different categories is disadvantageous to the reliability of the testimony.

The decisive importance in evaluating the reliability of the testimony of the witnesses can be ascribed to psychological factors which can be seen as the basis both for the introduction of the changes and for the stability of the testimony. A strong correlation, found during the examination, between individual properties of the witness and the presentation of the stable and reliable testimony is especially important. A strong influence on the presentation of this kind of testimony can be ascribed to such properties of the witness like high perception, low intensity of fear reactions, an average fear of social appraisal, striving for cooperation, absence of looking for being accepted by the others, a small intensity of openness in communication with the surroundings and an adequate level of aspiration.

In order to accept the testimony in which changes did occur as reliable the following individual properties of witnesses turned out to be significant - intellectual level, accentuated fear of social appraisal, heightened self-criticism.

A strong relationship between the introduction of changes in the testimony and individual properties and situational factors found in the research points to a considerable role of the way in which the witnesses who show certain psychic properties are interrogated.

Although the research included small groups of witnesses, the results obtained provide a certain insight into the complexity of the problem of the quantitative evaluation of changes in testimony and their situational and psychological conditioning. Needless to say that the full analysis of these factors and their mutual dependence can be made exclusively by the psychologist.

Reference

Arntzen, F. (1989). *Psychologia zeznan swiadkow*. Warszawa: PWN.

Expert Evidence in Child Sexual Abuse Criminal Cases in Canada and the United States

Hilary McCormack

Introduction

Sexual assaults, particularly those involving children, are difficult to prove. There is rarely corroborating evidence, either of an independent eyewitness or physical/medical evidence. The legal process can be traumatizing to a child and may inhibit a child from testifying or contribute to a child's refusal to testify at all. The repetition of details of the allegations to strangers in public, cross-examination, face-to-face confrontation with the accused and separation from a trusted and supportive parent or friend may adversely affect the child witnesses (Spencer & Flin, 1990, p. 283; Hornick & Bolitho, 1992) and can lead to erroneous conclusions with respect to the child's credibility.

Because there is rarely other confirming evidence, the complainant's testimony is central to a successful prosecution. The defence strategy most often centres on discrediting the child's credibility. It is therefore important to recognize that experts in the field can provide valuable assistance to the judge or jury in assessing the behaviour and credibility of child victims of sexual abuse. The expert can help explain conduct, which left unexplained, may result in the wrong inferences being drawn.

There are specific characteristics of intra-familial child sexual abuse which can reflect negatively on the child's credibility. Some of these include: failure to report the incident promptly; pressure from accused or family members not to testify or to retract the story; the child's ambivalence to criminal prosecution; the child's fear regarding potential incarceration of accused; ambivalent response or complete disbelief by other family members of child's revelation.

The growing recognition of characteristic indicators of intra-familial child sexual abuse has lead to the identification of what is called the child sexual abuse accommodation syndrome. There are said to be five characteristics of the syndrome: 1) secrecy, 2) helplessness, 3) entrapment and accommodation, 4) delayed, conflicting and unconvincing disclosure and 5) retraction (Summit, 1983).

The Nature and Requirement of Expert Evidence

Expert evidence is opinion evidence. The grounds for admission of expert opinion evidence are: the witness must be an expert in the field; expert witnesses cannot give their opinion upon matters not within their field; opinion evidence may not be given upon a subject matter within what may be described as a common-stock of knowledge; expert evidence will be admitted where it will be helpful to the jury in their deliberations and will be excluded only where the jury can as easily draw the necessary inferences without it; and where the jury can just as easily draw the necessary inferences without it then the intended opinion is superfluous.[1]

With a growing body of research and literature and a growing expertise in the characteristics and dynamics of child sexual abuse, experts in this area are being called to give opinion evidence in criminal cases. The following summary of the dynamics and behavioral indicators of child sexual abuse is intended as an overview to assist in understanding the evidence which experts have been permitted to give and which is referred to in the following case law analysis: it is not meant to be exhaustive. Interested readers may wish to consult some of the references cited.

Dynamics of child sexual abuse

a) *Progression of abuse* Sexual abuse often occurs progressively, from less intrusive to more intrusive behaviours. It may begin as exposure, progress through to touching and kissing and result in actual intercourse, anal or vaginal (American Bar Association, 1982; Sgroi, 1982).

b) *Duration of abuse* Intra-familial sexual abuse often occurs over a long period of time, from early childhood through to adolescence. Even infants have been sexually assaulted. Two peaks in the age of onset of child sexual abuse have been noted, age four and seven (Horsham, 1989). This observation is consistent with data from the Sexual Assault Clinic in Seattle where 50% of the children seen are under the age of five (Berliner, 1990). Children often endure the abuse because of bribes, fear of splitting up the family, misrepresentation of morality, fear of losing affection or of being blamed, parental psychological authority, and utter helplessness in the face of increasingly invasive assaults committed on them by a trusted adult, often a family member (Summit, 1983).

c) *Lack of force and physical injury* Because of the parents' psychological power over the child, force is often not necessary to accomplish the act or maintain the child's silence. Physical injury can and does occur, however, and can be very traumatic (Horsham, 1989).

d) *Timing of disclosure of abuse* There is a great deal of data to indicate that children will often delay in telling someone about the abuse. Often the child feels responsible for the abuse and is unlikely to disclose (Sorenson & Snow, 1991). Children tend to minimize their disclosures rather than fabricate things that didn't happen.

The delay will probably mean there is little or no medical evidence to support the child's allegation (American Bar Association, 1982). If the child discloses the abuse more than 24 to 48 hours after the occurrence, the likelihood of there being live sperm or other evidence is low. Vaginal and other mucous tissues heal quickly (Horsham, 1989).

e) *The role of the non-offending parent\other family members* In intra-familial sexual abuse, the non-offending parent, usually the mother, may or may not be aware that abuse is occurring. This must be evaluated on a case by case basis. If she is made aware, she is sometimes caught between believing her partner and believing her child.

Some non-offending mothers may have been abused themselves. Some, usually under threats or pressure from her partner, may even be involved as "co-offenders".

Perpetrators often include other family members, such as siblings, uncles, or grandparent, which can also result in an ambivalent response or complete disbelief by other family members of the child's disclosure and pressure from accused or family members not to testify or to retract the disclosure.

f) *Retraction and inconsistent statement* There is also literature to describe the phenomenon known as "recanting" where a child retracts the allegation of abuse after having disclosed it (Summit, 1983; Sorenson & Snow, 1991). With appropriate support the large majority of these children will reaffirm their statements (Sorenson & Snow, 1991). The family may pressurise the child to retract the story, by, for example, telling her she will split up the family, send the offender to jail, and\or cause her mother to lose financial support. The legal process can also exacerbate the situation and contribute to a child's retraction or refusal to testify. Moreover, the child may have ambivalent feelings toward the offender which could result in her changing the initial story at a later date or at trial (American Bar Association, 1982; Summit, 1983).

Behavioral indicators of sexually abused children

Although one cannot necessarily conclude that a child has been abused because she or he acts in certain ways, the following behaviours have been found to be highly significant in abused children:

a) excessive masturbation where the child cannot be distracted from the activity. The child may masturbate with an object or to the point of injury;
b) replication of adult sexual behaviours with dolls or other children;
c) age-inappropriate, sexually explicit drawings and\or descriptions;
d) bizarre, sophisticated or unusual sexual knowledge;
e) pseudo-mature seductive behaviours directed towards members of the opposite sex;
f) prostitution, promiscuity (Brier, 1989).

The Law

Canada

There are two rules of evidence which inhibit the introduction of evidence of dynamics of sexual abuse in child sexual assault prosecutions. Firstly, a party calling a witness cannot call evidence to bolster the credibility of it's own witness. Secondly, the expert's evidence cannot usurp the function of the trier of fact (either Judge or Jury as the case may be) in determining the issues.

Behavioral indicators of child sexual abuse should be tendered as constituting confirming evidence of the child's complaint in the same way as, for example, bruises or injury to the vagina. Expert evidence on the dynamics of sexual abuse should be tendered to explain conduct which is consistent with sexual abuse and which left unexplained might otherwise lead to the child being disbelieved.

Examining those cases where the use of expert evidence has been considered by Canadian courts, it is clear that where the questions have been put that go to deciding the ultimate issue, that is should the complainant be believed, then it is not admissible. Thus, in *Regina v. Kostuck*, the Manitoba Court of Appeal stated: "that a witness, expert or otherwise may not testify that an accused or any other witness, including a complainant, is likely telling the truth".[2]

The court took issue with the expert's opinion "that children very rarely lie about sexual abuse". Clearly this aspect of the expert's evidence offended the rule against "oath helping", however the Court did not comment on the broader issue of the admissibility of the remainder of the expert's evidence with respect to the dynamics of child sexual abuse. The court seemed to implicitly accept the admissibility of such expert evidence.

In *Regina v. Belliveau*, the British Columbia Court of Appeal made the distinction between the admissibility of expert evidence for the purpose of determining whether the child was sexually assaulted as opposed to such evidence being tendered to show that the complainant is telling the truth.[3] While the Court indicated that Crown counsel should not ask witnesses whether they consider the complainant to be a truthful person, the court accepted the admissibility of the expert's opinion that the child had been sexually abused, but not to establish that the child was a truthful witness. The court also held that the expert's evidence was capable of being, and in fact was, corroborative of the complainant's evidence.

The decision in *Beliveau* differs from the decision in *Kostuk* in the appropriateness of the expert expressing an opinion as to whether a child would lie about sexual abuse. Such an opinion was rejected in *Kostuk*. However, in *Belliveau*, the court did not disapprove of the expert's opinion that a child of that particular age is unlikely to have a motive for lying about sexual abuse, although the witness could not be asked whether this particular complainant was truthful.[4] The two cases can only be reconciled by making the fine distinction between commenting on credibility and commenting on a motive to make a false allegation of abuse.

The admissibility and limitations of this kind of evidence was first extensively addressed in *Regina v. Taylor*.[5] In this case the accused was convicted of two counts of sexual assault. During the trial the defence called a number of witnesses who testified they would not believe the testimony of the two complainants. The Crown in reply called, amongst others, two expert witnesses as to the propensity of young victims in sexual attacks to fantasize in the manner of the complainants.

The Ontario Court of Appeal concluded that it was appropriate for the Crown to call the reply evidence, particularly the expert evidence which tended to explain the stories of earlier sexual assaults related by the complainants. The court went on to say that the jury ought to be instructed that the medical explanation of the fantastic stories might, to some extent, reduce the impact this fantasizing might have had on the credibility of the complainants, if left unexplained. The court specifically ruled inadmissible the evidence of the expert, in response to a question posed by the trial Judge that, "in her experience only one or two percent of the children who complained of sexual abuse were lying".[6]

While there has been disagreement by other experts in the dynamics of child sexual abuse with respect to the validity of the expert evidence that it is characteristic of sexually abused to fantasize with regard to sexual incidents, as was tendered in *Taylor*, the case is one of the earliest to recognize this class of evidence and to attempt to articulate the proper use of such evidence and the limitations of its use. As with the evolution of any area of expertise, the body of knowledge is constantly growing and must be continually evaluated as this area of social science develops.

This decision was followed in *Regina v. Camilleri*.[7] There, the witness was permitted to give evidence that in her experience in interviewing child victims of sexual assault, it is not unusual to obtain different narratives from a victim, even a teenager, at different times, that usually disclosures become more detailed, very frightening events being disclosed last and that delay in disclosure is typical. The court ruled that the foundation for the admissibility of the evidence was to be found in the cross-examination of the complainants which established that they gave inconsistent or incomplete accounts of what had occurred at different stages in the proceedings. In this case, the witness was called as part of the Crown's case whereas the expert evidence in *Taylor* was reply evidence. Thus, *Camilerri* recognizes that where the foundation has been laid, for example by cross-examination, the expert evidence can be called as part of the Crown's case.

It may be appropriate to call expert evidence, not only where there is a perceived problem with the complainant's credibility, but also where a behavioral pattern of the complainant is indicative of, or consistent with, sexual abuse. In *R. v. Grenon*, Mercier, J. permitted a psychologist with an expertise in child sexual abuse to give evidence with respect to the dynamics of sexual abuse and to express her opinion that the complainant had been sexually assaulted.[8] There had not been any extensive cross-examination of the complainant with respect to the delay in reporting the evidence but she had exhibited "anxiety attacks". The expert concluded that she had been sexually assaulted based on a number of reasons, one of which was the anxiety attacks.

A similar approach was taken by the Saskatchewan Court of Appeal in *R. v. G.B. et al.*[9] The complainant's mother testified that her daughter had begun to wet her bed and experience nightmares. At trial, the Crown called Dr. Wollert who testified that sexually abused children go through a traumatic experience and that it is not uncommon for such a child to regress to bed wetting and show other signs of emotional stress. On the issue of the use of this expert evidence as corroboration of abuse, the court stated:

> I think it can now be taken that evidence of an expert ... is admissible.... This kind of testimony is helpful, because it provides a benchmark which can hardly be doubted, as it is entirely unlikely that such things as bedwetting and nightmares are the subject to be concocted or contrived by a youthful witness to support or buttress the reliability of any testimony that witness may later be called upon to give in court. It is always open to the trial judge to accept or reject expert testimony....[10]

In dismissing the accused's appeal to the Supreme Court of Canada, Madame Justice Wilson commented as follows on the admissibility of the expert evidence:

I need only say in dealing with this ground of the appeal that I agree with Wakeling J. A.'s conclusion that the expert evidence in this case was well within the bounds of acceptable and admissible testimony and that in cases of sexual assault against children the opinion of an expert proves invaluable.[11]

However, the Nova Scotia Court of Appeal came to the opposite conclusion in *R. v. Meisner*, where the court affirmed the refusal of the trial judge to permit a social worker to give the opinion that stomach cramps, flashbacks, nightmares and poor school grades, which the complainant suffered from after the assault, were consistent with the girl having been sexually assaulted. The court rejected the evidence on the basis that the sole purpose of the evidence was to bolster the credibility of the complainant.[12]

Expert evidence on the phenomenon of recanting was addressed in *Regina v. F.E.J.*[13] In this case, the defendant was charged with the sexual assault of his daughter. Shortly before the preliminary hearing the complainant wrote a letter to the Children's Aid Society worker, in which she said, "I am sorry but I lied about my dad". When cross-examined at trial about the letter, the child said that it was a lie and that she had written it to help her deal in her own mind with what had occurred and that the evidence that she gave at trial was true.

An expert testified that the letter was fairly typical of the recantations commonly seen among children who have been sexually abused when they realize the problems that their revelations have caused, and that the letter would be a typical one in a textbook on child sexual abuse. He further stated that in his experience he had not found one case in which a child was being truthful when recanting. The admissibility and use of that evidence was one of the grounds of appeal.

Galligan, J. A., writing for the Court, stated at p. 72:

I would think that it is probably not generally known that children who have been sexually abused, and have reported it, commonly recant their allegations. Thus, in order for the trial judge in this case to decide whether this child's testimony should have been disbelieved because of the letter, he was entitled to know that recantations are common.[14]

Galligan, J. A. cautioned against the expert commenting on the complainant's truthfulness and accordingly ruled that the expert's evidence that he had not seen one case where the recantation was truthful was inadmissible. His Lordship articulates the somewhat fine distinction between oath-helping and evidence that serves to support the witness's testimony. He points out, at p. 70, that:

The difference is that in the first case the witness gives his or her expert opinion about truthfulness. In the second, the evidence is only admitted to show a condition consistent with sexual abuse and, therefore, as being capable of supporting the witness's testimony. It remains for the court to decide as a question of fact whether the psychological or physical conditions, as interpreted by the expert, do in fact support the testimony of the child witness. The distinction is crucial and must always be borne in mind.[15]

A similar approach was taken by the British Columbia Court of Appeal in *R. v. R.A.C.* where a child sexual abuse worker was permitted to testify that two complainants whom she had counselled had a pattern of disclosure and behaviour that was "consistent with having been subject to sexual abuse".[16] The Court concluded that:

> Sora Davis ... explained the reason for lack of complaint and delay in disclosure. She explained why memory for detail of sexual abuse could improve in a protective environment. She explained why association between the complainants and the appellant could continue after sexual abuse had taken place. All of this evidence could, if accepted by the jury, be helpful in determining the issue of credibility. It was evidence which tended to show that inferences which might well be drawn on the basis of common sense and common experience should not be drawn as a matter of course in cases of sexual abuse.[17]

The court also pointed out that the jury had to be instructed that some of the complainant's behaviour might be caused by factors other than sexual abuse, such as physical abuse, and the expert's testimony had to be considered with "reservation and great caution".

More recently, the Nova Scotia Court of Appeal in *E.L.H. v. R.* ruled admissible the evidence of a social worker who had interviewed the child and concluded that the child showed symptoms often found in victims of sexual abuse.[18] These symptoms included depression, attempts to block out recollection of events, lack of trust in others and an inability to be specific as to time.

Although some of the cases are difficult to reconcile, the Supreme of Canada has clearly recognized the admissibility of this kind of evidence, not only to explain perceived frailties of the victim's evidence, but also to use psychological and physical symptoms to corroborate the child's testimony. Indeed, the Ontario Court of Appeal held in *R. v. Field* that expert evidence must be called on the issue of the child sexual abuse syndrome if there is to be reliance on the syndrome and that the judge cannot take "judicial notice" of it.[19]

The trend of the courts to look to experts in human behaviour to assess the reasonableness of certain conduct was demonstrated in Lavallée v. The Queen.[20] In this case the Supreme Court of Canada considered the admissibility of expert evidence on the battered wife syndrome. The court held that expert evidence could help the jury by dispelling the myths that battered women are not really as badly beaten as they claim, or that some women enjoy being beaten. Expert evidence pertaining to why an accused remained in a battering relationship may be relevant in assessing the nature and extent of the alleged abuse. Thus by providing an explanation as to why an accused did not flee when she perceived her life to be in danger, expert testimony may also assist the jury in assessing the reasonableness of the accused's belief that killing her batterer was the only way to save her own life.

Implicit in the reasoning of Wilson, J. was that the average juror would not be able to appreciate the accused's defence of self-defence without understanding why the accused would remain in an abusive relationship.

In *R. v. Millar*, the Ontario Court of Appeal admitted expert evidence in a physical child abuse case on the basis that the expert witnesses had "special knowledge and experience going beyond that of the trier of fact".[21] The experts were therefore permitted to give an opinion as to whether certain injuries were caused accidentally or intentionally, which were matters the trier of fact ultimately had to decide.

Experts may also be called by the defence to attack the credibility of the child, for example by commenting on a videotaped interview and suggesting that interviewer bias may have influenced the child. In *R. v. C.(A.)*, the accused called an expert who viewed the videotapes of the child's interview, listened to the child testifying and then testified that the child had been "manipulated and programmed".[22] The Crown was permitted to call it's own expert evidence to rebut this testimony.

In *R. v. Sanderson*, the court held that the accused had no statutory or constitutional right to have a child examined by his own expert.[23] Although the court was concerned that if the Crown is calling expert evidence, that this may place the accused in a difficult position making full answer and defence, the court was more concerned with "the potential for abuse, for oppression, and for intimidation" of the child if examination were allowed. In the United States, a similar application was rejected in *People v. Chard*.[24] The test that has been articulated in the majority of the states in the United States requires the accused to demonstrate a "compelling need or reason" for an involuntary psychological examination of a child in a sexual abuse case.

Thus the Supreme Court of Canada and the various provincial Courts of Appeal have accepted that expert evidence in the areas of both child abuse and spousal abuse can be of assistance to the jury by dispelling popular myths, so that the jury can evaluate the evidence, draw inferences, and make assessments of credibility on a more informed basis. It also recognized that it is the trier of fact and not the expert who must decide the issue of credibility.

The United States

The issue has also been dealt with by a number of states in the United States. The scope of this paper does not permit an in-depth analysis of the American jurisprudence, however, a quick review of how these courts have dealt with the issue is useful.

In *People v. Roscoe*, the California Court of Appeal ruled that the trial judge had erred in admitting testimony by a prosecution psychologist diagnosing the complainant as a victim of child molestation.[25] It further held that the rule authorizing the use of expert testimony to rehabilitate a complainant's credibility is limited to discussion of victims as a class supported by references to literature and experience and does not extend to discussion and diagnosis of the witness in the case at hand. It would be possible for an expert witness to tell the jury about various studies showing typical responses of victims in molestation situations without relying on a detailed analysis of the facts of the case at hand.

The Court referred to *People v. Bledsoe* where it was held that testimony that a victim suffered from rape trauma crisis syndrome was inadmissible to prove that a rape occurred, but can be introduced to rebut an inference of falsity arising from delay in reporting the incident, by providing the jury with findings of professional research on the subject of a victim's reaction to sexual assault.[26]

However, the same Court of Appeal reached a somewhat different conclusion in *Re Cheryl E.*, where the court ruled that the opinion of a psychiatrist that the complainant was abused was admissible.[27] However, the testimony that abusers are often passive dependent and that the defendant shared these traits was character evidence and inadmissible. The opinion that the defendant was the abuser was also not admissible.

Although the American cases differ on whether the expert can give the opinion that the particular complainant was a victim of abuse, they are consistent that an opinion cannot be given with respect to the credibility of the complainant, unless the area is specifically opened by defence. In *State v. Myers*, the psychologist's opinion as to characteristics of sexually abused children was admissible, but her opinion as to whether she believed the complainant was admissible only because defence had opened the door to such testimony by asking the child's mother if she believed her.[28] In *People v. Parks*, the teacher of a mentally handicapped witness was permitted to give objective information about the student's capabilities so as to assist the factfinder in evaluating her testimony, but not to render an opinion as to her credibility.[29] A contrary result was obtained in *State v. Kim*, where the court held that in view of the thoroughness of his evaluation, the testimony of a physician as to the believability of a 13-year-old's report of sex abuse was admissible.[30] It is hard to see how the thoroughness of the evaluation has any relevance to the admissibility of this kind of evidence and it is submitted that the better view is that set out in *State v. Keen*, where the court held that the opinion of psychiatrist that it was "reality" that adolescent victim had been attacked was de facto an opinion as to defendant's guilt and therefore inadmissible.[31] Testimony as to the credibility of the complainant was also rejected in *Wheat v. State*; *State v. Batangan*,; and *Commonwealth of Pennsylvania v. Harold Smith Jr.*.[32]

Expert evidence is admissible to explain certain perceived problems with the victims' credibility, for example, that victims of sexual assault frequently retract their statements or that sexually abused children frequently delay reporting. In *People v. McAlpin*, the Supreme Court of California concluded that expert evidence on the reactions of child victims of molestation was not admissible to prove that the sexual abuse had taken place, but could be used to rehabilitate the witness's credibility, where there was conduct, such as delay in reporting, that could be used to impeach the child's testimony.[33] Similarly, in *State v. Middleton*, testimony of social workers that abused children frequently retract their accusations was admissible, but the opinion as to whether the expert believed the accusations was not.[34] In *People v. Dunnahoo*, the court held that a police officer's testimony that sex abuse victims frequently retract their accusations was not based on common knowledge and was therefore admissible.[35] In *State v. Peterich*, testimony that sexually abused children delay reports was admissible, but testimony as to characteristics of abusers, that in 85%-90% of cases the offender is someone the victim knows, was inadmissible.[36] The same result was achieved in *State v. Maule*, where the court held that the testimony of a clinician as to characteristics of sexually abused children and as to whether the victims matched this profile may have been admissible, but statements as to characteristics of abusers, that they were typically "a male-parent figure", most commonly the biological father, were prejudicial and should not have been admitted.[37]

Conclusions

Historically, the law has approached all sexual offences with stereotypical misconceptions. Sexual offences involving children were approached with even greater scepticism because there was an assumption, derived without any empirical foundation, that all children were inherently unreliable and their evidence should therefore be viewed with great caution. Expert evidence can be helpful to the court to do away with widely held misconceptions about child sexual abuse, so that the trier of fact may evaluate the evidence free of the constraints of popular myths and make assessments on credibility on an informed basis.

The common law has traditionally viewed expert evidence with some suspicion. Undoubtedly, this has been in part due to a fear that the expert may usurp the function of the trier of fact and that the trial may be reduced to a battle of the experts with the side having the greatest resources to pay for the best expert having an unfair advantage. There is also a concern with respect to the objectivity of the expert. There is a recognition that even the best intentioned professional may have an unconscious bias and that certain experts, always testify for either the defence or the state.

Such fears should not blind the courts to the benefit to be derived from the advances in the fields of social science. In an increasingly complex world and with an increasing trend towards specialization, it is perhaps inevitable that judges and juries cannot be expected to be knowledgeable on every matter on which they are called to make assessments. The trend of the courts in Canada to recognize the value of the expertise of others can only add to the integrity of the criminal justice system. This is particularly so in the area of child sexual abuse where common experience may well lead to the wrong inferences being drawn. The courts have been careful to articulate the limitations of such evidence, to provide careful instructions to the jury on the use to which the evidence can be put and to emphasize that it is still up to the trier of fact to make the ultimate assessment on credibility. Judges have an important role in ensuring that this kind of evidence is properly used in the search for the truth.

References

American Bar Association. (1982). *Expert testimony on the dynamics of intra-family child sexual abuse and principles of child development.*

Berliner, L. (1990). The process of victimization: The victim's perspective. *Child Abuse and Neglect: The International Journal, 14,* 29-40.

Brier, J. (1989). *Therapy for adults molested as children: Beyond survival.* New York: Springer Publishing Co.

Hornick, J., & Bolitho, F. (1992, Sept.). *A review of the implementation of the child sexual assault legislation in selected sites.* Calgary: Canadian Research Institute for Law and the Family.

Horsham, P. (1989). *Practical guidelines to the assessment of the sexually abused child.* Ottawa: Canadian Public Health Association.

Spencer, J. R., & Flin, R. (1990). *The evidence of children: The law and psychology.* London: Blackstone Press.

Sgroi, S. (1982). *Handbook of clinical intervention of child sexual abuse* (Chapter 2). Lexington: Lexington Books.

Sorenson, T., & Snow, B. (1991, Jan-Feb). How children tell: The process of disclosure in child sexual abuse. *Child Welfare*, *LXX*, 3-15.
Summit, R. C. (1983). The child sexual abuse accommodation syndrome. *Child Abuse and Neglect: The International Journal*, *7*, 177-193.

Notes

[1] *Fisher v. the Queen* (1961), 130 C.C.C. 1 at 19, aff'd by S.C. at 24.
[2] *Regina v. Kostuck* (1987), 29 C.C.C.(3d) 190 at 192 (Man. C.A.).
[3] *Regina v. Belliveau* (1986), 30 C.C.C. (3d) 193 (B.C.C.A.).
[4] *Ibid.*, at 206.
[5] *Regina v. Taylor* (1987), 57 O.R.(2d) 737 (C.A.).
[6] *Ibid.*, at 206.
[7] *Regina v. Camilleri*, (D.C.O. unreported, May 1, 1987).
[8] *Regina v. Grenon*, (D.C.O. unreported, October 14, 1987).
[9] *R. v. G.B. et al.* (1988), 65 Saska. R. 134 (C.A.).
[10] *Ibid.* at 149.
[11] *R. v. G.B. et al.* (1990), 56 C.C.C.(3d) 200 at 219 (S.C.).
[12] *R. v. Meisner* (1992), 110 N.S.R.(2d) 270 (C.A.).
[13] *R. v. F.E.J.* (1990), 53 C.C.C.(3d) 64. (Ont.C.A.).
[14] *Ibid.*, at 72.
[15] *Ibid.*, at 70.
[16] *R. v. R.A.C.* (1990), 78 C.R.(3d) 350 (B.C.C.A.).
[17] *Ibid.*, at 399.
[18] *E.L.H. v. R.* (1991), 2 C.R. (4th) 186 (N.S.C.A.).
[19] *R. v. Field* (1990), 9 W.C.B. (2d) 736 (Ont.C.A.).
[20] *Lavallée v. The Queen* (1990), 55 C.C.C.(3d) 97 (S.C.C.).
[21] *R. v. Millar* (1989), 49 C.C.C.(3d) 193 at p.218 (Ont. C.A.).
[22] *R. v. C.(A.)* (1992), 71 C.C.C.(3d) 529 (Que.C.A.).
[23] *R. v. Sanderson*, [unreported], Nanaimo C.R. 3782 B.C.S.C.
[24] *People v. Chard*, 808 P.2d 351 (Colo. 1991).
[25] *People v. Roscoe*, 168 Cal.App.(3d) 1093.
[26] *People v. Bledsoe*, 36 Cal.App.(3d) 236.
[27] *Re Cheryl E.*, 153 Cal.App.(3d) 1098, 200 Ca.Rptr 789(2d) (Dist. 1984).
[28] *State v. Myers*, 359 N.W.2d 606 (Minn. 1984).
[29] *People v. Parks*, 41 N.Y.2d 36, 390 N.Y.S.2d 848, 359 N.E.2d 358 (1976).
[30] *State v. Kim*, 645 P.2d 1330 (Hawaii 1982).
[31] *State v. Keen*, 305 S.E.2d 535 (N.C.1983).
[32] *Wheat v. State*, 502 A.2d 253 (1983); *State v. Batangan*, 799 P.2d 48 (Hawaii 1990); *Commonwealth v. Harold Smith Jr.*, 567 A.2d 1080 (1989).
[33] *People v. McAlpin*, 812 P2d 563.
[34] *State v. Middleton*, 294 Or.427, 657 P.2d 1215 (1985).
[35] *People v. Dunnahoo*, 152 Cal.App.3d 561, 199 Cal.Rptr.796 2d (Dist. 1984).
[36] *State v. Peterich*, 101 Wash.App. 566, 683 P.2d 1973 (1984).
[37] *State v. Maule*, 35 Wash.App. 287, 667 P.2d 96 (1983).

Children's Disclosure of Secrets: Implications for Interviewing

J. Clare Wilson and Margaret-Ellen Pipe

The most common situation in which a child is interviewed is when a child is suspected to be the victim of abuse. One of the most pervasive aspects of abuse that makes interviewing a child victim difficult is the element of secrecy. Most victims of sexual abuse have been urged not to tell and hence may remain silent about the abuse for months, years or a lifetime (Burgess & Holstrom, 1975; Faller, 1984; Summit, 1983; Herman, 1981). Such is the prevalence of the element of secrecy in sexual abuse cases that if a child reports being told to conceal the abuse, this statement may be considered a validation that the abuse has occurred (Herman, 1981; Summit, 1983). Clinical commentaries on child sexual abuse (e.g. Summit, 1983) give the impression that young children are able to keep secrets in the situation of abuse. However, a deeper understanding of the nature of children's secrets is required before this information can be of any use to the interviewer. Do children understand the concept of secrets or, in the case of sexual abuse, are they merely responding to the fear of repercussions (Faller, 1984)? Is it a useful strategy to question children about secrets, and if so, from what age? Do non-abused children retract stories when repeatedly interviewed? It is important to address these questions empirically. For example, many sexual abuse prevention programs have targeted the need to educate children about "good" secrets and "bad" secrets (Gilbert, Berrick, Le Prohn, & Nyman, 1989), yet no research has been published to date showing that preschool children can understand such concepts.

The use of real life events to examine eyewitness testimony dates back to the turn of the century (Whipple, 1910), but it has been only recently applied to children's disclosure of secrets (Wilson & Pipe, 1989; Bottoms, Goodman, Schwartz-Kenney, Sachcenmaier, & Thomas, 1990). The results thus far have indicated that although children around the age of four have some understanding of secrets (Marvin, Greenberg, & Mossler, 1976) they do not necessarily keep them (Bottoms et al., 1990), whereas five- to six-year-olds are unwilling reporters of information deemed secret (Wilson & Pipe, 1989). Piaget (1932/1965) suggested that six-year-olds may be "rule bound", that is, if a child defines secrets as "don't tell", then that child will tell no one, irrespective of the secret. However, older children (e.g., older than eight years of age) may be more able to apply different rules to specific situations (Selman, 1980). Thus, nine-year-olds may judge the severity of the secret and choose whether or not to keep it.

A study by Pipe & Wilson (in press) compared the performance of six- and nine-year-olds in their disclosure of secrets during an event report. The interaction, about which the event report was obtained, involved children dressing up as magician's assistants and interacting in a ten minute magic show. This event was chosen for its wide ranging appeal to different age groups, thus ensuring the children would attend to and remember the event (c.f. Yarmey, 1979). The magic show had a second potential advantage in that the older children did not necessarily have a superior knowledge about the event compared to the younger children.

Eighty-eight six-year-olds (40 female and 48 male) and 88 nine-year-olds (53 female and 35 male) took part, in pairs, in the magic show. The magician randomly chose one child to be the magician's assistant and asked the other child to take a seat as the audience. The assistant was dressed up in a hat, cloak and a pair of white gloves, which were described as very special gloves, necessary to perform magic. The magician then demonstrated four tricks and allowed the assistant to try each trick demonstrated. Before the last trick, (the "rope trick") the magician took out a pen and began to tick off the tricks already performed and in doing so "accidentally" squirted ink onto the child assistant's gloves. The magician quickly took the child's gloves off and explained that the gloves would now be ruined. The gloves were placed under the table. The magician asked both children not to tell her boss about the ink spill as she might get into trouble for damaging the gloves. When the child assistant tried the rope trick, it failed to work which the magician attributed to the absence of the magic gloves. The interaction lasted approximately ten minutes.

The children were interviewed on two separate occasions about the magic show, first, two weeks after the show and again two months after the show. The interviews included free recall of the event and a series of questions (for a full description of the interviews see Pipe & Wilson, in press). The last question was "Finally, I found a pair of white gloves with ink spilt on them, do you know anything about them?". Those children who responded "Yes" to this question were then asked "What do you know?". This was the only specific question relating to the secret.

The results showed that children were more likely to give information about a secret in response to specific questioning than to spontaneously report it in free recall. Specific questioning also had the advantage that both age groups were more consistent in reporting the secret. The six-year-olds were significantly less likely to report the secret information compared to other aspects of the magic show. Thus, they did "keep the secret". There was no evidence that the nine-year-olds differentially concealed the ink spill as secret compared to their reporting of other aspects of the magic show. This suggested that they may not have considered the ink spill important enough to conceal or thought that the interviewer was not "the boss" (who they had been asked to keep the secret from) and hence it was permissible to reveal the secret to her. Interviewing both age groups twice did not increase the reporting of secret and highlighted potential inconsistencies (that is, those children who report the secret the first time and choose not to do so at the second interview), although such differences were non significant. Those children who acted as participants (the magician's assistant) were also significantly likely to report the secret during free recall than those who merely observed (the "audience"). Last, only six children (out of 176) reported being told to keep the ink spill secret.

Experiment 1

In the Pipe and Wilson study, the younger (five- to six- year-old) children kept the secret whereas the older (nine- to ten-year-old) children did not. Further, the children who were participants in the ink spill more frequently reported the secret than the observers. It is possible that the older children did not consider the ink spill as a secret but rather, as an accident and therefore may have not considered it necessary to conceal the incident from the interviewer. The present experiment aimed to clarify this issue. The effect of the magician explicitly labelling the incident as a secret or as an accident was therefore examined. This may not alter the way children define the incident but it may change whether the children conceal the information.

The participants in the Pipe and Wilson study had the ink spilt on their gloves and were the magician's assistant. It is unclear, however, whether the participants reported the secret more frequently than the observers due to the ink being spilt on their gloves or due to their being the magician's assistant. In the present study, all children took part in the magic show individually as the magician's assistant. When the ink spill occurred, half of the children watched as the magician spilt ink on her own gloves (hence, the children acted as observers), whilst the other half of the children had the ink spilt on their own gloves (as in Pipe & Wilson, in press). Further, there were no other witnesses to the ink spill. It was possible in the Pipe and Wilson study that the reason the participants reported the secret more frequently was that they feared the observers would report the secret and that the participants would be the one's to get into trouble for not telling.

Thirty-two five-year-olds (16 female and 16 male) and 34 nine-year-olds (20 female and 14 male) participated in this study. The procedure was similar to the Pipe and Wilson study with the following changes. First, the children interacted individually with the magician rather than in pairs. Second, the "ink spill" incident differed in that for half the children the ink was spilt on the magicians gloves while for the other half the ink was spilt on the child's gloves. Third, when the "accident" occurred the magician told half the children it was an accident and the other half that it was a secret. Fourth, free recall was followed by a number of questions with each child being asked "Finally, did anything odd happen during the magic show?" followed by "Its just that I found a pair of white gloves with ink on them. Do you know anything about that ?". Each child was individually interviewed one week after taking part in the interaction. The interview took place in the same room as the magic show.

To examine whether there were any age differences in the reporting of the secret, the three occasions when mentioning the secret was possible (during free recall, in response to the "Anything odd" question and in response to the "Ink spill" question) were added to obtain a total number of times each child reported the ink spill. Numbers of ink spill reports per child were submitted to a 2 (Age) by 2 (Accident versus Secret) by 2 (Magician's or Assistant's Gloves) ANOVA. There was a main effect of Age, $F(1,64) = 17.76$. The nine-year-olds reported the secret a mean of 1.4 times, whereas the five-year-olds reported the secret a mean of 0.75 times. Thus, the older children were more likely to repetitively report the secret than the younger children. No other main effects or interactions were significant.

Children's reporting of the secret was examined in more detail as follows. First, the number of reports of the secret in free recall were compared for the two age groups. The number of nine-year-olds who reported the secret in free recall was significantly higher than the number of five-year-olds who reported the secret (Chi square (1) =

8.6). Chi square analyses compared the Glove Conditions (Magician's versus Assistant's) and the Label Conditions (Accident versus Secret) separately for each age group. There were no significant effects. Second, responses to the question "Did anything odd happen?" were analysed using Chi square comparisons of age group by responses to the question. There was no significant effect. Very few children reported the secret in response to this question (overall mean = 0.15). Third, responses to the question "I found a pair of white gloves with ink spilt on them, do you know anything about it?" were analysed. The number of nine-year-olds who reported the secret in response to this question was significantly higher than the number of five-year-olds (Chi square (1) = 9.1). Chi-square analyses compared the Glove Conditions (Magician's versus Assistant's) and the Label Conditions (Accident versus Secret) separately for each age group. There was a significant effect of Gloves Conditions for the six-year-olds (Fisher Exact Test, $p < 0.02$). The group that had the ink spilt on the assistant's gloves reported the secret more frequently than the group that had the ink spilt on the magician's gloves. There were no other significant effects.

In summary, when specifically asked about the ink spill, the five-year-olds reported the secret less when they observed the ink being spilt on the magician's gloves compared to those who had the ink spilt on there own gloves. There was no significant effect of the ink spill being labelled as a secret or as an accident by the magician. It is therefore plausible that the children defined the incident irrespective of the label the magician used to describe it. Further, as both age groups reported the secret at significantly different rates, this may suggest that each age group defined the incident differently. The rate of reporting of the ink spill was, however, lower that than obtained in the study by Pipe and Wilson. It may be that due to the relatively low reporting rates, any affect of labelling the ink spill as an accident or as a secret is obliterated.

Experiment 2

In the previous experiments the to-be-kept-secret was an accidental ink spill which resulted in one of the magic tricks not working. The failure of the trick to work was attributed to the fact that, following the ink spill, either the child or magician was no longer wearing the magic gloves. Experiment 1 showed there was no significant effect of the magician overtly labelling the incident a secret or an accident on whether the children later reported the secret. The absence of a difference may be attributed to children defining accidents as events that you "don't tell" about. Thus, because the event was an accident, the effect of labelling it a secret or an accident may have been irrelevant - it may not have been reported anyway. In the present experiment, therefore, the event about which the secret was to be kept was changed as follows: at the same point in the magic show as that at which the accident had occurred in the previous studies (prior to the final trick), the magician complained of a sore leg and performed a series of leg exercises. She asked the children not to tell her boss as she might get fired for interrupting the magic show. The exercises were chosen as the alternative activity because they did not involve an accident, and they were incongruous with a magic show. An incongruous incident was important as it was necessary to attempt to make the incident salient without it being negative.

Forty-eight five-year-olds (23 females and 25 males) took part, in pairs, in the magic show. The procedure was similar to that of Experiment 1 with the following change. After the third trick, the confederate complained of "a sore leg". The confederate then began exercising the "sore leg" by doing star jumps and push ups. The confederate asked the children not to tell anyone about the exercising as her "boss" might not like it. Each child was interviewed about the interaction on three occasions. Each interview followed the same format of free recall followed by specific questions. Interview 1 took place four weeks after the initial interaction (the magic show). Interview 2 was conducted a week following Interview 1. Interview 3 was conducted four weeks after Interview 1. At the end of the third interview, seven questions were asked relating to the exercises the confederate performed during the magic show and to the children's reasoning as to whether withholding this information constituted a secret or a lie.

Only one child reported the secret during free recall or in response to the "Anything odd" question during any interview. To examine the possibility that the tricks were also recalled infrequently, the relative frequency with which the exercises (the "secret") were reported was compared to the other main actions which took place during the magic show, namely the trick components. Children were significantly more likely to recall a trick component from each of the tricks than they were to report the secret during free recall (Chi square (1) = 6.24).

Based on the lack of reports of the secret in free recall, one might reasonably conclude that children were either concealing the secret very well or that they had forgotten about it entirely. If they did forget it, they forgot it significantly more frequently than any major action in the magic show. To examine whether children could still recall the secret, at the end of Interview 3 all children were specifically interviewed about the exercises. The first question asked was, "Did the magician ever tell you NOT to tell anyone about something that happened during the magic show?". In response to this question, 25 children (54%) responded yes. When asked what the magician had done that was not-to-be-mentioned, 23 children (85% of those who said yes) went on to accurately disclose the exercise sequence.

The next question was very specific, "Did the magician do any exercises during the magic show?". All the children who had said "No" to the first question, also said "No" to this question. A Chi-square comparison, comparing the responding to Question 1 with Question 2, showed a significant difference, (Chi square (3) = 23.61). The children who responded affirmatively to Question 1 were equally likely to say either "yes" or "no" to this question. Having just answered Question 1 correctly, the children may have thought this question referred to something else. In total, 41% of children, replied "yes" to this question. The five-year-olds in the present study answered this question more frequently than the five-year-old children in Experiment 1 in response to the "Ink spill" question (Experiment 2 = 31%). Thus, it is unlikely that the children in the present study forgot the secret information any more than the children in the previous study.

The children were then told that the interviewer knew the magician had performed a number of exercises and it was okay to talk about it. The next question asked, "Exactly what exercises did the magician do again?" examined whether those children who had not reported the secret thus far, did remember what had happened. Only one child who had not disclosed the secret thus far now reported the exercises in response to this question.

The next question asked was "I don't think you ever mentioned the exercises in any other of the interviews, did you forget or did you just not want to tell me?". Of those children who had already reported the secret, six (23% of those who had already reported the secret) children said they did not want to tell on the magician whereas 17 children (85% of those who had reported the secret) said they had forgotten to mention it earlier. Two children who had not previously reported the secret responded that they did not want to tell, while the remainder reported that they had forgotten about the exercises.

The last question asked, "If you don't tell someone something even though you remember it, it that a lie or a secret?". Twelve of those 17 children who had not disclosed the secret reported it was a secret (70%), compared to nineteen of those who had disclosed the secret (61%). This difference was not significant.

In summary, the secret information was disclosed less frequently in free recall in the present study than in Experiment 1. There were four major changes in the present experiment which might account for this. First, the incident changed from an ink spill to a series of exercises. Thus, the saliency of the incident may have changed. Second, the exercises (unlike the ink spill) had no consequence for the magic show since the last trick worked in the present study. Thus, the children could discuss the magic show without having to explain the secret whereas in the previous study, the mentioning of the last trick not working sometimes cued the mentioning of the secret. Third, all children were observers. Fourth, the ink spill was essentially an accident whereas the exercises were an odd intrusion in the magic show.

It is a matter of speculation as to the relative impact of these changes. Some children were likely to have forgotten the incident, yet this was also likely in the previous studies. When asked specifically about the exercises, the six-year-olds in the present experiment disclosed the secret as frequently as those in the two previous studies in response to specific questioning. If the lack of consequence of the exercises on the magic show decreased the significance of the secret or resulted in the children not being cued into the reporting of the secret (and hence resulted in children forgetting it more frequently), then it might be expected that fewer children would have reported it in response to the specific questions asked in Interview 3. This was not the case.

Conclusions

The main findings of these experiments highlight some of the factors which aid the reporting of the information deemed secret. There appears to be an age influence on the disclosure of secrets. This may be due to five- to six-year-olds being in a "catch 22" situation developmentally, as they are old enough to understand and keep secret information but too young to understand what secrets should be kept or who to tell.

This may be due, in part, to their adherence to "rules" (Piaget, 1935/1965) in that a secret must not be told, irrespective of the secret. This is in contrast to the nine- to ten-year-olds who appeared to apply information more specifically to situations, thus they were able to keep secrets or disclose them as they saw fit.

One of the main concerns of interviewers is ensuring that children will accurately disclose information. These studies showed that the disclosure of secret information during free recall (i.e., unprompted) is rare with young children. The most effective disclosure question was "Do you know anything about the ink spill?", yet this question is both very specific and may be interpreted as leading the child. The "anything odd" question was too abstract for the young children to understand and hence did not increase disclosure. However, the question, "Did the magician ever ask you not to tell?" was effective in encouraging disclosure and was less leading than the very specific question.

References

Baker-Ward, L., Hess, T. M., & Flannagan, D. A. (1990). The effects of involvement on children's memory for events. *Cognitive Development, 5*, 55-69.

Bottoms, B. L., Goodman, G. S., Schwartz-Kenney, B., Sachsenmaier, T., & Thomas, S. (1990, March). *Keeping secrets: Implications for children's testimony.* Paper presented at the American Psychological and Law Society Meetings, Williamsburg, Virginia.

Burgess, A. W., & Holmstrom, L. L. (1975). Sexual trauma of children and adolescents: Pressure, sex and secrecy. *Nursing Clinics of North America, 10*, 551-563.

Faller, K. C. (1984). Is the child victim of sexual abuse telling the truth? *Child Abuse and Neglect, 3*, 473-481.

Gilbert, N., Berrick, J., Le Prohn., & Nyman, N. (1989). *Protecting children from sexual abuse: Does preschool training work?* Lexington, Massachusetts: Lexington Books.

Herman, J. L. (1981). *Father-daughter incest.* Cambridge, MA: Harvard University Press.

Marvin, R. S., Greenburg, M. T., & Mossler, D. G. (1976). The potential of children as eyewitnesses. *Law and Human Behaviour, 3*, 295-306.

Piaget, J. (1932/1965). *The moral judgement of the child.* London: Penguin.

Pipe, M-E., & Wilson, J. C. (In Press). Cues and secrets: Influence on children's event reports. *Developmental Psychology.*

Selman, R. L. (1980). *The Growth of Interpersonal Understanding: Developmental and Clinical Analyses.* New York: Academic Press.

Summit, R. C. (1983). The child sexual abuse accommodation syndrome. *Child Abuse and Neglect, 7*, 177-193.

Whipple, G. M. (1910). Recent literature on the psychology of testimony. *Psychological Bulletin, 7*, 365-368.

Wilson, J. C., & Pipe, M-E. (1989). The effects of cues on young children's recall of real life events. *New Zealand Journal of Psychology, 18*, 65-70.

Wimmer, H., Gruber, S., Perner, J. (1985). Young children's concept of lying: Moral intuition and the denotation and connotation of "to lie". *Developmental Psychology, 21*, 993-995.

Wimmer, H., & Perner, J. (1983). Beliefs about beliefs: Representation and constraining function of wrong beliefs in young children's understanding of deception. *Cognition, 13*, 103-128.

Yarmey, A. D. (1979). *The psychology of eyewitness testimony.* New York: MacMillan.

Three Dogmas Applied to Child Victims of Sexual Abuse: The Danish Perspective

Beth G. Nielsen

Cooperation between the criminal justice system, the social services and the medical profession in child sexual abuse cases is, generally, considered to be necessary. The appropriate authorities and professionals, in Denmark, are working together on particular cases or at a superior level within the administrative hierarchy. This does not, however, mean that multi-disciplinary work is operating smoothly and without problems. In particular, children's allegations of sexual abuse by a family member, as opposed to the alleged perpetrator's denial of that same abuse, give rise to controversy.

From a criminal justice point of view, the evidential problems in sexual abuse cases are considerable. The prosecutor must prove "beyond reasonable doubt" that the suspect/defendant is guilty. The standard of proof applied in civil proceedings differs from the one used in criminal proceedings. The social services have a statutory duty to intervene on behalf of the child if this child, based on the "balance of probabilities", is or has been exposed to sexual abuse. Adherence to these different standards of proof may result in situations where, on the one hand, it may be impossible to prosecute the alleged abuser or, if prosecution takes place, the defendant may end up receiving a judgement of acquittal and, on the other hand, the social services department may still find it justified to remove the child from her or his home.

Apparently, the existence of different standards of proof in criminal and civil proceedings has not been fully recognized by all social services departments or civil authorities. Consequently, civil cases involving charges of sexual abuse of children have been dropped - at least temporarily - when a parent (most often fathers or stepfathers), referring to a criminal discharge or acquittal, maintains his innocence, despite the fact that the child continues to allege or show symptoms of sexual abuse. The criminal standard of proof seems to affect the decision-making process of the child protection system. It is, of course, less surprising if parents do not understand the difference between the two standards. This ignorance will, however, often lead them to, although wrongly, believe that a non-conviction decision rendered by a criminal court of law, due to insufficient evidence, is to be equated with proof of innocence.

Social workers, psychologists and doctors etc., are often heard criticizing the legal profession (i.e., prosecutors, judges and defense counsels), for underestimating the validity and credibility of children's testimony and for putting too much emphasis on the adult's denials in child sexual abuse cases. The critics seem to ignore the fact that this has nothing to do with belief or disbelief, but instead with the valuable and well established principle of "the benefit of the doubt" which should rule in these sexual abuse cases as it does in murder cases. However, it may not be completely unfounded to assert that some criminal justice agents have an especially great lack of confidence in children. According to some studies conducted in the United States this description seems to, appropriately, fit on some defense attorneys (Saunders, 1988; Leippe et al., 1989).

A second kind of criticism is directed towards police investigations and criminal court proceedings. Both of these proceedings are claimed to be yet another form of child victim abuse. It is true that children are, sometimes, exposed to intimidating and embarrasing interviews regarding their own behavior and reactions in connection to sexual abuse. These interviews are, however, necessitated by the duty of the police and the court to establish whether there are any mitigating circumstances to be considered in the criminal case before them. To the child, unaware of the criminal procedure rules and the rules of evidence, these interviews may, quite often, give the impression of disbelief and/or a feeling of self-blame.

Some critics point to a third factor. They argue that the criminal justice system is oblivious to the psychological trauma suffered by the child as a result of sexual abuse.

Such assertions cannot be completely disregarded. There is reason to believe that in dealing with cases pertaining to sexual abuse of children, the Danish criminal justice system has been and still is, at least to some degree, applying the following three dogmas:

(1) children (girls) lie or fantasize about sexual abuse; (2) children (girls) precipitate sexual victimization; (3) children (girls) do not suffer from psychological trauma as a result of the sexual abuse.

Doctrines mentioned in legal textbooks and articles are developed through case law and practice. When "theoretical" experts study and describe children as victim-witnesses in sexual abuse cases, the resulting doctrines do, however, originate elsewhere.

This article will trace the origin and reproduction of these three dogmas throughout the Danish legal literature. The first dogma, "children lie or fantasize about sexual abuse", will be described in greater detail than the other two, because of the vital importance it has in answering the basic question posed during the criminal proceedings: is the suspect/defendant guilty? The second and third dogmas are important only if the question of guilt can be answered in the affirmative.

Before examining each doctrine separately, it seems relevant to explain a few characteristics of the Danish professional and legal fields. Denmark, being a country of five-and-a-half million inhabitants, has two law schools, but only a few scholars specializing in criminal procedure. There are two law journals, none of which specializes in criminal law and procedure. The situation is not any different within the medical and psychology professions. For years there was only one professor in child psychiatry. There are, of course, a number of clinical experts on child psychology, but among these only a few with a theoretical orientation. There is, however, no distinguished expert on witness psychology. Hence, the opinion of one expert will have an enormous impact on the theory as well as on the practice within this field. Thus, one unchallenged expert opinion will gradually become part of the common-sense beliefs held by lay persons including the criminal justice agents.

The first Dogma: Children Lie or Fantasize about Sexual Abuse.

The traditional view that children are imaginative and unreliable was legitimized by the studies on child witnesses that emerged in the beginning of the twentieth century in Germany and other European countries (Goodman, 1984). "False accusations" by girls against school teachers worried the establishment in Denmark as well as in other countries. A newspaper article published in 1936 contained the following headline: "Rely as little as possible on children's testimonies". Mr E. Kaper, Ph.D. and Lord Mayor, with the Copenhagen municipal schools as his special domain, emphasized that girls between 12 and 17 years of age were particularly untrustworthy (Bahnsen, 1936).

After the Second World War, the Danish criminal justice system gained its knowledge about child witnesses through the works of a Swedish witness psychologist, A. Wachtmeister. His book *För ung att tala sanning?* (*Too young to speak the truth?*) relied heavily on German studies. It was translated into Danish and published in Denmark in 1948 (Wachtmeister, 1948). The book received excellent reviews by the man who, a few years later, became the Chief Justice of the Danish Supreme Court (Trolle, 1944). The theories presented in this book were incorporated into the main textbook on criminal procedure which, until recently, was treated as the "bible" by all Danish law students and legal practitioners (Hurwitz, 1949).

Wachtmeister's theories further emphasized the already unanimous holding among leading European psychologists, that girls in the age of puberty are unreliable and dangerous. When, for instance, girls talk about "indecency" - Wachtmeister maintained - they may well have been touched, but the touching occurred in a way that, considering the real situation, should not have been misunderstood by the girls: "... a hand on the shoulder, a little push in the stomach etc., may by them be described as instances of fondling and touching of breasts and genitals". He goes on to explain: "The school master, while sitting at his desk, may have touched a girl's knee - and then she, stereotypically, asserts that he has touched her genital organs or put his hand between her legs. It is not, necessarily, a question of consciously lying..." (Wachtmeister, 1948, p. 53).

During the 1960s and 1970s similar opinions, although phrased differently, were being reproduced in textbooks and law journals by, for instance, the Chief Prosecutor and a distinguished Supreme Court defense counsel (Lindegaard & Trolle, 1975; Buhl, 1963). In 1969, an actual authority on children provided the criminal law profession with a reaffirmation of the theory on unreliable children in general and fantasizing pubescent girls in particular. Kai Tolstrup, the Director of the Child Psychiatric Ward at Copenhagen University Hospital (Rigshospitalet), stated in a law journal article:

> A characteristic problem in many of the cases presented for child psychiatric evaluation is the issue of trustworthiness; is the child telling the truth, lying or fantasizing. Direct lies may be acts of revenge and are extremely difficult to contradict but are, nevertheless, creating great inconvenience to the man being accused by the girl. Such cases are, however, much more palpable than cases where children fantasize without any conscious attempt to get themselves into focus or to

> hurt anybody by allegations of indecency. During the oidipal phase (age 3-5) in particular, the child's fantasy life is intensely pre-occupied by its own sexual role. Girls, especially, are so absorbed by their sexual relations to their fathers that the fantasies may assume, in the child's consciousness and presentation, the precise intensity of reality. This fact should be remembered, particularly in cases of alleged incest crimes. Taking such fantasies at face value may be even more unreasonable as times go by and many years have elapsed from the time of the alleged incident to the child's or young woman's recreated version. (Unauthorized translation).

Tolstrup referred to "the classic example" of the caution which has to be applied in the assessment of adult women's allegations of childhood sexual abuse: Sigmund Freud's account and later change of mind (Tolstrup, 1969). Tolstrup's opinion was the only one quoted in a 1971 governmental report on criminal investigation which also included a special section on child witnesses (Betænkning nr. 622/1971). Tolstrup's interpretation of lying and fantasizing has, since then, been repeated and the latest example of this is illustrated by the textbook which is currently being used at the Danish Police Academy. Hence, all Danish police officers have read the following as part of their training:

> The fantasy of pubescent girls is often strongly characterized by their erotic imagination and may result in strong exaggerations or direct lies when they testify on aspects of sex life. When interviewing girls of that age in sexual abuse cases, the policeman must remember this and be extremely skeptical about an imaginative account.

Against this background, it is hardly a surprise that more than 50% of all the sexual abuse cases, reported to the police, have never been prosecuted. Moreover, 25% of the prosecuted cases have resulted in acquittals. Although, not all of the non-conviction cases involve pubescent girls, a great many do. The rest of the cases involve child victims who are either mentally disturbed or too young to present any oral testimony.

Since the mid 1980s, scholars from the United States in particular have produced an increasing amount of research results, undertaken within the field of psychology, which stress the necessity to discard, at least in an absolute form. the above mentioned conception that children are unreliable.

Several Danish clinical psychologists are cognizant of the results derived from this research, and even some criminal justice agents seem to have perceived the shift. This awareness may, perhaps, be most apparent by comparing the defense lawyers' behavior and attitudes in the sixties with those of today. Several criminal cases show that lawyers, three decades ago, often asked the court to grant leave to call a child psychologist to testify as an expert witness on children's credibility in general or on the credibility of a particular child victim, whereas today the defense goes to extremes in order to prevent the prosecution from doing so. Expectations of what such expert witnesses may testify seem to have changed.

To date, the Danish legal literature has not embraced the new knowledge and assumptions regarding children's credibility. This may partly be due to a natural hesitation to accept the alterations of already well-established doctrines and partly because the old theories are still being vigorously defended by distinguished psychiatrists. Furthermore, it is a well known fact that psychiatry is held in higher esteem by the legal profession than is the field of psychology. One consequence of the close ties between the Danish professionals is that a statement by one active and outspoken psychiatrist from "the old school" may contribute to the delay of the adjustment to new psychological research results.

If the judge, during a criminal trial, is uncertain about which expert to believe or which theory to follow, then this uncertainty must provide the defendant with the benefit of that doubt and result in an acquittal. Doubt, however, is a subjective phenomenon. What seems convincing to one judge will not, necessarily, have the same effect on a fellow judge. This fact is illustrated by the dissenting opinions written by judges as well as by the situations where the outcome of a case may be different depending on whether the city courts or the appellate courts have decided the case. If the (majority of) judges find the explanations of the defendant and the plaintiff to be equally credible and no other evidence have been presented, then the criminal standard of proof ("beyond reasonable doubt") has not been satisfied. This will often be the case where the defendant is a grown man and the plaintiff/alleged victim is a (small) child. This tendency is further strengthened by the adherence to the notion that children are generally believed to be less trustworthy than adults.

There are indications, however vague, that the Danish courts, during the second half of the 1980s, have increased their conviction rate in child sexual abuse cases where the child's allegations were counteracted by the defendant's denial. Whether this trend is due to the above mentioned shift of opinions by psychologists on children's credibility and a corresponding change of mind among the judiciary is difficult to discern.

In the event that there might have been a change this is, however, being jeopardized by recent strong attempts to add a new aspect to the theory on children's fantasies. If the abuse stories are not a product of the children's own imagination, then they have had to be put into their minds by female psychologists who, evidently, must suffer from incest fixation. Since the beginning of 1992, the media - tabloid, broad-sheet and television alike - have advanced acrimonious attacks directed at one particular female psychologist who was involved, on the children's side, in the Danish "Orkney-case".

A small group, consisting of elderly male lawyers, psychiatrists and forensic experts, have tried hard to have the children's explanations interpreted as merely a matter of indoctrination by this female psychologist. This group, therefore, wanted to have the criminal case - in which several people, including the children's mother, were sentenced to imprisonment - reopened and succeeded. The case is also used by some psychiatrists in an attempt to discredit psychologists in general. It is interesting to note that any counter-balancing opinions from other psychiatrists have been, almost completely, absent from the public debate.

The aftermath of this case is now beginning to show. For instance, one board member of the Danish Social Workers Association has been quoted as saying "that for some years social workers were too keen on attending incest courses but, now, that has stopped". A few days later he claimed to have been misquoted, but the damage had already been done. Several social workers have, in private, told the author of this article that they have become afraid of public exposure and, therefore, hesitate to report any suspicion of child sexual abuse within the family.

The same is, unfortunately, also true for psychologists. According to one newspaper, the Danish Psychologist Association has found it necessary to advise its members to discuss what roles in the child sexual abuse controversy they should play. The chairman was quoted as having said that psychologists were easily perceived to be pointing a finger at every kind of physical contact between parents and children, and that psychologists, therefore, may have contributed to some parent's fear of touching their own children. These types of statement seem to acknowledge that incest fixation does in fact exist among psychologists.

In the wake of the indoctrination debate at least two adolescent girls have retracted their allegations of sexual abuse after their stepfathers had, already, served their prison sentences. One of the girls has accused the above mentioned female psychologist (the one crucified by the media) of having told her what to say to the police and in court. This should be seen against the theory of retraction as being one element in the so-called child sexual abuse accomodation syndrome (Summit, 1983). Moreover, the crime statistics for 1992 show a decrease by 50 per cent in the number of child sexual abuse cases reported to the police.

The present climate may lead to a revival of the doctrine on children's fantasies and incredibility or to its alternative: children's allegations are invented or heavily influenced by therapists. The difficulties in getting guilty perpetrators of child sexual abuse convicted may, once again, increase unless professionals - especially psychiatrists - supply the debate with more nuances.

The Second Dogma: Children Precipitate Sexual Victimization.

While, on the one hand, the doctrine of children's fantasies, due to the significance it has for the establishment of guilt, has a great impact on the criminal justice decision-making process, then, on the other hand, the doctrine of victim precipitation has a vital importance in cases where there is no doubt that sexual abuse has been committed, e.g. in cases where a confession has been obtained. Moreover, sexual acts with "consenting" children below a certain age are punishable. Similarly, sexual acts with biological offsprings are also punishable irrespective of consent. Consequently, even victim precipitated child sexual abuse is criminal. However, a sexual relationship between an adult and a minor, which is initiated or consented to by the latter, may constitute mitigating circumstances for the defendant at a criminal trial. This was emphasized in 1987 by a report on the general legal position of sexual abuse victims issued by the Standing Committee on Criminal Law (Betænkning nr. 1102/1982).

The theory on victim precipitation was an integral part of early victimology but like the doctrine on children's fantasies it was introduced into the Danish legal theory by psychologists and psychiatrists. In the above mentioned article by Kai Tolstrup, the leading child psychiatrist, the following cautionary instruction was given:

> One must be careful not to underestimate children's own role in acts of indecency. I am tempted to supplement the concept 'child seducer' with the expression 'adult seducer' about certain children. It is justified to claim that sometimes an act of indecency is the result of an interplay where it may be difficult to figure out who is the 'victim' and who is the 'criminal'. (Tolstrup, 1969).

Even Vladimir Nabokov's famous Lolita has been incorporated into the professional literature by Danish experts. Referring to a study conducted on sexual offenses committed in Copenhagen, a professor of forensic medicine claimed in 1974, in an article published in an international journal, that 4% of the very young girls and 54% of the other girls under the age of 15 who had been exposed to sexual assault were all physically well developed for their age. He added that it was not clear whether there was a preponderance of "Lolita types" among these girls (Voigt, 1972).

Quite recently, Danish criminal justice agents were reminded of "children's own role in acts of indecency". In two almost identical articles, one published in the police journal (*Dansk Politi*) and the other in the medical weekly (*Ugeskrift for Læger*), Th. Vanggaard, a retired professor of psychiatry and psycho-analysis, conveyed a case story of an adult woman whom he described as being "aggressive and psychopathic". This woman had told him about an incident which had happened when she was twelve years old. She had crawled between her father's knees as he was reading the newspaper and had "started working on him". The professor, honestly, claimed that he was unable to attach the woman's present emotional problems to the fact that the father "had not been able to resist her seduction" (Vanggaard, 1989, 1989, 1990). This expert did not seem to wonder who might have taught the twelve-year-old girl her "seductive behavior" in the first place.

Based on the above, it is understandable that the precipitation or seduction theory is still playing a role in the criminal justice proceedings. Occasionally, young girls are asked by the police or by the court about their initative to or enjoyment of having sex with their fathers/stepfathers, and a few verdicts also indicate that the victim's sexually provocative conduct has operated as a mitigating factor.

The Third Dogma: Children Suffer No Trauma From Sexual Abuse.

Like the first and second doctrines, this third one has also its origin in the psychological/psychiatric profession which, however, still continues to provide its support. In this context it may be appropriate to once again quote the child psychiatry expert Dr. Tolstrup as having stated:

> My material does not include one single example of a mentally healthy child who has become mentally ill due to a sexual crime.

After having consulted a colleague of his who is an expert on adult women, Dr. Tolstrup concluded:

> ... psychiatric experience of neurotic adult females shows that sexual trauma during childhood will only as an exception play a significant causal role in the later development of a neurosis (Tolstrup, 1969).

The previously mentioned article by Dr Tolstrup rejects the results of an interview study carried out in 1960 and led by E. Vestergaard, a female psychiatrist. Based on the results of this study, she did report on "lasting and very serious consequences of incestuous relationships especially when the daughter is in her puberty" (Vestergaard, 1960).

This was, however, not enough to convince Dr Tolstrup of the causal link between the sexual abuse and the trauma which these women subsequently experienced.

Tolstrup asserted that the statements made by these women should not be granted such power of evidence as Vestergaard obviously did. Interestingly enough, Vestergaard's study has never been mentioned in any legal or medical context until recently when this apparent neglect was criticized by feminist writers. Dr Tolstrup's work had instead been the inspirational source to the 1975 report on child sexual abuse and age limits, issued by the Standing Committee on Criminal Law. Additionally, the Counsel of Forensic Medicine has stated that knowledge about possible traumatic effects caused by an introduction to sexual life or sexual victimization during early childhood was scattered and incomplete (Betænkning nr. 747/1975).

Due to these kinds of expert opinions, the criminal justice system has until recently only rarely dealt with the possibility that sexual abuse may have damaging psychological effects on the child victims. A great deal of documentation on lasting emotional problems is slowly beginning to be considered seriously by the courts as well as by the Crime Compensation Board in cases concerning economic compensation to child victims. However, lawyers representing these children do not claim compensation for psychological damage suffered by their clients but instead, if at all, ask for "tort" damages. The Danish meaning of the concept of "tort" refers to the violation of a persons self-image and reputation. Thus, tort damages/compensation are awarded to a victim who has been subjected to humiliating and downgrading treatment by the offender. Damages are, however, not awarded for the direct effects suffered by the sexually abused victim due to the offense.

The causal relationship between abuse and damage must be established before any economic compensation can be granted. But as long as this causal connection is being rejected by the psychiatrists, it will be utterly difficult to receive compensation for psychological damages suffered as a result of the sexual offense. Professor Vanggaard has, on numerous occasions, claimed that during his 50 years of psycho-analytic practice he has never met a woman whose mental illness could be attributed to sexual abuse which had occured during childhood, nor has any of his "apprentices" ever described such a case. Defense lawyers who produce expert testimonies by psychiatrists of this school are hardly to blame if the courts hesitate to award compensation in these cases.

Summary and Conclusion

Until recently, three dogmas on children's behavior and reactions to sexual abuse have operated almost unopposed within the fields of law, medicine and psychology in Denmark: (1) children (girls) lie or fantasize; (2) they precipitate victimization; (3) they rarely suffer traumas as a result of sexual abuse. These doctrines are shown to have their roots in early twentieth century witness and child psychology studies. They were adopted by criminal law theory and were repeated and confirmed by experts of child psychiatry within suitable intervals.

Since the beginning of the 1990s, a new trend may be emerging: the doctrines seem to be used more cautiously by the criminal justice system, although a few distinguished psychiatrists continue to advance them in their original form or supplemented by equal theories.

The criminal justice system is required to make decisions - ultimately convictions or acquittals - often with the assistance of non-legal experts. Police, lawyers, judges, jurors and magistrates are specialists neither in children nor in the effects of sexual abuse. Not surprisingly, theory and practice of criminal law and procedure have mirrored the statements made by psychiatric and psychological scholars and practitioners for as long as these statements were unanimous and universal.

Disagreement among contemporary experts on children and child sexual abuse may possibly affect the criminal law theorists in such a way that they do not, at least not yet, want to reformulate the doctrines. Criminal justice practitioners cannot, however, wait for the experts to agree but will instead, in the meantime, be forced to make decisions to the best of their ability in cases before them. They must not convict innocent persons and they should not acquit guilty ones. But the legal guarantees against the first kind of miscarriage of justice are - and must be - stronger than the guarantees against the second kind.

The criminal justice system is in dire need of better expert assistance than it receives today, in order to avoid the second type of miscarriage of justice: acquittal of guilty offenders and consequently indirect labelling of the victims as liars.

It is particularly important for the theorists and practitioners of psychology and psychiatry, who have an understanding of the principles and functions governing the criminal justice system, to publish their present knowledge (and uncertainties) in ways which are easily accessible to the criminal justice agents.

References.

Bahnsen, P. (1936). *Vidneudsagnets upaalidelighed* [The unreliability of witness testimony]. København.

Betænkning nr. 622. (1971). [Governmental report No. 622].

Betænkning nr. 747. (1975). [Governmental report No. 747].

Betænkning nr. 1102. (1982). [Governmental report No. 1102].

Buhl, J. P. (1965). Afhøring af børn [Interrogation of children]. *Forhandlingerne på det treogtyvende nordiske juristmøde*. København.

Goodman, G. S. (1984). Children's testimony in historical perspectives. *Journal of Social Issues, 40*(2), 9-31.

Hurwitz, S. (1949). *Den danske Strafferetspleje*, 2. udg. [The Danish criminal procedure]. København.

Leippe, M. R., Brigham, J. C., Cousins, C., & Romanczyk, A. (1989). The opinions and practices of criminal attorneys regarding child eyewitnesses: A survey. In S. J. Ceci, D. F. Ross, & M. P. Toglia (Eds.), *Perspectives on children's testimony*. New York: Springer.

Lindegaard, P., & Trolle, J. (1975). *Procedure i straffesager*, 2. udg. [Procedure in criminal cases]. København.

Saunders, E. J. (1988). A comparative study of attitudes towards child sexual abuse among social work and juridical system professionals. *Child Abuse and Neglect, 12*. 83-90.

Summit, R. (1983). The child sexual abuse accomodation syndrome. *Child Abuse and Neglect, 7*, 177-193.

Tolstrup, K. (1969). Om skadevirkninger af sædelighedsforbrydelser mod piger [About damaging effects of sexual offences against girls]. *Juristen*.

Trolle, J. (1944). Om børns vidneforklaringer [About children's testimony]. *Juristen*.

Vanggaard, Th. (1989). Incest og fri fantasi [Incest and entire imagination]. *Dagbladet Politiken*, 15.1.1989; Incestvanvid [Incest madness]. *Ugeskrift for Læger*, 26/1989; Sund Politipraksis [Sound police practice]. *Dansk Politi*, 12/1990.

Vestergaard, E. (1960). Fader-datter incest [Father-daughter incest). *Nordisk Tidsskrift for Kriminalvidenskab*.

Voigt, J. (1972). Sexual offences in Copenhagen: A medico-legal study. *Forensic Science*, *1*.

Wachtmeister, A. (1948). *For ung til at tale sandhed?* [Too young to speak the truth?]. København.

Sexual Knowledge and Behavior of Children up to 12 Years - What is Age-appropriate?

Renate Volbert and Rianne van der Zanden

Introduction

In cases of alleged sexual abuse, the child's sexual knowledge and behavior are often considered crucial. Clinicians and researchers have frequently suggested that children may exhibit precocious sexual behavior and knowledge as a result of sexual abuse (e.g., Beitchman, Zucker, Hood, DaCosta & Akman, 1991; Browne & Finkelhor, 1986; Buffing & van der Zanden, 1992). In a recent review of the empirical literature Friedrich (1993) concluded, that sexual behavior is reported significantly more often in sexually abused children than in nonabused children. A study by Conte, Sorenson, Fogarty, and Dalla Rosa (1991) showed that professionals regard age-inappropriate sexual knowledge - besides physical indicators - as the most important indicator in sustaining a report of sexual abuse. On the other hand, defense attorneys sometimes argue that children who exhibit sexual behavior are also able to make up or fantasize a report of sexual abuse.

However, "sexualized behavior" is mostly treated as a broad category, and only examples for "abnormal sexual behavior" are given: such as aggressive sexual behavior against other children, excessive masturbation, provocative sexual behavior, insertion of objects into vagina or anus, and preoccupation with explicitly sexual material or with adults' private parts (e.g., Friedrich, Beilke & Urquiza, 1988; Hibbard & Hartman, 1992; Kolko & Moser, 1988; White, Halpin, Strom & Santelli, 1988). Studies, which systematically investigate the occurrence of different forms of sexualized behavior among abused and nonabused samples rarely exist (Friedrich et al., 1992). Since there is a lack of information about sexual behavior and knowledge of children in general, an understanding of the development of sexual behavior and knowledge in normal children is necessary as a first step. In the following, a survey of empirical studies on sexual behavior and knowledge of children up to 12 years of age is presented.

Several limitations must be emphasized here. Especially in the field of sexual behavior of children, numerous empirical studies are retrospective in nature: a restriction which must be particularly taken into consideration when examining information from the early years of a child. On the other hand, interviews with children are very often conducted with non-representative samples, for the reason that many parents do not consent to having their children interviewed on sexual matters. Most studies have not surveyed for a history of sexual abuse of their subjects, with the result that samples under investigation might not always consist entirely of nonabused children. Sexual behavior of children - and especially child knowledge on sexuality - may furthermore differ from culture to culture (e.g., Currier, 1981); results presented here are therefore applicable only within a cultural context similar to that in which the investigation was conducted. Not only has little empirical research been conducted in this field, but most studies available are also quite dated. Access to sexually explicit material - such as pornographic videos and magazines - has by now also become much easier. As a result, patterns of acquiring sexual knowledge and exhibiting sexual behavior may well have changed to some degree.

Sexual Behavior of Children

Upon review of the available literature, one of the most striking findings is the nearly total lack of definitions (see van der Zanden, 1992). Very often, no distinction is made among the ability of children's bodies to become aroused or to have pleasurable sensations, the behavior of children, or their knowledge and intentions (La Fontaine, 1990). There is no consensus as to whether children's behavior can be regarded as actually sexual when they are engaged in sexual activities. One standpoint is that the erotic significance of an act or a situation lies in the meanings which are applied to it, with the result that children who have not yet learned these meanings can not be regarded as fully sexual (Jackson, 1982). Despite definitional shortcomings, distinctions can in fact be drawn between auto-erotic and socio-sexual behavior. Existing empirical findings can be broken down into the following sources: a) observations of children by researchers, parents or teachers; b) retrospective research with adolescent or adult subjects; and c) interviews with children.

Auto-erotic Behavior

Observations Babies as young as six months discover their genitals (Galenson & Roiphe, 1974, 1979; Galenson, 1990; Kleeman, 1965, 1966, 1971). Already before they reach their first birthday, children touch, stroke, and rub their genitals, and rocking and pressing movements can often be observed (Bakwin, 1973; Lewis, 1965). According to Martinson (1980), this is merely reflexive behavior: it takes place "at random" and should not be considered as firm evidence of sexual capability (see also Rutter, 1980). In contrast to this more reflexive genital play, Martinson (1977) defines masturbation as genital play of volitional nature: the child is aware of erotic pleasure and actively seeks it. Genital play becomes increasingly volitional during the second year.

Galenson (1990) states that auto-erotic play begins to be accompanied by more intense sensations between 15 and 19 months. These observations are in accordance with those of Kleeman (1966, 1971), who considers genital play in the first year to be primarily a form of body exploration. From his standpoint, true auto-erotic elements develop at the end of the second year. However, Kinsey, Pomeroy, Martin & Gebhard (1953) report on masturbation behavior and orgasm-like responses in boys and girls only four months old.

Sears, Maccoby, and Levin (1957) and Newson and Newson (1963) questioned mothers on the auto-erotic behavior of their babies and toddlers. In both studies, about one-third of mothers reported observations of genital play or masturbation of their children. However, this did not necessarily involve masturbation in the sense of a rhythmic activity, which is probably much less frequent. In a more recent German study by Misgeld (1978), parents indicated that two-thirds of their boys up to three years old, and a quarter of the same-aged girls, played with their genitals. In contrast to these percentages, only 17% of mothers of four-year-old children reported observations of auto-erotic behavior (Newson & Newson, 1968). Friedrich, Grambsch, Broughton, Kuiper, and Beilke (1991) - who questioned a large sample of mothers about the sexual behavior of children between two and 12 years, and who screened for the absence of physical, psychological, and sexual abuse - found that about 20% of two- to six-year-old children masturbate and about 10% of seven- to 12-year-olds. The same developmental trend was revealed by Gagnon (1985), although with higher base rates: masturbation was observed by parents in 53% of three- to five-year-old boys and in 38% of girls of that age; afterwards a decrease was observed. However, it cannot be concluded that masturbation actually decreased, since older children might more frequently conceal such behavior. In their study, Gordon, Schroeder, and Abrams (1990a) reached findings similar to percentages found by Gagnon in 1985: 85% of parents of children between two and seven said that they had seen their children touching their genitalia, and that about 50% indicated their children had masturbated.

In a survey of 60 Norwegian kindergarten teachers, 85% reported observations of children masturbating, and 24% indicated that this behavior was observed often or very often (Gunderson, Melas & Skar, 1981). In about a quarter of reported cases, the teachers observed orgasm in masturbating children. Great individual differences in masturbation frequencies were reported: some children masturbated during long periods of the day, others hardly ever. Problems in the family were related to extreme preoccupation with masturbation. This appears contradictory to results by Spitz and Wolf (1949), who found genital play between 12 and 18 months to be an indicator for the positive quality of object-relation: children with beneficial attachment to their mothers engaged significantly more in genital play than children reared in institutions. The discrepancy might be due to the coverage of toddlers in one study and preschoolers in the other.

Studies reveal some evidence for sex differences, in indicating that genital stimulation is more common among boys than among girls (e.g., Friedrich et al., 1991; Misgeld, 1978; Newson & Newson, 1963; Rutter, 1971).

Retrospective research Auto-erotic behavior of children was one of the topics in the large-scale retrospective research by Kinsey, Pomeroy, and Martin (1948) and by Kinsey et al. (1953). It was found that the frequency of masturbation gradually increases during prepuberal years; 20% of male and 16% of female subjects reported to have masturbated before the age of 12. Several retrospective studies on childhood auto-erotic behavior which were conducted around 1970 in different countries (Denmark: Broderick, 1971; Germany: Giese & Schmidt, 1968; Israel: Hoch, Kubat, Fisher & Brandes, 1978) revealed slightly higher rates of masturbation behavior under the age of 12 than in the Kinsey studies. Highest percentages were found by Ramsey (1943a): 5% remembered to have masturbated at age five or younger, and 10% reported masturbation activity at age seven and 73% at age 12. The majority of the only male subjects were boys with lower-class status who, in several studies, were found to show relatively more sexual activities (e.g., Elias & Gebhard, 1974).

The German study of Giese and Schmidt (1968) was repeated after about 10 years (Clement, Schmidt & Kruse, 1984), and an increase in masturbation behavior for both sexes was found. In 1968, 32% of male and 18% of female respondents reported masturbation before puberty, compared to 42% and 31%, respectively, in 1981. However, it is not clear whether this reflects a real increase in masturbation activities, or merely more openness to talking about sex.

Interviews with children Elias and Gebhard (1974) analyzed interviews with four- to 14-year-old children, which revealed, that nearly half of the boys and one-third of the girls masturbated before puberty. Norwegian children under the age of 10 were interviewed by Langfeldt (1981, 1990), who found that 10% masturbate and reach an orgasm. Among pre-school children, some kind of mastubatory activities was common, and about 30% of two- to seven-year-old children masturbated regularly. Among children who did not masturbate, Langfeldt found a negative and in some cases even an aversive attitude to their sexuality and their genitals.

Socio-sexual Behavior

Observations Sexual behavior with others emerges around age three or four. Isaacs (1933) found a diversity of activities among pre-schoolers: 'Exhibitionistic and voyeuristic activities with both other children and adults are characteristic, masturbation occurs, children attempt to fondle their mother's breasts, and it appears from the nature of their play that urination is associated in children's mind with sex activities' (in Rutter, 1980, p. 325). Recent research, too, indicates that so called sex-play is quite frequent. In a study by Gordon et al. (1990a), 30% of parents indicated their two- to seven-year-old children had engaged in exploratory sexual play. Friedrich et al. (1991) found that mothers reported having witnessed a variety of sexual behavior among children between two and 12. For both sexes, a definite correlation between overt sexual behavior and age was found: there was a peak in overt sexual behavior between age three and five, and a decline in such behavior afterwards. Aggressive sexual behavior and action more imitative of adult sexual behavior were rarely established. Exhibition of several types of infrequent behavior was found to be extremely unusual. Although socio-sexual sexual play becomes more frequent around age three, interest in the genitals of the opposite sex can be observed already in the second year (Schuhrke, 1991).

The frequency of children touching parents' genitals in a non-clinical sample was explored by Rosenfeld, Bailey, Siegel, and Bailey (1986). At all ages until 10, over 30% of parents gave an answer other than "never" when asked if the daughter touched her father's genitals, and even 45% of the parents of eight- to 10-year-old boys answered other than "never" when asked if their son touched his mother's breasts or genitals. In general, children touched fathers' genitals less often than mothers' breasts and/or genitals. Intimately touching their parents declined significantly with increasing children's ages, with respect to both mothers and fathers.

Retrospective research Nearly half of the Kinsey et al. (1948) and the Ramsey (1943a) subjects reported socio-sexual play, both homo- and heterosexual, before age 12. Some subjects reported having experienced sexual arousal and/or an orgasm during these contacts. Most of these encounters occurred only once. They mainly took place with children of the same age and happened out of curiosity about the anatomy of the other child. Kinsey et al. (1948, 1953) found that most of the sexual contacts included showing, looking at, and touching genitals. Oral-genital contact was rarely reported, as was vaginal insertion. Some boys had ano-genital contacts. Lower percentages were presented by Misgeld (1978), who found that a total of approximately 20% of adults reported sexual play during childhood, and that 38% of them remembered having initiated sexual play during pre-school years, with another 44% between age six and nine. Of 1000 Australian students, 60% remembered sexual play with another child before the age of 12 (Goldman & Goldman, 1988). Again, these data reveal that most of the contacts consisted of showing, looking at, and touching genitals.

(Attempted) intercourse before age 12 was reported by nearly a third of the male subjects in the Ramsey study (1943a), and by about 20% in the sample of Kinsey et al. (1948). In the latter study, lower-social-class boys were overrepresented in the group who had experience with attempts at intercourse before age 12. The high percentages in the study conducted by Ramsey might be explained by the fact that the majority of the subjects were boys with lower-class status. Attempted intercourse without penetration was reported by 18% of the students interviewed by Goldman and Goldman (1988). Half of these cases were accompanied by mutual masturbation; 2% reported actual intercourse. All reported cases of (attempts at) intercourse took place between 10 and 12.

Sexual contacts with siblings were reported by 11% of the Goldman and Goldman (1988) sample. Finkelhor (1981) - whose data, however, were not restricted to children under 12 - found that 13% of the subjects had sexual contact with siblings; touching and stroking each other's genitals were the most frequently reported behavior, followed by looking at and showing genitals. Looking at each other's genitals and showing one's own genitals were more common in younger children. About a quarter of sexual encounters with siblings was indicated as involuntary. Involuntary sexual contacts with other children during childhood in general were reported by 18% of the Goldman and Goldman (1988) sample.

Interviews with children The percentages of sexual behavior before age 12 gained by interviews with four- to 14-year-old children (Elias & Gebhard, 1974) are in agreement with results in retrospective studies (Kinsey et al., 1948, 1953).

Sexual interest of school-age children was investigated in several studies by Broderick (1971). Most of what is described in these studies involves interest in the opposite sex, but relatively little entails concrete sexual behavior: i.e., most of the children between 10 and 12 are "in love" and are increasingly interested in the company of somebody of the opposite sex. According to studies by Broderick, Schoof-Tams, Schaegel & Walszal (1976) reported that almost 50% of children had been kissed by somebody of the opposite sex by the age of 11.

It is a controversial point whether the years between five and six and puberty are a sexually latent period with a repression of sex interest and little psychosexual development, as psychoanalytic theory suggests (see Fries, 1959). Empirical research does not fully support this hypothesis, since sex activities seem to be frequent during this period: Ramsey (1943a), for example, found an accumulative incidence of masturbation in boys - from 10% at seven to over 80% at 13 -, heterosexual play rose from less than 5% at five years to a third at eight years and to two-thirds at 13. Although masturbation starting in childhood was likely to carry on into adolescence among both boys and girls, prepubertal sex play with peers, by contrast, usually stopped in girls and frequently stopped in middle-class boys. Lower-class boys more actively continued sex play and were deemed three times as likely to have attempted intercourse (Elias & Gebhard, 1974). However, there seems to be a growing awareness by children of social taboos about sexuality during these years (Goldman & Goldman, 1982). There may be greater concealment of sex interests during middle childhood than during both the periods before and after (Rutter, 1980).

Sexual Knowledge

Most work in this area has focused on the development of gender identity and children's understanding of pregnancy and birth. Some studies have more explicitly investigated the knowledge of adult sexual behavior. Recent research has also explored children's understanding of sexual abuse. Although some investigations here are also retrospective, the children themselves were interviewed in most studies about their knowledge of these matters.

An early study by Hattendorf (1932) on the questions concerning sexuality asked by young children revealed that such questions first appeared as early as the second year, and reached peaks around ages five and nine for boys, and around ages five and nine and 13 for girls. Almost 50% of the children who had asked sexual questions did so between the ages of two and five. These ages correspond with the ages of children's questioning in general, so that it may be concluded that children become interested and begin asking about sex when they begin asking questions in general. Areas of sexual curiosity in declining order of frequency were: origin of babies, the arrival of another baby, intrauterine growth, process of birth, organs and functions of the body, physical sex differences, relation of the father to reproduction, and marriage. However, two-thirds of the 3,300 mothers approached for this study indicated that their children had not asked questions about sex. Most children under the age of two do not ask questions on sexual matters, but around two and three children start asking about genital differences. Children around age three and four seem to be interested mainly in the origin of babies. Many children at ages five and six show interest in their own having been a baby and wonder how babies feel inside the mother. Questions about birth become more prominent at that time. Around age eight, children are interested in sex information from their peers and in each parent's role in the reproductive process. Afterwards, around age eight or nine, interest in contacts with the opposite sex increases (e.g., Grassel & Bach, 1979; Malinowski, 1979). Broderick (1969) concluded that pre-schoolers are very interested in where babies come from, and show interest in sexual differences. However, he felt that they are rarely concerned with questions of sexual intercourse or conception.

Knowledge of genital differences Most comprehensive research has been conducted on knowledge of genital differences and the development of gender identity (e.g., Bosinski, 1989; Conn, 1940; Conn & Kanner, 1947; Bem, 1989; Emmerich, Goldman, Kirsh & Sharabany, 1977; Gesell, 1940; Goldman & Goldman, 1983; Slaby & Frey, 1975; Thompson & Bentler, 1971, 1973). These studies show a developmental progression in children's understanding of gender. By ages two to three, children learn to identify themselves as boys and girls, and shortly afterward they are able to identify the sex of others. Young children define sex primarily on the basis of visual salient cues such as clothing and hair, but most of them are aware of genital differences (e.g., Gordon et al., 1990a). It appears definite, however, that a child's gender identity is well developed before he or she has a proper appreciation of sex differences generally, and that gender identity clearly develops before full understanding of the genital basis of sex differences is gained. Under ordinary circumstances, gender identity is well established by three to four years (Rutter, 1980).

Bem (1989) found girls to have significantly more genital knowledge than do boys. Her female subjects had as much genital knowledge at age three as either males or females had by age five. In Bem's study, 58% of the girls and 15% of the boys could tell an expression for female genitals, and 67% of the boys and 68% of the girls, for male genitals. These results are in accordance with Bosinski (1989), who also found significantly better genital knowledge among four- to seven-year-old girls than among boys of the same age. Data by Moore and Kendall (1971) on three- to five-year-old children do not confirm a better total knowledge among girls, but they do verify the following overall pattern: children in general are better equipped with labels for male than for female genitalia (see also Gordon et al., 1990a; Victor, 1980), and the lowest knowledge can be found among boys on female genitals. Additional support for this pattern is provided by Fraley, Nelson, Wolf, and Lozoff (1991), who showed that little girls (one to four years old) were less likely than boys to receive a label for their own genitals by their mothers, whereas they seemed to be more likely than boys to receive a term for the genitals of the opposite sex. Terms employed for the female genitalia are often not distinctive or differentiated from terms given for the anus (Moore & Kendall, 1971). Parents still mislabel, nonlabel, or negatively label the sexual organs for the child, so that many children are left without a vocabulary with which to describe their physical or psychic experiences (see Moore & Kendall, 1971).

When questioned, children between two and seven seldom indicate any sexual function for genitalia. If they do so, these responses are primarily related to pregnancy and birth like "You make babies with it" (Gordon et al., 1990a).

Knowledge of pregnancy and birth Various studies show that children four to seven years old have a very basic knowledge of pregnancy, namely of intrauterine growth, but only very little knowledge of birth and almost no adequate knowledge of conception (Bernstein & Cowan, 1975; Bosinski, 1989; Cohen & Parker, 1977; Frasch & Grüninger, 1975; Goldman & Goldman, 1982; Gordon et al., 1990a; Grassel & Bosinski, 1983; Kreitler & Kreitler, 1966; Löwe, 1981; Moore & Kendall, 1971).

In earlier studies (e.g., Conn, 1947), however, pre-school children did not even refer to the mother's role in the coming of the baby, and the concept of the birth process was completely foreign for children of this age group. Conn concluded that it is inconceivable to pre-school children that the baby may be inside the mother. He reported beginning awareness of the mother's role around age eight. Accordingly, children around nine years of age may begin to think about various body apertures by means of which the baby may leave the mother. The average 10- to 12-year-old was found to believe that the baby was in the mother's stomach and required surgical removal. Out of 100 children between four and 11 years whom Conn interviewed, only six were aware that some form of genital contact occurred between the sexes and half of them appeared to be puzzled or in doubt as to the purpose of genital contact or penetration. Bosinski (1989) and Grassel and Bosinski (1983) emphasize that erroneous information - such as stories about the stork etc. - can primarily be found in older studies (e.g., Brückner, 1968; Grassel, 1967), where they covered up to 60% of cases. Retrospective research also shows that the primary years for learning of pregnancy in older samples were those from eight to 12, with the modal being 10. In a more recent sample, over half of the children knew of pregnancy before age seven, with the modal for boys being six and for girls, five (Gebhard, 1977).

Bernstein and Cowan (1975) stress the relevance of cognitive concepts to the understanding of the *origins of babies*, namely causality and identity. They suggest that children's concepts concerning the origin of babies follow a developmental sequence and are embedded in a matrix of cognitive-structural variables. At Level One, children are preformist and do not see the need for a cause of a baby. In Level Two, causes are assimilated from notions of people as manufacturers. At Level Three, two or three main factors are isolated by children, either social, sexual, or biological. Children at Level Four start coordinating the variables in a system of physical causes, but fail to grip with genetic transmission. Children at Level Five are able to understand genetic transmission, but conceptualize it as additive rather than interactive. At Level Six, children finally provide sophisticated theory of how people get babies. The authors conclude that children actively construct their notions about babies. "What is often taken as misinformation may largely be a product of their own assimilative processes at work on materials with too complex a structure for them to understand." (p. 90).

Goldman and Goldman (1983) found similar forms of children's explanations, although not in a clear progression. They categorized the children as geographers (the only explanation is that the baby is inside the mother), manufacturers (it is made outside and put inside the mother by non-sexual means), agriculturalists (the seed-in-the-soil-analogy is taken literally), reporters (who know the facts, but cannot explain them), the miniaturists (who believe the baby is fully formed in miniature in either the sperm or egg), and the realists (who have a reasonably accurate theory of fertilization and fusion). The authors assume that many of these stages could be eliminated. The fact that many children recognize sexual roles quite late seems not to be due to inherent difficulties in the problems posed, since some children at the age of seven not only knew the facts, but also provided adequate explanations (Goldman & Goldman, 1983).

Other studies further show that most young children (three to six years) either have no explanation when asked about the origin of babies (Bosinski, 1989; Moore & Kendall, 1971), or believe that the baby has always been inside the mother (Cohen & Parker, 1977). Kreitler and Kreitler (1966) found that the commonest theory among four- to five-year-old children is that the baby is created in the mother's belly from the food she eats, but this finding was not replicated in other studies. The assumption that pre-school children are able to understand gestation inside the mother is underlined by results of Bosinski (1989): out of 366 four- to seven-year-old children, 21% told that the baby eventually grows from an egg inside the mother's belly.

Children of this age group generally do not realize any causal relation between the father and the pregnancy and birth. The father's function is primarily seen in helping the mother (Kreitler & Kreitler, 1966; Moore & Kendall, 1971). Goldman and Goldman (1982) constructed a biological-realism scale to assess children's reports about *mother's and father's role in procreation.* They identified three levels of nonsexual, transitional sexual, and overtly sexual answers, with mainly nonsexual roles in procreation being perceived up to 11 years. Many younger children, however, knew some of the facts before, but they did not think of procreation in sexual terms. The authors assume that this is due to children's reluctance to view their parents as sexually active. While mothers appeared to be regarded as active in the presexual and nonsexual stages of thinking, they tended later to be seen as passive recipients in the sexual act, as compared with father's active role. Goldman and Goldman also showed cross-national differences in knowledge about pregnancy and birth. Results from a Swedish sample displayed much earlier insights into these processes, whereas North American children showed a much slower rate in development in the area of knowledge of birth and procreation in the pre-teen years. The authors conclude that children who are deprived of honest explanations will construct their own explanations and myths.

When regarding *theories of birth*, the commonest answer among four- to seven-year-old children in most studies involved reference to the opening of the belly (Bosinski, 1989; Grassel & Bosinski, 1983; Kreitler & Kreitler, 1966; Moore & Kendall, 1971). It was only in a study by Cohen and Parker (1977) that most children stated that the baby left the mother from a special hole, which was either called "vagina" - or "bottom" for children vague with terms. This refers to a problem connected with the psychoanalytic assumption that children provide a cloacal theory of birth (Freud, 1907). Agreement with such a theory differed among studies. Whereas in most studies evidence for such a theory was very scanty (Bosinski, 1989; Kreitler & Kreitler, 1966), Moore and Kendall (1971) found 20% agreement when the child had to consider whether this could be a possible exit. However, agreement might partly have occurred because children did not really differentiate between anus and vagina. Goldman and Goldman (1983) found anus responses to be evident among five- and seven-year-olds. The authors also showed that English-speaking children (from USA, Australia, and England) tended to declare a realistic birth exit by 11 years, and Swedish children, at nine years. More than one-third of the Swedish sample gave a realistic answer at age five.

Knowledge of birth-control cannot be found before sexuality is perceived as essential for procreation.

In the non-sexual cognitive period it is felt that nothing can be done or the manufacturers and agriculturalists simply do not continue their activities. Once sexual intercourse is seen as a cause, the abstention from sex is seen as one method of birth-control, but by 11 years one partner or the other (one-sex devices) is perceived as being able to do something. Awareness of both-sex devices is not normally known until 13 years. (Goldman & Goldman, 1982, p. 387).

Knowledge of adult sexual behavior Children have rarely been interviewed on their knowledge of sexual behavior independent of the reproduction process. The above-mentioned studies indicate that children around nine start to give notions about the sexual act when asked about procreation (although some children know about coitus before). In studies with pre-school samples, some children demonstrated knowledge about sexual intercourse, but these responses were in general very vague. It is therefore questionable whether these children had detailed knowledge about the sexual act.

Janus and Bess (1976) asked children from five onward to tell or write a composition about certain sexual topics. Kindergarten children indicated that kissing is what one does sexually with the opposite sex. Grade two and three children were most concerned with hugging, kissing, and dancing with the opposite sex. For grade four and five children, the following themes were predominant: touching and its connection with sex, shapes and personal tastes, awareness of intimate sexual activity, and privacy with the opposite sex. Grade six children provided specific knowledge of intercourse and its possible consequences. There was an increasing awareness of sex desires and drives in this age group. Thornburg (1985) asked 11- to 13-year-old children to define if possible a set of sexual concepts. More than 50% gave definitions for "abortion", "homosexuality", "prostitution", "veneral disease", "menstruation" and "intercourse", but with a lot of definitions being immature or inaccurate. Less than 25% gave any definition for "conception", "seminal emission", "contraception", and "ejaculation". The rest indicated that they did not know these terms at all. Almost half of 11- to 12-year-old children asked by Ripley, Burns, and Dickenson (1974) could not tell whether masturbation is harmful or not.

In a retrospective study, Gebhard (1977) found that knowledge of coitus steadily increases from early childhood until near puberty, when there is a marked acceleration in learning: in the Kinsey sample, more than half of the boys and girls learned of coitus in the years from 10 to 13; after early childhood, boys acquired this knowledge more rapidly than girls, and girls learned more at older ages. A more recent sample revealed that girls learn as readily as boys: over half of each sex reported to have learned of coitus by the end of their tenth year, and about 5% of the sample remembered to have known about coitus before age seven. In both samples, as well as in a study by Ramsey (1943b), most subjects did not learn about veneral disease before age 12. In the more recent sample, children generally learned about prostitution in the years between 12 and 15 - which is again in accordance with results by Ramsey (1943b) - but about a quarter reported to have learned of prostitution between eight and 11. All females in the more recent sample indicated that they did not know about penile erection before age eight and only 3% reported they knew about it before age 10. Most girls learned about it between age 12 and 15. About a quarter of the boys knew about penile erection before age eight, but even more than 50% of the males reported they were unaware of erections up to age 10. Whereas, in the Kinsey sample, males learned of nearly all sexual matters earlier than females, there were almost no sex differences in acquiring knowledge in the more recent sample (Gebhard, 1977).

Knowledge about sexual abuse Wurtele and Miller (1987) found that conceptualizations of sexual abuse, descriptions of abusers and victims, and perceptions of consequences of the abusive incident differ between five- to seven- and 10- to 12-year-old children. Whereas most of the younger children were unable to define the term "sexual abuse", half of the older children provided a fairly accurate description by implying sexual contact. Of the younger children, 50% believed that children are sometimes sexually abused; only 15% gave descriptions involving sexual touching. The young group was more likely to perceive the perpetrator as being their own age and as being a stranger, than was the older group. About 25% of the older group believed sexual abuse involves serious physical aggression.

Moderating variables As mentioned above, Goldman and Goldman (1982) found quite definite *cross-national differences* in children's sexual knowledge; the authors assume that this is due to different sex-education programs. Gordon et al. (1990a) showed that parents' reports of *sex education* were positively related to total sexual knowledge and to most areas of sexual knowledge of two- to seven-year-old children, but not for knowledge of adult sexual behavior. This may be because parents who do provide sex education mainly talk about pregnancy and birth, but not about intercourse (Finkelhor, 1984).

Gordon et al. (1990a) also found that *parents' attitudes to children's sexuality* were significantly correlated with some areas of child knowledge and with total knowledge, but not at the same time with children's knowledge about adult sexual behavior. Some *social-class differences* were found in this study: children from lower socioeconomic backgrounds demonstrated less total sexual knowledge, but this was not true for knowledge about the sexual behavior of adults. Mothers of these children also reported more restrictive attitudes about sexuality and less sex education with their children than those in middle and upper social classes. The child's age, social class, and sex education were significant predictors of child total sexual knowledge in the study by Gordon et al. (1990a). Elias and Gebhard (1974) found social class- and gender-interaction with boys from lower social classes providing knowledge about sexual behavior at an earlier age than among boys from upper classes. This contrasted with girls from upper social classes, who knew more about sexual behavior compared to girls from lower social classes. *Larger family size* and the presence of a *sibling of the other sex* might also be relevant factors for better sexual knowledge (Goldman & Goldman, 1982). Parents' reports of their *children's sexual experience* were found to be positively related to knowledge of sexual body parts and to total knowledge, but not to knowledge of adult sexual behavior (Gordon et al., 1990a).

Gordon, Schroeder and Abrams (1990b) conducted the only *comparison of sexual knowledge between sexually abused and nonabused children* and found no differences in any area of sexual knowledge. But children's information about adult sexual behavior was explored with very little explicit stimulus materials: e.g., a nude male and female in bed with covers up to their chests. Half of the abused children, however, gave unusually affective responses to the stimuli in the child interview, primarily reflecting affective distress during the interview - whereas none of the nonabused children did so. Material depicting sexual or possibly sexual interactions between adults and children was not used in this or in any other study.

Discussion

Knowledge about normal child sexual development (including sexual knowledge and behavior) is limited, since not much empirical research has been conducted. Although existing studies vary considerably in their characteristics - i.e., in their definitions of sexual behavior, kinds of sexual behavior under investigation, social and cultural backgrounds of the subjects, research methods, and in the historical periods during which studies were conducted - the actual results obtained have proved remarkably consistent.

Auto-erotic behavior (genital play and/or masturbation) is very common almost from the first months of life onward. Indicators of erotic arousal can be observed at latest at the end of the second year of life. In all age groups up to 12 years, 20% to 50% were reported to exhibit forms of auto-erotic behavior. A considerable percentage of children masturbate to the point of orgasm before puberty. While results suggest that auto-erotic behavior is likely to be carried on into adolescence, it is less frequently observed from around the age of five or six onward. Socio-sexual behavior starts around age three, and 20% to 60% of all children seem to be involved in exploratory sexual play. Most of these encounters take place with peers and do not occur frequently. Typical forms are showing one's own genitals, and looking at and touching or stroking others' genitals. Overt socio-sexual behavior is more frequent in the span between three and five years. Afterwards, a decrease is observed, but this may be only an indicator of greater concealment of sexual behavior. There seems to be a growing awareness by children of social taboos about sexuality during these years. Several forms of sexual behavior which are uncommon among children under 12 can be identified: aggressive sexual behavior, oro-genital contact, putting objects into the vagina or anus, and attempts at intercourse. The latter, however, was reported at a considerable rate for 10- to 12-year-olds in retrospective studies. From clinical experience, it seems reasonable that it is not a specific form of behavior which is indicative for sexual abuse, but the frequency of the exhibited sexual behavior and the context: i.e., where and with whom and under which conditions the behavior is shown. Occasional masturbation of a five-year-old girl seems to be part of normal sexual development, but the question remains as to how the same behavior should be assessed when it occurs very often in public, or when an unknown adult comes for a visit.

The sexual knowledge of children appears to be more extensively influenced by epochal changes. Earlier, it was assumed that it is inconceivable to pre-school children that the baby might be in the mother. Since, however, this assumption has been proven false. The fact that many children recognize sexual roles quite late is not due to inherent difficulties, but to a lack of information. In general, however, children's understanding of sexuality shows a progression related to cognitive development. By two to three, children learn to identify themselves and others as boys and girls. At that time, they also acquire knowledge of genital differences, although full comprehension of the genital basis of sex differences is not gained then. Even most recent studies show that parents still mislabel or nonlabel sexual organs for the child. Children in general are better equipped with labels for male than for female genitalia. Children between four and six have a basic knowledge of pregnancy - i.e., of intrauterine growth - but only very little knowledge of birth. Mainly nonsexual roles in procreation are perceived up to about nine years. However, some children at the age of seven can also provide adequate explanations. Pre-school children have almost no knowledge about adult sexual behavior independently of the reproduction process. Kowledge in this area increases steadily until near puberty, when there is a marked acceleration in learning. But even then many children are still very insecure about numerous sexual concepts: for example, about defining "intercourse" or "seminal emission" or "ejaculation".

If one compares results on child sexual knowledge with statements of allegedly sexually abused children - who can very often describe sexual interactions in a very vivid way - one might conclude that detailed knowledge about adult sexual behavior provided by young children should at least be regarded as a warning signal. To gain relevant information for assessing cases of alleged sexual abuse, further research should focus more on knowledge of children of concrete sexual acts and on knowledge of sexual interactions between adults and children. Knowledge in these areas should then be compared between sexually abused and nonabused children. With the availability of video tapes with explicit sexual content, there is a need for research on the effects on children who have been exposed to explicit sexual material. For obvious ethical reasons, however, this area would be very difficult to study systematically.

At present, studies on the sexual knowledge of children between two and six - including knowledge of adult sexual behavior and of sexual interactions between adults and children - are being conducted in Germany and in the Netherlands (Volbert & Buffing, in prep.). The child interviews are combined with parent questionnaires about sex education and the sexual behavior children had shown. Preliminary results have revealed that these children provided almost no knowledge of adult sexual behavior. The children also furnish no descriptions of sexual abuse when pictures of possibly sexual interactions between adults and children were shown. Data concerning sexual behavior support conclusions which indicate that looking at others' genitals is common, and showing and touching quite frequent - whereas other kinds of behavior are seldom reported. Only children's playing with their own genitals was reported as occurring often, with all other kinds of behavior observed with lower frequency by parents.

Results reported here indicate that careful assessment of sexual knowledge, behavior, and affect is essential. Simply being exposed to adult sexual behavior through watching adult movies, for example, might lead to demonstrations of precocious sexual behavior, but not to increased knowledge or displays of unusual affect.

> Even if the precocious sexual behavior is a result of sexual abuse (...) it may not necessarily be accompanied by increased understanding (...) a child's affective response to materials presented may be as important as what the child knows or how he or she behaves. (Gordon et al., 1990b, p. 57).

It is not to be expected that a certain form of sexual behavior or that the sexual knowledge of a child can ever be regarded as an ultimate proof of sexual abuse. But by identifying uncommon behavior and knowledge in different age groups - or uncommon contexts of exhibiting sexual behavior, or combinations of sexual behavior and uncommon affects - and by systematic comparisons between abused and non-abused samples, it will become clearer as to what kind of behavior and knowledge should raise concern. In any case, individual assessment is necessary concerning the origin of the uncommon behavior, knowledge, or affect. To meet this aim, more theoretical work on child sexual development will be necessary in the future.

References

Bakwin, H. (1973). Erotic feelings in infants and young children. *American Journal of Diseases of Children, 126*, 52-54.

Beitchman, J. H., Zucker, K. J., Hood, J. E., DaCosta, G. A., & Akman, D. (1991). A review of the short-term effects of child sexual abuse. *Child Abuse and Neglect, 15*, 537-556.

Bem, S. L. (1989). Genital knowledge and gender constancy in pre-school children. *Child Development, 60*, 649-662.

Bosinski, H. (1989). Zum aktuellen Stand der Geschlechtserziehung im Vorschulalter. *Ärztliche Jugendkunde, 80*, 290-297.

Bernstein, A. C., & Cowan, P. A. (1975). Children's concepts of how people get babies. *Child Development, 46*, 77-91.

Broderick, C. B. (1969). Normal sexual development. In C. B. Broderick & J. Bernard (Eds.), *The individual, sex and society* (pp. 23-41). Baltimore: John Hopkins University Press.

Broderick, C. B. (1971). *Kind, jeugd en seksualiteit.* Utrecht: Uitgeverij het Spectrum.

Browne, A., & Finkelhor, D. (1986). Impact of child sexual abuse: A review of the research. *Psychological Bulletin, 99*, 66-77.

Brückner, H. (1968). *Das Sexualwissen unserer Jugend.* Berlin: Deutscher Verlag der Wissenschaften.

Buffing, F., & Zanden, A. P. van der (1992). Signalen en signaleren van kindermishandeling. In H. E. M. Baartman & A. van Montfoort (Eds.), *Kindermishandeling. Resultaten van multidisciplinair onderzoek* (pp. 93-106). Utrecht: Data Medica.

Clement, U., Schmidt, G., & Kruse, M. (1984). Changes in sex differences in sexual behavior: A replication of a study on West German students (1966-1981). *Archives of Sexual Behavior, 13*, 99-121.

Cohen, B., & Parker, S. (1977). Sex information among nursery-school children. In E. K Oremland & J. D. Oremland (Eds.), *The sexual and gender development of young children: The role of the educator* (pp. 181-190). Cambridge: Ballinger Publishing Company.

Conn, J. H. (1940). Children's reactions to the discovery of genital differences. *American Journal of Orthopsychiatry, 10*, 747-754.

Conn, J. H. (1947). Children's awareness of the origins of baby's. *Journal of Child Psychiatry, 1*, 140-176.

Conn, J. H., & Kanner, L. (1947). Children's awareness of sex differences. *Journal of Child Psychiatry, 1*, 3-57.

Conte, J. R., Sorenson, E., Fogarty, L., & Dalla Rosa J. (1991). Evaluating children's reports of sexual abuse: Results from a survey of professionals. *American Journal of Orthopsychiatry, 61*, 428-437.

Currier, R. L. (1981). Juvenile sexuality in global perspective. In L. L. Constantine & F. M. Martinson (Eds.), *Children and sex. New findings, new perspectives* (pp. 9-19). Boston: Little, Brown and Company.

Elias, J., & Gebhard, P. H. (1974). Sexuality and sexual learning in childhood. In R. Rogers (Ed.), *Sexual education - rationale and reaction* (pp. 143-154). London: Cambridge University Press.

Emmerich, W., Goldman, K. S., & Sharabany, R. (1977). Evidence for a transitional phase in the development of gender constancy. *Child Development, 48*, 930-936.

Finkelhor, D. (1981). Sex between siblings: sex play, incest, and aggression. In L. L. Constantine & F. M. Martinson (Eds.), *Children and sex: New findings, new perspectives* (pp. 129-149). Boston: Little, Brown and Company.

Finkelhor, D. (1984). *Child sexual abuse. New theory and research*. New York: The Free Press.

Fraley, M. C., Nelson, E. C., Wolf, A. W., & Lozoff, B. (1991). Early genital naming. *Developmental and Behavioral Pediatrics, 12*, 301-305.

Frasch, H., & Grüninger, W. (1975). Das Sexualwissen von Schulanfängern - Ein empirischer Beitrag zur Sexualpädogogik. *Medien und Sexualpädagogik, 3*, 1-5.

Freud, S. (1907). *Zur sexuellen Aufklärung der Kinder* (Gesammelte Werke Bd. 7). Frankfurt: Fischer 1966.

Fries, M. E. (1959). Review of the literature on the latency period. In M. Levitt (Ed.), *Readings in psychoanalytic psychology*. New York: Appleton.

Friedrich, W. N. (1993). Sexual victimization and sexual behavior in children: A review of recent literature. *Child Abuse and Neglect, 17*, 69-66.

Friedrich, W. N., Beilke, R. L., & Urquiza, A. J. (1988). Behavior problems in young sexually abused boys. *Journal of Interpersonal Violence, 3*, 21-28.

Friedrich, W. N., Grambsch, P., Broughton, D., Kuiper, J., & Beilke, R. L. (1991). Normative sexual behavior in children. *Pediatrics, 88*, 456-464.

Friedrich, W. N., Grambsch, P., Damon, L., Hewitt, S. K., Koverola, C., Lang, R. A., Wolfe, V. & Broughton, D. (1992). Child Sexual Behavior Inventory: Normative and clinical comparisons. *Psychological Assessment, 4*, 303-311.

Gagnon, J. H. (1985). Attitudes and responses of parents to pre-adolescent masturbation. *Archives of Sexual Behavior, 14*, 451-466.

Galenson, E. (1990). Observation of early infantile sexual and erotic development. In M. E. Perry (Ed.), *Handbook of sexology: Vol. 7. Childhood and adolescent sexology* (pp. 169-179). Amsterdam: Elsevier.

Galenson, E., & Roiphe, H. (1974). The emergence of genital awareness during the second year of life. In R. C. Friedman, R. M. Richard, & R. L. van Wiele (Eds.), *Sex differences in behavior*. New York: Wiley.

Galenson, E., & Roiphe, H. (1979). Development of sexual identity: Discovery and implications. In T. B. Karasu & C. W. Socarides (Eds.), *On sexuality: Psychoanalytic implications* (pp. 1-28). New York: International Universities Press.

Gebhard, P. H. (1977). The acquisition of basic sex information. *Journal of Sex Research, 13*, 148-169.

Gesell, A. (1940). *The first five years of life*. London: Methuen.

Giese, H., & Schmidt, G. (1968). *Studenten-Sexualität. Verhalten und Einstellung*. Reinbek: Rowohlt.

Goldman, R., & Goldman, J. (1982). *Children's sexual thinking*. London: Routledge and Kegan Paul.

Goldman, R., & Goldman, J. (1983). Children's perceptions of sex differences in babies and adolescents: A cross-national study. *Archives of Sexual Behavior, 12*, 277-294.

Goldman, R., & Goldman, J. (1988). *Show me yours: What children think about sex*. London: Penguin Books.

Gordon, B. N., Schroeder, C. S., & Abrams, M. (1990a). Age and social-class differences in children's knowledge of sexuality. *Journal of Clinical Child Psychology, 19*, 33-43.

Gordon, B. N., Schroeder, C. S., & Abrams, M. (1990b). Children's knowledge of sexuality: A comparison of sexually abused and nonabused children. *American Journal of Orthopsychiatry, 60*, 250-257.

Grassel, H., & Bach, K. (Hrsg.) (1979). *Kinder- und Jugendsexualität*. Berlin: Deutscher Verlag der Wissenschaften.

Grassel, H., & Bosinski, H. (1983). Sexualwissen und Geschlechterrollen-Vorstellungen bei Vorschulkindern. *Ärztliche Jugendkunde, 74*, 110-120.

Gunderson, B. H., Melas, P. S., & Skar, J. E. (1981). Sexual behavior of pre-school children. In L. L. Constantine & F. M. Martinson (Eds.), *Children and sex. New findings, new perspectives* (pp. 45-61). Boston: Little, Brown and Company.

Hattendorf, K. W. (1932). A study of questions of young children. *Journal of Social Psychology, 3*, 37-65.

Hibbard, R. A., & Hartman, G. L. (1992). Behavioral problems in alleged sexual abuse victims. *Child Abuse and Neglect, 16*, 755-762.

Hoch, Z., Kubat, H., Fisher, M., & Brandes, J. M. (1978). Background and sexual experience of Israeli medical students. *Archives of Sexual Behavior, 7*, 429-441.

Isaacs, S. (1933). *Social development in young children*. London: Routledge and Kegan Paul.

Jackson, S. (1982). *Childhood and sexuality*. Oxford: Basil Blackwell.

Janus, S. S., & Bess, B. E. (1976). Latency: Fact or fiction? *The American Journal of Psychoanalysis, 36*, 339-346.

Kinsey, A. C., Pomeroy, W. B., & Martin C. E. (1948). *Sexual behavior in the human male*. Philadelphia: W. B. Saunders.

Kinsey, A. C., Pomeroy, W. B., Martin, C. E., & Gebhard, P. H. (1953). *Sexual behavior in the human female*. Philadelphia: W. B. Saunders.

Kleeman, J. A. (1965). A boy discovers his penis. *Psychoanalytic Study of the Child, 20*, 239-266.

Kleeman, J. A. (1966). Genital discovery during a boy's second year: A follow-up. *Psychoanalytic Study of the Child, 21*, 358-392.

Kleeman, J. A. (1971). The establishment of core gender identity in normal girls. *Archives of Sexual Behavior, 1*, 117-147.

Kolko, D. J., & Moser, J. T. (1988). Behavioral/emotional indicators of child sexual abuse in child psychiatric inpatients: A controlled comparison with physical abuse. *Child Abuse and Neglect, 12*, 529-241.

Kreitler, H., & Kreitler, S. (1966). Children's concepts of sexuality and birth. *Child Development, 37*, 363-378.

La Fontaine, J. (1990). *Child Sexual Abuse*. Cambridge: Polity Press.

Langfeldt, T. (1981). Process in sexual development. In L. L. Constantine & F. M. Martinson (Eds.), *Children and sex. New findings, new perspectives* (pp. 63-72). Boston: Little, Brown and Company.

Langfeldt, T. (1990). Early childhood and juvenile sexuality, development and problems. In M. E. Perry (Ed.), *Handbook of sexology: Vol. 7. Childhood and adolescent sexology* (pp. 179-200). Amsterdam/New York: Elsevier.

Lehman, H. C., & Witty, P. A. (1927). *The psychology of play-activities*. New York: Barnes.

Lewis, W. C. (1965). Coital movements in the first year of life. *International Journal of Psychoanalytics*, *46*, 372-374.

Löwe, B. (1981). Das Sexualkundliche Vorwissen von Schülern der Eingangsstufe der Grundschule - eine Pilotstudie an nordbadischen Grundschülern. In N. Kluge (Hrsg.), *Sexualpädagogische Forschung* (S. 59-88). Paderborn: Schöningh.

Malinowski, J. S. (1979). Answering a child's questions about sex and a new baby. *American Journal of Nursing*, *11*, 1965-1968.

Martinson, F. M. (1977). Eroticism in childhood: A sociological perspective. In E. K. Oremland & J. D. Oremland (Eds.), *The sexual and gender development of young children: The role of the educator* (pp. 73-82). Cambridge: Ballinger Publishing Company.

Martinson, F. M. (1980). Childhood sexuality. In B. B. Wolman & J. Money (Eds.) *Handbook of human sexuality*. Englewood Cliffs, NJ: Prentice Hall.

Misgeld, G. (1978). Die Entwicklung des Sexuellen im Kindesalter. In. H. Szewczyk & H. Burghardt (Hrsg.), *Sexualität* (S. 131-140). Berlin: Verlag Volk und Gesundheit.

Moore, J. E., & Kendall, D. C. (1971). Children's concepts of reproduction. *Journal of Sex Research*, *7*, 42-61.

Newson, J., & Newson, E. (1963). *Patterns of infant care in an urban community*. London: Allen & Unwin.

Newson, J., & Newson, E. (1968). *Four years old in an urban community*. London: Allen and Unwin.

Ramsey, C.V. (1943a). The sexual development of boys. *American Journal of Psychology*, *56*, 217-33.

Ramsey, C.V. (1943b). The sex information of younger boys. *American Journal of Orthopsychiatry*, *13*, 347-352.

Ripley, D. C., Burns, C., & Dickinson, V. A. (1974), Sexual knowledge and attitudes in Borehamwood. In R. Rogers (Ed.), *Sexual education - rationale and reaction* (pp. 155-167). London: Cambridge University Press.

Rosenfeld, A., Bailey, R., Siegel, B., & Bailey, G. (1986). Determining incestuous contact between parent and child: Frequency of children touching parents' genitals in a nonclinical population. *Journal of the American Academy of Child Psychiatry*, *25*, 481-484.

Rutter, M. (1971). Normal psychosexual development. *Journal of Child Psychology and Psychiatry*, *11*, 259-283.

Rutter, M. (1980). Psychosexual development. In M. Rutter (Ed.), *Scientific foundations of developmental psychiatry* (pp. 322-339). London: Heinemann Medical Books Ltd.

Sears, R. E., Maccoby, E. E., & Levin, H. (1957). *Patterns of child rearing*. New York: Harper and Row.

Schoof-Tams, K., Schlaegel, H., & Walczak, L. (1976). Differentiation of sexual morality between 11 and 16 years. *Archives of Sexual Behavior*, *5*, 353-370.

Schuhrke, B. (1991). *Körperentdecken und psychosexuelle Entwicklung*. Regensburg: S. Roderer Verlag.

Slaby, R. G., & Frey, K. S. (1975). Development of gender constancy and selective attention to same-sex models. *Child Development*, *46*, 849-856.

Spitz, R. A., & Wolf, K. M. (1949). Autoerotism: Some empirical findings and hypotheses on three of its manifestations in the first year of life. *This Annual*, *3/4*, 85-120.

Thompson, S. K., & Bentler, P. M. (1971). The priority of cues in sex discrimination by children and adults. *Developmental Psychology*, *5*, 181-185.

Thompson, S. K., & Bentler, P. M. (1973). A developmental study of gender constancy and parent preference. *Archives of Sexual Behavior*, *2*, 379-385.

Thornburg, H. D. (1985). Sex information as primary prevention. *Journal of Sex Education and Therapy*, *11*, 22-27.

Victor, J. S. (1980). *Human sexuality: A social psychological approach*. Englewood Cliffs: Prentice-Hall.

Volbert, R. & Buffing (in preparation). Sexual knowledge of pre-school children. Manuscript in preparation.

White, S., Halpin, B. M., Strom, G. A., & Santelli, G. (1988). Behavioral comparisons of young sexually abused, neglected and non-referred children. *Journal of Clinical Child Psychology*, *17*, 53-61.

Wurtele, S. K., & Miller, C. L. (1987). Children's conceptions of sexual abuse. *Journal of Clinical Child Psychology*, *16*, 184-191.

Zanden, A. P. van der (1992). Seksuel gedrag van kinderen: een literatuuroverzicht. *Tijdschrift voor Ontwikkelingspsychologie*, *19*, 133-155.

Sex, Lies and Video Tape

Richard Kemp, Nicola Towell, Carol Pearson, Donna Wright, Paul Donnelly, Justine Woods and David Milner

Introduction

Studying the use of video technology in courtroom proceedings is particularly important given recent changes in the British legal system. The 1988 Criminal Justice Act has made provision for children to give evidence via a "Videolink" in certain types of case, and in August 1992, the Lord Chancellor's Office welcomed the announcement that Scotland is to allow the televising of court cases. This has given rise to speculation that England and Wales will follow suit shortly. Davies and Noon (1992) have studied the introduction of Videolinks and have reached broadly favourable conclusions. It seems that the introduction of video-taped evidence is likely to ease the emotional strain on a distressed witness. Further evidence suggests no great disadvantages for videotaped over live presentations; no differences have been found in juror's verdicts, damage awards, retention of trial related information, perceptions of attorneys, juror's interest or motivations, or juror's perceptions of witnesses (e.g. Farmer, Williams, Lee, Cundick, Howell and Rooker, 1976; Miller, Bender, Boster, Florence, Fontes, Hocking and Nicholson, 1975; Juhnke, Vought, Pyszcynski, Dane, Losure and Wrightsman, 1979).

However, there is evidence from studies of communication that information retention is a function of the mode of presentation (e.g. Furnham, Benson and Gunter, 1987). It has been suggested that this effect might be due to changes in the level of interest in the subject. Importantly, Kaminski and Miller (1984) suggest that there is a positive relationship between juror's interest and information retention. It has also been shown that jurors will spend more time discussing, and will be more positively inclined toward, evidence presented on video (Thompson, 1989).

Armstrong (1976) and Grant (1987) have expressed concerns over whether different styles of video presentation will affect jurors' abilities to assess witness credibility. Miller et al. (1975), reported no substantial differences between split screen and full screen presentations, although jurors seeing monochromatic presentations recalled more detail than witnesses seeing colour presentations. Kaminski and Miller (1984) suggested that camera angle had no direct effect on jurors' perceptions of witnesses composure, credibility and degree of authoritarianism or on jurors' retention of trial related information.

One consequence of allowing video technology into courtrooms was recently seen in America when William Kennedy Smith's trial for sexual battery was broadcast live on television. The identity of Smith's alleged victim was masked in the television pictures, as can be seen in photographs 1 and 2. Comparing the masked and unmasked images of the witness giving evidence, it is striking how the images are qualitatively different, with the masked image lacking much of the emotional impact of the unmasked image.

Photographs One and Two Showing the Unmasked and Masked Faces of a Real Witness

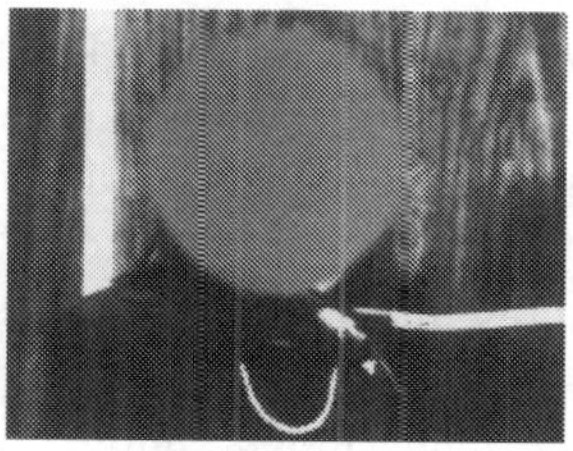

If video is to be used in legal proceedings there is a need to demonstrate two points. First, that its use will not alter the jurors' interpretations of the evidence; and secondly that any procedures adopted to mask the identity of a witness do not unduly affect either the jurors' perceptions of the witness or their recall of the testimony. The following experiments investigated these issues.

Experiment 1: A Comparison of Live and Video-taped Testimonies

The first study investigated the effect of four different modes of presentation of evidence on mock-jurors' immediate and delayed recall of trial related information.

Design and procedure Seventy-six undergraduate students studying at the University of Westminster acted as subjects. The 45 female subjects and 31 male subjects had a mean age of just under 23 years. All subjects were exposed to the testimony of an eyewitness to a minor mugging incident. One group of subjects watched a live enactment of the witness giving evidence; a second group watched a video recording of the enactment; a third group heard only the sound recording; while a fourth group read a typed transcript of the enactment. The recall of half the subjects in each group was tested immediately while the other half were tested one week later.

Results and discussion Analysis of the results showed no significant effect of mode of presentation. However, the main effects of delay and emotionality were significant. Subjects recalled less after the delay of one week ($F_{1,68} = 38.93$, $p<0.01$) and recalled more of the emotionally-charged details ($F_{1,68} = 30.97$, $p<0.01$). It was also found that subjects expressed no difference in how interesting they found the four modes of presentation.

These results seem to be in broad agreement with previous studies (e.g. Farmer et al., 1976; Miller et al., 1975; Juhnke et al., 1979), showing no obviously deleterious effects of varying the mode of presentation of evidence.

Experiments 2 and 3: Protecting the Identity of a Witness

Studying the pictures from the "Kennedy Smith rape trial" reproduced above would seem to suggest that masking the identity of a witness will affect our perception of that witness. In experiments 2 and 3, the effects of identity masking were investigated.

Design and procedure In the following studies, a "witness" was video-taped whilst recounting her evidence of an assault. Three versions of this evidence were prepared; in one the witness was seen unmasked, in the second her face was obscured by a "moving blob" and in a third the area of her face was obscured by a matrix of squares (pixelated). These three conditions are shown in photographs 3, 4 and 5.

Fifty-four undergraduate students at the University of Westminster acted as subjects. The 25 male subjects and 29 female subjects had an average age of about 23 years, and were equally distributed amongst three experimental conditions. They watched one of the three videos of the eyewitness's account of a fight in a pub and were then asked to read through a written statement supposedly presented by the accused and contradictory to the evidence on the video. Finally the subjects were presented with a questionnaire containing 13 questions about the subjects' perceptions of the credibility of the eye-witness's account, and 18 questions designed to test their recall of the details of the account given on the video.

Photographs Three, Four and Five Showing the Modes of Presentation Used in Experiments Two and Three

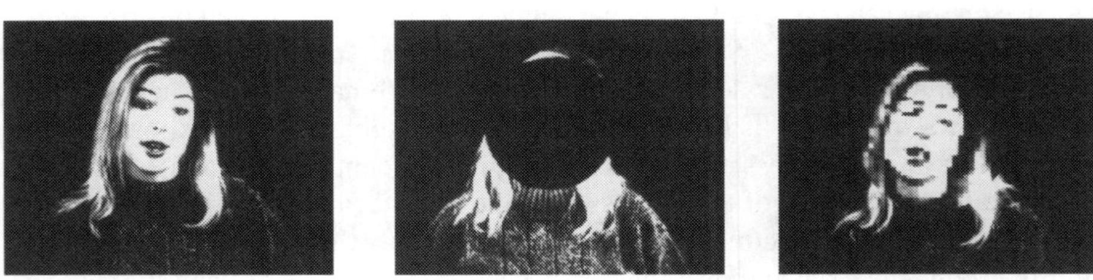

Results and discussion It was predicted that in the masked conditions the subjects would see the witness as less credible. While an overall assessment of the credibility of the witness did not significantly differ between the three masking conditions, two of the questions did reach significance. Both of these were quite specific questions: *Do you believe that the only time the speaker had met Tony, before that night, was once, when he sold her brother his car?* ($F_{2,51} = 4.12$, $p<.05$). *Do you think that the "victim" on the tape could have purposely left any details out?* ($F_{2,51} = 3.53$, $p<.05$) (see Figure 1).

The questions were directed at three different aspects of credibility, namely, how truthful the eye-witness was thought to be, how convincing she sounded, and the extent that she was thought to be telling the whole truth. In all three masking conditions, the mean for the "convincing" dimension was considerably higher than for either the "truthfulness" or "whole truth" dimension. In other words, regardless of mode of presentation, the subjects tended to see the witness as highly convincing but not telling the truth! These trends in the data seem to underline the difficulty in adequately measuring a complex construct like witness credibility.

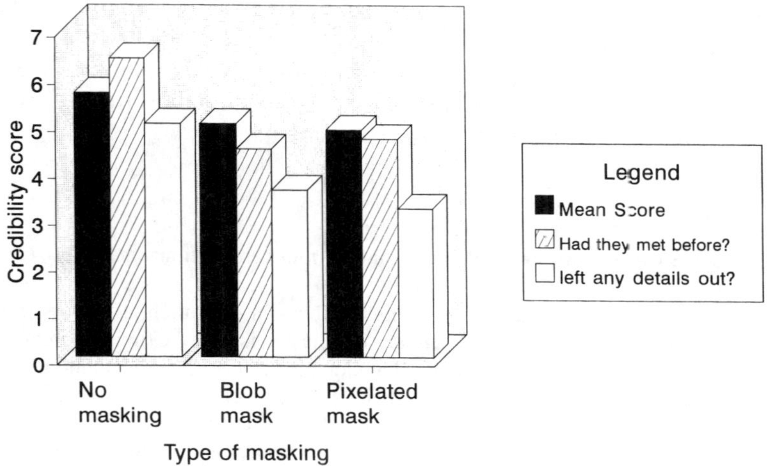

Figure 1. Witness Credibility by Type of Masking (Experiment 2).

It was also predicted that subjects' recall of the information contained in the original eye witness account would be impaired by masking the witness. In support, analysis showed that recall was significantly better in the unmasked condition than in either of the other two conditions ($F_{2,51} = 11.38$, $p<.05$). Subjects were also asked to rate how confident they were in the response they gave to each question. The confidence level was significantly higher for the unmasked condition ($F_{2,51} = 5.28$, $p<.05$), indicating that masking the identity of the witness depresses both jurors' memory and their confidence in their memory (see Figure 2).

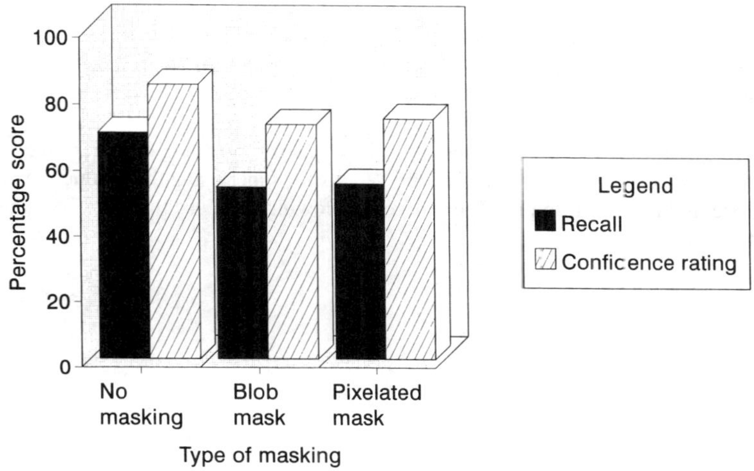

Figure 2. Recall and Confidence in Recall by Type of Masking (Experiment 3).

Conclusion

These findings suggest that there are no adverse consequences of permitting videotaped evidence in terms of the jurors' recall of the evidence. There may, however, be serious consequences when masking the identity of a witness on both the jurors' recall of information and their perception of the witness's credibility. Future research will attempt to replicate these findings by presenting testimonies from genuine eyewitnesses, as opposed to enacted eye-witness accounts.

References

Armstrong, J. J. (1976). The criminal videotape trial: Serious constitutional questions. *Oregon Law Review*, *55*, 567-585.

Davies, G., & Noon, E. (1992, March). Videolinks: Their impact on child witness trials. Paper presented at the 2nd Annual Conference for the Division of Criminological and Legal Psychology of The British Psychological Society, Harrogate, United Kingdom.

Farmer, L. C., Williams, G. R., Lee, R. E., Cundick, B. P., Howell, R. J., & Rooker, C. K. (1976). Juror perceptions of trial testimony as a function of the method of presentation. In G. Bermant, C. Nemeth, & N. Vidmar (Eds.), *Psychology and the law*. (pp. 209-237). Lexington, Mass: D.C. Heath & Co.

Furnham, A., Benson, I., & Gunter, B., (1987). Memory for television commercials as a function of the channel of communication. *Social Behaviour*, *2*, 105-112.

Grant, J. P. (1987). Face - to television screen - to face: Testimony by closed-circuit television in cases of alleged child abuse and the confrontation right. *Kentucky Law Review*, *76*, 273-299.

Juhnke, R., Vought, C., Pyszczynski, T. A., Dane, F. C., Losure, B. D., & Wrightsman, L. S. (1979). Effects of presentation mode upon jurors' reactions to a trial. *Personality and Social Psychology Bulletin*, *5*, 36-39.

Kaminski, E. P., & Miller, G. R. (1984). How jurors respond to videotaped witnesses. *Journal of Communication*, *34*, 88-102.

Miller, G. R., Bender, D. C., Boster, F., Florence, B. T., Fontes, N., Hocking, J., & Nicholson, H. (1975). The effects of videotape testimony in jury trials: Studies on juror decision making, information retention and emotional arousal. *Brigham Young University Law Review*, 331-373.

Thompson, D. M. (1989). Video recorded evidence: Psychological and legal issues. Paper Presented at the Police Powers Conference of the Society for the Reform of the Criminal Law, Sydney, Australia.

We would like to acknowledge the assistance of Janet Lewis for playing the part of the eye-witness in experiments 2 and 3, Tony Kerr and Edward Woods for supervising the production of the video films, and Stefan Sargent of Spitfire Television for allowing us to use the stills from the Kennedy Smith Rape Trial.

Detection of False Statements in First and Third Graders: The Development of a Nonverbal Detection Instrument

Aldert Vrij and Frans W. Winkel

Introduction

Interaction processes between interviewers and interviewees are not constrained to a verbal exchange of information. There will always be an exchange of information on the basis of the nonverbal behavior displayed by the parties as well (Vrij, 1991; Vrij & Winkel, 1991). Verbal information refers to the content of the interview, nonverbal information refers to the way the spoken information is presented: the gestures that accompany speech, head movements, trunk movements, gaze aversion, smiling, variation of pitch of voice, speech rate, speech disturbances (repetions of words, omissions of words) etc.

Therefore, in order to detect false statements of children three different types of detection instruments are possible: a "verbal detection instrument" (referring to the analysis of the verbal content of statements), a "nonverbal detection instrument" (referring to the analysis of nonverbal behavior displayed by children) and a "combination instrument" (referring to the analysis of both verbal and nonverbal information). Social psychological literature revealed several verbal detection instruments (Gardner, 1987; Steller, 1989; Undeutsch, 1989; Wegener, 1989; Yuille & Cutshall, 1989), although nonverbal detection instruments and combination instruments are not available yet.

Nowadays the "Statement Validity Assessment" (SVA) and the "Criteria Based Content Analysis" (CBCA) (Steller, 1989) are most often used. Both instruments refer to the analysis of the verbal content of a given statement using a set of defined criteria like the logical structure of the statements, the amount of unusual and superfluous details, the amount of spontaneous corrections etc. However, it is striking that empirical research on the ecological validity of these instruments is lacking (Wakefield, Underwager, Rossen, & Legrand, 1992). An exception is the study conducted by Lamers-Winkelman and Buffing (1992). They used the SVA-instrument in their research on sexually abused children in the Netherlands. Their (preliminary) results showed that the SVA-instrument failed to differentiate between true and false statements.

Nonverbal detection instruments and/or combination detection instruments are alternatives for (or completion of) the verbal instrument. There is very little research on nonverbal indicators of false statements in children. But the two studies we know do indicate nonverbal indicators. Lewis, Stranger and Sullivan (1989) showed that a false statement given by three year old children was associated by an increase in nervous touching. A study conducted by Feldman, Devin-Sheehan and Allen (1978) revealed, that telling untrue stories by third graders was associated with less smiling and longer pauses. However, many (social psychological) studies are conducted concerning nonverbal indicators of false statements in adults. Recent reviews (DePaulo, 1992; Ekman, 1989; Vrij, 1991) showed that false statements are associated with an increase in speech disturbances, changes in pitch of voice, a longer latency period (the period of silence between question and answer) and a decrease in movements (in particular hand movements). The control hypothesis and the cognitive hypothesis offer a possible explanation.

In the control approach (DePaulo & Kirkendol, 1989; Ekman, 1988) it is stated that expressing false statements is a stressful experience. Stress as a result of guilt, as a result of being aware of doing things which one is not allowed to do, or stress as a result of fear (fear of being caught). Therefore, while expressing false statements people tend to behave nervously. Indicators of nervous behavior include a high pitched voice, gaze aversion, smiling and liveliness (many hand and arm movements, self manipulations, trunk movements, foot and leg movements). However, people realize that those patterns of nonverbal behavior create an uncredible impression. For that reason, they are willing to control themselves and they want to behave as "natural" as possible. Therefore, they have to suppress nervous behavior. Interestingly, individuals can control certain parts of their body better than other parts. As a result some behaviors will betray false statements or - in terms of Ekman and Friesen (1974) - are leaking channels. People can not control their voice and speech very well. Therefore, hiding the truth results in changes in pitch of voice and in an increase in speech disturbances. It is difficult to control movements. When controlling their movements people tend to overcontrol them, which leads to inhibition of movements.

In the cognitive approach (Burgoon, Kelly, Newton, & Keely-Dyreson, 1989; Goldman-Eisler, 1968; Köhnken, 1989) it is stated that expressing false statements is a cognitive complexity. Presumably it is more difficult to fabricate a plausible and convincing false statement than it is to give a true statement. There is evidence to suggest that people engaging in cognitively complex tasks take longer to begin their response and speak more hesitantly once they do begin speaking (Goldman-Eisler, 1968).

The control approach implies that there may be differences in leaking channels between adults and children. This approach requires clear insight into how interviewees' nonverbal behavior will be interpreted by interviewers. Interviewees have to adopt the interviewer's viewpoint. Flavell and his associates have referred to this ability as "taking the role of the other" (Flavell, Botkin, Fry, Wright, & Jarvis, 1968).

Young children (up to six years) tend to be self-centered. Generally, they have great difficulty adopting another person's viewpoint. The ability seems to develop from the age of seven years (DePaulo & Jordan, 1982; Morency & Krauss, 1982; Saarni, 1982).

Based upon the foregoing, we hypothesized that expressing false statements by younger children (five and six years old) will be associated with a longer latency period and nervous behavior (like gaze aversion, smiling, many speech disturbances, changes in pitch of voice, and many movements). The nonverbal behavior indicators of false statements in older children (eight or nine years old) will highly correspond with the nonverbal indicators in adults (longer latency period, changes in pitch of voice, many speech disturbances and a decrease of movements). Therefore, we expect main effects of false statements with a longer latency period, changes in pitch of voice and more speech disturbances; and age by false statements interactions whereby younger children (five and six years old) show an increase in hand and arm movements while expressing false statements and older children (eight or nine years old) show a decrease in hand and arm movements. The increase could be attributed to arousal, the decrease could be attributed to overcontrol.

In the second study children tasted a bad drink (grapefruit juice) and a good drink (orange juice). This is the "classical" procedure derived from Feldman and White (1980). However, this procedure has a very experimental character and has hardly anything to do with regular interview situations. Therefore, in the first study, we used a procedure which a higher ecological validity: we asked children a leading or misleading question about a witnessed event.

Study 1

Method

Subjects A total of 39 boys and 30 girls participated in the study. Their average age was M=6 years and 9 months (SD=1.6). Thirty nine children were five or six years old (first graders), and 30 children were eight or nine years old (third graders).

Procedure The study was conducted in schools. The experimenter informed each class that they were going to watch a short videotape. The children were brought one by one into the interview room. A video fragment was then shown, following which the experimenter asked the child's opinion of the short movie. However, before the child could respond, the experimenter reported that she had to leave, but another woman (the interviewer) would like to discuss the videotape. The experimenter brought the child to the interviewer in a near-by classroom. The interviewer asked the child to repeat the content of the videotape as best as he/she could. Subsequently, the child was asked a leading or misleading question. All interviews were videotaped. On the videotapes the children were completely visible.

Interviewing the children was very strenuous. Therefore, the interviews were conducted by two interviewers. In order to determine the impact of the factor "interviewer" on the results, we included this factor in our design.

Content of the video fragment The video fragment lasted 61 seconds. A child, called Pippi, did several things which she was not allowed to do. As a result, a father of a girl-friend became angry at her.

Independent variables In our experiment two independent variables were manipulated, namely "interviewer style" and "question". The interviewer style is already introduced. The first interviewer took charge of 24 interviews, the second interviewer conducted 45 interviews.

The "question" was manipulated by asking a leading question ("Why did the father become angry at Pippi?", N=32 interviews) or a misleading question ("Why did the father beat Pippi?", N=37 interviews). The leading question will be used as a "control question". In order to determine nonverbal indicators of expressing false statements a comparison will be made between the children who agree with the misleading question (N=21 children) and the children who correctly answered the leading question (N=32 children).

Dependent variables First of all, we determined the verbal content of the answers given by the children. Moreover, the nonverbal behavior displayed by the children while answering the (mis)leading question was scored in detail by two independent coders. The average time of these answers was 12 seconds. After scoring the videotapes the coders compared their observations. The scoring was carried out once again if they disagreed substantially. Substantial differences were found (in 10% of the cases) with regard to head, trunk and foot/leg movements. Scoring was based upon scoring systems developed by Vrij (1991) and Vrij and Winkel (1991). The following 11 patterns of nonverbal behavior were scored:

(1) the frequency of *spoken words* (inclusive the ah- and non-ah speech disturbances);

(2) the frequency of *changes in pitch of voice*: the frequency of pitch raises and pitch falls;

(3) the frequency of *ah-speech disturbances*: the frequency of ahs;

4) the frequency of *non-ah speech disturbances*: the frequency of repetitions of words, omissions and corrections (the speech disturbances were scored on the basis of a typed verbatim text);

(5) *latency-period*: the period of silence beteen question and answer. Latency period was scored using a 5 point scale, varying from (1) very short to (5) very long;

(6) *gaze aversion*: the frequency of seconds the child did not look at the face of the interviewer;

(7) the frequency of *smiling and laughing*;

(8) the frequency of *hand and arm movements*. Simultaneous movements of hands and arms are scored as one movement, continuing movements were scored every two seconds;

(9) the frequency of *head movements*: the frequency of head nods and head shakes;

(10) the frequency of *trunk movements*. Trunk movements included clearly visible movements of the trunk (backward, forward or sideward);

(11) the frequency of *foot/leg movements*. Simultaneous movements of feet and legs are scored as one movement, continuing movements were scored every two seconds.

The reported duration and frequency of all categories of nonverbal behavior were corrected for the length of the answers or for the number of spoken words: "changes in pitch of voice" to "non-ah speech disturbances" were calculated per ten words, "gaze aversion" to "foot/leg movements" per one minute of answering.

Results

All 32 children answering the "leading question" gave a correct answer. A total of 21 out of the 37 children answering the "misleading question" agreed with this question. This implies that their answers were false. The other 16 children (ten first graders and six third graders) answered "I don't know" or told the interviewer that the father did not beat the child. This implies that their answers were true. Therefore, they are excluded from the analyses.[1] Five children of the remaining 53 children were excluded from the analyses as well, because of a bad quality of the videotapes, due to technical problems whilst recording these children.

A MANOVA was conducted in order to examine the extent to which the nonverbal behavior displayed by the children derives information about the falsity of their statements. A 2 (question: leading or misleading) X 2 (interviewer: A or B) X 2 (age: first graders or third graders) factorial design was used. Dependent variables were the 11 categories of nonverbal behavioral patterns. At a multivariate level the analysis revealed one significant effect, namely a significant "question X age" interaction effect $F(11,30) = 2.34$, $p < .05$. At a univariate level a significant effect occurred for hand and arm movements, $F(1,40) = 10.74$, $p < .01$ and marginal effects occurred for head movements, $F(1,40) = 3.59$, $p <.07$ and gaze aversion, $F(1,40) = 3.55$, $p <.07$. Answering the misleading question resulted in an increase in hand and arm movements (M=48.42 versus M=33.66) and head movements (M=24.48 versus M=18.48) in first graders and in a decrease in hand and arm movements (M=25.05 versus M=48.15) and head movements (M=10.62 versus M=18.24) in third graders. Answering the misleading question resulted in an increase in gaze aversion (M=34.79 versus M=19.56) in first graders while no difference emerged in gaze aversion between the two questions in third graders. All these results confirm the hypothesis.

At a multivariate level no significant effect emerged concerning the factor "question", $F(11,30) = 1.48$, n.s. However, we hypothesized several specific effects at a univariate level. Therefore, inspection of the univariate tests seems to be justified. As we hypothesized univariate tests showed a longer latency period in the misleading condition (M=2.67 versus M=1.69), $F(1,40) = 13.22$, $p <.001$.

Discussion

Results strongly underline the expectations. Expressing false statements was associated with nervous behavior (gaze aversion, many hand, arm and head movements) in first graders, third graders (over)controlled those behaviors.

Both first and third graders showed a longer latency period while answering the misleading question. There are three possible explanations. Firstly, the creation of a false statement is a more difficult task than recalling a certain event. Therefore, they had to think more about their answer, resulting in a longer latency period. Another possibility is, that children used the latency period to realize what was happening. Perhaps they asked themselves whether or not the present question was a misleading question, for they had no reasons to believe that the interviewer would deliberately ask a misleading question. Thirdly, the latency period could be used to formulate their strategy: to agree or disagree with the misleading question.

The expectations with regard to ah- and non-ah speech disturbances and changes in pitch of voice were not confirmed. The absence of a "speech disturbances effect" is possible due to the fact that the childrens' answers were very short. The occurrence of speech disturbances is more likely in extensive answers (Köhnken, 1989). The absence of a "pitch of voice effect" is possible due to our scoring method, which was not very punctual. In some research very small differences (a few hertz) were found between deception and speaking the truth (Scherer, 1986).

Study 2

Method

Subjects A total of 34 boys and 29 girls participated in the study. Their average age was M=6.78 years (SD=1.6). There were 36 five to six year olds (first graders), and 27 children were 8 or 9 years old (third graders).

Procedure and independent variables The study was conducted in schools. Each child tasted two drinks, grapefruit juice and orange juice. After each drink they were requested to convince the interviewer that both drinks tasted good, regardless of how the drinks actually tasted. The order in which the drinks were sampled was random. A camera (which could be seen by the children) recorded the child. After both interviews were completed, the children were asked about their true opinions of the two drinks.

Dependent variables The nonverbal behavior displayed by the children was scored by two independent coders. Both recordings of each child (lasting five seconds each) were observed simultaneously. The following ten patterns of nonverbal behavior were observed: leg/foot movements, self manipulations, hand and arm movements, trunk movements, head movements, gaze aversion, smiling/laughing, latency period, intonations and pitch of voice. Coders indicated for each category of nonverbal behavior the difference between the two videotapes.[2] Answers were given in terms of "shorter", "no difference" and "longer" (concerning latency period), "lower", "no difference" and "higher" (concerning pitch of voice) and "more", "no difference" and "less" (concerning the other nonverbal behaviors). The interagreement between the two coders (determined with a Pearson correlation) was sufficient for each pattern of nonverbal behavior. Correlations varying from $r= .77$ to $r= .93$.

Finally, we determined if every child kept to the instruction and how they actually liked both drinks.

Results

In the experiment, all children answered correctly that they liked both drinks. After asking the true opinions about the drinks, 60 children answered that they actually liked the orange juice and that they actually disliked the grapefruit juice. The remaining 3 children actually liked both drinks: they were excluded from the analyses.

Loglinear analyses were conducted to determine if possible differences in nonverbal behavior caused by the two drinks were influenced by the age of the children and the order in which the drinks were sampled. In the design only nonverbal behavior X age and nonverbal behavior X order interactions were included. Analyses concerning behavior X age interactions revealed significant effects for hand and arm movements and self manipulations ($X^2(2) = 10.03$, $p <.01$ and $X^2(2) = 6.84$, $p <.05$ respectively), and marginal significant effects for leg/foot movements and latency period ($X^2(2) = 4.82$, $p <.09$ and $X^2(2) = 5.34$, $p <.07$ respectively). Percentages are shown in Table 1.

Table 1: Nonverbal behaviour displayed by first and third graders

When lying	**More**	**No difference**	**Less**
hand and arm movements			
- first graders	39%	58%	03%
- third graders	11%	67%	22%
selfmanipulations			
- first graders	03%	97%	00%
- third graders	04%	81%	15%
leg and foot movements			
- first graders	12%	85%	03%
- third graders	15%	65%	20%
When lying	**Longer**	**No difference**	**Shorter**
latency period			
- first graders	64%	18%	18%
- third graders	33%	38%	29%

Table 1 revealed that false statements (i.e. pretending to like a drink which actually tasted bad) resulted in an increase in movements in many first graders and in a decrease in movements in many third graders. Moreover, false statements were associated with a longer latency period in many first graders and with a shorter latency period in many third graders. These results confirm the hypothesis. No nonverbal behavior X order interactions occurred.

We inspected the frequency scores to determine if there were differences in nonverbal behavior caused by the two drinks. Noteworthy differences emerged with regard to intonations and pitch of voice. False statements were associated with less intonations (5% more, 58% no difference, 37% less intonations) and with a higher pitched voice (32% lower, 63% no difference, 5% higher pitch of voice). These results confirm our hypothesis. With regard to the other nonverbal behavioral patterns it can be said that the "more" and "less" ratio was almost 1:1 and that high percentages of subjects (at least 67%) were classified in the "no difference" category.

Discussion

Results showed that false statements (i.e. pretending to like a drink with in fact tasted bad) was associated with an increase in movements (in particular hand and arm movements) in first graders and with a decrease in movements in third graders. This corresponds to the results of the first study. One note has to be made. High percentages of children showed no differences in movements between the two conditions. But in our view, since the videotapes lasted very short (only five seconds), the observed percentages can be considered as relatively high, because the children hardly have the opportunity to express large nonverbal differences in such a short period.

The shorter latency period as a result of false statements in third graders seems to be interesting. A possible explanation is, that children realize that a longer latency period will betray their lie. Therefore, they try to answer as soon as possible. Ironically, though, it could be just this unusual quickness of responding that is giving them away. In this case, the shorter latency period refers to a (not very succesful) attempted control of this behavior. Since results revealed an increase in latency period in the first study, results concerning latency period are conflicting in both studies. There are three possible explanations. Perhaps, the cognitive complexity of the false statement in the first study prevented a quick response. Another explanation is, that in the first study the latency period was not caused by cognitive complexity. As already mentioned before, perhaps children in that study used the latency period to realize what happened or to formulate a strategy how to react. Also another explanation is that in the second study the children had already been told how to act (i.e. positively to the taste) so they rushed to do so.

Unlike the first study, this study revealed differences in intonation and pitch of voice. Perhaps this is caused by the scoring method used in this study which was more punctual than the method used in the first study.

Final Conclusion

The results of both studies correspond to each other. Apparently, there exist nonverbal indicators of false statements in children. But which indicators reveal information about the falsity of statements depends on the age of children. False statements in first graders were associated with a longer latency period and "nervous behavior", such as an increase in movements, changes in pitch of voice, and gaze aversion. False statements in third graders were associated with a shorter latency period, changes in pitch of voice and a decrease in movements. A possible explanation is, that they tried to control their behavior and that this attempted control was only partially succesful.

Finally, four remarks will be made. Firstly, in the first study it remained unclear if those 21 children who agreed with the misleading question realize that their answers were wrong. Unfortunately, we did not ask the children following this question if they believed that statement or if they were just agreeing with the interviewer. However, we tend to believe that the children knew that their answers were wrong. For the results of the first study did overlap substantially with the results of the second study, in which we were sure that the children expressed false statements.

Secondly, the observed differences in nonverbal behavior are based upon a punctual and detailed scoring system. Therefore, it is still unknown how strong (i.e. clearly visible) these nonverbal indicators are. For instance, are observers able to classify true and false statements of children by analyzing the nonverbal behavior displayed by these children? Previous studies (for instance Westcott, Davies, & Clifford, 1991) showed that for untrained observers it is very difficult to detect false statements. It is our intention to conduct such an "observer study" with experts in the near future.

Thirdly, the present studies only dealt with behavioral differences. Processes causing these differences (stress, role taking, (over)control) were not inventoried. It seems worthwile to pay more attention to those processes in future experimental research, for instance by asking children about the reasons of their behavior.

Fourthly, on the basis of the present studies we still do not know if the obtained nonverbal indicators of false statements are suitable in cases of child sexual abuse. But, results showed that indicators derived from an experimental study (study 2) are quite similar to indicators derived from a study with a higher ecological validity (study 1). Therefore, it seems useful to replicate this kind of research in the context of child sexual abuse. The results of the present studies can be used as a key to select those behaviors which are possibly relevant to indicate false statements. In our view such a selection of behaviors is necessary. Sexual abuse interviews usually take a long time and analyzing nonverbal behavior is very time-consuming. From a practical point of view analyzing the total of nonverbal behavior displayed by the children seems to be impossible.

References

Burgoon, J. K., Kelly, D. L., Newton, D. A., & Keely-Dyreson, M. P. (1989). The nature of arousal and nonverbal indices. *Human Communication Research, 16*, 217-255.

DePaulo, B. M. (1992). Nonverbal behavior and self-presentation. *Psychological Bulletin, 111*, 2033-243.

DePaulo, B. M., & Jordan, A. (1982). Age changes in deceiving and detecting deceit. In R. S. Feldman (Ed.), *Development of nonverbal behavior in children*. New York: Springer-Verlag.

DePaulo, B. M., & Kirkendol, S. E. (1989). The motivational impairment effect in the communication of deception. In J. C. Yuille (Ed.), *Credibility assessment*. Dordrecht: Kluwer Academic Publishers.

Ekman, P. (1988). Lying and nonverbal behavior: Theoretical issues and new findings. *Journal of Nonverbal Behavior, 12*, 163-176.

Ekman, P. (1989). Why lies fail and what behaviors betray a lie. In J. C. Yuille (Ed.), *Credibility assessment*. Dordrecht: Kluwer Academic Publishers.

Ekman, P., & Friesen, W. V. (1974). Detecting deception from the body or the face. *Journal of Personality and Social Psychology, 38*, 270-277.

Feldman, R. S., Devin-Sheehan, L., & Allen, V. L. (1978). Nonverbal cues as indicators of verbal dissembling. *American Educational Research Journal, 15*, 217-231.

Feldman, R. S., & White, J. B. (1980). Detecting deception in children. *Journal of Communication, 30*, 121-129.

Flavell, J. H., Botkin, P. T., Fry, C. K., Wright, J. C., & Jarvis, P. T. (1968). *The development of role-taking and communication skills in children*. New York: Wiley and Sons.

Gardner, R. A. (1987). *The parental alienation syndrome and the differentiation between fabricated and genuine child sex abuse*. Cresskill, New Jersey: Creative Therapeutics.

Goldman-Eisler, F. (1968). *Psycholinguistics: Experiments in spontaneous speech*. New York: Doubleday.

Köhnken, G. (1989). Behavioral correlates of statement credibility: Theories, paradigms and results. In H. Wegener, F. Lösel, & J. Haisch (Eds.), *Criminal behavior and the justice system: Psychological perspectives*. New York: Springer-Verlag.

Lamers-Winkelman, F., & Buffing, F. (1992, May). *The use of Statement Validity Assessment by interviewing sexual abused children in the Netherlands*. Poster presented at the NAVO Advanced Study Institute "The child witness in context: Cognitive, social and legal perspectives", Il Ciocco Resort, Tuscany, Italy.

Lewis, M., Stanger, C., & Sullivan, M. W. (1989). Deception in 3-year-olds. *Developmental Psychology*, *25*, 439-443.

Morency, N. L., & Krauss, R. M. (1982). Children's nonverbal encoding and decoding deceit. In R. S. Feldman (Ed.), *Development of nonverbal behavior in children*. New York: Springer-Verlag.

Saarni, C. (1982). Social and affective functions of nonverbal behavior: Developmental concerns. In R. S. Feldman (Ed.), *Development of nonverbal behavior in children*. New York: Springer-Verlag.

Scherer, K. R. (1986). Vocal affect expression: A review and a model for future research. *Psychological Bulletin*, *99*, 143-165.

Steller, M. (1989). Recent developments in statement analysis. In J. C. Yuille (Ed.), *Credibility assessment*. Dordrecht: Kluwer Academic Publishers.

Undeutsch, U. (1989). The development of statement reality analysis. In J. C. Yuille (Ed.), *Credibility assessment*. Dordrecht: Kluwer Academic Publishers.

Vrij, A. (1991). *Misverstanden tussen politie en allochtonen: Sociaal-psychologische aspecten van verdacht zijn*. Amsterdam: VU Uitgeverij (diss).

Vrij, A., & Winkel, F. W. (1991). Cultural patterns in Dutch and Surinam nonverbal behavior: An analysis of simulated police/ citizen encounters. *Journal of Nonverbal Behavior*, *15*, 169-184.

Wakefield, H., Underwager, R., Rossen, B., & Legrand, R. (1992). Ondervraging van kinderen. In B. Rossen & J. Schuijer (Eds.), *Het seksuele gevaar voor kinderen: Mythen en feiten*. Lisse: Swets en Zeitlinger.

Wegener, H. (1989). The present state of statement analysis. In J. C. Yuille (Ed.), *Credibility assessment*. Dordrecht: Kluwer Academic Publishers.

Westcott, H. L., Davies, G. M., & Clifford, B. R. (1991). Adults' perceptions of children's videotaped truthful and deceptive statements. *Children and Society*, *5*, 123-135.

Yuille, J. C., & Cutshall, J. (1989). Analysis of the statements of victims, witnesses and suspects. In J. C. Yuille (Ed.), *Credibility assessment*. Dordrecht: Kluwer Academic Publishers.

Notes

[1] Another possibility to determine nonverbal indicators of false statements was to make a comparison between the 21 children who agreed with the misleading question and the children 16 children who disagreed with the misleading question. However, this option has two disadvantages. Firstly, the verbal content of those two types of answers differ from each other. Therefore, differences in nonverbal behavior could be caused by those different verbal contents. Secondly, "don't know" type of answers are usually very short, and it is impossible to make reliable analyses of nonverbal behavior on the basis of very short answers.

We can not rule out the possibility that those who agreed with the misleading question may well have believed they were answering correctly. We refer to this issue later in the final discussion.

[2] The recordings were too short to score the frequency of nonverbal behavior.

The Analysis of Family Dynamics in Child Custody Cases

Herbert L. Collier

What is in the best interest of the child? Our court systems (with our help) ultimately determine custody in accordance with the best interests of the child. The court may consider all relevant factors including: (a) the wishes of the child's parent or parents as to custody; (b) the wishes of the child as to his or her custodian; (c) the interaction and interrelationship of the child with a parent or parents, siblings, and any other person who may significantly affect the child's best interest; (d) the child's adjustment to home, school, and community; (e) the mental and physical health and parenting capacity of the adults; (f) the special needs of the children; and (g) which parent is more likely to allow the child frequent and continuing contact with the non-custodial parent.

The court, in determining custodians, does not prefer a parent as custodian because of the parent's gender. In addition, the court considers evidence of domestic violence as being contrary to the best interest of the child.

Divorce is definitely not an occurrence but a process. Far too often the process extends from pre-separation conflict to post-decree warring. The period represents for most litigants the most psychologically and financially stressful, contentious, fearful, and often angry period of their lives to date. We recognize that 5%-10% of parents who are contesting custody and visitation sometimes display grossly inappropriate behaviors (referred to as "divorce crazies") further exacerbated by paradoxical no fault divorce laws combined with an adversarial legal process.

P. G. Wodehouse (1959), the English humorist, using his best understatement characterized "the worst thing about Americans is they are always getting divorced and causing unpleasantness" (p. 10). The fallout from this behavior often creates disastrous effects on children's psychological development described by Wallerstein (1989). Essentially, her findings (Wallerstein, 1991) suggest that there is a growing consensus that significant numbers of children suffer for many years from psychological and social difficulties associated with continuing or new stresses within the post-divorce family. They experience heightened anxiety in the form of enduring attachments at later developmental stages including young adulthood.

Hetherington, Stanley-Hagan and Anderson (1989) state, "although the adjustment of children is related to the adaptation and behavior of the parents, what may be a positive life situation or coping strategy for one family member is not necessarily salutary for other family members" (p. 303). It has been argued that behavior problems exhibited by children in remarried families are attributable not to difficulties in adapting to remarriage, but to stresses associated with divorce and life in a single-parent household (Furstenberg, 1988; Zill, 1988).

Much has been written about attachment and bonding of children and the importance of determining, if possible, the nature of the psychological bonds with each parent (Rohman, Sales, & Lon, 1987). Commentators have argued that the court should concentrate upon discovering the psychological parent of the child and award custody to that "parent" (Goldstein, Freud, & Solnit, 1979).

A psychological parent has been defined as "one who, on a continuing, day to day basis, through interplay, and mutuality, fulfills the child's psychological needs for a parent, as well as the child's physical needs" (Goldstein et al., 1979, p. 98). However, Rohman et al. (1987) suggest that psychological parenthood is essentially a theoretical construct that may not reflect the realities of parent/child relationship dynamics. Furthermore, the doctrine may be of little value in the context of "difficult" child custody cases. "Existing psychological theories do not provide the basis to choose generally between two adults where the child has some relationship and some psychological attachment to each" (Mnookin, 1975, pp. 286-287).

It is not uncommon for parents to accuse the other of being physically, emotionally or sexually abusive. Such accusations send immediate red flags to examiners, lawyers and the court and as Schuman (1986) asserts, some unknown proportion of abuse reports are exaggerated if not false. Some of the latter group exists as a phenomenon separate from intentional malice i.e., lying or deliberate brainwashing.

Mutual parental accusations require additional time and careful investigation. The consequences for the psychologist are that the usual therapeutic and diagnostic techniques and roles need to be augmented to include a psycho/investigative approach. We become probing, inquiring, examiners, cross-validating mutual complaints. Psychological tests ordinarily relied on for describing dynamics are often abused or manipulated by highly motivated and driven parents. Results must be reevaluated in the light of the contentious frame of reference. "Faking good", not only seen in interviews but also on objective tests, is likely to be the rule rather than the exception.

The Minnesota Multiphasic Personality Inventory (MMPI) is perhaps still the most widely utilized objective instrument in these cases (Ollendick & Otto, 1984). Ollendick and Otto (1984) found in a retrospective study that parents ultimately receiving custody tend to represent themselves in a healthier fashion, cope with feelings of anger and impulsivity more effectively, and are more trusting and open toward others. They note the need to "focus on combining psychological test data with behavioral manifestations or symptoms directly" (Ollendick & Otto, 1984, p. 231).

Gardner (1982) warns that only in identifying those difficulties that actually interfere with parenting effectiveness is there assurance that the best interests of the children are met.

Obtaining valid data from children in the throes of high stress during custody and visitation disputes not only requires interviews but sometimes story-telling through the use of projective tests and play therapy. These techniques can provide important conceptual data for the children's positions.

For example, Miller and Veltkamp (1986) believe drawings have "allowed for psychometric analysis of ego functioning, the clarification and understanding of psychological dynamics inherent in the child and his or her relationship with others" (p. 275). "The use of doll play in evaluating interactive patterns of parents and their children has long been a technique valuable to the mediation process. Such efforts encourage expression of young children's feelings, attitudes and thoughts about how parents perceive them and how they perceive parental figures" (p. 277).

Every effort is made to assure fairness and objectivity. Appointments are alternated so that one parent may not complain of having to play "catch up".

Procedure for Evaluating Parents

Preparation and structuring During the initial session each parent is verbally informed and provided with a written account as to the nature of the study and the various tasks to be undertaken. These include interviews (structured and unstructured), psychological tests, joint sessions with their children and sessions with each child alone. Interviews by phone or in person are conducted with selected caretakers (including relatives, babysitters, counselors, physicians or teachers). If one or both parent has a serious committed relationship that person will be evaluated as well. The duration depends upon work schedules, court hearing deadlines, and the psychologist's schedule. Parents are admonished to avoid preparing the children in advance but simply inform them that all members of the family will be coming in to talk and to try to be as honest as possible. They are allowed latitude in prioritizing topics and presenting agendas which are woven into the outline below.

The parents are informed that the nature of the study is evaluative and not therapeutic and that our goal is not to diagnose but to obtain data. Every effort is made to be objective, reasonable, and data based.

Parenting data Information is collected describing the course of the marriage, the reasons for the divorce, and its impact on the children. The current visitation/temporary custody arrangement, each parent's involvement and personal responsibility for the children from birth to the present are outlined. Parents are asked to discuss their perceptions of their own and their spouses' strengths and weaknesses in parenting, as well as their perceptions of how the other spouse would appraise his or her own strengths and weaknesses. If a current significant other is involved, the parent is asked to discuss his/her strengths and weaknesses and that person's role with the children. Each parent is then asked for his or her perception of the spouses' current significant other and that individual's involvement with the child.

Employment Each parent is asked to briefly describe paid work experiences from past to present including attitudes about current employment, work hours, career or job satisfaction level, and long-term career goals.

Personal history interview: parents' family background Parents individually provide data on the role their own parents played in their growing-up years. Parents are questioned about their early histories particularly as they relate to their own parents' parenting styles, work schedules, time availability for them, parental influences or teachings, and observable dysfunctions such as alcohol or substance abuse, absence or neglect, or abuse (physical, sexual, or emotional). They are asked to describe current relationships with their respective parents, whether the parents are in good health, their marital status, and to what extent these parents are providing support or encouragement.

Data regarding siblings is recorded including the nature of their relationships and current contacts with the family.

Self perception Parents are asked to provide a self description: who they are, how they see themselves, and how do others see them.

Education They describe achievement levels, academic strengths and weaknesses, friendships, problems with authority, extracurricular activities, vocational school, or higher education.

Parenting values Parents are encouraged to describe their own thoughts, ideas, attitudes and feelings about a number of issues in an attempt to explore adequacy and appropriateness.

Medical/health attitudes How do the parents deal with health issues? What criteria or symptoms do they utilize to make a determination to contact a physician? Do they have some fundamental knowledge as to what constitutes illness?

Meeting the child's emotional needs How do they promote a feeling of security and continuity? How comfortable are they in emotional closeness and how perceptive are they in reading the child's status? How do they deal with inappropriate emotional responses?

Ideation What are the parents' expectations and goals for the child at successive education levels? How will they operationalize them?

Extracurricular activities/lessons To what extent do these activities have importance to them? How do they assess the child's interest and motivation? Do they over or underprogram the child's out of school time?

Daily management style How do they arrange mornings: breakfast, child care, preparation for school; lunches; the child's daytime schedule when apart; dinnertime? What is the evening scenario? How much time is allotted for homework, reading, play activity and bedtime rituals?

Teaching responsibility How do they teach the child self care? Is there a grasp for teaching accountability at different developmental levels? Do they over-expect or under-expect? What, if any, reinforcers do they utilize?

Discipline Can the parent explain a system which is congruent with the child's age and understanding? Is it absent, inconsistent or too harsh? Does it induce guilt?

Religious training Does the family have a religious belief system? If so, at what age do they anticipate the child's participation? If there is no formal religious training or education, what are their moral or ethical guidelines for self and for the child?

Acquisition of parenting skills Do they follow their own parents' approach; use intuitive strategies; consult with relatives, friends or colleagues; take parenting classes or read parenting books or magazines?

Attitude toward counseling If faced with a difficult intra-personal or inter-family problem, what is his/her attitude toward counseling for themselves and/or the child? What criteria would they utilize for making such a decision? What is the nature and duration of previous psychological counseling? By whom? Obtain permission to communicate with counselors.

Addictive behaviors Parents are also asked specific questions about possible habitual or addictive behaviors such as food, tobacco, prescription medications, alcohol, recreational drugs, substance abuse, gambling and workaholism.

Following a mental status exam, the parents' style and handling of strong, emotional stressors is assessed regarding (a) nervousness, anxiety, fear or worry, (b) depression, down periods, disillusionment, (c) anger, bitterness, hostility, and resentment, (d) rejection and hurt.

Parent/child interview and observations Each parent is requested to bring all the children in for one session. This provides the examiner the opportunity to observe (albeit in a clinical rather than "natural" setting) the interpersonal dynamics between the children and the parent and the children with each other. The first portion of this session is structured. The parent is initially and briefly asked some questions about each one of the children such as circumstances surrounding that child's birth or early development, schooling, likes and dislikes, or child's unique qualities. This approach places minimal stress on the children and allows smoother transitions into the child's session with the examiner.

In the unstructured part of the session the parent is encouraged to explore with the children play or activity opportunities including toys, games, a marking board, keyboard, dolls, puppets, bumper pool, and electronic games. In this framework the examiner may observe the parent's potential interactive, supportive, teaching, organizational, leadership style, and ability to set boundaries and be consistent.

Each parent and child are seen for a separate session in order to explore the way in which each child reacts one-on-one with the parent as well as observe the extent to which the parent is able to individualize.

Parent psychological testing The parent's test battery is divided into two sections (a) those tests relating to the adults themselves, and (b) those measures in which the parent is asked to record the child's development, behavioral and emotional functioning. The tests are chosen to supplement interview data relative to objectifying what is in the best interest of the child. This includes identifying their special needs, dynamics in relation to each parent and siblings, as well as determining parenting efficiency and capacity.

The adult test battery includes the Minnesota Multiphasic Personality Inventory (MMPI). It is incomparable in reliability and validity and thus is seldom questioned in legal contexts. This objective measure provides information about the validity or test taking attitude as well as psychodynamic measures of the individual. It is the most frequently employed measure utilized in the medical/legal context.

Tests which are routinely administered to parents to determine their perception of their children include the Vineland Adaptive Behavior Scales. These contain measures of communication, socialization, interpersonal relationships and provide both adjustment and maladjustment measures for the children. The scales are objectively normed. Each parent participates individually. It provides a good opportunity to observe how able the parents are to recall very specific developmental behaviors thus validating the degree of parental involvement.

The parents are requested to complete either the Personality Inventory for Children or the Child Behavior Checklist which allow them to assess emotional, behavioral, social, and academic functioning. A comparison of each parent's responses provides opportunities to determine to what extent parents' appraisals compare to clinical observation and evaluation of the child himself.

Procedure For Evaluating Children

Child interviews After there has been an opportunity for the child to become familiar and comfortable with the examiner, he or she is evaluated using a semi-structured interview. This consists of discussion about school, grade level, teacher, liked and disliked subjects, preferred peers, activities at school and in the neighborhood, and extracurricular activities.

Siblings The child discusses perceptions of siblings: what they are like, what they do for fun, what they argue about, and how they deal with conflict.

Parents The child describes each parent, enjoyable activities with each, what they do one-on-one, what each parent expects in the way of academic performance, extracurricular activity, chores, behavior, each parent's discipline style and the child's appraisal of its fairness.

Self-description The child describes himself or herself, favored activities, with whom, and long-term goals. They are encouraged to elaborate their thoughts and feelings about the parental separation and divorce process, what the divorce means personally, the visitation schedule, and its perceived fairness. Does the child feel divorced? Depending upon the circumstances and age of the children, they may be asked how they would arrange their schedule if they were in control.

The child is asked if a sister, brother, mom or dad (or any other relative with whom he or she lives or has frequent contact) has said what to say or not to say to the examiner. In addition the examiner asks if mom or dad say bad things about each other.

Child's recall of each parent's role In order to obtain a more detailed conception of each parent's caretaking/teaching involvement the child may be asked specific questions about who modeled or taught the child self-help skills, chores, games, and athletic activities; who delivers and picks the child up for doctor and dentist visits, school, friends, shopping trips, etc.

Child psychological testing Intelligence tests are not routinely administered unless there are specific concerns such as a suspected learning disability, over or underachievement or problems such as Attention Deficit Disorder. The WISC-III is the standardized, state-of-the-art scale which provides a breakdown of general ability with Verbal (cognitive) and Performance (non-verbal) components together with additional submeasures providing valuable data such as freedom from distraction, perceptual organization and verbal comprehension.

Objective personality measures Each child is routinely administered several objectively scored and normed measures.

The Piers-Harris Children's Self Concept Scale is a brief self-report measure designed to aid in assessment of self concept in children and adolescents. This test is one of the most frequently employed tests for self-esteem and is useful in custody disputes to determine conscious level self perceptions. It suggests the degree to which the child may be at risk due to parental conflict and interfamily stress. It focuses on conscious self-perceptions including behavior, intellectual and school status, physical appearance and attributes, anxiety, popularity and happiness and satisfaction.

The Revised Children's Manifest Anxiety Scale (RCMAS) is an objectively normed instrument designed to assess the level and nature of anxiety in children and adolescents including physiological anxiety, worry/over-sensitivity, social concerns, concentration and a lie scale. Used in an interview format, it provides an opportunity for the child to expand and clarify the nature of the anxiety.

The Parent Perception Inventory is used without the scoring format. Essentially it addresses children's perceptions of positive and negative parental behaviors. The results often elaborate the child's attitudes and feelings about each parent obtained in the interview section and/or from other test data.

The Parent Attachment Structured Interview (PASI) is a technique to evaluate children's attachment to the significant people in their lives. Although norms have not been forthcoming as yet, it elicits a range of information about these attachments including responsiveness, competence, security and hostility. This test, as well as the RCMAS, provide a broad range of opportunity for the child in a divorcing family to evaluate his and his parents' behaviors and interactions. These measures may be supplemented with projective tests. Although not employed routinely, these subjective measures sometimes provide hypotheses about the extent or depth of psychopathology. This data may not be accessible on a more conscious level. Children sometimes present a brave facade and deny problems and conflicts either out of a needed defense style or to protect one or both parents.

Draw A Person (DAP) The DAP may tell us how a child symbolically perceives and feels about himself.

Draw A Family (DAF) This drawing tells us how the child sees himself in relation to his family or the ideal family. The inquiry portion allows us to explore individual and inter-family dynamics.

Thematic Apperception Test (TAT) The TAT allows the child to project pre-conscious feelings, concerns, conflicts about personal, family and/or extra family issues.

Rorschach Ink Blots Content analysis may reflect the extent to which conflicts or worry may be pervasive.

Three fondest wishes If he or she had three wishes for anything wanted in the world, for anything in life to change (in self or in the family), or for any material thing, what would they be? The data obtained here tells us the extent to which worries or fears may have become fixed or obsessive and about other wants or needs.

Exploratory play therapy These are utilized with younger children with a sparsity of expressive language or those who are exceptionally defensive or oppositional. Puppet or doll play may elaborate personal or family dynamics and assist in determining whether there is any evidence of attempted alienation or maltreatment.

Outside nuclear family interviews If there are serious discrepancies between the parents' descriptions of the children or allegations about each other which need additional data to clarify, it may be necessary to interview others. At times, relatives or caretakers will be questioned. For educational issues, the teacher may be interviewed by telephone.

If the child has a chronic health problem the pediatrician or family doctor is contacted. The physician can provide data relative to how each parent cares for the child's medical needs, who is responsible for bringing the child in for appointments and if there are any problems with responsibility.

Family Evaluation Summary

After completing these tasks, a family summary is prepared for review with the parents (ideally together), the lawyers, and the court. It includes the following:-

1. A review of parental adequacy, skills and deficits. In this section, each parent's major concerns about the other's weaknesses, which they believe impinge on his or her efficiency versus capacity to parent, are discussed. These concerns, as well as the broader scoped investigative appraisal of their skills and deficits, is outlined.

2. The parents' ability to deal with special needs and problems of the children are outlined. These may be related to chronic health problems, academic achievement issues, behavior or emotional difficulties, or any other child problem which demands special or extra time and attention and the need to make arrangements and sacrifices.

3. A statement about each parent's motivation for custody and whether it meets the criteria for best interest of the children is discussed.

4. The age of each child, the child's perception and attachment to each parent and the child's preferences are detailed.

Recommendations At this point, the psychologist's role becomes less well defined. In some jurisdictions, the court assumes responsibility for considering the data and reaching its own conclusions and recommendations. In others, the court may look to the psychologist to make recommendations regarding custody or visitation scheduling. Care must be taken with respect to what specific recommendations should be made.

For example, Youngstrom (1992) describes the American Psychological Association's development of guidelines for custody evaluation and states although psychologists disagree over whether they should simply present their observations to the judge or actually make a custody recommendation, they all agree that any statements must be fully backed by hard evidence. And psychologists should hold their ground...in the face of lawyers and judges who want black and white conclusions (p. 24).

The reason for psychologists' hesitation is outlined by Grisso (cited in Youngstrom, 1991, p. 24) who states, "child custody evaluations sometimes prompt ethics complaints—to state psychological associations, to state licensing boards and to the APA". It is not uncommon for malpractice suits to follow in these cases particularly where the psychologist is not court appointed.

Time sharing suggestions are made on the basis of each parent's caretaking experience, capability, availability, and their geographic positioning to each other and to the school or child care facility. In some cases there will have been an opportunity to evaluate the children's ability to cope with various transitioning schedules. If not, their potential or capacity can be judged. Each parent's ability to adhere to a schedule and to complement that with some degree of flexibility in accommodating unforeseen changes is important to identify here. Accessibility is critical.

Conclusions

Psychologists continue to be handicapped at this time because of the lack of formal guidelines for custody evaluations. For this reason, it is important to obtain feedback from attorneys and the court in order to sharpen skills and provide the most appropriate information possible. In addition, membership in professional organizations and collaboration with colleagues struggling with the same issues assists in refining strategies.

References

Goldstein, J., Freud, A., & Solnit, A. (1979). *Beyond the best interests of the child.* New York: Free Press.

Hetherington, E. M., Stanley-Hagan, M., & Anderson, E. R. (1989). Marital transitions: A child's perspective. *American Psychologist, 44*, 303-328.

Miller, T. W., & Veltkamp, L. J. (1986). Use of fables in clinical assessment of contested child custody. *Child Psychiatry and Human Development, 16*, 274-285.

Mnookin, R. (1975). Child custody adjudication: Judicial function in the face of indeterminacy. *Law and Contemporary Problems, 39*, 226-293.

Okpaku, S. (1976). Psychology: Impediment or aid in child custody cases? *Rutgers Law Review, 29*, 1117-1153.

Ollendick, D. G., & Otto, B. J. (1984). MMPI characteristics of parents referred for child custody studies. *Journal of Psychology, 117*, 227-232.

Rohman, L. W., Sales, B. D., & Lon, M. (1987). The best interests of the child in custody disputes. In L. A. Weithorn (Ed.), *Psychology and child custody determinations* (pp. 59-105). Lincoln, NB: University of Nebraska Press.

Schuman, D. C. (1986). False accusations of physical and sexual abuse. *Bulletin of the American Academy of Psychiatry Law, 14*, 5-21.

Wallerstein, J. S. (1991). The long term effects on children: A review. *Journal of the American Academy of Child and Adolescence Psychiatry, 30*, 349-360.

Wallerstein, J. S., & Blakeslee, S. (1989). *Second chances.* New York: Ticknor and Fields.

Wodehouse, P. G. (1959). *The little nugget.* London: Penguin Books.

Youngstrom, N. (1992). APA develops guidelines for custody evaluations. *APA Monitor, 23*, 3.

Zill, N. (1988). Behavior, achievement, and health problems among children in stepfamilies: Findings from a national survey of child health. In E. M. Hetherington & J. D. Arasteh (Eds.), *Impact of divorce, single-parenting and stepparenting on children* (pp. 325-368). Hillsdale, NJ: Erlbaum.

The Factors Neutralizing Development Disorders in Children from Broken Families

Alicja Czerederecka and Teresa Jaskiewicz-Obydzinska

Introduction

For both partners the break-up of marriage usually brings about a low self-esteem, sense of damage, a negative evaluation of one's life's achievements and a sense of life disaster. The divorce proceedings usually make the conflict more acute and lead to pondering over grievances and leave a former partner with a feeling of being hurt. It is therefore very difficult to remain objective in such a situation as there exists an excessively negative image of the partner and the tendency to defensive idealization of one's own actions. Concentration on children can sometimes function as a neurotic satisfaction of needs; it provides a sense to one's life ("I must look after them and earn the living"), self-esteem ("I am OK - I am the one who is thinking about the child's well-being"), emotional contact ("I love and I am loved"). However, when both partners seek for the child's custody, they become competitors - there is a danger that the needs might not be satisfied. Partners who can not come to terms with parting are afraid of losing that significant substitute for the relationship.

This may be where the process of formation of child development disorders takes its origin when the family breaks up. The parents themselves, contrary to their intentions and declarations, give rise to disorders in the child's psychological development. They do it by involving the children in marital conflict. Very often they themselves unconsciously make sure that the child is the witness (and sometimes the partner) to their conflict with the spouse and press them to take the side of one of two loved parents. Projecting their own sense of emotional disappointment, they often feel obliged to provide a child with a negative image of the father or the mother; to convince the child that he is being emotionally rejected by him or her, or that the mother or father intend to hurt the child.

When the family breaks up the child is faced with the disorder of the sense of stability, with uncertainty and threat and with the distortion of the basic need for security. Despite a difficult situation those values can be rebuilt, at least to a large extent, but on condition that the parents work towards making it easier for the child to return to stabilization and balance without striving to disturb it.

Method

This study involved 50 children (26 girls and 24 boys) from 38 families at the Institute of Forensic Research in connection with formulating psychological expertise for the divorce court concerning the parental custody. The aim of the work was to establish factors which lessen the influence of stimuli harmful on the psychological development of a child in a broken family.

The group differed from other broken families as the conflict between the custodians was especially acute and prolonged. Both parents sought contact with the child and did not accept solutions proposed by the opposite side, forensic psychologists, and the court ruling including a series of appeals and not respecting the court decisions. In such situations, children are more frequently and more intensively subject to negative influences of the conflict between the parents than in other circumstances of a divorce case.

During the psychological examinations of the children the following tests were used: IQ test (46 children - Wechsler; 3 - Terman-Merrill; 1 - Raven); psychoorganic tests (mainly Bender - 36 persons); and personality tests (Rotter's free associations - 34 children; Gille's Film - 40 children; family picture - 45 children; CAT - 46 children; TAT - 4 children; Kugler-Thomas - 5 children). Interviews were conducted with every child, whose behaviours and spontaneous reactions were observed, especially while meeting the other custodian (in 49 cases). The obtained results constituted the basis for psychological development diagnosis of the children.

On the basis of the diagnosis the children were divided into three groups depending on the degree of the disorders:

(1) Children showing considerable disorders. The group encompassed children in which disorders, both emotional and social, were ascertained, relatively deep-rooted and found within different personality spheres.

(2) Children showing mild disorders. This group encompassed the children in which disorders concerned exclusively one personality sphere and one could ascertain a direct relationship of the disorder with a family situation as they either increased or decreased depending on the external circumstances.

(3) Children without disorders. The group encompassed children in which no disquieting changes or deviations from the correct personality development were noted, and no deprivations of their basic needs were found (security, support, emotional ties, affiliation, self-fulfilment). Incorrect behavioural patterns were rare.

There were 13 children in group 1, 31 children in group 2 and six children in group 3. The small number of children who did not show disorders is not surprising in such an unfavourable educational situation. The large number of children with considerable disorders may, however, be cause for concern.

As it was shown above, the degree of intensity of conflict between parents was similar in all cases, the level of disorders among children, on the other hand, varies considerably. This gives rise to a question - what makes it possible to lessen the negative effects of family situation.

The following hypotheses have been put forward: (1) among different forms of conflict between parents the one that involves manipulating the child seems to have the most negative influence on the child; (2) the lower the degree of involvement of the child in the conflict the greater is the chance for the correct development of the child.

The data concerning the family background were taken from the material needed for formulating the expert's opinion: case files, questionnaires of the interviews with the parents and observation of child-parent contact, conclusions included in expert witness opinions.

The level of child's involvement in the conflict was assessed by competent judges using a five-grade scale;

0 - positive attitude towards the other custodian;

1 - the isolation of the child from the conflict - secondary effects derived from self-identification with the way the parents reacted;

2 - showing discontent and lack of acceptance towards positive contact of the child with the other custodian;

3 - verbal prejudicing against the other custodian, deprivation of mutual contact;

4 - drastic forms of prejudicing - emotional and material blackmail, infliction of punishment, putting the other custodian in a very unfavourable light.

Characterization of the Examined Population

The population varied according to the legal and formal situation - 37 children were examined in connection with a divorce case, five - with the regulation of contact between the custodians and children, four - with the charge of ruling concerning the parental authority, three - deprivation of the parental authority, one - with the limitation of the parental authority.

The fact that most of the cases concerned divorce implies that the subject of the conflict between custodians is not only the regulation of parental custody. Frequently one of the sides would not agree for a divorce (40%), and property distribution was also contested (30%). The other subjects of the conflict were: abuse of alcohol by one of the parents (18%), abandonment of the spouse for another partner (18%), unfaithfulness without breaking-up (10%), in-laws interference (10%), and mental illness of one of the partners (12%). In some cases the following reasons were mentioned: criminal activity of the partner, forced sexual intercourse, and suspicion of sexual abuse of the child.

In the majority of the families the acute conflict had lasted for more than three years. In the cases of five children (three from group 2 and two from group 3) the conflict has lasted from one to three years.

The age of the children under examination varied from four years and a half to fifteen years. Half of the children were placed in the age limit seven years to ten years and eleven months. It is noteworthy that 66% of children without disorders were in the 4-6 years age range, (unfortunately one cannot exclude the possibility that the disorders have not manifested themselves yet because of the young age; they might appear at a later stage). However, this same age range constituted 46% of the group with greater disorders. Thus, they were the children either with numerous problems or very few. All other age ranges showed a normal distribution with most children being in the second category.

Personality disorders were found among boys more frequently (nine serious, 13 minor) than in girls (four serious and 18 minor). Disorders were absent in two boys and four girls.

The parents of the majority of children had at least secondary education (mothers of 82% of children and fathers of 72% of children). Twelve percent of mothers and 20% of fathers had vocational education, mothers of 6% of children and fathers of 8% of children were primary school graduates.

In 48% of families a high standard of living was found, in 44% an average one and in 18% a low standard of living was observed. One may assume that this is not accidental. The long duration of a divorce case is usually connected with a considerable financial strain which people having a lower standard of living cannot afford to bear.

One third of the children from the examined population showed various somatic disorders. The most common ones included: lower immunity to infections (four children), sight impairment (four children), meningitis (three children), vegetative symptoms of neurosis (three children), ear problems (two children), and disfigurement of the spinal cord (two children).

More than half of the number of the children with severe disorders showed somatic problems including one which was serious, whereas in the "no disorders" group somatic problems were found in only one person. When asked about neurotic symptoms of their children, the parents usually mentioned, behavioral disorders including aggression, educational problems at home and at school (30% of children), over-impulsiveness (22%), difficulties with concentration (20%), biting of nails (18%), phobias (16%), bad mood (16%), negativism (16%), self-isolation for the surroundings (10%), eating disorders (8%), speech impairment (8%).

The majority of children changed environment (e.g. by moving from mother to father, father to grandmother, etc.) at least once (86%), including 30% of the population which changed environment many times. Only 14% of the children remained continually in the same environment.

Mothers were the main custodians in 54% of the examined population and fathers in 40%. The contacts with the other side were often irregular or did not take place at all. Three children were an exception (6%). Two of them remained in the custody of both parents, and in the case of the third, the grandmother had the greatest influence (although the child met the parents quite often, albeit irregularly).

A statistically significant relationship was found between development disorders in children and the regulation of their contacts with custodians was found (analyzed separately for a mother r_p=0,53, for a father r_p=0,65). All children belonging to "no disorders" group remained in the mother's custody, and the contacts with the father was unequivocally determined: a regular one (33%) or lack thereof (67%) which suggests that such conditions give the greatest chance for correct development. All children remaining with the father showed disorders, and contact with the mother was frequently irregular.

The Effect of a Conflict on Children Disorders

There were nine forms of conflicts, which had been observed between the parents in the examined population. They were: verbal and physical aggression; manipulation of the child; refusing to consider the solutions proposed by the partner (negative attitude); presentation of inadequate, pathological forms of behaviour by one of the parents; inflicting corporeal punishment on children as a transfer of aggression towards the partner; isolation of one of the partners from the conflict (complete separation, lack of contact); involving a wider circle of people; being subject to other court cases (often of a criminal nature).

It was found that the simultaneous occurrence of many forms of conflict had an influence on the process of formation of disorders in children (r_p=0,5). It means that the more complex the conflict, the more likely the child is to experience a disorder.

Subsequently, a dependence between particular forms of conflict and the level of disorders presented by the children was examined. The results are shown in Table 1.

Table 1: The Forms of Conflict

Forms	Verbal aggression		Physical aggression		Manipulation of the child		Negative attitude		Presentation of inadequate		Corporal punishment		Isolation from the conflict		Involving the wider circle of people		Court cases	
Group	N	%	N	%	N	%	N	%	N	%	N	%	N	%	N	%	N	%
I	11	85	6	46	13	100	12	92	6	46	2	15	2	15	9	69	3	23
II	25	81	9	29	25	81	22	71	6	19	3	13	10	32	10	32	4	13
III	4	67	3	50	2	33	3	50	-	-	-	-	4	67	1	17	1	17
Total	40	80	18	36	40	80	37	74	12	24	5	10	16	32	20	40	8	16
r_p	0,18		0,25		0,61		0,39		0,45		0,25		0,42		0,49		0,17	

The results turned out to be quite interesting. A negligible relation between the disorders and the forms of conflict such as additional court cases, verbal aggression and corporeal punishment inflicted on the children was found. One should point out that the last of these forms did not appear at all in group 3. The most surprising, however, was the fact that there was no directly proportional relation between the appearance of physical aggression in the family and the level of disorders in children. Aggression appears most frequently in the group without disorders. The result suggests that we might overestimate the influence of such forms of conflict on a child, who is merely a passive observer and is not pressed to take sides. Much greater, directly proportional relation was found between disorders in children and negativism of the custodians towards each other, involving a greater number of people into conflict and inadequate and pathological forms of behaviour of one of the parents. When the latter issues arose, they always entailed disorders in children.

A negatively proportional relation was found between disorders in children and the isolation of one of the sides from the conflict. Although this phenomenon itself has a negative value, its immediate effects are advantageous: the more often the isolation took place the less frequent were the symptoms of personality development disorders in children.

The hypothesis put forward at the beginning has been confirmed. Out of different forms of conflict between parents, manipulating of the child in the conflict has the worst effect on the psychological development of the child. A high relationship between those two characteristics has been found (r_p=0,61). It turned out that manipulating took place in 100% of cases from the "severe disorder" group, 81% in "minor disorder" group and 33% in "no disorder" group.

Next, the phenomenon of manipulation was analyzed. By using a scale devised to measure the degree of involvement of the child into the conflict by the parents' manipulation was assessed. The results are shown in Table 2.

Table 2: The Level of Child's Involvement into the Conflict

Custodian	Mother										Father									
Level	0		1		2		3		4		0		1		2		3		4	
Group	N	%	N	%	N	%	N	%	N	%	N	%	N	%	N	%	N	%	N	%
I	-	-	-	-	3	23	6	46	3	23	-	-	-	-	3	23	4	31	6	46
II	1	3	1	3	10	32	19	62	-	-	-	-	2	6	7	23	20	65	2	6
III	2	33	-	-	4	67	-	-	-	-	-	-	1	17	3	50	1	17	-	-
Total	3	6	1	2	17	34	25	50	3	6	-	-	3	6	13	26	25	50	8	16
					rp = 0,5										rp = 0,5					

First, it was found that fathers, to a greater degree than mothers, involved the children in the conflict. None of the children remaining with a father showed a positive attitude towards a mother; in as many as eight cases fathers showed extremely drastic forms of involving children into the conflict and presenting a mother in a negative light. As far as mothers were concerned, there were three cases in which a father was presented in a favourable light and extremely negative conditioning of the child had been observed in three cases, too.

Within the group of children showing no disorders in psychological development, no direct involvement into the conflict was found (grades 3 and 4). It means that mothers appeared not to prejudice the children against the father in a direct way. They did not inform them about his negative features and did not expect from the children an unequivocal stand against the father. However, they often (four cases in six) used the method of indirect manipulation, that is, they demonstrated their own unwillingness toward the partner and discontent or uneasiness when the child met the father. The fathers did not show drastic forms of manipulation either; the only father who involved the child in an open way (grade 3) had been deprived of the contact with him for about three years.

In discussing the results of the children with disorders, correlation concerning the degree of involvement of the child by the main custodian proved to be very useful.

In the group of children with "minor disorders" of psychological development, direct involvement into conflict, grade 3, was most frequently observed. This was done by 19 mothers and 20 fathers. Moreover, it turned out that such forms of intervention were presented in 22 cases by main custodians of the children. There were also extreme, drastic forms of child manipulation (two fathers, of which one was the main custodian).

In all children showing serious disorders in psychological development there were found cases of manipulation on the part of the parents. The most drastic forms of involvement of a child into the conflict (grade 4) were presented by three mothers and six fathers; in six cases they were the main custodians. Mothers showed this form of intervention in six cases and fathers in four cases. "Only" the indirect form of manipulation (grade 2) was used by three mothers and three fathers, but only one of these persons (mother) was the main custodian.

The discussed results supported the second hypothesis which stated that the smaller the degree of involvement of the child into conflict, the greater is the chance for the correct development of the child.

Summary and Conclusions

In the research emphasis was laid on searching for factors which can have neutralizing effect in the situation of an acute conflict between the custodian and the fight for having custody.

The results of the research lead to the following conclusions. First it was rather surprising to find a considerable difference between a mother and a father as the main custodians. Fathers, to a greater extent involved both the children under their care and these children who were not into the conflict. All the children remaining in fathers' custody tended to have irregular contacts with mothers and showed disorders in psychic development.

This does not necessarily confirm the stereotyped view that fathers are unable to perform the duty of a custodian. The obtained results point out that it is just because of these stereotypes fathers feel unsure of themselves in their role and place too much emotion in their educational activities. This leads to quite an irrational behaviour, especially to a neurotic defense which finds its expression in creating in a child a negative picture of the mother, inflicting "emotional punishment" after the positive response of a child towards the mother.

Second, all children from the "no disorder" group remained in the mother's custody and had clearly defined contact with the father. They met him on a regular basis or did not have any contact at all. It turned out that such conditions gave a greater chance for normal development.

Third, the hypothesis put forward at the beginning proved to be correct - among different forms of conflict between parents the most important one is child manipulation. The obtained result passed the expectations of the researchers. It turned out that as long as the child is not forced to take sides and remains merely a passive observer he has a chance for correct development despite an acute conflict between parents.

In the population under examination the following factors has a negligible influence on disorders in children: physical and verbal aggression between parents - although these forms of behaviour are usually thought to be the main factors disturbing the correct psychic development of the child - which was also stressed by divorcing parents.

A considerable influence of inadequate patterns of behaviour on the part of the parents and of involving a greater number of persons into the conflict on the psychic well-being of the child was also found. An isolation of one of the partners from the conflict led to the diminishing of the disorders in the child. One should not, however, risk assuming` that in the situation of an acute conflict an isolation from one of the partners is called for. The beneficial result is only temporary and in the future such a situation may have a disturbing influence on the process of formation of self-image, psycho-sexual attitude patterns, models of family etc. in a child.

Fourth, the hypothesis that the lower the degree of involvement of the child in conflict, the greater is the chance for his normal development proved to be also correct.

It turned out that even in a situation of acute conflict it is possible to form a positive attitude towards a partner in a child. Unfortunately it has only been observed in the case of three mothers.

In the "no disorder" group there were fewest cases of negative interventions. The manipulation was limited to showing discontent towards positive relations with the partner.

In the "minor disorder" group active manipulation with the child - refusal to let the child meet the partner and presenting him in an unfavcurable light took place very often.

In the families of children with serious disorders active manipulation with a child was exclusively found - including the most drastic forms (forcing children to have an unequivocally negative attitude towards the partner).

The results of the research proved beyond any doubt that the isolation of the child from the conflict can be advantageous to his development. Once the family breaks up and the partners cannot come to an understanding, including educational matters, the parents should concentrate on the protection of the child. They usually declare such a point of view but their actions bring results contrary to expectations. Involved in the conflict, they are not able to evaluate the situation in an objective way and they blame the partner for the disorders in children. It seems that in such a situation family therapy should be called for. Suggesting therapy right after divorce court proceedings have started, or after an unsuccessful mediation effort, might give a greater chance for the correction of wrong attitudes of parents towards children. It especially concerns the fathers who show great interest in the custodian role, devote a lot of time to children, but cannot avoid serious educational errors.

Bullying or Peer Abuse in School: Intervention and Prevention[1]

Dan Olweus

Bullying or victimization among school children is certainly a very old phenomenon. The fact that some children are frequently and systematically harassed and attacked by other children has been described in literary works, and many adults have personal experience of it from their own school days. Though many are acquainted with the bully/victim problem, it was not until fairly recently - in the early 1970s - that efforts were made to study it systematically (Olweus, 1973a, 1978). For a number of years, these efforts were largely confined to Scandinavia. In the 1980s and early 1990s, however, bullying among school children has attracted attention also in other countries such as Japan, England, the Netherlands, Australia, Canada, and the USA. There are now clear indications of an increasing societal as well as research interest into bully/victim problems in several parts of the world.

This chapter gives an overview of some recent research findings on bullying or victimization among school children in Scandinavia. I will mainly confine myself to the effects of an intervention program against bullying that I developed and evaluated over a two-year period in 42 schools in Bergen, Norway, in connection with a nationwide campaign. I also briefly describe the content of the program and some of the principles on which it is based. A more detailed presentation of the program (and many of the research findings on bully/victim problems) is given in a small book *Bullying at school - what we know and what we can do* (Olweus, 1993) which has recently been published.

A number of findings concerning developmental antecedents of bullying problems, characteristics of typical bullies and victims, and the veracity of some popular conceptions of the causes of these problems are presented only briefly or not at all in this context, since these results have been described in detail in previous publications (e.g., Olweus, 1973a, 1978, 1979, 1980, 1981, 1983, 1984, 1986, 1987, 1991, 1993, in press). It should be mentioned, however, that the findings from this earlier research have generally been replicated in several different samples and were obtained with a number of different methods, including peer ratings, teacher nominations, self-reports, grades, projective techniques, hormonal assays, and mother/father interviews about child-rearing practices. Most of these results were derived from my Swedish longitudinal project (comprising approximately 900 boys) which started in the early 1970s and is still continuing.

Before embarking on the main theme of my presentation I will give a brief definition of what I mean by the term bullying or victimization. In addition, I will draw a sketchy portrait of typical victims and bullies as a background for the intervention program. (For more comprehensive overviews, see e.g., Olweus, 1986, 1991, 1993).

Definition of Victimization

I define *bullying or victimization* in the following general way: *a student is being bullied or victimized when he or she is exposed, repeatedly and over time, to negative actions on the part of one or more other students.*

The meaning of the expression *negative actions* must be specified further. It is a negative action when someone intentionally inflicts, or attempts to inflict, injury or discomfort upon another - basically what is implied in the definition of aggressive behavior (Olweus, 1973b). Negative actions can be carried out by physical contact, by words, or in other ways, such as making faces or dirty gestures, and intentional exclusion from a group.

It must be stressed that the term bullying or victimization is not (or should not be) used when two students of approximately the same strength (physical or psychological) are fighting or quarrelling. In order to use the term bullying, there should be an *imbalance in strength (an asymmetric power relationship)*. The student who is exposed to the negative actions has difficulty defending him/herself and is somewhat helpless against the student or students who harass.

It is useful to distinguish between *direct bullying* -with relatively open attacks on the victim - and *indirect bullying* in the form of intentional social isolation and exclusion from a group. It is important to pay attention also to the second, less visible form of victimization. In the present chapter the expressions bullying, peer abuse, victimization, and bully/victim problems are used synonymously.

Prevalence

In connection with a nationwide campaign against bully/victim problems in Norwegian primary and secondary/junior high schools, launched by the Ministry of Education in 1983, data were collected with a questionnaire[2] measuring different aspects of victimization from more than 700 schools from all over Norway (Olweus, 1985, 1986, 1991).

On the basis of this survey, one can estimate that some 84,000 students, or 15% of the total in Norwegian comprehensive schools (568,000 in 1983-84), were involved in bully/victim problems "now and then" or more frequently (autumn 1983) - as bullies or victims. This percentage represents one student out of seven. Approximately 9%, or 52,000 students, were victims, and 41,000, or 7%, bullied other students "now and then" or more frequently. Some 9,000 students were both victim and bully (17% of the victims).

It can thus be stated that *bullying is a considerable problem in Norwegian primary and secondary/junior high schools*, a problem that affects a very large number of students. Data from other countries such as Sweden (Olweus, 1986), Finland (Lagerspetz, Björkqvist, Berts, & King, 1982), England (Smith, 1989), and USA (Perry, Kusel, & Perry, 1988) indicate that this problem exists also outside Norway and with similar or even higher prevalence rates.

Characteristics of Typical Victims and Bullies

The picture of the typical victim emerging from the research is relatively unambiguous (see Olweus, 1978, 1993). Victims of bullying are more anxious and insecure than students in general. They are often cautious, sensitive, and quiet. When attacked by other students, they commonly react with crying (at least in the lower grades) and withdrawal. They have a negative view of themselves and their situation. They often look upon themselves as failures and feel stupid, ashamed, and unattractive.

Further, the victims are lonely and abandoned at school. As a rule, they do not have a single good friend in their class. They are not aggressive or teasing in their behavior; accordingly, one cannot explain the bullying as a consequence of the victims themselves being provocative to their peers (see below). If they are boys, they are likely to be physically weaker than boys in general.

In summary, the behavior and attitude of the victims seem to signal to others that they are insecure and worthless individuals who will not retaliate if they are attacked or insulted. A slightly different way of describing the typical victims is to say that they are characterized by *an anxious reaction pattern combined* (in the case of boys) *with physical weakness*.

This is a sketch of the most common type of victim, whom I have called *the passive or submissive victim*. There is also another, smaller group of victims, *the provocative victims*, who are characterized by a combination of both anxious and aggressive behavior patterns. (See Olweus, 1973a, 1978, for more information about this kind of victim.)

A distinctive characteristic of *typical bullies* is their aggression towards peers; this is implied in the definition of a bully. They are, however, often also aggressive towards teachers, parents, and siblings. Generally they have more positive attitudes to violence and the use of violent means than students in general. They are often characterized by impulsivity and strong needs to dominate others. They have little empathy with victims of bullying. If they are boys, they are likely to be physically stronger than boys in general, and victims in particular.

In contrast to a fairly common assumption among psychologists and psychiatrists, we have found no indications that the aggressive bullies (boys) are anxious and insecure under a tough surface. Data based on several samples and using both direct and indirect methods such as projective techniques and hormonal assays all pointed in the same direction: the bullies had unusually little anxiety and insecurity or were roughly average on such dimensions (Olweus, 1981, 1984). And they did not suffer from poor self-esteem.

In summary, the *typical bullies* can be described as having *an aggressive reaction pattern combined* (in the case of boys) *with physical strength*.

As regards the possible psychological sources underlying bullying behavior, the pattern of empirical findings suggests at least three, partly interrelated motives. First, the bullies have a strong need for power and dominance; they seem to enjoy being "in control" and subduing others. Second, considering the family conditions under which many of them have been reared (see Olweus, 1980, 1993), it is natural to assume that they have developed a certain degree of hostility towards the environment; such feelings and impulses may make them derive satisfaction from inflicting injury and suffering upon other individuals. Finally, there is an "instrumental component" to their behavior. The bullies often coerce their victims to provide them with money, cigarettes, beer, and other things of value. In addition, it is obvious that aggressive behavior is in many situations rewarded in the form of prestige (e.g., Bandura, 1973).

Bullying can also be viewed as a *component of a more generally conduct-disordered, antisocial and rule-breaking behavior pattern*. From this perspective, it is natural to predict that youngsters who are aggressive and bully others in school run a clearly increased risk of later engaging in other problem behaviors such as criminality and alcohol abuse. Several studies confirm this general prediction (e.g., Loeber & Dishion, 1983; Magnusson, Stattin, & Duner, 1983).

In my own follow-up studies we have also found strong support for this view. Approximately 60% of boys who were characterized as bullies in grades 6-9 had been convicted of at least one officially registered crime by the age of 24. Even more dramatically, as much as 35-40% of the former bullies had three or more convictions at this age, while this was true of only 10% of the control boys (those who were neither bullies nor victims in grades 6-9). Thus, as young adults the former school bullies has a fourfold increase in the level of relatively serious, recidivist criminality as documented in official crime records.

It may be mentioned that the former victims had an average or somewhat below average level of criminality in young adulthood.

A Question of Fundamental Democratic Rights

The results obtained in my research demonstrate convincingly that bullying is a considerable problem in Scandinavian elementary and junior high schools, that the teachers (in 1983) did relatively little to counteract it, and that the parents knew too little about what their children were exposed to or engaged in. The *victims* of bullying are a large group of students who are to a great extent neglected by the school. We know that many of these youngsters are the targets of harassment for long periods of time, often for many years (Olweus, 1977, 1978). It does not require much imagination to understand what it is to go through the school years in *a state of more or less permanent anxiety and insecurity and with poor self-esteem*. It is not surprising that the victims' devaluation of themselves sometimes becomes so overwhelming that they see suicide as the only possible solution.

Bully/victim problems have even broader implications than those suggested in the previous paragraph. They really concern some of our *fundamental democratic principles: every individual should have the right to be spared oppression and repeated, intentional humiliation, in school as in society at large*. No student should be afraid of going to school for fear of being harassed or degraded, and no parent should need to worry about such things happening to his or her child!

Bully/victim problems also relate to a society's general attitude to violence and oppression. What kind of view of societal values will a student acquire who is repeatedly bullied by other students without interference from adults? The same question can be asked with regard to students who, for long periods of time, are allowed to harass others without hindrance from adults. *To refrain from actively counteracting bully/victim problems in school implies a tacit acceptance.*

In this context, it should be emphasized that it is of great importance to counteract these problems also for the sake of the aggressive students. As reported above, school bullies are much more likely than other students to follow an antisocial path. Accordingly, it is essential to try to redirect their activities into more socially acceptable channels. And there is no evidence to suggest that a generally "tolerant" and permissive attitude on the part of adults will help bullies outgrow their antisocial behavior pattern.

Against this background, it is now appropriate to briefly describe the effects of the intervention program that I developed and evaluated in connection with the campaign against bully/victim problems in Norwegian schools.

The major goals of the program were to reduce as much as possible existing bully/victim problems and to prevent the development of new problems.

The Intervention Program

Subjects and design

Space limitations prevent detailed presentation of methodological information including sampling scheme, definition of measuring instruments and variables, and significance tests. Only summary descriptions and main results will be provided in this context (for more details, see Olweus, 1991, 1992; Olweus & Alsaker, 1991).

Evaluation of the effects of the intervention program is based on data from approximately 2500 students originally belonging to 112 grade 4-7 classes in 42 primary and junior high schools in Bergen (modal ages at Time 1 were 11, 12, 13 and 14 years respectively). Each of the four grade/age cohorts consisted of 600-700 subjects with a roughly equal distribution of boys and girls. The first time of date collection (Time 1) was in late May 1983, approximately four months before introduction of the intervention program. New measurements were taken in May 1984 (Time 2) and May 1985 (Time 3),

Since the campaign was nationwide, it was not possible to set up a strictly experimental study with random allocation of schools or classes to treatment and control conditions. Instead, a quasi-experimental design (sometimes called an age cohort or selection cohort design, see Cook and Campbell, 1979) was chosen, making use of "time-lagged contrasts between age-equivalent groups". In particular, for three of the cohorts data collected at Time 1 (see Figure 1) were used as a base line with which data for age-equivalent cohorts at Time 2 could be compared. The latter groups had then been exposed to the intervention program for about eight months. To exemplify, the data for the grade 5 cohort at Time 1 (modal age 12 years) were compared with the Time 2 data for the grade 4 cohort which at that time had reached the same age as the base line group. The same kind of comparisons were made between the grade 6 cohort at Time 1 and the grade 5 cohort at Time 2, and between the grade 7 cohort at Time 1 and the grade 6 cohort at Time 2.

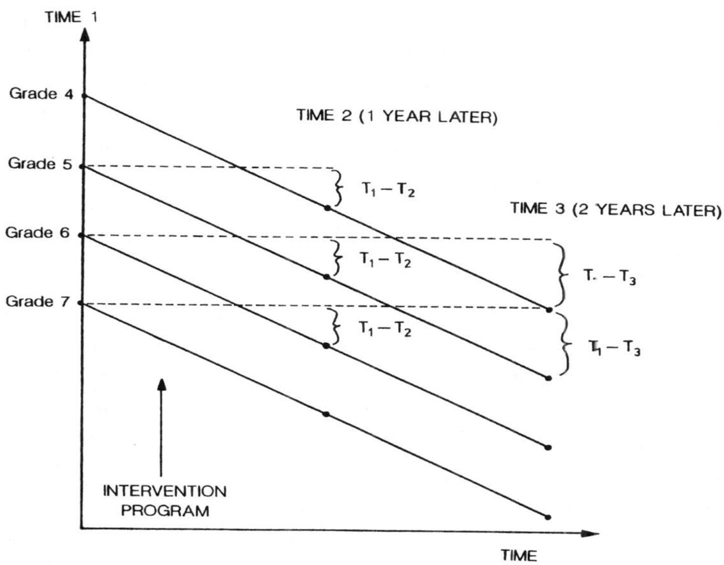

Figure 1: Design for evaluation of effects of intervention program. Fictitious data (which to some extent reflect the general trend of the empirical findings).

Comparisons of data collected at Time 1 and Time 3 permit an assessment of the persistence or possible decline or enhancement of the effects over a longer time span. For these comparisons data for only two of the cohorts could be used as a base line, those of the grade 6 and grade 7 cohorts, which were contrasted with data collected at Time 3 on the grade 4 and grade 5 cohorts respectively. The latter groups had been exposed to the intervention program during approximately 20 months at that time.

An attractive feature of the design is the fact that two of the cohorts serve as a base line group in one set of comparisons and as a treatment group in another. This is the case with the grade 5 cohort at Time 1 the data for which are used as a base line in comparison with the grade 4 cohort data collected at Time 2 (after eight months of intervention). In addition, the grade 5 cohort data obtained at Time 2 serve to evaluate the possible effects of eight months of intervention when they are compared with the data for the grade 6 cohort at Time 1. The same situation applies to the grade 6 cohort in comparisons with the grade 5 and grade 7 cohorts respectively.

The advantage of this aspect of the design is that a possible bias in the sampling of the cohorts ("selection bias") would operate in opposite directions in the two sets of comparisons, thus making it much more "difficult" to obtain consistent (apparent) "intervention effects" across cohorts as a consequence of such bias. There are, however, no grounds for expecting such bias since the classes/schools were distributed on the different cohorts by a basically random procedure. Accordingly, the cohorts should be essentially equivalent in important respects at Time 1. This aspect of the design would provide the same kind of protection against faulty conclusions in case the base line data for one or both of these cohorts were unusually high or low simply as a function of chance.

To avoid erroneous conclusions due to possible selective attrition (more extreme or deviant individuals may be more likely to drop out in longitudinal studies), analyses were restricted to students for whom there were valid data at both time points in a particular comparison (both for the base line and the intervention groups). In the present research, however, the results were basically the same whether we controlled or did not control for such attrition.

Statistical analyses

Since classes rather than students were the basic sampling units (with students nested within classes), it was considered important to choose a data analytic strategy that reflected the basic features of the design. Accordingly, data were analyzed with ANOVA (analysis of variance) with students nested within classes nested within schools nested within times/occasions (Time 1 versus Time 2, Time 1 versus Time 3). Sex of the subjects was crossed with times, schools (within times), and classes (within schools). (For additional information, see Olweus, 1991; Olweus & Alsaker, 1991).

Properties of the outcome variables analyzed are discussed elsewhere in some detail (Olweus, 1991). Generally, it was concluded that the evidence available attests to the adequacy and validity of the data employed.

Main results

Results for the variable "Being exposed to direct bullying" and "Bullying other students" are presented separately for boys and girls in Figures 2-5. In Figure 6, the results for the variable "Total antisocial behavior" is shown for boys and girls combined (only Time 1-Time 2 comparisons).

Since the design of the study is relatively complex, a few words about how to read the figures are in order.

The panel to the left in, for example, Figure 2 shows the effects after eight months of intervention, while the one to the right displays the results after 20 months. The upper curves (designated "Before") show the base line data (Time 1) for the relevant cohorts (the grade 5, grade 6, and grade 7 cohorts in the left panel and the grade 6 and grade 7 cohorts in the right). The lower curves (designated "After") display data collected at Time 2 (after eight months of intervention) in the panel to the left and at Time 3 (after 20 months of intervention) in the right-hand panel for the age-equivalent cohorts (the grade 4, grade 5 and grade 6 cohorts at Time 2 and the grade 4 and grade 5 cohorts at Time 3). Figure 6 refers only to the effects after eight months of intervention.

The main findings of the analyses can be summarized as follows:

(1) There were marked reductions in the levels of bully/victim problems for the periods studied, eight and 20 months of intervention respectively. By and large, reductions were obtained for both boys and girls and across all cohorts compared. See Figures 2-5.

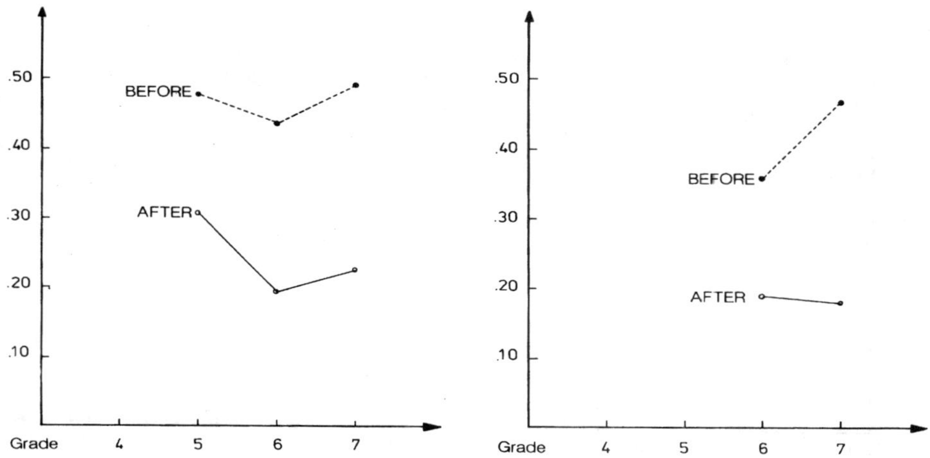

Figure 2: Effects of intervention program on "Being exposed to direct bullying" for boys. Panel to the left shows effects after eight months of intervention, and panel to the right displays results after 20 months of intervention. Upper curves (designated "Before") show base line data (Time 1), and the lower curves (designated "After") display data collected at Time 2 in the left panel and at Time 3 in the panel to the right.

(2) Similar reductions were obtained for the aggregated "peer rating" variables "number of students being bullied in the class" and "number of students in the class bullying others". There was thus consensual agreement in the classes that bully/victim problems had decreased during the periods studied.

(3) In terms of percentages of students reporting being bullied or bullying others, the reductions amounted to approximately 50% or more in most comparisons.

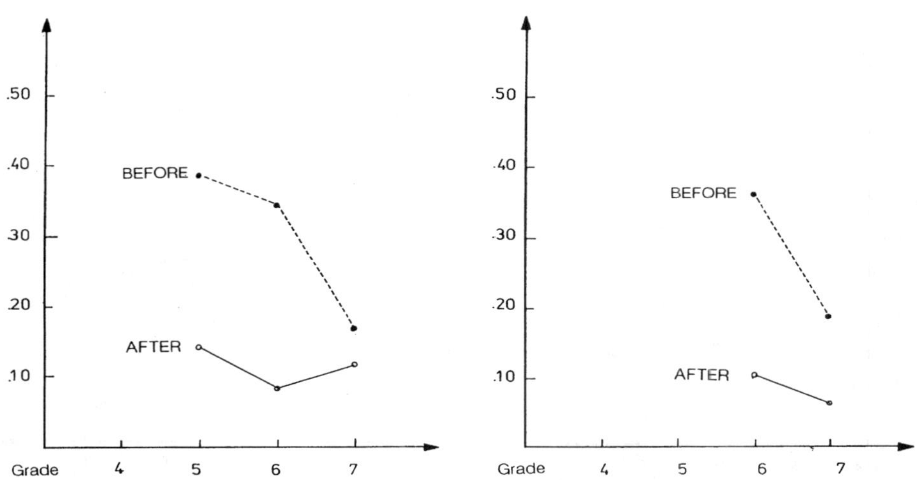

Figure 3: Effects of intervention program on "Being exposed to direct bullying" for girls. See Figure 2 for explanation of the figure.

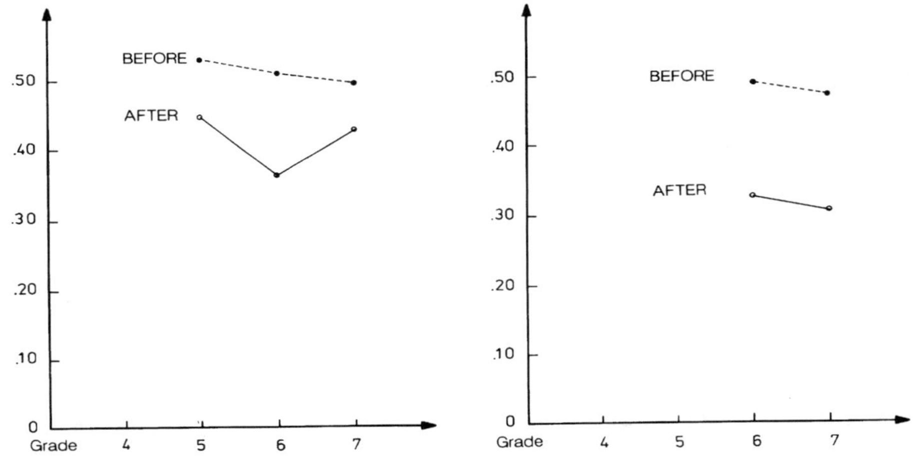

Figure 4: Effects of intervention program on "Bullying other students" for boys. See Figure 2 for explanation of the figure.

(4) There was no displacement of bullying from the school to the way to and from school. There were reductions or no changes on the items measuring bully/victim problems on the way to and from school.

(5) There was also a reduction in general antisocial behavior such as vandalism, fighting, pilfering, drunkenness, and truancy (see Figure 6). (For the grade 6 comparisons, the effects were weak for both time periods. See Olweus, 1989, for details about the construction of the 23-item scale.)

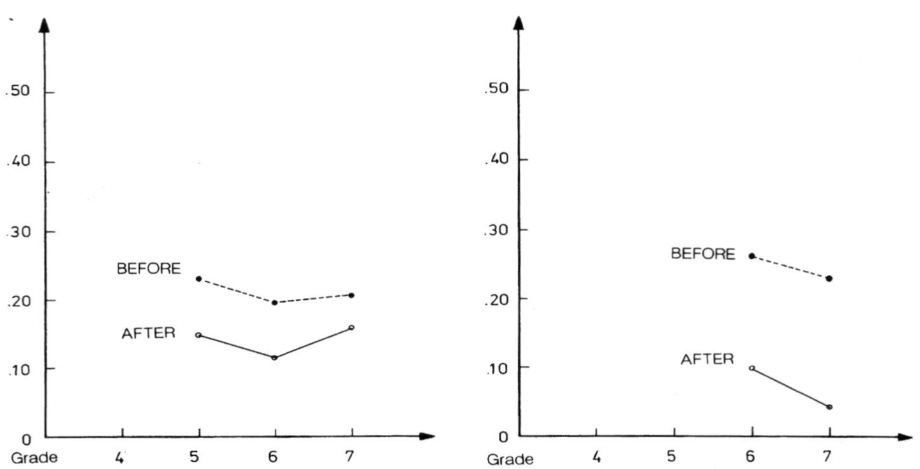

Figure 5: Effects of intervention program on "Bullying other students" for girls. See Figure 2 for explanation of the figure.

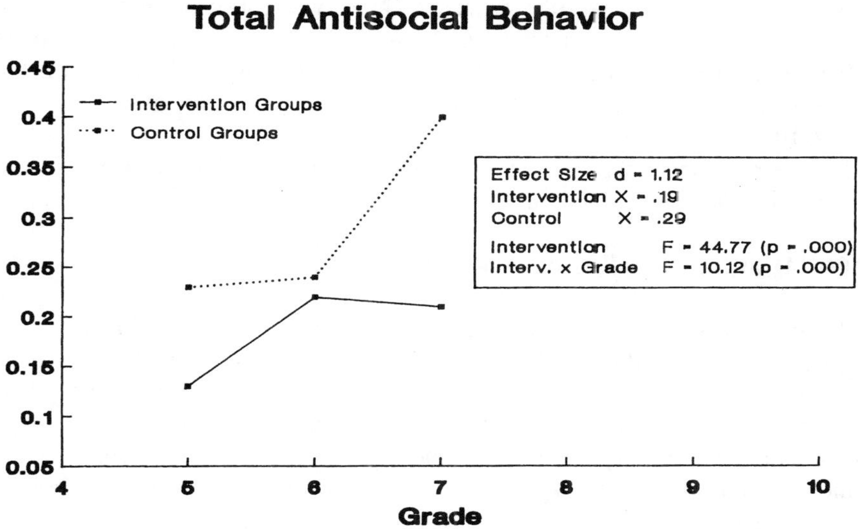

Figure 6: Effects of intervention program on "Total antisocial behavior" for boys and girls combined. Time 1 (Control Groups) verses Time 2 (Intervention Groups).

(6) In addition, we could register marked improvement as regards various aspects of the "social climate" of the class: improved order and discipline, more positive social relationships, and a more positive attitude to school work and the school.

(7) At the same time, there was an increase in student satisfaction with school life as reflected in "liking recess time".

(8) For several of the variables, the effects of the intervention program were more marked after two years than after one year.

In the majority of comparisons for which reductions were reported above, the difference between base line and intervention groups were highly significant or significant.

Prevention of new cases of victimization

By combining information from two questionnaire items it was possible, given certain reasonable assumptions, to estimate which victimized individuals at a certain time point were "new cases" and which were not. In this way, incidence rates (number and percentage of new cases, see Olweus, 1989) could be calculated for each cohort and time point, to be related to incidence data from the relevant comparison cohort.

At baseline (Time 1 in Figure 1) - before the intervention - the percentage of new victimization cases (out of the total number of subjects) was estimated at 2.6% for the boys and 1.7% for the girls. After the intervention program (Times 2 and 3 in Figure 1), corresponding figures were considerably lower, approximately .6% for the boys and .5% for the girls. These results indicate that the intervention program did not only affect already existing victimization problems but also reduced considerably the number/percentage of new cases. On the basis of these analyses it can be concluded that the *intervention program had both primary and secondary prevention effects* (Cowen, 1984).

It may be mentioned that, at Time 1, the new cases estimated in this way constituted approximately 20% of the total number of victimized children.

Quality of data and possible alternative interpretations

It is beyond the scope of this chapter to discuss in detail the quality of the data collected and the possibility of alternative interpretations of the findings. An extensive discussion of these matters can be found elsewhere (Olweus, 1991). Here I limit myself to summarizing the conclusions in the following "point statements":

Self-reports, which were implicated in most of the analyses conducted so far, are in fact the best data source for the purposes of this study. (It should be noted, however, that largely parallel results were obtained for the peer rating variables mentioned above and for teacher ratings of bully/victim problems at the class level; in the latter case, however, the effects were somewhat weaker.)

It is very difficult to explain the results obtained as a consequence of (a) underreporting by the students; (b) gradual changes in the students' attitudes to bully/victim problems; (c) repeated measurement; and (d) concomitant changes in other factors, including general time trends. All in all, it is *concluded that the reductions in bully/victim and associated problems described above are likely to be mainly a consequence of the intervention program and not of some other "irrelevant" factor.*

In addition, a clear "dosage-response" relationship ($r = .51$, $n = 80$) has been established in preliminary analyses at the class level (which is the natural unit of analysis in this case): those classes that showed larger reductions in bully/victim problems had implemented three presumably essential components of the intervention program (including establishment of class rules against bullying and use of class meetings) to a greater extent than those with smaller changes (additional information on these analyses can be found in Olweus and Alsaker, 1991). This finding certainly provides corroborating evidence for the effects of the intervention program. It will be followed up with more systematic and comprehensive analyses.

Brief comments

The reported effects of the intervention program must be considered quite positive in particular since most previous attempts to systematically reduce aggressive and antisocial behavior in pre-adolescents/adolescents have been relatively unsuccessful (e.g., Dumas, 1989; Gottfredson, 1987; Kazdin, 1987). The importance of the results is also accentuated by the fact that there has occurred a highly disturbing increase in the prevalence of violence and other antisocial behavior in most industrialized societies in the last decades. In the Scandinavian countries, for instance, various forms of registered criminality have typically increased by 400-600% since the 1950s or the 1960s.

As mentioned above, we can estimate that approximately 80,000 students in Norwegian comprehensive schools were involved in bully/victim problems in 1983. On the basis of the reported results the following conclusion can be drawn: *if all primary and secondary/junior high schools in Norway used the intervention program in the way it was used in Bergen, the number of students involved in bully/victim problems would be reduced to 40,000 or less in a relatively short period of time.* Effective use of the intervention program would also result in lower levels of theft, vandalism, and other antisocial behavior, which would save society large amounts of money.

Basic principles

Having described the design of the intervention program and reported on some of its effects, it is now natural to present its underlying principles and major sub-goals.

The intervention program is built around *a limited set of key principles* derived chiefly from research on the development and modification of the implicated problem behaviors, in particular aggressive behavior. It is considered important to try to create a school (and ideally, also home) environment characterized by *warmth, positive interest, and involvement from adults* on one hand and *firm limits to unacceptable behavior* on the other. Third, in cases of violations of limits and rules, *non-hostile, non-physical sanctions* should be consistently applied. Implied in the latter two principles is also a certain degree of *monitoring and surveillance* of the students' activities in and out of school (Patterson, 1986). Finally, adults are supposed to *act as authorities at least in some respects*. In a sense, the present intervention program is based on an *authoritative adult-child interaction, or child rearing, model (cf. e.g., Baumrind, 1967) applied to the school setting*.

The first three of these principles largely represent the opposite of the child rearing dimensions that have been found in our research to be important in the development of an aggressive reaction pattern (Olweus, 1980); negativism on the part of the primary caretaker, permissiveness and lack of clear limits, and use of power-assertive methods.

The principles listed above were translated into a number of specific measures to be used at the *school, class*, and *individual levels*. It is considered important to work on all of these levels, if possible. Space limitations prevent a description of the various measures but such an account can be found in the book *Bullying at school -what we know and what we can do* (Olweus, 1993). Figure 7 lists a set of core components which are considered, on the basis of statistical analyses and our experience with the program, to be particularly important in any implementation of the program.

With regard to implementation and execution, the program is mainly based on a *utilization of the existing social environment*: teachers and other school personnel, students and parents. Non-mental health professionals thus play a major role in the desired *restructuring of the social environment*. "Experts" such as school psychologists and social workers may also serve important functions such as planning and coordinating, counselling teacher and parent groups, and handling more serious cases.

General Prerequisites

++ **Awareness and involvement on the part of adults**

Measures at The School Level

++ **Questionnaire survey**

++ **School conference day**

++ **Better supervision during recess**

+ **Meeting staff - parents (PTA meeting)**

Measures at the Class Level

++ **Class rules against bullying**

++ **Class meetings**

Measures at the Individual Level

++ **Serious talks with bullies and victims**

++ **Serious talks with parents of involved students**

+ **Teacher and parent use of imagination**

Figure 7: Overview of core components of the Olweus anti-bullying intervention program (++ core component; + highly desirable component).

Additional characteristics

Further understanding of the program and its way of working can be gained from a brief description of four major sub-goals.

To increase awareness of the bully/victim problem and advance knowledge about it including to dispel some of the myths about it and its causes. Use of the questionnaire is an important step in obtaining more specific knowledge about the frequency and nature of the problems in a particular school.

To achieve active involvement on the part of teachers and parents. This implies among other things that the adults must recognize that it is their responsibility to control to a certain degree what goes on among the children at school. One way of doing this is to provide adequate supervision during recess time. Further, the teachers are encouraged to intervene in possible bullying situations and give a clear message to the students: bullying is not accepted in our school. Teachers are also strongly advised to initiate serious talks with victims and bullies, and their parents, if a bully/victim problem has been identified in the class. Again, the basic message should be: we don't tolerate bullying in our school and will see to it that it comes to an end. Such an intervention on the part of the school must be regularly followed up and closely supervised; otherwise the situation may easily become worse for the victim than before the intervention.

To develop clear rules against bullying behavior such as: (a) we shall not bully others; (b) we shall try to help students who are bullied; (c) we shall make a point to include students who become easily left out. Such a set of rules may serve as a basis for class discussions about what is meant by bullying behavior in concrete situations and what kind of sanctions should be used for students who break the rules. The behavior of the students in the class should be regularly related to these rules in class meetings ("social hour"), and it is important that the teacher make consistent use of sanctions (some form of non-hostile, non-physical punishment) in cases of rule violations and also give generous praise when the rules have been followed.

To provide support and protection for the victims. If followed, class rules against bullying certainly support children who tend to be victimized. In addition, the teacher may enlist the help of "neutral" or well-adjusted students to alleviate the situation of the victims in various ways. Also, teachers are encouraged to use their imagination to help victimized students to assert themselves in the class, to make them valuable in the eyes of their classmates. Parents of victims are exhorted to help their children develop new peer contacts and to teach them in detail how to make new acquaintances and to maintain a friendship relation.

It may be added that the present intervention program has been evaluated by more than 1000 Norwegian and Swedish teachers. In short, their reactions have generally been quite favorable, indicating among other things that the teachers see the proposed principles and measures as useful and realistic. Furthermore, possible reasons for the effectiveness of the program have been discussed in some detail in Olweus, 1992.

Concluding Words

The basic message of our findings is quite clear: it is definitely possible to reduce substantially bully/victim problems in school and related problem behaviors with a suitable intervention program. Thus, whether these problems will be tackled or not no longer depends on whether we have the knowledge necessary to achieve desirable changes. It is much more a matter of our willingness to involve ourselves and to use the existing knowledge to counteract these problems.

References

Bandura, A. (1973). *Aggression: A social learning analysis*. Englewood Cliffs, N. J.: Prentice-Hall.

Baumrind, D. (1967). Child care practices anteceding three patterns of preschool behavior. *Genetic Psychology Monographs*, *75*, 43-88.

Cook, T. D., & Campbell, D. T. (1979). *Quasi-experimentation*. Chicago: Rand McNally.

Cowen, E. L. (1984). A general structural model for primary program development in mental health. *Personnel and Guidance Journal*, *62*, 485-490.

Dumas, J. E. (1989). Treating antisocial behavior in children: Child and family approaches. *Clinical Psychology Review*, *9*, 197-222.

Gottfredson, G. D. (1987). Peer group interventions to reduce the risk of delinquent behavior: A selective review and a new evaluation. *Criminology*, *25*, 187-203.

Kazdin, A. E. (1987). Treatment of antisocial behavior in children: Current status and future directions. *Psychological Bulletin, 102*, 187-203.

Lagerspetz, K. M., Björkqvist, K., Berts, M., & King, e. (1982). Group aggression among school children in three schools. *Scandinavian Journal of Psychology, 23*, 45-52.

Loeber, R., & Dishion, T. (1983). Early predictors of male delinquency: A review. *Psychological Bulletin, 94*, 69-99.

Magnusson, D., Stattin, H., & Dunér, A. (1983). Aggression and criminality in a longitudinal perspective. In K. T. Van Dusen & S. A. Mednick (Eds.), *Prospective studies of crime and delinquency*. Boston: Kluwer-Nijhoff.

Olweus, D. (1973a). *Hackkycklingar och översittare: Foskning om skol-mobbning*. Stockholm: Almqvist & Wiksell.

Olweus, D. (1973b). Personality and aggression. In J. K. Cole & D. D. Jensen (Eds.), *Nebraska symposium on motivation, 1972: Vol. 20* (pp. 261-321). Lincoln: University of Nebraska Press.

Olweus, D. (1977). Aggression and peer acceptance in adolescent boys: Two short-term longitudinal studies of ratings. *Child Development, 48*, 1301-1313.

Olweus, D. (1978). *Aggression in the schools: Bullies and whipping boys*. Washington D. C.: Hemisphere (Wiley).

Olweus, D. (1979). Stability of aggressive reaction patterns in males: A review. *Psychological Bulletin, 86*, 852-875.

Olweus, D. (1980). Familial and temperamental determinants of aggressive behavior in adolescent boys: A causal analysis. *Developmental Psychology, 16*, 644-660.

Olweus, D. (1981). Bullying among school boys. In N. Cantwell (Ed.), *Children and violence* (pp. 97-131). Stockholm: Akademilitteratur.

Olweus, D. (1983). Low school achievement and aggressive behavior in adolescent boys. In D. Magnusson & V. Allen (Eds.), *Human development. An interactional perspective* (pp. 353-365). New York: Academic Press.

Olweus, D. (1984). Aggressors and their victims: Bullying at school. In N. Frude & H. Gault (Eds.), *Disruptive behavior in schools* (pp. 57-76). New York: Wiley.

Olweus, D. (1985). 80000 barn er innblandet i mobbning. *Norsk Skoleblad* (Oslo, Norway), *35*, 18-23.

Olweus, D. (1986). *Mobbning - vad vi vet och vad vi kan göra*. Stockholm: Liber.

Olweus, D. (1987). Bully/victim problems among school children. In J. P. Myklebust & R. Ommundsen (Eds.), *Psykologprofesjonen mot ar 2000* (pp. 395-413). Oslo: Universitetsforlaget.

Olweus, D. (1991). Bully/victim problems among school children: Basic facts and effects of a school based intervention program. In D. Pepler & K. Rubin (Eds.), *The development and treatment of childhood aggression* (pp. 411-448). Hillsdale, N. J.: Erlbaum.

Olweus, D. (1992). Bulling among school children: Intervention and prevention. In R. D. Peters, R. J. McMahon, & V. L. Quincy (Eds.), *Aggression and violence throughout the life span* (pp. 100-125). Newbury Park, C. A.: Sage.

Olweus, D. (1993). *Bullying at school: What we know and what we can do*. Oxford: Blackwell Publishers.

Olweus, D. (in press). Annotation: Bullying at school: Basic facts and effects of a school based intervention program. *Journal of Clinical Psychology and Psychiatry*.

Olweus, D., & Alsaker, F. D. (1991). Assessing change in a cohort longitudinal study with hierarchical data. In D. Magnusson, L. Bergman, G. Rudinger, & B. Törestad (Eds.), *Problems and methods in longitudinal research*. New York: Cambridge University Press.

Olweus, D., & Smith, P. K. (in press). *Manual for the Olweus Bully/Victim Questionnaire*. Oxford: Blackwell Publishers.

Patterson, G. R. (1986). Performance models for antisocial boys. *American Psychologist, 41*, 432-444.

Perry, D. G., Kusel, S. J., & Perry, L. C. (1988). Victims of peer aggression. *Developmental Psychology*, *24*, 807-814.

Smith, P. (1989). *The silent nightmare: Bullying and victimization in school peer groups*. Paper presented at the meeting of the British Psychological Society, London, England.

[2] There is an (expanded) English version of this questionnaire (one version for grades 1-4, and another for grades 5-9 and higher grades). This questionnaire will soon be available from Blackwell (Olweus & Smith, in press).

[3] The updated "package" related to the intervention program consists of the Bully/Victim Questionnaire, a 20-minute video cassette showing scenes from everyday lives of two bulied children (with English subtitles; for European or North American current), and a copy of the book *Bullying at school - what we know and what we can do* (Olweus, 1993; this book is sold in bookstores or through direct order from the publisher) which describes in detail the program and its implementation. The video can be ordered from the author. For more information, please write to the author at the University of Bergen, Oysteingate 3, N-5007 Bergen, Norway.

[1] The research reported in this chapter was supported by grants from the William T. Grant Foundation, the Norwegian Research Council for Social Research, the Swedish Delegation for Social Research (DSF), and in earlier phases, from the Norwegian Ministry of Education which is gratefully acknowledged.

Part IV

Legal Decision Making

Anchored Narratives: a Theory of Judicial Reasoning, and its Consequences

Willem A. Wagenaar

In criminal trials the finder of fact is often confronted with problems that have no logical solution. This is because sometimes the evidence is incomplete or contradictory. Sometimes statements are probabilistic, in the sense that they contain expressions like "maybe", "possibly", and similar quantifiers of uncertainty; other statements are mistakes or even lies. There is no *algorithm* for solving such ill-defined problems, and judges and juries must find their own personal ways. The law, especially rules of evidence, may give some guidance, but the final criterion for acceptance of a solution is purely subjective: the "beyond reasonable doubt" criterion in Anglo-Saxon countries, the inner "conviction" in many countries on the European continent. How are such problems solved, and how is it decided that the criterion of subjective certainty is met?

The Theory of Anchored Narratives

I will skip over a number of theoretical traditions and their proponents, and introduce the notion of the *evaluation of narratives*. This theory proposes that judges evaluate the quality of narratives, offered by the prosecution and the defense. Narratives are accepted as true if they meet a number of criteria, that determine their "goodness". Bennett & Feldman (1981), for instance, proposed that the goodness of a narrative is determined by two factors: the presence of a coherent central action, and a setting that makes the action understandable. Pennington & Hastie (1986, 1988) and others have elaborated upon this idea, and provided empirical evidence for it. A further adaptation of the narrative theory was presented by Crombag, Van Koppen, & Wagenaar (1992), and Wagenaar, Van Koppen, & Crombag (1993). The present contribution summarizes this adaptation, some of the supporting evidence, and a few, possibly surprising consequences.

Good narratives are not sufficient in the courtroom: on top of being "good" they must be tied to reality by means of evidence. No matter how clear the theme is of John's purported murder of his wife, no matter how compelling the description of the circumstances in which the murder occurred, there must be evidence that John actually did it. I propose, however, that evidence is nothing else but another narrative. Let us assume that the evidence against John is the fact that the murder weapon contained his fingerprints. To the court that is not a fact, it is a narrative told by a witness, possibly a police officer. The witness tells how he analyzed traces on the weapon, how he compared the fingerprints to those of John, why he thinks the prints are identical, etc. The truth of this narrative depends again on its consistency and the compellingness of circumstances. For instance, why should the court believe that this weapon was the actual murder weapon? Because it was found next to the body? That is only a compelling argument when it is believed, as a general rule, that weapons found close to bodies are always (or almost always) murder weapons. Once this rule is doubted, the whole story about the fingerprints falters, and there is no evidence. The problem can be solved by another expert witness, who explains that he performed some tests on the weapon, and discovered that it had fired the fatal bullet. That evidence seems to complete the proof of John's guilt, but again: it is a narrative. The expert tells the story of a weapon and a bullet that were given to him, how he performed tests, how he compared traces on various bullets, etc. We may believe his story, but many questions remain unanswered. How do we know that he is talking about the same weapon, and about the actual bullet found in the body? How do we know he is competent and honest? There may be additional evidence that provides answers to all these questions but that evidence consists again of narratives and nothing else. The ever regressing process of finding evidence for narratives ends only when all parties share a general belief, of which the narrative is a special case. For instance, when a ballistic expert claims that two bullets were fired by the same weapon, his narrative may be accepted because all parties have absolute faith in ballistic experts. The reasoning then is:

- All ballistic experts tell the truth when they testify within the domain of their expertise.
- This is a ballistic expert, testifying about ballistics.
- Therefore his testimony is true.

The theory of anchored narratives claims that finders of fact are doing this: judge the quality of the narratives offered to them, and try to anchor them to generally accepted beliefs. Usually the beliefs are stated in an uncertain form: "Most ballistic experts tell the truth". This leaves an opportunity for asking further questions. In what conditions are ballistic experts not speaking the truth; why should we believe the testimony of this particular expert? A lawyer may engage in an infinite regression of such questions, till a stop-rule dictates the end. Examples of stop-conditions are:

- Both parties share the belief that is reached.
- The trial judge prevents further questioning because he trusts the general belief that is reached.
- The law offers the belief as a certain fact.

A schematic representation of the theory is presented in Figure 1. Here it is seen that the narrative is divided into a number of sections; each section needs it own anchoring. Examples of themes that qualify for independent anchoring are:

Identity; who did it?

Actus reus; what did he do?

Mens rea; did he do it intentionally?

In Figure 1 it is seen that all three themes are anchored in some manner, but the complexity of the anchoring constructions varies. One anchoring is direct, the other two contain various levels of evidence. One anchoring branches out considerably. The mass of beliefs assumed to be shared by most people is sketched as a rugged landscape, with peaks and hollows. This is the representation of what the court (judges or jury members) believes to be shared by most *others*. On some topics the court is rather credulous; it assumes that most people hold something for true that, in fact, deserves further questioning. Such a belief is a peak in the belief landscape, which is

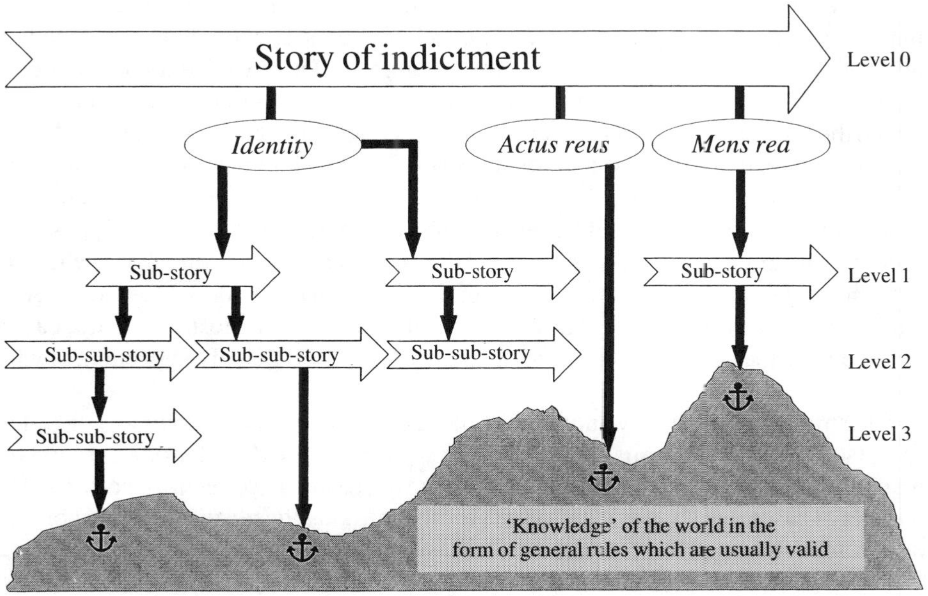

Figure 1: Theory of Anchored Narratives

easily reached by an anchor coming from above. In other cases the court is rather critical, and needs to be convinced by a detailed exposition, involving many levels.

Testing by Anomalies

How does one test such a theory of judicial reasoning? One may simply ask judges how they reason. Or one may collect think-aloud protocols. In some countries, like the Netherlands, one may read the verdicts, because law requires that they contain explicit reasons. One may present artificial cases to judges or jury members, in order to study their reactions to experimental manipulations hidden under the cover of a case description.

For various reasons we decided not to use any of these methods. Instead we resorted to a somewhat unusual method: the prediction of anomalies. Anchored narratives is a heuristic; like all naturally evolved heuristics it works well in the majority of the situations, and goes awry in some exceptional cases. These exceptions are probably not representative, but they are highly revealing. All theories of judicial reasoning predict about the same result in the majority of the cases; therefore the majority of cases does not help to discriminate among theories. We studied a particular small minority of cases, whose existence is predicted by the theory of anchored narratives, while other theories predict that they cannot possibly occur. If the anomalies do occur, they constitute a support for our theory. For example, theories that propose some form of *logical inference* as the vehicle of judicial reasoning, predict that there can be no conviction just on the basis of the strength of the narrative, without any further evidence. Anchored narratives predicts that in some extreme cases the story is so plausible that it is anchored directly to the belief structure, without any intermediate level of evidence (like the second theme in Figure 1). Theories that assume a logical analysis of all possible explanations of the facts, accepting guilt only if all versions in which the accused is innocent are falsified, predict that nobody will be convicted when there is another equally or even more likely suspect. Anchored narratives predicts that such convictions will happen, because plausibility and anchoring do not require the logical exclusion of other and better narratives. Theories that propose some sort of probabilistic revision of opinion predict that there can be no conviction when the evidence in favour of innocence is more diagnostic than the evidence favouring guilt. Anchored narratives, on the other hand, predicts that very diagnostic evidence can be omitted from the anchoring structure, without affecting the perceived strength of what remains.

The strategy of testing by anomalies is not unlike the use of neurological disorders as tests of theories of normal functioning of the brain. One disorder of a certain type may prove the operation of mechanisms that are not easily discernable in normals. The number of cases that show the disorder is irrelevant, and indeed, considerable portions of theoretical work are accepted on the basis of a few extraordinary neurological cases. In the same way it is not important whether in our analyses of criminal trials we find many examples of a certain anomaly; just one is enough to demonstrate the working of anchored narratives. The collection of anomalies to which I will refer throughout this paper was collected by Crombag, Van Koppen, and me (cf. Wagenaar, Van Koppen, & Crombag, 1993) by using two selection criteria. We asked lawyers to present us with cases in which:

- A client was first convicted, but acquitted on appeal, or
- A client was convicted although the lawyer was convinced of the client's innocence.

Thirty-five such cases were minutely analyzed, to see whether they were examples of the anomalies listed below. All of them were, and quite often a case was an example of many anomalies. In the discussion below I will present only one or two examples for each anomaly, although the collection of 35 cases contained many more. But, as argued before, one case is enough to demonstrate an anomaly's existence.

Eight Anomalies

1. Narratives are believed although there is no evidence Anchored narratives predicts that a narrative can be anchored directly, without any intervening evidence. An example is the case of *Henkemans*. He was convicted of smuggling 16 kilos of heroin. Before Henkemans arrived at Amsterdam Airport the police were tipped off by an informer that he carried heroin in his suitcase. They decided not to arrest him immediately, but instead, to follow him till he made contact with a local drug gang. Henkemans took his suitcase to a hotel, where he met with two Chinese. A few hours later the Chinese left the hotel, and took the suitcase (presumedly the same, but we cannot be sure of that) to their house. When the police raided the house they found 16 kilos of heroin. There is no logical proof that all or even a portion of this heroin had been in the suitcase, which contained no traces of heroin. The house of the two Chinese was built as a "safe house", which means that it was designed for hiding drugs. One may infer that the two Chinese had owned heroin before. How then, can it be proved that the heroin in their house came from Henkemans? We propose that Henkemans was convicted just because the story was too good. He came from Thailand on a ticket that was given to him by a friend whose name and address he could not remember. The police were tipped off about him. The first thing he did in Amsterdam was contact two professional dealers. What else could he be but a drug courier? His own account of the facts was highly unsatisfactory. He claimed that giving away free tickets is normal among friends in Thailand; in exchange he had carried a suitcase with delicatessen which his friend wanted to present to his Chinese relations in Amsterdam. Henkemans was convicted, although there was no evidence that he had ever carried heroin.

Henkemans' story is an example of what we have labelled "dissociation of conviction and proof". A court can be convinced by circumstances that will never be accepted as legal proof. Dutch law specifies clearly that the conviction should be based upon the facts that are presented as legal proof. The reasoned verdict, required by law in The Netherlands, should list the elements of proof that are both legal and convincing. Such elements are absent in Henkemans' case; how was he then convicted? In the course of time the presentation of a coherent reasoning has been reduced to a mere listing of the elements of proof, without a logical context that explains what these elements prove, and why. Such a listing is meaningless if it just mentions something like "The finding of the heroin in the safe house, the behaviour of Henkemans after his arrival in Amsterdam, and his own statements". It does not explain why the court was convinced that Henkemans' suitcase contained 16 kilograms of heroin.

Another example of dissociation occurred in the case of Carroll accused of being one of the IRA-members who killed two Australian tourists in Roermond. The only evidence relating Carroll to the scene of the murder was an identification made by two witnesses who had seen the terrorists escape in a car. The witnesses had looked into the car for about 1.5 sec., as it passed their house. It was dark, the car had tinted windows, and the one man that was visible was seen from the side, while he was turning his face away. Moreover the face of the defendant had been shown on TV and in the newspapers, and the witnesses had seen this. The prosecutor concluded that, maybe, the recognitions were not convincing, but they were not illegal. The convincing evidence consisted of a large number of suggestive circumstances that made a good story but that could never be used as legal evidence. Thus the prosecutor asked the court to convict Carroll on the basis of a narrative, not supported by evidence. The court obliged him readily, although later, on appeal, Carroll was acquitted.

2. *The narrative that wins the battle is clearly false* A court may compare the quality of two opposing stories, instead of comparing the quality of their anchorings. Thus it may happen that the winning story is insufficiently anchored, as in the case of Henkemans, above. A stronger case, however, is one in which the winning narrative,

although a better story, is clearly disproved by the facts. An example is the case of Karakaya, accused of killing an old man Ekkers, who lived in the same apartment building.

The prosecution's story was that Karakaya killed Ekkers with the intention of robbing him. Indeed around 2 p.m. Karakaya tried to sell some goods that were stolen from Ekkers' flat. But that does not prove that he killed the old man: there were a few other suspects, like Karakaya's wife Cemile, and Ekkers' son Sietze. Karakaya's own account of the facts was changed six times, with the effect that his story was totally incredible at the end. In some of these versions he confessed to the crime, but his successive descriptions followed closely the changing information available to the police, thus suggesting that the police pressed him to confess. Karakaya's later protestations that he was forced to confess were not accepted. His narrative simply lost against the much better narrative of the prosecution. Still, the prosecution's account contained a clear impossibility. It claimed that Ekkers was killed around noon. The other suspects had an alibi for that time, while Karakaya had not. But three witnesses had seen Ekkers alive at two o'clock in the afternoon. One of them even spoke with him; he had said that he expected a visit from his son Sietze, and that there was a quarrel about money. A fourth witness stated that he spoke to Ekkers on the phone at about 12.45 pm. Quite a few people saw Karakaya selling the stolen goods before two o'clock, which can be squared with the other testimony only if he returned to kill Ekkers *after* selling the stolen property. But that is not the prosecution's story. The court accepted that Ekkers was murdered around noon, although there was no single piece of evidence to confirm this time slot. It failed to explain on what grounds the testimony by four witnesses was rejected.

The theory of anchored narratives predicts that falsifications of the narrative play no significant role (cf. Anomaly 5, below) so that a battle between stories is not decided by the fact that one of the two is impossible. The decision of guilt is a two-step process: first the battle between narratives is waged, in which the quality of the stories is the prevailing factor. The subsequent anchoring occurs through a selection of supporting evidence, which in a complicated case is always available in sufficient amounts. The falsifying evidence is discounted with or without further reasons. There is no attempt to anchor the narrative that lost the battle, so that a difference in quality of anchoring will never become evident. For instance, in the case of Henkemans the police never searched for delicatessen in the 'safehouse', although such a find would have provided an anchor to Henkemans' story.

3. Important sections of the narrative are not anchored Above it was argued that each narrative should contain details with respect to, at least, three themes: *identity*, *actus reus*, and *mens rea*. Anchored narratives predict that an attempt will be made to provide enough anchors to make the narrative convincing, but not necessarily anchors for each of the three themes. Thus it may happen that the *actus reus*, the criminal act, is not anchored at all, such as in the case of Henkemans, in which it was never proved that he actually smuggled heroin. Another example is the case of Mr *Helder*, in which the *mens rea*, the intention to commit a crime, was not proved.

Mr Helder was the driver of a wealthy, old, and extremely ill lady. The lady wanted him to inherit her fortune, and decided to marry him. Six weeks later she was dead. Rumours said that Helder had poisoned her, and he was arrested. The pathologist's report stated that the old lady had died from the combination of drugs and a high dose of alcohol. Helder had administered these on the evening of her death, but there was nothing unusual about this; the lady was an alcoholic and the doctor had prescribed her the drugs in full awareness of this fact. Helder had simply performed a routine action, like on all previous evenings. Even when the lady had died from the combination, there is no reason to believe that Helder intended this to happen. Eight years later it was discovered that the lady had died from a disease called Conn's syndrome, and that the drug-alcohol combination had nothing to do with it. Thus, initially the criminal intention was not proved, while later even the criminal act appeared to be absent. Helder was sentenced to 12 years in prison; the new information did not lead to a revision of the verdict. The appeal court reasoned in its verdict that Helder had strongly *willed* the death of the old lady and that, for that reason, he was the cause of her death. The story of the butler who kills his wealthy employer won again; the total absence of any anchoring for one important theme did not strike the court as a relevant problem.

4. Alternative suspects are not ruled out Since anchoring constructions are only made for the one narrative that is finally accepted by the court, it is not always realised that similar or better constructions can be made to support the guilt of other suspects. The case of Karakaya, described above, is an example of this: there were at least two other suspects, and the courts never explained why Karakaya was a more likely suspect than the others. An almost classical example is the case of the *Graanhout* family.

Mr and Mrs Graanhout were driving through the night, with their baby girl of 18 months sleeping in the back. They stopped because Graanhout wanted to urinate. From this point the stories of the two diverge. Maria claims that Ahmet took the baby and returned later with the dead body in his arms. Ahmet says that Maria had the dead child in her arms when he returned to the car. From this point they agree again: Ahmet tried to resuscitate the baby, they went to find a doctor and ended up in a nearby hospital, where a nurse called the police. The police immediately arrested Ahmet and accepted Maria as a witness. It is not clear on what evidence this decision was based. The nurse had overheard Maria saying that they should get away before the police were informed: clearly she was not the innocent outsider that she pretended to be in a later stage. The statements of both parents are unreliable because they had used a fair amount of drugs on that particular night. But, with a body and a clear accusation from an eyewitness, the case was legally proven, even though the alternative narrative with Maria in the role of the perpetrator, has the same quality of anchoring. But Ahmet was a likely enough suspect to prevent the analysis of other narratives: he was not the real father of the child, he was a black man and a drug addict, and he had a prior conviction for abusing the same child.

In our collection of 35 cases many have one or more quite likely suspects, other than the accused. Who will be treated as the suspect and who will be the witnesses, often depends upon the very first decision by the police. The case of *Rijkbloem* is a clear demonstration of the ensuing problems.

Danny Rijkbloem was arrested for shooting the father of his girlfriend Nicole. His defense was that Nicole had come to his house with her parents, in order to fetch her clothes. There was a quarrel, in which the mother suddenly produced a gun. Rijkbloem hit the mother on the wrist, the gun went off, and the bullet hit the father by accident. Rijkbloem called the police, but when they arrived he was arrested, while Nicole and her mother were accepted as witnesses. Their hands were never tested for traces of gun powder, and they were not searched, so that they could have smuggled out the murder weapon, which was never found. The two women stated that Danny had shot the old man from a distance of about 50 cm, but forensic expertise showed that this was definitely not true, while Rijkbloem's version was borne out by the tests. That marked the two women as likely suspects, but it was too late for the collection of the relevant evidence. Rijkbloem was convicted, to a considerable extent through this early decision of the police at the scene of the crime. Such decisions go uncriticized, because the construction of anchored narratives does not require the analysis of alternatives.

5. Falsifications of the narrative do not prevent its acceptance Logically speaking falsifications of the narrative should lead to its rejection, unless it can be shown that the falsifying evidence is wrong. According to our theory, however, it may happen that the falsifications are not openly contested, while the narrative is still accepted. This is brought about in three different ways. One is that the falsification is not noticed because the anchoring construction contains only verifications. The second is that falsifications are declared unsupported. Falsifications are themselves narratives; without proper anchoring they have no absolute value. A court may decide that the falsifications presented by the defense are not properly anchored, without explaining why this is so. In the case of Karakaya, discussed above, there were four witnesses who had seen the victim after he was supposedly killed. The discounting of these falsifications was probably based on the consideration that these witnesses were not reliable. But the court never explained why they were less reliable than other witnesses, on whose testimony Karakaya was convicted. The third way of discounting falsifications is by constructing a new narrative that fits with the falsifications, but that is not mentioned in the reasoned verdict. This must have happened in the case of *Buendia*.

Pablo Buendia was accused of stabbing his ex-wife Aureliana with a flick knife, and killing her brother Alfredo. The fight had been an almost Shakespearean drama in which Pablo had supposedly first stabbed himself through the heart, and thereafter his ex-wife and her brother. The problem was that the witnesses gave vastly different accounts of what had happened, in which order the various actions had taken place, and who had been present. The court must have made its own compromise story, because the evidence was mutually irreconcilable. In the last stage of the trial the court ordered a forensic analysis of the clothes of the two victims. It appeared that the clothes contained traces of the blood of two men, other than Pablo and Alfredo. Obviously these two had taken part in the fight and had been injured. Who were they? Why had the witnesses not talked about these others? The forensic expertise showed also that Aureliana's and Alfredo's wounds were not made by Pablo's knife. What other knife was there? Who had removed it from the scene and why? The narrative of the prosecution, in which the fighting was among Pablo, Aureliana, and Alfredo, and nobody else, was clearly falsified. There were others, and there was no reason why these others could not have killed Alfredo. But the court convicted Pablo without explaining why the forensic expertise, produced on its own request, was irrelevant or incorrect.

One may attempt a reconstruction of the court's reasoning in this case. It must have been aware of the falsifying evidence; it did not simply overlook it. Also, since the evidence came from the National Forensic Laboratory, the court cannot have failed to accept it as reliable. Hence we must assume that the court tacitly reconciled the conflicting evidence by composing its own narrative. Possibly it supposed that the two unknown men came to the assistance of Aureliana and Alfredo. Pablo attacked them with his flick knife, and they defended themselves with another knife (indeed Pablo had sustained some superficial scratches and not the deep stabbing mentioned in the original story). Pablo had then grabbed their knife and attacked Aureliana and Alfredo with it. This narrative is entirely different, but it fits most facts. Since in this version Pablo is still the murderer of Alfredo, the difference with the prosecutor's narrative does not matter, so that Pablo can be convicted on the same charge.

Our 35 cases abound with falsifications that were not considered in the verdict, and indeed, Dutch law does not prescribe a reasoned rejection of falsifications, no matter how strong they are.

6. The major portion of the evidence may not fit with the narrative The anchoring construction consists of evidence that connects the narrative to general beliefs. The evidence is selected so that it fits this purpose, and it may happen that, in fact, only a small portion of the evidence can be used in this manner. But the anchoring construction will look reliable enough, even when the major portion of the evidence does not fit. In a complicated case it is usually impossible to accommodate all evidence; hence selection is almost dictated by the nature of the task, and there is no law prescribing what proportion of evidence may be ignored.

Once information is lost in the selection process, it is not likely to be considered again. In simple run-of-the-mill cases the reason for omission is not contradiction but redundancy. The advantage of selection would be lost if all rejected information had to be considered again. It is much more practical to evaluate the quality of what is retained. As a consequence it may not be noticed that the rejected information is plentiful and in conflict with the adopted narrative. The case of *Carroll* supplies an example.

Carroll was accused of belonging to the IRA-group that killed two Australian tourists in Roermond. The evidence against Carroll consisted of identification by a married couple, Mr and Mrs Averkamp. There were many problems with these identifications (see above). The picture of Carroll had been shown on television and in the major newspapers before the Averkamps attempted their identification. The identification was by means of exactly the same picture that had been published. Mr Averkamp admitted that he had seen the TV program and the newspaper. Although the newspaper had been lying about, Mrs Averkamp denied seeing the picture, "because it did not interest her". This is at least surprising, since she knew that she was one of the few witnesses to a crime that attracted international interest. Worse was that according to Mr Averkamp's testimony, his wife *did* see the picture and had discussed it with him! Another problem was that the photographic lineup was presented at 11 am to Mr Averkamp, and at 5 pm to Mrs Averkamp. In between they had lunch together. Mrs Averkamp stated that they did not discuss the lineup, Mr Averkamp said that "of course" they discussed it; there was little else they were discussing those days! The court convicted Carroll on the basis of these recognitions and quoted the statements by Mr and Mrs Averkamp. But the quotes ended exactly in the middle of the sentences that contained the contradictions between the witnesses, so that the reasoned verdict revealed nothing of the conflict. With a Dutch court, consisting of professional judges, one may not suppose malevolence. The selection of evidence was probably directed at getting a coherent picture of what actually had happened. Afterwards it was difficult to see that the cited evidence was wholly invalidated by the sections that were left out.

7. The danger of suspect-driven search is not recognized In principle, when a crime has been committed, the facts are used to deduce the identity of the perpetrator. For instance, when fingerprints are found in the vicinity of the body, they may lead to the detection of the only person who has such fingerprints. This is called crime-driven search. The reverse strategy is called *suspect-driven* search. One starts with a suspect; it is unimportant why that person is a suspect, and it needs no further justification. The strategy is to collect as much information about this person as is possible, in the expectation that something will emerge that links him to the crime, or to any crime. A nice example is the case of *Speckman*.

Mr Speckman was recognized as the bankrobber whose face was recorded by a video camera in a bank; the recording was shown in a nation-wide broadcast. Speckman confessed to this robbery. The investigation is an example of crime-driven search: the beginning was a recording and the end result was Speckman's identity. But then he was shown to witnesses of five other robberies. Apart from the fact that the lineup procedures were highly irregular, the recognitions are questionable because they are the product of suspect-driven search. What are the chances that a person is identified at least several times when he is shown to a mass of witnesses from five robberies? A test can be obtained through the presentation of *target-absent* lineups, but this is never done outside the psychological laboratory.

Suspect-driven search is like trawling with a very wide net: you will always catch at least one fish. Examples of such trawling methods abound in our set of 35 cases. In the case of Alderman *Schuddeboom* the real reason for the investigation was a political feud between Schuddeboom and the police; Schuddeboom had ruled against the acquisition of a radar speed control installation. The police started an investigation on Schuddeboom's use of proxy votes. The voting system required that proxies were given on a special form, signed by the Mayor. In fact roughly 700 out of 1000 proxies in Schuddeboom's town were given on illegal forms. Since it is not permitted to receive more than four proxies, the 700 illegal proxies must have been collected by more than 175 different people. The Mayor investigated all the proxies by contacting the voters personally. In the end he accepted only 349 proxies. The only matter that surfaced in the investigation was that irregular procedures were followed by many people; there was no special link to Alderman Schuddeboom. Two of the rejected votes had been given to the wife of Schuddeboom's gardener, Mrs Hol. But her signature on the form was forged. Mr Hol confessed that he had made the forgery. This is what had happened. Schuddeboom had found two brothers, Isaac and Bartolemew Blattgerste, who were willing to let somebody vote for them by proxy. Since Schuddeboom had already four proxy votes, he needed somebody to receive the two new votes. He asked his gardener (who also had received four proxies) whether his wife would vote for the two brothers. Schuddeboom gave him the form and explained where Mrs Hol should place her signature. Hol did not want to go home during lunch time and copied his wife's signature. Clearly, the only criminal act in this story was performed by Hol, not by Schuddeboom. Hol was never prosecuted, although he confessed, but Schuddeboom *was*, allegedly because he had been present and had abetted the crime. These two facts were never proven.

Schuddeboom's case is an example of trawling. The major portion of the initial 1000 proxy votes were collected by members of Schuddeboom's party. It is quite unlikely that a close scrutiny of all votes would *not* have produced an irregularity like the incident with Mrs Hol's signature. Placed within the context of the vast fishing expedition the facts seem insignificant. But the anchored narrative makes another impression. It does not explain that the police wanted to get at Schuddeboom anyway, and that they needed an analysis of 1000 proxy votes before they were able to pin him down on something.

Similar trawling exercises were found in at least five other of our 35 cases. Suspect driven search appeared to be the rule rather than the exception: in 33 out of 35 cases the investigation started with a suspect who was suspected for unclear reasons, or for reasons that were not at all related to the crime. Subsequent evidence was collected that linked the suspect to the crime. It is surprising how easily such evidence is found, once the police are convinced that they have their man. Since the anchored narrative does not reflect the actual proceedings, the court will not be sensitive to the difference between crime-driven and suspect-driven search, and accept highly questionable investigations.

Identity tests like lineups and showups are in principle suspect-driven. The test does not produce a suspect but may link an already available suspect to a crime. It is of some importance to realise *why* the suspect was suspected in the first place; was that on the basis of crime-driven search, in which case the identity test may serve as a confirmation, or will the test itself constitute the major ground for suspicion? In the last case it must be realised that many others, placed in the position of the suspect, may be "recognized", especially when they are selected on the basis of their outer appearance. In a recent study by Wagenaar (1993) it was shown that innocent suspects are far more likely to be identified in otherwise fair target-absent lineups, when they are only more similar to the real perpetrator than the foils. That is exactly what happens when suspects are suspected because of their appearance. This effect is usually neglected, even in the scientific literature. Navon (1990), for instance, argued that lineups need not be perfect because even with flaws in the procedure it may be highly diagnostic when a suspect is recognised. Well, it is not when the suspect was suspected because of his outer appearance.

Another example of suspect-driven search is the selection of witnesses on the basis of the suspect's appearance. This happens when a picture of the suspect is published on TV or in a newspaper, and the public encouraged to report to the police if they recognize this person as the perpetrator of a particular crime. Witnesses selected in this manner are almost certain to identify the suspect in later confrontations, but the evidence is not logically compelling unless it is mounted in a plausible narrative.

Gross (1987) reported that in 60% of identification suspects are preselected on the basis of such procedures as the two described above. Ten cases in our set of 35 involved identification tests; in four out of these ten, suspects were preselected in the way described above.

8. Anchors are attached to blatantly wrong beliefs The challenge of implicit beliefs is an important aspect of the defense strategy. All evidence against the accused derives it evidentiary value from the connection to a general belief; destruction of that belief removes the evidence. When the defense is not successful in this respect, it may happen that evidence remains connected to erroneous beliefs. A clear example in the previous section was the belief that criminals will not lie about the identity of their accomplices. In The Netherlands the law forbids suspects in the same case to testify against each other. Obviously the legislator feared that suspects might be tempted to lie about each other's role. Unfortunately it is not forbidden for suspects to testify in each other's trial, if the cases are treated separately. Hence the routine practice, approved by our Supreme Court, is to split cases with more than one suspect, so that the accused may legally testify against one another. Obviously the Supreme Court trusted the honesty of witnesses under oath, even when they have a clear interest in lying. Challanging this belief in the courtroom will have little or no effect; not only because there is a Supreme Court ruling, but above all, because judges tend to think in the same way: they really believe that in such conditions witnesses will speak the truth, and also that they can spot a lie when it is told.

Many unsafe or even clearly false beliefs remain unchallenged because they are not made explicit. An extreme case is the trial against Mr *Castelyn*, who was accused of sexually abusing two little girls, Nancy and Gwenny, aged two-and-a-half years and eight months, respectively. Castelyn was convicted on both charges, although the evidence was scanty. In the case of eight months old Gwenny the evidence consisted of an affidavit written by a police officer. According to Dutch law a statement by a police officer needs no further proof; hence the abuse of Gwenny was legally established. But once the belief that police officers do not make mistakes is challenged we are confronted with a whole series of more and more absurd beliefs. The police officer related the story as it was told to him by Gwenny's mother. Thus the underlying belief is that the affidavit is an accurate reproduction of the mother's story, and that the mother spoke the truth. In fact the mother had all sorts of reasons to lie; she had accused Castelyn falsely at a previous occasion. Apart from that, did the mother actually see the abuse? No, she had been told about it by little Nancy, aged two-and-a-half. Thus a further belief is that the mother understood what Nancy tried to say, and that Nancy gave an accurate representation of what actually had happened. According to the affidavit Nancy had said: "Kees stick in belly; Gwenny also ouch". It is not clear what this means. The official interpretation is that "Kees" means the accused, Castelyn, and that stick in belly means an actual penetration. Further that the reference to Gwenny means that Kees did the same to the baby. Let us believe that this is what Nancy meant, even though it requires some mental elasticity; then still the question remains how Nancy could know what Castelyn did to Gwenny. The prosecution's narrative is that Castelyn abused the baby when he changed her diapers in the middle of the night, with nobody present. Hence Gwenny must have communicated her pain and its origin to Nancy. Babies do not talk; they may cry, but their cries are not easy to interpret. We are asked to believe that Gwenny, aged eight months, communicated the abuse by Castelyn to her sister of two-and-a-half. Even when we accept the safety of the triple hearsay construction (from Nancy to mother; mother to police officer; police officer to court by means of a written statement), then still the initial step from Gwenny to Nancy is based upon a clearly absurd belief. The case was tried by a District Court, then by a Court of Appeal, then by the Supreme Court which referred the case back to a second Court of Appeal. None of the learned lawyers in these four colleges pronounced their doubt that Gwenny gave accurate information about the sexual abuse by Castelyn. Not that they would explicitly endorse such an absurd belief: they were simply not forced to analyze their beliefs at a sufficiently deep level.

The reason why narratives are anchored to wrong or even absurd beliefs is not that these beliefs are really shared by the courts. Judges only do not always make the beliefs, presupposed by the evidence, explicit.

The purpose of collecting anomalies was to test some extreme predictions of our theory. Other theories of judicial reasoning do not make such a collection of extreme predictions; therefore I consider the plentiful occurrence of the predicted anomalies as a challenge to other theories, and as support for the theory of anchored narratives.

Universal Rules for the Use of Evidence

The heuristic of anchored narratives is probably the best strategy that a court can follow when evidence is incomplete, probabilistic, and conflicting. But the anomalies, even when they represent the exception rather than the rule, demonstrate that there should be some protection against the possible pitfalls of the heuristic. It is my strong opinion that rules of evidence, trial procedures, and legal precedence have the important role of protecting the accused against the errors introduced by the heuristics that a court may use. Such rules should therefore be based upon a psychological analysis of how courts think, rather than on a logical or legal analysis of problems of evidence. The theory of anchored narratives can therefore be used as a basis for the derivation of *universal* rules for the use of evidence. By "universal" I mean that the rules apply to all systems of criminal law, be they adversarial or inquisitorial, with or without juries, based on common law or on state law. The reason for the claim to universality is that the heuristic of anchored narratives is assumed to operate within the minds of jurors and judges in every system, and in the same manner.

The reader will notice that some of the universal rules proposed are remote from the current practice and may, indeed, be impossible to implement within some of the existing systems. An example is the requirement that courts, whether they consist of professional judges or lay juries, give reasons for their verdict. This is not impossible with lay juries, but it does not happen in any jury system known to me at this moment. It is also not likely that such a practice will be introduced, because juries, who find it already difficult to agree about the decision of guilt, will find it almost impossible to agree about their *reasons*. I will not use practicality as a criterion for the generation of universal rules, however. In a conflict between theory and practice I give preference to our theory because it is based upon a systematic analysis of the problem. If it is impossible to implement a theory-based rule in practice, it means that practice contains a built-in weakness of which we should be aware.

1. Prosecution must present at least one well formed narrative and no more than a limited set of narratives The reason for this rule is clear. The defense cannot attack the narrative that makes the guilt of the accused plausible when that narrative is vague, or when it changes all the time. Examples of vagueness abound in our cases. There are, for instance, indictments making such general claims as that the accused committed a murder on the evening of 23rd March 1990, or at least on the 23rd, or at least in March, or at least in 1990. In other cases the definition of the crime is broad and not specific, such as in the case of *Rabout*.

Franklin Rabout was accused of stabbing his wife with a pair of scissors. Forensic expertise proved convincingly that *she* had stabbed *him* with the scissors. Rabout was subsequently convicted for *biting* his wife, even though biting was never mentioned in the indictment or at the trial. But biting is a form of "grievous bodily harm", and that was the term used in the indictment. But if this term includes such a broad variety of acts, it is impossible to defend the accused against all interpretations that it may get in the hands of a court.

Rule 1 states that courts should not be permitted to construct their own narratives in their deliberations, so that they are not openly discussed at the trial. The prosecution must explain what, in its vision, the accused did and why that is a criminal act; the court decides only whether the claim is sufficiently supported by the facts. In the case of Rabout it was explained afterwards what narrative the court believed to be true: not the prosecutor's story, but something entirely different. Hence, in a way, the prosecution lost its case. But Rabout was convicted nevertheless.

2. Essential components of the narrative must be anchored The central components of the narrative are

- identity (who did it?)
- *actus reus* (what did he do?)
- *mens rea* (did he do it with criminal intent?)

Not only should the narrative describe these components, but the prosecution should also present anchorings for each of them. That is: there should be at least three pieces of evidence, each creating a connection to a general belief. For instance, in the case of Mr Helder who was accused of killing the old lady by giving her a combination of medicine and alcohol, there is no anchoring for the mens rea component. That means that this aspect is linked directly to a general belief that husbands always administer medicines to their wealthy spouses with the intention to kill them. For some of the charges against the bankrobber Speckman there is no evidence related to the identity component. In the case of Henkemans, suspected of smuggling drugs into Amsterdam Airport, there is no evidence that he carried drugs. In many legal systems there is a requirement as to the minimum amount of evidence, but there is never a formal requirement that there is a minimum amount of evidence for *each component*.

3. Anchors for different components should not all be attached to a single belief It is possible that all three components are anchored to one and the same belief. An example is a confession in which the accused confesses that he committed the crime, with full intention to do harm, and in full awareness of its criminal character. The weakness of such an anchoring is that it rests upon the single belief that the confession is true. The "*unis testis*" rule, which is generally accepted throughout the world, requires that the proof of guilt rests upon at least two independent pieces of evidence when the evidence consists of witness testimony. It is logical to extend this requirement to the anchoring of narratives: the narrative should be anchored to at least two different beliefs. Apart from the obvious example of a single all-comprising confession, there are cases in which all evidence is collected by a single police officer, which anchors the narrative to the belief that this one officer has no secret motive for lying. Still another example is the case in which all evidence is produced by a single witness, such as in cases of child abuse or rape. One might argue that such cases are violations of the *unis testis* rule, so that they should be rejected even without Rule 3. In the Netherlands, however, one has discovered several ways for getting around the *unis testis* rule. For instance by letting the victim make her statement in front of a police officer, who acts in court as a second witness. Or by engaging an expert psychologist who assesses the veridicality of the victim's statement. These circumventions violate the universal rule that not all anchors should be attached to the same belief.

A direct consequence of Rule 3 is that confessions cannot be accepted as complete proof, quite contrary to the custom in many countries. Again, this does not mean that my rule is wrong; it merely signifies that the rules of evidence in such countries are based upon unsafe premises.

4. The verdict must contain a reasoned account that specifies the narrative in which the court believes, and its anchors (evidence plus beliefs) A check upon the use of the anchored narratives heuristic is only possible when the narrative and its anchors are made explicit. In The Netherlands there is a rule that courts must give reasons for their verdicts. But this rule is clearly insufficient, since Dutch courts make a mockery out of this sensible requirement. These days they have adopted the general habit of producing "head-and-tails" verdicts, in which they repeat the indictment and add the sentence that this is proven by the evidence; no reasoning why and how the evidence proves anything at all. Apparently a much stricter rule is needed.

We suspect that many of the cases cited above would have ended differently if the courts had been forced to write down their reasoning. They would have discovered that the underlying reasoning was sloppy, incomplete, or wholly illogical; they would have noted that in many cases the evidence rested upon beliefs that, if made explicit, they themselves did not share. A nice example is the case of *King*.

Andrew King was accused of attempted burglary in the house of the Zomerdijk family. Nobody had actually seen him in the house, but father and mother Zomerdijk had heard a toy in their son's bedroom being disturbed. Apparently the narrative believed by the court was that King had entered the bedroom through the garden door, stumbled over the toy, and fled the house before anybody saw him. But the Zomerdijk's evidence constitutes an anchor only if it is believed that nothing or nobody else could have stirred the toy. No other person, no dog (there were two dogs in the house), nor the wind (there was a strong wind and Mrs Zomerdijk admitted that she had not closed the door properly). A minute attempt to exclude all other possibilities in a written account of the verdict might have convinced the court that there was sufficient doubt.

The presence of a reasoned account is essential for the preparation of an appeal, because otherwise it is not clear against what reasoning the accused should defend himself. The purpose of an appeal procedure is not simply to get a second chance, but to correct the faulty reasoning of a lower court, if it occurred. Without a reasoned account there is a too high likelihood of a *common mode error*; the conditions that caused the error in the first instance, may cause the same error in the appeal procedure. A nice example is the case of Castelyn (the talking baby) discussed above. Four learned colleges failed to appreciate that babies don't talk; if one of them had written down the narrative of how the baby complained to her sister of two-and-a-half about the sexual abuse by Castelyn, it would have transpired that the underlying belief is absurd.

5. A court's decision about the level of analysis must be supported by an explicitation of the underlying belief The regressive process of tracing the beliefs that underlie seemingly convincing evidence can be stopped when the court decides that further prodding is useless. For instance, the court may decide that expert opinion on eyewitness memory is not needed, because it believes that jury members have sufficient knowledge of the fallibility of memory. This decision limits the level of analysis. Statements by eyewitnesses are linked directly to the beliefs of the jury members; deeper levels, such as the evaluation of the qualities of the expert, the empirical evidence supporting his claims, the applicability to the case at hand, etc, are excluded. Such decisions are clearly in the province of a judge. But they are based upon a belief which from thereon will form a part of the anchoring construction. The jury members are being tacitly told that they can trust their intuitions about eyewitness memory.

In Dutch courts many decisions about the level of analysis are taken by the judges: which witnesses will appear, what experts are needed, whether additional investigations will be ordered, what questions may be asked by the defense counsel. The reasons for these decisions are sometimes far from clear. For instance, in the case of

Rijkbloem the only two eyewitnesses were not permitted to testify. Rijkbloem was accused of killing the father of his girlfriend Nicole. His defense was that Nicole's mother had shot her own husband by accident. Forensic expertise supported Rijkbloem's account and falsified the version of the two women. Naturally the defense wanted to examine the two women. The court refused and used the women's affidavits as evidence against Rijkbloem. Why was the level of analysis limited to a stage in which the affidavits were believed and the forensic expertise discounted? Was it the belief that eyewitnesses are less likely to make errors than forensic scientists? In the appeal procedure it would have helped if this belief, or what other belief inspired the court's decision, was made explicit. But it was not.

6. There should not be a competing narrative with equally good or better anchors If the facts can be fitted in another narrative in which the accused does not commit a criminal act, there is sufficient doubt about the question of guilt. It is not the task of a court to generate a complete set of alternative narratives, but if the defense produces one that meets the requirements, the reasoned verdict should contain an explicit explanation of why this narrative is rejected. A simple example is the case of Henkemans, accused of smuggling heroin. Nobody saw the heroin in his suitcase. The only evidence is that he contacted some Chinese drugdealers, in whose house heroin was found. Henkemans' story is that he transported delicatessen, which were a present from a friend in Thailand to his Chinese relations in Amsterdam. That story is far-fetched and a frequently encountered excuse, but it was not disproved by a single fact.

The rule becomes somewhat problematic when testimony of an interested party forms part of the evidence. For instance, in the cases of Graanhout, Rabout, and Rijkbloem, all cited above, the key evidence consisted of testimony by the only witnesses, who would naturally become suspects themselves if they did not accuse the defendant. The testimony does not agree with the alternative narrative, and for that reason one might think that Rule 6 does not apply. But the fact that these witnesses accuse someone else fits precisely in the alternative account. If Mrs Graanhout killed her own baby, it is not surprising that she tried to saddle her husband with it. Forensic expertise proved that Mrs Rabout stabbed her husband with the scissors; but she tried to incriminate him. Rijkbloem claimed that Nicole's mother killed her own husband; is it unnatural, if this were true, that the women accused the man who started their troubles? If testimony by interested parties is discounted, Rule 6 is applicable to many of our 35 cases. If Rule 6 is not applied because of the testimony of witnesses who may be suspects themselves, there must be very good anchors for the claim that those interested witnesses did not lie.

7. There should be no falsifications of anchors used in the court's reasoning Selection of evidence makes it possible that falsifications are discounted, even when they render an essential anchor totally invalid. For instance, in the case of Karakaya there were four witnesses who saw the victim after the purported time of his death. These testimonies falsified Karakaya's (withdrawn) confession. Using the confession in the anchoring construction is only permitted if there is a detailed account of why the four witnesses are wrong. Another well-known example is the conflict between identifications and alibis. Quite often an identification is believed and the alibi rejected, but without a clear reason. Rattner (1988) demonstrated that about 50% of wrongful convictions in the United States are caused by too much reliance on identifications. I fear that in a fair proportion of these cases alibis were rejected without good reason. An excellent example is the case of Ted Larwood described by Wagenaar & Loftus (1990).

Rule 7 is again in conflict with practices in countries that have trial by jury. Juries do not explain why they believe some portions of the evidence, and why they reject other parts. The danger is, of course, that they bolster the plausible narrative with evidence, without a worry about the fact that the story is disproved by other evidence. To some extent the problem can be solved in the trial judge's summing up; he may explain the conflict and urge the jury to accept the incriminating evidence only if they have good reasons to reject the conflicting information. But we will never know what these good reasons are.

8. There should be no anchoring to absurd beliefs The rule is clear; the obvious problem, though, is that beliefs are never made explicit. I will just mention one of the issues. In many countries it is forbidden to present the accused's criminal record, because one fears the belief "Once a thief, always a thief". There are, however, quite a few situations in which the record is revealed to jury members and judges; for instance, when the accused takes the witness stand in his own case. In The Netherlands it is even done as a rule. If the fear of a false belief in this respect is justified, why is it suddenly removed when the accused takes the stand, or when the accused is tried in a Dutch court?

Another example is the worrying role of psychologists as experts in criminal trials. In Dutch courts psychologists are allowed to testify about the personality of the defendant, even before a decision about guilt or innocence is reached. In the case of Rabout, accused of stabbing his wife with a pair of scissors, the psychologist described him as an aggressive man. This is probably as prejudicial as the revelation of a criminal record. To make things worse, the psychologist described Rabout as "implicitly aggressive", by which he meant that one cannot see his aggressiveness. He smiles a lot and is very polite, but underneath there is an enormous amount of dormant aggression. Thus it became impossible for Rabout to correct the expert opinion through decent behaviour; on the contrary, smiles and polite answers confirmed the psychological analysis. In fact it appeared that Rabout's wife Irene was the aggressor and Rabout the victim. But he was convicted nevertheless, for biting Irene, a charge that had never been discussed at the trial. Is it far-fetched to suppose that the conviction was anchored to the belief that an aggressive man must have committed at least some sort of crime? The belief that personality analyses are diagnostic for the question of guilt is absurd. But many judges think that appearance of the accused in court is important, because that way one may assess what sort of person he is.

Conclusion

As far as I know there has never been an attempt to devise universal rules for the use of evidence, based upon a psychological model of judicial reasoning. There are of course some sets of rules based upon legal or humanitarian principles, such as those in Article 6 of the European Declaration of Human Rights. It will be noted that my rules are different; they are more difficult to implement, maybe even not implementable at all. On the other hand they point to weaknesses that pervade many or all systems of criminal law; even when a rule cannot be implemented, it will be wise to consider the consequences carefully, and to investigate what sort of other precautions have been taken to avoid the pitfalls against which the rule was to present a safeguard.

I do not claim that the theory of anchored narratives is the only one that may generate universal rules, nor even that my set of rules is the only or even the best one that can be derived from the theory. I do claim, however, that "anchored narratives" accounts for a varied set of anomalies in criminal litigation, by relating them to a single reasoning heuristic. One may consider these anomalies as the few instances in which the heuristic goes wrong. The set of universal rules proposed above follows logically from the theory and would, in practice, have prevented almost every one of the anomalous cases in our corpus. Even when they cannot all be implemented,the rules offer a logical basis for the comparison and evaluation of the different systems of criminal law that exist in Europe. It is hoped that they even constitute a basis for suggesting improvement for some of these systems. My own country is an obvious candidate.

References

Bennett, W. L., & Feldman, M. S. (1981). *Reconstructing reality in the courtroom*. London: Tavistock.

Crombag, H. F. M., Koppen, P. J. van, & Wagenaar, W. A. (1992). *Dubieuze zaken: De psychologie van strafrechtelijk bewijs*. Amsterdam: Contact.

Gross, S. R. (1987). Loss of innocence: Eyewitness identification and proof of guilt. *Journal of Legal Studies, 16*, 395-453.

Navon, D. (1990). How critical is the accuracy of an eyewitness memory: Another look at the issue of lineup diagnostics. *Journal of Applied Psychology, 75*, 506-510

Pennington, N., & Hastie, R. (1986). Evidence evaluation in complex decision making. *Journal of Personality and Social Psychology, 51*, 242-258.

Pennington, N., & Hastie, R. (1988). Explanation-based decision making: Affects of memory structure on judgment. *Journal of Experimental Psychology: Learning, Memory, and Cognition, 14*, 521-533.

Rattner, A. (1988). Convicted but innocent: Wrongful conviction and the criminal justice system. *Law and Human Behavior, 12*, 283-293.

Wagenaar, W. A. (1993). *The forensic context of lineup tests*. Submitted for publication.

Wagenaar, W. A., & Loftus, E. F. (1990). Ten cases of eyewitness identification: Logical and procedural problems. *Journal of Criminal Justice, 18*, 291-319.

Wagenaar, W. A., Koppen, P. J. van, & Crombag, H. F. M. (1993). *Anchored narratives. The psychology of criminal evidence*. Hemel Hempstead: Harvester Wheatsheaf.

Psychosocial Investigation in Death Penalty Mitigation: Procedures, Pitfalls and Impact[1]

Sandra B. McPherson

Conceptual Aspects

In *Furman v. Georgia* (1972), the U.S. Supreme Court invalidated the death penalty on the basis of discriminatory applications and mandated the remedy of mitigation in any subsequent capital legislation. Nonetheless, research continues to show discrimination reflecting pervasive system bias (Hilliard, 1982). In a capital case, there is a guilt and a penalty phase, with defense and prosecution juxtaposed at both levels. As the Ohio law is currently drafted, there is a legislative concern for misuse or overuse of the death penalty in that the standard of proof is set at the highest level (beyond reasonable doubt) and the burden is on the prosecution. In the course of the trial, the state must prove the specified aggravating factors and that these factors outweigh mitigating ones.[2]

In spite of this structure, the current weight of precedent and appellate decision-making favors prosecution. For example, regarding constitutionality of the death penalty under the 8th Amendment concept of cruel and unusual punishment (1791), appellate decisions have been unfavorable. Specifically, in *Stanford v. Kentucky* (1989), it was held that capital punishment administered to a 16 or 17 year old person was not cruel and unusual on the basis that 22 of 37 states allow 16 year olds to be executed (although Ohio is not one of them). In *McClesky v. Kemp* (1987), in spite of acknowledging that statistical studies have shown that defendants who murder whites are four times as likely to get the death penalty than defendants who murder blacks, there was no Constitutional issue. The court indicated that if a jury was properly selected and state legislatures did not adopt the death penalty knowing and intending it to be discriminatorily applied, then no issues of discrimination arose, regardless of statistical findings.

One of the more critical issues in the context of appellate decisions has been that of dangerousness. As Schoots (1989) indicates, the scientific basis for making judgments as to fitness for punishment does not meet adequate standards for expert testimony and results may be prejudicial to the defendant. Similarly, Green (1984) raises complex issues as to unreliability of predictions of dangerousness, criteria for diagnosis of antisocial personality, and admission of opinion based on hypothetical issues which may foreclose mitigation. Citing *Jurek v. Texas* (1976) and *Barefoot v. Estelle* (1983), he notes the jury has the specific task of evaluating the future potential of the defendant and that the presence of a battle of the experts, should testimony as to dangerousness be allowed, prejudices in favor of prosecution since the jury will look for and be swayed by any expert willing to take on the burden of prediction. In *Barefoot v. Estelle* (1983), following the Supreme Court decision upholding expert testimony as to dangerousness, Barefoot was duly executed. One psychiatrist testified he was 100% accurate in his predictions; the other claimed reasonable medical certainty. Neither examined Barefoot in making their predictions (Smith & Meyer, 1987).

Another Supreme Court decision favoring prosecutorial interests is *Payne v. Tennessee* (1991) which overruled the decision in Booth v. Maryland (1987) and admitted victim impact testimony. In general, decisions have not only favored prosecution by validating procedures and rulings made in cases at bar, but decisions have also acted to limit habeas corpus and narrow bases of appeal to substantive over procedural errors (Smith, 1992).

Mitigation factors listed in the Ohio statute include whether the victim induced or facilitated the crime; whether the offender was under duress, coercion, or strong provocation; or was mentally ill or defective and lacked substantial capacity to appreciate the criminality of the act or to conform his conduct to requirements of the law; youth of offender; lack of significant prior criminal history; offender was not the principal participant in the offense; other relevant factors; nature and circumstances of offense, and history, character and background of the offender (Ohio Revised Code [ORC 2929.04]).

Various decisions have conflicted in the interpretation of factors (Kelleher et al., 1992). Under youth of the offender, it has been suggested that age 20 is "entitled to some weight", (*State v. Montgomery*, 1991), but that age 19 was of little importance (*State v. Powell*, 1990). Lack of significant criminal record has been construed as important only where there is no record (*State v. Stumpf*, 1987; *State v. Steffen*, 1987; and *State v. Beuke*, 1988). While diminished responsibility based on mental condition will not serve as a primary defense (*State v. Wilcox*, 1982), in *State v. Cooey* (1989), the courts limited expert testimony unrelated to the insanity defense to the mitigation phase.

Procedural Aspects

Formal procedure initiates with an indictment, flowing from which is the process of pretrial, plea bargaining[3] and trial. Defendant may opt for a trial by jury or by a three judge panel. Defendant may raise the issue of age at the time of the act; if found guilty but under-age, a sentence of 20 years of life may be imposed. If the defendant is found guilty of aggravated murder without an age factor, a mitigation phase trial takes place before the jury or three judge panel which heard the case in chief. Penalty options are 20 or 30 years to life, with most sentences augmented by a three year mandatory gun specification penalty, or death. If the jury finds beyond reasonable doubt that aggravating outweigh mitigating factors, a recommendation for death follows. If the three judge panel in a non-jury trial or the judge following a jury recommendation of death concurs that aggravating outweigh mitigating factors, the death sentence is imposed. Because the prosecution has the burden and the standard is the highest, it has been held that prosecution is allowed both opening and closing statements to the jury/judge panel (*State v. Buell*, 1986). As part of mitigation, the defendant may request pre-sentence investigations under ORC 2929.024 or 2929.03. In the latter case, the pre-sentence investigation shall be furnished to the court, jury, prosecutor, and defendant's counsel, although none of the contents of that investigation can be used in evidence during the guilt phase. Further, the court may delete erroneous information which could mislead the jury (*State v. Cooey*, 1989). By contrast, under 2929.024, the information is protected from all access except as defense determines appropriate. Since the actual processing of a mitigation case depends upon a high level of trust existing between the defendant and investigators, 2929.024 is the best defense option. However, the court may or may not authorize funds for an indigent client under this provision (*State v. Esparza*, 1988).

Mitigation defenses are often intensely psychosocial and psychological, the purpose of which is to explain "the life of the defendant ... and why he was in the situation where he could kill another human being" (Stebbins, 1988). General psychological assessment and/or specialized evaluation are conducted as appropriate to explain defendant behavior. The task is more broadly based than sanity or competency evaluations which seek to answer why an individual fits in one legal category versus another. Social history information is compiled and potential witnesses for the mitigation hearing are identified. The importance of beginning investigations early has been emphasized by many workers (Stebbins, 1988). In the first cases processed, investigation was often conducted after a finding of guilty, leaving only a few days to develop and prepare the mitigation defense. It was quickly apparent that mitigation investigation needs time to pursue leads and obtain additional expert witnesses as needed. Presuming investigation under 2929.024, the mitigation specialist, expert witness, and any other persons brought in on a case become part of the defense team (Hudson et al., 1987).

Pitfalls

Although procedures derive from state law, outcomes reflect local factors. Thus, one-third of one county's indictments result in death sentences, whereas in another, only 3 to 4% do. In the county with the largest center of urban crime, 10% of indictments with death penalty specifications get a death outcome (Eisenberg, 1992). Mitigation pitfalls are found in aspects of jury behavior, the law, strategies of the defense team, in characteristics of defendants and cases, and in underlying societal racism.

Jury research Some people over-attribute cause to "internal disposition" and under-estimate situational factors (Costanzo & Costanzo, 1992) making punitive responses more likely. Another factor involves death qualification: juries in death trials have been purged of members who cannot bring themselves to vote for a death penalty. The result is a jury pool which tends towards authoritarian attitudes (Bray & Noble 1987; Cox & Tanford, 1989; Kadane & Powers, 1987; Luginbuhl & Powers, 1987; Thompson, 1989). Death qualified juries frequently indicate a lack of com-prehension of the task of weighing aggravating versus mitigating factors, some jurors believing that death is mandatory (Geimer & Amsterdam, 1988; Luginbuhl, 1992).[4] Recent research also indicates cognitive processing of written and oral information is poorer for high than low authoritarian mode subjects (Wegman, 1992), which may facilitate pre-existing bias to favor death verdicts. Finally, research suggests remorse, confession, and perceived redemption potential are important determiners of life over death recommendations (Costanzo & Costanzo, 1992). These factors interact to the defendant's detriment where innocence is maintained.

Legal findings Appeals decisions are complex.

(1) In states where dangerousness is raised as an aggravating factor, a defendant is entitled to mental health experts. Given that the prosecution cannot compel a defendant to provide insight into his mental functioning at the time of the act, nor compel close and intimate observers of his behavior to provide evidence relating to his history, experts cannot always obtain the kind of data that Monahan (1984) and others say are necessary for any prediction.

(2) Defendants are not denied their right to effective assistance of counsel by forcing a choice between presenting a defense in the case in chief (which requires a plea of not guilty to the charges as specified, even though the defendant may be guilty of the act or acts) or retaining credibility for the sentencing hearing (where the prior plea of not guilty may be viewed as evidence of intransigence, lying, and/or lack of remorse) (*State v. Shields*, 1984).

(3) In Ohio, age is defined as chronological and not mental. Furthermore, although retardation is viewed as a possible mitigating factor, it may not outweigh aggravating conditions, and retarded persons may be viewed as understanding the wrongfulness of their acts and therefore responsible for them (*State v. Hill*, 1989; *State v. Rogers*, 1985).

(4) Failure to summon witnesses to speak to an abusive childhood and to positive contributions constituted reversible error (*State v. Scott*, 1989).

(5) A recent Supreme Court decision upheld the right of prosecution to present victim impact evidence. In Ohio, there has been a decision that victim impact may be presented if there is a direct connection to the defendant's personal responsibility and guilt (*Payne v. Tennessee*, 1991; *State v. Huertas*, 1991).

Considerations of strategy Death penalty work begins with considerations of plea bargains. In some cases, defense teams have obtained an expert in jury selection to minimize death proneness.[5] A special concern pertains to the factor of a mental disorder on the basis of which the individual "lacks substantial capacity to appreciate the criminality of his conduct or to conform his conduct to the requirements of the law". Especially in cases where sanity was raised, juries and judges may negate the importance of the mental disorder on the basis that it was already argued. However, a different kind and degree of disorder is contemplated in the mitigation phase. Special questions of competence can be raised. Many people on death row lack judgment and social competence and cannot collaborate in a mitigation defense (Core et al., 1992).

In approaching testimony, specific strategies are developed. For example, defense may wish to avoid the presentation of a prior criminal record; the whole issue of psychological history may have to be omitted in testimony. In effect, a strategy decision must be made as to whether a complete explanation of the person and the crime will weigh positively in a cost benefit analysis against the impact of a prior criminal and juvenile history. Hearsay objections to the mitigation data base may have to be overcome. The psychologist may interview those persons who were primary providers of material or may rest upon the team approach as a proper procedure for the development of psychological conclusions; all members of the investigative effort must have substantial mental health credentials in such cases. Psychological reportage is an issue; it may be preferable to communicate entirely by conference, but the risk of discovery objections presents.[6] A very brief report which lists only conclusions and sources provides latitude for courtroom strategy, but even so may open up territory where defense counsel may wish to preserve last minute prerogatives. Especially where the defense expert opposes the death penalty, prosecution may imply the testimony is biased in that it does not include psychological factors supporting the death penalty. Response on cross-examination can note that the task is not to present data which supports an execution, but only that which supports the presence of mitigation factors. However, the psychologist must support the system and the truth it demands. The court may permit inquiry into areas omitted by defense. In such instances, psychological testimony may be harmful to the defendant. It is then up to the appeals process to evaluate as to reversible error.

The defendant has the option of presenting an unsworn statement or testifying under oath. Prosecution has the option of characterizing the former as potentially self-serving (*State v. Mapes*, 1985). Some defendants maintain innocence with attendant problems. In a few cases, defendants have expressed no remorse and in one well known case, the defendant (a cult leader) chose instead to spend five hours haranguing the jury on the scriptural basis validating killings - a strategy with a foregone conclusion. Questions of defendant competence and effectiveness of counsel might be raised in such a situation, but *State v. Tyler* (1990) upheld results where a defendant decided not to call mitigation witnesses and instructed his counsel he was going to present an unsworn statement; failure to ask for a competency hearing was not ineffective assistance.[7]

Defendant characteristics Most defendants in aggravated homicide cases are intrinsically unattractive to the average juror or judge and often come from a social context which contains many repugnant features. Other problems include family pride and the need for members to glorify or idealize the defendant. Thus, even where a defendant has admitted to significant drug-alcohol involvement, family members will maintain that there has been little or no substance use. Where problems are identified, serious questions arise as to which of these should be paraded in front of the jury. Sometimes the presentation of negative family history only serves to further identify the defendant as beyond redemption. There is also the possibility of subsequent libel suits where references to extremely socially unacceptable behaviors are made in a public forum. Where defendants maintain innocence, the psychologist must avoid invalidating the residual doubt position. Focusing on favorable personality, family and situational data may be ineffective as Ohio death row opinions indicate judges discount psychological factors which do not bear a direct relationship to the crime. Another difficulty arises when defendants have a death wish; an issue of competence presents in this context, but to pose this dilemma as a mitigating factor is to invite the rebuttal that a self-serving and unverifiable argument has been made.

In some ways, given that the mitigation expert must explain and define defendant and crime, the best cases may also be the worst. Such crimes are so heinous and personality characteristics and functioning of the criminals so horrendous as to cause a reactive need for psychological distance by juries and judges.

Crime characteristics Some crimes are sufficiently abhorrent that sympathy for the criminal is difficult to elicit. Such crimes may involve victims whose behavior does not lend itself to (inappropriate) construal as contributory to their plight - for example, the rape and killing of a woman on her way to work as opposed to a woman involved in a drug deal dispute. In most serial, mass or rape murders, ritual killing, or murders for hire, saving the defendant is unlikely. Highly arousing photographs during guilt phase condition mitigation outcomes. Current research indicates it is not uncommon for juries to decide well before the end of the case in chief whether they will vote life or death at the penalty phase, influenced by the presentation of evidence before any weighing of mitigation factors can occur (Sandys, 1991).

Racism In Ohio, as of 25 March 1992, 113 persons were on death row. Of that sample, complete data as to race, sex and age of defendant[8], and victims' race were available for 98 defendants. Table 1 gives the breakdown for Ohio death penalty (DP) offenders as contrasted with homicide rates in the U.S. (1990 Uniform Crime Reports, 1991).

Table 1: Race as a factor in death row occupancy

Defendant Race	**Victim**				**Total**	
	Black		**White**			
	Ohio DP	**US Homicides**	**Ohio DP**	**US Homicides**	**Ohio DP**	**US Homicide**
Black %	31	49	29	3	59	51
White %	1	6	40	43	41	49
Total %	32	54*	68*	46	100	100

*rounding error for column

Statistical evaluation supports racial biases noted in other studies (χ^2 =219.02, 1 df; p=.001). Intriguingly, Hilliard (1982) notes the current law has specified aggravating factors which contain within them characteristics likely to generate more black than white defendants (1982).

Case Related Data - The Variable Impact of Mitigation

Life vs. death sentence opinions Fifty four life and 112 death sentence opinions were evaluated. Life opinions were found from 1982 to 1990 and from 22 of Ohio's 88 counties; 38 (70%) were decided by a three judge panel. Death opinions reflected primarily jury trials (N=91 or 81%) and represented almost all death cases to date.

Table 2 contrasts the two samples on statutory factors. Death opinions are broken down into those where the judge acknowledged the presence of a factor and qualified it as mitigating versus those where the factor was mentioned but discounted.

Table 2: Frequency of cited statutory provision for life and death opinions

Provision	Life opinions		Death opinions			
			Factor allowed		Factor disallowed	
	N	%*	N	%	N	%
1. Victim facilitation	7	13	1	0	–	–
2. Offender duress	4	7	1	1	3	3
3. Mental defect, disease	19	35	13	12	19	17
4. Youth offender	17	31	11	10	47	42
5. No significant prior criminal history	21	39	12	11	0	0
6. Offender not the primary actor	1	02	2	2	2	2
Total opinions	54		112		112	

*Percentages do not total to 100 because each case had different numbers of cited provisions

Some interesting content is found. In life opinions IQ varied from 60 to "below average". Personality disorders and depression were cited as qualifying. Youth of the offender involved ages from 18 to 30 years, most being 18 to 21. Absence of violence or use of weaponry was noted. In the case of death opinions, low IQs might be cited as mitigating; three allowed major mental illnesses and five allowed personality disorders. However, in 19 similar cases, evidence raised under this factor was acknowledged but found to be non-qualifying. In cases allowing age as a factor, seven stated the age involved, averaging 19.9 years. Average age of the non-allowed group was 28.5, with five being 19 or 20 years of age; chronological age on its own does not constitute a mitigating factor in the minds of many judges. As to background and character, circumstances of the crime, and any other factors, the following appeared most frequently in the life opinions: drug-alcohol abuse; no prior planning; the state and/or victim's family recommended life; acknowledgement of guilt and expression of remorse; co-defendants who plead out to or received life or lesser sentences; amenability to treatment; length of sentence; and early environment/socialization/ psychological factors, including the presence of abuse and neglect and the lack of positive parental guidance and involvement. In the death opinions, judges gave some weight to negative family history, especially childhood abuse, but family history for violence could lead a judge to believe there was no rehabilitation potential, or judges would note that other persons had survived under equally horrendous circumstances without criminal acts. Similarly, positive family history could be mitigating or not; where it could be shown that the defendant had played some positive role, the judge might suggest some mitigating weight, but positive family history could easily become a basis for pointing out depravity of the offender and lack of response to reasonable and positive input. Expressions of remorse might be noted favorably but could be viewed as self-serving. Maintaining innocence and residual doubt were not acknowledged; in general, a stance of innocence was held to be intransigence. Identified psychopathology could be negative. For example, one defendant was identified as a sexual sadist, and although important to explaining and understanding the crime, it was in no way mitigating insofar as the judge was concerned. Finally, a count of factors considered mitigating results in an average of 5.32 for life over 2.25 for death opinions (Life N=37; Death N=109).

Case example Procedures for one case included interviews; psychological testing; and collection of extensive background information including medical, agency and prior criminal justice system records. At the hearing, the appearance of relatives, the defendant's unsworn statement, and finally expert testimony was carefully organized. Testimony included research findings as to recidivism for persons in extended incarceration. Pictorial representations of his family tree showing dsyfunctionality in relationships and chemical dependency were presented. Highlighted was the defendant's success in his personal life situation. However, completely unexpected and unplanned events played a part. This defendant had shown up on the first day of his trial dressed in his best suit - a powder blue formal. At the time of his mitigation phase, he showed up wearing clothing he was alleged to have worn at the time of the killing. He maintained since there were no blood stains, he couldn't have committed the crime. His impact on the jury and how he acted during that unsworn statement, backed up as it was by his initial way of approaching his situation, served to confirm for them that the mental deficits noted in the psychological and social history testimony were clearly present, and the man deserved some sympathy; possibly consideration was given to residual doubt.

Conclusions

Both casework and research illustrate mitigation as a creative process wherein formal assessment, informal modes of evaluation, investigatory techniques, and sometimes serendipitous events combine to allow the development of a defense which diverts from a death penalty outcome. The work requires close communication and strategy-building between mental health professional and lawyer. Mitigation is an arena within which psychological data can be helpful, even determining the outcome, but there must be both professional skill and conservatism in order to avoid legal and ethical problems, not least of which is the mandate to do no harm.

References

Barefoot v. Estelle. 1983. 463 U.S. 880.
Booth v. Maryland. 1987. 482 U.S. 496.
Bray, R. M., & Noble, A. M. (1987). Authoritarianism and decisions of mock juries. In S. Wrightsman, S. Kassin, & C. Willis (Eds.), *In the jury box*. Beverly Hills: Sage.
Core, J., Shorr, S., & Pudvan, L. (1992). Personal communications.
Costanzo, M., & Costanzo, S. (1992). Jury decision making in the capital penalty phase: Legal assumptions, empirical findings, and a research agenda. *Law and Human Behavior, 16*(2), 185-202.
Cox, M., & Tanford, S. (1989). An alternative method of capital jury selection. *Law and Human Behavior, 13*(2), 167-184.
Eighth Amendment, 1791, U.S. Constitution.
Eisenberg, J. R. (1992). Personal communication.
Furman v. Georgia. (1972). 408 U.S. 238.
Geimer, W. S., & Amsterdam, J. (1988). Why jurors vote life or death: Operative factors in ten Florida death penalty cases. *American Journal of Criminal Law, 15*(1,2), 1-54.
Green, W. (1984). Capital punishment, psychiatric experts, and predictions of dangerousness. *Capital University Law Review, 13*, 533-553.
Hilliard, E. C. (1982). Capital punishment in Ohio: Aggravating circumstances. *Cleveland State Law Review, 31*, 495-528.
Hudson, J., Core, J., & Shorr, S. (1987). Using the mitigation specialist and the team approach. *Champion*, June, 33-36.
Jurek v. Texas. 1976. 428 U.S. 262, 274.
Kadane, J., & Powers, T. (1987, August). *Penalty supports and conviction proneness*. Paper presented at the Annual Meeting of the American Psychological Association, New York.
Kosko, J. R. (1992). *Ohio statutes and cases*. Presentation at Cleveland Bar Association Seminar: Not guilty by reason of insanity. Cleveland, Ohio.
Kelleher, V., Snyder, P., & Eisenberg, J. (1992). Penalty phase investigations: Discovering why this happened. Unpublished guidelines.
Luginbuhl, J. (1992). Comprehension of judges' instructions in the penalty phase of a capital trial: Focus on mitigating circumstances. *Law and Human Behavior, 16*(2), 203-218.
Luginbuhl, J., & Powers, J. (1987, August). *Jurors' death penalty support and conviction proneness*. Paper presented at the Annual Meeting of the American Psychological Association, New York.
McClesky v. Kemp. 1987. 481 U.S. 279.
Monahan, J. (1984). The prediction of violent behavior: Toward a second generation of theory and policy. *American Journal of Psychiatry, 141*, 10-11.
Morgan v. Illinois. 1992. 60 U.S.L.W., 4541.
Ohio Revised Code, Section 2929.
Payne v. Tennessee. 1991. 59 U.S. L. W., 4814.
Sandys, M. (1991). *The life or death decisions of capital jurors: Preliminary findings from Kentucky*. Paper presented at the Annual Meeting of the American Society of Criminology, San Francisco, CA.
Schoots, N. (1989). Overde voodrtrat ethische dilemmas in de gezindherdszorg. [On the death penalty: Ethical dilemmas in medicine]. *Psycholoog, 24*(10), 504-507.
Smith, S. R. (1992). 1991-92 Supreme Court term: Cases of interest to psychologists. *Bulletin of the American Academy of Forensic Psychology, 13*(1), 1-2.
Stanford v. Kentucky. 1989. 492 U.S. 361.
State v. Beuke. 1988. 38 05 3d 29.
State v. Buell. 1986. 22 OS 3d 124.

State v. Cooey. 1989. 46 OS 3d 20.
State v. Esparza. 1988. 39 OS 3d 8.
State v. Hill. 1989. 11th Dist. Ct. App., Trumbull, Nos. 3720, 3745.
State v. Huertas. 1991. 51 OS 3d 22.
State v. Mapes. 1985. 19 OS 3d 108.
State v. Montgomery. 1991. 61 OS 3d 410, 419.
State v. Powell. 1990. 49 OS 3d 255, 263.
State v. Rogers. 1985. 17 OS 3d 174.
State v. Scott. 1989. 63 App., 3d 304.
State v. Shields. 1984. 15 OA pp 3d 112.
State v. Steffen. 1987. 31 OS 3d 111.
State v. Stumpf. 1987. 32 OS 3d 95.
State v. Tyler. 1990. 50 OS 3d 24.
State v. Wilcox. 1982. 70 OS 2d 182.
Stebbins, D. C. (1988). Psychologists and mitigation: Diagnosis to explanation. *Champion*, April, 34-38.
Thompson, W. C. (1989). Death qualification after Wainwright v. Witt and Lockhart v. McCree. *Law and Human Behavior*, 13(2), 185-216.
Uniform Crime Reports for the United States. (1991). Federal Bureau of Investigation, U. S. Department of Justice, Washington, DC.
Wegman, M. F. (1992). *Information processing deficits of the authoritarian mind*. Dissertation, The Fielding Institute, California.

Notes

[1] This paper is largely based on Ohio statute.

[2] This burden contrasts with the shift in Ohio law favoring the state in not guilty by reason of insanity pleas, where post-Hinckley changes shifted the burden of proof onto the defendant (Kosko, 1992). Statutory aggravating specifications are assassination of political or elected officials or candidates, murder for hire, murder to escape legal consequences of another offense, murder while a prisoner, murder with a prior conviction for attempted murder or murders, murder endangering two or more people, murder of a police officer, felony murder, and murder of a witness (ORC 2929.04[A]).

[3] An estimated 80% of death row residents were offered a plea but did not take it (Eisenberg, 1992).

[4] Such a misconstruction may reflect defensive operations to handle unconscious conflicts about rendering a death recommendation rather than naivete or inadequate instructions - the author.

[5] In *Morgan v. Illinois* (1992), the Supreme Court has held that jurors who state they will automatically recommend the death penalty upon conviction must be excused.

[6] In U.S. procedures, there are theoretically no surprises. Any known evidence presented must be announced in advance. Attempts to avoid this process can result in objections at trial.

[7] Ineffective assistance is a basis for mistrial and reversal in U.S. courts and refers to situations where legal representation was so substandard as to cause prejudice.

[8] Consistent with other data on violent crime, there were only three females and most persons were ages 19-28.

Attitude and Behavior of Male and Female Judges Concerning the Punishment of Offenders

Margit E. Oswald and Regine Drewniak

Women do not only break the law more seldom than men but they also have a more lenient attitude toward punishment - that is at least what the stereotypes of sex roles imply, and what has caused several politicians and social scientists to attach much hope but also fears and anxiety to the fact that the proportion of female judges increases steadily (1965: 4%; 1991: 18%) (cf. Augstein, 1989; Menkel-Meadow, 1989; Sessar, 1989).

In a longterm study we were the first to analyze data from the Federal Central Register (BZR) in Berlin with respect to the unappealable sentences of single judges from 1989/1990 (Oswald, 1994). We sampled male and female criminal court judges of three magistrates' courts in larger cities in different states of the former Federal Republic of Germany. For methodological reasons we analyzed only those cases where the major offence was petty theft (§242 StGB). Only this group of offences is large enough to allow the application of multivariate analysis, in order to take into account features of cases which legally influence sentencing behavior, e.g., previous convictions of the offender.

The sentences passed were transformed into measures of punitivity (severity of sentences) by means of a punitivity scale. In the framework of the General Linear Model (cf. Cohen & Cohen, 1983), each judge was assessed an average punitivity score (adjusted means).

With respect to petty theft *there were no differences* between female and male criminal court judges in sentencing.

How to explain this result? Numerous studies on the relation between attitude and behavior unveil, above all, that the actual behavior of a person differs from his or her respective attitude (cf. Canary & Seibold, 1984). A discrepancy between attitude and behavior can be expected, e.g., if there are strong normative influences upon the behavior situation, i.e. specific expectations with respect to behavior (cf. Fishbein & Ajzen, 1975; Gibson, 1978). Thus, it may hold just for female judges that they orientate their sentences less by their own attitude toward punishment but also by prevailing punishment standards, either because of their status of minority (cf. Kanter, 1978), or because of a generally higher tendency to adapt (cf. Model A in Figure 1). But it may be as well possible, that female criminal court judges neither differ from their male colleagues in sentencing behavior nor in attitude toward punishment.

Given this assumption, the question rises whether the coincidence of attitudes toward punishment of female and male judges can be generalized to all female judges, or only to the subset of female judges at criminal courts. Both possibilities seem feasible. Thus, it could be that female judges acquired an attitude toward punishment similar to that of their male colleagues due to their professional socialization (cf. Model C in Figure 1). As well, it could be that female judges in total do have a more

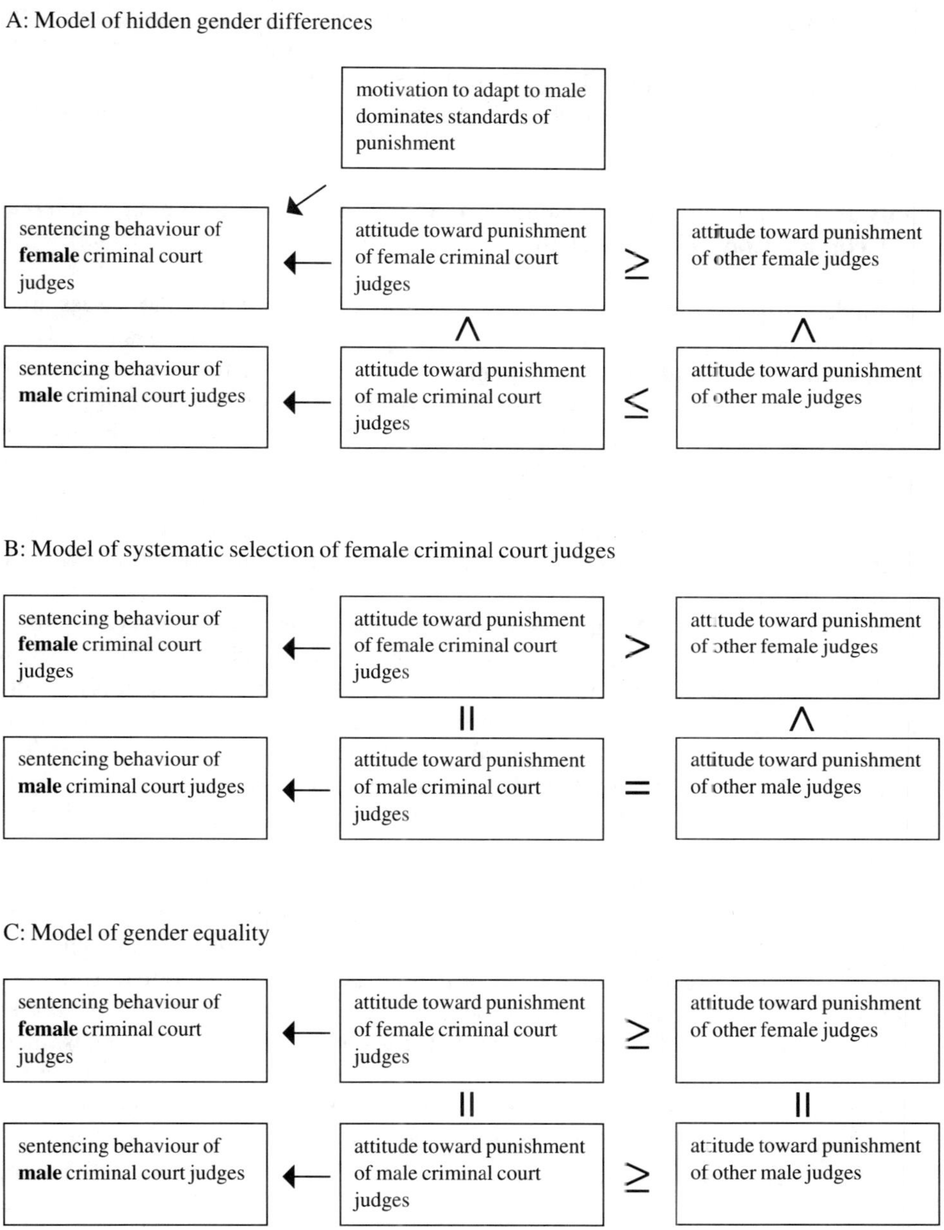

Figure 1: Three models to explain why female and male judges at magistrates' criminal courts do not differ with respect to their sentencing behaviour

lenient attitude toward punishment, but that the field of prosecution of criminal offences is mainly chosen by those female judges who show a relatively harsh attitude toward punishment (cf. Model B in Figure 1). In the following we will describe two studies on attitudes toward punishment of female and male judges at magistrates' courts.

Study 1: Attitudes toward Punishment of Female and Male Judges at Magistrates' Criminal Courts in Three Cities.

The models displayed above are severely simplified. Above all, it cannot be assumed that attitude toward punishment is a homogeneous one-dimensional construct. Thus, in connection with attitude toward punishment several constructs are discussed: authoritarianism, attribution of responsibility, justification of punishment, political ideology, etc. (cf. Carroll et al., 1987; Oswald, 1994). On the other hand, Fishbein & Ajzen's suggestion to define "attitude" only in relation to behavior seems too narrow to cope with the cognitive structures of a person related to the application of punishment. An attitude is defined by these authors as the (weighted) sum of positively and negatively evaluated consequences associated to a given behavior (cf. Ajzen & Fishbein, 1980).

In the study 56 criminal court judges at three city magistrates' courts (21 of them female) were individually interviewed to assess several subdimensions of their attitude toward punishment, like e.g. attribution style or intention to apply severe punishments. The sub-dimensions and also the respective theoretical assumptions on how they interrelate cannot be explained more detailed here for lack of space. The most important predictor of sentencing behavior as measured by means of data from the BZR (cf. Oswald, 1994), however, was a dimension called "offender-society-orientation".

This dimension refers to a central conflict in punishing: assessing the kind and severity of a sentence involves considerations which are often not compatible with each other, and which take into account concern for the offender on one hand, and concern for "non-offenders" or society in the largest sense on the other. Thus, in a given case it could be that a very lenient sentence would be the best alternative for the resocialization of the offender, but contradicts the (anticipated) need for punishment displayed by non-offenders. The respective position on the dimension "offender-society-orientation" unveils how the judge evaluates the different concerns. Individual positions on this dimension can be interpreted as specific tendencies of behavior, or as cognitive strategies which people have developed when handling such conflicts (cf. Oswald, 1994).

This construct was operationalized by confronting the judges at criminal courts with two corresponding conflict situations. Their elaborations with respect to offender and society were recorded both by open and by structured questions, and processed by means of a given schema.

At a correlation of .48 the offender-society-orientation proves to be the best predictor of the average sentencing severity of individual judges.

Above all, the offender-society-orientation is interesting with respect to our question for gender differences in sentencing severity: the conflict of judges described above, to consider more the offender's, or more the society's concern, is very similar to the well known moral dilemmata and it is not by accident that these often refer to criminal cases (cf. Kohlberg, 1981/84). Previous studies seem to corroborate the theoretical assumption that women, in these conflicts, tend to neglect the concern of society in favor of the concern of the persons involved (cf. Haan, 1978; Gilligan, 1982; Lyons, 1983). Contrary to this, our study has shown that female judges at criminal courts do not display a higher orientation toward the offender. Thus, these results do not support Model A but leave open whether Model B or Model C is more correct (cf. Figure 1).

Study 2: Attitudes toward Punishment of Male and Female Judges in Various Fields of Actions at Magistrates' Courts.

This study which was supported by the German Research Foundation (DFG) and mainly accomplished by Mrs Drewniak included female and male judges in different fields of action at magistrates' courts. The sample size was 557: all female judges (N = 233), and a random sample of male judges at all 31 middle sized magistrates' courts in states of the former Federal Republic of Germany. The response rate was 43%. With respect to the distribution of sexes and assignment of actions, the distribution of the respondents reflects the distribution of the judges asked.

Since also judges not at criminal courts have been included in this study, we could not assess any actual sentencing behavior. However, we do have information with respect to the intention to punish more or less severe. Relevant variables in this study were: offender-society-orientation, assessed this time by means of a standardized questionnaire (cf. Table 1), intention to punish more or less severe, and interests of judges towards the activity in criminal courts. As can be seen from Table 1, the offender-society-orientation was assessed twice, each time after the description of a conflict situation. One of these situations deals with a case of severe property offence (§ 243 StGB), and in the other a case of dangerous assault (§ 223a StGB). The intention to punish was also asked separately for each of these cases. The interest in the activity in criminal courts was ascertained in three different ways: (1) records of the judges about their former and/or actual activity as a criminal court judge; (2) a questionnaire concerning the acceptance of the activity as a criminal court judge; and (3) rank order of the different fields of magistrates' courts according to the judges personal preference.

Also in this study, the offender-society-orientation turns out to be the best predictor of the intention to punish: the higher the orientation toward society, the more increases the intention to punish. Although the offender-society-orientation of a judge controls more of the variance of the intention to punish if the conflict relates to a dangerous assault (51.5%) than to a property offence (29.7%), the main results hold for both offences. For the sake of simplicity we will therefore refer in the following only to the average scores on the respective dimensions.

Table 1: Items to measure offender-society orientation

	PROPERTY OFFENCE			DANGEROUS ASSAULT		
	Factor loadings (43.1% expl. Var.)	Item analysis		Factor loadings (41.5% expl. Var.)	Item analysis	
		r_{it}	r_{tt}		r_{it}	r_{tt}
Even if the risk of the offender's recidivism is small the protection of society must be considered	.698	.62	.88	.657	.57	.87
If there is a chance for the offender to be law abiding in future it has to be taken in priority	.635	.55		.574	.49	
Obedience to norms in general wouldn't pay if the violation of norms remains unpunished	.720	.64		.731	.65	
In the given case a compensation of injustice may be possible by other means than punishment	.737	.66		.787	.70	
The offender should not get away unpunished	.642	.55		.703	.60	
With respect to potential offenders, the sentencing decision is not problematic because sentencing decisions don't become public	.587	.51		.529	.46	
Even a criminal offence which is quite harmless as a single act gains in importance as part of a whole trend	.760	.69		.696	.62	
In criminal offences of this kind the victim gets nothing out of the punishment of the offender	.631	.54		.552	.45	
In comparison to other offenders, it would be unjust if an offender is not punished	.753	.67		.735	.64	
The meaning of punishment should primarily be to cause a positive change in the offender	.479	.40		.525	.43	
To stabilize norms, there should be not too many exceptions from punishing deviant behaviour	.671	.59		.717	.63	
An increasing frequency of delinquency should not have any effect upon sentencing	.493	.42		.411	.35	

Gender, Different Fields of Action, and Offender-society-orientation

What are the differences between judges in the different fields of action with respect to their offender-society-orientation; are female judges at criminal courts highly selected? If we classify judges according to their actual or former experience as a criminal court judge and their preference for this activity (Factor 1), we find four groups. If we furthermore separate judges with respect to gender (Factor 2), we obtain a 2x4 table (cf. Table 2). An ANOVA demonstrates that the groups classified by Factor 1 differ significantly with respect to their average offender-society-orientation but that there is no significant effect of gender. Judges who work at a criminal court, at the time being, and who also prefer this activity to other ones do have a higher society orientation than judges who never worked in criminal courts and never preferred to do so: not gender but the fact whether a judge works in a criminal court or wants to do so has a significant effect upon the attitude variable "offender-society-orientation" which in turn is relevant to the intention to punish.

Table 2: Items to measure offender-society orientation. Classification of judges according to their experience as a criminal court judge and their preference for this activity

	Group 1: actual experience as criminal court judge & preference for this activity	**Group 2: at least no actual experience as criminal court judge & preference for this activity**	**Group 3: actual or former experience as criminal court judge & no preference for this activity**	**Group 4: neither actual nor former experience as criminal court judge & no preference for this activity**
♂	.549 (.88) N=5	.157 (1.27) N=39	–.042 (1.24) N=39	–.042 (1.08) N=28
♀	.804 (1.16) N=17	.037 (.91) N=18	–.132 (.95) N=26	–.178 (1.07) N=37

ANOVA

source of variance	QS	df	MS	F
gender of judges	.078	1	.078	.065
group	18.792	3	6.265	5.205*
gender * group	1.275	3	.425	.353

Gender, Different Fields of Action, and Intention to Punish

If we classify judges as we did in the preceding analysis (cf. Table 2) and look how the groups differ in their average intention to punish, we find the following picture: Factor 1 "Experience as a criminal court judge and preference for this activity" is again an important grouping variable to predict the intention to punish ($F=2.998$; $df=3$; $p< .05$). Contrary to the former results, however, the gender factor also seems to be important. Female judges do have significantly less intention to punish than male judges (F=10.074, df=1, p<.01). Planned comparisons though show that significant gender related differences only appear in group three.

Gender and Systematic Self-selection to Different Fields of Action

So far, the method of analysis of variance does not unveil the interesting fact that the percentage of female judges in the four groups formed by Factor 1 differ systematically ($\chi^2 = 10.42$; df = 3; p < .05). Female judges in group 1 and 2 are under-represented, in group 4 however over-represented. This fact points to the relevant question, whether female judges in general are less represented in criminal courts and whether this is due to their lower interests in this kind of activity. This question can be answered in the affirmative: the percentage of female judges at criminal courts is much lower than the percentage of females among all judges at the 31 magistrates' courts (22.3%) (cf. Figure 2). Additionally, female judges accept the activity as a criminal court judge to a smaller degree than their male colleagues (t=4.06; df=233; p<.001), and their preference for this field of action is also much lower than that of male judges (t = 3.78; df = 1; p < .001).

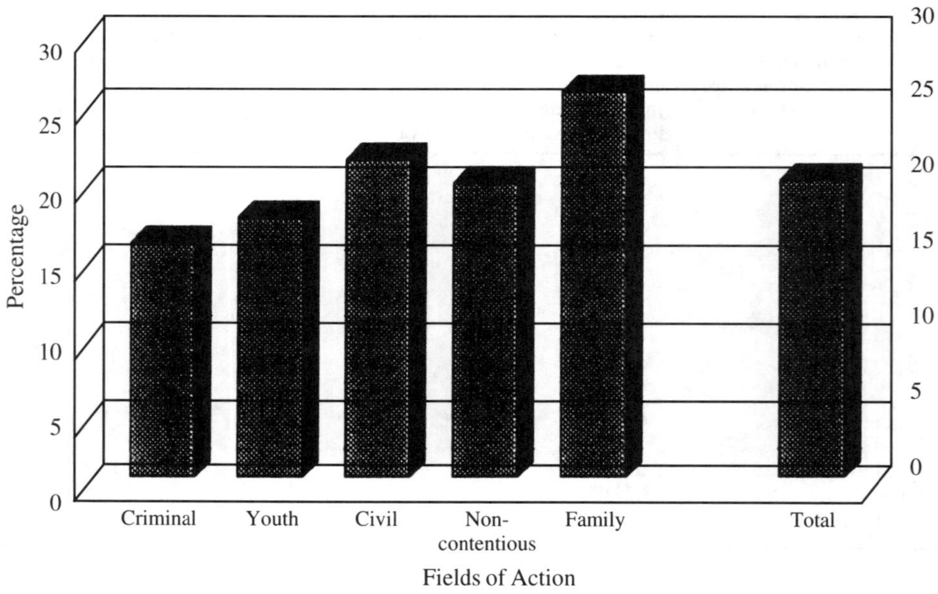

Figure 2: Percentages of female judges in different fields of magistrates' courts

Multiple Regression Model and the Relative Importance of Gender

Because of the problem of self-selection it appears more adequate to analyze the gender related effect by multiple regression analysis. Considering, in summary, the correlation between all relevant, non-redundant variables, we performed two multiple regression models to predict the average intention to punish (cf. Figure 3). In the first model we only analyzed the gender related effect, in the second model we analyzed the effects of all the relevant variables. In the second model we then removed the gender variable. Based on the difference of the proportion of variance explained (R^2), we exactly get the proportion attributed to gender. As we see (Model 1), the effect of gender explains at most 4.8% of the variance, while all the predictors in sum (Model 2) explain a proportion of 53%. Of this proportion, the gender related effect not further explained is 2.4%.

Intercorrelation of relevant, non-redundant variables

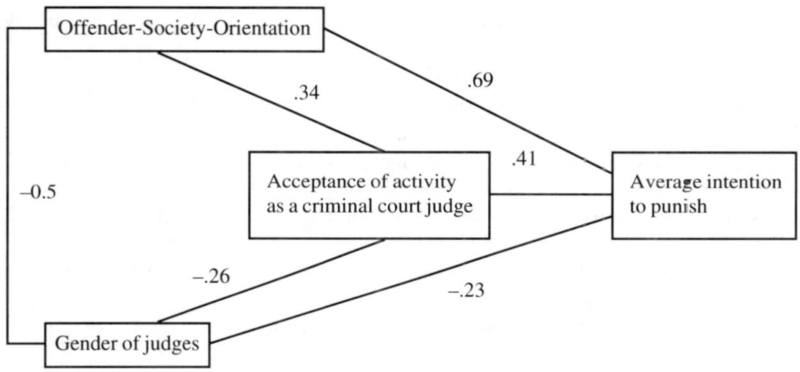

	Model 1			Model 2		
Variable	Coefficient	Std. Error	F-value	Coefficient	Std. Error	F-value
Gender	.719	.203	12.558***	.520	.148	12.264**
Acceptance of activity as a criminal court judge			.266	.085	9.783**	
Offender-Society-Orientation				.874	.067	170.873***
adjusted R^2		.0478			.530	
adjusted R^2 without Gender		.000			.506	

Figure 3 Intercorrelations of relevant variables and multiple regression models predicting average intention to punish

Which Model Proves Most Adequate?

Since we found that female judges, in general, express a somewhat lower intention to punish, it is not immediately obvious to decide between the models of explanation (cf. Figure 1). In total, however, the equality model (cf. Model C) proves most adequate: we could neither confirm that female criminal court judges are significantly more lenient than male criminal court judges (cf. Model A), nor did we find a significant interaction effect according to which groups of female judges (criminal court judges vs. judges in other fields of activity) differ much more in their intention to punish than the respective groups of male judges (cf. Model B). The gender effect discovered has much to do with the different interests of male and female judges. Female judges are simply over-represented in that group of judges who neither work as a criminal court judge nor prefere that activity. And this group of judges in general demonstrates a more lenient attitude towards punishment.

References

Ajzen, J., & Fishbein, M. (1980). Understanding attitudes and predicting social behavior. Englewood Cliffs, NJ: Prentice Hall.

Augstein, F. (1989). Frauen im Recht. Zeitmagazin, 24, 30-38.

Canary, D. J., & Seibold, D. R. (1984). Attitudes and behavior. New York: Praeger.

Carroll, J. S., Perkowitz, W. T., Lurigio, A. J., & Weaver, F. M. (1987). Sentencing goals, causal attributions, ideology, and personality. Journal of Personality and Social Psychology, 52(1), 107-118.

Cohen, J., & Cohen, P. (1983). Applied multiple regression/correlation analysis for the behavioral sciences. Hillsdale, NJ: Lawrence Erlbaum.

Fishbein, M., & Ajzen, J. (1985). Belief, attitude, intention, and behavior: An introduction to theory and research. Reading, MA: Addison-Wesley.

Gibson, J. L. (1978). Judges' role orientations, attitudes, and decisions: An inter-active model. The American Political Science Review, 72, 911-924.

Gilligan, C. (1982). In a different voice. Psychological theory and women's development. Cambridge: Harvard University Press.

Haan, N. (1978). Two moralities in action contexts: Relationships to thought, ego regulation, and development. Journal of Personality and Social Psychology, 36, 286-305.

Kanter, R. M. (1978). Reflections on women and the legal profession: A sociological perspective. Harvard Women's Law Journal, 1, 1-17.

Kohlberg, L. (1981/84). Essays on moral development: Vol. 1/2. San Francisco: Harper & Row.

Lyons, N. P. (1983). Two perspectives: On self, relationships, and morality. Harvard Educational Review, 53, 125-145.

Menkel-Meadow, C. (1989). Exploring a research agenda of the feminization of the legal profession: Theories of gender and social change. Law and Social Inquiry, 14(2), 289-319.

Oswald, M. E. (1994). Psychologie des richterlichen Strafens. Stuttgart: Enke.

Sessar, K. (1989). Die Frau vor den Toren der Jurisprudenz. In W. Melnizky & O. F. Müller (Hrsg.), Strafrecht, Strafprozeßrecht und Kriminologie. Festschrift für Franz Pallin zum 80. Geburtstag, (pp. 401-418). Wien: Manz.

Predicting Court Sentences: A Perilous Exercise

Catherine Fitzmaurice, Donald Rogers and Paula Stanley

Introduction

This paper is concerned with predictions of court sentences. The research project on which it is based spread over some five years. Our aim is not to report on all of its findings but to outline some of the problems which we encountered.

As the project developed, we discovered that predicting court sentences was a perilous exercise. Some of the perils pertain to the actual task of prediction, others to the interpretation of predictions and the third to the use of predictions

So, first, we want to describe briefly the aim, method and some of the results of the project. Secondly, we want to discuss the issues which pertain to the interpretation of the predictions. Thirdly, we want to examine, in the context of the introduction of the new Criminal Justice Act (CJA), the issues associated with the production and use of such predictions.

Predicting Sentences: Why and How?

The initial project can be said to be the direct consequence of the introduction, by the Criminal Justice Act of 1982, of a new Order. Under its Schedule 11, it introduced a Specified Activities Order which imposes specific conditions on an offender. The reactions of probation services to this Order were varied.

One of the issues it raised is central to the research project we undertook and concerns the position of this new Order in the overall sentencing tariff. In other words, probation services were, by and large, eager to ensure that Specified Activities Orders were ONLY recommended in court by probation officers when a custodial sentence was likely.

To be in a position to know that a sentence of imprisonment is likely requires a means of assessing risks. By then, services had had considerable experience with Community Service Orders and knew of the problems which result from inappropriate targeting: in other words, if an order, which was meant to be an alternative to custody, was recommended or given in cases which did not warrant custody, subsequent offending or non-completion of the order was likely to lead to immediate imprisonment.

Of course, officers made judgments about the risk of custody. They did and do so, on the basis of their experience of the courts they served. However, a need emerged in probation for a more "objective" indication of custodial risk. The most famous example of this development is due to David Bale (1990) who constructed the Cambridgeshire Risk of Custody Scale. Within a few years, this scale, based on the sentencing practice of Cambridgeshire, had been adopted by many probation services with or without modifications.

Following the development of the Cambridgeshire scale, three main issues arose amongst probation practitioners: the first concerned the need to adopt a scale at all rather than to keep on relying on the officers' judgement of risks in courts. The second concerned the statistical construction of the Cambridgeshire scale itself which was seen as problematic by some. The third centred on the relevance of a scale based on Cambridgeshire courts to courts which were not in Cambridgeshire.

The research project reported here stems largely from the last two concerns. One of its aims was to ascertain whether it was possible to develop a predictive instrument which rested on a different methodology. Another was to find out whether such a predictive instrument could be developed which also reflected individual court practices.

The next two aims had little to do with the concerns of the time. One was to ascertain whether sentences other than custody could also be predicted and the other, if predictions could be updated so as to keep reflecting the sentencing patterns of courts over time.

Hence, the research project aimed to develop and assess a predictive instrument which would offer an indication of risks for different sentences including custody and which could be updated so as to keep on reflecting the current sentencing practices of courts.

A first scale which fulfilled these objectives was developed on a limited number of cases and has been reported elsewhere (Fitzmaurice, 1990). Later, the same method was used on a much larger sample and it is those results which are reported here.

The Method

The choice of the method presented few problems originally. There existed a predictive method which had been used previously and with success in a criminological setting. The Parole Index, developed by Chris Nuttall and his team in 1977, provided estimates of the likelihood of reconviction of individual parole applicants. The Parole Index was repeatedly tested and its reliability was verified over time (Sapsford, 1978; Ward, 1987). The method it uses was also compared to other statistical techniques by Farrington and Tarling (1985) and found to be robust in relation to criminological predictions. Consequently the same method was adopted.

The sample was made up of some 4000 cases. On each of these cases 32 variables were collected. These 4000 cases had received one of eight sentences available to adult offenders: discharge; fine; probation order; Community Service Order; Schedule 11 Order; fully suspended sentence; partially suspended sentence; and custody.

Understandably, given the number of cases, the number of outcomes and the number of variables, the whole process was computerised. Individual predictions based on the statistical model were also computerised. The resulting software became known as the Sentencing Prediction Scale (SPS) (Fitzmaurice and Biddle, 1990). Once the information about an offender has been keyed in, SPS produces a set of predictions, one for each sentence. When the offender had been sentenced, both the recommendations and the sentence are entered into the database. Periodically, the system can be updated using the cases recently sentenced so that predictions keep on reflecting the sentencing patterns of courts.

Initially, the first scale used 32 "predictive" variables. The next step consisted in developing different models which required fewer variables and in ascertaining how these different models affected the accuracy of predictions. In fact, the question was to know if eight different sentences could be predicted with a much smaller number of variables.

We selected variables which were closely associated with the eight sentences and eliminated those which were likely to be redundant given their degree of association with one or more other variables. We tentatively identified three models: Models 7, 9 and 12 which, as their name indicate, involved respectively seven, nine and twelve variables. The probation area which acted as host to the project suggested we run two others, Models 16 and 17, which required 16 and 17 variables.

We constructed each model, ran them and analysed the performance of each of these models for each of the eight outcomes. What stemmed from the varied measures we used was a fairly simple and consistent message: some models performed better than others in predicting certain sentences but no single model towered above the rest in terms of its performance.

It is clearly not possible here to review in detail the results so we have summarised in Table 1 some of the information we obtained on each of the six general models.

Table 1: Comparison of 6 models for 7 sub scales (when selection ratio = base rate)

	MODEL					
	7	**9**	**12**	**16**	**17**	**32**
DISCHARGE						
Cutoff	69	70	67	60	63	70
% True Positives	38.4	38.4	40.0	40.5	40.8	39.4
% True Negatives	91.3	91.6	91.5	91.5	91.6	91.4
% Total successes	84.6	84.4	85.1	85.1	85.2	84.9
Phi (and RIOCC)	0.30	0.29	0.31	0.32	0.32	0.31
Odds ratio	6.46	6.33	7.16	7.30	7.47	6.89
FINE						
Cutoff	50	46	40	43	45	40
% True Positives	67.3	66.8	67.4	61.1	60.4	66.1
% True Negatives	88.8	88.6	88.9	87.0	86.5	88.3
% Total successes	83.3	83.0	83.4	80.5	79.8	82.6
Phi (and RIOC)	0.56	0.55	0.56	0.48	0.47	0.54
Odds ratio	16.3	15.5	16.5	10.5	9.68	14.6
PROBATION						
Cutoff	56	55	49	56	57	53
% True Positives	46.5	44.8	48.9	41.1	41.3	51.6
% True Negatives	88.1	87.7	88.9	86.5	87.1	89.2
% Total successes	80.5	79.8	81.5	78.0	78.8	82.3
Phi (and RIOC)	0.35	0.32	0.38	0.28	0.28	0.41
Odds ratio	6.41	5.77	7.48	4.47	4.74	8.74

Table coninued over

Table 1 continued

	MODEL					
	7	**9**	**12**	**16**	**17**	**32**
COMMUNITY SERVICE						
Cutoff	55	58	56	55	60	58
% True Positives	41.6	43.5	43.7	41.4	38.1	46.1
% True Negatives	90.3	90.6	90.4	90.1	90.0	90.8
% Total successes	83.4	83.9	83.6	83.0	82.8	84.2
Phi (and RIOC)	0.32	0.34	0.34	0.31	0.28	0.37
Odds ratio	6.51	7.40	7.31	6.38	5.56	8.37
SPECIFIED ACTIVITIES						
Cutoff	72	70	76	76	75	77
% True Positives	20.6	22.7	18.5	20.5	23.6	21.3
% True Negatives	98.4	98.5	98.3	98.2	98.4	98.3
% Total successes	96.7	97.1	96.7	96.4	96.7	96.7
Phi (and RIOC)	0.19	0.21	0.17	0.19	0.22	0.20
Odds ratio	15.2	19.9	13.0	13.6	18.1	15.6
FULLY SUSPENDED						
Cutoff	64	65	60	61	59	57
% True Positives	25.7	26.7	24.9	27.0	26.0	23.9
% True Negatives	92.7	92.8	92.6	92.6	92.5	92.4
% Total successes	86.6	86.9	86.5	86.6	86.4	86.2
Phi (and RIOC)	0.18	0.20	0.17	0.20	0.18	0.16
Odds ratio	4.36	4.70	4.14	4.65	4.32	3.81
CUSTODY						
Cutoff	45	46	43	40	41	45
% True Positives	57.6	56.6	55.7	57.5	56.5	52.7
% True Negatives	91.2	91.0	90.9	91.2	91.0	90.3
% Total successes	85.4	85.1	84.8	85.3	85.0	83.8
Phi (and RIOC)	0.49	0.48	0.47	0.49	0.47	0.43
Odds ratio	14.1	13.1	12.6	13.9	13.0	10.3

Table 1 provides five measures associated with the optimal cut-off point. This has been defined (Copas and Tarling, 1986) as the case where the selection ratio and the base rate are the same. In other words, the optimal cut-off point corresponds to a situation where the proportion of the sample which is predicted to get a disposal equals the proportion of the sample which actually gets this disposal. The first three measures in the Table are percentages. "True positives" are those cases which were predicted to receive a given sentence and received it. "True negatives" are those cases which were predicted *not* to receive the given sentence and did *not* get it. The third, "total success", has been included here largely because it has been extensively used as a measure of accuracy with other risk of custody scales.

However, this measure is, in our opinion, potentially misleading. The reason for this is that "total success" is calculated by adding all "true positives" and all "true negatives" and dividing the sum by the total number of cases. Hence the measure is likely to give an over-optimistic picture of accuracy.

To illustrate, let us take the example of custody in our sample. If we try to predict who will get a custodial sentence, we are effectively trying to identify the 685 people who got custody out of the 3975 who were sentenced. This means that 83% of the offenders did not get custody. The chances are that whatever the predictive instrument one uses, a greater percentage of non-custody cases would be identified as such. Consequently, the percentage of "true negatives" is always likely to be very high. Here it is of the order of 91%.

Since the percentage of "total success" is an average based on "true positives" and "true negatives", it will be biassed by the high "true negatives". Indeed, if we look at all "total success" values for each of the disposals predicted by the best model for that disposal, they range from 82% to 97%. It would be at best misguided in our view to claim that the accuracy of our scale varied between these "total success" percentages. As we said earlier, these have largely been included as a point of comparison for those scales which rely on this measure.

Table 1 also provides the odds ratio. This measure compares the successful and unsuccessful predictions above and below the cut-off point. It gives an indication of how well differentiated the cases are which fall on either side of the cut-off point. An odds ratio of 14.1 (as in the custody example) means that cases falling above the cut off point are 14 times more likely to get custody than cases falling below.

Finally, Phi is a measure which varies in this particular case (2×2 tables) from zero to one. In cases where the selection ratio is equal to the base rate, as is the case here, Phi is equal to another measure called "relative improvement over chance" (RIOC). Hence, a Phi value of .56 (fines) means that using the information from the scale provides an improvement of 56% over predictions made by chance.

Even with this reduced amount of statistical information on the models, it is possible to see why it was said earlier that some models worked better for some disposals than for others. So, looking at each disposal in turn, Model 17 is better at predicting discharges, Model 12 at fines, Model 32 at probation and CSOs, Model 9 is better for Schedule 11 and fully suspended sentences whilst Model 7 is better for custody.

However, in many instances, there is little difference between models. So, for example Model 12 is better than Model 7 for fines but only marginally so: the percentages of "true positives" and "true negatives" are virtually the same; the Phi values are the same and the odds ratio are respectively of 16.5 and 16.3 which is far from constituting a large difference.

This is not to mean that there are no sizeable difference between models for each disposal: the difference in odds ratio for CSO for example is 8.37 with Model 32 but only 5.56 for Model 17 and the respective percentages of "true positives" are 46.1% as opposed to 38.1%.

We mentioned earlier that predicting court sentences was a perilous exercise. The nature of the first peril is that, unfortunately, there is no simple solution to the question of accuracy.

What the data tell us is that the choice of a given model entails an acceptance of the strengths and limitations inherent to that model over the advantages and limitations of the others. If practitioners are going to use the tool to make decisions or to monitor practice, then that decision, to a degree, belongs to them. At least, the data give them a means of making an informed decision about accuracy over all disposals and hence about the trade-off between models.

Predicting the Predictable

The perils are not limited to the choice of models. It is clear that whatever the model used, certain disposals are quite difficult to predict. This may be related to the method itself; it may also and importantly be related to the degree of consistency of the sentencers.

So, for example, it is quite difficult to predict discharges and suspended sentences. However, closer scrutiny of the actual scores indicates that discharges and suspended sentences cases are not always treated as very different sentences in the tariff. Interestingly, it would appear from our data that in many instances suspended sentences were used by sentencers instead of a discharge.

This had very significant consequences, of course, as further offending following a suspended sentence was likely to lead to an immediate sentence of imprisonment whilst further offending following a discharge was very unlikely to have the same result.

It also means that regardless of the model used, the ability to predict will be severely restricted. The greater the randomness in the initial decisions, the more difficult predictions become. In essence, we can only predict what is predictable.

Policy and Practice

Another of the perils we encountered is that predictions can reveal the quirky nature of interaction between policy and practice. Here, the case in point concerns Community Service Orders and Specified Activities Orders (also referred to as Schedule 11). In the service which provided our data, the policy concerning these two disposals had been consistent over time.

It was to recommend both orders as a high tariff disposal which could be used instead of imprisonment. The main difference revolved around the notion of social need: when such a need was identified by officers, a Specified Activities Order was seen as a more desirable and effective form of intervention.

The overall number of Schedule 11 cases is much smaller than for Community Service Orders. It is consequently more difficult to predict Schedule 11 than it is to predict CSOs. However, it is clear, from our data, that the practice differs: the two orders were not used in the same way either in terms of tariff position or in the extent of their use by the courts. To put it another way, the information on which the scores are based highlights, at times, the divergence between policy and practice. Here, the nature of the peril is that, often, neither practioners nor policy makers find it comforting to discover such discrepancies!

So far, we have reviewed some of the perils which are related to the prediction task itself and to the interpretation of the predictions.

In summary, it is clear from our data that predictions enabled by the scale improve considerably our ability over chance to predict sentences. The data also suggest that the choice between models will be a trade-off and that some disposals will always be difficult to predict especially when their number is small or when the sentencing pattern which underpins them lacks in consistency.

Incidentally, it is worth stressing that the difficulty is not limited to a statistical instrument. The odds of being able to predict accurately, for example, 575 cases of CSO or 685 custody cases out of 4000 cases constitute a formidable task for human beings. Evidence would suggest that their ability to do so would be more limited than that of the models we tried.

The last point of this summary, as was exemplified by our example of CSO and Schedule 11, illustrates that the information the scale holds is useful in understanding the nature of the risks offenders face in court and their relationship to policy.

Predictions and the Criminal Justice Act 1991

Finally we want to turn to the issues associated with the production and use of such predictions. It has been argued that the implementation of the Criminal Justice Act 1991 rendered redundant any effort at sentencing predictions. It is worth looking at this view.

The CJA 1991 is a challenging act. Its central tenet is that penalties should be proportional to the seriousness of the crime. Two consequences follow. The first relates to previous convictions. We simplify, but, basically, one of the Articles of the CJA specified that they should not be considered when sentencing. This could be said to be internally consistent with a just desert philosophy. The offender is simply punished for the crime which was committed. However, the following Article did free sentencers from this restriction in certain instances which were not clearly specified. The question remains as to how sentencers could integrate these two articles into their sentencing practices. Moreover, when previous convictions are taken into consideration, the extent to which they influence sentence will inevitably vary across sentencers.

The second consequence concerns offence seriousness. The notion of proportionality is central to the Act's philosophy. Sentencers will be expected to give a penalty commensurate with the seriousness of the offence. This means that sentencers will need to assess how serious they believe an offence to be. The Act has provided no guidance on the subject.

The literature does indicate that there exists some consensus about the seriousness of crimes. However, what Fitzmaurice and Pease (1986) demonstrated is that sentencers vary amongst themselves not only in their assessment of offence seriousness but also in the way they translate their assessment of seriousness into a penalty.

In other words, even if the Act (or anyone else for that matter) had provided a very fine grading of offence seriousness, discrepancies could still be expected because sentencers are very likely to translate these estimates differently into a penalty.

Given the lack of clarity concerning previous convictions and the question of seriousness and its translation, what are the likely consequences of the Act on sentencing practice? The most likely outcome is that courts will vary amongst themselves in their use of previous convictions, in their assessment of offence seriousness and in their translation of this assessment into a penalty.

Since the Act has not taken the form of clear guidelines about levels of penalties for specific categories of offences over the whole of the spectrum of offences, the leeway for discretion within the new Act is still considerable. This is more than ever the case for community based disposals as the Act offers sentencers the possibility of combining orders and imposing specific and new restrictions.

In many ways, the next five years are likely to be fascinating. A new and more complicated "tariff" relying heavily on community based disposals will emerge and custodial rates will also be affected. Because of this, probation officers are likely to keep wanting to use some kinds of predictive tools. We would argue that predictive scaling should continue, not in isolation and so as simply to inform probation practice *but* to enable a reflection on developing sentencing patterns.

Clearly, the use of predictions offered by ROC scales or by SPS and based on pre CJA 1991 should be discontinued as the Act becomes implemented. Their continued use could be very damaging to the emergence of new sentencing practices. But what do we do after that?

Shaping Sentencing Practice by Default

We believe that what we have learned about predictive scaling and its use enables us to reflect on what is probably its biggest peril: that of a shaping of sentencing policy which is carried out, by default, by the probation services.

Proportionality and consistency are central to justice. Different means can be adopted to achieve these aims. The guidelines movement, the existence in other countries of fairly prescriptive criminal codes or the formation of a sentencing council constitute some of the options. These options rely on sentencers' views or sentencers' practice. Indeed, statistical scaling could be a powerful help to these kinds of development.

Interestingly, the current use of sentence predictions stemmed primarily from probation services which were concerned with diversion from custody. The concern is a legitimate one. It is understandable that, given the pressures on resources and the attachment to non custodial disposals, services should have turned to predictive tools. They give a baseline on which, at least, consistent recommendations can be ensured.

However, if we look at it differently, the reliance on predictive scaling by services is an aberration. If clear guidelines or a code existed to limit discretion, such instruments would never have been needed. The use of predictions by services have taken place largely because of the absence of clear directions about sentencing policy and hence discrepancies in sentencing practices.

Moreover, services have, by and large, used predictive scores in isolation from the magistracy and the judiciary. Policy decisions by services to recommend only certain disposals according to the level of predicted risk of custody, however laudable the intentions, are problematic precisely because they constitute unilateral decisions.

Given the absence of guidelines or codes and the likely discrepancies in sentencing practice to which the new Act is likely to give rise, the need for predictive instruments related to sentence is unlikely to abate amongst probation practitioners.

Since the CJA 1991 offers such a potential for new sentencing patterns, it also offers the opportunity to open the discussion. We would argue that sentencers should have access to the information which comes from predictive scaling, be it on patterns of offending or patterns of sentencing. Moreover, we would also argue that this information should be shared and used to facilitate a joint reflection and a joint shaping of sentencing policy.

In most areas, there already exist fora where sentencers and services meet. Other structures which facilitate and foster the liaison with sentencers are likely to be created at regional and national levels. In such contexts, the information derived from sentencing patterns and their predictability, constitutes an invaluable starting point for concerted discussions about proportionality and consistency which are so important to the new Criminal Justice Act and more generally, to justice.

References

Bale, D. (1990). The Cambridgeshire risk of custody. In G. Mair (Ed.), Risk prediction and probation: Papers from a Research and Planning Unit Workshop (Home Office Research and Planning Unit Paper No. 56). London: HMSO.

Copas, J., & Tarling, R. (1986). Some methodological issues in making predictions. In A. Blumstein (Ed.), Criminal careers and 'career criminals': Vol. 2. National Academy Press.

Farrington, D., & Tarling, R. (Eds.), (1985). Prediction in criminology. Albany: State University of New York Press.

Fitzmaurice, C., & Pease, K. (1986). The psychology of judicial sentencing. Manchester: Manchester University Press.

Fitzmaurice, C. (1990). Predicting risks in courts: The Staffordshire Sentencing Prediction Scale. In G. Mair (Ed.), Risk prediction and probation: Papers from a Research and Planning Unit Workshop (Home Office Research and Planning Unit Paper No. 56). London: HMSO.

Fitzmaurice, C., & Biddle, F. (1990). SPS: Sentencing prediction scale [Software package].

Nuttall, C., Barnard, E., Fowles, A., Frost, A., Hammond, W., Mayhew, P., Pease, K., Tarling, R., & Weatheritt, M. (1977). Parole in England and Wales (Home Office Research Unit Study No. 38). London: HMSO.

Sapsford, R. (1978). Further research applications of the 'Parole Prediction Index'. International Journal of Criminology and Penology, 6, 247254

Ward, D. (1987). The validity of the Reconviction Prediction Score (Home Office Research Study No. 94). London: HMSO.

Communication Channels and Gender Differences in Decoding and Integration of Cues in Legal Decision-Making[1]

Gerhard Kette and Vladimir J. Konečni

Introduction

It has been frequently asserted that judges and juries integrate non-evidentiary and extra-legal elements into their verdict decisions. In civil-law cases, the verdicts - perhaps of necessity - often involve ambiguous personal and psychological data about the litigants, so that such cases may be especially vulnerable to extra-legal biasing influences.

Gender of legal participants, as a particularly controversial extra-legal factor, has been the subject of an especially large amount of researchers' attention. In this paper, we consider the gender of the "judge" as an extra-legal factor in civil-law (small-claims) cases. However, we do so in the context of examining the extent to which the decoding and decision-making strategies dealing with emotion-laden information are differentially affected by gender. We shall first consider the potential biases induced by the sex of judge, and culprit, as well as any that may be induced by the differential weighing and processing of emotional information.

The experimental data in which the *sex of the juror* served as an independent variable established few consistent differences between the decisions of the male and female jurors. The bulk of the data suggest that men are more active in jury deliberations than women and thus may be more influential in determining verdicts (for a summary see Kette, 1994). Most of the actual trial data relating to gender were based upon civil suits. Jurors favored plaintiffs of their own sex in verdicts, but consistently awarded higher damages to men than to women. When the sex of the juror does significantly predict decision behavior, the results sometimes go in one direction (e.g. females acquit more than males) and sometimes in the opposite one.

Studies Examining Gender-Related Issues in Judges' Decision Making

In reviewing the experimental jury research, few studies have examined the relationship between the sex of the judge and his or her sentencing behavior (most of the latter research was conducted with archival data). This reliance on archival methodology reflects, in part, the absence of information about the sentencing behavior of female judges. In most jurisdictions the majority of judges is male and thus relatively few offenders are sentenced by female judges. Most of the results of these archival analyses must therefore be considered tentative. In the past, researchers have mainly focused on interactions between the sex of the judge and three case characteristics: the offense of which the defendants are convicted and the sex and race of defendants.

In an archival study using more than 27,000 cases, Myers and Talarico (1987) found that contrary to expectation, the prison sentences (of both black and white offenders) tended to be longer in courts where female judges presided. They also considered the issue of whether female judges treated certain types of offenders differently than males judges. The general expectation was that, with the exception of rape, female judges would sentence more leniently than male judges. In actuality, they found considerable similarity in the sentences imposed by male and females judges. Where significant differences existed, they suggested that female judges may be more severe than male judges toward both violent and property-crime offenders.

Despite small sample sizes of female judges, their data also provided some support for the expectation that female judges sentenced rape offenders more harshly than male judges. Rape offenders would more likely be imprisoned and receive longer prison sentences if sentenced by female judges. Surprisingly, however, they received more lenient split sentences (time in jail, followed by probation) from female judges. Finally, they found that male judges did not treat female offenders more leniently than females judges. In fact, male judges appeared to sentence female offenders significantly more harshly than did female judges, and there was also some evidence that male judges sentence male offenders more leniently than female judges. Again, samples were small, and these differences are suggestive rather than definitive.

The most detailed information about sex differences in sentencing behavior is based on archival research by Kritzer and Uhlmann (1977). They developed competing expectation about the sentencing behavior of female judges, arguing, on the one hand, that female judges may be more threatened than male judges by normative violations and for this reason be more punitive, and, on the other, that because of differences in sex-role socialization, females judges may be more lenient. Previous evidence of "chivalrous" or paternalistic attitudes toward female offenders led Kritzer and Uhlmann to expect that male judges would punish female offenders more leniently than would their female colleagues.

Virtually no support was found for these hypotheses. In general, the sentencing behavior of male and female judges was more alike than different. Most notably, there were no significant differences in the way male and female judges treated female (or male) offenders. Male judges did not appear to be paternalistic toward female offenders, nor did females judges appear to be more empathetic. Although female judges treated rape offenders more harshly than did male judges, the differences were not significant. Only one difference in sentencing behavior was noteworthy: female judges punished larceny offenders more harshly than did male judges. Other differences in sentencing behavior existed, but could be traced to legally relevant facts.

More recent work with archival data (Gruhl, Spohn, & Welch, 1981; Myers & Talarico, 1987) has demonstrated a slight (but statistically non-significant) tendency for female judges to use the prison option more frequently than do male judges. Although sentencing behavior differed depending on the type of offender, there was no consistent tendency for female judges to be lenient or male judges to be more severe. Contrary to expectation, female judges were less likely to imprison rapists. Male judges sentenced female offenders more leniently than did female judges. They were less likely to send female offenders to prison, and imposed slightly less severe sentences. In contrast, female judges treated male and female offenders similarly.

Thus, the literature on sex biases in judges' decision-making provides a quite inconsistent picture about the behavior of male and female judges, especially when the gender of the defendant is also considered. The gender differences appear only occasionally, are of varying intensity, though they emerge in civil- as well as criminal-law decision-making. Quite unexplained are the strength and direction of these effects and their causes.

Furthermore, the vast majority of these studies failed to consider the gender of the probation officers who recommend sentences to judges in criminal cases. Yet, in archival research with over 1200 cases, Konečni and Ebbesen (1982) found the probation officers' recommendations and the judges' sentencing decisions to be identical 87% of the time and there was considerable evidence that the causal arrow went from probation officers to judges. This suggests the need to understand a 2 (female vs. male) × 3 (probation officer vs. judge vs. defendant) pattern and nothing is at present known about this (not to mention further possible interactions of this 2 × 3 pattern with the type of crime, strength of evidence, prior criminal record of the defendant, and his/her in-jail vs. out-on-bail status - which factors were identified by Konečni and Ebbesen (1982) as causally affecting the probation officers' recommendation (and only *indirectly* the judges' sentences)).

Studies Examining Gender-Related Issues in Decoding Non-Verbally-Communicated Information

The research on sex differences in decoding non-verbal behavior suggests that females are better at it than males (cf. Hall's (1978) meta-analysis of 75 studies). Furthermore, Rosenthal and DePaulo (1979) supported the hypothesis that non-verbally women are more interpersonally accommodating than men. They are superior decoders and encoders, principally when reacting spontaneously (Fujita, Harper, & Wiens, 1980) and particularly with regard to positive messages (Noller, 1980). A longitudinal and cross-sectional examination of the acquisition of females' superiority in decoding non-verbal cues, indicated what with age, females lost more of their advantage for the less controllable, or more covert channels, but gain more advantage for the less "leaky" channels (Blanck, 1981). In the context of an interview procedure, Christensen and Rosenthal (1982) illustrated the importance of gender and non-verbal decoding skills as determinants of interpersonal expectancy effects in communication. Here, males were more biased by their expectations and produced stronger behavioral confirmation in their communication partners (interviewees) than females, with female interviewees more readily showing "behavior confirmation". More recent studies have attempted to clarify this phenomenon by adding new variables such as measures of personality (Kombos & Fournet, 1985; Schneider & Schneider-Duker, 1984), factors of socialization and attitudes (Noller, 1986), or by methodological criticism (Eisenberg & Lennon, 1983).

In the courtroom, non-verbal communication (facial expression, gestures, body movement, and paralinguistic elements such as variation of voice pitch, speech rate, and loudness) may subtly affect the proceedings and outcome of a trial, yet the participants may be unaware of this.

Hypotheses

The present study examined the relevance of gender in the decoding, integrative and "verdict" decision-making activities by simulated judges to whom civil-law case information was communicated in four different ways: Video and Sound; Video Only; Sound Only; and Transcript Only. The focus was especially on the role of extra-legal emotion-laden information. Specifically, we tentatively hypothesized, on the basis of the literature review, that female decoding and decision-making processes may be disproportionately influenced by intense emotional information, especially when the content and emotionally-colored information are inconsistent (hence the four-communication-channel experimental design).

In part, these hypotheses were based on a study by Kette and Brandstätter (1990) which demonstrated - using the multiple-time-series methodology - that pure emotionally-laden information (entirely excluding legal facts) influenced verdicts and that for females non-verbal cues were a stronger predictor of verdicts than for males.

Our specific hypotheses were: (a) women are better than men at *decoding* non-verbally-communicated information of a predominantly emotional nature in a legal context; (b) therefore, women are more accurate in *predicting* the outcomes of civil-law cases in the Video Only condition; (c) women tend to put more emphasis on non-verbal cues than men do, which leads them to weigh that kind of information to greater extend in arriving at verdicts.

Method

Research participants The research participants were 72 male and 72 female graduating (social science) students from the University of California, San Diego, ranging in age from 22 to 31, with a mean of 25 years. All of them participated as part of their introductory psychology course requirements. The subjects were tested in groups of two to five, with each subject in a group randomly assigned to experimental condition. (Data from a further nine subjects were not analyzed because these individuals had previously viewed parts of the case materials.) There were 18 subjects in each condition of the basic 2 (gender) × 4 (mode of presentation) design.

Stimulus case materials The stimulus materials were 15 different videotaped civil-court cases which were presented in the long-running TV series "The People's Court". Each "episode" consists of a short introduction (giving the title of the case and a description of the plaintiff's complaints), followed by the presentation of the evidence (testimony by the plaintiff, defendant, and witnesses), and the judge's verdict. The judge was male and in all the cases the same person. In the episodes, the camera typically focused on the courtroom participant who was talking. Therefore, accurate observation of non-verbal cues (both facial and body) could be made by the subjects.

It should be noted that the judge is a real (retired) judge, not an actor, and that the litigants are similarly not actors, but persons involved in a real-life litigation. Finally, the judge's decision is binding, in that a contract to that effect is previously signed by the litigants. In the 15 cases that were used, the range of amounts sued for by the plaintiffs was \$24.47 to \$1,500.00 (the upper limit being fixed by law for small-claims courts), with a mean of \$877.36.

The introduction to a case and a portion of the evidence presentation were used as stimulus materials. The period of evidence presentation (which lasted from four to 12 minutes across the 15 cases used, with an average of seven minutes) was split into segments of 30 seconds each. Each such segment was defined as a "piece of evidence". After each segment, the subjects were given five seconds to rate it on two scales (described below). To prevent a biased selection of the 15 cases from the total pool of episodes, the sequence of the five cases presented to the subjects was determined by the sequence in which the programs had been aired. The 15 cases were divided into three blocks of five cases and balanced for episode length, and the gender and credibility of the plaintiffs.

Video and sound condition was considered as one containing both legally relevant and emotionally relevant information. In the Video Only and Sound Only conditions, information was presented on the respective channels. The Video Only condition was assumed to present exclusively emotional (non-factual) information in terms of behavioral and facial cues. In contrast, the Audio Only condition presumably involved the presentation of paralinguistic emotionally relevant cues, as well as evidentiary information. The Transcript Only condition involved emotionally relevant information only to the extent that the content itself was emotionally colored.

The four conditions thus represented a gradual series of emotionally/substantively relevant information communicated to the subjects. Some of the issues arising from the use of these different communication channels have been previously investigated. For example, facial cues have been shown to convey emotional information to a large degree (Fujita et al., 1980; Rosenthal & DePaulo, 1979; Harris & Rosenthal, 1985). Different studies have shown that visual cues alone can transmit experimenter expectations (Blanck & Rosenthal, 1984). Kraus, Apple, Moency, Wenzel, and Winton (1981) showed that verbal, paralinguistic and visual factors play a role in the judgements of another's affect (see also Ekman, 1980).

Design, procedure and dependent measures A 2 (sex of "judge") × 4 (modes of presentation: Video and Sound, Video Only, Sound Only, Transcript Only) design was used. Each subject was randomly assigned to a block of cases and thus viewed and rated five cases, all in one mode. The subjects were told that the experiment was designed to answer the question of "how accurately a lay person can predict the outcome of civil liability cases when the evidence is presented on different channels". The subject's task was to indicate on a 120 mm rating scale, anchored by 0.00\$ and the full amount that the plaintiff was suing for in the case in question, the extent of a defendant's liability for the damages allegedly suffered by the plaintiff. The subjects were instructed to rate quickly and to use all available information.

A measure of the subject's accuracy in predicting the real judge's verdicts was obtained by subtracting the "People's Court" judge's verdict in a particular case from the subjects' "verdicts". Because of the different demands (in $) in every case the values were transformed into units of the 120 mm graphic rating-scale. A measure of the subject's accuracy in predicting the real judge's verdicts was obtained. An analysis of disparity within gender groups was also carried out. For both of these measures the *last* of the subjects' sequential dollar verdicts in the series (consisting of 30 second segments) was used (in units of the graphic rating scale).

Another dependent variable was a measure of the influence of emotionally-laden (non-legal) information on the two sexes' verdicts using multiple time series analyses in which different channels of information could be conceptualized as independent and dependent variables, respectively.

Results

"Judges'" verdict accuracy Accuracy of an *individual* verdict is defined as the absolute difference (in mm of the graphic rating scale) between the verdict of a particular subject and the actual verdict of the "People's Court" judge. The *accuracy* of a *group* of six male or female subjects is defined as the *disparity* among their verdicts (within a particular case and a single mode of presentation). The individual accuracy measure indicates how much an individual of either sex differs from the real world outcome, the disparity reflects the homogeneity of the verdicts within the two gender groups. It is notable that the correlations between the two measures are higher for females and that they are the lowest in the two conditions that can be thought of as the most difficult conceptually (Video Only and Sound Only).

An analysis of variance of the individual accuracy scores (see Table 1) revealed a main effect of the mode of presentation ($F(3,719) = 2.78$, $p = 0.04$)[2] which was due to the fact that the Video Only condition resulted in the lowest accuracy: the average absolute deviation - for the two sexes combined - from the "People's Court" judge's verdicts was 43.8 (in mm of the 120 mm graphic rating scale) or 37%. The other three conditions did not differ from each other (the range, for the two sexes combined, was from 40 mm for the Video and Sound condition to 42 mm for the Sound Only condition).

Table 1: Means and standard deviations for accuracy as a deviation from the actual verdict as a function of the sex of "judge" and experiment condition

	Video & Sound	Video Only	Sound Only	Transcript
Female "Judge"				
M	42.7	49.7	45.7	44.1
SD	36.6	41.0	40.5	41.6
Male "Judge"				
M	37.6	52.7	38.9	38.4
SD	36.7	44.9	43.5	37.8

Note: The deviation between the individual verdict and the actual verdict is the absolute difference of the two ratings (in mm of the 120 mm graphic rating-scale). High numbers indicate a larger difference from the actual verdict, that is low accuracy.

Both the main effect of the gender of "judges" ($F(1,719) = 1.48$, p - 0.23) and the interaction ($F(3,719) = 0.55$, p - 0.65) were not significant. The latter was true even though in three of the four conditions, those including verbal information, men's verdicts approximated "People's Court" judge's verdicts more closely than did women's. The only reversal occurred in the Video Only condition, with women more accurate than men.

If a significant gender difference were to be obtained in the analysis of *group disparity*, that would imply a gender difference in factual/emotional processing, or differential within-gender variability in response to the type and difficulty of tasks, decision-making strategies, and possibly other factors (our experiment was not designed to distinguish between such differences), or both. Disparity was defined as the standard deviation of the verdicts by male and female subjects, respectively, calculated for each of the 15 cases (120 standard deviations: 2 (gender in groups of six) × 4 (modes of presentation) × 15 (cases)). There was, in fact, no main effect of gender, $F(1,119) = 0.10$, $p > 0.05$; the interaction was not significant ($F(3,119) = 1.25$, $p > 0.10$). However, a marginally significant interaction between these two factors emerged in a theoretically important analysis: 2 (gender) × 2 (contrast of the three communication channels involving factual information, Video and Sound + Sound Only + Transcript vs. only non-verbal information (Video Only): $F(1,119) = 3.49$, p - 0.06. As can be seen from Table 2, the interaction is due to the considerably greater variability in verdicts reach by men, as opposed to women, in the Video Only condition, in the context of a mode-of-presentation main effect that was due mainly to the Video and Sound condition resulting in the least variability for both men and women, especially compared to the Video Only condition.

Table 2: Means and standard deviations for disparity of verdicts as a function of the sex of "judge" and experiment condition

	Video & Sound	**Video Only**	**Sound Only**	**Transcript**
Female "Judge"				
M	31.6	36.5	35.3	37.4
SD	13.2	8.9	16.1	14.2
Male "Judge"				
M	28.9	46.0	35.6	33.8
SD	13.1	8.0	19.8	11.7

Note: Disparity is the standard deviation of the individual verdicts (in mm of the 120 mm graphic rating-scale) within one cell and one case; that is, the means in the table are calculated from the 15 standard deviations according to the 15 cases.

Weighing of emotional information The central issue of the degree of weighing of emotionally-laden information, especially in the light of the assumption that such information may be differentially used by the two sexes, was approached by time-series analyses. We employed the multiple time-series method (cf. Möbus & Nagl, 1983), such that two "independent" (Video Only and Transcript Only) and one

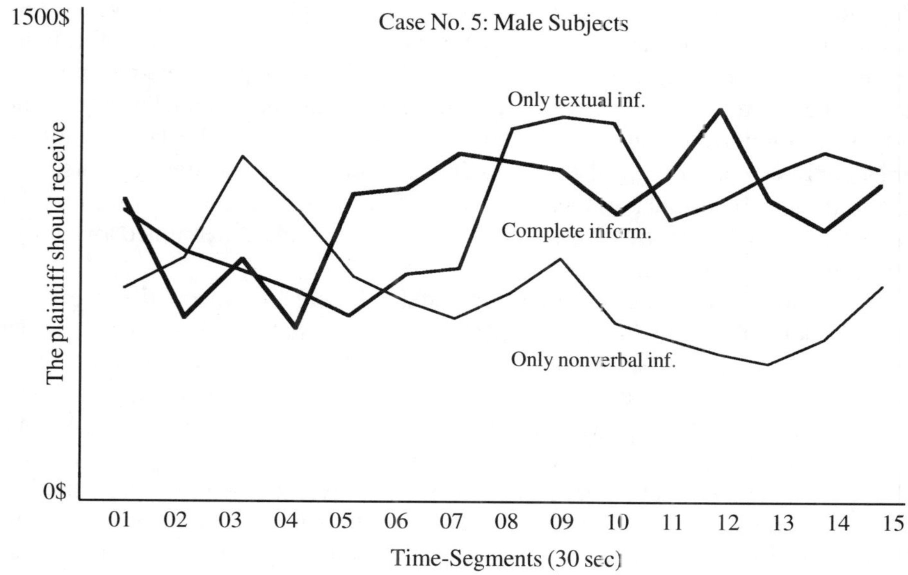

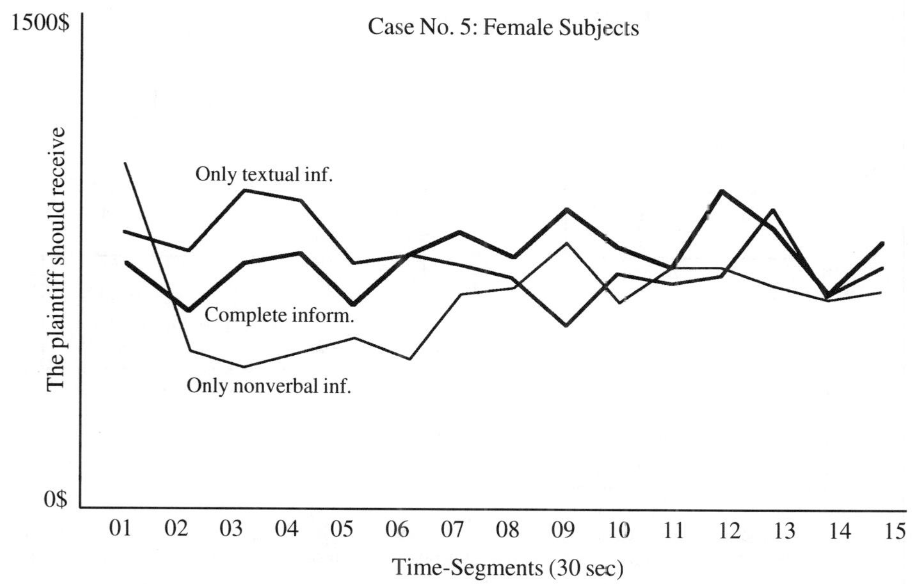

Figure 1: Sample time series for male and female subjects in one case and three presentation modes; independent series: only nonverbal and only textual information; dependent: condition with complete information (video & sound).

"dependent" variable (Video and Sound) were conceptualized.[3] The Video Only condition was construed as providing exclusively emotionally-relevant information, whereas the Transcript Only condition was assumed to provide predominantly factual, legally-relevant information. The dependent-variable channel was the Video and Sound condition which combines both types of information. The data for the time-series analyses were obtained by averaging, for males and females separately, the ratings at each 30-second point, in each of the 15 cases. Another way of putting this is that individual subjects' time-series data in the three channels mentioned above were averaged, separately for each sex.[4]

The statistical procedures used are illustrated in Figure 1 for one of the 15 cases. In the top panel of this figure are presented the averaged data for male subjects' verdicts in the Video Only, Transcript, and Sound and Video conditions across the 15 30-second segments. The bottom panel presents the data for female subjects. In the analysis, the "predictive" power (σ-coefficients) of the two "independent" variables was compared in the data for the two sexes. Whereas in female subjects the non-verbal (Video Only) and textual (Transcript) information are equally good "predictors" of the "dependent" variable, the male subjects' verdicts in the complete-information channel (Video and Sound) were "predicted" only by factual/legally-relevant information (Transcript), as evidenced by the divergence of the Audio Only time-series line. In 11 out of 15 cases, women weigh the non-verbal/emotional information more than did men. The σ-coefficients and the appropriate t-test documenting these statements are presented in Figure 2.

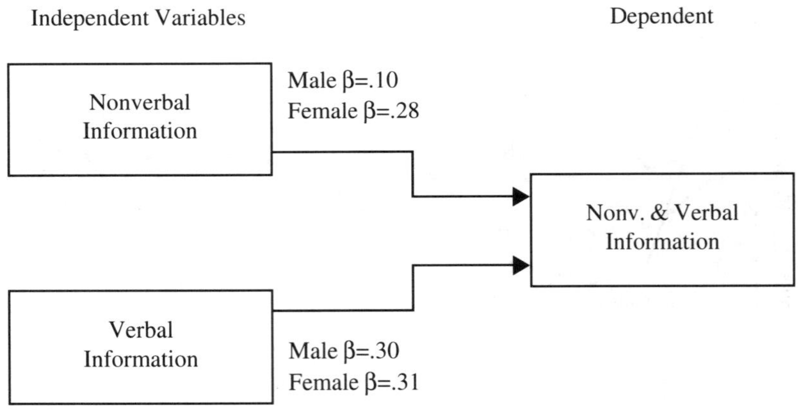

Figure 2: Sample time series for male and female subjects in one case and three presentation modes; independent series: only nonverbal and only textual information; dependent: condition with complete information (video & sound).

Time-series auto-correlations An analysis of the autocorrelations of the 720 (144 subjects rating five cases each) individual time series was also carried out. The Function of Auto-Correlations (ACF) or Function of Partial-Auto-Correlations (PACF, see Mobus & Nagel, 1983) can be interpreted as "memory" of events in the time series (at time-lags t minus 1, t minus 2, ... t minus n), that is, the memory of previously seen "pieces of evidence" (or previously *given ratings* of those "pieces of evidence", i.e. "consistency": these two interpretations cannot be separated easily). Such data can perhaps clarify any observed gender X mode-of-presentation interactions, in that a different pattern of auto-correlations would be observed in the relevant cells.

High auto-correlations could, of course, also be caused by the nature and order of the introduction of evidence. (For example, if the presented evidence favored one side throughout, then each new piece would cause a move to that side, and there would be a pseudo-trend in the time series.[5]) To separate "memory" effects from the irrelevant, contaminating type-of-case effects, such trends have to be statistically eliminated (by differentiation). If auto-correlations remain statistically significant, this suggests that the previous verdict decisions are "dragged along". One implication of this is that a superior memory for certain types of previously presented information (for example, in the Video Only channel) would substantially influence the subsequent verdict-related decision-making process.

The 720 auto-correlations were used as data in a 2 (sex of subject) × 4 (mode-of-presentation) design: no significant effects emerged. An attempt was then made to focus on the two communication channels which repeatedly differentiated between men's and women's verdicts in other analyses. In a 2 (sex of subject) × 2 (Video Only vs. Transcript Only) design, 360 auto-correlations served as data points. This analysis yielded no main effects, but a statistically significant interaction, $F(1,359) = 3.82, p = .05$. There were lower auto-correlations for men than for women in the Video Only condition, and a reversal in the Transcript condition (see Table 3). This pattern exactly parallels the results obtained with other dependent measures.

Table 3: Means of autocorrelations of the individual time-series of $-amount-ratings as a function of the sex of "judge" and experiment condition

	Video & Sound	**Transcript**
Female "Judge"		
M	.39	.28
SD	.29	.29
Male "Judge"		
M	.33	.34
SD	.31	.33

Note: The autocorrelation (time lag minus 1) indicates the "memory" of the individual (differenced) time series. N=90 (18 Ss per cell, rating five cases each).

Discussion

For men, in contrast to women, facial configurations, gestures and body language of the litigants did not "predict" the decision-making process and its outcomes (verdicts over time; Figures 1 and 2). In addition, women's relative reliance on non-verbal behavior was not associated with greater decoding accuracy: if anything the data (Table 1) indicate that men were somewhat (though not significantly so) more accurate than women in three of the four mode-of-presentation conditions - all those involving verbal/factual information. To the extent that the litigants were likely to engage in all sorts of non-verbal simulation and dissimulation, women's apparent (conscious and unconscious) greater sensitivity to, and attempts to capitalize on, the non-verbal "leakage" resulted in poorer accuracy.

Furthermore, women were mor homogeneous than men in responding to the information in the Video Only channel (Table 2), yet their greater homogeneity (smaller disparity) was associated with greater accuracy only in the conceptually most difficult (or unreliable) circumstances (Video Only, Sound Only)

There was thus no evidence in our data to suggest that women's relatively more homogeneous, more non-verbally-sensitive judgements led to objectively "better" decisions - in terms of fairness or equity. In fact, one could conclude that their reliance on emotionally-colored information (presumably for the most part conveyed non-verbally) was "unfair" to the litigants. However, such a statement is based on the assumption that the "People's Court" judge's verdicts are "fair" by some objective criterion - a tentative supposition indeed. Besides, the lone "People's Court" judge is male and it is entirely possible that female reliance on non-verbal information would bring them closer to the verdicts of female judges.

Nevertheless, the observed sex differences should be explored in further research to examine the possibility of differential utilization of emotion- vs. content-based information in legal contexts. Such research, directed specifically at the relative weights given to emotional expression as opposed to verbal content (whether true or false) might explain the differences between female and male jurors (and perhaps judges) noted in the introduction.

The fact that measures of accuracy in terms of a quasi-real world legal outcome were obtained in the present study is significant because of the existing literature that suggests that, in general, people rely more on non-verbal cues than verbal content in certain situations, including legal contexts, especially when, for example, the tone of voice and verbal contents are in conflict (e.g. Domangue, 1978; Efran, 1974; Ekman & Friesen, 1974; Kulka & Kessler, 1978; Littlepage & Pineault, 1981; Mehrabian & Wiener, 1967). To the extent that one is willing to grant the "People's Court" judge the status of an objective and fair (or at least highly trained) arbiter, the juror's reliance on non-verbal or emotional input (provided by the accused, the victim, the witnesses or civil-law litigants) is perhaps detrimental to fairness and justice (cf. Maier and Thurber, 1968). If so, the question is whether this state of affairs can be improved (for example, by instructions to the jury).

With regard to the essential Video Only vs. Audio Only vs. Transcript contrasts, one might note that the symbol of justice stands with a sword in her right hand, scales in her left, and a blindfold: she can only hear.

References

Blanck, P. D. (1981). Sex differences in eavesdropping on nonverbal cues: Developmental changes. *Journal of Personality and Social Psychology, 41*(2), 391-396.

Blanck, P. D., & Rosenthal, R. (1984). The mediation of interpersonal expectancy effects: The counselor's tone of voice. *Journal of Educational Psychology, 76*, 418-423.

Christensen, D., & Rosenthal, R. (1982). Gender and nonverbal decoding skill as determinants of interpersonal expectancy effects. *Journal of Personality & Social Psychology, 42*(1), 75-87.

Domangue, R. (1978). Decoding effects of cognitive complexity, tolerance of ambiguity, and verbal-nonverbal inconsistency. *Journal of Personality, 46*, 519-522.

Efran, M. G. (1974). The effect of physical appearance on the judgment of guilt, interpersonal attraction, and severity of recommended punishment in a simulated jury task. *Journal of Research in Personality, 8*, 45-54.

Eisenberg, N., & Lennon, R. (1983). Sex differences in empathy and related capacities. *Psychological Bulletin, 94*(1), 100-131.

Ekman, P. (1980). Relative importance of face, body and speech in judgements of personality and affect. *Journal of Personality and Social Psychology, 38*, 270-277.

Ekman, P., & Friesen, W. V. (1974). Detecting deception from the body or face. *Journal of Personality and Social Psychology, 29*, 288-298.

Fujita, B. N., Harper, R. G., & Wiens, A. N. (1980). Encoding-decoding of nonverbal emotional messages: Sex differences in spontaneous and enacted expressions. *Journal of Nonverbal Behavior, 4*(3), 131-145.

Gruhl, J., Spohn, C., & Welch, S. (1981). Women as policymakers: The case of trial judges. *American Journal of Political Sciences, 25*, 308-322.

Guilford, J. P. (1954). Psychometric Methods (2nd ed.). New York: McGraw.

Hall, J. A. (1978). Gender effects in decoding nonverbal cues. *Psychological Bulletin, 85*(4), 845-857.

Harris, A., & Rosenthal, R. (1985). The mediation of interpersonal expectancy effects. *Psychological Bulletin, 97*, 363-382.

Kette, G. (1994). *Die Signalerkennengstheorie als Modell der laienrichterlichen Urteilsbildung*. Wien: Springer.

Kette, G., & Brandstätter, H. (1990). Times series analysis of a murder trial. *Journal of Social Behavior, 5*, 15-31.

Kombos, N. A., & Fournet, G. P. (1985). Effects of dominance-submissiveness and gender on recognition of nonverbal emotional cues. *Educational and Psychological Research, 5*(1), 19-28.

Konečni, V. J., & Ebbesen, E. B. (1982). An analysis of the sentencing system. In V. J. Konečni & E. B. Ebbesen (Eds.) *The criminal justice system: A social-psychological analysis*. San Francisco: W. H. Freeman.

Kraus, R. M., Apple, W., Moency, N., Wenzel, C., & Winton, W. (1981). Verbal, vocal and visible factors in judgements of another's affect. *Journal of Personality and Social Psychology, 40*, 312-320.

Kritzer, H. M., & Uhlmann, T. M. (1977). Sisterhood in the courtroom: Sex of judge and defendant in criminal case disposition. *Social Science Journal, 14*, 366-379.

Kulka, A., & Kessler. (1978). Is justice really blind? The influence of litigant physical attractiveness on juridical judgement. *Journal of Applied Social Psychology, 8*, 366-379.

Littlepage, F., & Pineault. (1981). Detection of truthful and deceptive interpersonal communications across information transmission modes. *Journal of Social Psychology, 114*, 57-65.

Maier, E., & Thurber, G. (1968). Accuracy of judgements of deception when an interview is watched, heard and read. *Personnel Psychology, 21*, 23-40.

Mehrabian, A., & Wiener, M. (1967). Decoding of inconsistent communications. *Journal of Personality and Social Psychology, 6*, 108-123.

Möbus, C., & Nagl, W. (1983). Messung, analyse und prognose von veranderungen. In J. Bredenkamp & H. Feger (Eds.), Hypothesenprüfung. *Enzyklopädie der Psychologie* BI5 (pp. 239-470). Göttingen: Hogrefe.

Myers, M. A., & Talarico, S. M. (1987). *The Social Context of Criminal Sentencing*. New York: Springer.

Noller, P. (1980). Misunderstanding in marital communication: A study of couples' nonverbal communication. *Journal of Personality and Social Psychology, 39*(1-6), 1135-1148.

Noller, P. (1986). Sex differences in nonverbal communication: Advantage lost or supremacy regained? *Australian Journal of Psychology, 38*(1), 23-32.

Rosenthal, R., & DePaulo, B. M. (1979). Sex differences in eavesdropping on nonverbal cues. *Journal of Personality and Social Psychology, 37*(2), 273-285.

Schneider, J., & Schneider-Duker, M. (1984). Sex roles and nonverbal sensitivity. *Journal of Social Psychology, 122*(2), 281-282.

1. This study was sponsored by the Österreichischer Forschungsfond Project Nr.: J70 to Gerhard Kette and by various research grants at UCSD to Vladimir J. Konečni. We thank Mag. Gernot Fillip for assistance in the statistical analysis and also Professor Hermann Brandstätter for a helpful discussion of the methodological and theoretical questions of the study. Correspondence should be addressed to Gerhard Kette at the Department of Psychology, University of Linz, A-4040 Linz, Austria or Vladimir J. Konečni at the Department of Psychology, University of California, San Diego, La Jolla, California 92093, USA.
2. Mixed-design ANOVA: 18 Ss rating five episodes each in each cell of the 2 (gender) × 4 (mode of presentation) design.
3. As an indication of the reliability of ratings, the average intercorrelation was used, which is known as the intraclass correlation (Guilford, 1954, p. 395). The reliability of the ratings in all four modes is acceptable. The reliability of judgements of one rater ranged from, r 1/1=.30 to .54, while the reliability of the averaged judgements of the nineteen rater per cell ranged from r 18/18=.61 to .90. Therefore it was possible to integrate the individual time series into one group time series.
4. Since trends in this type of data may cause artificially high correlations between the "independent" and "dependent" times-series, reflecting nothing more interesting than certain case and evidence-presentation features (e.g. cases may differ in how gradually the pro-plaintiff evidence is introduced), such trends were statistically removed - a procedure common in multiple time-series methodology.
5. We attempted to minimize an unduly large effect of each new piece of information by printing the following instruction above the rating scales: "Considering all available information thus far, the plaintiff will receive:".

Juror Decision-Making and the Trial Process

John Jackson

Introduction

In recent years there has been no shortage of debate in the United Kingdom about the role and function of the jury and there has been growing concern about a number of features of the jury system - for example, the eligibility requirements, the selection process, the phenomenon known as "eyeballing" and the problem of understanding evidence in complex cases such as fraud trials. But there has been a general absence of empirical research to inform these issues, although there has been no shortage of anecdotal accounts from individual jurors (see Barber & Gordon, 1976; The Times, 1988; Lofthouse, 1992). A certain amount of jury research was carried out in the 1970s mostly comparing jury verdicts with the verdicts of shadow or mock juries and with the views of professional participants in cases (see, eg, Zander, 1974; McCabe & Purves, 1972, 1974; Baldwin & McConville, 1979). But the findings of the research tended to be somewhat inconclusive on the central question which prompted many of the studies, whether juries were doing their job properly. One problem was that there was considerable controversy about what kind of job jurors should do. There were and arguably still are two competing conceptions about the function of the jury (Findlay & Duff, 1988). On one view jurors should bring in a "correct" verdict in terms of the law and the facts. Against this is the view that the jury's function is not merely to apply the law to the facts - jurors also have an important function in mediating between the law and community values. This division of opinion about the function of the jury made it difficult for researchers to come to conclusive judgements about the performance of juries and although much useful information was gleaned about their operation, conflicting findings emerged on the question of jury competency and the research provoked criticism from protagonists in the jury debate on the ground that the methods used could not be an adequate measure of jury competency.

In an earlier paper it was argued that what was needed was a programme of research that could inform the concerns aroused about the jury system without being necessarily defined by these concerns and it was suggested that the focus of research should shift away from directly assessing the quality of the verdicts reached by juries towards looking at the needs, difficulties and perceptions of jurors themselves (Jackson, 1990). Research of this kind could not only inform existing concerns about the jury system (for example, the extent to which jurors are competent to decide complex cases) but would also be likely to raise other concerns such as the suitability of present trial procedures and the rules of evidence for jury decision making.

The Crown Court survey carried out in February 1992 under the auspices of the Royal Commission on Criminal Justice which sent detailed questionnaires to jurors as well as other participants in every trial which reached a verdict over a two week period in England and Wales is a valuable step in this direction (see Zander & Henderson, 1993). Although section 8 of the Contempt of Court Act 1981 prevented questions being asked about the deliberation process, the Commission's research asked useful questions about whether jurors could remember and understand the evidence and the judge's instructions on the law. The Commission's (1993) call for section 8 to be amended to enable research to be conducted into juries' reasons for their verdicts is also to be welcomed.

This paper concentrates on the results of what is believed to be the first survey in the United Kingdom to monitor the perceptions of actual jurors. Questionnaires covering a number of aspects of jury service were given to all jurors who attended for jury service over a six month period at Belfast Crown Court. Sixty percent of jurors responded and 237 questionnaires were analysed. Section 8 of the Contempt of Court Act 1981 applies in Northern Ireland as in England and Wales and the survey was unable to ask jurors directly about their discussions in the jury room. The survey was part of a larger survey designed to elicit the views and experiences of lay participants in the Belfast criminal courts (see Jackson et al. 1991). The research was motivated by the absence of any data in Northern Ireland concerning the experiences of victims, witnesses, defendants and jurors in the courts and by a desire to discover the extent to which the "ordinary" criminal justice system as opposed to the so-called Diplock system which operates in terrorist cases was working in the Northern Ireland situation.

The Survey

Problems have been associated with the operation of the jury system in Northern Ireland and these persuaded the Diplock Commission (1972) to recommend the adoption of juryless trials in terrorist cases. The extent to which our survey supports the view that the peculiar exigencies of the Northern Ireland situation are having an adverse effect on the workings of the jury system is discussed in a previous paper (Jackson & Doran, 1992). The concern in this paper is more generally with jurors' perceptions of the trial process and the jury system. A note of caution must first be entered because although 237 jurors responded to the questionnaires, only just over a quarter (63) were sworn in to hear a particular case. This is because large numbers of jurors were never called to the jury box to hear a particular case or if they were called they were challenged by either the prosecution or defence. (Defendants still have an individual right to challenge up to 12 jurors peremptorily in Northern Ireland.)

Jury comprehension One basic question that was asked was whether jurors could understand what the trial participants were saying. Overall, jurors reported a high level of comprehension (see Table 1). Professional participants, such as judges, counsel, expert witnesses and police witnesses, were claimed to be understood more than lay witnesses. Ninety percent of jurors said they understood most or all of what the professional witnesses said; only 77% said they understood most or all of what lay witnesses (including defendants) said. These responses ought obviously to be treated cautiously so far as the level of comprehension was concerned as there may well have been a tendency on the part of jurors to over-estimate their ability to comprehend the evidence. At the same time few commented on the inability of other jurors besides themselves to comment on the evidence. The consistently higher levels of comprehension given to professional participants is perhaps surprising. Researchers noted that judges intervened frequently during the examination of expert (mostly medical or forensic science) witnesses to ensure that their testimony was comprehensible and a number of jurors commented on how helpful judicial interventions were.

Table 1: Understanding the Evidence

How much could you understand of what was said by the following?	All %	Most %	Some %	None %
Judge	65	25	8	2
Prosecution counsel	57	30	10	3
Defence counsel	57	34	6	3
Police witnesses	70	19	11	-
Civilian witnesses	55	29	14	2
Accused	60	17	21	2
Expert witnesses	80	13	7	-

Jury instructions Concern has been expressed in the United States about both the timing and content of jury instructions. A common complaint is that jurors are presented with a mass of factual evidence before they even know what the rules are (Wrightsman et al, 1987). The Morris Committee on Jury Service (1965) suggested that judges give some guidance and directions to jurors at the commencement of a trial but this has not been adopted at least in Northern Ireland and it is left to prosecution counsel in their opening address to tell the jury about the respective functions of the judge and the jury as well as about the specific charges in the case. Ninety percent of jurors in our survey said that the function of the jury had been explained and 81% said they received an explanation of the charges but some commented that they would have liked more written information on what the charges meant.

Another concern is that when instructions are given to jurors there is frequently difficulty in comprehending and following them (Hans & Vidmar, 1986; Kassin & Wrightsman, 1988). This was borne out so far as instructions on the rules of evidence are concerned in the LSE Jury Project in 1973 (Cornish & Sealy, 1973). The researchers found that directions on the limited use to be made of evidence of recent complaint in a rape case were not understood, that mock juries given corroboration warnings were more likely to convict than those who were not given the warning and that certain mock jurors were readier to convict when directed on the beyond a reasonable doubt standard of proof than on the balance of probabilities standard.

Jurors in our survey were not asked whether they understood specific directions given to jurors during the judge's summing up. Ninety seven percent said they understood the summing up and 93% said they found it useful. Again, caution is needed in respect of jurors' self-assessment of their comprehension of instructions. One foreman reported that "we didn't understand the alternative charges". Thirty two percent said that the judge had told them to disregard information of some kind or another (hearsay evidence or details about an accused's history). Eighty four percent said that they understood why they had been told to disregard the information, and 68% they had been able to disregard it. This left almost a third who admitted that they were not able to disregard the information given.

The sufficiency of evidence Although jurors made few complaints about their comprehension of the evidence and the directions given to them, they did complain about wanting more information on a number of matters. Before retiring to reach their verdict 20% said that they would have liked more information such as "more witnesses", "more questions to be asked of witnesses", "more prosecution evidence" and whether the defendant had a criminal record. Theoretically, any member of a jury can ask questions during the trial but this is a practice which is commonly thought to be fraught with dangers. The Morris Committee said that if questioning was encouraged there was a risk of questions prejudicial to the accused being asked inadvertently as well as a danger of the proceedings getting out of hand. Recent research from the United States did not find that these dangers actually materialised when jurors were encouraged to ask questions (Heuer & Penrod, 1988, 1992). Eighty two percent of jurors in our survey said they were given no information about asking questions and only 8% said that questions were asked during the proceedings. A majority thought that with hindsight it would have been useful if the jury had asked questions. As one juror put it:

> I did not know we could (ask questions) - In fact one member could not make her decision and if she could have asked it (her question) then maybe it would have been easier for our jury to agree.

Thirty one percent thought that there had been an attempt to hold back information from them during the trial. An example given by one juror concerned particular information about the defendant which the judge stopped the prosecution giving. This juror said that he would have very much liked to hear information which the prosecution was going to mention. The dissatisfaction felt about information being held back was linked to a fairly strong perception among a number of jurors that they had been "left out" of the trial proceedings.

Note-taking and memory aids It is commonly suggested that jurors would be helped in their decision-making if they took notes of what they have heard during the trial. Against this, it is sometimes argued that note-taking may distract jurors from concentrating on the evidence. Recent research in the United States suggests that both the advantages and disadvantages of note-taking may be exaggerated (Heuer & Penrod, 1988, 1992). In 1965 the Morris Committee recommended that jurors be provided with adequate facilities to take any notes they wish in jury boxes and in line with this virtually all jurors in our survey said that facilities for note-taking had been provided. However, jurors were not encouraged to take notes. Only 20% said they were told they could take notes, 73% said they were not told and seven per cent were not sure. Thirty three percent said they had actually taken notes.

Almost all jurors said that the documentation they had been given in their cases was useful but 40% said that further written information would have been helpful. Jurors were not very specific about what exactly they would have liked but a number said they would have liked to have seen copies of witness statements.

The verdict The view of a number of commentators that the deliberation phase is over-estimated in importance because jurors have made up their minds during the trial and they rarely change their minds during deliberation was confirmed in our survey (see Hans & Vidmar, 1986). Ninety four percent said that the discussion had either no influence on their verdict, or had reaffirmed their own opinion. Only three jurors said that discussion had altered their opinion, two from not guilty to guilty and one from guilty to not guilty.

Ninety one said they agreed with the verdict and 9% said they disagreed. Those who disagreed did not indicate that they disagreed because of any perversity on the part of the jury. Two jurors who explained their disagreement suggested that this was due to genuine and reasonable disagreement about the guilt of the accused.

Confidence in the jury system Fifty percent of all jury respondents thought the jury system was fair, 15% thought it was unfair and 35% were not sure. These proportions were virtually identical for Catholic and Protestant jurors. When asked whether their view of the court system had changed as a result of jury service, 70% said "no" and 30% said "yes" with most of the latter group indicating that their views had changed for the worse. The most frequent complaints were the delays and organisation involved in jury service and an unfair system of selection jurors. Various adverse comments were made about the challenging system which still exists in Northern Ireland and the competence of jurors to decide cases:

> I think people should be asked to sit a type of aptitude test. Although I realise this would be difficult, if not impossible, it would be fair to any defendant hoping for a jury of average intelligence.

> Jurors should be selected from persons interested in the workings of the law, sifting through evidence and who will not be taken in by appealing towards looks, etc. Because they would be smaller in number than the present system they could be kept permanently in the books and given a uniform fee for their service.

Particular concern was expressed about young people on the jury:

> I feel that persons under the age of 25 may not have enough experience of life to give fair and impartial results.

> I don't know if there is a lower age limit for jurors. If not, I feel there should be. In two cases a couple of jurors took the cases light-heartedly.

A few jurors also stated that the appearance of the defendant prejudiced the jury:

> Seeing the defendant unconsciously causes one to 'judge a book by its cover'. This often biases a decision for both innocent and guilty.

Another juror expressed concern about seeing defendants in handcuffs and suggested that jurors should not see the accused until the jury has been sworn in. This was an important comment in the light of one case where jurors sitting in the public gallery saw a defendant plead guilty to a charge of buggery and were then sworn in to determine his plea of not guilty to rape. The outcome of this case caused concern in court and was one example of what other trial participants saw as the unpredictability of juries. Although few of the lay witnesses and defendants in the survey as a whole ended up having their cases tried by jury, a number of defendants expressed concern about the competence of jurors and jurors were compared unfavourably with judges.

The Role of the Jury in the Trial

It would be unwise to draw too many conclusions from this limited survey largely because of the small sample involved. Nevertheless, there are certain signs which suggest that it is wrong to place too much confidence in the present jury system. Much of the focus to date has been on reforming the process of selection of the jury. It is argued that too many people are exempt or excused from jury service and that juries are therefore rarely a random selection of the adult population. We were unable to shed much light on the question of the representativeness of jury panels as the response rate to our questionnaires was 60%, thereby leaving an "unknown" 40% for whom we had no demographic details whatsoever. So far as the respondents who participated in the survey were concerned, there was a slight under-representation of the 55-70 year old age group, an under-representation of Catholics and an over-representation of the unemployed. Although complaints were made about the challenging system, there was no evidence that this led to any tendency towards perverse verdicts in favour of defendants.

More worrying was the fact that although the general level of the responses was such as to give a certain confidence in the competence of jurors, there were complaints about the competence of young people on the jury and about the prejudices of certain jurors coupled with some evidence of the unpredictability of certain verdicts. This suggests that there is a need to review the composition of juries but it also suggests that there may be a need to re-think the role of jurors during the trial.

Hastie, Penrod and Pennington (1983) have characterised the ideal juror during the trial as a relatively passive record-keeper who encodes the events of the trial verbatim. This representation of the juror as a tape-recorder corresponds to an underlying assumption of the legal system that jurors suspend judgement and evaluation until all the evidence has been presented and until after they have been instructed at the end of the trial on how to evaluate and what to judge. A fundamental distinction is made between the evidence, what is reported at first hand by witnesses, and inferences drawn from the evidence, judgements and conclusions. This distinction is rooted in what Twining (1982) has called the rationalist tradition of evidence scholarship, one of the assumptions of which is that knowledge is based on direct sense experience, that an object outside the observer simply imprints its character on the observer. Knowledge about past events is then decided by drawing inferences from the testimonial evidence presented directly to the trier of fact at the trial. Not all evidence that the parties wish to be considered by the trier of fact, of course, is considered. Judges put evidence through a filter of positive probative utility and where the prejudicial effect of evidence outweighs its probative value it is not admitted, although if such evidence is revealed accidentally this is erased from the mind of the jury by the device of directing juries to ignore it.

In fact, of course, perception is no longer thought of as a passive process of encoding external stimuli. Cognitive scientists now almost universally recognise that human beings play an active role in the acquisition of sensory information and there is always, as Hastie, Penrod and Pennington put it, "extensive cognitive activity by the perceiver in comprehension and memory tasks" (pp. 18, 19). Jurors therefore do not come to the evidence with a clean slate; instead they make sense of the evidence by fitting it within existing thought patterns. Hastie, Penrod and Pennington have shown how at the stage of analysis of evidence stories and schemas guide jurors and lawyers now recognise that rather than building up their case piece by piece they must present an overall story with a clear sequence of events (Binder & Bergman, 1984). But the problem is that their communication with jurors is essentially one way only. So lawyers do not know for sure if their presentation is making sense as jurors are not encouraged to ask questions requesting clarification or further information about the stories that are presented to them. As a result they may misunderstand parts of the story, distort what they have heard or speculate unnecessarily about gaps which have been left out.

Not surprisingly, certain jurors in our survey felt frustrated by their inability to engage in the kind of two-way communication that is natural in ordinary conversation when the narrator tells a story (see also Lofthouse, 1992). Of course, judges may act as a conduit for jurors by putting questions to counsel and witnesses themselves and jurors reported that they found judicial interventions helpful. But judges do not have a privileged glimpse into jurors' minds and they cannot therefore be relied upon to deal with the difficulties which jurors may be experiencing. Even when jurors pluck up the courage to ask a question, this must be done through the judge who may not always understand what is meant. A good example of this occurred in one case where the jury passed a note up to the judge asking whether rape could be committed in the absence of evidence of a sexual assault. The judge seemed to consider that the question had legal implications and after consultation with counsel he told the jury that the definition of the offence of rape would be explained to them in due course. In fact the question had medical implications as the question seemed prompted by the testimony of a medical witness that there was very little medical evidence of a sexual assault in the case.

It is difficult to assess what effect the encouragement of this passive role has on the jury's decision-making performance. Jurors in our survey complained more about being unable to follow up further lines of inquiry than about failing to understand the evidence. A recent field experiment in the United States, however, suggests that jury questioning promotes juror understanding of the facts and that it is particularly helpful in trials involving complicated testimony or legal issues (Heuer & Penrod, 1992). It proved less helpful, on the other hand, in getting at the truth or in opening up further lines of inquiry.

Another consequence of encouraging jury passivity is that it is very hard to know what is going on in jurors' heads during the trial. We have seen that certain jurors were concerned about the prejudices of jurors against the defendant and a number of jurors also indicated that they wanted to know more about the defendant's past. At present problems of prejudice are generally only dealt with, if at all, at the end of the trial in the judge's charge to the jury, although juries are warned to ignore prejudicial evidence if it is wrongly admitted during trial. It has been suggested that there are two kinds of prejudice that may work against an accused person in the criminal trial (Zuckerman, 1989). There is first of all the problem that the jury may exaggerate or underestimate the probative force of the evidence. Juries may believe, for example, that because the accused committed a similar offence in the past to the one he is now charged with, he must also be guilty on this occasion. This kind of prejudice can be countered quite effectively at the end of the trial because all that is necessary is to point out the dangers of making this kind of inference and it can then be assumed that the jury will take heed, for as Zuckerman has put it, "many of us make mistakes of inference at times, but it is not the case that we insist on continuing to make the same mistakes once we have been persuaded of the shortcomings of our reasoning" (pp. 231-232).

The other kind of prejudice is more insidious and cannot be erased so easily. This occurs when certain evidence leads juries to take a hostile attitude towards the defendant with the result that they are more inclined to convict him than they might otherwise be. Evidence of a defendant's previous convictions, for example, may lead juries to convict not as the result of any mistaken inference but simply because of his previous bad character. Alternatively, any doubts in the evidence may be resolved against him rather than in favour of him because the jury may have few regrets about convicting him wrongly. This kind of prejudice may have occurred in the rape case where the jury were already privy to the accused's conviction for buggery. The defendant commented:

> They closed their minds as soon as they heard the charges ... They didn't even listen to the judge ... who did his best for me.

Since conviction is itself a form of punishment, it is understandable that a jury should wish to know not only whether the accused committed the offence but also what sort of character he is and whether he deserves to be punished. The courts permit defendants to adduce evidence of their good character before the jury. However, the problem with permitting bad character to be taken into account in conviction is that it offends two central principles of criminal evidence - what Zuckerman has called the principle of confining verdicts to the charge and the principle of full proof. Accused persons are only entitled to be convicted when there is proof beyond reasonable doubt on the charges brought.

This other kind of prejudice may be much more difficult to dislodge by instructions at the end of the trial. If evidence of bad character can be kept from the jury, so much the better. But the problem as we saw in the rape case above is that the jury can all too easily acquire knowledge about an accused's past and instructions at the end of the trial may be ineffective to dislodge any prejudices already formed. Recent American research suggests that instructions before the trial may have much greater impact than instructions delivered at the end of the trial (Kassin & Wrightsman, 1987). An alternative method for dealing with problems of prejudice would be to encourage jurors to ask questions and if jurors displayed prejudice or if they wanted answers to prejudicial matters to give jurors instructions when the questions were asked.

Of course, there are risks in encouraging juries to participate more in trial proceedings and more fieldwork needs to be done to see what impact pre-trial instructions and jury questioning would have. But if, as our survey suggests, jurors make up their minds about a case during the course of a trial and if certain jurors form prejudicial judgements which are not later displaced, then it would seem wiser to try to counteract these prejudices before the trial starts or to have these prejudices brought into the open during the trial so that they can be dealt with by the judge rather than left to fester in the minds of the jurors until they are brought out in the deliberation phase.

Conclusion

Our survey suggests that certain jurors may become prejudiced against defendants at an early stage of the trial. There may be a number of reasons for this. The UK courts make no attempt to discover the attitudes of jurors before they are selected to sit in a case. Once they are selected they are presented at the beginning of the trial with the sight of the defendant in the dock, a picture of legal guilt, and given no judicial instruction on the presumption of innocence. More must be done to try to deal with these prejudices as they offend against the principle that defendants are entitled to be tried only on the evidence against them. One approach would be to move more towards the American system of conducting a pre-trial voir dire to determine the juror's capability to try the case. But this only deals with jurors' pre-trial prejudices and does nothing to counteract prejudices that may emerge from the trial process. Another approach is to try to unearth these prejudices during the trial and to deal with them there and then. Failure to deal with the problem of prejudice may further diminish the confidence that there is in the jury system.

References

Baldwin, J., & McConville, M. (1979). *Jury trials*. Oxford: Oxford University Press.

Barber, D., & Gordon, G. (1976). *Members of the jury*. London: Wildwood House.

Binder, D.A., & Bergman, P. (1984). *Fact investigation: From hypothesis to proof*, St Paul, Minnesota: West.

Cornish, W. R., & Sealy, A. P. (1973). Jurors and the rules of evidence. *Criminal Law Review*, 208-223.

Diplock Commission (1972). *Report of the Commission to consider legal procedures to deal with terrorist activities in Northern Ireland*, Cmnd. 5185. London: HMSO.

Findlay, M., & Duff, P. (1988). *The jury under attack.* Sydney: Butterworths.

Hans, V. P., & Vidmar, N. (1986). *Judging the jury.* New York: Plenum.

Hastie, R., Penrod, S., & Pennington, N. (1983). *Inside the jury.* Cambridge: Harvard University Press.

Heuer, L., & Penrod, S. (1988). Increasing jurors' participation in trials. *Law and Human Behaviour, 12*, 231-261.

Heuer, L., & Penrod, S. (1992). *Juror notetaking and question asking during trials.* Paper presented at Reform of Evidence Conference, Vancouver.

Jackson, J. D. (1990). Jury confidence in jury service: A new impetus to jury research. *Social Behaviour, 5*, 139-153.

Jackson, J. D., Kilpatrick, R., & Harvey, C. (1991). *Called to court: A public view of criminal justice in Northern Ireland.* Belfast: SLS Legal Publications.

Jackson, J. D., & Doran, S. (1992). Diplock and the presumption against jury trial: A critique. *Criminal Law Review*, 755-766.

Kassin, S. M., & Wrightsman, L. S. (1988). *The American jury on trial: Psychological perspectives.* New York: Hemisphere.

Lofthouse, S. (1992). The trials of a juryman. *New Law Journal, 142*, 561-562.

McCabe S., & Purves, P. (1972). *The jury at work.* Oxford: Blackwell.

McCabe, S., & Purves, P. (1974). *The shadow jury at work.* Oxford: Blackwell.

Morris Committee (1965). *Report on jury service*, Cmnd 2627. London: HMSO.

Royal Commission on Criminal Justice (1993). Cmnd 2263. London: HMSO.

The Times (1988). *The jury on trial.* 24-27 October.

Twining, W. L. (1982). The rationalist tradition in evidence scholarship. In E. Campbell & L. Waller (Eds.), *Well and truly tried* (pp. 101-131). Sydney: Law Book Co Ltd.

Wrightsman L. S., Kassin, S.M. & Willis, C. E. (1987). *In the jury box: Controversies in the courtroom.* London: Sage.

Zander, M. (1974). Are too many professional criminals avoiding conviction? A study of Britain's two busiest courts. *Modern Law Review*, 37, 28-61.

Zander, M., & Henderson, P. (1993). *The Crown court study.* The Royal Commission on Criminal Justice Research Study No. 19.

Zuckerman, A. A. S. (1979). *The principles of criminal evidence.* Oxford: Oxford University Press, Oxford.

From Juror to Jury Decision Making: A Non-Model Approach

Ramon Arce, Francisca Fariña and Jorge Sobral

Introduction

Since the judicial world knows no absolute truth, we must resort to other means in order to identify decisions deviating from "normality". Two concepts that have sometimes been confused in the literature on the performance of juries should be distinguished: bias and error. Jury error (e.g. finding the innocent guilty) is difficult to establish, because the majority of cases are brought with uncontestable evidence (including those whose contestable aspects are avoided by plea bargaining); such cases seldom reach a jury trial. In the minority of cases that do come before a jury, the evidence is almost always subject to at least two interpretations (depending in part on the number of alternative verdicts available). Our thesis is that it is in conditioning the interpretation of the evidence that jury bias can play a role in possible judicial error.

If individual jurors were totally unbiased, juries would invariably reach swift unanimous decisions. Such is not the case: 5.6% of juries are deemed hung (Kalven & Zeisel, 1966), and in only a very small minority of cases is the jury of one mind without deliberation (Hans & Vidmar, 1986). In other words, different jurors assess evidence differently and reach different verdicts. The failure of early attempts to investigate this phenomenon (Hastie et al., 1983) was followed by the equally unsuccessful application of statistical methods: Pennington and Hastie (1986) found no quantitative relationship between verdict and evidence, and Dane (1985) even found only moderate agreement (77%) between jurors' verdicts and their estimates of the probability of guilt or of reasonable doubt. What does seem clear is that jurors evaluate evidence in a global fashion (Pennington & Hastie, 1986), i.e. their accounts of events are not strictly determined by the evidence but are constructed in accordance with principles of cognitive consistency - which is not to say that these coherent accounts may not be accompanied by a greater or lesser degree of uncertainty (Arce, in preparation).

The approach taken in this paper is to analyse jury function into distinct component tasks, and after separate investigation of each facet to proceed to their integration in an overall scheme. In this way, each jury task can be investigated by the means most appropriate to its nature.

Performance of Individual Jurors

Our findings regarding the decision processes of individual jurors show firstly that the presumption of innocence is general in that the degree of certainty accompanying guilty verdicts is almost always greater than 50%. When the influence of judges' instructions in this respect was investigated in a study involving two timings for the instructions (before and after evidence giving), four certainty requirements (the balance of evidence, clear and convincing evidence, evidence beyond all reasonable doubt, and "it is ten times better to free a guilty person than to convict an innocent one") and two ways of defining certainty levels (numerical and semi-quantitative), jurors receiving instruction were more certain of the correctness of their verdicts than those given no instructions, though the verdict itself was unchanged except in certain conditions.

Another finding concerns the factors that can interfere with the concept of reasonable doubt. We presented cases of rape, criminal negligence, theft and currency smuggling to 189 subjects, asked them to state the level of certainty they would require to convict the accused in each case, and investigated the influence of the following factors on their replies in each case: sex, locus of control, attitude toward delinquency, conservatism, dogmatism and self-conscious political stance. We found that the level of certainty required varied from case to case (multivariate $F_{4,181}=1391$; $p<.001$) and that much of this variance was attributable to the case-dependence of the requirements of the individual subjects (multivariate $F_{3,182}=5.15$; $p<.002$). In some cases, the factors being investigated significantly affected certainty requirements; for example, the sex of the subjects significantly influenced their certainty requirement in the rape case ($F_{1,183}=13.9$; $p= .000$).

Analysis of subjects' reconstructions of the events at issue showed three kinds of interpretation: one in favour of the accused being found guilty; another in favour of the accused being found not guilty on the basis of the evidence; and a third in favour of the accused being found not guilty on the basis of the lack of incriminating evidence, i.e. by appeal to the presumption of innocence. Some subjects did not understand why we asked for a reconstruction of the events, because they failed to entertain the possibility of alternative pictures; a similar finding was reported by Pennington and Hastie (1986).

When asked to give not only a verdict, but also a recommended sentence and an estimated probability of guilt, some subjects were inconsistent or lied (Alonso-Quecuty & Arce, 1992). However, analysis of the content of reconstructions of events showed that reconstructions were consistent regardless of whether the subject was consistent in the above sense, and reconstructions were also unaffected by the certainty of the subject in his or her verdict. This finding is taken as reflecting the subject's interpretation of all evidence in the light of a pre-existing decision or bias; the possibility of its being due to the subjects not remembering the evidence correctly does not appear to be tenable (Cowan et al., 1984).

We also investigated the relationship between the individual characteristics of the subject and his or her verdict. Hitherto, studies in this area have sought, on the basis of a single case each, to identify variables capable of predicting predisposition to give a verdict of guilty or not guilty. Though variables were found which correlated significantly with verdicts in certain cases, the results obtained in different studies were inconsistent, and in none was more than about 15% of the variance in verdict explained. In view of this, we hypothesized (a) that the problem was multivariate rather than univariate (Hans & Vidmar, 1982), and (b) that interaction between subject variables and case type would have to be taken into account (Bem & Allen, 1974). Our results showed the existence of predictive psychosocial profiles we labelled internal attribution, external attribution, conservative and progressive, and interaction between subject variables and case type was confirmed, but explicative power was again low, with variance of around 12%, and discriminant analysis failed to identify a profile distinguishing clearly between subjects tending to find guilty and subjects tending to find not guilty.

Group Decisions

Hypothesizing that groups that were homogeneous as regards the psychosocial characteristics of their members might reach biased decisions due to their members sharing the same bias, we presented the same four cases to mock juries selected on the basis of the psychosocial profiles mentioned above. We found that juries of opposite profile arrived at the same verdict in some cases but not in others (Arce et al., 1992). Sequential analysis of the juries' deliberations showed that psychosocial profiles influenced both the content and style of deliberation (Arce et al., 1990a; Arce et al., 1992).

In a second study, the consistency of our results was tested by presenting a rape case to single-sex juries. The verdicts of male and female juries differed significantly (Table 1), even though the proportions of men and women in mixed juries has been reported not to influence their verdict (Nelligan 1988). This suggests that the presence of different points of view improves jury performance by removing systematic bias.

Table 1: Verdict of single sex juries in a rape case by sex of jury

	Not guilty	Guilty	Hung
Men	6	2	2
Women	1	7	2
Mixed (men/women)	5	3	2

Not mixed group included in the analysis, chi of sex (men and women) by verdict (guilty and not guilty) (1)=6.34921; $p<.01$

Decisions of Individual Jurors after Joint Deliberation

Hitherto, the decisions of the individual jurors after joint deliberation have not generally been considered in work in this area, possibly because joint deliberation was assumed to bring about a conversion process in which some jurors changed their decisions as the result of being convinced by others that their initial decision was wrong. When we investigated this question, we found that, although conversion was indeed the usual process followed, over 10% of jurors changed their vote under pressure from the other jurors while retaining unchanged their real opinion. This tendency to conform almost always favoured a verdict of not guilty, and may be one of the reasons why the phenomenon sometimes known as the leniency of the jury is not observed in studies of individual jurors.

Identifying Erroneous Decisions

We mentioned above that the psychosocial profile of psychosocially homogeneous juries affected their deliberation style, as characterized by the form and function of the juror's "speeches" during deliberation (for more details: Arce et al., 1990b). The styles of the ideologically homogeneous (conservative and progressive) juries differed from those of the "attributionally" homogeneous (internal and external attribution) juries. Furthermore, juries of opposing ideology or opposing attributional locus exhibited the same style when their verdicts agreed, but differed in style when they reached different verdicts (Arce et al., 1990a). This latter result appears to be significant, because in both the ideological and attributional jury pairs it was the jury that failed to maintain a single deliberation style which emitted a verdict differing from that of other juries and from that of experienced collaborating magistrates. These findings suggest that, depending on the kind of case being tried, certain psychosocial biases may favour verdicts that are erroneous or at least socially deviant.

Conclusions

Jury bias not only, apriori, prevents the jury from fulfilling its purpose of representing society in the judicial process, and thereby brings the jury into disrepute; we have found that, specifically, jury bias can affect the content and style of the jury's deliberations, and that as a result it can affect the verdict. In heterogeneous juries, on the other hand, the presence of various different points of view leads to longer deliberations with more varied content, and hence to verdicts that are more representative of society.

According to our findings, there are no "universal" markers of jury bias, i.e. variables indicative of bias in a given direction (guilty or not guilty) in all kinds of trial: a jury with psychosocial bias of the progressive type appeared to err towards a not guilty verdict in a rape and murder case, not to influence the verdict outcome in a criminal negligence case, and to err towards a verdict of guilty in a currency smuggling case. The type of psychosocial bias of this jury led to judicial error in different directions, depending on the kind of case, but other types of bias are related more directly with the very concepts of guilt and innocence rather than with particular kinds of offence: a jury with a psychosocial profile of internal attribution type was sometimes biased towards guilty verdicts, and a jury with an external attribution profile towards not-guilty verdicts. Thus one may usefully distinguish between profiles defined in terms of "content variables" such as sex or political ideology which determine mental contents, and profiles defined in terms of "stylistic variables" such as the locus of control. These different types of variable determine different types of filter used by the individual in the assessment of evidence.[1]

The evaluation of evidence by the individual juror depends on that juror's preconceptions, which bias his or her reading of evidence that is not 100% sure. In other words, evidence is interpreted, and integrated in a coherent scheme, in accordance with the prejudices determined by variables such as the stylistic and content variables mentioned above. Numerous studies have found that jurors do not in general differ as regards their remembrance of the evidence presented (Cowan et al., 1984); however, because of their different assessments of this evidence, they do differ as regards their accounts of the events involved in the case (Pennington & Hastie, 1986). The reconstruction of events depends, inter alia, on the relative importance given to each element of proof and on the credibility given to each witness; both depend on the predisposition of the juror (Cowan, et al., 1984). With regard to credibility, it should be borne in mind that many cases depend essentially on the evidence of the sole witness of the offence being tried.

Many previous studies of jury bias have concluded that bias in one direction due to one subset of the individual juror's characteristics will generally be offset by bias in the opposite direction due to another subset. This is in keeping with our finding that juror's individual pre-deliberation verdicts bore no strong correlation with their biasing psychosocial characteristics. A case in point is that of a juror who in trying a case of theft induced by need was biased towards a not guilty verdict by his external attribution characteristics and towards a guilty verdict by his conservatism (Arce, 1992). Notwithstanding this, our results suggest that even when the individual juror is balanced, i.e. when his or her biases in some sense cancel each other out, one or another may gain ascendancy over the others when the juror is included in a jury that is homogeneous for that particular bias, since the biases of the individual jurors may then act synergically to determine the content and style of deliberation, which can influence the verdict. By comparison, heterogeneous juries were found to indulge in longer, richer deliberations.

Research on jury bias is undertaken in the hope of finding mechanisms to avoid the all-too-frequent occurrence of highly polemical decisions. Though some of these apparent errors seem, at least on the surface, to involve obvious racial or sexual bias (a recent case in point was the release of the assailants of Rodney King in Los Angeles), it seems that existing jury selection mechanisms (voir dire, standby, etc.) are incapable even of the apparently simple task of preventing the selection of racially and/or sexually homogeneous juries (Van Dyke, 1977). Though nationwide the numbers of black or white, or male or female persons serving on juries in any one year may faithfully reflect the make-up of the population, this is insufficient; it is in the jury hearing each specific case that the plurality of society must be represented. In any event, in other cases of polemical verdicts there is no evident socio-demographic jury bias, and the offending jury is sometimes vaguely described as incompetent (Jackson, 1990); in these cases the cause may lie in psychosocial bias of the kinds I have discussed earlier, which is completely ignored by current jury selection procedures.

It also seems clear that existing or proposed mechanisms to counteract jury bias once the jury has been formed are also of limited efficacy. Judicial instructions regarding the standard of proof tend, as we have seen above, to be interpreted differently in different cases due to juror bias, and in any case serve only to reduce the risk of erroneous guilty verdicts, not that of erroneous not guilty verdicts (Kagehiro, 1990). A second mechanism that has been proposed (Janis, 1972) is for jurors to set down in writing their personal verdicts before joint deliberation, and for them to be obliged to defend these verdicts and to give an explicit account of the events at issue, the idea being that in this way socially or logically unacceptable hidden bias would be avoided; however, our results suggest that, because of individual jurors giving in to group pressure, this mechanism too would be ineffective, and it is hard to see how such yielding to pressure could be avoided by judicial instructions.

The conclusion must be that jury selection be performed on a more scientific basis than at present - in saying which we naturally have in mind a selection procedure forming part of the judicial system, not biased "scientific selection" by the parties involved in the case (Hans & Vidmar, 1982). Specifically, we propose a procedure in which firstly a randomly selected group of possible jurors is purged of members with financial, sentimental or other specific relationships with the accused; and secondly, a professional legal psychologist scientifically selects a balanced, socio-demographically and psychosocially heterogeneous jury from among the remaining members of the group. A jury selected in this way would be more likely to be a faithful cross-section of society, and hence more likely to fulfil its purpose, than is at present guaranteed by existing jury selection procedures.

References

Alonso-Quecuty, M., & Arce, R. (1992). *Jurados mentirosos: Análisis de la reconstrucción de la evidencia.* Unpublished paper. Universidad de La Laguna.

Arce, R., Sobral, J., & Fariña, F. (1990a). *Attribution and deliberation style.* Paper presented at 2nd European Conference on Law and Psychology, Nürnberg.

Arce, R., Sobral, J., & Fariña, F. (1990b). Una aproximación al análisis de la interacción de jurados. In *Libro de Simposios del III Congreso Nacional de Psicología Social* (pp. 183-189). Santiago: Tórculo.

Arce, R., Sobral, J., & Fariña, F. (1992). Verdicts of psychosocially biased juries. In F. Lösel, D. Bender, & T. Bliesener (Eds.), *Psychology and law.* Berlin: Walter de Gruyter and Co.

Bem, D., & Allen, A. (1974). On predicting some of the people some of the time. *Psychological Review, 81*, 506-520.

Cowan, C., Thompson, W., & Ellsworth, P. (1984). The effects of death qualification on jurors' predisposition to convict and on the quality of the deliberation. *Law and Human Behavior, 8*(1/2), 53-79.

Dane, F. (1985). In search of reasonable doubt. A sistematic examination of selected quantification approaches. *Law and Human Behavior, 9*(2), 141-158.

Hans, V., & Vidmar, N. (1982). Jury selection. In N. Kerr & R. Bray (Eds.), *The psychology of the courtroom.* New York: Academic Press.

Hans, V., & Vidmar, N. (1986). *Judging the jury.* New York: Plenum Press.

Hastie, R., Penrod, S., & Pennington, N. (1983). *Inside the jury.* Cambridge, Mass.: Harvard University Press.

Janis, I. (1972). *Victims of groupthink.* Boston: Houghton Mifflin.

Kagehiro, D. (1990). Defining the standard of proof in jury instructions. *Psychological Science, 1*(3), 194-200.

Nelligan, P. (1988). The effects of the gender of jurors on sexual assault verdicts. *Sociology and Social Research, 72*(4), 249-251.

Pennington, N., & Hastie, R. (1986). Evidence evaluation in complex decision making. *Journal of Personality and Social Psychology, 51*, 242-258.

Simon, R., & Mahan, L. (1971). Quantifying burdens of proof: A view from the brench, the jury, and the classroom. *Law and Society Review*, *5*, 319-330.
United States vs. McDaniels, 379f. Supp. 1243 (E. D. La).
Van Dyke, J. (1977). *Jury selection procedures*. Cambridge, Mass.: Ballinger Publishing Company.

[1] Selective reconstruction of the evidence, anchoring and perseverance among other strategies, are only means towards the predetermined solution.

The Influence of the Size and Decision Rule in Jury Decision-Making

Pilar de Paul Velasco

Introduction

In Spain trial by jury is not a current reality. For this reason, the interest of some Spanish psychologists in jury research may seem surprising.

In 1978 the Spanish Constitution considered the possibility of juries in the Administration of the Justice System. Since then, some projects have been developed, all of which have restricted the right to trial by jury in criminal cases. But, for the moment, juries in Spain are a juridicial dream. We do not have any laws that determine the number of members nor the consensus requirement.

Both structural factors have been analysed in research in law and psychology, particularly in the United States during the 70s. Many studies of the jury size and decision rule have centred on the influence of this structural variation on the verdict. The general conclusion is that there are no significant differences between different juries (Davis et al., 1975; Kerr et al., 1976; Nemeth, 1977; Saks, 1977; Foss, 1981 Hastie et al. 1983).

Some studies show the advantages of small juries over larger ones: deliberation in smaller juries is more likely to reflect a high juror participation and a relatively equal participation of all members. Other evidence indicates that larger juries might have an advantage over smaller ones. Deliberation in larger juries is more likely to lead to an exchange of information and opinions about the case. Relative to the decision rule, a unanimous decision is more likely to reflect an increase in the exchange of opinions and information with an increase in the possibility of conflict. These findings can help to determine the best jury composition and could be useful for the development of the jury in Spain.

After a review of the research and literature on jury size and decision rule, an empirical study was designed. It was necessary to base this on simulated panels. The mock juries varied in size (with 12 or six members, in order to reproduce the traditional jury size studies) and decision rule required (unanimous or two-third majority decision, in order to reproduce the traditional rule variations). In this study interest centred on the jury decision-making process. In this sense, the current study was conducted in order to check the effects of size and rule variation on the dynamics of social interaction: the give-and-take of information and opinion, disagreement, conflict, and so on.

Method

Subjects Most of the psychological experiments with simulated juries use students as subjects. This study is no exception. Two hundred and sixteen students at the

Universidad Complutense of Madrid (144 females and 72 males) served as mock jurors. All subjects participated voluntarily in the experiment.

Design Subjects were randomly assigned to six or 12 member juries and the juries of each size were divided into two: one-half was required to reach a unanimous verdict and the other was required to reach a two-third majority veredict. Thus yielding a 2x2 factorial design with six juries in each of the four cells. In each jury one-third of the members were males (in order to represent the sex distibution in psychology students).

Procedure The general procedure adopted in mock jury studies employ a 'courtroom' that really is an ordinary classroom and a brief written summary of the facts (be they true or false). In the present study the simulated juries were put into an actual courtroom and listened to a real trial in a magistrate court, in order to achieve the highest possible degree of realism. Since it was not possible for all subjects to listen simultaneously to a trial, the experience was repeated six times. Three were robbery cases, one a drug-trafficking case, one injury case and one sexual abuse case. Each case was judged by the four jury types.

At each session, after listening to the case, the subjects were conducted to an experimental room. Before each deliberation the experimenter instructed the juries about the presumption of innocence and the beyond reasonable-doubt standard. The instructions given to the subjects differed only with respect to the rule manipulation. The total deliberation time set was one hour and at some time during deliberation the jury selected a foreman. In each jury, the foreman recorded the vote of each juror (guilty, or not guilty) and was instructed to consider the jury as hung if the group had not reached a verdict within the 60 minutes.

The decision-making process was videotaped without the knowledge of the subjects. Jurors were identified by lettered cards on the table. The videotaped deliberations of our 24 groups were analyzed by means of a Bales Interaction Analysis (Bales, 1950). Each comment was coded in terms of who initiated the comment, to whom and which of the 12 Bales categories it represented (positive reactions, attempted answers, questions and negative reactions). The percentage of acts in each of the categories was computed and for each group we constructed the interaction profile. The level of inter-scorer reliability was 75% by means of the Kappa statistic.

Participation by each juror was obtained by dividing the number of comments made by that juror by the total number of comments made by all members. The twelve-member average was doubled to obtain the participation comparison.

A nonparametrical analysis of variance was applied in order to explore the effects of structural variation in deliberation time, juror participation and social interaction during group discussion. (In each case a significance level of 5% was applied.)

Results

Neither assigned rule nor jury size had a significant effect on the veredict or deliberation time. One statistically significant finding was obtained for the jury size factor. The average percentage of juror participation in six-member juries was more than in twelve-member juries.

No juror on six-member juries remained silent. This did occur in over half of those on twelve-member juries. However there were no statistical differences in equality participation of all members between different jury sizes.

All decision-making processes showed a general interaction profile. The jury groups were more work-oriented with higher rates in task-orientated categories and less emphasis in socio-emotional acts. Neither the assigned rule nor jury size had a significant effect upon Attempted Answers (B Acts), Positive Reactions (A acts) and Negative Reactions (D acts).

Analyses of variance showed that jury size had a main effect on Bales categories 7, 8 and 9 (C acts, Named Questions). In the larger juries deliberation was more likely to involve asking for opinions, information and suggestions.

Table 1: Effect of Jury Size on Number of Questions

	V.I	H Kruskall-Wallis	
	12	8.33	0.0039*
	6		

*p<0.05

Other results highlight the high participation of the foreman. In 56% of juries the member who spoke the most was the foreman. This was selected by a random procedure in only two groups. Thirty percent of the juries were presided over by the man at the head of table.

Also, the differences between judge and jury show a disagreement level of 50%. This finding could be attributed to the different level of access to case information between magistrates and mock juries. The Spanish Justice System is an inquisitorial system and the oral trial has little importance. Therefore, in some cases written information is not reproduced in the trial.

It is not possible to conclude that larger unanimous juries are more likely to be hung. There were only three hung juries, all from the unanimous condition (two six-member and one twelve-member).

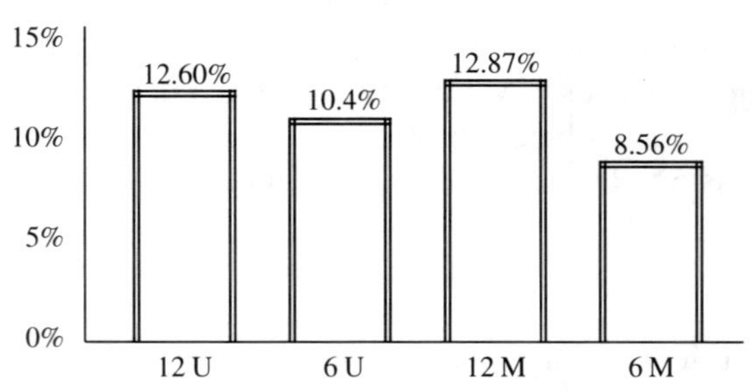

Figure 1: Average percentage of questions in different type juries

Discussion

This study found two statistically significant effects of jury size: one relating to juror participation and the other to the interaction process during decision-making.

The higher level of juror participation in six-member juries is consistent with the existing literature. This, however, is not necessarily relevant to real juries. The relevance of this result could be dismissed because there is no fixed time limit on real deliberation. We can conclude, in accordance with Diamond (1974) and Lempert (1975), that the larger jury is more likely to have jurors who find no need to add their opinions because it has been offered first by another. When a juror remains silent, the jury decision-making will not suffer in its fact-finding function, and it is not possible to conclude that the group is being deprived of ideas or information. Also, any comment made during deliberation, even if it is only one, has an affect on the decision-making and may be helpful if it forces other jurors to reconsider their opinions.

The jury size had a substantial effect on the number of questions acts during deliberation. The attempted answers were the same between six- and twelve-member juries. Consequently we can conclude that an advantage of decision-making in larger juries is more likely to represent higher fact-finding activity.

The lack of significant effects from assigned decision rule could be explained by the tendency to adopt an implicit rule (Davis, 1973; Davis et al. 1976). Half of the groups from the two-thirds decision rule continued the discussion until all individuals agreed with the verdict. If other studies corroborate this tendency, the advantages of non-unanimous rules would be lacking in the decision-making of Spanish juries.

This exploratory study is obviously limited in generalizability but it is hoped that it might stimulate further research into the factors affecting jury decision-making and that it will be useful to the future development of the Spanish jury.

References

Bales, R. F. (1950). *Interaction process analysis*. Cambridge, Mass : Addison-Wesley.

Davis, J. H. (1973). Group decision and social interaction: A theory of social decision schemes. *Psychological Review*, 80, 97-125.

Davis, J. H., Kerr, N. L., Atkin, R. S., Holt, R. W., & Meek, D. (1975). The decision processes of six and twelve person mock juries asigned unanimous and two-thirds majority rules. *Journal of Personality and Social Psychology*, *32*, 1-14.

Davis, J. H., Stasser, G., Spitzer, C. E., Holt, R. W. (1976). Changes in group members' decision preferences during discussion: An illustration with mock juries. *Journal of Personality and Social Psychology*, *34*, 1177-1187.

Diamond, S. S. (1974). A jury experiment reanalyzed. *University of Michigan Law Review*, *7*, 520-532.

Foss, R. D. (1981). Structural effects in simulated jury decision making. *Journal of Personality and Social Psychology*, *40*(6), 1055-1062.

Hastie, R., Penrod, S. D., Pennington, N. (1983). *Inside the jury*. Cambridge: Harvard University Press.

Kerr, N. L., Atkin, R. S., Stasser, G., Meek, D., Holt, R. W., & Davis, J. H. (1976). Guilt beyond a reasonable doubt: Effects of concept definition and assigned decision rule on the judgments of mock jurors. *Journal of Personality and Social Psychology*, *34*, 282-294.

Lempert, R. O. (1975). Uncovering non-discernible differences: Empirical research and the jury size cases. *Michigan Law Review*, *73*, 644-708.

Nemeth, C. (1977). Interactions between juror as a function of majority vs. unanimity decision rules. *Journal of Applied Social Psychology*, *7*, 38-56.

Saks, M. J. (1977). *Jury verdicts: The role of group size and social decision rule*. Lexington: Heath.

The Jury in the United Kingdom: Juries and Jury Research in Context

Sally Lloyd-Bostock

Jury research has been one of the major topics of legal psychology. Indeed, it was arguably Kalven and Zeisel's seminal (sociological) study of the American jury that gave the initial impetus to the very rapid growth in law and psychology research during the 1970s and 1980s (Kalven & Zeisel, 1966). At the same time, some jury research by psychologists has come in for sharp criticism from psychologists, sociologists and others for low external validity, for concentrating on a narrow range of questions about juror decision-making, and for lack of awareness of the realities, debates and controversies surrounding the institution of the jury, sometimes to the point of naivety (e.g. Vidmar, 1979; Baldwin & McConville, 1979; Bankowski, 1988). Moreover, the field has been dominated by research on the jury in the United States. Its relevance to the jury in Britain and elswhere cannot be taken for granted.

It is obviously important that jury researchers should pay attention to the external validity of their research, in the particular jurisdiction in question. Perhaps less obvious to experimental psychologists is the importance of recognising the political and philosophical assumptions on which they base their research, and the view of juries and jury trials they are (usually implicitly) adopting. Writers such as Bankowski (e.g. 1988) have argued that most research has taken juries and jury trials at face value and investigated the "rationality", "reliability" etc of juries as decision-makers in a "strict" legal sense. As a result jury research has been less rich than it might have been - for example, focussing narrowly on juror deliberations and ignoring the way in which the wider context of the trial provides cues to jurors about what they ought to be doing (Bankowski & Mungham, 1976; Bankowski, 1988). Twining (1984) has similarly argued for a broader "contextual approach" in another major area of legal psychology, eyewitness research. He suggests that "the problems" of misidentification in legal processes have been too narrowly defined, so that the main relevance of psychology has been seen as relating to the cognitive processes of the individual witness, rather than to other participants and to interactive aspects of legal processes.

As jury research by psychologists confronts these criticisms, and goes beyond implicit assumptions and "strict" legal models, it becomes more embedded in the broader context of the jury and the jury trial. The powers and role of the jury in the particular jurisdiction, and the realities of jury decision-making become centrally relevant. This paper describes some central features of the jury in the United Kingdom that distinguish it from the US and other juries; and outlines some current debates about the jury in the United Kingdom, and the attitudes of some commentators and critics to reforms.

The Declining Role of the Jury in the UK

There has been a marked erosion of the role and powers of the jury in the UK over the past 20 or so years: a book on the jury published in 1988 was entitled *The Jury Under Attack* (Findlay & Duff, 1988). The language in which reforms and changes have been proposed reflects the ascendance of values of efficiency and crime control. Juries have been viewed as expensive and time consuming, and as undermining the criminal justice system by inappropriate acquittals. Juries are used far less often in the UK than in the US. The right to trial by jury is not enshrined in a constitution, and it has virtually disappeared altogether in civil cases.

Criminal cases

In England criminal juries are used for all cases that are tried by the crown courts where the accused pleads not guilty. This is about 2% of all criminal trials. The vast bulk of criminal cases are not tried in the crown court, but in the magistrates court; and of those that are tried in the crown court, the majority plead guilty to all charges. For example, in 1986 there were 28,000 contested trials in the crown courts (which implies a jury). Of the 110,000 defendants dealt with in the crown courts 67% peaded guilty to all counts (*Judicial statistics*, 1986).

Growth of scope of Magistrates Courts at expense of jury trials

The division of business between the crown courts and the magistrates courts is based on the "seriousness" of the offence. The right to a jury trial has been removed for several series of classes of offence. For example, the Criminal Law Act 1977 removed the defendant's right to choose jury trial in cases of criminal damage below £200. The Criminal Justice Act of 1988 further extended the powers of the magistrates courts: for example, taking and driving away a car without the owners consent, and common assault and battery were changed from triable-either-way to summary offences.

The main justification put forward for these changes is the expense and delay involved in jury trials. The crown courts have a backlog of cases, and it appears that defendants are increasingly opting for a jury trial. Thus, when the James Committee in 1975 recommended the removal of the right to choose a jury trial for several new categories of offence, the justification was that jury trials were too time consuming and expensive for such "trivial" offences; it would be much more "efficient" to process such cases through the magistrates courts. It has also been suggested that the wish to increase conviction rates was a central consideration (e.g. Blake, 1988). At the time of the Criminal Law Act 1977, the police - and in particular Sir Robert Mark, the Chief Commissioner of the Metropolitan Police -had been arguing that the jury system resulted in the acquittal of far too many defendants. Blake (1988) suggests that the police were delighted with the recommendations of the James Committee, and observes that it is interesting to see how the police make use of the measures that were eventually enacted. He notes that charges of assault occasioning actual bodily harm on police officers (which carries a right to jury trial) have been dropped in favour of a charge of assaulting the police, which does not; or the damage any individual was charged with kept below the value that would allow the defendant to choose a jury trial (Blake, 1988, p. 146).

The Diplock Courts

A significant exception to the rule that more serious cases are tried before a jury are the so-called Diplock Courts in Northern Ireland. These are courts which try certain categories of serious crime without a jury. Following an enquiry by Lord Diplock (Diplock Commission, 1972), they were set up under the Northern Ireland Emergency Provisions Act in 1973 to deal with alleged problems of intimidation of jurors and perverse acquittals in terrorist trials. The categories of "scheduled" offences that may be tried without jury include murder, manslaughter, most offences of violence against the person, arson, malicious damage, riot, firearms and explosives offences, armed robbery, aggravated burglary, and various other offences that might be thought likely to be committed by members of paramilitary organisations. The Diplock courts have generated a significant literature of their own (see e.g. Walsh, 1983; Jackson & Doran, 1992).

Scots juries

There are several differences between English and Scots juries. In England juries consist of 12 members, but in Scotland there are 15. A further peculiarity of the Scottish jury is that there are not two but three possible verdicts - "guilty", "not guilty", or "not proven". "Not proven" is a form of general verdict for acquittal.

The majority rule also works differently in Scotland. In England, Wales and Northern Ireland, unanimous verdicts were abolished in 1967, as a result of police concern about bribery and intimidation in a series of trials of London gangsters. Now, if the jury has been unable to reach a unanimous verdict after two hours, they may bring a majority verdict of 10-2. Scotland has had majority verdicts for a long time. In Scots law there must be a majority decision for a verdict, but that means at least eight out of 15 for either acquittal or conviction (not proven and not guilty are lumped together). A hung jury is impossible - there will be a majority one way or the other.

Civil cases

The use of juries in civil cases in England began to decline in the middle of the last century, and continued to fade until it has now to all practical purposes been abolished. The picture is not totally clear cut because the civil jury was not simply abolished in one fell swoop. What happened was a process of atrophy which accelerated this century apparently as a result of the huge growth of claims and actions for personal injury and death. In 1933 the right to a jury trial in most cases - notably personal injury - became a decision at the discretion of the judiciary.

The final fatal blow to the civil jury in England is generally considered to have been a personal injury case in 1966 (*Ward v. James*). Lord Denning gave strong advice against the use of juries in personal injury cases. The case caused a furore - the Court of Appeal, it was said, had attacked a fundemental right to trial by jury. But the civil jury was to all intents and purposes already dead and appears to be little lamented. All that remains today is an occasionally used statutory right to jury trial in certain cases (specified in the Administration of Justice Act 1981) namely actions for libel, slander, malicious prosecution and false imprisonment; and allegations of fraud. There are so few such cases that statistics are no longer published in the Annual Judicial Statistics. Zander (1988) estimates that there have been of the order of one or two dozen per year since *Ward v. James*; and even before that, in 1963 for example, there were only 27 jury trials out of a total of 962 in the Queens Bench Division.

The civil jury in personal injury cases survived for much longer in Northern Ireland, and was only abolished in 1987. The abolition was long expected but was strenuously opposed by both the Law Society in Northern Ireland and the Northern Ireland Bar. The change took away a substantial part of the work of the Northern Ireland Bar.

Debates over the Functioning of Juries

Do juries make larger awards?

In *Ward v. James* in 1966, Denning was negative about the advisability of a plaintiff asking for a jury in a civil case. He said for example:

> [Solicitors advise their clients] If I were you I should not ask for a jury. I should have a judge alone. You know where you are with a judge, and if he goes wrong you can always go to the Court of Appeal. But as for a jury, you never know what they will do, and if they do go wrong there is no putting them right .... So the client decides on judge alone. That is why jury trials have declined. It is because they are not asked for ....

However, the general perception now seems to be that the plaintiff is likely to get a higher award with a civil jury - or at least in a system that retains a jury in personal injury cases, which is not quite the same thing since the vast majority of claims are settled without trial. A jury trial may be expensive, but the potential for larger awards at trial puts the plaintiff into a stronger position in negotiations. A series of very large awards and settlements in libel cases involving well known people such as Elton John have been widely publicised in the past few years. In 1989 a libel jury awarded the astonishing sum of £600,000 to the wife of the Yorkshire Ripper Peter Sutcliffe. Juries are always a rich source for the cartoonist. This time a cartoon in *The Times* portrayed a man looking despairingly at a pile of bills, and a woman saying to him "Can't you get someone to libel you?".

The expectation that juries are likely to be generous is popularly thought to explain the high levels of compensation paid in the US. It does seem clear that awards are indeed higher in the US, but there may be other explanations than a straightforward tendency of juries to award large sums. Much depends on exactly what role juries play, and what information and guidance they have. This is an area where empirical data and informed argument are lacking and research might be done, especially given recent interest in contingent fee systems in Britain. We do not have a clear basis for understanding and predicting how a similar system might work in Britain.

Challenging jurors

The rules in Britain for challenging jurors are very different from those in the US. Anything approaching "scientific" jury selection as practised in the US has gone from being virtually impossible to totally impossible in England, for the defence at least. The defence's right of peremptory challenge was abolished in the Criminal Justice Act of 1988. This is a very significant change. (Peremptory challenges survive in Northern Ireland.)

Under the peremptory challenge procedure, after the clerk had asked 12 members of the jury in waiting to step into the jury box, counsel for the accused (or the accused if unrepresented) called out "Challenge" immediately before the juror took the oath. No reason needed to be given, and the juror was replaced by another. The right dates back to the 15th century when it was introduced to redress the balance in the defendant's favour. It has been steadily eroded. In 1925 the number of challenges was reduced from 25 to 12. In 1949 the number was further reduced to seven (seven per defendant where several were tried together). In 1977 the number was fixed at three. In 1989, it was removed altogether.

The changes appear to have come in response to particular cases, or even to rumours about defence practices, rather than any more systematic evidence. The reduction in 1977 was evidently precipitated by a case in which a number of youths, mainly black, were tried for causing criminal damage and disorder. The defence used their challenges to try to achieve a representation of ethnic minorities on the jury. The youths were acquitted, and there were mutterings about the defence tactics.

Prior to the more recent changes, there was particular concern about multi-defendant trials, in which the defendants pooled their challenges. In particular, there was a notorious trial in 1986 in which eight RAF men were charged with offences under the Official Secrets Act. Their counsel (it is said) agreed to exercise their peremptory challenge to get a young, male jury. In the event they were acquitted (whether because of the composition of the jury is highly questionable; the case was weak) - and once again mutterings about defence tactics fuelled the campaign for the abolition of peremptory challenges.

There were in fact more reliable data available to the government. A study based on over 2,500 cases was conducted by the Crown Prosecution Service, and the report released in 1987, while all the debate was going on. It showed that use of peremptory challenges was not associated with an increased likelihood of acquittal. However, the government refused to drop the clause abolishing peremptory challenge from the Bill.

The use of peremptory challenge to attempt to achieve a more sympathetic jury has been discussed by its opponents as if it were an attempt to pervert the true nature of a jury trial, with a "random" jury. The Fraud Trials Committee in 1986, for example, writes: "The existence of the peremptory right of challenge must necessarily .... tend to erode the principle of random selection, and may even enable defendants to ensure that a sufficiently large part of a jury is rigged in their favour" (Roskill, 1986, p. 126).

The right to challenge for cause remains. But it is a somewhat empty right, since nothing is known about the jurors except their names and addresses; and the lawyers are not supposed to ask questions. The challenging party must adduce *prima facie* evidence to support the challenge before the juror may be questioned about his or her suitability. But the defence has practically no information on which such a challenge may be based, and no right to ask all members of the jury in waiting exploratory questions about their backgrounds, attitudes, etc., with a view to showing that they should not be on the jury. Not surprisingly challenges for cause are extremely rare.

The right to ask questions was removed after the so-called Angry Brigade Trial in 1972, which involved charges arising from, amongst other things, bombings of the houses of Conservative MPs. The judge allowed the defence to ask jurors such questions as whether they were members of the Conservative Party. A large number of jurors were challenged. Shortly after the case the Lord Chief Justice issued a Practice Note designed to stop such questions. Jurors' occupations used to be available, but that was changed in 1973, because the Lord Chancellor decided that there was evidence of "abuse" by the defence of the right of peremptory challenge in cases with political overtones - i.e. the defence were making use of the information in the exercise of peremptory challenge.

Roskill (1986) conceded that if the right to peremptory challenge went, there would be a case for returning to the practice of including jurors' occupations; but "beyond this we do not think that any further disclosure of information about prospective jurors need be made available to the defence as of right" (p. 129). He refers to worries that abolition of the right of peremptory challenge might lead to increased use of the challenge for cause, and that that might lead to "the kind of protracted proceedings which sometimes take place in the United States ... the so-called voir dire". He is confident that "no such practice would ever be entertained by the judiciary in this country ... we would expect judges to continue to be firm and adhere to well-established principles in carrying out their statutory duty of determining the propriety of a challenge for cause and of following the well established practice of not permitting such a challenge ... [without the prima facie evidence referred to above]" (Roskill, 1986, p. 128-29).

Roskill's whole discussion of the issue is unpersuasive. It seems that peremptory challenge is an abuse if based on relevant information and an abuse if based on superficial information. Roskill writes:

> The exercise of peremptory challenge .... especially if done as appears too often to be the case by reference only to superficial appearance - for example, dress, manner, age, and the carrying of particular newspapers - must be to further erode the principle of random selection ... (p. 125).

As we have seen, "superficial information" is all that is available. A few pages later Roskill writes that information about occupation was excluded as described above "because of evidence that the defence were sometimes using this knowledge to decide whether to make a peremptory challenge". He goes on to suggest that information about occupation might be restored because "risks of abuse would be far less than they were [if peremptory challenge were abolished]" (p. 129).

A serious consequence of the abolition of peremptory challenges is that one possible means of ensuring a racial mix on juries has been lost. This is frequently desired. It is widely accepted amongst the judiciary that it is reasonable for the defence to desire that a certain proportion of the jury should come from a minority racial group; or be women; or from a certain age group. Judges have expressed their willingness to help achieve a reasonable balance in cases of racial disturbances and demonstrations. This has been achieved in various ways. In spite of the Practice Note putting a stop to questions, the judge does sometimes allow questions, or puts questions himself, or invites jurors to disqualify themselves if they hold strong views against certain groups. But this kind of adjustment will be much more difficult without peremptory challenge.

Stand-by for the prosecution and jury vetting

The defence right of peremptory challenge is paralleled by the prosecution right to stand a juror by. The effect of standing a juror by is to remove him or her without showing cause, and there is no limit on the number who may be stood by. Although it was widely expected that if peremptory challenge went, so would the prosecution right of stand by, that has not in fact happened. The government argued that in practice the right was being used sparingly, and in the absence of information that it was being used improperly there was no need to abolish it.

In addition to retaining this advantage, the prosecution has also had the possibility of access to information on jurors obtained by the CID or Special Branch for the purposes of jury vetting. It is known that jury vetting takes place at least occasionally, and indeed, in 1978 the Attorney-General revealed the guidelines, in response to public pressure. The guidelines allow that in cases where strong political motives are involved the panel of jurors may be investigated. If anything indicating "disloyalty" is found, the juror is to be stood by.

Jury vetting as currently practised makes use of the right to stand by, which means that no reason is given publicly. It is up to the Director of Public Prosecutions to decide whether the case falls into the vettable category - in other words, to authorise vetting. The practice has been condemned by the National Council for Civil Liberty (Liberty), and is disliked as much because of the clandestine way in which it is con-ducted as for the principle of vetting itself.

We now have a potentially serious imbalance between prosecution and defence in their relative abilities to influence the composition of the jury. Unlimited rights of stand by for the crown, aided by the police and intelligence services; random selection for the defence. It is remains to be seen whether developments will occur to restore the balance - perhaps in the use of challenge for cause.

Jury competence

A major focus of attention regarding juries in recent years has been their competence or otherwise to try complex cases. In particular, a Royal Commission was set up in Britain under Lord Roskill to look into fraud trials, on the premise that the public no longer believe that the legal system is capable of dealing effectively with frauds. The Roskill Committee reported in 1986 (their report has been quoted above), and recommended amongst other things that juries should be dispensed with in complex fraud cases. The government did not adopt this proposal, but incorporated several others in the 1988 Criminal Justice Act, not only for fraud cases - for example regarding the use of visual aids and glossaries to assist juries.

These latter recommendations arose partly from research carried out by psychologists in connection with the Commission. The Medical Research Council's Applied Psychology Unit at Cambridge University was commissioned to investigate the extent to which jurors' understanding could be enhanced by changes in the way in which information was presented to them in fraud trials. They showed clearly that significant improvments in comprehension could be achieved quite easily by the use of charts, visual aids, summaries, etc.

It is very probable that jurors' ability to ensure that they understand could be enhanced by encouraging them to ask questions. Juries can in fact ask questions (through the judge) but they rarely do so and do not usually know that they can. The Morris Committee on Jury Service considered whether juries needed more help to arrive at their decisions, and reported in 1965. They recommended that prospective jurors should be sent some general guidance in a pamphlet, but thought there was "some peril in encouraging" jurors to ask questions. It was left to the judge conducting the case.

Questionable verdicts

Juries have a long history of occasionally acquitting in a case where the accused is technically clearly guilty. The borderline between verdicts where the jury is exerting its power to defy, say, the judge or government, and verdicts where the jury has been confused or incompetent or prejudiced is a hazy one. As several commentators have pointed out (e.g. Bankowski, 1988) the notion of a "wrong" verdict is premised on a certain view of the nature of truth and of jury trials; and may mean little more than "a verdict I disagree with", whoever "I" may be.

The lack of concensus amongst "experts" as to what is a questionable verdict comes out clearly in data Baldwin and McConville collected during their study of the Birmingham Crown Court in England (Baldwin & McConville, 1979). (They explicitly avoid the expression "perverse verdicts".) They adopted a method similar to that used by Kalven and Zeisel (1966), obtaining opinions of the verdict from lawyers and police involved in cases. Looking at acquittals, there is a clear pattern whereby involvement in the case for the defence is related to seeing acquittals as justified; and conversely, involvement for the prosecution is related to seeing acquittals as questionable. Thus, for example, the defence solicitor expressed "serious doubts" about 10% of acquittals; whereas the police expressed serious doubts about 44% and the prosecuting solicitor 26%. Acquittals were regarded as fully justified 83% of the time by defence solicitors, compared with 48% by the police and 62% by judges.

When they looked at doubtful convictions, Baldwin and McConville found that the pattern was reversed for the lawyers; prosecuting solicitors least often doubted convictions, and defence solicitors most often. However, it is not simply a matter of thinking your own side should have won. The police expressed more doubts than all the other respondents about convictions as well as acquittals. They seem to be generally sceptical about jury verdicts.

Doubtful convictions are perhaps more serious in their consequences than are doubtful acquittals. Baldwin and McConville suggest that their figures are worrying. They find that 15 out of 256 convictions were doubted by two or more respondents. Baldwin and McConville comment that rather little research attention has been given to the question of jury convictions, and suggest that findings such as theirs raise doubts about the very basis of trial by jury. Some of the convictions do indeed seem hard to justify. Several are cases where the judge has indicated they ought to acquit. Baldwin and McConville write: "it seems possible that in some cases the jury failed, through confusion, ignorance or stupidity to pick up cues from the judge's summing up" (p. 80).

Quite different considerations are raised by those jury acquittals which can be interpreted as the jury performing the vital function so often claimed for it, of mediating between law and the people, formulating norms for society, injecting "lay acid" into legal proceedings, and bringing ordinary common sense to bear in legal decisions. Baldwin and McConville reserve judgment as to whether any of the questionable acquittals in their study fall into this category. But there is little doubt that they occur. Throughout the history of the jury juries (including coroners' juries) have occasionally defied governments or judges, and not only in Britain. Freeman (1981) lists several. As he describes it:

> ... juries may and do infuse non-legal values into the trial process. They are the conscience of the community; they represent current ethical conventions. They are a constraint on legalism, arbitrariness and bureaucracy. (1981, p. 88).

One of his examples is that of the Oxford hot dog salesman who was provoked by a group of youths and wounded one of them. The judge directed the jury that provocation was no defence. However, the jury returned a verdict of not guilty. They appeared to be saying that if provocation wasn't a defence, it ought to be. Lord Goff (1988) describes a case heard before him of "glassing" in which the jury appeared to reject the legal definition of murder. The defendant rammed a jagged glass into his victims face, severing his jugular vein. Though horrified at his victim's death, he clearly intended to cause "really serious bodily harm", which was sufficient mens rea for murder. The jury, despite being directed to that effect, acquitted him of murder. As Lord Goff put it, they could not bring themselves to call him a murderer (a feeling with which Goff himself entirely sympathised).

A much more celebrated case is the trial of Clive Ponting. Ponting was a civil servant accused of leaking information about the sinking of the Belgrano in the Falklands war. There was widespread public sympathy for Ponting's position of conscience. He was acquitted by a jury in 1985 of charges under the Official Secrets Act, in spite a strong indications from the judge that they should convict. This time *The*

Times published a cartoon following the verdict, showing the jury delivering a verdict of "Not guilty, so there!".

It is important to remember that when juries take the law into their own hands they do not always take a civil libertarian or liberal point of view. For example, jury acquittals of allegedly corrupt police officers; or of those accused of disseminating racist material, have caused concern in Britain.

Conclusion

As observed at the outset of this paper, the vast bulk of jury research relates to the US jury. Furthermore, although it is a major topic within the field of psychology and law, research on juries has been criticised for its low external validity, and for its narrow focus on the "rationality" of jury decision-making. Researchers have been urged to take a broader view, and locate jury research more explicitly in its context. This paper has outlined the role and powers of the jury in the United Kingdom, and various controversies and reforms that would form the part of the context of any jury research in this country.

There has been rather little empirical jury research carried out in Britain in recent years (see, e.g., McCabe, 1988), but it may be reviving (see, e.g., Jackson, 1990). A significant hindrance to research has been that the Contempt Act of 1981 made it contempt to publish, or to solicit for publication what happens in the jury room - whether or not the case is identified. One project at least was stopped as a result. Others may have been deterred. (Incidentally, Roskill complained quite bitterly about not being able to ask jurors in fraud trials anything about their experience.) The possibilities may be opening up again with signs of a greater willingness to allow members of juries to be approached. The recent Royal Commission on Criminal Justice (1993) has recommended that the contempt rule should be amended to allow for research into jurors' reasons for their verdicts.

References

Baldwin, J., & McConville, M. (1979). *Jury trials*. Oxford: Clarendon Press.

Bankowski, Z. (1988). The jury and reality. In M. Findlay & P. Duff (Eds.), *The jury under attack*. London: Butterworths.

Bankowski, Z., & Mungham, G. (1976). The jury in the legal system. In P. Carlen (Ed.), *The sociology of law*. Keele: University of Keele Monograph.

Blake, N. (1988). The case for the jury. In M. Findlay & P. Duff (Eds.), *The jury under attack*. London: Butterworths.

Diplock Commission (1972). *Report of the Commission to consider legal procedures to deal with terrorist activities in Northern Ireland*, (Cmnd.5185). London: HMSO.

Findlay, M. & Duff, P. (Eds.) (1988). *The jury under attack*. London: Buterworths

Freeman, M. (1981). The jury on trial. *Current Legal Problems*, 65-111.

Goff, Lord (1988). The mental element in the crime of murder. *Law Quarterly Review*, 30-59.

Jackson, J. (1990). Jury confidence in jury service: A new impetus to jury research. *Social Behaviour*, *5*, 139-153.

Jackson, J., & Doran, S. (1992). Diplock and the presumption against jury trial: A critique. *Criminal Law Review*, 755-766.

James Committee (1975). *The distribution of criminal business between the Crown Courts and the Magistrates Courts*, (Cmnd. 6323). London: HMSO.

Kalven, H., & Zeisel, H. (1966). *The American jury*. Boston: Little Brown.

McCabe, S. (1988). Is jury research dead? In M. Findlay & P. Duff (Eds.), *The jury under attack*. London: Butterworths.

Morris Committee (1965). *Report of the Morris Departmental Committee on jury service*, (Cmnd. 2627). London: HMSO.

Roskill, Lord (1986). *Report of the Fraud Trials Committee*. London: HMSO.

Royal Commission on Criminal Justice (1993). (Cmnd. 2262). London: HMSO.

Vidmar, N. (1979). The other issue in jury simulation research: A commentary with special reference to defendant character studies. *Law and Human Behavior (Special issue: Simulation research and the law), 3*, 95-106.

Twining, W. (1984). Identification and misidentification in legal processes: Redefining the problem. In S. Lloyd-Bostock & B. R. Clifford (Eds.), *Evaluating witness evidence*. Chichester: Wiley.

Walsh, D. (1983). *The use and abuse of emergency legislation in Northern Ireland*. London: Cobden Trust.

Zander, M. (1988). *Cases and materials on the English legal system*. London: Weidenfeld & Nicolson.

Part V
Perceptions and Reactions to Criminality

Coping with Burglary: The Effects of a Police Service on Victims' Emotional Readjustment[1]

Frans W. Winkel and Aldert Vrij

Introduction

Becoming a victim of crime "forces" individuals to come to terms with the event and its consequences. Victimisations or stressors result in coping processes. Two dimensions are discernable, namely problem and emotion focused coping. The first concept refers to, either cognitive or behavioral, activities aimed at "eliminating" the stressor as such. A central question here is how to prevent a re-occurrence of the event. One could think of taking all sorts of preventive measures reducing the future likelihood of becoming a victim again of this event or something similar. Emotion focused coping relates to activities aimed at controlling the emotional impact of the event, like feelings of fear and concern about crime or anger. Psychological distress is generally considered to be a central and dominant response to victimisations (Cook, Smith, & Harrell, 1987). Emotion focused coping is aimed at countering this. A central issue here thus is how to manage these emotions or how to reduce them to a psychologically tolerable level.

The quality and speed of these two sorts of coping processes are theoretically linked to three general determinants, namely pre-victimisation, victimisation, and post-victimisation variables (Sales, Baum, & Shore, 1984; Winkel, 1990; Winkel & Steinmetz, 1990). The first concept refers to (bio- and socio-graphical, or psychological) victim attributes that were already present prior to the victimisation. Examples include relatively stable traits like hardiness (Kobassa, 1979) and styles of (causal) attribution (Janoff-Bulman, 1979; Miller & Porter, 1983; Peterson, Semmel, Abramson, Metalsky, & Seligman, 1982), or prior negative life events (Cook et al., 1987). The second concept refers to aspects of the crime, like type of crime and its surrounding situational circumstances (e.g. inside or outside, day or night, weapons or not, familiarity with perpetrator; Burt & Katz, 1985; Lurigio, 1987; Resick, 1987). The last concept represents third party responses to the event. These include both responses by significant others in the direct social environment of the victim, of victim assistance workers and other social service providers, as well as those of police officers and criminal justice personnel (Frieze, Greenberg, & Hymer, 1987). Here, we will focus on the police role, and consider in particular the relation between police functioning and the quality of both sorts of coping processes.

The important role of the police vis a vis crime victims is underlined in several international documents (APA, 1984), like the UN Declaration of Basic Principles of Justice for Victims of Crime and Abuse of Power, and in our national Dutch victim-oriented guidelines "Vaillant". It is frequently noted in this context that the police are usually the first (and often the only) agency with which victims have contact.

Rosenbaum (1987, p. 504) observes that the police are thus in a unique position to influence victims' perceptions. Following Bard and Sangrey (1980, p. 32) he assumes that "minutes of skillful support by any sensitive person immediately after the crime can be worth more than hours of professional counseling later".

In the scholarly literature on police-victim interactions two issues are noteworthy: (1) a preponderance of negative, critical comments on police functioning; and (2) an almost total lack of empirical evaluation studies on the impact of police crisis intervention programmes. Regarding the first issue police-victim relations are often considered from the perspective of secondary victimisation. In commenting on the genesis of the US victims movement Smith, Sloan, and Ward (1990, p. 89) for example note: "the early goals of the movement were oriented toward healing the second wound" (Symonds, 1980), the "secondary or second victimisation" (Hagan, 1982; Knudten & Knudten, 1981), the "second injury" (APA, 1984) or "revictimisation" (Viano, 1987). These parallel concepts reflect a belief that the justice system "revictimised" the original victim through mistreatment at the hands of police, attorneys, or judges as the victim progressed through the system (Viano, 1987). Some went so far as to argue that adverse treatment of certain classes of victims (e.g. those who were female, non-white, young or poor) occurred regularly (Meyers, 1977; Meyers and Hagan, 1979; Elias, 1986).

Although at different locations there is an intensive search for alternatives, aimed at improving the quality of the first contact between police officers and victims (cp Winkel, Vrij, Koppelaar, & V.d Steen, 1991; Winkel & Koppelaar, 1991) - in several US states for example experiments were conducted with victim assistance workers driving along with surveillance-teams, that were directed to crisis situations - the number of empirical studies is remarkably low (Skogan & Wycoff, 1987). Particularly absent are studies on crisis interventions, that is interventions conducted directly following the victimisation experience. Studies presently available (Skogan & Wycoff, 1987; Van den Boogaard & Wiegman, 1991; Winkel & Koppelaar, 1988, Zwanenburg & Winkel, 1990, Winkel, 1989, 1991) either concern a later point in time (re-contact-programs), or relate to non police officers (Davis, 1987; Roberts, 1990).

Obviously, there is sufficient ground for analysing the impact of police crisis intervention programmes in more detail. However, several studies examining the usefulness of interventions aimed at relieving the adverse impact of crime reveal a rather pessimistic picture. Lurigio (1987) noted that the police programmes discussed by Skogan and Wycoff (1987) and by Rosenbaum (1987) both failed to produce favorable changes in victims' problem- and emotion-focused coping with the event. The former programme even backfired: it hampered victim readjustment. Consistent with these studies, Davis (1987), evaluating interventions conducted by victim support workers, also reports null findings, i.e., treated victims fared no better than untreated victims. In explaining these null findings generally two issues are salient: the ingredients of the intervention are simply ineffective - an issue we will deal with in the next section - or the analyses conducted to evaluate programme impact are insensitive to small effect sizes. Variation in coping processes appeared to result from three types of variables; assistance programmes merely representing one of those types. These other sources of naturally occurring (as opposed to experimentally induced) variation in the coping processes disturb the outcome measures, utilised to evaluate programme impact (Judd & Kenny, 1981; Skogan & Wycoff, 1987). By controlling for these sources one can improve the efficiency of the estimates of the impact of the treatment. If other known sources of variation are accounted for, the remaining variation in outcomes that might be related to the intervention can be estimated more accurately. Empirically, prior life stress (representing a pre-victimisation variable) and perceived seriousness of the victimisation (a victimisation variable) appear to be rather powerful predictors of coping. Various studies (Cook et al., 1987; Skogan & Wycoff, 1987; Winkel, 1989) revealed substantial correlations between these variables and measures of coping with victimisations. In order to clarify programme impact it is thus advisable to introduce these variables as covariates.

The Intervention Programme

The present study was conducted in cooperation with two police forces, namely Hoorn (experimental group) and Alkmaar (control group). The intervention programme now constitutes regular policy of the force, and was introduced after intensive information and consultation sessions. When a burglary is reported on the telephone the victim is visited *at home* by a couple of uniformed police officers forming part of the local surveillance team involved. In principle the visit took place within *half an hour* after the telephone call (cp. crisis intervention). Prior to the visit officers have agreed upon a division of tasks, in such a way that one of the officers will focus on the technical aspects of the incident (and is charged with conducting a *technical criminal investigation*) and the other officer on the victim. This victim-oriented officer is charged with *filing the burglary report at the victim's home*, giving the victim both oral and written *crime prevention information*, and with conducting a *security inspection*. A final characteristic of the programme evaluated is that all participating police officers were *trained* beforehand. This training programme entailed the participation in a basic course on criminal investigation, a basic course on crime prevention and a crime prevention refresher course. The refresher course was given by members of the crime prevention department, just before the start of the present study.

A central element of the first course was getting acqainted with conducting a criminal investigation. Attention was given to fingerprints, foot(im)prints, methods to secure these traces (powder method, chemical means, gypsum, plastic foil), securing blood traces and the possible transportation of excrements. During the second course attention was given to organisational, architectural and electronic measures to prevent burglary, to giving preventive information and to victim assistance. The refresher course particularly focused on the task of the victim-oriented officer. The important steps he is supposed to take during visiting the victim were elucidated. The following points ("face it, please"- model) were addressed:

a) preparation phase:

* File charges of a burglary and hand out the pre-structured card, on which the victim can later record missing property;

* Assess the victim's psychological condition during the initial contact; try to find out whether the victim is strongly emotionally affected by the event or not, and is thus ready to process preventive information effectively;
* Communicate openness, if the victim is emotionally upset and provide room for emotional expression;
* Educate and inform the victim about the true nature of the event utilising statistical background information: for example perpetrators are generally youngsters employing simple "technical" resources, their likelihood of returning to the victim's home is generally quite low, violent perpetrator-victim interactions sporadically occur in cases of burglary, etc.
b) communication phase:
* Positive communication strategy: in giving preventive information utilize a positive communication strategy. That is: explicitly link positive behavioral consequences to preventive behaviors expected from the victim. Make clear to the victim that behavioral performance yields positive returns in the form of reducing the likelihood of future re-victimisation (cp. opportunity reduction; giving the burglar a hard job, etc);
* Limitative strategy: utilise a limitatative communication strategy by making clear to the victim that the expected preventive measures are sufficient. More extreme preventive options, barricading one's doors, buying a watchdog, etc. should be rejected;
* Explain your expectations and make explicit which type of preventive measures you want victims to take. Focus on simple preventive measures, like closing doors and windows, installing other locks, and try to fit the advice to the specific situation of the victim;
* Advertise and sell crime prevention;
* Security check: perform a security check in the victim's home and hand out written crime prevention information. Refer to and illustrate the crime prevention leaflets during the security check;
* End the conversation by informing victims about further procedures or victim assistance facilities. Hand out your id-card, which the victim may use in case of any trouble or if the victim has or wants any further information.

Important elements of the intervention programme - training, a home visit, the use of particular communication strategies, and conducting a security inspection - directly follow from guidelines resulting from previous studies (Winkel, 1991, 1991a). For example, particularly a positive strategy is expected to stimulate victims to actually take preventive measures (Winkel, 1989a), while it also contributes to reducing feelings of concern about burglary (Winkel, 1989b). Furthermore, a limitative strategy is utilised in order to counter the phenomenon of response generalisation, which refers to the easily elicitated tendency to react to preventive communications with extreme preventive options (Winkel, 1987). However, regarding other elements, such as "time" and a "criminal investigation on the spot" the empirical discussion so far is far from clear. At best, there is only anecdotal evidence for the beneficial impact of conducting a criminal investigation in the victim's home. Showing respect for, attention to and involvement with victims are generally considered to be favorable conditions in the victimological literature. Conducting a criminal investigation might reflect such an attitude. Furthermore, one could argue that conducting a criminal investigation created a certain order and structure in the victim's perceptual chaos. The idea that the officer involved knows precisely what to do in these possibly confusing circumstances might have a reassuring impact on victims. Regarding "time" we further note that especially adherents of the recontact-model (Winkel 1989c) frequently suggest that a later intervention is probably more effective because the likelihood of confusing the victim through "over-informing" him or her is diminished. However, such a speculation has never been tested empirically. Moreover, we would like to note that in the present program the likelihood of over-informing the victim is controlled for by having the provision of informational support (crime prevention information) preceded during the "preparatory phase" by emotional support (cp emotional expression), if needed.

Hypotheses Various hypotheses, describing the intervention's impact on police related variables, on problem focused coping and on emotion focused coping, were experimentally tested. Due to space limitations, here, we will only consider the last one. This hypothesis states: (1) the intervention will facilitate emotional coping with the event, in the sense that perceived police protection against crime will be considered sufficient more strongly, perceived safety of the living environment will be strenghtened, and concern about crime will be reduced. These effects will be particularly visible with regard to burglary and will not generalise to violent crime outside.

Method

Procedure Subjects constituted a random sample of persons reporting a burglary to the police forces of Hoorn (experimental group) and Alkmaar (control group). These cities were selected because of similarities both in terms of (objective) crime rates and in (subjective) citizens' perceptions of crime problems (Winkel, 1986a, 1986b, 1987a). The lower limit of the sample size was set in advance at N=150, and broken down to 90 controls and 60 experimental subjects. These limits were assisgned to reach an acceptable statistical power (.80), given small effect sizes and conventional levels of significance (Cohen, 1977). At a random basis, police personnel requested victims to participate in a study on perceptions of crime. The hit rate of these requests was close to 100%; only a few victims refused to participate. Those willing to participate were given a questionnaire directly following their report. All questionnaires were gathered within three days, either through a pollster, or through members of the Alkmaar crime prevention department. Experimental victims were exposed to the above programme: reporting took place at the victim's home, a criminal investigation and a security inspection were conducted there, if necessary emotional support was provided, and all victims were given oral and written crime prevention information. Such a program was absent with control victims. These latter victims were exposed to a strongly divergent procedure. After a telephone report of a burglary members of the surveillance team requested victims to report their burglary at a police station and to take relevant insurance papers with them. In case of very clear traces a "technical investigation unit" was called in, and this unit could refer to a crime prevention official or to victim assistance agencies. At the police station the report was filed by civilians in a room where crime prevention material was available.

Measures In the questionnaire various background characteristics of the victim were recorded, such as age, sex, educational level, living situation, and prior victimisation experiences. The relevant covariates were measured, too. To assess prior life stress victims were asked how things had gone in the past year in four areas, namely financially, physically, socially, and emotionally. Responses were in terms of seven point rating scales ranging from very bad to very good. An identical measure was used by Cook et al. (1987). To measure perceived seriousness nine questions were asked about the expected somatic (headaches, loosing appetite, sleeping disturbances) and psychic (degree of intrusion, distrusting others, fright responses, impact on emotions) consequences of the event. Responses were in terms of seven point rating scales ranging from very weak to very strong. The somatic items were taken from the stress-scale, utilised by Cook et al. (1987). The psychic items were based on the modified Symptoms Checklist (Arrindell & Ettema, 1986).

Measures related to emotion focused coping were based on the Coping with Crime Monitor (Winkel, 1981, 1983, 1987a), specifically on the CCM's Fear of Crime scale. In particular the 10 highest loading items on its three subscales were included in the present questionnaire. These subscales relate to perceived (un)safety of the living environment (e.g. how safe or unsafe do you feel when you are at home alone during the day; how safe or unsafe do you feel when you are walking alone on the streets in this neighborhood at night), feelings of concern about (burglary or violent) crime (how concerned or unconcerned are you that somebody will break into your house at night, when you are not at home; how concerned or unconcerned are you that you will be assaulted in this neighborhood during the day), and to the perceived protection the police offer against crime (e.g. to what degree do you feel protected by the police against burglary; against a violent crime on the streets). Responses were again in terms of seven point rating scales running from very safe, very unconcerned, and sufficient to very unsafe, concerned and insufficient.

Results

Sample The total sample comprised 165 victims of burglary. The control group consisted of 101 subjects, the experimental group of 64. Mean age was 43 years. About 60% were male and 39% female. A majority lived together with others (n=125; 76%), 24% (n=39) lived on their own. Regarding educational level 28% (n=46) formed part of the low, 41% (n=68) of the middle, and 26% (n=42) of the high level. Prior victimisation experiences were present in 30%; 70% did not have such experiences. Regarding type of burglary 2% (n=3) were victims of an unlawful entry, no loot, 21% (n=35) of an unlawful entry with "loot", 16% (n=27) of a burglary without loot and 59% (n=97) of a burglary with loot. No significant differences emerged on any of these measures between experimental and control group.

Hypotheses Data were first analysed at an aggregate level, using a factorial design representing the intervention, while controlling for two covariates, namely prior life stress and perceived seriousness of the event. ANCOVA's on the three overall scales (having acceptable reliablities) revealed significant differences both with regard to problem- and emotion-focused coping. Inter alia, a main effect emerged on the overall scale for emotion focused coping (F (1,145)= 3.82; p <.05).

To assess the programme's impact on emotion focused coping in more detail ANCOVA's were conducted on the relevant subscales. Table 1 presents an overview of the means in the experimental and control group on these scales. The pattern of means in this table is generally in line with hypothesis 1. Significant differences emerged on the overall scale for perceived police protection against crime ($F(1,153)= 2.81$; $p<.05$) and on the overall scale for concern about crime ($F(1,148)= 2.86$; $p<.05$). Perceived safety of the living environment was not significantly affected ($F <1$; ns). Hypothesis 1 is thus confirmed with regard to perceived police protection and concern about crime. However, this conclusion must be qualified. In line with the hypothesis experimental victims report less concern about burglary ($F(1,150)= 5.82$; $p<.01$), while experimental and control subjects do not report differences in concern about violent crime outside ($F<1$; ns). Contrary to hypothesis 1, though, the outcomes on perceived police protection against burglary and violent crime are reversed. Experimental subjects qualify the protection the police offer against violent crime outside as significantly more sufficient than controls ($F1,150)= 2.80$; $p< .05$); while such an effect is absent on the perceived protection against burglary ($F(1,150)= 2.23$; $p=.07$). At best there is only a statistical trend suggesting that victims exposed to the intervention feel better protected by the police against burglaries.

Table 1: Means on outcome measures in experimental and control group

Emotion-focused coping.	**Control group *M***	**Experimental group *M***
Perceived police protection	4.97	4.53*
N = 2 items; alpha = .85		
sufficient (1) - insufficient (7)		
- burglary	4.98	4.51
- violent crime	4.97	4.56*
Perceived safety of living environment	2.57	2.66
N = 4 items; alpha = .79		
safe (1) - unsafe (7)		
Concern about crime		
N = 4 items; alpha = .79	3.93	3.69*
unconcerned (1) - concerned (7)		
- burglary	5.03	4.43**
- violent crime	2.88	2.92

* = $p < .05$; ** = $p < .01$

Analyses revealed that some victims in the control group received elements of the intervention, and moreover that not all experimental victims received the full intervention. In order to statistically control for this overlap between experimental and control group a number of additional ANCOVA's were performed, enabling comparisons across "pure" groups. In comparing controls who were not exposed at all with experimental victims exposed to all components of the intervention a rather clearcut picture emerged: F-values related to emotion focused coping were lower than the ones reported above. The "all or nothing" analyses point to the following conclusion: as far as victims' coping processes are concerned some programme components appear to be ineffective, suggesting that doing more does not necessariliy result in better victim re-adjustment. In order to explore which programme components were responsible for a reduced effect on emotion focused coping two additional ANCOVA's were conducted, comparing subjects exposed to preventive communication with those not so exposed, and one comparing victims exposed to a criminal investigation with those not exposed to that component. These ANCOVA's were based on a 2 (control / experimental) x 2 (criminal investigation absent / present) x 2 (preventive communication absent / present) model. None of the twoway interactions, nor the threeway interaction were significant. Subsequently several designs were processed: (a) main effects due to crime prevention and criminal investigation were estimated after pooling the treatment effect, the relevant 2nd order and 3rd order interactions; and (b) a more simple preventive communication by criminal investigation design without such pooling. Both designs resulted in similar outcomes. On variables related to emotion focused coping these analyses revealed the following picture. On perceived police protection no significant main effects emerged, neither due to conducting a criminal investigation ($F(1,151)= 1.80$; ns) nor to providing preventive communication ($F < 1$; ns). Opposing effects emerged on concern about crime. Preventive communication significantly reduced concern about crime ($F(1,150)=4.96$; $p<.01$), while conducting a criminal investigation did not have an impact ($F< 1$; ns). However, in the latter case the relevant means were reversed: criminal investigations thus tended to stimulate concern about crime. On perceived safety of the living environment both main effects were insignificant ($F<1$; ns). Here too, the means associated with conducting a criminal investigation were reversed. This pattern again suggests that safety perceptions were negatively related to conducting a criminal investigation, while the relation with preventive communication was in a positive direction.

Discussion

Supportive responses from the police, immediately following the victimization appear to make a difference. A sensitive approach to victims appears to facilitate emotion focused coping with the event. Our findings do not support the contention, advanced by adherents of the re-contact model, that early interventions run a high risk of confusing victims through over-informing him or her, at this point in time. On the contrary, programme impact is clearly beneficial.

The present intervention programme encompassed a set of components, the efficacy of which were demonstrated in previous experiments, excercising more stringent control than the present field study. The above results appear to re-emphasize their usefulness in daily police practice, not only during victim-recontacts, but also during intial contacts, directly following the victimisation. Conducting a criminal investigation was here added to this set of effective initiators of coping processes, mainly for two reasons. Firstly, it gives expression to the notion of increased police attention to crime victims, and was thus assumed to be of value in further stimulating victims' coping with the event. Our results appear to underscore this notion's validity: victims highly valued the component. However, the emanating assumption was clearly challenged by our data. Our additional analyses suggested that criminal investigations may backfire, and thus thwart the initiation of coping processes. However, we would not advice to exclude this component completely from future intervention programmes. This has to do with our second reason for its introduction in the present programme. Although accepted and appreciated, many police officers actually still consider victim oriented programmes to belong to the softer types of police work. Criminal investigations do not share this quality, but are generally perceived to be part of the real job. Criminal investigations may thus serve as a foot in the door for succesfully implementing victim oriented programmes in police forces, and as a guarantee for their longer term adoption. From this perspective, the component merits further research attention. Future experiments should examine whether its potentially adverse impact could be avoided or reduced, for example by making explicitly clear to victims that criminal investigations substantially increase the clearance rate. The positive returns for victims of conducting criminal investigations should be stressed, one way or another. The present results suggest that a criminal investigation is only beneficial to victims, if it is combined with the provision of crime prevention information. Besides examining specific components, future studies might also profit from assessing the impact of the components discussed here by several "programme providers". The "source magnification effect" (Winkel, 1984) suggests that the overall impact of intervention programmes can be enhanced if different service providers combine their efforts. An obvious possibility here would be to combine inputs into the programme from victim assistance workers with inputs from the police (cp Winkel & Vreeburg, 1992). Finally, we would like to note that the measures used in this study to assess program impact were limited both in terms of range and time. To assess longitudinal effects future studies should add repeated measures at different points in time. As to range, in particular cognitive elements were relatively ignored. Our insights in program impact might be enriched by incorporating in future studies the cognitive dimensions of victims' coping processes (self-views, views of the world, future plans, relationships, and activities/priorities following victimisation) as suggested by Collins, Taylor and Skokan (1990).

References

American Psychological Association. (1984). *Final report of the task force on victims of crime and violence (A. Kahn).* Washington DC: Government Printing Office.

Arrindell, W. A., & Ettema, J. H. M. (1986). *Handleiding bij een multidimensionele psychopathologie indicator.* Lisse: Swets & Zeitlinger.

Bard, M. & Sangrey, D. (1979). *The crime victim's book.* New York: Basic Books.

Bard, M. & Sangrey, D. (1980). Things fall apart: Victims in crisis. In L. Kivens (Ed.), *Evaluation and change.* Minneapolis: Minnesota Medical Research Foundation.

Burt, M. R., & Katz, B. L. (1985). Rape, robbery and burglary: Responses to actual and feared criminal victimization, with special focus on women and the elderly. *Victimology*, *10*, 325-358.

Cohen, J. (1977). *Statistical power analysis for the behavioral sciences*. New York: Academic Press.

Collins, R. L., Taylor, S .E., & Skokan, L. A. (1990). A better world or a shatttered vision? Changes in life perspectives following victimization. *Social Cognition*, *8*(3), 263-285.

Cook, R. F., Smith, B. E., & Harrell, A. V. (1987). *Helping crime victims: Levels of trauma and effectiveness of services*. Washington DC: NIJ, US Department of Justice.

Davis, R. C. (1987). Studying the effects of services for victims in crisis. *Crime and Delinquency*, *33*, 520-531.

Elias, R. (1986). *The politics of victimisation*. New York: Oxford University Press.

Frieze, I. H., Greenberg, M. S., & Hymer, S. (1987). Describing the crime victim: Psychological reactions to victimization. *Professional Psychology: Research and Practice*, *18*, 299-315.

Hagan, J. (1982). Victims before the law: A study of victim involvement in the criminal justice process. *Journal of Criminal Justice*, *73*, 317-330.

Janoff-Bulman, R. (1979). Characterological versus behavioral self-blame: Inquiries into depression and rape. *Journal of Personality and Social Psychology*, *35*, 351-363.

Judd, C. M., & Kenny, D. A. (1981). *Estimating the effects of social interventions*. New York: Cambridge University Press.

Knudten, M., & Knudten, R. (1981). What happens to crime victims and witnesses in the justice system. In B. Galaway & J. Hudson, (Eds.), *Perspectives on crime victims* (pp. 52-61). St Louis: Mosby.

Kobassa, S. C. (1979). Stressful life events, personality and health: An inquiry into hardiness. *Journal of Personality and Social Psychology*, *37*, 1-11.

Lurigio, A. J. (1987). Are all victims alike? The adverse, generalized and differential impact of crime. *Crime and Delinquency*, *33*, 452-469.

Meyers, M. M. (1977). *The effects of victim characteristics on the prosecution, conviction and sentencing of criminal defendents*. PhD dissertation. Ann Arbor, Michigan: University Microfilms.

Meyers, M., & Hagan, J. (1979). Private and public trouble: Prosecutors and the allocation of court resources. *Social Problems*, *26*, 439-451.

Miller, D. T., & Porter, C. A. (1983). Self-blame in victims of violence. *Journal of Social Issues*, *39*, 139-152.

Peterson, C., Semmel, A., Abramson, L. Y., Metalsky, G. I., & Seligman, M. E. P. (1982). The attributional style questionnaire. *Cognitive Therapy and Research*, *6*, 287-300.

Resick, P. A. (1987). Psychological effects of victimisation: Implications for the criminal justice system. *Crime and Delinquency*, *33*, 468-479.

Roberts, A. R. (1990). *Helping crime victims: Research, policy and practice*. Newbury Park: Sage.

Sales, E., Baum, M., & Shore, B. (1984). Victim readjustment following assault. *Journal of Social Issues*, *40*, 117-136.

Skogan, W. G., & Wycoff, M. A. (1987). Some unexpected effects of a police service for victims. *Crime and Delinquency*, *33*(4), 490-501.

Smith, B. L., Sloan, J. J., & Ward, R. M. (1990). Public support for the Victims' Rights Movement: Results of a statewide survey. *Crime and Delinquency*, *36*, 488-502.

Symonds, M. (1980). The second injury to victims. *Evaluation and Change*, *7*, 36-38.

Viano, E. (1987). Victim's rights and the constitution: Reflections on a bicentennial. *Crime and Delinquency*, *33*, 438-451.

Winkel, F. W. (1981). Angst voor criminaliteit: Verklarende modellen. *Tijdschrift voor Criminologie*, *23*, 289-308.

Winkel, F. W. (1983). Onrust over criminaliteit: Een empirische toetsing van enkele predictormodellen. *Tijdschrift voor Criminologie*, *24*, 40-53.

Winkel, F. W. (1984). Changing misconceptions about rape through informational campaigns: A model. *Victimology*, *9*, 262-272.

Winkel, F. W. (1986a). *Probleemgeorienteerd politieren in Hoorn: Bevindingen uit de bevolkingspeiling*. Amsterdam: Stichting Mens & Recht.

Winkel, F. W. (1986b). *Probleemgeorienteerd politieren in Zaanstad: Bevindingen uit de bevolkingspeiling*. Amsterdam: Stichting Mens & Recht.

Winkel, F. W. (1987). Response generalisation in crime prevention campaigns: An experiment. *British Journal of Criminology*, *27*, 155-173.

Winkel, F. W. (1987a). *Politie en Voorkoming Misdrijven: Effecten en Neven-effecten van Voorlichting*. Amsterdam: Mens & Recht.

Winkel, F. W., & Koppelaar, L. (1988). Police information for victims of crime: A research and training perspective from the Netherlands. *Police Studies*, *11*, 72-82.

Winkel, F. W. (1989). Responses to criminal victimisation: Evaluating the impact of a police assistance programme and some social psychological correlates. *Police Studies*, *12*, 59-73.

Winkel, F. W. (1989a). Police crime prevention campaigns: A social-psychological perspective on effective preventive messages. *Journal of Police and Criminal Psychology*, *5*, 11-21.

Winkel, F. W. (1989b). Increased fear of crime and related side-effects of persuasive communication: The pricetag of burglary prevention campaigns? In E. C. Viano (Ed.), *Crime and its victims: Research and public policy issues* (pp. 273-297). Washington DC: Hemisphere.

Winkel, F. W. (1989c). Preventieve voorlichting als vorm van slachtofferhulp: De kunst van het voorlichten. In J. Soetenhorst-de Savornin Lohman (Ed.), *Slachtoffers van misdrijven: Ontwikkelingen in hulpverlening, recht en beleid* (pp. 69-97). Arnhem: Gouda Quint.

Winkel, F. W. (1990). *Slachtofferhulp: Verkenning en sociaal-psychologische analyse*. Amsterdam: Swets & Zeitlinger.

Winkel, F. W., & Steinmetz, C. H. D. (1990). Slachtofferschap en angst voor criminaliteit: Een schokverwerkingsmodel. In F. W. Winkel & A. v.d. Wurff (Eds.), *Angst voor criminaliteit: Theorie, onderzoek en interventie* (pp. 22-47). Amsterdam: Swets & Zeitlinger.

Winkel, F. W. (1991). Police, victims and crime prevention: Some research based recommendations on victim orientated interventions. *British Journal of Criminology*, *31*, 250-266.

Winkel, F. W. (1991a). Police communication programmes aimed at burglary victims: A review of studies and an experimental evaluation. *Journal of Community and Applied Social Psychology*, *1*, 275-289.

Winkel, F. W., Vrij, A., Koppelaar, L., & V.d. Steen, J. (1991). Reducing secondary victimisation risks and skilled police intervention: Enhancing the quality of police-rape victim encounters through training programmes. *Journal of Police and Criminal Psychology*, *7*(2), 7-15.

Winkel, F. W., & Koppelaar, L. (1991). Rape victims' style of selfpresentation and secondary victimisation by the environment. *Journal of Interpersonal Violence*, *6*, 29-40.

Winkel, F. W., & Vreeburg, E. A. M. (1992). *Slachtoffer-gerichte preventie van criminaliteit: De samenwerking tussen politiele Bureaus Criminaliteitspreventie en Bureaus voor Slachtofferhulp*. 's Gravenhage: VNG-Reader.

Zwanenburg, A., & Winkel, F. W. (1990). Oog voor angstgevoelens: Observaties vanuit de praktijk van de afdeling voorkoming misdrijven. In F. W. Winkel & A. v.d. Wurff (Eds.), *Angst voor criminaliteit: Theorie, onderzoek en interventie* (pp. 165-179). Amsterdam: Swets en Zeitlinger.

[1] This study was supported by a grant from the Directie Criminaliteitspreventie (DCP) of the Ministry of Justice.

Reactions to Criminal Victimization: A Field Study of the Cognitive Effects on Victims and Members of Their Social Network[1]

Adriaan J. M. Denkers and Frans W. Winkel

Introduction

Every year 8.7% of the Dutch population is personally confronted with a serious crime (Steinmetz, 1990). The notion that victimization can have its social and psychological consequences is widely accepted. The emotional effects have elaborately been documented by clinical and social psychologists (Frieze, Greenberg, & Hymer, 1987). However, the cognitive effects of victimization have received remarkable little attention (Catlin & Epstein, 1992). Janoff-Bulman's World Assumptions Model (1989) offers an approach to assess such cognitive consequences. She states that people, in day to day life, hold certain implicit assumptions about the world of which they are hardly aware. These assumptions model the way in which we interpret the world around us and how we function in it. Consequently, people are generally reluctant to change their basic beliefs. Only traumatic events, like criminal victimizations, can dramatically effect the basic assumptions about the world (Janoff-Bulman, 1985; Janoff-Bulman & Frieze, 1983). The resulting change of perspective influences the way everything is observed; how good-bad, normal-abnormal and pleasant-unpleasant every-day events are. These changed assumptions can thereby influence the victim's wellbeing. Janoff-Bulman (1989) proposes three primary categories of vulnerability-related basic assumptions: (1) "benevolence of the world" (the impersonal world and people); (2) "meaningfulness of the world" (just world, control over outcomes and chance); and (3) "worthiness of the self" (self-esteem, self-control and luck). In accordance with studies on various negative life-events, we expect that criminal victimization will negatively influence these assumptions. Next, we presume that such cognitive effects will not exclusively arise among the direct victims, but will also contaminate those who are indirectly confronted with victimization, such as relatives, friends and acquaintances of the victim (Steinmetz, 1990; Winkel, 1990). That is, as victims search for social support, they automatically confront the approached members of the social network with assumptions-threatening information. These members of the social network might consequently be labelled indirect victims.

Due to the dominant "victim blaming model", victimologists are generally quite pessimistic about the contents of the reactions from the social network (Beijk, 1986; Van Dijk, 1989). Central to this model is the idea that members of the social network will mainly blame the victim and/or provide the victim with internal attributions in order to safeguard their own belief in a just world (Lerner & Miller, 1978). According to this "satanic scenario" "*the chance of receiving warmth and comfort diminishes with the magnitude of the victim's need*" (Van Dijk, 1989. p. 14). We believe that there are good reasons to doubt the validity of the "victim blaming" model in the present context. Effectively an arguable generalization is made when assuming that the reactions of subjects in an experiment, who do not know and are unlikely to ever meet the victim, are interchangeable with the reactions of members of the victim's social network, who have invested time and energy in establishing a good relationship with the victim. From our perspective it seems more plausible that members of the social network will react empathically towards their unfortunate relative, friend or acquaintance and will likewise rather provide external instead of internal explanations. Some empirical support for this hypothesis is offered by the experiments conducted by Lerner and Simmons (1966) and Chaikin and Darley (1973). These experiments indicate that others who get the opportunity to compensate the victim and respectively identify with the victim, describe the victim in much more positive terms.

Hardly any empirical data are available on the exact relation between the different types of explanations provided by members of the social network and the victim's wellbeing (Hirsch, 1980; Buunk & Jansen, 1987). To complicate matters, opposing predictions can be formulated from a theoretical point of view. Two renowned social psychological models - the Abramson/Seligman Model (Abramson, Seligman, & Teasdale, 1978; Abramson, Matalsky & Wortman, 1989) and the Janoff-Bulman Model (Janoff-Bulman & Wortman, 1977) - offer conflicting predictions. The first model predicts a negative influence of internal and a positive influence of external attributions on the victim's wellbeing. The second model gives reversed predictions. Janoff-Bulman (1979) distinguishes two types of internal attributions, namely character and behaviour attributions. Behaviour attributions are expected to be associated with good adjustment and character attributions with maladjustment. The two considered models base their predictions on different psychological mechanisms: the first model assumes that internal attributions impair self-esteem; the second model assumes that character attributions reduce perceived control over outcomes, while behaviour attributions increase this perceived control. Concerning the empirical foundation of both models, Tennen and Afflick (1990) and Winkel and Vrij (1992a) tend to deny support for the Abramson/Seligman Model. Subsequently, Meyer and Taylor (1986), Frazier (1990) and Winkel and Vrij (1992b) suggest that character attributions are maladaptive, while the results regarding behaviour attributions are paradoxical.

In concluding this section we note that the following general hypotheses were formulated.

(1) First, the reports on the world-assumptions will be more negative among both direct and indirect victims than the reports of non-victims.

(2) Opposed to the dominant theory of victim-blaming, we expect members of the social network to react empathically and mainly with external explanations. Internal explanations towards the victims character or behaviour will occur less frequently.

(3) External explanations from members of the social network and explanations addressing the victims character will negatively influence victims' well-being. A possible positive influence might be expected of explanations directed towards the victim's behaviour.

Method

Subjects Interviews were conducted among 152 inhabitants of Amstelveen: 50 victims of crime, 49 members of the social network and 53 persons who had not been (directly or indirectly) victimized during the past year. An almost identical distribution of crime-types was found in the victim and the social network group: 25.3% reported a burglary, 23.0% a person-orientated crime, 21.1% theft and 30.6% reported an other crime (sex-related crime, car-related crime, bag-snatching, etc.).

Subjects averaged 40 years of age; 47% were male and 52.7% female. A significant age-difference ($F(2,147) = 10.25, p < .00$) was found between the three groups: $M^{\text{non-victims}} = 48$ years, $M^{\text{victims}} = 37$ years and $M^{\text{social network}} = 34$ years.

Procedure A team of interviewers conducted the interview door to door in Amstelveen. Subjects were asked if they, during the past year, had been victimized by a more serious crime than for instance "the theft of a bike". If they answered in the affirmative they were given the victim questionnaire. If the answer was negative the interviewer asked if someone they are close to, for example a relative, friend or acquaintance, had been a victim of such crime during the past year. If the answer was in the affirmative the social-network questionnaire was presented. If this answer was negative too, the subject was given the non-victim questionnaire. Some time later the interviewer collected the filled in questionnaire.

Measures To assess the psychological impact of victimization a Dutch translation of Janoff-Bulman's (1989) "Assumptive Worlds Scale" was used. This scale consists of eight sub-scales: just world; benevolence of the people; benevolence of the world; random; luck; self- worth; self-control; and controllability. All these scales consist of four items.

Victims and members of the social network were asked to report the frequency of different types of verbal reactions they had respectively received or given, distinguishing (1) internal explanations: behaviour ("the way you behave evokes this sort of event"); character ("you are the type of person that attracts these events"); (2) external explanations ("these sort of events can be expected in that place or situation" and "that is the way society is"); and (3) an empathic reaction ("it is awful what happened to you").

The questionnaire also entailed a general cognitive evaluation scale for "subjective well-being": a Dutch translation (Heesink, 1989) of the "Satisfaction With Life" Scale of Diener, Emmons, Larsen and Griffon (1985) (five items). Some representative items are: "in most ways my life is ideal" and "the most important things that I expected out of life I have already got". According to the researchers this scale correlates highly with other measures of well-being.

All responses were in terms of seven-point rating scales:
Assumptive Worlds Scale (1) = no, definitely not; (7) = yes, definitely;
reactions from the social network (1) = never; (2) = almost never; (3) = seldom; (4) = now and then; (5) = regularly; (6) = often; (7) = very often; and
life-satisfaction (1)= do not agree at all, (7)= agree totally.

Reliabilities: Cronbach's Alpha of the assumptive world sub-scales varies between .60 and .69; for the total Assumptive Worlds Scale alpha is .74, and for life satisfaction alpha=.85.

Results

On the eight Assumptive Worlds sub-scales a MANOVA was conducted to investigate the differences between victims (both direct and indirect) and non-victims. This analysis showed a significant multivariate effect: $F(8,123)=2.85$, $p<.01$. Univariate differences were found on the assumptions about the *benevolence of the impersonal world* ($F(1,130)=10.69$, $p<.01$), self-controllability ($F(1,130)=6.84$, $p<.05$), *control over outcomes* ($F(1,130)=3.65$, $p<.05$), and *luck* ($F(1,130)=3.28$, $p<.05$).

Table 1: Assumptions about the World means of Victims, members of their social network and non-crime victims.

	Victims	Social network	Non-victims
Benevolence of the World			
- of the impersonal world	4.30_a	3.92_a	4.65_b
- of people	4.50_a	4.47_a	4.80_a
Meaningfulness of the World			
- just world	3.01_a	3.09_a	3.07_a
- controllability of outcomes	4.05_a	4.16_{ab}	4.43
- chance	4.04_a	4.10_a	4.08_a
Worthiness of Self			
- self-worth	4.68_a	4.53_a	4.51_a
- self-control	4.91_a	4.79_a	5.34_b
- luck	4.27_a	4.50_{ab}	4.72_b

(Between subscripts a, b and c: $p < .05$)

To further explore the differences between the three groups, contrast analyses were conducted (Table 1). These analyses further revealed a linear pattern on the assumptions *luck* ($F_{lin.}(1,141)=5.64$, $p<.05$; $F_{dev.lin.}(1,141)=.002$, $p<.1$) and *control over outcomes* ($F_{lin}(1,141)=3.67$, $p=.058$; $F_{dev.lin.}(1,141)=.212$, $p>.1$). Victims reported the least *luck* and *control over outcomes* and non-victims the most, with indirect victims in the midpoint. These results correspond with the expectation that victimization can cognitively effect both direct and indirect victims.

To inspect the frequencies of network-reactions a multivariate analysis of variance was conducted based on a mixed 2 (group: direct/indirect victim) x 4 (reaction type) design, of which the later is a within-subjects factor. This analysis revealed a significant reaction-type effect ($F(4,89)=58.33$; $p<.01$). The results indicate, as expected, that members of the social network mainly meet their unfortunate friend or relative with empathic reactions and external explanations (see Figure 1). Internal attributions, both those that are directed towards the victim's character and those that are directed towards the victim's behaviour, are relatively uncommon. The absence of a group effect indicates that victims and members of their social network did not report different frequencies on the reactions that they had received (victim) or given (social network).

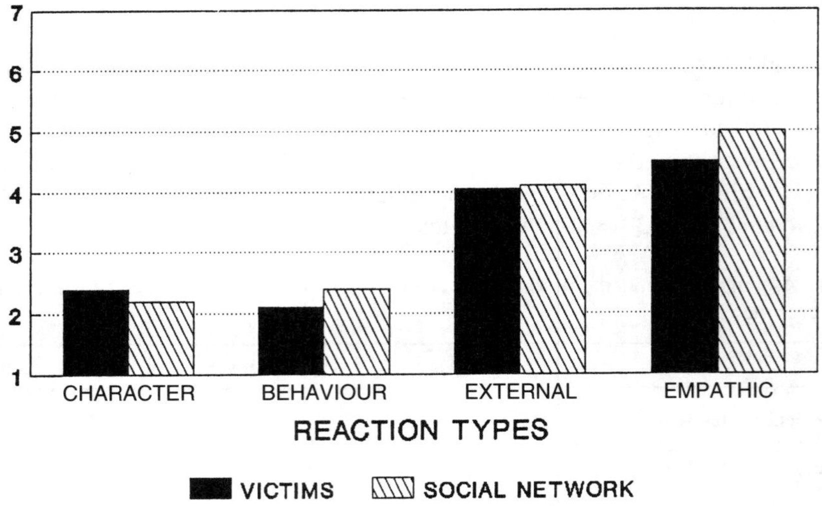

Figure 1: Type of network reactions: received (victims) and given (network).

To acquire insight in the psychological mechanisms postulated by the Abramson/ Seligman and Janoff-Bulman models, the correlations between the network-reactions (attributive and empathic) and several basic assumptions were inspected. Counter to the first model, self-esteem has been found to correlate negatively with external network attributions (r=-.44, p<.01). This implies that external attributions certainly do not buffer positive self-esteem. Further, empathic reactions do not correlate with self-esteem (r=.09, *ns*), whereas empathic reactions do correlate with self-control (r.41, p<.01). In accordance with the Janoff-Bulman Model self-esteem does not correlate with external attributions (r=.09, *ns*), but does (marginally) correlate negatively with character attributions (r=-.21, p=.08). However, contrary to the Janoff-Bulman Model no positive relationship is found between behaviour attributions and self-control (r=.01, *ns*).

To examine the influence of the different types of explanation given by the social network on the life-satisfaction of the victims and their social network, mean splits were conducted on each "explanation-variable". Unfortunately, the resulting dichotomy gave an almost identical distribution for character and behaviour explanations. Guided by this and the observed high intercorrelation between character and behaviour attributions (r=.59, p<.01), we decided to join both into one internal variable. Next an explanation-type variable was created consisting of four categories: (1) more than average external and more than average internal; (2) more than average external and less than average internal; (3) less than average external and more than average internal; and (4) less than average external and less than average internal. With life-satisfaction as dependant variable, an ANOVA was conducted with a mixed 2 (group: direct/indirect victim) x 4 (explanation-type) design, of which the later is a within-subjects factor. A significant group x explanation interaction effect emerged (F(3,86)=2.813, p<.05). The results are graphically presented in Figure 2.

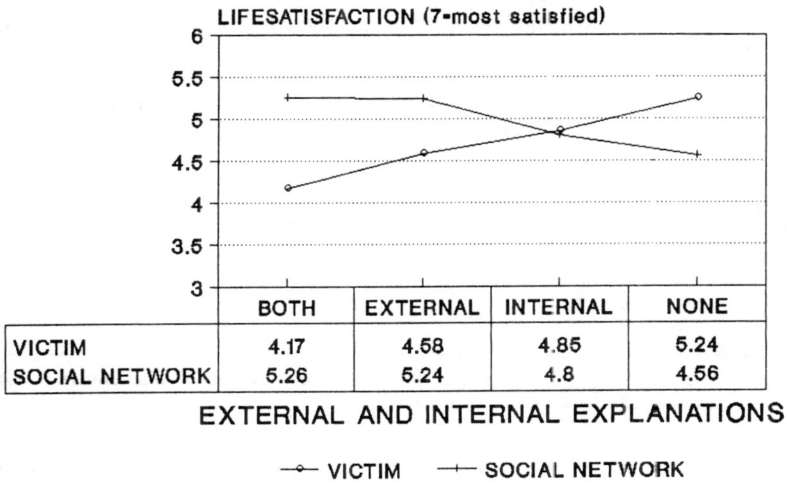

Figure 2: Life satisfaction and external/internal explanation

Figure 2 indicates that members of the social network benefit most from giving both explanations and least from giving no, neither internal nor external, explanations. This pattern runs counter to the observed effects of these explanations on the victims' life-satisfaction. Victims benefit most from receiving no explanations and least from hearing both types of explanation. Victims are better off when only internal explanations than when only external explanations are given. These results support our third hypothesis.

To examine the relation between the assumptions about the world and satisfaction with life, correlation analyses were conducted. These analyses showed that none of the assumptions from the *meaningfulness of the world* category correlate significantly with satisfaction with life ($r_{\text{just world}}$=.05, $r_{\text{controllability of outcomes}}$=.03 and r_{chance}=-.02; all *ns*). All the assumptions out of the categories *benevolence of the world* ($r_{\text{impersonal world}}$=.26, p<.05; and r_{people}=.36, p<.01) and *worthiness of self* ($r_{\text{selfesteem}}$=.45, p<.01; $r_{\text{self-control}}$=.55, p<.01; and r_{luck}=.21, p<.05) do correlate significantly. An overall scale, in which all assumptions are represented, also correlates strongly with life-satisfaction (*r*=.45; p<.01).

Separate factor-analyses within the victim and social network groups were conducted on the overall scale of assumptions, satisfaction with life and the original seven-point rating scales of the internal and external explanations. Both analyses resulted in a solution with two factors (eigenvalue > 1). The explained variance in both groups was over 70% (victims 73.4% and members of the social network 70.7%). The VARIMAX-rotated solutions are represented in Table 2.

Table 2: Varimax rotated solution of factor-analysis on victims and members of their social network's satisfaction with life, Assumptions about the World and internal and external explanations

	Victims		Social Network	
	Factor 1	**Factor 2**	**Factor 1**	**Factor 2**
Factor 1: Explanations				
External explanations	.87		.60	.40
Internal explanations	.80		.90	
Factor 2: Cognitions				
Assumptions about the world		.92		.89
Satisfaction with life	-.45	.69		.78

(eigen-value > 1; Loadings less than .30 are excluded from this table; explained variance of victim and social network factor-analysis are: 73.4 and 70.7)

At first sight the two solutions appear to be identical: one factor (explanations) consists of both types of explanations. The other (cognitions) includes assumptions about the world and life-satisfaction. A closer look reveals that there are differences between victims and their social network in the way both scales relate to one another. Within the victim-group there is a negative relation between the factor "explanations" and life-satisfaction. This indicates that receiving explanations from the social network has a negative influence on the victims satisfaction with life. This result is analogous to the findings represented in Figure 1.

Within the social network group a positive relation is found between external explanations and the factor "cognitions". An interpretation, analogue to the findings represented in Figure 1, could be that members of the social network can positively influence their cognitions by giving the victim external explanations for the event.

Discussion

Both direct and indirect experiences with crime appear to affect one's basic assumptions about the world. Taking into account that satisfaction with life, utilized here as a general measure of wellbeing, appeared to be associated with these assumptive worlds, one may conclude that the cognitive impact of crime stretches far beyond those directly involved as a victim: by sharing victim experiences with friends, relatives and acquaintances, they may also be cognitively "contaminated" (indirectly victimized). In this study various differences emerged between victims and members of their social network, and non-victims in the way they perceive the world. These differences were found in all three primary categories distinguished by Janoff-Bulman (1989): benevolence of the world ("benevolence of the impersonal world"); meaningfulness of the world ("control over outcomes"); and worthiness of self, ("self-control" and "luck"). Both victims and their social network reported a more negative impression of the impersonal world and a reduced sense of control over outcomes. Moreover, linear patterns were observed on the assumptions about self-control and luck: non-victims reported more positive and victims more negative cognitions than members of the social network did.

As to attributions, this study suggests that the success of psychological adaptation is influenced by the type of explanations that one receives or gives. Victims are more successful, or are more satisfied with their life, if no explanations are given by their relatives, friends or acquaintances. If any are given, internal explanations seem to be least harmful. Counter to this, members of the social network, who have been "indirectly victimized" by their unfortunate relative, friend or acquaintance, adapt most successfully if they provide both types of explanations, and more so when only external than when only internal explanations are given.

Possibly because of this positive influence on their satisfaction with life, external explanations from the social environment outweighed the internal explanations. Furthermore, members of the social network generally reacted empathically. These results run counter to the dominant theory of victim blaming. In our view, the victim-blaming perspective rests too heavily on the idea that members of the social network react in a way identical to people who do not even know the victim. Knowing the victim thus appears to be an important determinant of the type of response elicited in the social environment. This variable should be examined more closely, because reactions of members of the social network obviously are of much greater importance to the process of de-victimization than the reactions of people who never had or will have contact with the victim.

Another possible reason for not blaming the victim could be that members of the social network just do not want to hurt their unfortunate relative. friend or acquaintance. It might be a natural response to protect, comfort and help someone from your in-group, yet if people indeed act according to this less selfish reasoning, they may unwillingly and unknowingly harm the victim in the process.

In view of the findings, this study offers more support for the Janoff-Bulman Model (1979) than for the Abramson/Seligman Model (1978). Explanations from the social network that elicit external attributions have a more negative influence on the victim's satisfaction with life than explanations that lead to internal attribution. It must be noted, however, that victims who received no explanations were most satisfied with life. Unfortunately the present data did not permit a sensible analysis of the differential impact of character- and behaviour-attributions.

From an applied perspective, we finally note that recently developed victim-oriented training programmes for police officers, victim assistance workers and criminal justice personnel might profit from taking the cognitive impact of victimization more explicitly into consideration. Cognitive restructuring techniques, aimed at restoring the victims' assumptive worlds, in our view, should be a regular component of such programmes.

References

Abramson, L. Y., Matalsky, G. I., & Wortman, C. B. (1989). Hopelessness depression: A theory-based subtype of depression. *Psychological Review*, *96*, 358-372.

Abramson, L. Y., Seligman, M. E. P., & Teasdale, J. D. (1978). Learned helplessness in humans: Critique and reformulation. *Journal of Abnormal Psychology*, *87*, 49-74.

Beijk, J. (1986). Het geloof in de rechtvaardige wereld. *Psychologie*, *5*, 18-21.

Buunk, A. P., & Jansen P. (1987). Sociale ondersteuning in de thuissituatie en psychosociale stress op het werk. *Gedrag en gezondheid, 15*, 147-154.

Catlin, G., & Epstein, R. A. (1992). Unforgettable experiences: The relation of life events to basic beliefs about self and world. *Social Cognition, 10*, 189-209.

Chaikin, A. L., & Darley, J. M. (1973). Victim or perpetrator: Defensive attribution or responsibility and the need for order and justice. *Journal of Personality and Social Psychology, 25*, 268-275.

Diener, E., Emmons, R. A., Larsen R. J., & Griffon S. (1985). The satisfaction with life scale. *Journal of Personality Assessment, 49*, 71-75.

Frazier, P. A. (1990). Victim attributions and post-rape trauma. *Journal of Personality and Social Psychology, 59*, 298-304.

Frieze, I. H., Greenberg, M. S., & Hymer, S. (1987). Describing the crime victim: Psychological reactions to victimisation. *Professional Psychology; Research and Practice, 18*, 299-315.

Heesink, J. (1989). *Schaalanalyses voor het project 'het proces van sociale integratie van jong-volwassenen' II: Werk, opleiding en welzijn*. Amsterdam: Vrije Universiteit.

Hirsch, B. J. (1980). Natural support systems and coping with major life changes. *American Journal of Community Psychology, 8*, 159-172.

Janoff-Bulman, R. (1979). Characterological versus behavioral self-blame: Inquiries into depression and rape. *Journal of Personality and Social Psychology, 37*, 1798-1809.

Janoff-Bulman, R. (1985). The aftermath of victimization: Rebuilding shattered assumptions. In C. R. Figley (Ed.), *Trauma and its wake*. New York: Brunner/Mazel.

Janoff-Bulman, R. (1989). Assumptive worlds and stress of traumatic events: Applications of the schema construct. *Social Cognition, 7*, 113-136.

Janoff-Bulman, R., & Frieze, I. H. (1983). A theoretical perspective for understanding reactions to victimization. *Journal of Social Issues, 39*, 1-17.

Janoff-Bulman, R., & Wortman, C. B. (1977). Attributions of blame and coping in the real world: Severe accident victims react to their lot. *Journal of Personality and Social Psychology, 35*, 351-363.

Lerner, M. J., & Miller, D. T. (1978). Just world research and the attributional process: Looking back and ahead. *Psychological Bulletin, 85*, 1030-1051.

Lerner, M. J., & Simmons, C. H. (1966). The observer's reaction to the "innocent victim": Compassion or rejection? *Journal of Personality and Social Psychology, 22*, 202-210.

Meyer, C. B., & Taylor S. E. (1986). Adjustment to rape. *Journal of Personality and Social Psychology, 50*, 1226-1234.

Steinmetz, C. H. D. (1990). *Hulp aan slachtoffers van ernstige misdrijven, effecten van slachtofferhulp en primaire opvang*. Arnhem: Gouda Quint.

Tennen, H., & Afflick, G. (1990). Blaming others for threatening events. *Psychological Bulletin, 108*, 209-232.

Van Dijk, J. (1989). Eigen schuld, dikke bult? Over de neiging om het slachtoffer verantwoordelijk te stellen voor zijn/haar lot. In J. Soetenhorst-de Savorin Lohman (Ed.), *Slachtoffers van misdrijven ontwikkelingen in hulpverlening, recht en beleid*. Arnem: Gouda Quint.

Winkel, F. W. (1990). *Slachtofferhulp: Verkenning en sociaal-psychologische analyse*. Amsterdam: Swets en Zeitlinger.

Winkel, F. W., & Vrij, A. (1992a). Televisie en de opsporing van daders van criminaliteit: Differentiele publieksacties als functie van het informatie-aanbod en de geprefereerde preventie-strategie. *Gedrag en Gezondheid, 5*, 56-70.

Winkel, F. W., & Vrij, A. (1992b). Crime victims' attributional attitudes and differential psychological responses to victimization: The influence of behaviour, character and external explanations. In N. Clark & G. Stephenson (Eds.), *Issues in criminological and legal psychology*. Leicester: British Psychological Society.

[1] This study was subsidised by the C.D.W.O. of the Dutch Department of Justice.

[2] We should note that both models don't consider the effects of network attributions - explanations given by members of the social network - on the victim's wellbeing, but only the effects of attributions provided by the victims themselves. We thereby assume that the effects are identical.

The Criminal Justice Response to Sexual Assault in Canada

Julian V. Roberts

Rape reform has become an important issue in criminal justice in North America and elsewhere over the past decade, resulting in a great deal of legislative activity. The wave of rape law reform which swept across the United States in the 1970's reached Canada in 1983. The reform bill in Canada had several aims, and these included (but were not restricted to) the following: increasing the number of sexual assault victims who would report to the police; increasing the efficiency of police processing (i.e., increasing the percentage of cases that were cleared by the laying of a criminal charge); increasing the conviction rate in cases of sexual assault and changing conceptions of crimes of sexual aggression.

This chapter presents an overview of the empirical research upon the sexual assault in Canada, beginning with the evaluation of the 1983 rape reform. Specifically, I summarize data relating to seven critical issues: (a) reporting sexual assaults to the police; (b) the founding of complaints; (c) the laying of criminal charges; (d) the relative attrition rates of sexual assault compared to other serious crimes of violence; (e) the conviction process; (f) the sentencing of offenders convicted of sexual assault and (g) the impact of the legislation upon public opinion. Within the scope of a brief chapter, it is not possible to explore each issue in depth. Instead, I attempt to convey an overview of the most important findings.

Rape Reform in Canada

In 1983, the offences of rape, attempt rape, indecent assault (of a male victim) and indecent assault (female) were replaced by a tripartite classification of sexual assault. The new classification defined three levels of seriousness: (a) sexual assault (S. 271); (b) sexual assault with a weapon, threats to a third party or causing bodily harm (S. 272); and (c) aggravated sexual assault (S. 273). (Hereafter the three levels will be referred to as sexual assault I, II and III.) The maximum penalties for the three levels of sexual assault are: 10 years; 14 years and life imprisonment. The sexual assault offences correspond in structure to the three assault offences created at the same time (assault (S. 266); assault with a weapon or causing bodily harm (S. 267); aggravated assault (S. 268)). The maximum penalties for the three assault offences are: five years; 10 years and 14 years, respectively. The new offences of sexual assault were placed in the Offences Against the Person Section of the Canadian *Criminal Code*; prior to 1983 the offences of sexual aggression were located in the Sexual Offences Section. The idea behind this change was to stress the assaultive in addition to the sexual nature of crimes of sexual aggression.

In addition to creating these new offences to replace the earlier ones, the legislation made a number of important changes to the law relating to the prosecution of cases of sexual aggression. The spousal immunity provision which had prevented a husband from being charged with raping his wife was abolished. The law became gender-neutral in the sense that men and women were afforded the same legal protection regarding sexual assault. As well, certain idiosyncrasies (such as the fact that indecent assault had carried a higher maximum penalty if the victim had been a male) were repealed. Henceforth the law treated assaults against male and female victims in the same way. Finally, a number of important changes were made to the conduct of sexual assault trials (e.g., the rule regarding recent complaint was repealed). (For further information on the legislation and the new offences, see Watt, 1986.)

As Marsh, Geist and Caplan (1982) conceptualize criminal law reform, three factors are critical: the law; the criminal justice system responsible for implementing the law; and the advocacy groups responsible for provoking reforms in the first place. From the Canadian perspective, in 1983 the indications for a positive response to the reforms were propitious. First, the law (Bill C-127) was passed expeditiously, and with a considerable amount of positive publicity in the Canadian news media. Second, the Federal Department of Justice (with responsibility for criminal law reform) invested a great deal of resources in a public legal education initiative to inform the people of the importance of the reforms. Third, the criminal justice system in Canada appeared responsive to reform in the area of the treatment of victims of sexual aggression. Thus special facilities such as sexual assault units were set up in police forces across the country. As well, there was an increase in the number of sexual assault centres and in special teams located in hospitals to deal with sexual assault victims. Fourth, a number of prominent advocacy groups had worked strenuously to promote the creation and passage of the reform legislation. In addition, the Minister of Justice indicated his personal support for the reform legislation. Finally, the Canadian reforms were more far-reaching than some of the American reforms (see Backhouse and Schoenroth, 1984, for a comparison of the Canadian and American reforms). There was cause therefore for optimism that the legislative reforms which were enacted in 1983 would change both the criminal justice system as well as the negative perception of that system held by victims of sexual assault.

Evaluating the Rape Reform Legislation

The federal government recently completed an ambitious, multi-year evaluation of the rape reform legislation. Research studies examined all the areas of criminal justice affected by the reform legislation. This research included: in-depth site studies which focused upon the processing of cases of sexual assault, and which looked at issues such as the attrition of cases (e.g., Baril, Bettez and Viau, 1988); studies of criminal justice statistics (Roberts, 1990a); an examination of sentencing patterns (Roberts, 1990b); surveys of front-line personnel such as sexual assault crisis centre workers (CS/RESORS Consulting Ltd., 1991); public surveys to assess knowledge of, and attitudes towards the new legislation (Department of Justice Canada, 1988); reviews of the case law relating to sexual assault that has evolved over the past few years (Department of Justice Canada, 1992), and finally a special study on sexual homicide (Roberts and Grossman, 1991). (For an annotated bibliography of sexual assault in Canada, see Roberts and Grossman, 1992b.) In all, the Canadian legislative evaluation was an ambitious examination of the effects of the new legislation, one that was more comprehensive than any other rape reform legislative evaluation to this point in North America or anywhere else. In this chapter I review some of this research.

Method

Reporting trends

The analyses include all reports of crimes of sexual aggression made to the police between January 1, 1979 and December 31, 1988. This period includes the year of implementation plus five years, a post-intervention period that in light of other evaluations should be sufficient to detect a gradual effect and also to determine whether the impact was transitory. The unit of analysis was monthly, national totals of all the offences of sexual aggression (rape and indecent assault prior to 1983; sexual assault after 1983). Monthly totals were used to achieve greater sensitivity to any possible treatment effects.

The "founding" of reports

Once an incident is reported to the police, a preliminary investigation is conducted, as a result of which a percentage of all reports are classified as "unfounded". Considerable criticism has been directed at this process: in the past, the unfounded rate for crimes of sexual aggression such as rape was higher than for other personal injury offences. Accordingly, one of the explicit aims of the reform legislation was to decrease the percentage of reports that are declared by the police to be "unfounded".

Clearing cases by charge

Cases that remain (after "unfounded" reports are dropped) are classified as "actual offences". A charge is laid against a suspect in only a proportion of actual offences. The rate at which cases of the earlier offence of rape were cleared by charge was decried by many observers who found that the police were more reluctant to lay charges in rape cases than in other personal injury offences. It was anticipated that one of the collateral benefits of stressing the aggressive rather than the sexual aspect of crimes of sexual aggression would be an increase in the percentage of cases "cleared by charge".

Court processing issues

The aforementioned issues (reporting; founding; charg-ing) are all examined using data derived from the Uniform Crime Reporting Database. Questions relating to court processes (conviction rates; sentencing trends) can only be examined by special studies, as there are no national conviction or sentencing statistics currently available in Canada (although this is likely to change in the near future).

Results and Discussion

Reporting trends before and after the reform

Examination of the reporting data of the pre-reform sexual offences (rape; attempt rape; indecent assault) revealed only modest increases in all categories for the five-year period prior to the reforms. The overall reporting rate of all three levels of sexual assault increased 22% over the five-year period. Over the same period, reports of non-sexual assault increased by 20% (Roberts, 1990a). However, there was a statistically significant increase in the number of reports of sexual aggression following passage of the rape reform legislation. The national sexual assault rates more than doubled over the period examined. It is also important to note that the increase in reports of sexual assault far exceeds the increase in reports of non-sexual assault over the same period. The difference between the two slopes is statistically significant ($t(46) = 6.1, p < .001$). Thus the increase in sexual assault reports was not part of a generalized increase in reporting of personal injury offences over the same period. To summarize, we can conclude that (a) reports of crimes of sexual aggression were relatively stable in the pre-reform period; (b) after 1983 there was a significant increase in monthly totals of sexual assault across the country; (c) while the number of assaults also increased, the rate of increase was less than half that of sexual assault (see Roberts and Gebotys, 1992, for further information).

Can the increase in reporting statistics be unequivocally attributed to the 1983 legislation rather than some other influence, such as a general change in social attitudes to reporting (as appears to have been the case in Michigan)? In Canada, the co-occurrence of the legislation and the relatively sharp increase in reporting in 1983 would seem to rule out such explanations. However, this does not explain the mechanism by which the legislation changed reporting patterns. The weakness of a time-series design (such as the one employed here) is that there are many aspects of the reform legislation that may have had an effect upon sexual assault statistics (see Campbell and Stanley, 1963). Thus there may be several alternate explanations for the increase in reporting; these have been explored elsewhere and will only be summarized here.

One possibility is that the increase in the number of reports may simply reflect the fact that the law now speaks to a wider range of victims. However, other research carried out at the same time however shows that the number of cases of sexual assault in which either the suspect was a woman or the husband of the complainant is under 5% (e.g., University of Manitoba Research Ltd., 1988). This explanation can therefore be discarded. Another hypothesis relates to recording patterns: incidents classified as sexual assault now include cases formerly recorded as a sexual offence other than rape or indecent assault. However, the incidence of these other sex crimes has increased steadily at a rate unchanged since prior to the 1983 legislation. This shows that the rise in reporting was not associated with all sexual offences, but rather was specific to the crimes of sexual assault. Thirdly, it might be argued that acts which before 1983 were not brought to the attention of the police are now being reported as sexual assaults. Research reveals that the incidents now reported as sexual assault do not differ significantly from the kinds of incidents formerly reported as indecent assault or rape (Department of Justice, 1990). Finally, it is possible that the 1983 legislation has had no effect upon the reporting behaviour of adult victims, but that there has been a significant impact upon the reporting of assaults committed against juveniles. The evidence on sexual assault reporting from the Department of Justice studies seems to suggest that an increase in juvenile complainants has taken place but that the magnitude of the increase cannot explain the substantial increase in reports of sexual assault.

To summarize, none of these alternate explanations seem sufficient to explain the increase in reporting that occurred after 1983. This was in all probability due to a change in victims' attitudes, brought about by the reform legislation and the publicity surrounding its passage.

Recent reporting trends

At this point we focus on the reporting trends since 1983. Several trends are apparent. First, the overall increase in reports of sexual aggression is clear: in 1983 there was a total of 13,851 reports made; this figure rose to 32,861 in 1990, an increase of 137%. This is more than double the increase of reports of non-sexual assault (Roberts, 1990a). Second, the increase in the number of reports (any level) made since 1983 is confined to the first level of seriousness (sexual assault I). Thus there were 12,241 reports classified at the first level in 1983. This rose to 31,401 in 1990, an increase of 156%. By comparison, over the same period, reports classified at the second level rose a modest 13%, while reports classified as aggravated sexual assault actually *declined* by 39%. Third, the percentage of all reports accounted for by the first (i.e., least serious) level rose from 88% in 1983 to 96% in 1990 (see Roberts and Grossman, 1994, for further analysis).

Taken together, these last two findings are intriguing. There are two explanations for the high percentage of cases classified at the first level of seriousness. Assuming that the law had an effect in attracting victims who previously would not have turned to the police, it is unlikely that the increase in reporting would be uniform across all levels of seriousness. In all probability, the more serious cases of sexual aggression were always more likely to be reported to the police. Legislation which attracts more victims is probably going to attract a proportionately greater number of cases at the least serious level (sexual assault I). Thus a growing percentage of all sexual assaults accounted for by sexual assault level I is consistent with the hypothesis that the legislation (and publicity surrounding its passage) had changed victims' attitudes towards reporting. However, the decline in the proportion of reports classified as aggravated sexual assault also suggests that there has been a significant transformation in the classification procedures used by police forces across the country. Some reports that would have been classified as aggravated sexual assault in the first years after the reforms were introduced are now being classified as level II or perhaps even level I. And, since the initial classification is likely to be highly predictive of the eventual charge laid, as well as any subsequent conviction, this shift in police practices has consequences for the entire criminal justice process as well as for victims.

It is noteworthy that this trend is restricted to cases of sexual assault. This is clear from comparisons with the assault offences. In terms of the distribution of reports across the three levels however, there is an important difference. For the most recent year for which data are available, of all reports of assault recorded by the police, 80% were classified as assault I. Thus a greater percentage of assault reports (compared to sexual assault reports) are classified at the higher levels of seriousness.

Founding rates

The average unfounded rate for sexual offences prior to 1983 (1979-1982) was 15%. The average unfounded rate for the three offences of sexual assault in the post-reform period was also 15%. Thus there is no evidence that the reform legislation increased the percentage of reports declared to be founded. How does the unfounded rate of 15% for the new offences of sexual assault compare to the unfounded rates for other crimes against the person? The overall unfounded rate for the assault offences in 1988 was 7.5% (Canadian Centre for Justice Statistics, 1989). Relative to other crimes of violence then, the sexual assault offences result in a higher percentage of reports being dismissed as unfounded.

Clearance rates

In 1982, the last year in which rape and indecent assault existed, the overall clearance rate for these offences was 38% (Canadian Centre for Justice Statistics, 1983). Within five years of the passage of the legislation, the clearance rate had risen to 48%. However, this increase cannot be attributed to the reform legislation, for there was a corresponding increase in the clearance rates for the non-sexual assault offences, as well as for the more general category of crimes of violence.

Attrition rates

The clearance data raise a much-discussed issue in the sexual assault literature: attrition of cases as they make their way through the criminal justice process (e.g., Caringella-MacDonald, 1985). These data describe case attrition occurring as a consequence of police decision-making, the first official stage at which filtering takes place. The issue of attrition addresses more than just police decision-making. However, the absence of national conviction data, and of integrated criminal justice data-bases in Canada, means that we are restricted to examining the attrition of cases from the initial report to the laying of a charge. Using more recent (1991) data, it is clear that just over half the reports of sexual assault (all levels combined) do not proceed to the point at which a charge is laid. The cleared by charge statistic of 48% cited above is based upon actual offences (reports minus incidents designated as "unfounded"). However, basing clearance rates upon actual offences, rather than the initial pool of reports made to the police may be to take too much for granted. Thus if we examine what happened to the number of initial reports (not "actual offences") of sexual assault for the year 1991 (35,570), charges were laid in 15,715 (42%) of the cases in the original pool of reports. From the perspective of individuals making a report of sexual assault to the police, this figure may be a more appropriate statistic. Thus over half the cases do not proceed to the laying of a charge. This national statistic suggests that the process of attrition is even higher than suggested by research drawing upon a single site (e.g., Minch, Linden and Johnson, 1987). By comparison, of all *reports* of one of the three levels of non-sexual assault for the same year, 48% resulted in the laying of a charge. Attrition rates for sexual assault then are higher than for reports of non-sexual assault. In fact the attrition rate for sexual assault is one of the highest examined in a recent study, which yielded the following clearance rates:- assault police officer: 95%; attempt murder: 77%; homicide: 66%; sexual offences (other than sexual assault): 61%; other crimes of violence (other than assault or sexual assault): 47% (see Roberts and Grossman, 1994). Thus, if one of the aims of the rape reform was to decrease the attrition rate of sexual assault cases, it does not appear to have been particularly successful.

Conviction rates

As noted above, national data are not currently available on con-viction rates, therefore we have to turn to the special studies conducted in several sites across the country in order to obtain an idea of the effect of Bill C-127 on this critical variable. The results vary from province to province, but one thing is clear: pre-post comparisons fail to show consistent increases in the conviction rate following passage of the reform legislation. For example, in British Columbia the conviction rate changed a mere 3%, while in Manitoba, Ontario and Quebec, the conviction rate actually declined after the reforms were implemented (see Department of Justice, 1990, for further information). The rape reform legislation has not had an effect upon the likelihood of obtaining a conviction.

Sentencing trends

Although reforming sentencing trends was not one of the princ-ipal goals of the rape reform legislation, a great deal of concern has arisen around the issue of sentencing in cases of sexual assault in Canada (see Roberts and Mohr, 1994). At the present time, national sentencing statistics are not routinely published in Canada. Accordingly, in order to obtain an idea of sentencing trends we have to draw upon a sub-national data-base. Roberts (1990b) examined sentencing trends before and after the rape reform legislation was passed. Results indicated that there had been little change in the overall severity of sentences imposed for crimes of sexual aggression since 1983. In terms of sentencing severity, approximately 60% of convictions for the first level of sexual assault resulted in a period of incarceration. The two more serious levels of sexual assault resulted in incarceration of the offender in almost all (over 90%) of cases. Examination of sentences imposed in British Columbia revealed an incarceration rate of 78% for sexual assault I, and 99% for sexual assault II and III. How do these incarceration rates compare to incarceration rates for other personal injury offences? Assault I generated an incarceration rate of 22%, while the two higher levels of assault resulted in a sentence of custody in 63% of cases. Of the serious crimes against the person other than murder, only attempt murder, criminal negligence causing death and manslaughter resulted in higher incarceration rates than sexual assault level I. Thus there does appear to be a degree of ordinal proportionality in terms of sentencing severity. That is, the relative seriousness of the different offences is reflected in the ordering of the incarceration rates (see Roberts, 1990b for further information). It should be pointed out that these data come from a single province, and are not necessarily representative of the rest of Canada.

Before concluding this discussion of criminal justice statistics, I draw attention to a phenomenon that is relevant to almost all the issues examined in this chapter: inter-jurisdictional variation. Although the rape reform legislation is federal in nature, and applies to all provinces and territories, the administration of criminal justice is a matter of provincial jurisdiction. Moreover, the diverse nature of Canada's provinces means that both crime rates, and the criminal justice response to crime, vary considerably. Some examples will illustrate the point.

Crime reporting rates vary greatly across the country. For the most recent year for which data are available at the time of writing (1991), while the national rate of sexual assaults reported to the police was 132 per 100,000 residents, this masks considerable diversity. Thus in Quebec the rate was 63 incidents of sexual assault per 100,000 population, while in the NorthWest Territories the rate was 1,020 incidents per 100,000 population. Even adjoining provinces have very different rates of sexual assaults reported to the police. The same is true for the unfounded rate, which is twice as high in some provinces (e.g., 18% in New Brunswick) than in others (9% in Quebec). Different police forces across Canada also seem to have different levels of success in clearing crimes. Thus the clearance rate for sexual assault varies from 41% in New Brunswick to 75% in the Yukon. Finally, this pattern of diversity extends to the sentencing stage as well. While there is a high degree of variability in sentencing for all kinds of offences in Canada (judges have a great deal of discretion, and little guidance) there appears to be more disparity in sentences imposed for sexual assault than for other offences against the person. For example, comparing just four provinces, the incarceration rate for sexual assault I varied from a low of 58% in one to 90% in another.

Public knowledge of the sexual assault law

Finally, I deal with the issue of public awareness of the rape reform legislation. Law reform in the area of sexual aggression cannot take place if the public are unaware of the reform. As noted in the introduction, one of the goals of Bill C-127 was to change perceptions of the crimes of sexual aggression. All too often, the public seem unaware of even well-publicized legal interventions (see Roberts, 1992 for a review of this literature). Accordingly, it was important to know how much the Canadian public had learned about the rape reform legislation. A nation-wide telephone survey of Canadians took place in 1988, five years after the rape reform legislation was passed.

Respondents were asked a series of questions about sexual assault, the criminal justice response, and their attitudes towards reporting to the police, if they were victimized. The results revealed widespread awareness of the substantive changes to the law. For example, 83% of respondents were aware that a man could now be charged with the sexual assault of his wife. A similar percentage were aware of the definitional changes, for example that a sexual assault could take place in the absence of sexual intercourse. Over three-quarters were aware that both sexes could be charged with the crime of sexual assault. In terms of attitudes towards the system, the Canadian public appeared to have more positive than negative views of the criminal justice response to sexual assault. Finally, it is important to note that almost nine out of ten respondents indicated that they would turn to the police if they had been sexually assaulted. This result supports the interpretation offered earlier, that victims have a more positive view of the system, and this explains the dramatic increase in the numbers of sexual assaults reported to the police in recent years (see earlier section on reporting trends). (For further information on the survey, see Department of Justice, 1988.)

Conclusion

These findings suggest that the rape reform legislation introduced in Canada in 1983 was successful in achieving one of its goals, namely attracting more victims into the criminal justice system. In this regard, it appears to have succeeded where some other rape reform initiatives (e.g., Michigan, see Marsh, Geist and Caplan, 1982) have failed. Ironically, its success has been in attracting more victims into the system, rather than in changing the way that the system processes cases of sexual aggression. The reforms have had no significant effect upon the decision as to whether a particular case is founded, whether a charge is laid in the case or whether a conviction is eventually recorded. We have to conclude that Canada's reform legislation, while it has attracted a larger number of victims to report victimizations, has failed to change the processing of those reports by the police, or the courts. Accordingly, although it was regarded at the time as a bold step towards reform of the criminal justice system, empirical research suggests a rather more cautious interpretation. The danger is that victims who are now coming forward in record numbers may be disillusioned by the criminal justice response. This may in turn lead to a reduction in the reporting rate of crimes of sexual aggression, and we would be back where we started in 1983. Bill C-127 should be seen then as the first step, rather than the last word in terms of reforming the criminal justice response to crimes of sexual aggression in Canada.

The challenge now to researchers is to understand why the reform legislation had such meagre impact upon the criminal justice response to crimes of sexual aggression. This is obviously the first step towards preparing further legislation which will affect criminal justice processing of these kinds of cases.

References

Backhouse, C. and Schoenroth, L. (1984). A comparative study of Canadian and American rape law. *Canada-US Law Journal*, 7, 173-213.

Baril, M., Bettez, M.-J., & Viau, L. (1988). *Sexual assault before and after the 1983 reform: An evaluation of practices in the judicial district of Montreal, Quebec.* Ottawa: Department of Justice Canada.

Campbell, D., & Stanley, J. (1963). *Experimental and quasi-experimental designs for research.* Chicago: Rand McNally.

Canadian Centre for Justice Statistics (1983). *Canadian Crime Statistics: 1982.* Ottawa: Supply and Services Canada.

Canadian Centre for Justice Statistics (1989). *Canadian Crime Statistics: 1988.* Ottawa: Supply and Services Canada.

Caringella-MacDonald, S. (1985). The comparability in sexual and nonsexual assault case treatment: Did statute change meet the objective? *Crime and Delinquency, 31,* 206-222.

CS/Resors Consulting Ltd. (1988). *The impact of legislative change on survivors of sexual assault: A survey of front-line agencies.* Ottawa: Department of Justice Canada.

Department of Justice Canada (1988). *Canadian attitudes towards justice issues.* Ottawa: Research Section, Department of Justice Canada.

Department of Justice Canada (1990). *Overview. Sexual assault legislation in Canada: An evaluation.* Ottawa: Department of Justice Canada.

Department of Justice Canada (1992). *A review of the sexual assault case law. Sexual assault legislation in Canada: An evaluation.* Ottawa: Department of Justice Canada.

Marsh, J., Geist, A., & Caplan, N. (1982). *Rape and the limits of law reform.* Boston, Mass: Auburn House.

Minch, C., Linden, R., & Johnson, S. (1987). Attrition in the processing of rape cases. *Canadian Journal of Criminology, 29,* 389-404.

Roberts, J. (1990a). *An analysis of national statistics. Sexual assault legislation in Canada: An evaluation.* Ottawa: Department of Justice Canada.

Roberts, J. (1990b). *Sentencing patterns in cases of sexual assault. Sexual assault legislation in Canada: An evaluation.* Ottawa: Department of Justice Canada.

Roberts, J. (1992). Public opinion, crime and criminal justice. In M. Tonry (Ed.), *Crime and justice: An annual review of research, Vol. 16.* Chicago: University of Chicago Press.

Roberts, J., & Gebotys, R. (1992). Reforming rape laws: Effects of legislative reform in Canada. *Law and Human Behavior, 16,* 555-573.

Roberts, J., & Grossman, M. (1992a). *Homicide and sexual assault. Sexual assault legislation in Canada: An Evaluation.* Ottawa: Department of Justice Canada.

Roberts, J., & Grossman, M. (1992b). *Sexual assault: An annotated bibliography.* Ottawa: Crime and Justice Research Centre.

Roberts, J., & Grossman, M. (1994). *Criminal justice processing of sexual assault cases.* Ottawa: Canadian Centre for Justice Statistics.

Roberts, J., & Mohr, R. (1994). *Confronting sexual assault. A decade of social and legal change.* Toronto: University of Toronto Press.

University of Manitoba Research Ltd. (1988). *Report on the impact of the 1983 sexual assault legislation in Winnipeg, Manitoba.* Ottawa: Department of Justice Canada.

Watt, D. (1986). *The new offences against the person.* Toronto: Butterworths

Social Beliefs About Recidivism in Crime

Santiago Redondo, Eulalia Luque and Jaume Funes

Introduction

Recidivism of offenders is one of the factors which is most frequently examined when we refer to the effectiveness or ineffectiveness of preventive action or treatment applied to offenders. As with other social issues which the population is concerned about (such as unemployment, drug addiction, abortion, health, etc.), recidivism is a phenomenon often referred to by the mass media, and one which people tend to form opinions about, opinions which may be either close to or far from existing knowledge about its true dimensions.

Similarly, the feelings and beliefs which a population has regarding the volume of crime which exists in the society it lives in, and about the levels of recidivism of convicted offenders, are probably related, in an interesting way, to the expectations citizens build up as to what kind of criminal policy should be applied, about whether penal measures should be more lenient or severe, their belief in and support for reformatory programmes, and whether or not resources should be allocated to deal with the rehabilitation of offenders. This has been underlined by research which has established a close link between certain cognitions, attitudes, beliefs and emotions of people - such as the feeling of collective identity, the feeling of respect for others, obligation, or negative emotions such as hate, envy or resentment - and the ideas and expectations which these same people have about justice (Montada & Schneider, 1989; Rivera, 1989; Solomon, 1989).

Besides this interaction between emotional elements and beliefs about justice, which could be said to be general for all citizens, it has also been suggested that the upbringing of individuals could have a decisive influence on the opinions people have about justice (Hoffman, 1989).

The present research was prompted by a Seminar on the problem of recidivism in crime in which the authors presented the main findings of a research piece about recidivism in Spain. We aimed to investigate the estimates of recidivism which, before knowing the "true" information about recidivism rates, were made by the participants in this Seminar. These estimates were examined in relation to a series of respondent's personal and social variables, as well as with the criminal act itself.

More precisely, the following three objectives were set: (1) to evaluate the possible differences which exist between the beliefs about the recidivism rates of our sample, and the beliefs of other populations, which had already been assessed; this comparison would be made with a Canadian sample population, researched by Roberts and White (1986); (2) to evaluate the differences between these beliefs and the "actual" recidivism figures in our country (Redondo et al., 1991; Redondo, Funes, & Luque, 1993); and finally (3) to assess the importance attributed by the subjects to the influence which different factors (such as criminal typology, age, employment situation, etc.) could have on crime, recidivism, or the rehabilitation of the offenders.

Method

Sample The participants in the sample were professionals and students selected from three courses of criminology (which the authors taught on), two of which were held in Barcelona (XLVI International Course of Criminology, Barcelona, 28-31 of October, 1991; and students from the Seminar of Juvenile Delinquency, from the Institute of Criminology of the University of Barcelona, 1991-92 academic year) and one in Albacete (Master in Criminology of the University of Castilla-La Mancha, 1991-92 academic year).

The final sample consisted of 106 subjects, with an average age of 32.3 (ranging from 21 to 65). As far as the academic background of the sample participants is concerned, 38% held higher degrees, 38% held an ordinary degree, 19% held Higher Certificates of Education or were studying the first years of diplomas or University degrees (six subjects did not answer the academic background item). Regarding academic modalities, the biggest group was made up of those who held degrees in Law (22%), followed by those with Diplomas in Criminology (17%), and psychologists (7.5%). The most common professions were prison staff (31%), police officers (13%) and lawyers (8.5%). Other professions included administrative workers, university lecturers, social workers, bank workers, educators, private researchers and teachers.

Instruments A questionnaire was drawn up for the purpose of data collection. In it the subjects were requested to make different percentage estimates about the recidivism of groups of offenders, after being released from prison and having served a prison sentence. To this end the subjects were asked to consider determined conditions and factors which are normally supposed to be related to crime. This questionnaire consisted of a section on personal details and 32 questions, with a wording similar to the one used in the Canadian research of Roberts and White (1986), which went as follows: "Out of one hundred first offenders (who had never been in prison before), convicted of offences against property (with no personal violence), what percentage do you think will be convicted of another offence in the five years following their release from prison?" In each one of the 32 questions the following elements were gradually modified: (1) factors related to the criminal record and actions committed by the subjects (first offenders /recidivists /multi-recidivists; property offences /against people/ sexual offences /drug trafficking); (2) factors related to the sentence and how it is served or penitentiary factors (less than two-year sentence /six-year sentence / over 10 years; sentence completed in no-privilege status /ordinary /open /parole status); and (3) social and environmental factors (returning to a deprived area / middle class area; having no paid job to go to after release from prison / having a paid job; being a drug addict /or not a drug addict; have support from social services / have no support).

Results

Comparison of estimated and actual recidivism rates for Spanish and Canadian samples

Regarding the first two objectives, Table 1 allows us to compare the differ-ences between the recidivism estimates by Spanish and Canadian subjects, as well as to assess the existing differences, in the Spanish sample, between recidivism estimates and the actual recidivism figures.

Table 1: Differences between the beliefs held about recidivism by Spanish and Canadian subjects (in percentages), contrasted with the "actual" recidivism in crime figures in countries. Three columns appear for each group of offenders (first, recidivists and multi-recidivists) and country (Spain and Canada): the recidivism percentages estimated by the population studied appear in the "EST" column; the actual crime recidivism percentages appear in the "Actual" column, whereas the "aR" column[1] represents the accuracy rate for the estimates with regard to the actual recidivism figures.

	First offenders						**Recidivists**						**Multirecidivists**			
	Spain			**Canada**			**Spain**			**Canada**			**Spain**			**Canada**
	EST	Actual	aR	EST	Actual	aR	EST	Actual	aR	EST	Actual	aR	EST	Actual	aR	EST
Against property	50.4	23.4	0.46	49	27.3	0.56	73.5	35.9	0.49	47.9	47.5	0.99	84.8	55.7	0.66	51.9
Against people	32.8	7.7	0.23	55.8	16.7	0.30	47.8	25	0.52	53.2	43.7	0.82	55.2	16.6	0.30	56.7
Sexual offences	31.1	0	0	57.6	13.5	0.23	45.4	0	0	53.9			52.3	0	0	55
Drug traffic offences	60.8	11.1	0.18				88.6	0	0				100	44.4	0.44	

[1] The "aR" column (accuracy ratio) was calculated by dividing each "actual" score by its corresponding "estimated" score. The closer the accuracy ratios are to 1, the greater the harmony which exists between the "estimated" and "actual" recidivism figures.

Recidivism of offenders against property

With regard to offenders who had committed offences against property, in the case of first offenders, the subjects of the Spanish sample "estimated" a recidivism rate of 50.4%, whereas the "actual" recidivism rate for these offenders was 23.4% (which gives us an "accuracy ratio", or aR, of 0.46). On the other hand, the Canadian sample of Roberts and White's study (1986) had produced, for property offenders, and also in the case of first offenders, an "estimated" recidivism rate of 49%, whereas the "actual" recidivism percentage was in the order of 27.3% (aR=0.56).

For the recidivists - offenders who had committed a previous offence - the Spanish sample "estimated" a subsequent recidivism rate of 73.5%, whereas the "actual" recidivism rate was 35.9% (which gives an 0.49 aR). In Canada, the "estimate" had been 47.9% with a "actual" recidivism of 47.5% (aR=0.99).

In the case of multi-recidivist offenders - those who had already committed more than one offence - the average "estimate" made by the Spanish sample was 84.8%, compared to an "actual" figure of 55.7% (aR=0.66). The Canadian sample had "estimated" subsequent recidivism to be 51.9%, with no data on "actual" recidivism being available.

Recidivism of offences against people

The subsequent recidivism of first offenders against people was "estimated" at 32.8% by the Spanish sample, compared to an "actual" figure of 7.7% (aR=0.23). The Canadians had "estimated" this recidivism at 55.8%, with the "actual" figure standing at 16.7% (aR=0.30).

In the case of recidivists against people, the Spanish sample "estimated" a 47.8% rate of subsequent recidivism, whereas the "actual" figure stood at 25% (aR=0.52). The Canadian sample "estimated" this recidivism at 53.2%, with the "actual" figure being 43.7% (aR=0.82).

The Spanish sample estimated for multi-recidivists against people a subsequent recidivism of 55.2%, in contrast with a "actual" recidivism rate of 16.6% (aR=0.30). The Canadian sample "estimated" recidivism in this group at 56.7%.

Recidivism of offenders in sexual offences

The Spanish sample "estimated" the subsequent recidivism of first offenders in sexual offences at 31.1%, that of recidivists at 45.4% and that of multi-recidivists at 52.3%, whereas in the "actual" figures no case of recidivism had been recorded for any of these groups of offenders (aR=0 in all cases). Canadian research "estimated" that recidivism by first offenders in sexual offences at 57.6%, against an "actuality" of 13.5% (aR=0.23); that of recidivists at 53.9%; and that of the multi-recidivists at 55%, with no "actual" data being available for the latter two groups.

Recidivism of offenders in drug trafficking offences

In this case we have no Canadian data. Our Spanish sample "estimated" the subsequent recidivism of first offenders for drug traffic offences at 60.8%, the "actuality" being 11.1% (aR=0.18). The "estimate" for recidivists was 88.6% and the "actual" figure was 0 (aR=0). The subsequent recidivism of multi-recidivists was "estimated" to be 100%, whereas "actual" data gave a percentage of 44.4% (aR=0.44).

Age and recidivism

The sample as a whole estimated that offenders under 30 are more likely to relapse into crime (53.9%) than those above 30 (39.3%).

Previous convictions and recidivism

Where those with previous convictions are concerned, the sample estimates subsequent recidivism in percentages which are inversely proportional to the time spent previously in prison: 47.9% for offenders who had previously been sentenced to less than two years, a level of 39.6% for those who had been sentenced to six years, and 29% for those who had been given a sentence of more than 10 years.

Social reinstatement factors and recidivism

Subjects were asked to estimate the recidivism of offenders taking into account a series of factors which we have called reinstatement factors. These factors had been dichotomised into their more and less favourable aspects.

When the most favourable pole is considered, the factor to which the sample attributes greatest importance in the social reinstatement of subjects, once they have served their sentence, is that of employment: if they have a job, recidivism is estimated in only 21.5% of the cases. If they have no job, an important increase is assigned to levels of recidivism (67.8%). The difference between either assignation means that the job factor is afforded greater importance as an element of integration: there is a difference of 46.3 points between the two extremes.

If, on the other hand, we pay attention to the less favourable aspects of the factors considered, the condition of dependence on drugs is seen as the element which would lead to the highest rate of recidivism: the sample considered that 73.4% of drug addicts would go back to prison. Nevertheless, greater importance is attached to having a job than not taking drugs in terms of social reinstatement: the sample estimated that 30.5% would recidivate even although they aid not take drugs.

The kind of area to which the offender returns follows drugs in the negative stereotype. If offenders returned to a deprived area, their recidivism was estimated at 71.7%. If they returned to live in a middle-class area, 39.3% of the cases would recidivate.

Finally, on being released from prison, having or not having the help of the social services would swing the recidivism rate from 30.8% to 52.6%, respectively (a difference between both poles of 21.8 points).

As far as the evaluations made by different sample subgroups are concerned, some significant differences appear in the estimates of recidivism with the drug addiction /non-addiction factor taken into consideration. The prison staff presented recidivism evaluations for non-addicts which were significantly lower (22.1%) than the rest of the professions as a whole (33.9%) (confidence level 95%). Men overestimated the recidivism of drug addicts (77%) as opposed to women (66.7%) (significant difference at a confidence level of 95%). The rest of the subgroups and sample categories produced no significant differences.

The estimates of the levels of recidivism - both in terms of the criminal activity and of the age of those convicted - present no significant differences if we consider the profession or the level of the use of the mass-media held by the subjects who completed the questionnaire. The level of distortion, of "constructed actuality", common to prison staff is no lower than that of students of criminology or other professionals. We are not questioning the strong influence which the mass-media have in the building of social representations, but - perhaps because of the way it was asked - we found no significant differences of estimation between individuals who do not read newspapers, or do not watch television, and those who do. Nevertheless, it may be that the beliefs and social representations we are analyzing are founded on rumours, fears and worries in which the influence of access to the mass-media cannot be measured directly.

The women who completed the questionnaire tend to exaggerate somewhat the levels of recidivism. The biggest differences between men and women were found in the estimation of the recidivism of first offenders against sexual freedom (36.2% in the estimate made by women, 27.5% as estimated by men). Nevertheless, none of the differences found have statistical significance.

With a view to obtaining complementary information, the subjects were asked simply to estimate what importance some offences, age or sex, had, in the totality of sentences which courts of law pass in one year. The distortion we commented on previously regarding recidivism was maintained even amongst professionals who come into contact with prisoners, when dealing with offences such as drug trafficking (about 45% in the estimates, when the true figure stands somewhere around 8.9%).

Generally speaking, the negative decreasing impact which a closed penitentiary status and the deprivation of parole would have on recidivism was appreciated correctly. However, estimates on returns to crime were far higher than the actual figures (the estimates for individuals on parole were around 30%, when in the study by Redondo, Funes, Giménez Salinas, González and Roca (1991), the figure was found to be 19.8%. Going back to what we mentioned previously, the people who completed the questionnaire considered that the circumstance or the context which had the greatest influence on the production of recidivism was drug addiction, predicting that three out of every four such cases would return to prison. Along with this stereotype, and in similar proportions, they estimated that those who returned to live in a deprived area would easily become recidivists upon leaving prison. Additionally, it was believed that recidivism would be far lower if the convicted person had a job to go to after leaving prison, and if he were attended by social services resources.

No statistically significant differences were found in the evaluation of the weight of social factors, or those related to the type of punishment, amongst professionals or between levels of information. On the contrary, it was found that women underestimated significantly the impact of the closed prison, whereas they were able to consider more deeply the condition of drug addiction (significant at the level of confidence of 95%).

Discussion

Regarding the evaluation of the differences between the beliefs of the Spanish sample about recidivism figures and the estimates made by the Canadian sample (Objective 1), globally speaking the Spanish results are not particularly different from those obtained in Canada. In both countries actuality is distorted. The general public, even when it consists of professionals or learned individuals, tends to consider recidivism as a phenomenon of vast magnitude. Beliefs relating to complex social phenomena, including crime, tend to be systematically distorted to almost inexplicable limits, transforming them into independent actualities which can have an ever greater influence than the objective offences themselves.

For first-time offenders against property, beliefs or prejudices place recidivism at a rate which is almost twice the actual one (aR around 0.5). People think that one out of every two offenders goes on to commit further offences, when the truth is that only one in four does so.

For subjects who commit offences against people, the data from the Canadian research differ somewhat from the Spanish sample. In Spain, the estimated recidivism for this criminal typology is less than that for property offenders, whereas the opposite is true for Canada. However, in both research studies - Spanish and Canadian - these data are far from the truth (for the Spanish sample aR=0.23; Canada, aR=0.30).

It is not easy to make comparisons in the case of sexual offences. The actual rate of recidivism is very low (partly due to the characteristics of the offence, and partly because of the effect of preventive imprisonment), but collective estimates are still far from actuality.

But it is in the case of drug-trafficking offences where collective beliefs would appear to have little or nothing to do with actuality. Like the rest of the components of the "drug problem", almost everything is "constructed actuality", hardly anything is "actual reality". People believe that recidivism is practically six times greater than it actually is (aR=0.18).

When trying to evaluate whether or not offenders with previous convictions will commit further offences, the appreciation begins to take on more realistic proportions, although the tendency to distort is still maintained. Nevertheless, it is not easy to explain the differences which can be observed between the Canadian study (Roberts & White, 1986) and our own.

References

Hoffman, M. (1989). Empathetic emotions and justice in society. *Social Justice Research*, *3* (4), 283-311.

Montada, L., & Schneider, A. (1989). Justice and emotional reactions to the disadvantaged. *Social Justice Research*, *3* (4), 313-344.

Redondo, S., Funes, J., Giménez-Salinas, E., González, C., & Roca, M. (1991). *Justicia penal i reincidencia a Catalunya: Factors personals, udicials i penitenciaris*. Lecture at Interlabo Meeting, held in Barcelona on "La Crise Des Systèmes de Sanction".

Redondo, S., Funes, J., & Luque, E. (1993). *Justícia penal i Reincidència*. Collecció "Justícia i Societat". Barcelona: Generalitat de Catalunya.

Roberts, J. V., & White, N. R. (1986). Public estimates of recidivism rates: Consequences of a criminal stereotype. *Revue Canadienne de Criminologie*, *28* (3), 229-241.

Rivera, J. de (1989). Introduction: Emotions and justice. *Social Justice Research*, *3* (4), 277-281.

Solomon, R. (1989). The emotions of justice. *Social Justice Research*, *3* (4), 345-374.

Law and Psychology in the Perception of Crime Seriousness: Towards a Joint Approach

David J. Main, Julian C. W. Boon, and Harry McAllister

Introduction

Crime is of central concern to us all, be it as victims, potential victims or routinely conducting our affairs in a manner adjudged by the law to be proper. In broad terms the law and legal system of a country should reflect the views of the citizens of that country, and as these views change so too should the law. Potentially this means de-criminalizing some behaviours (e.g. prostitution) and introducing new laws where necessary (e.g. speed limits). In the West in recent years, there has been increasing controversy relating to the issue of the de-criminalization of drug usage. All shades of opinion have been advanced on the subject from strictly maintaining the status quo of allowing only drugs which are already legal (e.g. alcohol), through partial de-criminalization of certain currently illegal substances (e.g. cannabis), to complete de-criminalization of all substance use.

However, while there has been no shortage of views advanced on the subject there has been little in the way of systematic psychological investigation into how drugs are perceived in relation to the law. This in turn means that anecdote aside, little is known about such things as group and regional differences in the perception of drugs and the law, and similarly almost nothing is known about how the newer drugs such as Crack and Ecstasy are perceived. Clearly systematically gathering information is very important both in formulating future policy relating to drugs and the law, and to the targeting of groups which may benefit from public education relating to drugs.

In this paper a study is presented which explores how drugs are perceived with particular reference to individual differences and how different drug offences are rated in relation to each another in terms of their perceived seriousness. The study was conducted in three British cities using undergraduate and non-undergraduate participants. In this way it was hoped to explore the consistency in the perceptions of drugs as a function of geographical location and participant characteristics.

Method

Subjects

All participants were tested in one of three locations: Leicester in England, Dundee, and Aberdeen in Scotland. A total of 163 males and 296 females from Aberdeen (females = 158, males = 105), Dundee (females = 83, males = 37) and Leicester (females = 55, males =21) participated in the study. With the exception of the Dundee sample, subjects were all university undergraduates with an average age of approximately 19 years. In Dundee the subjects were a mixture of university and technical college students (74), with an average age of 22. The sample also included a variety of non-students (46) ranging in age from 22 to 69 years, with an average age of 38 years. The overall average age for the Dundee sample was 28 years for both males and females.

Materials

As part of a larger study into the perceptions of crime, a questionnaire was developed, a section of which comprised a range of 38 diverse prototypic offences which were similar in style to those adopted by Hansel (1987) and Forgas (1980). This allowed the offences to be described in words or phrases which were readily understood by the public, rather than as precise legal definitions. The offence descriptions were presented to subjects in alphabetical order. Of critical interest to this study were the six offences relating to drugs namely the illegal substance use of Heroine, Crack, Ecstasy, Glue sniffing, and Cannabis, together with the legal substance use offence of being Drunk and Disorderly. It is important to reiterate that these offences all concern the personal use of drugs rather than pushing or selling drugs to others. Subjects were asked to rate each item on a scale from one to five in terms of what they personally felt about the crimes rather than what they felt society in general or the courts felt about the offences. As all the 38 offences to be rated were prototypic rather than specifically detailed, the following instruction was inserted as a guideline: "Of course there are different degrees of seriousness within any one crime type, but what we would like you to do is to rate for the seriousness of what you consider is the most typical instance or version of each crime type". Responses were then made by ringing one of the five numbers opposite the item e.g.:

Cannabis (illegal substance use) 1 2 3 4 5

Subjects were informed that the five points on the scale corresponded to: 1 = Relatively Trivial; 2 = Moderately Serious; 3 = Serious; 4 = Very Serious; and 5 = Extremely Serious.

Procedure

Subjects were recruited to the study on a voluntary basis by being asked whether they would take part in a study investigating people's perceptions of crime. Subjects were variously tested on an individual or group basis depending on their availability and they were assured of the complete anonymity of their responses. No time limit was imposed on completing the questionnaire although subjects were encouraged to work through the 38 items in a fluid way and not to pause unduly long on any one item. All the data were collected between February and June 1992.

Results

The three geographical areas were each analysed separately and the data were categorised on the basis of subject gender. The Dundee sample of the study (N=120) contained a total of 46 participants (15 males and 31 females) who were non-students. To examine the differences between the students and the non-students of this sample, a rank order of offences was compiled based on mean scores for the two groups. The resultant correlation of rank orders was 0.964. Two tail t-tests were then conducted between the student and non-student groups on the drug offences and none was found to be significantly different. Accordingly the student and the non-student data were merged to form a unitary Dundee sample.

For each of the three geographical areas the means for the ratings for the six critical items were calculated and then placed in rank order. As can be seen in Table 1, all the mean ratings but one (Leicester male ratings for Crack and Heroine) showed complete consistency in terms of the mean average ranking of the six crimes. Heroine illegal substance use (ISU) was rated most seriously ranging from a minimum average rating of more than "Serious" (Aberdeen males) to more than "Very Serious" (Dundee females). The next on the ranking was Crack ISU which none of the groups on average rated as being "Very Serious". Thereafter on the mean rating rankings came Ecstasy ISU which the majority of the groups rated as being less than a "Serious" crime but more than a "Moderately Serious" crime. Glue sniffing was likewise rated by all but one group - the Dundee female group who on average rated it as more than "Serious". All three male groups and one female group (Leicester) on average rated the crime of Cannabis ISU as being between "Trivial" and "Moderately Serious" while the remaining two female groups considered it to be more than "Moderately Serious". All groups on average considered the Drunk and Disorderly offence to be between "Trivial" and "Moderately Serious".

Table 1: Mean scores for Drug Offences

	Fem.	**Male**	**Sig.**
Aberdeen			
Heroine	3.646	3.238	p=0.0068 **
Crack	3.242	3.143	p=0.4913
Ecstacy	3.051	2.629	p=0.0052 **
Glue Sniffing	2.905	2.3520	p=0.0002 ***
Cannabis	2.335	1.724	p=0.0000 ***
Drunk & Disorderly	1.772	1.543	p=0.0185 *
Dundee			
Heroine	4.048	3.757	p=021
Crack	3.675	3.514	p=0.5
Ecstacy	3.373	2.838	p=0.04 *
Glue Sniffing	3.325	2.816	p=0.058 (NS)
Cannabis	2.687	1.578	p=0.0000 ***
Drunk & Disorderly	1.940	1.730	p=0.23
Leicester			
Heroine	3.491	3.300	p=0.493
Crack	3.250	3.350	p=0.695
Ecstacy	2.821	2.600	p=0.432
Glue Sniffing	2.589	2.500	p=0.767
Cannabis	1.714	1.600	p=0.646
Drunk & Disorderly	1.670	1.450	p=0.257

While there did appear to be a strong trend for females to rate the crimes as being more serious than males, subsequent *t*-testing on the basis of gender showed this to be statistically significant in only seven of the 18 cases (Aberdeen - Heroine t (261) = 2.74 , p<.01; Ecstasy t (261) = 2.83, p< .01; Glue sniffing t (261) = 3.74, p< .001; Cannabis t (261) = 4.43, p< .001; Drunk and Disorderly t (261) = 2.37, p< .05; Dundee - Ecstasy t (118) = 2.10, p< . 05; Cannabis t (118) = 5.42, p< .001). These results echo robust trends in the literature for females to tend to rate crimes as being more serious (Pease, 1988; Rossi, Waite, Bose, Berk 1974; Toseland, 1982; Wolfgang, Figlio, Tracy, & Singer, 1985) possibly reflecting the higher fear of crime expressed by women (see for example Gomme, 1986; 1988).

Discussion

This discussion will not be directed towards either supporting or opposing the de-criminalization of currently illegal drugs. Instead the main purpose will be to articulate the contribution that psychology can make in identifying corollaries stemming from deceptively complex legal issues. In so doing, it attempts to show how this could improve policy decision making, and lead to legal revisions which are responsive to, and representative of, citizen opinion.

To demonstrate this we can initially distinguish between two hypotheses which have polarised opinions in the ISU de-criminalization debate. The first could be described as the "stepping stones" view which portrays the "soft" drugs (e.g. glue sniffing and cannabis usage) as being the harbingers of usage to the harder drugs (e.g. heroine) (Krug, Sokol, & Nylander 1964; Winick, 1964). The latter hard drugs are usually characterised as being more addictive and destructive than the soft drugs by the authorities and for this reason warrant more powerful deterrents/punishments (though see Davies, 1992 for an incisive critique of the concept of addiction). The second and opposing view, is that soft drugs do not necessarily per se provide the impetus to progress to harder drugs but can be characterised as a flirtation or be maintained as a behaviour without extending further (see Krug et al., 1964 for a discussion of this).

For the stepping-stone theorists, the implications of the data presented here would seem to be very alarming. They clearly demonstrate that the soft drugs are regarded as being of lesser significance - being rated on average as being little more than "Trivial" in terms of crime seriousness. The findings also suggest that males in particular will be susceptible to this belief. To the extent that the males' perception of ISU crime seriousness can be linked with their perceptions of the drugs' harmfulness, then clearly this group could be seen as being at particular risk to long term hard drug abuse. Such findings would therefore militate for a targeted education campaign aimed at: (i) capitalising on the negative perceptions held by women especially of incompetent males who erroneously believe that they know what they are doing (Touhey, 1974); and (ii) characterising feelings of control in drug related contexts being akin to illusory fools' paradises etc.

Alternatively these data would have a very different set of conclusions for the proponents of de-criminalization of current ISU. Specifically, they show people to be highly consistent and discerning in their perception of drugs in relation to the law. From this perspective, these findings argue that if a mood for ISU de-criminalization does exist, then it is for partial de-criminalization of specific drugs such as cannabis, rather than an all encompassing blanket withdrawal of legislative jurisdiction. In the Dundee male sample cannabis ISU was rated as being no more serious than fare dodging, poll tax evasion, TV License Evasion or being drunk and disorderly ($t(36) < 1$, n.s.; $t(36) = 1.4$, n.s.; $t(36) < 1$, n.s.; $t(36) < 1$, n.s.) while in the Leicester male sample it was rated as being no more serious than parking on a yellow line or TV License Evasion ($t(19) = 1.79$, n.s.; $t(19) = 1.00$, n.s.).

While it would seem from these data the hard drugs appear to be regarded as being of sufficient seriousness as to be off-limits for reform we wish to re-iterate that, geographically speaking, these data represent only three snap shots relating to a controversial legal issue. As such they represent neither a complete nor a sufficient justification for drawing solid conclusions regarding a nation's aggregate viewpoint. A nation-wide picture would require a large-scale fully randomised study.

As noted above, it is not the prime purpose of this paper to enter the arena of the ISU de-criminalization debate, rather it is to promote awareness of the applied potential of a psychological approach and contribution to understanding people's perceptions of the law. The potential usefulness of crime seriousness studies has been remarked upon before (for examples see Corbett & Simon, 1991; Levi & Jones, 1985; Miethe, 1984) and we are not alone in calling for the regular and diverse sampling of crime seriousness to provide feedback on attitude changes (see for example Pease, 1988). A systematic and informed approach to gauging people's perceptions on legal matters can only be to the benefit of government and policy makers, both in accurately reflecting public opinion in legal decision making, and where deemed appropriate, in effectively targeting educational campaigns.

References

Corbett, C., & Simon, F. (1991). Police and public perceptions of the seriousness of traffic offences. *British Journal of Criminology*, *31*, 153-164.

Davies, J. B. (1992). *The myth of addiction: Attributional perspectives on the nature of addiction*. Reading: Harwood Academic Press.

Forgas, J. P. (1980). Images of crime: A multidimensional analysis of individual differences in crime perception. *International Journal of Psychology*, *15*, 287-299.

Gomme, I. M. (1986). Fear of crime among Canadians: A multi-variate analysis. *Journal of Criminal Justice*, *14*, 249-258.

Gomme, I. M. (1988). The role of experience in the production of fear of crime: A test of a causal model. *Canadian Journal of Criminology*, *30*, 67-76.

Hansel, M. (1987). Citizen crime stereotypes normative consensus revisited. *Criminology*, *25*, 455-485.

Krug, D. C., Sokol, J., & Nylander, I. (1964). Inhalation of commercial solvents: A form of deviance among adolescents. In E. Harms (Ed.), *Drug addiction in youth*, (pp. 36-45). Oxford: Pergamon Press.

Levi, M., & Jones, S. (1985). Public and police perceptions of crime seriousness in England and Wales. *British Journal of Criminology*, *25*, 234-250.

Miethe, T. D. (1984). Types of concensus in public evaluations of crime: An illustration of strategies for measuring consensus. *Journal of Criminal Law and Criminology*, *75*, 459-473.

Pease, K. (1988). *Judgements of crime seriousness: Findings from the 1984 British Crime Survey.* (Research and Planning Unit Paper 44). London: Home Office.

Rossi, P. H., Waite, E., Bose, C. E., & Berk, R. E. (1974). The seriousness of crimes: Normative structure and individual differences. *American Sociological Review*, *39*, 224-237.

Toseland, R. W. (1982). Fear of crime: Who is the most vulnerable? *Journal of Criminal Justice*, *10*, 199-209.

Touhey, J. C. (1974). Effects of dominance and competence on heterosexual attraction. *British Journal of Social and Clinical Psychology*, *13*, 22-26.

Winick, C. (1964). Marihuana use by young people. In E. Harms (Ed.), *Drug addiction in youth* (pp. 19-35). Oxford: Pergamon Press.

Wolfgang, M., Figlio, R. M., Tracy, P. E., & Singer, S. J. (1985). *The national survey of crime severity* (NCJ-96017). Washington, DC: U.S. Government Printing Office.

Part VI
Correlates of Offending

Deviance or Resilience? A Longitudinal Study of Adolescents in Residential Care[1]

Doris Bender, Thomas Bliesener, and Friedrich Lösel

Introduction

Developmental research on delinquent behavior has shown that the prevalence of most types of offenses increases across childhood, peaks in adolescence and early adulthood, and then decreases again in the third decade of life (Blumstein, Cohen, & Farrington, 1988; Farrington, 1992). This pattern has been confirmed in cross-sectional and longitudinal studies using both self-reports and official statistics. Delinquency can be viewed as a typical problem behavior in male adolescents and, to some extent, it can be interpreted as an expression of the attempt to cope with the demands of this phase of development (Jessor, 1987; Lösel & Bender, 1991). However, the phenomenon of transitional delinquency cannot hide the fact that some juvenile delinquents develop into relatively persistent criminals who continue to commit a great number of offenses over time (Farrington & West, 1990; Wolfgang, Figlio, & Sellin, 1972).

With respect to the conditions underlying persistent and serious juvenile delinquency, a number of consistent findings from a variety of countries particularly point to social influences of the background milieu, e.g., parents' childrearing behavior, such as poor supervision or monitoring, erratic or harsh parental discipline, parental rejection, parental discord, and so forth (Farrington, 1989, 1990; Loeber & Stouthamer-Loeber, 1986).

Besides identifying risk factors increasing interest in research has focused on developmental causes and has revealed that juvenile delinquency is frequently preceded by antisocial behaviors that can manifest in various ways at different ages (Bell, 1986; Farrington, Loeber, & Van Kammen, 1990; Loeber & Stouthamer-Loeber, 1987). Furthermore, "developmental paths" have been identified for specific types of juvenile delinquency (Loeber, 1990). These include, for example, an aggressive/versatile path, an nonaggressive path, and an exclusive substance abuse path (see Chaiken & Chaiken, 1984; Loeber, 1988; McCord, 1981). The ways in which these developmental paths differ include when problematic behavior is first exhibited and how far it is accompanied by aggressiveness, attention problems, poor relationships to peers and adults, troublesome behavior at school, school dropout, and drug usage (Kelso & Stewart, 1986; Loeber, 1982; Werner, 1990; Wolfgang, 1985).

As well as describing typical courses of delinquent behavior (see, also, Peterson, 1982; Robins, 1978), atypical courses have also been studied (Rutter & Giller, 1984). These are particularly (a) delinquent adolescents from low risk backgrounds and (b) adolescents from high risk backgrounds who do not have a criminal record. A closer inspection of the latter group reveals that some non-delinquents also exhibited impairments that could be diagnosed as internalizing disorders (see Achenbach & Edelbrock, 1983; Garmezy & Streitman, 1974). They exhibited, for example, social isolation and, at a later age, a high divorce rate. Others were nervous, withdrawn, and unmarried.

However, a substantial part of the risk group has coped with life without developing serious emotional and behavioral problems. Risk research on delinquency has only begun to focus on these relatively "unpredictable" and "inexplicable" outcomes in recent years, although they are particularly interesting from a preventive perspective. This focus of research is embedded in a general trend within developmental psychopathology in the last decade. In general, this phenomena of increasing interest in research is defined as the ability of an individual to cope successfully with and adapt to aversive life conditions or life events. It is described with terms such as resilience, stress resistance, invulnerability, buffering and so forth (e.g., Anthony, 1987; Block & Block, 1980; Cohler, 1987; Felsman & Vaillant, 1987; Garmezy, 1985, 1987; Masten, 1989; Masten, Best, & Garmezy, 1990; Rutter, 1985, 1990; Werner, 1989; Werner & Smith, 1982). Well-designed cross-sectional and longitudinal studies have contributed to the understanding of factors and mechanisms involved in these positive outcomes. However, our knowledge on resilience in delinquency-prone contexts is still sparse. Part of the resilience studies were performed in only middle deprived milieus and addressed coping with single, critical life events or specific psychiatric family problems. Studies in the high-stress multi-problem milieu, which is responsible for persistent delinquency and other severe disorders, are rare. Only a few have specifically investigated factors that protect against antisocial and delinquent behavior (e.g., Pulkkinen, 1988; Werner, 1990). Studies on criminality have paid particular attention to single variables such as intelligence as a protective factor (see Kandel et al., 1988; White, Moffit, & Silva, 1989).

These and other research orientations form the background for our Bielefeld-Erlangen Study on Resilience (e.g. Lösel & Bliesener, 1990; Lösel, Bliesener, & Köferl, 1989). The main goals of our project are: (1) to study resilience in adolescence under conditions of a particularly high risk of developing disorders (multi-problem milieu); (2) to investigate resilience also outside the family context; (3) to study heterogeneous protective factors simultaneously and integratively; (4) to test the consistency of findings by multiple group definitions and operationalizations; and (5) to estimate the stability of findings during adolescence.

We proceed from a concept of resilience that views personal and social resources as protective factors. In the sense of Rutter's (1985) moderator concept, a factor should only be considered as protective if it differentiates between persons who face a comparatively high risk of psychological disorder, but, in one case, become deviant, while, in the other case, they remain healthy. Protective factors may operate through both direct and indirect effects. Resilience results from complex nature-nurture interactions and is not conceived as a fixed quality but can vary across time and circumstances.

Our theoretical approach is oriented toward the balance models proposed e.g. by Werner and Smith (1982), Pickenhain (1989) and others. According to Werner and Smith it is the balance between (a) biological risk factors and stressful life events that heightens children's vulnerability, and (b) the protective factors in their lives that enhance their resiliency. As long as the balance between stressors and protective factors is manageable, an individual can cope successfully. Behavioral or emotional disorders may result from changes in both domains. Those concepts agree with the findings that it is not individual, critical life events or short-term stressors that markedly increase the risk of disorder but only accumulated and long-lasting stressors and strains (Coyne & Downey, 1991; Thomas & Chess, 1984).

To specify the content, we have not chosen special resilience constructs such as "hardiness" (Kobasa & Puccetti, 1983) or "sense of coherence" (Antonovsky, 1987), although we have taken aspects of these constructs into account. Instead we are more concerned with those personal and social resources that have previously proved to be protective in different research contexts. According to Rutter (1985, 1990), Garmezy (1985), Werner (1985, 1989), Cohler (1987), Masten (1989), Masten et al. (1990) and others this probably includes: (a) the way in which the individual deals with stressors, particularly actively trying to cope; (b) cognitive competences (e.g. an at least average level of intelligence); (c) experiences of self-efficacy and corresponding self-confidence; (d) temperament characteristics that favor effective coping (e.g flexibility, approach orientation); (e) stable emotional relationships with at least one parent or other reference person; (f) open supportive educational climate that encourages constructive coping; (g) social support from outside the family.

In the following we present a comparison of our cross-sectional and longitudinal findings on a selection of personal and social resources. It is tested whether they are able to function as protective factors in the very riskful background of a multi-problem milieu and the setting of social welfare institutions.

Method

Sample

We chose adolescents from residential institutions as our target groups. According to a great number of empirical findings, such persons are particularly faced with a high risk of developing long-term behavioral and emotional problems, particularly delinquency. They frequently come from very stressful, underprivileged, multi-problem milieus with poverty, childrearing deficits, problems with alcohol and violence, divorce, unmarried mothers, and so forth.

In our sampling procedure, we contacted 60 residential institutions for adolescents in North-West Germany. In order to be as close as possible to everyday life in our assessment of resilience phenomena, we chose a "naturalistic" approach. The educators or social workers were given a detailed explanation of the concept of resilience. If they thought that suitable cases were present in their residential home, these adolescents were then discussed in a case conference. Resilient adolescents could be named in 27 residential homes. In this way we were able to obtain 66 adolescents aged between 14 and 17 for the group of resilients. The comparison group was a sample of 80 adolescents who were diagnosed by the educators as having developed especially marked behavioral disorders while having been exposed to an equally high risk load. Entries in the home records revealed that the majority of these adolescents had already committed offenses before being sent to the homes and also during their residence there. The average age of the resilients (R) was 15.5 years, that of the deviants (D) was 15.7 years. The ratio of boys to girls was 3:2.

Instruments

In the first wave of data collection, we used semi-structured interviews, standardized questionnaires and tests. Four domains of variables were assessed in the adolescents: (a) biographical risk load; (b) problem behavior; (c) personal resources; and (d) social resources. To obtain additional information, we also gave interviews and questionnaires to the educators. The major instruments are sketched briefly in the following.

Risk load The index consisted of 71 items dealing with stressful life events and circumstances like deaths, divorces and separations, problems in setting up the family, changes in the place of residence and school, parental unemployment and financial problems, time spent in residential institutions and hospitals, experiences with extreme parental childrearing, marital conflicts, drug and alcohol abuse in the family, and so forth. Each item's significance as a risk factor was rated by six experts, and the items were summated to form our risk index.

Problem behavior In order to obtain a more detailed assessment of the criterion of resilience - mental health instead of behavioral and emotional problems - we adapted the various versions of the Child Behavior Checklist (CBCL) from Achenbach and Edelbrock (1983, 1986, 1987; see Lösel, Bliesener, & Köferl, 1991). We used our adaptations of the Teacher's Report Form (TRF) for the educators and the Youth Self Report (YSR) to obtain a more precise assessment than the naturalistic group diagnosis.

Personal resources (a) Intelligence. We used a short form of the Prüfsystem für Schul- und Bildungs-beratung (PSB; Horn, 1969). This instrument assesses Verbal Intelligence, Reasoning and the Technical/Spatial factor.

(b) Temperament. We adapted the Revised Dimensions of Temperament Survey (DOTS-R; Windle, Hooker, Lenerz, Easter, Lerner, & Lerner, 1986; Windle & Lerner, 1986) with the scales Approach/Avoidance, Rigidity/Flexibility, and Task Orientation.

(c) Coping style. We used a short version of Seiffge-Krenke's (1984, 1989) Coping Questionnaire containing the three scales Active Problem Solving, Internal Coping Strategies, and Problem-Avoiding Behavior.

(d) Self-esteem. We used the scale on Self-esteem from Hörmann's (1986) German adaption of Marsh and O'Neill's (1984) Self-Description Questionnaire (SDQ).

(e) Achievement orientation. We used the Achievement Orientation Scale from the Mehrdimensionaler Persönlichkeitstest für Jugendliche (MPT-J; Schmidt, 1981).

(f) Self-efficacy and helplessness. We used the Self-efficacy and Helplessness Scales from Jerusalem and Schwarzer (1986).

Social resources (a) Social support. We developed a semi-structured instrument that uses ten problem situations to assess various types of social support (material, emotional, evaluative, and informative support). In addition, the support givers were named and the frequency and quality of the support provided was rated (see Bliesener, 1991). These reports were used to determine reliable indices of frequency of social support, netsize and satisfaction with support.
(b) Social climate. We assessed the perceived social climate in the direct environment with the Familiendiagnostisches Testsystem from Schneewind, Beckmann and Hecht-Jackl (1985). This is based on the scales of Moos and Moos (1981). These scales were subjected to factor analysis. Two factors could be extracted. The first factor (33% of variance) correspond to the socio-emotional dimension (see Schneewind et al., 1985) of educational climate with the marker variables Cohesion (.83), Openness (.74), Tendency for Conflict (-.76) and Autonomy (.58). The second factor (18% of variance) marked the dimension of norm orientation and supervision with the scales Achievement Orientation (.66), Religious Orientation (.63), and Control (.56). The instructions were adapted for the situation in a residential home.
(c) Social relationships in family and non-family domains. The adolescents' reports on their biography and their current life conditions were assessed in a semi-structured interview. It also contained questions on the adolescents' relationships to their families, to the residential home, and to school.

We used some of these instruments along with others to perform a second wave of data collection two years later. Because of legislation on the protection of individual data, contact could only be made through the residential institutions. This led to extensive search procedures. We were able to regain contact with 114 adolescents, 101 of whom had taken part in two investigations of about five hours duration. The remaining adolescents had either moved away without leaving an address, had run away from the institution, or refused to participate.

Results

The naturalistic group diagnoses proved to be sufficiently valid (see Bliesener & Lösel, 1992). The resilient (R) and the deviant (D) group had a similar risk load, and the resilients' scores were even somewhat higher (R: M=29.03, SD=14.96; D: M=27.10, SD=14.39; p=ns). Both groups were highly at risk when compared to a "normal sample" of 628 school students (M=10.28, SD=8.75, $p \leq .001$; see Lösel et al., 1991). Their mean score was close to the 90th percentile of the normal sample's distribution. In the Achenbach scales (the YSR and TRF) the D group's scores were about one standard deviation higher in the externalizing syndrome (aggression and delinquency scales) than the scores of the resilient group. The difference in the internalizing score was much lower (but significant). This indicates that we are mainly dealing with conduct disorders. However, there are more heterogenous multiple disorders as well.

Table 1: Mean comparison of Personal and Social Resources for the Resilient (R) and Deviant (D) Adolescents at Wave 1 and Wave 2 (d-indices)

		Wave 1 (37/46)			**Wave 2 (18/19)**		
	Expected direction R:D	**Empirical direction R:D**	**d**	**p**	**Empirical direction R:D**	**d**	**p**
Personal resources							
Intelligence							
Verbal	>	>	.18		>	.10	
Reasoning	>	>	.10		>	.14	
Technical/Spatial	>	>	.49	*	>	.43	
Temperament							
Approach orientation	>	>	.43	*	>	.28	
Flexibility	>	>	.68	***	>	.61	*
Task orientation	>	>	.18		>	.52	
Coping style							
Active problem solving	>	>	.49	*	>	.75	*
Internal management	>	>	.18		>	.06	
Problem avoiding	<	<	.52	*	<	.32	
Self-related cognitions							
Achievement orientation	>	>	.20		>	.41	
Self esteem	>	>	.54	**	>	.47	
Self efficacy	>	>	.20		>	.02	
Helplessness	<	<	.75	***	<	.70	*
Mean *d* (corrected for direction)			.38			.37	
Social resources							
Social support							
Frequency	>	>	.08		>	.02	
Netsize	>	>	.24		>	.02	
Satisfaction	>	>	.61	***	>	.80	*
Social climate							
Socio-emotional orientation	>	>	.80	***	>	1.19	***
Norm orientation	>	>	.35		>	.80	*
Mean *d* (corrected for direction)			.42			.57	

* $p(t) \le 0.5$ ** $p(t) \le 0.1$ *** $p(t) \le .005$.

The naturalistic group diagnosis was used as a basis to test how far the variables that were assumed to be protective factors actually differentiated between the resilients and the deviants. But we also tested the consistence of findings across different operationalizations of resilience by using a multiple gating procedure (Loeber, Dishion, & Patterson, 1984). This contained three, increasingly stricter definitions of the resilient and deviant groups: (1) naturalistic diagnosis; (2) naturalistic diagnosis validated by the YSR; (3) naturalistic diagnosis validated by the YSR and TRF, and

(4) groups matched for age and gender (see Bliesener, Köferl, & Lösel, 1990; Bliesener & Lösel, 1992; Lösel & Bliesener, 1990; Lösel, Bliesener, & Köferl, 1990; Lösel et al., 1989; Lösel, Kolip, & Bender, 1992). The group definition was also of fundamental importance when analyzing our second wave of measurement. We used the following procedure. On the basis of the naturalistic group definition in the first wave, adolescents were only retained in the resilient group for whom (a) recent psychiatric or legal data from case analyses did not indicate any serious problem behavior, and (b) the scores on all YSR scales did not indicate any deviance at the second measurement timepoint (scores below the 85th percentile on all scales). In the deviant group, at least one scale on the broadband syndrome (externalizing and internalizing scale) had to score above the 85th percentile.

A selection of our *cross-sectional findings* of quantitative instruments and interview data are presented in Table 1 and Table 2. Groups were defined according to the "naturalistic group definition" validated by the YSR. For simplicity of presentation, group differences obtained with t-tests and χ^2-tests are presented as Cohen's (1988) d-indices. The d-index of effect size expresses the difference between group means in units of the standard deviation in the population. This standardization permits direct comparisons of effect sizes with differently scaled features.

In all variables of the quantitative instruments (Table 1, left), the mean differences take the anticipated direction. Among the personal resources, the resilients are better in the technical/spatial factor of intelligence, they are much more flexible in temperament and more approach-oriented, had a more positive self-esteem, considered themselves to be less helpless and had a more active and less avoiding approach to problem solving in their coping style than the deviants. Among the social resources, the resilients reported much more satisfaction with the social support they received and they described the climate in the residential institutions as being more socio-emotional oriented, that is, characterized by cohesion, openness, autonomy, and low tendency for conflict. Comparing the corrected mean effect sizes (d-indices) the figures show nearly equal effect sizes for the group differences on personal versus social resources.

The variables of the interview data that are assumed to be protective factors within and outside the family are presented in Table 2 (left).

Anticipated differences were found, for example, regarding the presence of a reference person in addition to the family care-giver. Resilients evaluate the relationship to their mother less positive and have less contact with their father. They identify more strongly with the school: they have a better relationship to school, have a higher grade secondary education, and are more satisfied with their school performance. They name fewer friends at the institutions and they have a more realistic estimation of their vocational and private future.

The *longitudinal findings* are presented in Table 1 and 2 (righthand columns). Comparing the findings of the quantitative instruments to the cross-sectional data (see Table 1) in all variables, the mean differences take the same direction as in the first wave. Groups were defined with the naturalistic group definition validated by the YSR at the first and second wave. The following considers only longitudinally stable resilients and deviants.

Table 2: Differences Between Resilient (R) and Deviant (D) Adolescents in Interview Data at Wave 1 and Wave 2 (Percentages and d-indices)

Variables	Wave 1 (37/46) R:D	d	p[a]	Wave 2 (18/19) R:D	d	p[a]
Family domain						
Positive evaluation of relation to mother[b]	64/89	.61	*	71/77	.14	
Contact with mother (more than 1/month)[b]	60/48	.26		53/53	.00	
Mother with chronic physical disease	28/20	.20		29/11	.50	
Positive evaluation of relation to father[b]	69/75	.12		75/73	.06	
Contact with father (more than 1/month)[b]	26/43	.37	*	29/44	.32	
Father with chronic physical disease	47/26	.45		47/16	.72	*
Handicapped person in family	30/15	.37		22/11	.32	
Care of relatives	24/24	.01		17/32	.35	
Positive evaluation of family compared to institution	22/35	.28		33/21	.28	
Non-family domain						
Reference person outside core family	87/59	.65	**	94/58	.95	**
Second reference person outside core family	30/22	.18		33/11	.58	
Positive evaluation of institution compared to family	38/20	.41		39/21	.41	
Naming of 1-2 friends at institution	41/74	.72	**	44/74	.63	
Higher grade secondary education	30/4	.75	**	39/5	.90	*
Good relationship to school[b]	86/56	.70	**	94/58	.93	*
Satisfaction with school performance[b]	89/62	.63	**	89/58	.75	*
Taking on official posts at school	30/20	.22		33/21	.28	
Naming of 1-2 friends at school	70/59	.24		67/58	.18	
Creation of a private sphere within institution	71/59	.26		81/59	.52	
Realistic view of occupational future	91/67	.58	*	80/67	.30	
Realistic view of private future[b]	76/42	.72	**	88/41	1.12	**

Note: [a]χ^2 tests, $df=1$ $^*p \leq 0.5$ $^{**}p \leq 0.1$.
Note: [b] Dichotomized variables of originally rank or interval scaled measures.

Across the two measurement times the effect sizes (d-indices) of several resilience characteristics remain remarkably stable. For example, resilients have a more flexible temperament, feel themselves less helpless, and take a more active approach to solving their problems. The d-indices on intelligence differences, approach oriented temperament, and problem-avoiding coping style are weaker and no longer discriminate significantly between groups. Among social resources, there are good predictor effects in satisfaction with social support and as in the cross-sectional comparison we find a strong and significant effect size for a socio-emotional oriented social climate. In contrast to the cross-sectional data, there is also a comparable predictor effect of a norm oriented social climate.

The differences in the interview variables (see Table 2) correspond well with the picture obtained with quantitative variables. The direction and magnitude of effect sizes retain a certain stability. In the non-family domain most differences even become higher. For example, the existence of a reliable reference person outside the family, higher grade secondary education, a good relationship to school, satisfying school performance and realistic private future perspectives show predictor effects over the two year interval. Differences in the evaluation of the relationship to mother and contact with father become weaker and no longer discriminate significantly between the two groups. More clearly than in the cross-sectional findings, those adolescents who had reported that they had a father with chronic physical disease at Wave 1 proved to be resilient at Wave 2.

Discussion

This study focused on identifying protective factors against antisocial behavior and delinquency in resilient adolescents from residential institutions. In line with Rutter (1985), we define protective factors as those variables that discriminate between resilient and deviant outcomes in adolescents from high risk backgrounds. Accordingly, protective factors moderate the direct negative impact of risk factors. Our study in a multi-problem milieu is targeted towards this constellation. It is unable to test whether, in contrast, factors show no differences in groups from low-risk backgrounds. It should be emphasized that our resilient adolescents are a highly selective sample with severe and, in part, long-term deprivation and stress (5% of the population of the residential homes studied). Resilience and deviance are operationalized relatively validly with multiple instruments. The basis is a dichotomous global rating performed by educators or social workers. To avoid overlooking potential internalizing problems, which are difficult for external observers to recognize, this naturalistic group definition is validated with self-ratings.

The differences between the two groups in personal and social protective factors agree with major findings and hypothesis in this field (see Garmezy, 1985; Rutter, 1990; Werner, 1989). This holds for both the cross-sectional and longitudinal perspective. In the comparison of cross-sectional and longitudinal data, fewer significant effects are found in *personal resources*. This seems to be due to the smaller sample size at Wave 2. Nonetheless, group differences are completely identical in direction. The mean protective effect size found at Wave 1 remains stable over a period of two years. This is remarkable when we consider that the retest reliability of questionnaire scales is frequently only moderate. It should be noted that several of the personality traits are already relatively stable at the ages of 14 to 17 (e.g. intelligence, temperament, achievement motivation). Thus, for example, numerous findings suggest that temperament traits, such as the greater flexibility among our resilient adolescents, depend on genetic factors (Buss & Plomin, 1984; Thomas & Chess, 1984). It is conceivable that the more active way of approaching and dealing with problems is also related to temperament traits. In addition, when forming our groups, we focused particularly on persistent deviants and stable resilients. This means that our research tends to address the aspect of stability rather than the aspect of change across development.

We find it particularly remarkable that, the differences in *social resources* not only retain completely the same direction but also that the mean effect size actually increases. The greater satisfaction of resilient adolescents with the social support they receive proves to be a good predictor of resilience two years later. However, this social support does not differ in frequency and extent from the scores of deviant adolescents. The adolescents' perspectives of the social climate in the residential home proves to have even greater predictive power. Resilients perceive the social climate in the home to be less conflictual, more open, and characterized by stronger cohesion and autonomy. This discriminating factor, which represents the quality of social relationships and the potentials for personal growth in the residential home (Moos & Moos, 1981; Schneewind et al., 1985), even shows a longitudinal increase in effect size. At the same time, the interview data reveal that resilient adolescents more frequently have a reference person outside the family. One half of these reference persons are professional educators at the residential home, about one third, relatives of the juveniles. In contrast to the cross-sectional effect, Wave 2 also shows a stronger effect on the second climate dimension. Those adolescents who had perceived the home climate two years before as not only more positive on the emotional dimension but also more structured, more norm-oriented, more achievement-oriented, and having a religious orientation remain resilient in the long-term.

As in the other variables, the increase in effect sizes is partially due to the more concise longitudinal group definition. Nonetheless, content-related reasons should also be considered. The norm- and achievement-oriented aspect may only show its protective effect on education after a delay. Adolescents from very problematic backgrounds who achieve stable resilience seem to require not only security and autonomy but also structure, control, and an orientation towards values and norms. Research has shown that deficits in norm orientation and not just in socio-emotional climate are found, for example, in the family or school milieu of delinquent or aggressive adolescents (e.g. Farrington, 1992; Olweus, 1990). This aspect should become increasingly important when there are many changes during a biography, that is, when an adolescent needs more orientation and security. Therefore, this normative aspect of education in the sense of aids to orientation may be particularly significant at Wave 2 during the many changes in the transition to the age of majority.

This is supported by the fact that our resilient adolescents cope better not only in the residential home but also in an academic context. As we know from risk research, poor academic performance and school dropout are risk factors for persistent antisocial and delinquent behavior (Farrington, 1992; Loeber, 1990). In contrast, attending a more advanced secondary school, a better relationship to the school, and greater satisfaction with academic performance predict resilience and socially adaptive behavior in our study. The present findings indicate that these differences are not due primarily to intelligence, although this seems to be a protective factor against criminality (e.g., Kandel et al., 1988; White et al., 1989). Our study shows only specific and small differences in intelligence, which, nonetheless, increase when problem behavior is assessed with the educators' ratings in the TRF (Lösel & Bliesener, 1990) instead of the YSR. Motivation factors need to be taken into account alongside ability factors. Our resilient adolescents tend to be, for example, more task- and achievement-oriented. According to social learning and control theories (see Bandura, 1979; Hirschi, 1969), good school grades gives adolescents positive reinforcement, encourage identification with the academic context, and contribute to socially adaptive behavior.

However, this finding also illustrates the problems involved in defining protective factors that sometimes can only appear as the opposite face of risk factors (see Lösel, in press; Masten, 1985; Rutter, 1990). Rutter's (1985) moderator function mentioned above provides an important basis for our interpretation. It is also helpful to not just view the variable statically but to pay more attention to the process that raises or lowers a risk. This removes the need to discriminate in general terms between "positive" and "negative" factors in the sense of protective and risk factors. It is the effective mechanisms in the context of other variables that is important. It is not only just that which superficially "does you good" that necessarily has a protective effect. In the field of medicine, it is sometimes the bad-tasting drug that is most effective. Hence, individual variables that are viewed as risk factors may, in low dosage, have an indirect protective effect, as found in the process underlying immunization (see Rutter, 1985; Werner, 1985). The protective effect is then adaptive changes after successfully coping with the limited (not overdosed) stress or threat (see, also, the aspect of challenge in coping with critical life events; Lazarus & Folkman, 1984).

A similar indirect protective effect is suggested, for example, in the finding that stable, resilient adolescents more frequently have a father with chronic disease. This is also a variable that can be a risk factor in research on developmental psychopathology. Its protective effect may be due to adolescents' experiences of responsibility and duties at an earlier stage. This can lead to early self-reliance and realistic attitudes as long as the stress is not too much for the child (see Werner, 1990). Our resilient adolescents' better hold on reality is also reflected in, for example, their more realistic estimation of their private future prospects.

If we try to use the results to draw a picture of stable resilient adolescents in comparison to persistent deviant adolescents from multi-problem milieus, we can summarize as follows. Resilient adolescents perceive themselves as being less helpless, have a more positive self-image, and try to cope with their problems more actively. They have accepted the residential home situation better. A flexible temperament makes it easier for them to adapt. They have a reference person outside the family (often in the residential home), and are satisfied with the support they receive. They perceive the climate in the home as warm, open, and developmentally stimulating, as well as being structured, achievement-oriented, and oriented towards norms and values. They are contented with their academic performance, have a good relationship with the school, and a realistic estimation of what they can personally achieve in the coming years.

The changes in the size of some of the effects when we move from the cross-sectional to the longitudinal perspective may not be due only to reliability problems of instruments or to delayed protective effects of factors. For example, extreme cases in the sample are also subject to selection effects. Very positive cases of resilience have sometimes moved far away and are mastering their own lives, while some extremely troublesome and delinquent adolescents have run away from the residential home and cannot be contacted. Furthermore, changes in the life context need to be taken into account. For example, effect sizes in the interview data suggest that the non-family domain gains in importance the greater the temporal distance to the family of origin.

The fact that the prospective longitudinal study produces similar findings to the cross-sectional study naturally does not permit causal interpretations in the strictest sense. However, it qualifies one of the main criticisms addressed to cross-sectional results in such studies; that differences in protective factors are only correlates or consequences of problem behavior in deviants (see Lösel & Bliesener, in press; Luthar & Zigler, 1991). Even longitudinal correlation designs, cannot test this strictly. However, the more process-oriented integration of our findings reveal mechanisms of protective factors that are of theoretical and practical importance. We anticipate more information from the analysis of non-stable resilients and deviants as well as from further waves of measurement.

References

Achenbach, T. M., & Edelbrock, C. (1983). *Manual for the Child Behavior Checklist and Revised Child Behavior Profile*. Burlington, VT: University of Vermont.

Achenbach, T. M., & Edelbrock, C. (1986). *Manual for the Teacher's Report Form and Teacher Version of the Child Behavior Profile*. Burlington, VT: University of Vermont.

Achenbach, T. M., & Edelbrock, C. (1987). *Manual for the Youth Self Report Profile*. Burlington, VT: University of Vermont.

Anthony, E. J. (1987). Children at high risk for psychosis growing up successfully. In E. J. Anthony & B. J. Cohler (Eds.), *The invulnerable child* (pp. 145-184). New York: Guildford Press.

Antonovsky, A. (1987). *Unravelling the mystery of health: How people manage stress and stay well*. San Francisco: Jossey-Bass.

Bandura, A. (1979). The social learning perspective: Mechanisms of aggression. In H. Toch (Ed.), *Psychology of crime and criminal justice* (pp. 198-236). New York: Prentice Hall.

Bell, R. O. (1986). Age-specific manifestations in changing psychosocial risk. In D. C. Rarran & J. D. McKinney (Eds.), *Risk in intellectual and psychosocial development* (pp. 169-185). Orlando, FL: Academic Press.

Bliesener, T. (1991). Soziale Unterstützung im Jugendalter: Konstruktion und Validierung eines Instruments zu ihrer Erfassung. *Psychologische Beiträge*, *33*, 1-29.

Bliesener, T., & Lösel F. (1992). Resilience in juveniles with high risk of delinquency. In F. Lösel, D. Bender, & T. Bliesener (Eds.), *Psychology and law. International perspectives* (pp. 62-75). Berlin, New York: De Gruyter.

Bliesener, T., Köferl, P., & Lösel, F. (1990). Protektive Faktoren bei Jugendlichen aus "Multi-Problem-Milieus" mit hohem Risiko der Delinqenzentwicklung. In S. Höfling & W. Butollo (Eds.), *Psychologie für Menschenwürde und Lebensqualität*, Bd. 3 (S. 80-93). Bonn: Deutscher Psychologen Verlag.

Block, J. H., & Block, J. (1980). The role of ego-control and ego-resiliency in the organization of behavior. In W. A. Collins (Ed.), *The Minnesota symposia on child psychology: Vol. 13. Development of cognition, affect, and social relationships* (pp. 39-101). Hillsdale, NJ: Erlbaum.

Blumstein, A., Cohen, J., & Farrington, D. P. (1988). Criminal career research: Its value for criminology. *Criminology*, *26*, 1-35.

Buss, A., & Plomin, R. (1984). *Temperament: Early developing personality traits*. Hillsdale, NJ: Erlbaum.

Chaiken, M. R., & Chaiken, J. M. (1984). Offender types and public policy. *Crime and Delinquency*, *30*, 195-226.

Cohen, J. (1988). *Statistical power analysis for the behavior sciences* (2nd ed.). Hillsdale, NJ: Erlbaum.

Cohler, B. J. (1987). Adversity, resilience, and the study of lives. In E. J. Anthony & B. J. Cohler (Eds.), *The invulnerable child* (pp. 363-404). New York: Guildford Press.

Coyne, J. C., & Downey, G. (1991). Social factors and psychopathology: Stress, social support, and coping processes. *Annual Review of Psychology*, *16*, 401-425.

Farrington, D. P. (1989). Long-term prediction of offending and other life outcomes. In H. Wegener, F. Lösel, & J. Haisch (Eds.), *Criminal behavior and the justice system: Psychological perspectives* (pp. 26-39). New York: Springer.

Farrington, D. P. (1990). Implications of criminal career research for the prevention of offending. *Journal of Adolescence, 13*, 93-113.

Farrington, D. P. (1992). Psychological contributions to the explanation, prevention, and treatment of offending. In F. Lösel, D. Bender, & T. Bliesener (Eds.), *Psychology and law. International perspectives* (pp. 35-51). Berlin, New York: De Gruyter.

Farrington, D. P., Loeber, R., & Van Kammen, W. B. (1990). Long-term criminal outcomes of hyperactivity-impulsivity-attention deficit and conduct problems in childhood. In L. N. Robins & M. R. Rutter (Eds.), *Straight and devious paths to adulthood* (pp. 62-81). New York: Cambridge University Press.

Farrington, D. P., & West, D. J. (1990). The Cambridge study in delinquent development: A long-term follow-up of 411 London males. In H. J. Kerner & G. Kaiser (Eds.), *Criminality: Personality, behavior, and life history* (pp. 115-138). Berlin: Springer.

Felsman, J. K., & Valliant, G. E. (1987). Resilient children as adults: A 40-year study. In E. J. Anthony & B. J. Cohler (Eds.), *The invulnerable child* (pp. 289-314). New York: Guildford Press.

Garmezy, N. (1985). Stress resistant children: The search for protective factors. In J. E. Stevenson (Ed.), *Recent research in developmental psychopathology. Journal of Child Psychology and Psychiatry, Book Supplement No. 4* (pp. 213-233). Oxford: Pergamon Press.

Garmezy, N. (1987). Stress, competence, and development: Continuities in the study of schizophrenic adults, children vulnerable to psychopathology, and the search for stress-resistant children. *American Journal of Orthopsychiatry, 57*, 159-174.

Garmezy, N., & Streitman, S. (1974). Children at risk: The search for the antecedents of schizophrenia. Part I: Conceptual models and research methods. *Schizophrenia Bulletin, 8*, 14-90.

Hirschi, T. (1969). *Causes of delinquency*. Berkeley: University of California Press.

Horn, W. (1969). *Prüfsystem für Schul- und Bildungsberatung - PSB*. Göttingen: Hogrefe.

Hörmann, H-J. (1986). Selbstbeschreibungsfragebogen. In R. Schwarzer (Ed.), *Skalen zur Befindlichkeit und Persönlichkeit* (pp. 47-83). FU Berlin: Forschungsbericht.

Jerusalem, M., & Schwarzer, R. (1986). "Selbstwirksamkeit" und "Hilflosigkeit" (Skalenbeschreibung). In R. Schwarzer (Ed.), *Skalen zur Befindlichkeit und Persönlichkeit* (pp. 15-42). FU Berlin: Forschungsbericht.

Jessor, R. (1987). Problem-behavior theory, psychosocial development, and adolescent problem drinking. *British Journal of Addiction, 82*, 435-446.

Kandel, E., Mednick, S. A., Kirgegaard-Sorensen, L., Hutchings, B., Knop, J., Rosenberg, R., & Schulsinger, F. (1988). IQ as a protective factor for subjects at high risk of antisocial behavior. *Journal of Consulting and Clinical Psychology, 2*, 224-226.

Kelso, J., & Stewart, M. A. (1986). Factors which predict the persistence of aggressive conduct disorder. *Journal of Child Psychology and Psychiatry, 27*, 77-86.

Kobasa, S. C., & Puccetti, M. C. (1983). Personality and social resources in stress resistance. *Journal of Personality and Social Psychology, 45*, 839-850.

Lazarus, R. S., & Folkman, S. (1984). *Stress, appraisal, and coping*. New York: Springer.

Loeber, R. (1982). The stability of antisocial and delinquent child behavior: A review. *Child Development, 53*, 1431-1446.

Loeber, R. (1988). The natural history of juvenile conduct problems, delinquency, and associated substance use: Evidence for developmental progressions. In B. B. Lahey & A. E. Kazdin (Eds.), *Advances in clinical child psychology: Vol. 11* (pp. 73-124). New York: Plenum.

Loeber, R. (1990). Disruptive and antisocial behavior in childhood and adolescence: Development and risk factors. In K. Hurrelmann & F. Lösel (Eds.), *Health hazards in adolescence* (pp. 233-257). Berlin, New York: De Gruyter.

Loeber, R., Dishion, T. J., & Patterson, G. R. (1984). Multiple gating: A multistage assessment procedure for identifying youths at risk for delinquency. *Journal of Research in Crime and Delinquency, 21*, 7-32.

Loeber, R., & Stouthamer-Loeber, M. (1987). Prediction. In H. C. Quay (Ed.), *Handbook of juvenile delinquency* (pp. 352-382). New York: Wiley.

Lösel, F. (1994). Protective effects of social resources in adolescents at high risk for antisocial behavior. In H. J. Kerner & E. Weitekamp (Eds.), *Cross-national longitudinal research on human development and criminal behavior*, (pp. 281-301). Dordrecht: Kluwer.

Lösel, F., & Bender, D. (1991). Jugend und Gesundheit. In J. Haisch & H-P. Zeitler (Eds.), *Gesundheitspsychologie* (pp. 65-86). Heidelberg: Asanger.

Lösel, F., & Bliesener, T. (1990). Resilience in adolescence: A study on the generalizability of protective factors. In K. Hurrelmann & F. Lösel (Eds.), *Health hazards in adolescence* (pp. 299-320). Berlin, New York: De Gruyter.

Lösel, F., & Bliesener, T. (in press). Why do high-risk adolescents not develop conduct problems? A study on protective factors. *International Journal of Behavioral Development.*

Lösel, F., Bliesener, T., & Köferl, P. (1989). On the concept of "invulnerability": Evaluation and first results of the Bielefeld Project. In M. Brambring, F. Lösel. & H. Skowronek (Eds.), *Children at risk: Assessment, longitudinal research, and intervention* (pp. 186-219). Berlin, New York: De Gruyter.

Lösel, F., Bliesener, T., & Köferl, P. (1990). Psychische Gesundheit trotz Risikobelastung in der Kindheit: Untersuchungen zur "Invulnerabilität. In I. Seiffge-Krenke (Ed.), *Jahrbuch der Medizinischen Psychologie: Bd. 4. Krankheitsverarbeitung von Kindern und Jugendlichen* (pp. 103-123). Berlin: Springer.

Lösel, F., Bliesener, T., & Köferl, P. (1991). Erlebens- und Verhaltensprobleme bei Jugendlichen: Deutsche Adaptation und Kulturvergleichende Überprüfung der Youth Self-Report Form der Child Behavior Checklist. *Zeitschrift für Klinische Psychologie, 20*, 22-51.

Lösel, F., Kolip, P., & Bender, D. (1992). Stress-Resistenz im Multi-Problem-Milieu. Sind seelisch widerstandsfähige Jugendliche "Superkids"? *Zeitschrift für Klinische Psychologie, 21*, 48-63.

Luthar, S., & Zigler, E. (1991). Vulnerability and competence: A review of research on resilience in childhood. *American Journal of Orthopsychiatry, 1*, 6-22.

Marsh, H. W., & O'Neill, R. (1984). Self-description Questionnaire III: The construct validity of multidimensional self-concept ratings by late adolescents. *Journal of Educational Measurement, 21*, 153-174.

Masten, A. S. (1985). Risk, vulnerability, and protective factors in developmental psychopathology. In B. B. Lahey & A. E. Kazdin (Eds.), *Advances in clinical child psychology* (pp. 1-52). New York: Plenum.

Masten, A. S. (1989). Resilience in development: Implications of the study of successful adaptation for developmental psychopathology. In D. Cicchetti (Ed.), *The emergence of a discipline: Rochester symposium on developmental psychopathology. Vol. I* (pp. 261-294). Hillsdale, NJ: Erlbaum.

Masten, A. S., Best, K. M., & Garmezy, N. (1990). Resilience and development: Contributions from the study of children who overcome adversity. *Development and Psychopathology, 2*, 425-444.

McCord, J. (1981). Alcoholism and criminality. *Journal of Studies on Alcohol, 42*, 739-748.

Moos, R. H., & Moos, B. S. (1981). *Family Environment Scale Manual.* Palo Alto: Consulting Psychologists Press.

Olweus, D. (1990). Bullying among school children. In K. Hurrelmann & F. Lösel (Eds.), *Health hazards in adolescence* (pp. 259-298). Berlin, New York: De Gruyter.

Patterson, G. R. (1982). *Coercive family process*. Eugene, OR: Castalia.

Pickenhain, L. (1989). *The range of disturbance of higher nervous functions in man understood by synergetic principles*. Paper presented at the First International Conference on Higher Nervous Functions, Osaka, Japan.

Pulkkinen, L. (1988). Delinquent development: Theoretical and empirical considerations. In M. Rutter (Ed.), *Studies of psychosocial risk: The power of longitudinal data* (pp. 184-199). Cambridge: Cambridge University Press.

Robins, L. N. (1978). Sturdy childhood predictors of adult antisocial behavior: Replications from longitudinal studies. *Psychological Medicine*, *8*, 611-622.

Rutter, M. (1985). Resilience in the face of adversity. Protective factors and resistance to psychiatric disorder. *British Journal of Psychiatry*, *147*, 598-611.

Rutter, M. (1990). Psychological resilience and protective mechanisms. In J. Rolf, A. S. Masten, D. Cicchetti, K. H. Nuechterlein, & S. Weintraub (Eds.), *Risk and protective factors in the development of psychopathology* (pp. 181-214). New York: Cambridge University Press.

Rutter, M., & Giller, H. (1984). *Juvenile delinquency: Trends and perspectives*. New York: Guilford Press.

Schmidt, H. (1981). *Mehrdimensionaler Persönlichkeitstest für Jugendliche (MPT-J)*. Braunschweig: Westermann.

Schneewind, K. A., Beckmann, M., & Hecht-Jackl, A. (1985). *Das Familienklima - Testsystem*. Universität München: Forschungsbericht Nr. 8.1.

Seiffge-Krenke, I. (1984). *Problembewältigung im Jugendalter*. Habilitationsschrift. Universität Giessen.

Seiffge-Krenke, I. (1989). Die Bewältigung alltäglicher Problemsituationen: Ein Coping-Fragebogen für Jugendliche. *Zeitschrift für Differentielle und Diagnostische Psychologie*, *21*, 210-220.

Thomas, A., & Chess, S. (1984). Genesis and evolution of behavioral disorders: From infancy to early adult life. *American Journal of Psychiatry*, *141*, 1-9.

Werner, E. E. (1985). Vulnerability and resiliency: A longitudinal perspective. In M. Brambring, F. Lösel, & H. Skowronek (Eds.), *Children at risk: Assessment, longitudinal research, and intervention* (pp. 157-172). Berlin, New York: De Gruyter.

Werner, E. E. (1990). Protective factors and individual resilience. In S. J. Meisel & R. Shonkoff (Eds.), *Handbook of early childhood intervention* (pp. 97-116). New York: Cambridge University Press.

Werner, E. E., & Smith, R. S. (1982). *Vulnerable but invincible*. New York: McGraw-Hill.

White, J., Moffitt, T., & Silva, P. A. (1989). A prospective replication of the protective effects of IQ in subjects at high risk for juvenile delinquency. *Journal of Consulting and Clinical Psychology*, *6*, 719-724.

Windle, M., Hooker, K., Lenerz, K., East, P. L., Lerner, J. V., & Lerner, R. M. (1986). Temperament, perceived competence, and depression in early- and late-adolescents. *Developmental Psychology*, *22*, 384-392.

Windle, M., & Lerner, R. M. (1986). Reassessing the dimensions of temperamental individuality across the life span: The Revised Dimensions of Temperament Survey (DOTS-R). *Journal of Adolescent Research*, *1*, 213-230.

Wolfgang, M. E. (1985). From boy to man - from delinquency to crime. In S. Mednick, M. Harway, & M. Finnelo (Eds.), *Handbook of longitudinal research*. New York: Praeger.

Wolfgang, M. E., Figlio, R. M., & Sellin, T. (1972). *Delinquency in a birth cohort*. Chicago: University of Chicago Press.

[1] This research was funded by the German Research Council (Deutsche Forschungsgemeinschaft) at the Research Center "Prevention and Intervention in Childhood and Adolescence", University of Bielefeld, Germany.

Psychosocial Influences on the Development of Antisocial Personality

David P. Farrington

Antisocial Personality

Robins (e.g. 1986) has consistently shown how a constellation of indicators of childhood antisocial behaviour predicts a constellation of indicators of adult antisocial behaviour. The childhood indicators include illegal acts such as stealing and vandalism, resistance to authority, physical aggression, impulsivity, precocious drinking and sexual behaviour, running away from home, truanting from school, lying and cruelty to animals. The adult indicators include crime and violence, excessive drinking, a poor employment record, marital break-ups, child neglect, reckless driving and failure to pay debts. In several longitudinal studies, Robins showed that the number of childhood symptoms predicted the number of adult symptoms, rather than any specific childhood factor predicting a specific adult factor (Robins & Ratcliff, 1978, 1980; Robins & Wish, 1977).

Robins' research had an important influence on the classification of childhood conduct disorder and adult antisocial personality disorder in the *Diagnostic and statistical manual* (DSM-IIIR) of the American Psychiatric Association (1987). Each of these is defined according to explicit diagnostic criteria. *Conduct disorder* is diagnosed when a child's disturbed behaviour persists for at least six months and includes at least three of the following elements:

(1) has stolen (without confronting the victim) more than once;
(2) has run away from home overnight more than once;
(3) often lies;
(4) has deliberately engaged in fire-setting;
(5) often truants;
(6) has broken into buildings or cars;
(7) has destroyed other people's property;
(8) has been cruel to animals;
(9) has forced someone into sexual activity;
(10) has used a weapon in more than one fight;
(11) often starts physical fights;
(12) has stolen while confronting the victim;
(13) has been cruel to people.

According to DSM-IIIR, about 9% of American males under age 18 show conduct disorder. In Canada, the prevalence was 7% for males aged four-11 and 10% for males aged 12-16 in a large-scale epidemiological survey (Offord et al., 1986).

Antisocial personality disorder is diagnosed when an adult aged 18 or over displays at least four of the following symptoms:

(1) has an unstable employment history, including unemployment for six months or more within five years;
(2) has repeatedly committed crimes such as stealing and vandalism;
(3) has repeatedly been involved in physical fights, including violence to a spouse or child;
(4) repeatedly defaults on debts or fails to support dependents;
(5) fails to plan ahead or is impulsive;
(6) repeatedly lies;
(7) drives recklessly or while drunk;
(8) if a parent, neglects children;
(9) has not sustained a totally monogamous relationship for more than one year;
(10) lacks remorse.

For the diagnosis to be given, the antisocial adult must also have shown conduct disorder before age 15. This requirement was included in DSM-IIIR because Robins' research (e.g. 1986: 228) showed that, while only about half of conduct disordered children became antisocial adults, virtually all antisocial adults had previously shown at least one symptom of childhood conduct disorder. According to DSM-IIIR, 3% of American adult males show antisocial personality disorder. However in the recent large-scale multi-site Epidemiological Catchment Area programme, Robins et al. (1991) reported that the life-time prevalence for American adult males was 7%.

Robins' conclusions about the continuity of antisocial personality have essentially held up in the Epidemiological Catchment Area programme. Looking forwards, 27% of males showing three or more childhood symptoms also showed four or more adult symptoms, and the prevalence of adult antisocial personality disorder increased to 49% for the more extreme category of males showing six or more childhood symptoms. Looking backwards, 95% of males with four or more adult symptoms had at least one childhood symptom, and 76% had three or more childhood symptoms (Robins et al., 1991).

The category of adult antisocial personality disorder is closely related to the construct of *psychopathy*. The best known psychometric measure of this latter construct is the "Psychopathy Checklist" of Hare (1980, 1986). This focuses slightly more on personality factors in comparison with DSM-IIIR, which focuses more on indicators of antisocial behaviour. The Psychopathy Checklist includes criteria such as: superficial charm or conning; an inflated ego; boredom, risk-taking and excitement-seeking; pathological lying; lack of remorse; cold, lacking emotions and lacking empathy; a parasitic lifestyle; easily becoming angry and aggressive; promiscuous sexual behaviour; child behaviour problems and delinquency; impulsivity and failure to honour financial and family commitments; failure to accept responsibility for actions; and a variety of different offences committed. Despite its slightly different emphasis, Psychopathy Checklist scores in adults are highly correlated with the diagnosis of antisocial personality disorder (e.g. a point-biserial correlation of .67 was reported by Hare, 1985). While Hare's research was carried out in Canada, Raine (1985) showed that similar results were obtained in England (with important factors of impulsivity, emotional detachment, egocentricity and superficial relationships).

Current research focuses on the extent to which psychopathy should be regarded as a unitary construct. Harpur et al. (1988, 1989) have shown that Psychopathy Checklist scores could reflect two correlated factors, one defined by personality traits such as low emotionality, guilt, remorse and empathy, and the other defined by a chronically unstable and antisocial lifestyle. Blackburn (1988) pointed out that an antisocial lifestyle may or may not reflect an antisocial personality. He has consistently distinguished between "primary" or non-anxious psychopaths and "secondary" psychopaths who show anxiety.

In Great Britain, definitions of psychopathy are more subjective than North American ones, and explicit diagnostic checklist criteria have not been developed. In the 1959 and 1983 Mental Health Acts, psychopathic disorder is defined as a persistent disorder "which results in abnormally aggressive or seriously irresponsible conduct". According to Walker (1985), British psychiatrists reserve the label of "psychopath" for persons who show unusual (e.g. sadistic) impulses, or who have unusually weak self-control, or who commit crimes without anxiety about the consequences or remorse. Davies and Feldman (1981) found that the key symptoms were: not profiting from experience, low impulse control and chronic antisociality. Generally, the concepts of psychopathy and antisocial personality seem to be measuring much the same underlying syndrome. It would be desirable for British psychiatrists to use explicit diagnostic criteria in diagnosing psychopathy or antisocial personality.

Large-scale epidemiological studies (e.g. Offord et al., 1986, 1989; Robins et al., 1991) and literature reviews (e.g. Kazdin, 1987; Robins, 1991) suggest that the most important precursors and correlates of childhood conduct disorder and adult antisocial personality disorder include: low family income, parental unemployment, poor housing, low socio-economic status, large family size, convicted parent, poor parental education, harsh or erratic parental discipline, poor parental supervision, broken home, single parent families, low intelligence, low school achievement and early school leaving. However, many of the previous studies focus only on clinic samples or only on delinquency and crime. The main aim of the present paper is to measure the antisocial personality syndrome in a general population sample at different ages from childhood (age 10) to adulthood (age 32) and to investigate its psychosocial correlates and precursors.

The Cambridge Study in Delinquent Development

The present research uses data collected in the Cambridge Study in Delinquent Development, which is a prospective longitudinal survey of the development of offending and antisocial behaviour in 411 London males. At the time they were first contacted in 1961-62, these males were all living in a working-class area of London. The sample was chosen by taking all the boys who were then aged eight to nine and on the registers of six state primary schools within a one-mile radius of a research office that had been established. Hence, the most common year of birth of these males was 1953. In nearly all cases (94%), their family breadwinner at that time (usually the father) had a working-class occupation (skilled, semi-skilled or unskilled manual worker). Most of the males were white in racial appearance and of British origin. The study was originally directed by Donald J. West, and it has been directed since 1982 by David P. Farrington, who has worked on it since 1969. The major results can be found in four books (West, 1969, 1982; West & Farrington, 1973, 1977), and in more than 60 papers listed by Farrington and West (1990).

A major aim in this survey was to measure as many factors as possible that were alleged to be causes or correlates of offending. The males were interviewed and tested in their schools when they were aged about eight, 10, and 14, by male or female psychologists. They were interviewed in a research office at about 16, 18 and 21, and in their homes at about 25 and 32, by young male social science graduates. At all ages except 21 and 25, the aim was to interview the whole sample, and it was always possible to trace and interview a high proportion: 389 out of 410 still alive at age 18 (95%) and 378 out of 403 still alive at age 32 (94%), for example. The tests in schools measured individual characteristics such as intelligence, attainment, personality, and psychomotor impulsivity, while information was collected in the interviews about such topics as living circumstances, employment histories, relationships with females, leisure activities, drinking, fighting, and offending behaviour.

In addition to interviews and tests with the males, interviews with their parents were carried out by female social workers who visited their homes. These took place about once a year from when the male was about eight until he was aged 14-15 and was in his last year of compulsory education. The primary informant was the mother, although many fathers were also seen. The parents provided details about such matters as family income, family size, their employment histories, their child-rearing practices (including attitudes, discipline, and parental discord), their degree of supervision of the boy, and his temporary or permanent separations from them. Also, when the boy was aged 12, the parents completed questionnaires about their child-rearing attitudes and about his leisure activities.

The teachers completed questionnaires when the males were aged about eight, 10, 12, and 14. These furnished data about their troublesome and aggressive school behaviour, their attention deficits, their school attainments and their truancy. Ratings were also obtained from their peers when they were in the primary schools, about such topics as their daring, dishonesty, troublesomeness and popularity.

Searches were also carried out in the central Criminal Record Office in London to try to locate findings of guilt of the males, of their parents, of their brothers and sisters, and (in recent years) of their wives and cohabitees. Convictions were only counted if they were for offences normally recorded in the Criminal Record Office, thereby excluding minor crimes such as common assault, traffic infractions and drunkenness. The most frequent offences included were thefts, burglaries and unauthorized takings of vehicles, although there were also quite a few offences of violence, vandalism, fraud and drug abuse. In order not to rely on official records for information about offending, self-reports of offending were obtained from the males at every age from 14 onwards.

For the present analyses, each variable was dichotomized, as far as possible, into the "worst" quarter of males (e.g. the quarter with lowest income or lowest intelligence) versus the remainder. This was done in order to compare the importance of different variables and also to permit a "risk factor" approach. Also, with dichotomous independent variables, it is easy to study interactions. Because most variables were originally classified into a small number of categories, and because fine distinctions between categories could not be made very accurately, this dichotomizing did not usually involve a great loss of information. The one-quarter/three-quarters split was chosen to match the prior expectation that about one-quarter of the sample would be convicted as juveniles. Variables were not included in the analysis if more than about 10% of the sample were not known on them. (For more information about all the variables discussed here, see the books on the Study listed above.)

Summarizing, the Cambridge Study in Delinquent Development has a unique combination of features. Eight face-to-face interviews have been completed with the subjects over a period of 24 years, between ages eight and 32. The attrition rate is unusually low for such a long-term survey. The main focus of interest is on crime and delinquency, but the survey also provides information about alcohol and drug abuse, educational difficulties, poverty and poor housing, unemployment, sexual behaviour, and other social problems. The sample size of about 400 is large enough for many statistical analyses, but small enough to permit detailed case histories of the males and their families. Information has been obtained from multiple sources, including the males themselves, their parents, teachers, peers, and official records. Generally, the data came from parents, teachers, peers or tests completed by the males between ages eight and 14, but primarily from interviews with the males between ages 16 and 32. Information has been collected about a wide variety of theoretical constructs at different ages, including psychological (e.g. intelligence, impulsivity), family (e.g. parental supervision and discipline), and social (e.g. income, employment) factors.

Measures of Antisocial Personality

Farrington (1991) devised scales for different ages (10, 14, 18 and 32) that were the best measures available in this project of the personality and behavioural features included in the definitions of conduct disorder, antisocial personality disorder and psychopathy. For convenience, these scales were termed "antisocial personality" (AP) scales, although they measured behaviour as well as personality. Variables were only included in a scale if they were theoretically distinct but intercorrelated, and if they seemed to reflect different components of antisocial personality. As far as possible, component variables at each age were drawn from different sources (the males, peers, mothers, teachers and records), although at ages 18 and 32 most variables were derived from interviews with the males.

Table 1 summarizes the variables included in each scale. More details about the variables measured at ages 10, 14 and 18 can be found in West and Farrington (1973, 1977), while those at age 32 have been described in detail by Farrington (1989). Most variables at age 10 were derived from teacher, peer or parent ratings, and were actually combinations of measures at ages eight and 10. The "has stolen" and "gets angry" ("I get so angry I can't talk") variables were derived from items of the New Junior Maudsley Inventory, while impulsiveness was based on scores on three psychomotor tests. The reliability of the AP scale at age 10 was .67. This is inevitably lower than in many psychological tests, because of the elimination of overlapping or redundant

Table 1: Components of Antisocial Personality Scales

Age 10	**Age 14**	**Age 18**	**Age 32**
Troublesome (T,P)	Convicted (R)	Convicted (R)	Convicted (R)
Conduct problem (M)	SR delinquency (B)	SR delinquency (B)	SR delinquency (B)
Difficult to discipline (T)	Steals outside home (M)	SR violence (B)	Involved in fights (B)
Dishonest (P)	Disobedient frequently (T)	Antisocial group (B)	Taken drug (B)
Has stolen (B)	Lies frequently (T,M)	Taken drug (B)	Heavy drinker (B)
Gets angry (B)	Bully (B)	Heavy smoker (B)	Poor relationship with parents (B)
Truant (T)	Hostile to police (B)	Heavy drinker (B)	Poor relationship with wife (B)
Daring (M,P)	Truant (T)	Drunk driver (B)	Divorced/Child elsewhere (B)
Lacks concentration/ Restless (T)	Regular smoker (B)	Irresponsible sex (B)	Unemployed frequently (B)
Impulsive (B)	Had sex (B)	Heavy gambler (B)	Anti-establishment (B)
	Daring (T)	Unstable job record (B)	Tattooed (B)
	Lacks concentration/ Restless (T)	Anti-establishment (B)	Impulsive (B)
		Tattooed (B)	

Key: R=Records, B=Boy/Man, T=Teacher, P=Peer, M=Mother, SR=Self Report.

variables. At age 10, each male was scored according to his percentage of adverse ratings out of 10. (Where a male was not known on one or more variables, the percentage was based on less than 10 items.) The "worst" quarter of the males on the AP scale at age 10 were the 98 (24%) with four or more adverse features.

At age 14, "convicted" referred to convictions between ages 10 and 14 inclusive. The teacher ratings were all combinations of measures at ages 12 and 14. "Regular smoking" referred to under age 14, while "had sex" referred to sexual intercourse by age 14. The reliability of the AP scale at age 14 was .75, and the worst quarter were the 88 males with four or more adverse features out of 12.

At age 18, "convicted" referred to convictions between ages 15 and 18 inclusive, and most self-report items referred to the same time period. Antisocial group activity included violence, vandalism and hanging about on the streets. The "drunk driver" category included motoring convictions. "Irresponsible sex" referred to having intercourse without using contraceptives (or ensuring that the girl was using contraceptives). An "unstable job record" reflected periods of unemployment, several short-lived jobs, and getting sacked. "Anti-establishment" attitudes were those negative to police, bosses, school, rich people and civil servants, while the impulsiveness measure was based on items such as "I generally do and say things quickly without stopping to think". The reliability of the AP scale at age 18 was .74, and the worst quarter were the 88 males with six or more adverse features out of 14.

At age 32, "convicted" referred to convictions between ages 27 and 32 inclusive, and most self-report items referred to the same time period. A poor relationship with a wife or cohabitee was based on either hitting her or not getting on well with her. Being divorced or separated and having a child living elsewhere were closely related, so these items were combined. Frequent unemployment meant 10 or more months unemployed in the previous five years. Drunk driving was too common at age 32 to be considered deviant (53% of drivers had driven after consuming at least five pints of beer or equivalent other amounts of alcohol), and heavy smoking and gambling were no longer associated with other measures of antisocial personality at this age. Conversely, a poor relationship with one's parents, which was not related to other measures of antisocial personality at age 18, was related at age 32. The reliability of the AP scale at age 32 was .71, and the worst quarter were the 92 males with four or more adverse features out of 12.

In accordance with the diagnostic criteria for adult antisocial personality disorder in DSM-IIIR, and with the Psychopathy Checklist, measures of impulsivity were included in the AP scales. However, impulsivity is not included in childhood conduct disorder in DSM-IIIR, but in attention deficit-hyperactivity disorder (American Psychiatric Association, 1987). Farrington et al. (1990) argued that hyperactivity-impulsivity-attention deficit and conduct disorder were differently related to early background factors and later criminal outcomes, even though they often co-occurred in the same children, and hence that they should be distinguished as different constructs. Whether impulsivity should better be regarded as an element of antisocial personality or as a risk factor is a key theoretical issue that needs to be resolved.

Similar problems arise with other components. Again in accordance with the diagnostic criteria, an unstable job record and frequent unemployment are included as components of AP scales, although it might also be argued that unemployment could cause antisocial behaviour (e.g. Farrington et al., 1986). Equally, other components, such as heavy drinking, could be indicative or causal (or even indicative and causal). In order to avoid tautological findings, indicators are not studied as risk factors. In this paper, I have followed psychiatric criteria in distinguishing between indicators of AP and risk factors, but the current psychiatric classifications may not be optimal. Longitudinal and experimental research is needed to distinguish among causes, consequences and indicators (see e.g. Farrington et al., 1986; Tonry et al., 1991).

The behavioural manifestations of antisocial personality are inevitably different at different ages. For example, a person cannot have an unstable job record at age 10 or be a frequent truant (at least from school) at age 32. However, it is interesting that the meaning of variables also seems to be different at different ages. As already mentioned, drunk driving, heavy smoking and heavy gambling were related to other indicators of (and hence presumably reflected) antisocial personality at age 18 but not at age 32.

The full AP scales at the four ages were all significantly intercorrelated (10 vs. 14, $r = .50$; 10 vs. 18, $r = .38$; 10 vs. 32, $r = .30$; 14 vs. 18, $r = .58$; 14 vs. 32, $r = .42$; 18 vs. 32, $r = .55$; all $p < .0001$). These significant intercorrelations show that the AP scores of the males stayed relatively constant over long time periods. While, as expected, the lowest correlation was between the most widely separated ages 10 and 32, the correlation between ages 18 and 32 was remarkably high, suggesting stabilization of personality over the adult ages.

When the antisocial males were defined as the worst quarter of the sample at each age, it was generally true that about half of those who were antisocial at one age were still antisocial at a later age, and conversely that about half of those who were antisocial at one age had been antisocial at an earlier age. For example, 49% of antisocial males at age 10 (48 out of 98) were still antisocial at age 14, compared with only 13% of the non-antisocial males at age 10 (40 out of 313); and 55% of antisocial males at age 14 (48 out of 88) had been antisocial at age 10, compared with only 15% of the non-antisocial males at age 14 (50 out of 323; see Farrington, 1991).

As the odds ratio (OR) is used as the main measure of the strength of relationships later in this paper, it is helpful to explain it now in connection with the relationship between AP at 10 and AP at 14. The odds of antisociality at 14 given antisociality at 10 are 48/50 or .96. The odds of antisociality at 14 given no antisociality at 10 are 40/273 or .147. Hence, the odds ratio is .96/.147 or 6.55. (Unfortunately, the OR published for this comparison in Farrington, 1991, was incorrect.) The chance value of the OR is 1, and its significance can be tested using chi-squared. In a 2x2 table, the logarithm of the odds ratio is related through a mathematical approximation to the phi correlation (and hence chi-squared), so conclusions drawn from odds ratios are likely to be essentially the same as those drawn from correlations. The OR is the most meaningful statistic, since it basically shows increases in risk associated with a risk factor. Roughly speaking, antisociality at 10 increased the risk of antisociality at 14 six times.

Up to age 32, 153 males (37%) were convicted. Possibly because convictions were especially prevalent between ages 15 and 18 (94 males being convicted during this age range), convictions were most closely related to AP at 18. As many as 83% of the 88 antisocial males at 18 were convicted up to 32, compared with only 25% of the remainder (OR = 14.93). In contrast, 62% of the 98 antisocial males at 10 were convicted, compared with 29% of the remainder (OR = 3.96); 76% of the 88 antisocial males at 14 were convicted, compared with 27% of the remainder (OR = 8.79); and 74% of the 92 antisocial males at 32 were convicted, compared with 25% of the remainder (OR = 8.58). These results reflect the considerable overlap between offending and antisocial personality.

Risk Factors for Antisocial Personality

Table 2 shows the major risk factors or predictors of the antisocial personality measures at ages 10, 14, 18 and 32 (identifying the worst quarter of the boys as antisocial at each age). Variables measured at age 8-10 are, strictly speaking, correlates of AP at age 10, but they are shown in Table 2 as possible predictors. All the other relationships shown in Table 2 are genuinely predictive, since the risk factors were measured before the AP outcomes. Ages of measurement typically extend over two years rather than one; for example, the variables measured at age eight were actually measured at age 8-9, the variables measured at age 18 were actually measured at age 18-19, and so on.

It is not unambiguously clear in all cases that the risk factors are possible causes of AP as opposed to consequences or indicators. Low family income and the education of the father beyond the minimum school leaving age clearly seem to be possible causes. However, poor parental supervision could conceivably be a consequence of having an antisocial child, if the parents give up trying to monitor and control the child in the face of his antisocial behaviour. Also, the boy's low school attainment might possibly be another indicator of his antisocial personality, to the extent that his low attainment was caused by his disruptive school behaviour. Despite these conceptual problems, all the risk factors shown in Table 2 could conceivably be explanatory factors for AP through some causal chain, and none of them directly measures any of the components of the AP scales. Hence, they will be treated here as possible explanatory factors.

Since regression analyses were planned to investigate the extent to which each risk factor predicted AP measures independently of other risk factors, highly intercorrelated risk factors were removed from the analyses. Specifically, when two risk factors had a phi correlation of .5 or greater, one of them was removed. For example, at age eight-10 low family income was retained in the analysis in preference to an erratic job record of the father, poor parental supervision in preference to physical neglect of the boy, low attainment in preference to low verbal IQ, and height in preference to weight. When risk factors at age 8-10 were highly intercorrelated with the same risk factors at age 12-14, the age 8-10 risk factors were retained in the analysis. Thus, family size, social class and height at age 14 were deleted, and family size, social class and height at age 8-10 were retained. The regression analyses were based on 28 risk factors at age 8-10, six at age 12-14, and four at age 18. There were few explanatory variables at later ages partly because most variables were arguably indicators of AP and partly because later variables were deleted in favour of earlier ones.

Table 2 shows the risk factors that were significantly related to at least one AP measure (all except church attendance of the boy, education of the mother, nervousness of the boy and nervousness of the father at 8-10, which were not related to any AP measure). For example, 23% of the boys came from low income families, and low family income at eight significantly predicted all four AP measures (e.g. OR for AP at 10 = 3.17). Negative odds ratios signify negative relationships; for example, boys with mothers who worked full-time when they were eight tended not to be antisocial. One-tailed statistical tests were used, because all predictions were directional.

The strongest correlates of AP at age 10 were poor parental supervision, low family income, a delinquent older sibling, low junior school attainment, poor parental child-rearing behaviour (a combination of harsh or erratic discipline, cruel or neglecting attitude and parental disharmony), a lack of interest in the child by the father, large family size (four or more siblings), being relatively small in height and transferring to a high delinquency rate secondary school at 11. Small height may possibly be a risk factor because of its association with poor nutrition in childhood (and hence socio-economic deprivation). The "vulnerable" measure was a combination of low family income, large family size, a convicted parent, poor parental child-rearing behaviour and low non-verbal IQ (90 or less) at 8-10 (see West & Farrington, 1973: 131). Of 63 boys possessing three or more of these adverse features, 52% (33) were antisocial, compared with only 19% of the remainder (65 out of 348; OR = 4.79, chi-squared = 31.54, $p < .0001$).

Table 2: Risk Factors for Antisocial Personality

Variable (% Identified)	Odds Ratios			
	AP10	AP14	AP18	AP32
Age 8-10				
Low family income (23)	3.17**	3.02**	3.47**	2.03*
Working mother (23)	-1.76*	-1.34	-1.35	-1.20
Poor housing (37)	1.85*	1.90*	2.04*	1.39
Low social class (19)	1.64*	1.98*	2.11*	2.06*
Large family size (24)	2.46**	1.78*	3.54**	2.52**
Father well educated (35)	-2.07*	-1.55	-2.52*	-1.12
Nervous mother (32)	1.49	1.88*	2.47**	1.26
Convicted parent (25)	2.09*	2.13*	4.79**	3.86**
Delinquent sibling (11)	3.14**	2.17*	3.55**	1.79
Behaviour problem sibling (38)	1.11	1.56	2.80**	1.71*
Poor child-rearing (24)	2.92**	2.07*	2.70**	1.29
Authoritarian parents (24)	1.74*	1.39	1.20	1.06
Poor supervision (19)	3.93**	2.04*	2.39*	2.12*
Separated (22)	1.99*	3.70**	2.38**	2.46**
Father not interested (12)	2.50*	1.48	2.72*	1.41
Uninterested in education (17)	2.09*	2.63**	2.13*	1.88*
Catholic family (21)	1.32	2.02*	1.95*	1.76*
Delinquent school (21)	2.35*	1.80*	2.61**	1.92*
Low non-verbal IQ (25)	1.76*	3.22**	2.98**	2.12*
Low attainment (23)	2.99**	3.22**	3.00**	2.47**
High neuroticism (29)	2.08*	1.78*	2.16*	1.58*
Unpopular (32)	1.52	1.16	1.33	1.64*
Few friends (12)	-1.25	-2.36*	-2.10	-1.34
Small (18)	2.41**	2.30*	1.88*	1.11
Vulnerable (15)	4.79**	4.18**	9.67**	4.03**
Antisocial (24)	–	6.55**	3.81**	2.29*
Age 12-14				
Father unemployed (11)	–	–	5.25**	4.48**
Poor child-rearing (29)	–	–	2.49**	2.08*
Father not involved (28)	–	–	2.97**	2.29*
Low non-verbal IQ (29)	–	–	2.56**	1.87*
Stayed at school (39)	–	–	-4.59**	-3.92**
High neuroticism (25)	–	–	1.93*	2.23*
Antisocial (21)	–	–	8.56**	5.81**
Age 18				
Unskilled manual job (16)	–	–	–	4.71**
No girlfriend (42)	–	–	–	-1.80*
Hospitalized for illness (14)	–	–	–	2.35*
Wears glasses (20)	–	–	–	-1.90*
Antisocial (23)	–	–	–	9.35**

*=p<.05, **=p<.001 (based on chi-squared, corrected for continuity, one-tailed test).

The strongest predictors of AP at age 14 were separation from a parent (for reasons other than death or hospitalization), low non-verbal IQ, low junior school attainment, low family income, parents who were not interested in the boy's education, not having few friends, being relatively small, a delinquent older sibling and a convicted parent. The composite "vulnerable" measure at 8-10 was a significant predictor (OR = 4.18) as was AP at 10 (OR = 6.55).

Risk factors measured at 12-14 were then added as predictors of AP at 18. The strongest predictors of AP at 18 were periodic unemployment of the father at 14, a convicted parent at 10, not staying on at school beyond the minimum school-leaving age (of 15), large family size at 10, a delinquent sibling at 10, low family income at eight, low junior school attainment, low non-verbal IQ at eight-10, and the father not being involved in the boy's leisure activities at 12. Vulnerability at 8-10 predicted AP at 18 (OR = 9.67) better than did AP at 10 (OR = 3.81) or AP at 14 (OR = 8.56).

Risk factors measured at 18 were then added as predictors of AP at 32. The strongest predictors of AP at 32 were an unskilled manual job at 18, periodic unemployment of the father at 14, not staying on at school, a convicted parent at 10, large family size at 10, low junior school attainment, separation from a parent at 10 and hospital treatment for illness at 18. AP at 18 was a better predictor of AP at 32 (OR = 9.35) than was AP at 14 (OR = 5.81), AP at 10 (OR = 2.29) or vulnerability at 8-10 (OR = 4.03).

Independently Important Risk Factors

In attempting to explain the development of antisocial personality, an important first step is to establish which risk factors were independent predictors. Two methods of investigating independent predictors were used, namely ordinary least squares (OLS) regression and logistic regression. In practice, the two methods tend to produce similar results with dichotomous data (e.g. Cleary & Angel, 1984). The main differences between them follow from the fact that missing cases can be deleted variable by variable in OLS regression (thereby using as much of the data as possible), whereas in logistic regression a case that is missing on any one variable has to be deleted from the whole analysis, causing a considerable loss of data. The most reliable predictors are those identified by both methods. The OLS regression analyses were carried out first, beginning with all significant predictors. Because they were computationally more intensive, the logistic regression analyses were then carried out second with all independent predictors identified in the OLS regression together with the next three or four predictors that would have entered the OLS equation.

A systematic search was then carried out for all two-way interaction effects between independent predictors identified by either OLS or logistic regression. It was not feasible to investigate all possible interaction effects (i.e. involving variables not identified as independently important in the regressions), because of the large number of possibilities. Essentially, two independent predictors were entered in a mini-logistic regression and then the interaction effect. With dichotomous data, the interaction effect is constructed by scoring 1 if both variables are present (e.g. poor supervision and low attainment) or if both variables are absent (e.g. satisfactory supervision and satisfactory attainment) and 0 for other combinations (e.g. poor supervision and satisfactory attainment or satisfactory supervision and poor attainment). Since only six significant two-way interaction effects were discovered in four separate analyses (predicting AP at 10, 14, 18 and 32), higher-order interaction effects were not investigated. Where an interaction effect was significant, it was then included as a variable in the larger OLS and logistic regressions, entering the equation after all main effects. One-tailed tests were used for main effects and two-tailed tests for interactions.

Table 3 shows that the independently important risk factors for AP at 10 were poor parental supervision, low junior school attainment, poor parental child-rearing behaviour and high neuroticism (on the New Junior Maudsley Inventory). A father who was not well educated (not staying on at school beyond the minimum leaving age) and a delinquent sibling also entered the OLS regression, while separation from a parent also entered the logistic regression. There was one significant interaction, between supervision and attainment, largely caused by the fact that the boys who had both poor supervision and low attainment were less likely to be antisocial (26%) than those who had only poor supervision (50%) or only low attainment (47%). This is not easily interpretable, and may be a chance finding, since there were only 19 boys with both poor supervision and low attainment. (Unlike most risk factors, poor supervision and low attainment were not significantly intercorrelated.)

In predicting AP at 14, 18 and 32, the previous measure of AP was included as a predictor. (It was always the best predictor.) It was easier to interpret the results by studying firstly what predicted AP at 10 and then what added to AP at 10 in predicting AP at 14, what added to AP at 14 in predicting AP at 18, and what added to AP at 18 in predicting AP at 32. If the only effect of a risk factor was in predicting AP at 10, for example, this would be clear, because it would not appear as a predictor of AP at a later age independently of AP at 10. If AP at 10 had not been included as a predictor of AP at 14, a risk factor that only predicted AP at 10 could nevertheless appear also as an independent predictor of AP at 14, essentially as a secondary consequence of the continuity in AP over time. (The composite "vulnerable" measure was not included in the regression analyses, since its individual component variables were included.)

Table 3 shows that the independently important predictors of AP at 14, in addition to AP at 10, were separation from a parent, low non-verbal IQ, not having few friends and low junior attainment. Coming from a Roman Catholic family (which tended to be associated with Irish origin) was significant in the OLS regression but not in the logistic regression. None of these risk factors had significant interaction effects.

The independently important predictors of AP at 18, in addition to AP at 14, were a convicted parent at 10, the father not involved in the boy's leisure activities at 12, periodic unemployment of the father at 14, the father not staying on at school beyond the minimum school leaving age, the boy not staying on at school beyond the minimum school leaving age and not having few friends. A delinquent sibling at 10, high neuroticism at 10, poor parental child-rearing at 8 and large family size at 10 were significant in one regression analysis but not in the other. The interaction between the father's unemployment and the father's education was significant in both regressions. This interaction was significant because the father's unemployment predicted the boy's AP much more strongly if he had stayed on at school (OR = 28.8) than if he had not (OR = 3.2). Hence, unemployment seemed to have a worse effect for the better educated fathers. The interaction between the father's unemployment and the boy's education was significant in only one regression.

Table 3: Regression Analyses for Antisocial Personality

Variable at Age	OLS Regression F Change	p	Logistic Regression LRCS Change	p
AP10				
Poor supervision	25.07	.0001	16.38 (2)	.0001
Low attainment 10	14.86	.0001	19.26 (1)	.0001
Poor child-rearing 8	8.01	.002	4.60 (4)	.02
High neuroticism 10	3.55	.03	3.38 (5)	.03
Father well educated 10 (-)	3.66	.03	–	–
Delinquent sibling 10	2.96	.04	–	–
Separated 10	–	–	6.31 (3)	.006
Supervision × Attainment	25.24	.0001	16.35 (6)	.0001
AP14				
Antisocial 10	53.86	.0001	50.40 (1)	.0001
Separated 10	17.05	.0001	16.24 (2)	.0001
Low non-verbal IQ 8-10	12.90	.0002	9.84 (3)	.0009
Few friends 8 (-)	4.53	.02	4.17 (5)	.02
Low attainment 10	4.83	.01	3.90 (4)	.02
Catholic family 8	2.83	.05	–	–
AP18				
Antisocial 14	63.17	.0001	39.97 (1)	.0001
Convicted parent 10	24.86	.0001	9.06 (3)	.001
Father not involved 12	9.67	.001	3.49 (8)	.03
Father unemployed 14	5.83	.008	6.42 (5)	.006
Father well educated 10 (-)	4.62	.02	8.17 (4)	.002
Delinquent sibling 10	4.46	.02	–	–
High neuroticism 10	3.18	.04	–	–
Stayed at school 14 (-)	2.81	.05	4.85 (6)	.01
Few friends 8 (-)	2.58	.05	4.07 (7)	.02
Poor child rearing 8	2.64	.05	–	–
Large family size 10	–	–	20.01 (2)	.0001
F unemployed × F educated	6.20	.01	9.67 (9)	.002
F unemployed × Stayed	–	–	5.89 (10)	.02
AP 32				
Antisocial 18	93.84	.0001	66.01 (1)	.0001
Convicted parent 10	9.40	.001	6.36 (3)	.006
Stayed at school 14 (-)	7.44	.003	10.29 (2)	.0007
Hospitalized for illness 18	6.23	.007	4.54 (4)	.02
Unskilled manual job 18	5.49	.01	4.93 (5)	.01
High neuroticism 14	2.63	.05	–	–
Stayed × Unskilled	5.20	.02	5.92 (6)	.02

Notes: OLS=Ordinary Least Squares, LRCS=Likelihood Ratio Chi-Squared, AP=Antisocial Personality, (-) indicates negative weightings. Numbers in parentheses indicate the order of entry in the logistic regression. The variables are listed according to their order of entry in the OLS regression.

The independently important predictors of AP at 32, in addition to AP at 18, were a convicted parent at 10, the boy not staying on at school, hospital treatment for illness at 18 and an unskilled manual job at 18. High neuroticism at 14 was an independent predictor only in the OLS regression. The interaction between not staying at school and an unskilled manual job was significant in both regressions. This interaction was significant because early school leaving predicted AP only for those who did not have unskilled manual jobs (OR = 5.47) and did not matter at all for those who had unskilled manual jobs (OR = -1.07). Hence, poor education had a worse effect for boys in higher status jobs.

It is interesting to compare these results with the independently important predictors of other types of antisocial behaviour discovered in this study in previous regression analyses. For example, conviction up to age 32 was best predicted at 8-10 by large family size, a convicted parent, daring, poor housing, not having few friends, separation from a parent and low junior attainment (Farrington, 1993a). A composite measure of social dysfunctioning at age 32 was best predicted at 18 by a poor relationship with the parents, an unskilled manual job, no examinations taken and nervousness (Farrington, 1993a).

Soccer hooliganism at age 18 was best predicted at 14 by being relatively small, a father not interested in the boy, early school leaving and not being nervous (Farrington, 1994). Spouse assault at age 32 was best predicted at 14 by a convicted parent, unpopularity, daring and separation from a parent (Farrington, 1994). Bullying at age 14 was best predicted by a convicted parent, not having few friends, low school attainment and not attending church (Farrington, 1993c). Having a child who was a bully (when the male was aged 32) was best predicted at 18 by bullying at 14 (showing the intergenerational transmission of bullying), poor reading, heavy gambling and unpopularity (Farrington, 1993c).

It is perhaps worth commenting on the protective influence of having few friends. Farrington et al. (1988a, 1988b) investigated the vulnerable boys who were not convicted up to age 32, and found that the most characteristic feature of these boys was that they had few or no friends at age eight. While they were genuinely well-behaved at age 32, they were often leading relatively unsuccessful lives, for example living in dirty home conditions, not being home owners, living alone, never having married, having large debts, and having low status, lowly paid jobs. Therefore, for boys from vulnerable backgrounds, social isolation may act as a protective factor against offending and antisocial behaviour (possibly because this often involves group activity) but not against other kinds of social dysfunctioning.

The relationships among having few friends at eight, neuroticism at 10 and 14, and hospital treatment for illness at 18 were puzzling. Few friends, neuroticism and illness were not significantly intercorrelated. Having few friends was negatively related to AP, while neuroticism and illness were positively related to AP. In regard to the components of the AP scales, having few friends was significantly correlated with not having sex and not being daring at 14 and with not being violent, not drinking heavily and not taking drugs at 18. Neuroticism was significantly correlated with troublesomeness, dishonesty, getting angry, impulsivity, truancy, being convicted, heavy gambling, self-reported delinquency, fighting and anti-establishment attitude. Illness at 18 was significantly correlated with drug use, a poor relationship with the wife, self-reported delinquency and fighting at 32.

In regard to other risk factors, having few friends was significantly correlated (positively) with poor parental child-rearing, low family income and going to a high delinquency rate school. Neuroticism was significantly correlated with poor parental supervision, the father not joining in the boy's leisure activities, low intelligence and attainment, and early school leaving of the boy and his father. Illness was significantly correlated (negatively) with a low social class family, although it was almost significantly positively correlated with a nervous father and being relatively small. It is plausible to argue that neuroticism was a risk factor for AP while having few friends was a protective factor. The significance of illness remains puzzling. It may be that these relationships might be clarified by distinguishing between physical and psychological illness and even by distinguishing between neurotic and non-neurotic antisocial personalities (cf. Blackburn, 1988), but this was not possible within the scope of this paper.

Explaining the Development of Antisocial Personality

Figure 1 attempts to summarize the results of all the regression analyses in one diagram (after Farrington, 1986). The middle of the diagram, reading down, shows the continuity from AP at 10 to AP at 14, 18 and 32. Parent-child interaction factors predicted AP at 10 (supervision, child-rearing), 14 (separation) and 18 (the father not involved in the boy's leisure activities). A convicted parent at 10 had lasting effects, predicting AP at 18 and 32. School failure had persistent effects, predicting AP at 10 and 14 (junior school attainment) and AP at 18 and 32 (early school leaving). Periodic unemployment of the father predicted AP at 18, while an unskilled manual job of the boy predicted AP at 32. While neuroticism at 10 predicted AP at 10 and hospital treatment for illness at 18 predicted AP at 32, not having few friends at eight predicted AP at 14 and 18.

Farrington (1990) concluded that the most important independent predictors of convictions fell into six categories: socio-economic deprivation, poor child-rearing, antisocial family members, school failure, impulsivity and antisocial child behaviour. Impulsivity and antisocial child behaviour are included in the AP measures, but most of the risk factors shown in Figure 1 fall into the other four categories, which are arguably the most important continuing influences on antisocial personality at different ages.

Farrington (1986, 1992, 1993b) proposed a theory to explain the development of offending which might also be used to explain the development of antisocial tendency and behaviour. The theory explicitly distinguishes between energizing, directing, inhibiting, and decision-making stages of offending, and explicitly distinguishes between influences on an underlying antisocial tendency or personality and influences on the behavioural manifestation of that personality in offending (or antisocial behaviour). It also emphasizes the need to distinguish between influences on the onset, persistence, and desistance of offending and antisocial behaviour. Antisocial personality concerns between-individual differences, whereas the behavioural manifestation concerns within-individual differences. Differences between individuals are assumed to be in degree rather than in kind; it is postulated that individuals can be ordered on a single dimension of antisocial personality, and that their relative positions on this dimension tend to remain consistent over time.

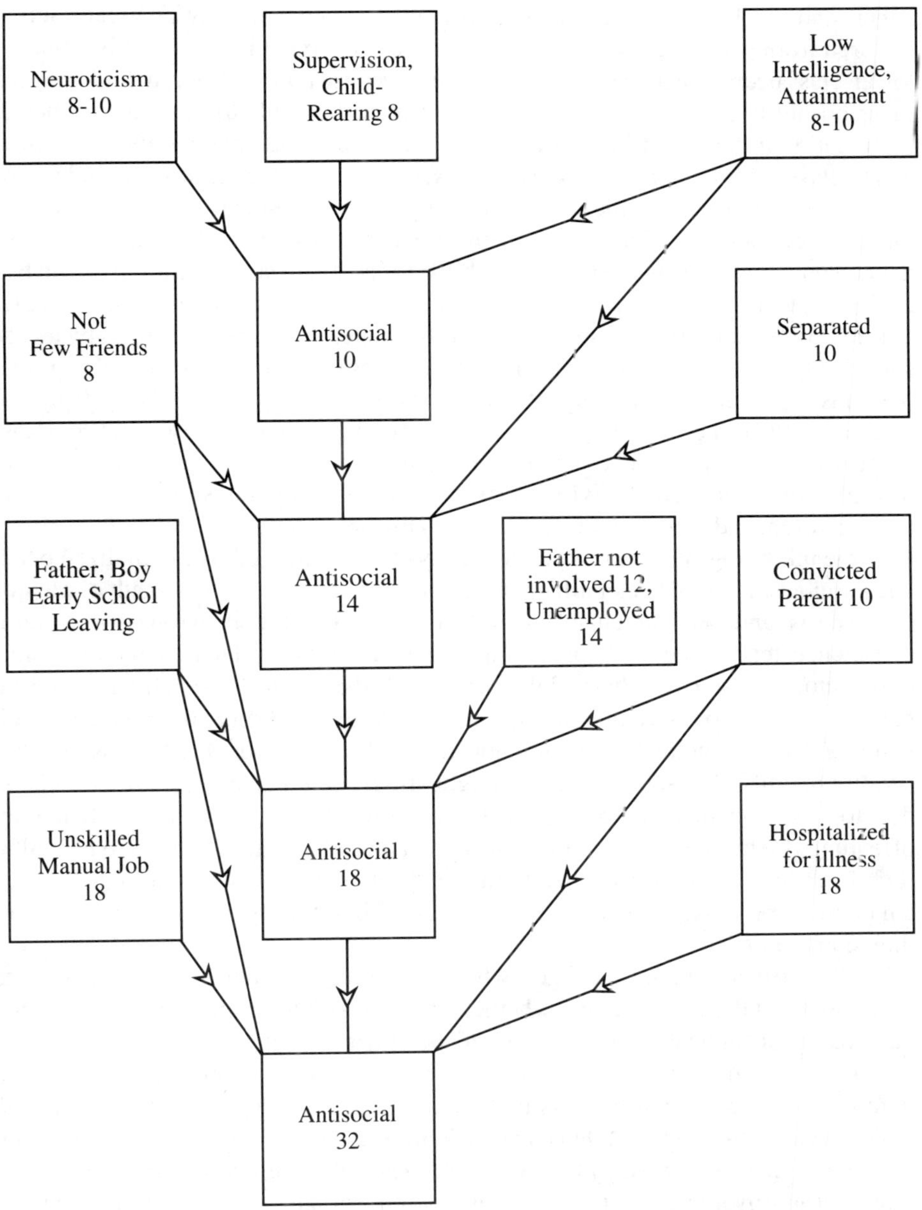

Figure 1: Stepping Stones to Antisocial Personality

The theory proposes that the main long-term energizing factors that ultimately lead to between-individual variations in antisocial tendency are desires for material goods, status among intimates, and excitement. The main short-term energizing factors that lead to within-individual variations in antisocial behaviour are boredom, frustration, anger, and alcohol consumption. The desire for excitement may be greater among children from poorer families, perhaps because excitement is more highly valued by lower-class people than by middle-class ones, because poorer children think they lead more boring lives, or because poorer children are less able to postpone immediate gratification in favour of long-term goals (which could be linked to the emphasis in lower-class culture on the concrete and present as opposed to the abstract and future).

In the directing stage, these motivations produce antisocial tendency if socially disapproved methods of satisfying them are habitually chosen. The methods chosen depend on maturation and behavioural skills; for example, a five-year old would have difficulty stealing a car. Some individuals (e.g. children from poorer families) are less able to satisfy their desires for material goods, excitement and social status by legal or socially approved methods, and so tend to choose illegal or socially disapproved methods. The relative inability of poorer children to achieve goals by legitimate methods could be because they tend to fail in school and tend to have erratic, low status employment histories. School failure in turn may often be a consequence of the unstimulating intellectual environment that lower-class parents tend to provide for their children, and their lack of emphasis on abstract concepts.

In the inhibiting stage, antisocial tendency can be inhibited by internalized beliefs and attitudes that have been built up in a social learning process as a result of a history of rewards and punishments. The belief that offending is wrong, or a strong conscience, tends to be built up if parents are in favour of legal norms, if they exercise close supervision over their children, and if they punish socially disapproved behaviour using love-oriented discipline. In addition, a strong conscience might be fostered by a genetically or biologically high degree of fearfulness, or high conditionability. Antisocial tendency might also be inhibited by empathy, which may develop as a result of parental warmth and loving relationships. The belief that offending is legitimate, and anti-establishment attitudes generally, tend to be built up if children have been exposed to attitudes and behaviour favouring offending (e.g. in a modelling process), especially by members of their family, by their friends, and in their communities.

In the decision-making stage, which specifies the interaction between the individual and the environment, whether a person with a certain degree of antisocial personality or tendency commits an antisocial act in a given situation depends on opportunities, costs and benefits, and on the subjective probabilities of the different outcomes. The costs and benefits include immediate situational factors such as the material goods that can be stolen and the likelihood and consequences of being caught by the police, as perceived by the individual. They also include social factors such as likely disapproval by parents or spouses, and encouragement or reinforcement from peers. In general, people make rational decisions. They choose to commit antisocial acts if the net benefits (expected benefits minus expected costs) of these acts exceed the net benefits of alternative acts. However, more impulsive people are less likely to consider the possible consequences of their actions, especially consequences that are likely to be long delayed. Impulsive people give relatively more weight to immediate rather than longer-term outcomes, and hence are more likely to commit antisocial acts.

The consequences of offending feed back to antisocial personality and to the cost-benefit calculation in a learning process. If the consequences include official labelling, stigmatization, and isolation with other offenders or antisocial people, this may make it more difficult for an offender to achieve his aims legally, and hence it may lead to an increase in his antisocial tendency. If the consequences of crime are reinforcing (e.g. gaining material goods or peer approval) or punishing (e.g. legal sanctions or parental disapproval), this may affect the person's future subjective estimation of costs, benefits and probabilities.

The relative ordering of people on antisocial personality tends to stay reasonably consistent over time, because internalized beliefs are built up in childhood and thereafter do not change much or change rather slowly. However, absolute levels of antisocial tendency are probably lower in adulthood than in the teenage years, partly because the strength of long-term energizing factors declines and partly because there is more opportunity to satisfy desires in socially approved ways. Different behavioural manifestations of antisocial personality at different ages depend partly on behavioural skills (e.g. maturation) and partly on environmental factors (e.g. opportunities).

Applying the theory to explain some of the risk factors for antisocial behaviour and delinquency, children from poorer families may be likely to offend because they are less able to achieve their goals legally and because they value some goals (e.g. excitement) especially highly. Children with low intelligence may be more likely to offend because they tend to fail in school and hence cannot achieve their goals legally. Impulsive children, and those with a poor ability to manipulate abstract concepts, may be more likely to offend because they do not give sufficient consideration to the possible long-term consequences of offending. Children who are exposed to poor parental child rearing behaviour, disharmony or separation may be likely to offend because they do not build up internal controls over socially disapproved behaviour, while children from criminal families and those with delinquent friends tend to build up anti-establishment attitudes and the belief that offending is justifiable. The whole process is self-perpetuating, in that poverty, low intelligence, and early school failure lead to truancy and lack of educational qualifications, which in turn lead to low status jobs and periods of unemployment, both of which make it harder to achieve goals legitimately.

Conclusions

While antisocial personality is a meaningful concept, it is not clear what indicators of it are the most appropriate and whether variables are causes, consequences or indicators. In particular, research is needed on the link between impulsivity and antisocial behaviour, and future research should also distinguish indicators of personality from indicators of antisocial behaviour. The most important psychosocial influences on the development of antisocial personality in this research were socio-economic deprivation, school failure, poor parenting and antisocial family members. Similar results were obtained in research on offending and on specific types of antisocial behaviour such as bullying and spouse assault.

Generally, there was continuity in antisocial personality from childhood to adulthood, since about half of antisocial males at one age continued to be antisocial at a later age. Future research should focus on the half of the males who do not continue and seek to identify protective factors. In particular, research is needed on the links between antisocial personality and indicators of neuroticism and social isolation, as risk and protective factors. To the extent that antisocial personality is caused by poor parenting, school failure and socio-economic deprivation, it might be prevented by parent training, pre-school intellectual enrichment programmes and income maintenance programmes. These types of prevention experiments are urgently needed.

References

American Psychiatric Association. (1987). *Diagnostic and statistical manual of mental disorders* (3rd Ed., Revised). Washington, DC: Author.

Blackburn, R. (1988). On moral judgements and personality disorders: The myth of psychopathic personality revisited. *British Journal of Psychiatry, 153*, 505-512.

Cleary, P. D., & Angel, R. (1984). The analysis of relationships involving dichotomous dependent variables. *Journal of Health and Social Behaviour, 25*, 334-348.

Davies, W., & Feldman, P. (1981). The diagnosis of psychopathy by forensic specialists. *British Journal of Psychiatry, 138*, 329-331.

Farrington, D. P. (1986). Stepping stones to adult criminal careers. In D. Olweus, J. Block, & M. R. Yarrow (Eds.), *Development of antisocial and prosocial behaviour* (pp. 359-384). New York: Academic Press.

Farrington, D. P. (1989). Later adult life outcomes of offenders and non-offenders. In M. Brambring, F. Losel, and H. Skowronek (Eds.), *Children at risk: Assessment, longitudinal research and intervention* (pp. 220-244). Berlin: De Gruyter.

Farrington, D. P. (1990). Implications of criminal career research for the prevention of offending. *Journal of Adolescence, 13*, 93-113.

Farrington, D. P. (1991). Antisocial personality from childhood to adulthood. *The Psychologist, 4*, 389-394.

Farrington, D. P. (1992). Explaining the beginning, progress and ending of antisocial behaviour from birth to adulthood. In J. McCord (Ed.), *Facts, frameworks and forecasts: Advances in criminological theory: Vol. 3* (pp. 253-286). New Brunswick, NJ: Transaction.

Farrington, D. P. (1994). Childhood, adolescent and adult features of violent males. In L. R. Huesmann (Ed.), *Aggressive behaviour: Current perspectives* (pp. 215-240). New York: Plenum.

Farrington, D. P. (1993a). Childhood origins of teenage antisocial behaviour and adult social dysfunction. *Journal of the Royal Society of Medicine, 86*, 13-17.

Farrington, D. P. (1993b). Motivations for conduct disorder and delinquency. *Development and Psychopathology, 5*, 225-241.

Farrington, D. P. (1993c). Understanding and preventing bullying. In M. Tonry (Ed.), *Crime and justice: Vol. 17* (pp. 381-458). Chicago: University of Chicago Press.

Farrington, D. P., Gallagher, B., Morley, L., St Ledger, R. J., & West, D. J. (1986). Unemployment, school leaving and crime. *British Journal of Criminology, 26*, 335-356.

Farrington, D. P., Gallagher, B., Morley, L., St Ledger, R. J., & West, D. J. (1988a). A 24-year follow-up of men from vulnerable backgrounds. In R. L. Jenkins & W. K. Brown (Eds.), *The abandonment of delinquent behaviour* (pp. 155-173). New York: Praeger.

Farrington, D. P., Gallagher, B., Morley, L., St Ledger, R. J., & West, D. J. (1988b). Are there any successful men from criminogenic backgrounds? *Psychiatry, 51*, 116-130.

Farrington, D. P., Loeber, R., & Van Kammen, W. B. (1990). Long-term criminal outcomes of hyperactivity-impulsivity-attention deficit and conduct problems in childhood. In L. N. Robins & M. Rutter (Eds.), *Straight and devious pathways from childhood to adulthood* (pp. 62-81). Cambridge: Cambridge University Press.

Farrington, D. P., Ohlin, L. E., & Wilson, J. Q. (1986). *Understanding and controlling crime*. New York: Springer-Verlag.

Farrington, D. P., & West, D. J. (1990). The Cambridge Study in Delinquent Development: A long-term follow-up of 411 males. In H. J. Kerner & G. Kaiser (Eds.), *Criminality: Personality behaviour and life history* (pp. 115-138). Berlin: Springer-Verlag.

Hare, R. D. (1980). A research scale for the assessment of psychopathy in criminal populations. *Personality and Individual Differences, 1*, 111-119.

Hare, R. D. (1985). Comparison of procedures for the assessment of psychopathy. *Journal of Consulting and Clinical Psychology, 53*, 7-16.

Hare, R. D. (1986). Twenty years of experience with the Cleckley psychopath. In W. H. Reid, D. Dorr, J. I. Walker, & J. W. Bonner (Eds.), *Unmasking the psychopath: Antisocial personality and related syndromes* (pp. 3-27). New York: Norton.

Harpur, T. J., Hakstian, A. R. & Hare, R. D. (1988). Factor structure of the Psychopathy Checklist. *Journal of Consulting and Clinical Psychology, 56*, 741-747.

Harpur, T. J., Hare, R. D., & Hakstian, A. R. (1989). Two-factor conceptualization of psychopathy: Construct validity and assessment implications. *Psychological Assessment: A Journal of Consulting and Clinical Psychology, 1*, 6-17.

Kazdin, A. E. (1987). *Conduct disorders in childhood and adolescence*. Newbury Park, California: Sage.

Offord, D. R., Alder, R. J., & Boyle, M. H. (1986). Prevalence and socio-demographic correlates of conduct disorder. *American Journal of Social Psychiatry, 6*, 272-278.

Offord, D. R., Boyle, M. H., & Racine, Y. (1989). Ontario Child Health Study: Correlates of disorder. *Journal of the American Academy of Child and Adolescent Psychiatry, 28*, 856-860.

Raine, A. (1985). A psychometric assessment of Hare's checklist for psychopathy on an English prison population. *British Journal of Clinical Psychology, 24*, 247-258.

Robins, L. N. (1986). Changes in conduct disorder over time. In D. C. Farran & J. D. McKinney (Eds.), *Risk in intellectual and social development* (pp. 227-259). New York: Academic Press.

Robins, L. N. (1991). Conduct disorder. *Journal of Child Psychology and Psychiatry, 32*, 193-212.

Robins, L. N., & Ratcliff, K. S. (1978). Risk factors in the continuation of childhood antisocial behaviour into adulthood. *International Journal of Mental Health, 7*, 96-116.

Robins, L. N., & Ratcliff, K. S. (1980). Childhood conduct disorders and later arrest. In L. N. Robins, P. J. Clayton, & J. K. Wing (Eds.), *The social consequences of psychiatric illness* (pp. 248-263). New York: Brunner/Mazel.

Robins, L. N., Tipp, J., & Przybeck T. (1991). Antisocial personality. In L. N. Robins & D. Regier (Eds.), *Psychiatric disorders in America* (pp. 258-290). New York: MacMillan/Free Press.

Robins, L. N., & Wish, E. (1977). Childhood deviance as a developmental process: A study of 223 urban Black men from birth to 18. *Social Forces, 56*, 448-473.

Tonry, M., Ohlin, L. E., & Farrington, D. P. (1991). *Human development and criminal behaviour*. New York: Springer-Verlag.

Walker, N. (1985). *Sentencing: Theory, law and practice*. London: Butterworths.

West, D. J. (1969). *Present conduct and future delinquency*. London: Heinemann.
West, D. J. (1982). *Delinquency: Its roots, careers and prospects*. London: Heinemann.
West, D. J., & Farrington, D. P. (1973). *Who becomes delinquent?* London: Heinemann.
West, D. J., & Farrington, D. P. (1977). *The delinquent way of life*. London: Heinemann.

A Critical Look at the Conceptual Models Explaining Drug Use and Crime[1]

Serge Brochu

The link between drug[2] use and crime has been a very popular topic of discussion among scientists throughout the last 20 years. These discussions, based on numerous studies, brought a number of conceptual models to the forefront which primarily aimed at explaining the nature of the relationship between these two deviant behaviors. Based on a thorough literature review, this paper will discuss the principal conceptual models and will provide a critical evaluation of their utility in understanding drug use and crime.

Method

In order to carry out this research, a literature review of the past 20 years (1972-1992) was conducted. To perform this task, four procedures were required: (1) five international data bases (PSYLITT, SOCIOFILE, MEDLINE, NCJRS, and SOCIAL SCIENCES INDEX) were consulted from SILVER PLATER (these documents were located and obtained by the inter-library loan services of the University of Montreal when they were not on the premises); (2) letters were sent to scientists in this field enabling us to obtain their most recent research; (3) five large libraries specializing in either the field of addiction or criminology were visited in order to obtain unpublished documents; and (4) the bibliographies of former literature reviews were taken into consideration to ensure the review of previous studies. Two judges read these manuscripts and classified them according to the to the nature of the study.

A total of 927 studies on drugs and crime were found (see Table 1). Fifteen percent (N=134) discussed drug policies (legalization, mandatory drug testing, and drug enforcement strategies). Twenty percent (N=185) of the studies focused on prevalence of drug use among offenders or prevalence of crimes among addicts or drug users. Another 20% (N=187) evaluated the impact of different types of drug abuse treatment on the criminality of addicts during a follow-up period. Finally, almost half (45%; N=421) of the studies attempted to reach a better understanding of the nature of the link between drugs and crime.

Table 1: Studies on Drugs and Crimes published during the last 20 years (1972-1992)

	N	%
Policy	134	15
Prevalence	185	20
Treatment	187	20
Link	421	45
Total	927	100

From the 421 studies looking at the link between drug use and crime, two-thirds (N=282) discussed original data. These studies were classified according to the conceptual model they were supporting. Six percent (N=16) were supporting the expectancy model; 11% the personality model (N=31); 11% (N=32) the systemic model (N=32); 13% (N=37) the psycho-pharmacological model; 16% (N=46) the economico-compulsive model; and 43% (N=120) of the studies were supporting the joint occurence model (see Table 2).

Table 2: Models supported by Studies on Drugs-Crime Link (1972-1992)

	N	%
Expectancy	16	6
Personality	31	11
Sytemic	32	11
Psycho-pharmaco.	37	13
Economico-comp.	46	16
Joint occurence	120	43
Total	282	100

Note: Psycho-pharmaco. = Psycho pharmacological
Economico -comp. - Economico-compulsive

One must add that the number of studies supporting a model is not necessarily linked to the veracity or the power of the model but rather to its popularity among scientists and/or government. We must then carefully review these studies in order to evaluate their utility in understanding drug use and crime.

The Conceptual Models

Many conceptual models have been elaborated in order to understand the nature of the relationship between drugs and crime. We will now briefly describe the most important ones. Basically, these models are produced from one of three hypothesis: (1) intoxication or addiction cause criminal activities; (2) criminal involvement precipitates drug use; and (3) drugs and crime are not causally linked.

Drugs cause crime

Let us look at the conceptual models which fall under the first hypothesis which states that intoxication or addiction is a major cause of criminal activities. We found two models: psycho-pharmacological; and economico-compulsive.

The psycho-pharmacological model is concerned with the relationship between intoxication and violence. We have become accustomed to reading reports which indicate that alcohol, sometimes in combination with other drugs, has been involved in over 50% of violent crimes. According to this model, as a result of short- or long-term ingestion of specific drugs, an individual may exhibit violent (impulsive) behaviors. The most relevant drugs in this regard are alcohol, barbiturates, cocaine, other stimulants, and Phencyclidine (PCP) (Miller & Potter-Efron, 1989). There are many ways that drug induced aggression might occur. Those most often discussed are ego-control diminution; the deterioration of judgement; the induction of irritability and impulsiveness; the production of paranoid thought; and the induction of feelings of omnipotence. These explanations have now replaced the discredited disinhibition theory (Gottheil et al., 1983).

Numerous studies give some support to this model. Researchers have found subjects' shock delivery to be a function of alcohol ingested (Taylor & Gammon, 1975). In studies of incarcerated delinquents, Tinklenberg et al., (1974; 1981) identified barbiturates (secobarbital) as the single substance most likely to increase assaultiveness. Data presented by Brody (1990) suggest that more than half of the cocaine-involved patients admitted to a hospital emergency department were combative and agitated with symptoms of paranoia and delirium at the time of admission. PCP has also been associated with assaultive behaviors (Simonds & Kashani, 1979; 1980).

The economico-compulsive model, extremely popular among police officers, examines the connection between the addiction to hard drugs (heroin and cocaine) and acquisitive crimes (drug selling, shoplifting, prostitution, etc.). This model has its origin in the observation that most heroin addicts are deeply involved in criminal activities (Ball, Shaffer & Nurco, 1983; Faupel, 1991; Johnson et al., 1985; Nurco, et al., 1988a, 1988b and 1988c). Numerous studies have shown that 95% or more of male narcotics addicts reported obtaining income from illegal activities (Ball et al., 1981; Johnson et al., 1985). This involvement in a criminal career is believed to be due to the addiction to an expensive drug. Heroin or cocaine addicts are seen as people who must be involved in money-producing crimes in order to satisfy their dependency.

In support of this position, studies have shown that crime levels increase from a period of pre-addiction to addiction (Anglin & Speckart, 1986; Ball et al., 1981; Nurco et al., 1984). Moreover, it appears that addicts display higher crime rates during a period of high consumption while a period of treatment or a period of lower drug intake corresponds to a decrease in crime involvement (Anglin & Speckart, 1986; Nurco et al., 1988a, 1988b, 1988c; Speckart & Anglin, 1986).

According to this model heroin or cocaine addicts are not motivated by impulse to act violently but rather by the desire to obtain money to purchase drugs.

Drugs cause crime, but crime causes drugs

Systemic model The third model refers to the "normal" aggressive patterns of interactions within a black market. The systemic model observes the interaction among a criminogenic milieu, a delinquent-prone individual, and the drug market. The milieu of drug dealing is conducive to violence: drug dealing attracts individuals willing to engage in violent behaviors, which thus increase the likelihood of violence. In this model, violence is intrinsic to involvement with the traffic of illicit substances. It includes business disputes over territory, enforcement of organizational discipline, robberies of traffickers usually followed by retaliation, elimination of informers, disputes over drugs, punishment for selling inferior quality drugs, punishment for failing to refund debts ("messing up the money") and so on (Adler, 1985; Fagan, 1989; Fagan & Chin 1990; Goldstein, 1990; Goldstein et al., 1987). Systemic criminality represents, according to Collins (1990), the most important violent outcomes associated with drug use. This systemic violence tend to occur in (a) socially disorganized areas, which (b) have traditionally high rates of violence, and (c) are economically disadvantaged. Drug traffickers appear to come disproportionately from these milieu (Collins, 1990).

Drugs are only co-related to crime

According to this third hypothesis, one has to look at other factors in order to explain the nature of the link between drug use and crime. These two variables would not be related in the classical causal way. Three conceptual models fall under this hypothesis: the personality model; the joint occurence model and the expectancy model.

The personality model looks for a third factor to explain both drug use and crime. According to this model the third factor is defined as an antisocial personality. In 1925, Kolb wrote:

> Habitual criminals are psychopaths, and psychopaths are abnormal individuals who, because of their abnormality, are especially liable to become addicts. (Kolb, 1925, p. 89).

Many studies have supported this viewpoint and found that both alcoholism and illicit drug use were significantly associated with antisocial personality (Gibbs, 1982; Hammersley, Lavelle, & Forsyth, in press; Hill, Haertzen, & Glaser, 1960; Kolb, 1927; Lewis, Cloninger, & Pais, 1983).

The joint occurence model took its origin in the observation that minor delinquency often occured before drug use. In these cases, drug use is certainly not the cause of the beginning of a criminal career (Brochu and Douyon, 1990; Leblanc, 1986). In fact, prospective longitudinal studies show that delinquency and drug use are linked to a similar set of social, psychological, and démographic variables. Delinquency, drug abuse and other types of deviant behaviors would present some partial commonality in etiology, while some unique causal factors would be linked to specific types of problem behaviors. However, these problem behaviors are linked in a pattern of mutual reinforcement. One of these behaviors increases the probability of others, but they are not causally linked or, if they are, there is a bidirectional causal relationship between them: one influences the other. As mentioned above, delinquent behavior usually precedes drug use, however, there is some evidence that drug use subsequently influences delinquent activities (e.g. reducing the probability of dropping out of crime) (Elliott, in press; Elliott, Huizinga, & Menard, 1989).

The expectancy model is a critical reaction to the psycho-pharmacological model. The roots of this model are found in a study produced by Lang et al., (1976) which shows how the behaviors of subjects who believed they had comsumed alcohol became more aggressive even though they had received a placebo (see also George and Marlatt, 1986). This model views the effects of drug use as a self-fulfilling prophecy. More specifically, some drugs, for example alcohol, have acquired a reputation for stimulating aggressiveness, and anticipation of intoxication would then act as a social signal which permits the expression of aggressive impulses. Users who may wish to engage in a violent act ingest the drug in order to be freed of their responsibility. This would be true for some wife abusers (Coleman and Strauss, 1983) as well as some sex offenders (McCaghy, 1968). Brochu and Lévesque (1990) noted that these relaxed standards of accountability in relation to intoxication are often used by clever offenders capitalizing on a drug's reputation by claiming that they were not responsible for their criminal actions. More recently, Fagan (1990) refined this conceptual model. Briefly, according to this author:

> intoxication affects the cognition processes that shape perceptions of both one's own physiology (i.e., expectancy) and the associated behavioral response. The cognitive processes themselves are influenced by cultural and situational factors that determine the norms, beliefs, and sanctions regarding behaviors following intoxication. (Fagan, 1990, p. 299).

Thus, a violent-prone person who believes that alcohol stimulates aggression will interpret the physiological changes induced by the intoxication as signs of hostility. If the sanctions and the norms permit him to express this violence, and if the situation is appropriate (for him), this person will have great difficulty in seeing an alternative response to the situation, and will probably become hostile. When this individual returns to a sober state, there will be a tendency for him to blame the intoxication for his behavior.

In short, aggression following intoxication is not considered a linear process, but is rather perceived as a reciprocal process in which expectancies, physiological factors, social norms, and situations all play an important role in the conduct of aggressive or non-agressive behaviors (Fagan, 1990).

A critical look

Let us critically re-examine these explanation models.

The psycho-pharmacological model only explains one type of criminality: violence. The majority of the studies have been done with alcohol, however, only a minority of drunk people become violent. In fact, the research literature in general indicates that drug-induced psycho-pharmacological violence is uncommon (Abram & Teplin, 1990; Collins, 1990; Fagan, 1990; Fagan & Chin, 1990; Miller, 1990; Wish, 1986). Moreover, some of the physiological effects of alcohol which are well known (slowed reaction time, difficulty of concentration) do not lead directly to violent behaviors. In fact, most studies do not support a direct association between alcohol intoxication and violence.

It is usually assumed that intoxication leads to the crime, however, Cordelia (1985) found that some offenders drink before their offense to calm their nerves. Scientists must look at the set and the setting of the intake. With respect to other drugs, the data do not prove that pharmacological effects of PCP, amphetamines, cocaine or other stimulants are major factors accounting for interpersonal violence, when demographic and other conditions for violence are controlled.

The economico-compulsive model sees a causal link between drug use and crime. However, many studies indicate that, with regard to the onset, there is no causal link between drug use and crime (Carpenter et al., 1988; Elliott, in press; Elliott, Huizinga, & Menard, 1989). In addition, many studies do not prove without doubt that crimes (especially acquisitive crimes) committed by addicts are motivated by the compulsion to get money to purchase heroin or cocaine. In some cases the reverse could be true. What would a young offender, who does not go to school, and has a lot of free time, like to buy with the money he has stolen? A sound system; a nice pair of jeans; some jewellery; and ... alcohol and drugs in order to party. A lifestyle characterized by lots of free time and money could be the causal factor in drug use. It is not because offenders are drug users that drug use causes crime. Results from Elliott, Huizinga and Menard (1989) suggest that: "Minor offending is a necessary cause or precursor of marijuana and polydrug use" (p. 188).

Criminal activities as result of heroin addiction could be the reality of a sub-group of addicts. Results obtained by Faupel (1991) indicate that heroin use could be seen as a career with temporal character (four phases).

(1) The *occasional-use* phase is characterized by participants who are just beginning their addiction careers. At this stage, subjects are experimenting with both drug use and crime. There is no evidence for a causal relationship at this point.

(2) The *stable-addict* phase is typified by "specialization" in drug used as well as their involvement in crimes. During this stage, the level of drug consumption is a function of their capacity to afford it.

(3) The *freewheeling-addict* phase is characterized by the loss of control (diminished life structure). Consumption will be limited only by the availability of the drug. This availability is in relation to their success in the crime business. At this stage, "crime causes drugs".

(4) The last career phase, called "*street junkie*" is determined by tolerance to heroin, low availability, and diminished life structure. Their crime involvement is strongly linked to their addiction. At this stage, "drug use causes crime". It is usually at this stage that they meet treatment specialists if they have not been previously arrested and incarcerated.

These results indicate that an empirical association between drug use and crime does not necessarily determine a causal link.

The systemic model studies deal almost exclusively with violence and drug distribution, an approach which has featured prominently in the mass media in the last decade. However, little research has been done on this model. Collins (1990) mentioned that drug distribution and violence tend to occur in areas that: "are socially disorganized ... have traditionally high rates of interpersonal violence; and are economically disadvantaged." (p. 266). However, supporters of this position have considerable difficulty explaining exactly how social and economic factors are involved. With regard to this model, we must agree with Collins (1990) in that it needs further elaboration in order to incorporate multiple factors such as social, economic and cultural variables.

The personality model was, during the last decade the target of many criticisms. This model does not put enough emphasis on cultural, economic and social factors accompanying drug use and crime. If the only cause of drug use and crime were an antisocial personality, how then can we explain why these behaviors vary with social and environmental factors? In addition, antisocial personality cannot account for variations of these behaviors over time, for example declining involvement in crime and increasing involvement in drug use during late adolescence (Elliott in press).

Only a few empirical studies have been done on this model, with conflicting results. Recent studies have found that antisocial personality accounts for a negligible amount of the variance when the effects of other variables are considered independently (Jaffe, Babor and Fishbein, 1988; Muntaner et al., 1990).

The joint occurence model is a relatively new one. Many studies from the early 70s support this idea, but the conceptualization occurred, for the most part, in the last 10 years. Prospective longitudinal studies and ethnological studies using some qualitative methods offer a new perspective on the nature of the drugs/crime nexus. There is only limited evidence to support this model, largely due to the difficulties with such a multi-causal position. Some of the data are relatively weak, and factors involved have yet to be specified. Some researchers argue that the joint occurence model is too opportunistic to account for the highly structured sequences observed (Kandel, 1988).

More studies should be done in order to examine carefully the different types of deviant behaviors across sex, race, age, social class and place of residence.

Research on the *expectancy model* is almost exclusively concerned with alcohol and family violence. Researchers must recognize the empirical and the conceptual complexity of the relationship, and take into account both the role of alcohol as an excuse for crime, and psycho-pharmacological effects. For example, Gustafson (1985; 1986; 1992) has conducted a series of studies using balanced placebo designs that lend support to the view that even when expectancy is carefully controlled, it is possible to demonstrate a pharmacological effect of alcohol on aggressive behaviors. In addition, more interviews with individuals who behave violently are needed to help to understand how their cognitive processes function and what their beliefs about alcohol entail.

The Need For An Integrative View

It appears from the literature that drug use is neither a necessary nor a sufficient cause of crime. A simple equation does not represent the complexity of the nature of human interactions.

Goldstein (1985) understood this problem when he proposed his tripartite scheme. According to this framework, there are three ways that drugs and violence can be related to each other: psycho-pharmacologically; economic-compulsively, and systemically. Clearly, there are situations in which these factors may overlap, and some factors may be more important with different drugs. For example, barbiturates, amphetamines, and alcohol may promote psycho-pharmacological violence, whereas heroin and cocaine will be associated with economically compulsive violence. However, any illicit drug trade may be associated with systemic violence.

Goldstein's (1985) concept of the tripartite framework helped refine thinking about the link between drug use and crime. It clearly indicates that the models we discussed earlier are not mutually exclusive. Rather than being conceptualized as models, they should be viewed as etiological factors explaining offences committed by drug users.

However, this tripartite framework fails to incorporate data from new studies indicating that a large proportion of crimes committed by drug users are not directly motivated by psycho-pharmacological, economic compulsive, or systemic reasons. In this sense, we should add to this famework a fourth factor: co-occurring delinquency. Faupel (1991) indicates that this co-occurring concept is a good explanation of crimes committed by addicts up to the point they become more tolerant (fourth phase) to heroin.

This fourth factor needs more research in order to understand how this co-occurring delinquency interplays with drug use and how personal and social environments predispose individuals to crime and drug abuse. With regards to personal environment, there is evidence, for example, that personality types and expectancies could be considered as risk factors. Social factors such as community disorganization and social control are known to be linked with both delinquency and drug abuse. The inclusion of this fourth factor in Goldstein's concept needs more formal development but it is an attempt to interpret some results from past studies.

This literature review of the last two decade clearly supports the notion of a link between drugs and crime. It is extremely important now that we move beyond simple prevalence studies of drug use and crime to achieve a real understanding of how drugs contribute to the process of delinquency. This will only be achieved through intensive interviewing of drug addicts, as well as fieldwork studies in this area. Researchers must begin to recognize the importance and need for systematically gathered life history data. This is the only way to gain knowledge about the complexity of the elusive relationship between drug use/abuse and criminal behaviors.

References

Abram, K. M., & Teplin, L. A. (1990). Drug disorder, mental illness, and violence. In NIDA Research Monograph Series, *Drugs and violence: Causes, correlates, and consequences: Vol. 103* (pp. 222-238). Rockville, MD: National Institute on Drug Abuse.

Adler, P. A. (1985). *Wheeling and dealing: An ethnography of an upper-level dealing and smuggling community*. New York: Columbia University Press.

Anglin, M. D., & Speckart, G. (1986). Narcotics use, property crime, and dealing: Structural dynamics across the addiction career. *Journal of Quantitative Criminology*, *2*, 355-375.

Ball, J. C., Rosen, L., Flueck, J. A., & Nurco, D. N. (1981). The criminality of heroin addicts: When addicted and when off opiates. In J. A. Inciardi (Ed.), *The drug-crime connection* (pp. 39-65). Beverly-Hills, CA: Sage.

Ball, J. C., Shaffer, J. W., & Nurco, D. N. (1983). The day to day criminality of heroin addicts in Baltimore - a study in the continuity of offence rates. *Drug and alcohol dependence*, *12*, 119-142.

Brochu, S., & Douyon, A. (1990). *La consommation de psychotropes chez des jeunes de 13 à 18 ans en centre de réadaptation*. (Toxicomanie 3). Montréal: Association des intervenants en toxicomanie du Québec.

Brochu, S., & Lévesque, M. (1990). Treatment of prisoners for alcohol or drug abuse. *Alcoholism Treatment Quarterly*, *7*, 15-21.

Brody, S. L. (1990). Violence associated with acute cocaine use in patients admitted to a medical emergency department. In NIDA Research Monograph Series, *Drugs and violence: causes, correlates, and consequences: Vol. 103* (pp. 44-59). Rockville, MD: National Institute on Drug Abuse.

Carpenter, C., Glassner, B., Johnson, B. D., & Loughlin, J. (1988). *Kids, drugs, and crime*. Toronto: Lexington.

Coleman, D. H., & Strauss, M. A. (1983). Alcohol abuse and family violence. In E. Gottheil, K. Druley, T. E. Skoloda, & H. M. Waxman (Eds.), *Alcohol drug abuse and aggression*, (pp. 104-124). Springfield, IL: Charles C Thomas.

Collins, J. J. (1990). Summary thoughts about drugs and violence. In NIDA Research Monograph Series, *Drugs and violence: Causes, correlates, and consequences: Vol. 103* (pp. 265-275). Rockville, MD: National Institute on Drug Abuse.

Cordilia, A. (1985). Alcohol and property crime: Exploring the causal nexus. *Journal of Studies on Alcohol*, *46*, 161-171.

Elliott, D. S. (in press). Health enhancing and health compromising lifestyles. *Adolescent Health Promotion*. Carnegie Corporation.

Elliott, D. S., Huizinga, D., & Menard, S. (1989). *Multiple problem youth: Delinquency, substance use, and mental health problems*. New York: Springer-Verlag.

Fagan, J. (1989). The social organization of drug use and drug dealing among urban gangs. *Criminology*, *27*, 633-667.

Fagan, J. (1990). Intoxication and aggression. In M. Tonry, & J. Q. Wilson (Eds.), *Drugs and crime, crime and justice: A review of research: 13* (pp. 241-320). Chicago: The University of Chicago Press.

Fagan, J., & Chin, K. L. (1990). Violence as regulation and social control in the distribution of crack. In NIDA Research Monograph Series, *Drugs and violence: Causes, correlates, and consequences: Vol. 103* (pp. 8-43). Rockville: National Institute on Drug Abuse.

Faupel, C. E. (1991). *Shooting dope: Career pattern of hard-core heroin users*. Gainesville, FL: University of Florida Press.

George, W. H., & Marlatt, G. A. (1986). The effects of alcohol and anger on interest in violence, erotica, and deviance. *Journal of Abnormal Psychology*, *95*, 150-158.

Gibbs, J. T. (1982). Psychosocial factors related to substance abuse among delinquent females: Implications for prevention and treatment. *American Journal of Orthopsychiatry*, *52*, 261-271.

Goldstein, P. J. (1985). The drugs/violence nexus: A tripartite conceptual framework. *Journal of Drug Issues*, *15*, 493-506.

Goldstein, P. J. (1990). Drugs and violent crime. In N. A. Weiner, & M. E. Wolfgang (Eds.), *Pathways to criminal violence* (pp. 16-48). London: Sage.

Goldstein, P. J., Brownstein, H. H., Kurlander, L. T., Glasel. D., & Martinez, J. (1987). *Drug related crime analysis*. Washington: National Institute of Justice.

Gottheil, E., Druley, K. A., Skoloda, T. E., & Waxman, H. M. (1983). Aggression and addiction: Summary and overview. In E. Gottheil, K. Druley, T. E. Skoloda, & H. M. Waxman (Eds.), *Alcohol, drug abuse and aggression* (pp. 333-365). Springfield, IL: Charles. C. Thomas

Gustafson, R. (1985). Alcohol and aggression: Pharmacological versus expectancy effects. *Psychological Reports*, *57*, 955-966.

Gustafson, R. (1986). Alcohol, frustration, and aggression: An experiment using the balanced placebo design. *Psychological Reports*, *59*, 207-218.

Gustafson, R. (1992). Alcohol and aggression: A replication study controlling for potential confounding variables. *Aggressive Behaviors*, *18*, 21-28.

Hammersley, R., Lavelle T., & Forsyth, J. M. (in press). Adolescent drug use, health and personality. *Drug and Alcohol Dependence*.

Hill, H. E., Hartzen, C. A., & Glaser, R. (1960). Personality characteristics of narcotic addicts as indicated by the MMPI. *Journal of General Psychology, 62*, 127-132.

Jaffe, J. H., Babor, T. F., & Fishbein, D. H. (1988). Alcoholics, aggression and antisocial personality. *Journal of Studies on Alcohol, 49*, 211-218.

Johnson, B. D., Goldstein, P. J., Preble, E., Schmiedler, J., Lipton, D. S., Spunt, B., & Miller, T. (1985). *Taking care of business: The economics of crime by heroin abusers*. Toronto: Lexington.

Kandel, D. B. (1988). Issues of sequencing of adolescent drug use and other problem behaviors. *Drugs and Society, 3*, 55-76.

Kolb, L. (1925). Drug addiction in its relation to crime. *Mental Hygiene, 9*, 74-89.

Kolb, L. (1927). Clinical contribution to drug addiction. The struggle for cure, and the conscious reasons for relapse. *Journal of Nervous and Mental Disease, 66*, 22-43.

Lang, A. R., Groeckner, D. J., Adesso, V. J., & Marlatt, G. A. (1976). Effects of alcohol on aggression in male social drinkers. *Journal of Abnormal Psychology, 84*, 508-518.

LeBlanc, M. (1986). *Drogue et délinquance chez les adolescents et les pupilles du tribunal de Montréal: Épidémiologie et politique sociale*. Conseil des services de santé et des services sociaux du Montréal métropolitain: Mémoire présenté à la commission administrative sur l'alcoolisme et la toxicomanie.

Lewis, C. E., Cloninger, C. R., & Pais, J. (1983). Alcoholism, antisocial personality and drug use in a criminal population. *Alcohol and Alcoholism, 18*, 53-60.

McCaghy, C. H. (1968). Drinking and deviance disavowal: The case of child molesters. *Social Problems, 16*, 43-49.

Miller, B. A. (1990). The interrelationships between alcohol and drugs and family violence. In NIDA Research Monograph Series, *Drugs and violence: causes, correlates, and consequences: Vol. 103* (pp. 177-207). Rockville, MD: National Institute on Drug Abuse.

Miller, M. M., & Potter-Efron, R. T. (1989). Aggression and violence associated with substance abuse. *Journal of Chemical Dependency Treatment, 3*, 1-36.

Muntaner, C., Walter, D., Nagoshi, C., Fishbein, D., Haertzen, C. A., & Jaffe, J. H. (1990). Self report vs. laboratory measures of aggression as predictors of substance abuse. *Drug and Alcohol Dependence, 25*, 1-11.

Nurco, D. N., Ball, J. C., Shaffer, J. W., & Hanlon, E. (1988a). Narcotic addiction and crime. In J. M. Scher & M. Segal (Eds.), *Perspectives in drug abuse: Drugs and the law: Vol. 1* (pp. 197-205). London: Freund Publishing House.

Nurco, D. N., Hanlon, T. E., Kinlock, T. W., & Duszynski, K. R. (1988b). Differential criminal patterns of narcotic addicts over an addiction career. *Criminology, 26*, 407-423.

Nurco, D. N., Kinlock, T. W., Hanlon, T. E., & Ball, J. C. (1988c). Non-narcotic drug use over an addiction career. A study of heroin addicts in Baltimore and New York City. *Comprehensive Psychiatry, 29*, 450-459.

Nurco, D. N., Shaffer, J. W., Ball, J. C., & Kinlock, T. W. (1984). Trends in the commission of crime among narcotic addicts over successive periods of addiction and non-addiction. *American Journal of Drug and Alcohol Abuse, 10*, 481-489.

Simonds, J. F., & Kashani, J. (1979). Drug abuse and criminal behavior in delinquent boys committed to a training school. *American Journal of Psychiatry, 136*, 1444-1448.

Simonds, J. F., & Kashani, J. (1980). Specific drug use and violence in delinquent boys. *American Journal of Drug and Alcohol Abuse, 7*, 305-322.

Speckart, G., & Anglin, M. D. (1986). Narcotics use and crime: An overview of recent research advances. *Contemporary Drug Problems, 13*, 741-769.

Taylor, S. P., & Gammon, C. B. (1975). Effects of type and dose of alcohol on human physical aggression. *Journal of Personality and Social Psychology (SP 51402), 32*, 169-175.

Tinklenberg, J. R., Kopell B. S., Roth W. T., & Darley C. (1974). Proceedings: Drugs, delinquency, and aggression. *Psychopharmacology Bulletin, 10*, 62-3.
Tinklenberg, J. R., Murphy, P., Murphy, P. L., & Pfefferbaum, A. (1981). Drugs and criminal assaults by adolescents: A replication study. *Journal of Psychoactive Drugs, 13*, 277-287.
Wish, E. D. (1986). PCP and crime: Just another illicit drug? In NIDA Research Monograph Series, *Phencyclidine: An update: Vol. 64* (pp. 174-189). Rockville, MD: National Institute on Drug Abuse.

Notes

[1] Support for this study was provided by the *Conseil québécois pour la recherche sociale*
[2] Alcohol is understood as a psycho-active drug and will be included under the generic term 'drug'.

Part VII
Prevention and Treatment of Offending

Absence from School: Research and Practical Management

Ian Berg

It would be nice to think that research findings are quickly put into practice. This is by no means always so. Studies by Clarke (1980) on absconding from residential approved schools, reported about 20 years ago, are examples of how simple practical measures to prevent and remedy running away, which were suggested by scientific investigations of the problem, were not adopted. It was found that buildings which were easy to leave unobserved, times of day and weather conditions when the light was poor, and other circumstances that made it relatively easy to get away from the school premises, made it more likely that absconding would occur. Absconding was also encouraged by putting together those children who had run away before. Absconding was more frequent shortly after admission. A tendency to abscond was conceptualised as a learned response to environmentally induced stress. The research suggested that simple practical measures would have the effect of reducing the problem. Less stressful admission procedures, greater surveillance, and buildings that were more difficult to get out of, secure accommodation for children who made a habit of running off, and care not to reward those who had gone away and been brought back, suggested themselves as procedures that would reduce the size of the problem. A decade after completing the work he could find little evidence that any notice had been taken of it. Dismally, Clarke attempted to explain this failure to implement his findings. One reason was that institutions, from which children frequently absconded, were being radically reorganised. It was a time of change. There was an idealistic view prevalent, that by making institutions more acceptable to children, they would be less likely to want to run away from them. He found it particularly galling, that new legislation no longer required abscondings to be recorded, thereby removing a useful measure of an important problem. For the rest, the failure to act on the research findings was attributed to inertia in institutions, conflicting theoretical view points and a general lack of understanding by practitioners of research publications.

Those of us who worked on the Leeds Truancy Project have similar gloomy feelings about the reception given to our findings (Berg et al., 1988). The research arose out of the dissatisfaction of juvenile court magistrates, in the city of Leeds, in the 1970s, with the standard procedure for dealing with children taken to court for failure to go to school, namely the Supervision Order which immediately passed the child over to a social worker. The Leeds magistrates preferred to hang on to the problem themselves. They began to adjourn the proceedings repeatedly and have the child come back to court over and over again so that they could monitor progress in getting back to normal school attendance. A retrospective survey carried out in 1973 looked at children dealt with by repeated adjournments compared with those put on Supervision Orders. It appeared that, despite similar circumstances, the adjourned group did substantially better than those on supervision as far as improved school attendance was concerned. In 1977, a controlled trial of adjournments versus

Supervision Orders, was carried out by the magistrates. Random allocation ensured that any child included in the trial had an equal chance of being managed by either procedure. Beforehand, the average attendance of both groups of children was 25%. In the six month period afterwards, the adjourned group attended 65% of the time on average and the supervised children just under 50% of possible attendances. There was also good evidence that the children in the adjourned group were committing criminal offences less frequently than those in the other group. Adjournments did not result in significantly more Care Orders than did supervision. As researchers, those of us involved were greatly encouraged by the fact that magistrates, there and then, virtually abandoned the use of the Supervision Order as totally discredited. Subsequent work led us to the view that the Supervision Order actually worsened the situation, since we considered that if nothing had been done, the school attendance of those put on Supervision Orders would have actually been better. We didn't expect social workers to be happy with our findings, nor were they. A group of them complained to the Lord Chancellor. We were encouraged by the willingness of Leeds magistrates to abandon the use of Supervision Orders as a general rule. Particular aspects of the adjournment system were looked at by further randomly controlled trials. Flexible adjournments which enabled children, who responded well, to come back to court less often, were compared with inflexible monthly appearances, and both were compared with a system of letters excusing the child coming to court at all after one or two appearances, if school attendance was satisfactory. This was done in 1980. The results indicated no difference between the four methods of handling truancy. We wondered if it was the process of coming to court which had the desirable effect, rather than what happened after the child appeared there. When the ten week period before coming to court was looked at in the middle of which the summons was issued, it was found that there was a 20% improvement in school attendance in the five weeks prior to the appearance in court. Another randomly allocated trial was carried out to see if those who had responded well by the time of their appearance in court required any further attendances at court to maintain their progress. Those who had at least 85% school attendance at this stage of the proceedings were randomly allocated to either "no order made" or "continued court appearances". For both groups of children school attendance averaged 75% without any significant difference between them. It looked as if it was the procedure of taking children to court which produced the desired effect and not repeated visits. Those who responded well to coming to court, which was roughly half of those summoned, had a significantly greater precourt improvement in attendance than those whose level of attendance wasn't good enough for them to be included in the study. Those who didn't improve as much and were not included in the trial still had roughly 70% attendance after repeated adjournments and in some instances an Interim Care Order, which required a stay of three weeks in a Local Authority Observation and Assessment Centre.

There was a widespread and mistaken belief that the adjournment system led to too many children being taken into care. This misapprehension was partly due to the fact that official records failed to distinguish between Interim Care Orders and Full Care Orders. Whenever children were put on Full Care Orders it was at the request of the social services department and on grounds other than absence from school.

Nevertheless, we were uneasy about the small proportion of children coming to court for difficulties going to school who were put on Interim Care Orders (ICOs). The magistrates considered the possibility of an ICO to be an essential part of the adjournment procedure. Between 1985 and 1987 a fourth randomly allocated trial was undertaken to see whether the Interim Care Order was an effective ingredient of adjournment (Brown et al., 1990).

About 80 children were included in the trial whose attendance was less than 80%. Half had an Interim Care Order with three weeks spent away from home in an Assessment Centre and half came to court after adjournment of the proceedings once a week for four weeks. They were essentially a group of failures of the adjournment procedure and were dealt with in one of these ways about two months after first coming to court. There was no overall significant difference between the two groups over six months as far as school attendance was concerned. It remained about 70% which was double the school attendance in a 10 week period before first coming to court. Although it could be that the possibility of an Interim Care Order was an important part of the adjournment system, the making and carrying out of an ICO was shown not to be necessary.

Having demonstrated the value of court appearances under care proceedings in failure to go to school, it was upsetting to find that this was totally disregarded in the recent Children's Act which brought to an end the whole system. This Act, which makes provision for an "Education Supervision Order" enshrines in statute the procedure which we found least helpful in dealing with unsatisfactory school attendance. It remains to be seen what will happen, but school attendance figures of 10 years ago and more recently for Leeds in our possession suggest that things are getting worse. The Education Department in Leeds had abandoned the system a few years in advance of the new law coming into force.

Although it was gratifying to pursue a series of studies each refining an effective method of getting defaulters back to more normal school attendance, whilst showing how courts could get the same results with greater economy, the most important outcome of the investigation was the finding that the adjournment procedure appeared to have an impact on delinquency. Many surveys including our own in Leeds have shown a connection between truancy and delinquency. The first of our randomly allocated trials produced good evidence for adjournment being associated with less delinquency than a Supervision Order. It could of course reflect a damaging effect of supervision on delinquency as we suspect in the case of school attendance, but three subsequent trials have all indicated less delinquency than would otherwise have been expected in those responding to coming to court in their school attendance suggesting a positive effect of adjournment on delinquency. One would have thought that the Government would have seized on any procedure which might have some effect on reducing criminal offending.

Looking at the way education welfare worked in Leeds, it was encouraging to find that the vast majority of children attending less than 70% of the time over a longish period had been visited by an educational welfare officer and also to find that the chances of being taken to court increased exponentially with the severity of the school attendance problem.

Attempts were sometimes made by those dealing with severe school attendance problems to identify children with features suggesting special requirements such as referral to child psychiatry (Bools et al., 1990). To provide some guidelines we interviewed the mothers of 100 severe school attendance problems in Leeds and carried out a cluster analysis of responses to a standard interview scale. About one in ten were boys who truanted and displayed severely antisocial behaviour. One in five of the others stayed home refusing to attend school and showed symptoms of anxiety and depression on having to go to school and sometimes more generally. Although the remainder truanted and had evidence of conduct problems in many instances, other factors such as social circumstances appeared more relevant to the poor school attendance than a conduct or an emotional disorder affecting the child.

Hoping that our findings published in 1990 might have had some effect, we carried out the survey of 80, 13- to 15-year-old children in the nearby city of Bradford who were attending school less than 40% of the time (Berg et al., 1992). Interviews with mothers and the children themselves confirmed the existence of a group of 15 emotionally disturbed children who had DSMIIIR anxiety/mood disorders. There was little evidence that referral for psychiatric assessment had been seriously considered in their case. The study found 25 DSMIIIR disruptive behaviour disorders. However, half the group had little in the way of psychiatric features.

The poor attenders as a whole were characterised by materially disadvantaged home backgrounds. The Leeds studies suggested that the substantial group of non disturbed severe school attendance problems in Bradford would have responded well to juvenile court appearances but these had rarely happened.

There is some consolation in the outcome that no-one seriously questioned the research methods of the various random trials. But we are sorry that the various Government departments concerned with the Children's Act chose to ignore the results.

References

Berg, I., Brown, I., & Hullin, R. (1988). *Off school in court.* Heidelberg: Springer-Verlag

Berg, I., Butler, A., Franklin, J., Hayes, H., Lucas, C., & Sims, R. (1993). DSM IIIR disorders, social factors and management of school attendance problems in the normal population. *Journal of Child Psychology and Psychiatry*, 34, 1187-1203.

Bools, C., Foster, J., Brown, I., & Berg, I. (1990). The identification of psychiatric disorders in children who fail to attend school: A cluster analysis of a non-clinical population. *Psychological Medicine*, *20*, 171-181.

Brown, I., Berg, I., Hullin, R., & McGuire, R. (1990). Are Interim Care Orders necessary to improve school attending in truants taken in juvenile court? *Education Review*, *42*, 231-245.

Clarke, R. (1980). Absconding from residential institutions for young offenders. In L. Hersov & I. Berg (Eds.), *Out of school. Modern perspectives in truancy and school refusal.* Chichester: John Wiley.

The Prevention of Delinquency in Spain

Vicente Garrido Genoves

In recent years, psychologists and educators have been interested in studying the possibilities of cognitive methods for the prevention of antisocial attitudes and behaviors in adolescence. Guided by the social competence construct (e.g. Barth, 1986), several investigators have oriented their efforts towards the teaching of systematic ways of thinking and the improvement of interpersonal cognitive abilities.

Based on the works of Ross and Fabiano (1985) and Shure and Spivack (1978), among others, it can be shown that it is possible to manage appropriate programs for preventing the involvement in habits and behaviors predictive of future delinquency careers. Burchard and Burchard's book (1987) *The prevention of delinquency* is a good example of the efforts made by psychologists and educators for equipping children with more social and personal resources as a way of avoiding a delinquent career. Our work uses different components of the program designed by Ross and Fabiano (1985) in the treatment of delinquency. Although Ross and Fabiano did not use their program in prevention - their review was based on the kinds of interventions that were successful in treatment - we have selected components of their program with the addition of elements from other cognitive programs, in a combination for preventing deliquency. In this case we have used the Think Aloud Program developed by Camp and Bash (1981).

Our research presents the implementation of a cognitive and behavioral program in a center that contains young males and females at social risk. The Monteolivete District House is one of many that the Valencia authorities have recently created for taking care of boys and girls that have suffered abuse and/or neglect in their family, or have shown several disruptive behaviors which have not been stopped because the family do not have the personal and social resources for its resolution. All of them present school failure, for which the center personnel and the school district teachers try to compensate. The district houses are open centers, with various educators and a social worker supervising the socio-cultural activities and the daily routines of the young people. Most of them return home every evening.

Method

A quasi-experimental design was used: eight males and four females in the experimental group, and six males and three females in the control, matched for familial and personal characteristics. The mean age of the subjects was 11.5 years.

The following evaluation instruments were used:

(1) the Wechsler Intelligence Scale for Children (WISC) (the following subtests: arithmetic, keys, digits and incomplete figures);

(2) the Means-End Problem-Solving Procedure (MEPS), a test created by Spivack, Shure and Platt (1985) "to measure the ability of a person to conceptualize the

means or sequence of steps that may be necessary to carry one from a point of having a need or a problem requiring solution, to the point where the need is satisfied or the problem is resolved" (p. 2);

(3) the Matching Familiar Figures (MFF), a classic reflexivity-impulsivity test in which two different measures are taken: time and errors (Kagan et al., 1964).

(4) A self-report measure of perceived self-efficacy in social interaction with other children, designed by Wheeler and Ladd (1982)

Social skills training was evaluated by four trained judges who watched two videotapes, one as the pre-test and the other as the post-test. In both of them the children performed three social skills, without training in the pre-test and with training in the post-test. The three selected skills were: to say a nice thing to somebody, to ask for a change of behavior, and to ask for a favour. Four children from the experimental group and four from the control group took part in these role-plays. Judges evaluated the tapes on verbal criteria (spontaneity, use of appropriate words, clarity, tone of voice), and non-verbal criteria (posture, distance, eye-contact).

Our research team trained three educators over two months to provide them with the expertise required to teach the children the cognitive program.

The program comprised: (1) the Thinking Aloud Program of Camp and Bash (1981), a 23 lesson kit designed to improve reflexive and problem-solving thinking; (2) the Kohlberg moral dilemmas, using group discussions for enhancing moral reasoning, used in our case for raising empathy and social perspective skills; and (3) 13 social skills imparted in 10 one-hour sessions.

Results

(a) Social skills training With regard to social skills training, the results are, in general, very promising. Among the experimental subjects, two improved in the non-verbal subtotal (15 in the pre-test vs. 22 in the post-test, 12 vs. 24), three in the verbal subtotal (23 vs. 31, 13 vs. 32 and 45 vs. 54), and three got better results in the total score (46 vs. 62, 27 vs. 65 and 90 vs. 101). So, three of the four subjects in the experimental group showed a better social performance in relation to the pre-test. In the case of the subjects in the control group, with the exception of one boy, the children deteriorated in their social performance in the two sub-totals (non-verbal: 22 vs. 18, 14 vs. 10 and 34 vs. 23; verbal: 27 vs. 23, 18 vs. 10, and 40 vs. 23) as well as in the total (56 vs. 48, 36 vs. 23, and 85 vs. 53).

(b) Cognitive intervention No significant differences between groups were found in the pre-test cognitive measures (see Table 1). With respect to the pre-test/post-test differences, the control group did not show any significant positive changes. In fact, the means-ends thinking (MEPS) decreased to 2.33 in the post-test from a score of 3.55 in the pre-test (see Table 2) ($p < .02$).

Table 1: Comparison of Groups on Pre-test Measures.

Tests	Exp. Group Mean	S.D.	Control Group Mean	S.D.	t	p
WISC						
(a) Keys	34.33	11.71	34.00	7.93	.07	.94
(b) Arithemic	7.66	2.80	7.22	1.64	.42	.67
(c) Digits	7.25	1.86	7.88	2.52	-.67	.51
(d) I. Figures	11.83	2.55	12.88	2.08	-1.01	.32
MEPS	2.41	1.37	3.55	1.13	-2.02	.058
MFF						
(a) Time	10.60	3.61	11.23	4.51	-.36	.72
(b) Errors	12.50	5.74	8.88	4.70	1.54	.14
Self-report	34.83	8.63	38.22	7.04	-.96	.34

Table 2: Comparison of Pre-test and Post-test Scores for the Control Group (N = 9).

Tests	Pre-test Mean	Post-test S.D.	Mean	S.D.	t	p
WISC						
(a) Keys	34.00	7.93	30.55	10.53	1.77	.11
(b) Arithemic	7.22	1.64	8.11	1 26	-1.8	.10
(c) Digits	7.88	2.52	7.77	2.68	.55	.59
(d) I. Figures	12.88	2.08	13.33	1.50	-.46	.65
MEPS	3.55	1.13	2.33	1.58	2.82	.02
MFF						
(a) Time	11.23	4.51	11.84	6.22	-.32	.75
(b) Errors	8.88	4.70	9.66	2.87	-.42	.68
Self-report	38.22	7.04	39.77	9.16	-.82	.43

In the experimental group, subjects have improved significantly in the following variables: Keys ($p < .01$) and Incomplete Figures ($p < .02$) from the WISC; the time measure of the MFF ($p < .005$); the MEPS ($p < .03$); and the self-report of self-efficacy ($p < .01$) (see Table 3).

Table 3: Comparison of Pre-test and Post-test Scores for the Experimental Group (N = 12).

Tests	Pre-test Mean	Post-test S.D.	Mean	S.D.	t	p
WISC						
(a) Keys	34.33	11.71	40.08	11.36	-2.80	.01
(b) Arithemic	7.66	2.80	8.33	2.30	-1.08	.30
(c) Digits	7.25	1.86	8.08	1.88	-1.76	.10
(d) I. Figures	11.83	2.55	13.16	3.58	-2.68	.02
MEPS	2.41	1.37	3.58	1.08	-2.46	.03
MFF						
(a) Time	10.60	3.61	19.13	7.38	-3.52	.005
(b) Errors	12.50	5.74	9.25	5.13	1.97	.07
Self-report	34.83	8.63	43.66	9.88	-3.08	.01

Discussion

It is important to remark, in the discussion of this program, that these results are the product of a course that lasted 40 hours, over two months. It is not too much to ask teachers and practitioners in the social services and justice system to implement this kind of intervention, which seems to hold great promise in correcting the social-cognitive deficits of children at social risk. Of course, booster sessions will be necessary, but it can be concluded that time invested in socio-cognitive programs can support other efforts in the prevention of antisocial behavior and broader social failure.

It is interesting to ask generally what we have learned from cognitive programs (mainly the Robert Ross "R & R" program) applied up to now in several countries (see Ross, 1992; Ross, Fabiano & Garrido, 1990; Garrido & Sanchis, 1991).

In general, we can say that:

(1) We are able to improve the skills targeted in the treatment: reflexivity, role-taking, cognitive problem-solving abilities, and so on (see Ross & Fabiano, 1985).

(2) The cognitive model has a positive influence upon academic progress (Berrueta-Clement et al., 1987), which is a major predictor of later adjustment, and therefore a resilience factor against delinquency.

(3) The cognitive model has proved its adaptability to a great variety of subjects - children, youths, adults, men and women, of various ethnic groups - and with different types of problems like drug-addiction, robbery, and violence. However, there still remains a dearth of outcome evaluation studies of the effectiveness of cognitive programs with different groups of people and different types of problem.

(4) Cognitive programs have also been readily accepted by practitioners in various fields - psychologists, social workers, probation officers, and so on.

(5) Finally, the research has showed that some programs are effective in the reduction of the recidivism (Ross & Fabiano, 1985; Ross, 1992; Ross, Fabiano, & Diemer-Ewles, 1988; Garrido, 1992).

If we want to progress towards more effective offender rehabilitation we must direct future research toward answering several important questions.

1. Theoretical background Is it now possible to elaborate a theoretical model that will support and improve the research? The experience accumulated in social sciences teaches us that theory is essential in order to integrate and develop knowledge. Jack Katz's (1988) *Seductions of crime* and Yochelson and Samenow's (1976) *Criminal thinking patterns* have been two good attempts, but in our opinion not totally successful. Perhaps Walters' (1990) *Criminal lifestyle* is an interesting and worthwhile path to follow in the nineties.

2. Assessment We do not have good instruments to assess with confidence the intermediate cognitive variables which are supposed to be influenced in the intervention. Neither are all the constructs used well defined, nor do they have unequivocal operational definitions (e.g., "empathy", "problem-solving skill"). It is true that the tests we are using are able to detect the changes we predicted would appear as a consequence of the intervention, but it is not clear that those tests are really measuring the things we say they do. For example, does the Means-Ends Problem-Solving Procedure (MEPS) measure also optional thinking, and not only planning? Finally, the relationship between interpersonal or social intelligence and academic or impersonal intelligence needs more research, especially the ways in which both of them can mutually compensate to obtain an adjusted socialization process.

3. Intervention We do not know yet which of the modified components of the intervention are really essential in this process of prosocial change. Probably empathy is a basic element, but is it also a sufficient one? In this sense, it might be very useful to investigate if the R & R program could specialize in different programs for different kind of offenders.

4. We need also to investigate the relationship between the operant and cognitive aspects of the rehabilitation program. For example, do we know what happens if we punish the criminal thinking patterns? Do the same effects appear as when we punish observable behaviors?

The R & R model will be only tested in all its integrity when the network of services for treatment, both inside and outside institutions, share the principles and action guides involved in that model. In the meantime, it is necesary to continue working; it does not matter that we do not have all the answers to all those questions.

References

Barth, R. (1986). *Social and cognitive treatment of children and adolescents*. San Francisco: Jossey-Bass.

Berrueta-Clement, J., Schweinhart, L., Barnett, W., & Weikart, D. (1987). The effects of early educational intervention on crime and delinquency in adolescence and early adulthood. In J. Burchard & S. Burchard (Eds.), *Prevention of delinquent behavior* (pp. 220-240). Beverly Hills, CA: Sage.

Burchard, J., & Burchard, S. (Eds.) (1987). *Prevention of delinquent behavior*. Beverly Hills, CA: Sage.

Camp, B., & Bash, M. (1981). *Think aloud*. Champaign, Ill: Research Press.

Garrido, V. (1992). Education for social competence in the treatment of juvenile delinquents. In B. Rowson & J. McGuire (Eds.), *What works* (pp. 27-37). Manchester: Greater Manchester Probation Service.

Garrido, V., & Sanchís, J. R. (1991). The cognitive model in the treatment of Spanish offenders. *The Journal of Correctional Education, 42*, 111-118.

Kagan, J., Rosman, B. L., Day, D., Albert, J., & Phillips, W. (1964). Information processing in the child: Significance of analytic and reflective attitudes. *Psychological Monographs, 78*(578).

Katz, J. (1988). *Seductions of crime*. New York: Basic Books.

Ross, R. (1992). Reasoning and rehabilitation of offenders. In B. Rowson & J. McGuire (Eds.), What works (pp. 21-26). Manchester: Greater Manchester Probation Service.

Ross, R., & Fabiano, E. (1985). *Time to think*. Johnson City: Institute of Social Sciences and Arts.

Ross, R., Fabiano, E., & Diemer-Ewles, C. (1988). Reasoning and rehabilitation. *International Journal of Offender Therapy & Comparative Criminology, 32*, 29-36.

Ross, R., Fabiano, E., & Garrido, V. (1990). El pensamiento prosocial. *Delincuencia/delinquency, 1*.

Shure, M., & Spivack, G. (1978). *Problem-solving techniques in childrearing*. San Francisco: Jossey-Bass.

Spivack, G., Shure, M., & Platt, J. (1985). *Means-ends problem solving (MEPS)*. Philadelphia, PA: Hahnemann University.

Walters, G. D. (1990). *The criminal life-style*. Newbury Park, CA: Sage.

Wheeler, V. A., & Ladd, G. W. (1982). Assessment of children's self-efficacy for social interactions with peers. *Developmental Psychology, 18*, 795-805.

Yochelson, S., & Samenow, S. E. (1976). *The criminal personality: A profile for change*. New York: Aronson.

The Social Competence of Young Offenders: A Return to Basics

Clive R. Hollin

While there are several models of social competence in the social psychology literature, the social skills and cognitive-behavioural models have attracted particular attention in the field of delinquency. These two models are important not only at a theoretical level, but also because of the way that they inform the efforts of practitioners who work with delinquents. My purpose in this paper is fourfold: 1) to give a brief overview of these two models; 2) to discuss the empirical research these theoretical models have generated in the study of young offenders; 3) to consider the conclusions from the outcome studies of practice based on these models; 4) finally to return to basics in suggesting where we turn next as both researchers and practitioners.

Social Skills

As detailed by Argyle (1967), the social skills model is illustrated in Figure 1.

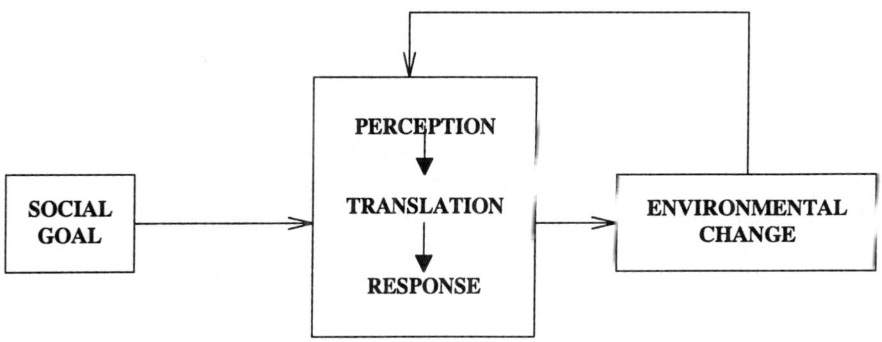

Figure 1: Social Skills Model (Argyle & Kendon, 1967)

In order to achieve a social goal, the model suggests that the socially competent individual will be skilled in three areas of functioning: 1) *social perception*, in which the person detects and understands a social signal, either verbal or non verbal, in their environment; 2) the process of *translation* during which the person makes decisions about their course of action; 3) based upon their perception of the situation and their social decision-making, the individual finally makes an observable *response*. This response then impacts upon the social environment, typically the other people involved, and the changes precipitated by the response close the system in the form of a feedback loop.

Yet further, Argyle suggests that these social processes can be conceived of as skills, acquired through learning like any other skill. It therefore follows that those who lack social skills can be helped through social skills training (SST) to improve their social competence (Hollin & Trower, 1986a, 1986b, 1988).

Social skills and delinquency

Is there any evidence to show that delinquents have particular difficulties in any of the components of the social skills model as described by Argyle?

Social perception I know of only one study of social perception in delinquents. McCown et al. (1986) investigated the ability of delinquents to recognise emotion from facial expression. They found that, compared to non-delinquents, the delinquents could recognise happiness, anger, and fear equally well; but were less able to detect sadness, surprise, and disgust.

Translation In the social skills model the translation stage is characterised, following perception, by the cognitive processes of deciding on a suitable response. This process of social problem solving demands the ability to generate feasible courses of action, consider alternatives, and make plans towards achieving the desired outcome. Several studies have suggested that young offenders experience difficulties with this aspect of social cognition. For example, Freedman et al. (1978) found that young offenders gave less competent responses than non-offenders to a series of social problems, as assessed using the Adolescent Problem Inventory (API). The delinquents used a more limited range of alternatives to solve interpersonal problems, and relied more on verbal and physical aggression. In a similar study, Veneziano and Veneziano (1988) used the API to define three groups of delinquents: those offenders classified as "incompetent" in their knowledge of social skills, "moderately competent", and "competent". It was found that these groups differed significantly in the number of behavioural difficulties they experienced, on measures of personality, and on measures of social values and morality. In general, the group with less knowledge was disadvantaged compared to their peers. Overall, the delinquents showed a lower knowledge of social skills than a sample of "good citizens". Similarly, Gaffney and McFall (1981) developed the Problem Inventory for Adolescent Girls (PIAG), a self-report measure of social competence in dealing with awkward social situations. They found that delinquent girls gave less socially competent statements as to their probable actions in the various social situations.

Attempts to determine the relationship between these measures and offending have provided mixed results. Some studies have not found a relationship between API scores and offending (Hunter & Kelley, 1986; Veneziano & Veneziano, 1988). However, Ward and McFall (1986), using the PIAG, found that female young offenders gave less competent responses to the problem situations, and that a lower PIAG score was significantly related to higher rates of self-reported offending.

Response Spence (1981a) compared the social performance skills of 18 young male offenders with 18 non-delinquent controls matched for age, academic performance, and social background. The delinquents showed significantly less eye contact and speech, but more "fiddling" and gross body movements - an aggregation of behaviours known to relate to poor ratings of social skill (Spence, 1981b). Indeed, on global ratings of social skill, social anxiety, and employability the delinquent group were rated less favourably than the non-delinquents.

In summary, the force of much of the research is that delinquents do experience difficulties some with social skills. However, three points remain to be made. The first is that the range of empirical evidence with young offenders is not great, there are relatively few studies. Thus any conclusions that may be drawn should, at best, be tentative in nature - especially given the artificiality of many experimental situations.

The second point concerns the heterogeneity of the delinquent population. Veneziano and Veneziano (1988) suggest that their findings show that: "Delinquents are diverse group with respect to social skills, with a wide range of knowledge and presumably behavior" (p. 167). It is unwise to assume that all young offenders will exhibit similar deficits in social ability. Further, the point should be made that the population in question - as defined by the studies in the literature - includes delinquent young people who have committed minor offences and young offenders convicted of serious crimes. The hypothesis remains to be tested that the degree and type of offending are related to social functioning and ultimately treatment outcome.

The final point concerns the further assumption, important when it comes to intervention, that some young people behave in a delinquent fashion because they lack the skills necessary for prosocial behaviour. As noted, there is only limited evidence that social skills are related to offending (Ward & McFall, 1986); with some studies finding no relationship (Furnham, 1984; Hunter & Kelley, 1986; Veneziano & Veneziano, 1988). As Gaffney and McFall (1981) state: "Although the data show a relationship between a lack of competence in social situations and delinquent behavior, the research does not provide evidence that delinquency is caused by a lack of social skills" (p. 967).

Nonetheless, a body of research has looked at the effects of training delinquents in social skills (for reviews see Hollin 1990a; Hollin & Henderson, 1986). There are several texts available to inform the practice of SST with offenders (e.g., Priestly et al., 1984; Priestley & McGuire, 1985).

Social skills training and delinquency

Micro-skills training Some training programmes have successfully improved delinquents' "micro-skills", that is specific nonverbal and verbal behaviours such as eye contact and questioning (e.g., Spence & Marzillier, 1981).

Macro-skills training Complex "macro-skills", rather than "micro" behaviours, have been a target in some SST programmes. Thus, for example, SST has been used successfully used to teach complex negotiation and agreement skills to delinquents and their parents (Serna et al., 1986). Similarly, Werner et al. (1975) used STT to train young offenders in a number of skills known to be crucial in police-juvenile encounters. The improvement in skill level was reflected in more favourable ratings from police officers of the offenders' level of politeness and respectfulness.

Institutional behaviour As many training programmes have been conducted within institutions, several studies have examined the effects of SST on the trainees' institutional behaviour. Hollin and Henderson (1981) monitored offending against discipline as indices of institutional behaviour in a penal establishment: following SST there was a significant improvement on this measure for the young offenders who took part in the training. Similarly, Hollin and Courtney (1983) used skills training techniques to attempt to change institutional rule-breaking behaviour. Whilst a decrease in self-reported institutional offending was found, official rates of rule breaking were not changed.

The crucial question, however, is whether SST can affect recidivism.

Recidivism Several studies have looked at the long-term effectiveness of SST by examining recidivism rates. Acknowledging the difficulties in measuring recidivism, the conclusion with regard to recidivism is that SST seems to have little impact in those few studies where it is measured (see Hollin & Henderson, 1984; Henderson & Hollin, 1986). Of particular interest here is the work of Spence and Marzillier (1981) who found that six months after a successful training programme, the SST group showed the lowest level of official police convictions (although the difference between the SST group and the control groups was not statistically significant). Importantly, Spence and Marzillier also measured self-reported offending, and found that the SST group reported a numerically *higher* incidence of offending than the controls.

In summary, it can be seen that the use of SST with delinquents has met with mixed success. With some targets, principally the "micro" and "macro" social behaviours, there has been considerable success. However, with recidivism the outcome evidence is less than encouraging.

Should we be surprised at these mixed findings of generally less well developed social competence among delinquent samples, improved social competence through SST, but no effect of SST on recidivism? At one level clearly not: inherent in the assumption that SST can change criminal behaviour is the theoretical position that delinquency can be explained in terms of individual skill deficits. Such a view is clearly at odds with mainstream theories from criminology, and with contemporary psychological theory that holds that crime is a function of the *interaction* between the individual and their environment (Hollin, 1989, 1992). However, as I will explore later, rather than dismiss the role of social competence in explaining delinquency, an alternative approach can be formulated by returning to basics.

Cognitive-Behavioural Approaches

While the social skills model generated a substantial body of evidence, the cognitive revolution in psychology had an impact upon both models of social functioning and research with young offenders. Theoretically, for example, there were advances such as that proposed by McFall (1982) that elaborated upon the role of cognition in social interaction skills. More recently, Dodge (1986) has defined a sequence of steps in effective social information processing and performance: 1) encoding social cues; 2) cognitive representation and interpretation of these social cues; 3) searching for appropriate ways to respond in a given situation; 4) choosing the optimum response; 5) enacting the selected response. Yet further, another body of research has accumulated on the cognitive style - the attitudes, beliefs, and values - of delinquent samples.

Information processing

The impact of theories such as that advanced by Dodge has been most keenly felt in the study of aggressive and violent behaviour. There is a growing body of research that strongly suggests that aggressive and violent people search for and perceive fewer social cues that non violent people; are more likely to interpret the behaviour of other people in a hostile manner; generate fewer options for dealing with a social situation; and believe that violent conduct is legitimate behaviour (e.g., Slaby & Guerra, 1988). Yet further, it is now generally taken that emotional arousal can have a complex interaction with cognition, intensifying the individual's aggression and increasing the likelihood of a violent outburst (e.g., Novaco & Welsh, 1989).

Cognitive style

Research here has highlighted trends among delinquent populations in cognitive style. Thus, delinquent samples do not score highly on measures of empathy and self-control; are characterized by a marked delay in the development of moral reasoning; and show a tendency to external locus of control (Ross & Fabiano, 1985).

Cognitive-behavioural intervention

A range of intervention programmes with delinquents - generally referred to as cognitive-behavioural programmes - followed the resurgence of interest in cognition. Some of these were elaborations of familiar social skills procedures, such as SST plus self-instructional training (Hollin et al., 1986), while others began to develop in new directions. These latter programmes included innovations such as moral reasoning development, training in role-taking skills, self-control and self-instructional training, anger control, and social problem solving skills training (for reviews see Hollin, 1990b; Ross & Fabiano, 1985). Even more recently there has been the development of the multimodal programmes: packages that contain a combination of the techniques listed above. A typical example is to be found in Aggression Replacement Training (ART) (Goldstein & Keller, 1987). ART consists of structured learning training that incorporates both SST and social problem solving skills training; anger control training; and moral development education.

It is clear from the meta-analyses that cognitive-behavioural programmes do offer an optimum approach to reduce recidivism among young offenders (Lipsey, 1992). Having said that, there is no room for complacency and we need to consider ways of improving still further the effectiveness of cognitive-behavioural intervention programmes with delinquents.

Next Steps

I think we have reached a stage at which we are ready for the second generation of research in this area. The first generation of research has clearly defined the areas with which we should be concerned. The second generation must build on this I think by returning to basics in two ways: 1) to search more deeply *within* models of social competence; 2) to research *across* the full complexity of a model rather than look at parts of a model in isolation. Let me give examples of both approaches.

Increasing depth

Taking the social skills model, one approach to increase the depth of findings is to look more closely at the traditional measures of social competence. An excellent example of this is to be found in the recent study by Simonian, Tarnowski, and Gibbs (1991) of the API scores of delinquents. The merit of this study is that, unlike previous studies, they looked systematically, using a principal components analysis, at the API scores. Simonian et al. found three distinct factors within the API that corresponded to the demand characteristics of different social situations: 1) *Immediate Response Demand*, associated with situations that demanded a quick response; 2) *Deferred Response Demand*, in situations in which there is time to contemplate one's response; and 3) *Antisocial Peer Influence*, in situations in which there was peer pressure to behave in an antisocial manner. Interestingly, the delinquents' API scores on these three factors were then found to correlate with different types of antisocial conduct. The first factor correlated with serious aggressive delinquent acts, perhaps suggesting mediation of situational demands through angry arousal to violent conduct. The second factor correlated with drug taking, suggesting a recourse to artificial stress reducing agents, perhaps mediated by poor social problem solving skills. The third factor was correlated with a wide range of low level delinquent acts, clearly reflecting an inability to resist peer group pressure to offend.

Increasing breadth

The second approach to generating new research lies in designing research that will look at the relationships between different components of social functioning. A study by Hollin and Swaffer (in press) provides an illustration of this strategy. In what was essentially a pilot study, we used three measures of social competence - one of social perception, one of social problem solving, and one of response skills - with a group of young offenders. As expected, we found that the young offenders gave less than optimum performance on each measure. However, if we follow the original model, it is not unreasonable to predict that there should be a relationship between these three measures. Our results showed a significant correlation between delinquents' scores on measures of social perception and social response skills. However, the social problem solving skills measure did not correlate with either of the other measures. There are several possible explanations for this, some methodological others theoretical, but the point is made that we need to undertake some basic research in area of social competence in delinquents.

Conclusion

The time is right for a considered review and appraisal of the research in this field. The trend towards research that examines the full complexity of the relationship between social competence and delinquent behaviour must continue. Following the lead of practitioners who have developed multimodal intervention programmes, researchers would do well to adopt multimodal research designs. Rather than a rejection of any link between social competence and delinquent behaviour, we need new research designs and new data to allow old models to be fully explored.

References

Argyle, M. (1967). *The psychology of interpersonal behaviour*. Harmondsworth, Middlesex: Penguin Books.

Dodge, K. A. (1986). A social-information processing model of social competence in children. In M. Perlmutter (Ed.), *Minnesota symposium on child psychology: Vol. 18* (pp. 77-125). Hillsdale, NJ: Erlbaum.

Freedman, B. J., Rosenthal, L., Donahoe, C. P., Schlundt, D. G., & McFall, R. M. (1978). A social-behavioral analysis of skills deficits in delinquent and non-delinquent adolescent boys. *Journal of Consulting and Clinical Psychology*, *46*, 1448-1462.

Furnham, A. (1984). Personality, social skills, anomie and delinquency: A self-report study of a group of normal non-delinquent adolescents. *Journal of Child Psychology and Psychiatry*, *25*, 409-420.

Gaffney, L. R., & McFall, R. M. (1981). A comparison of social skills in delinquent and nondelinquent adolescent girls using a behavioral role-playing inventory. *Journal of Consulting and Clinical Psychology*, *49*, 959-967.

Goldstein, A. P., & Keller, H. (1987). *Aggressive behavior: Assessment and intervention*. Elmsford, NY: Pergamon Press.

Henderson, M., & Hollin, C. R. (1986). Social skills training and delinquency. In C. R. Hollin & P. Trower (Eds.), *Handbook of social skills training: Vol. 1. Applications across the life span* (pp. 79-101). Oxford: Pergamon Press.

Hollin, C. R. (1989). *Psychology and crime: An introduction to criminological psychology*. London: Routledge.

Hollin, C. R. (1990a). Social skills training with delinquents: A look at the evidence and some recommendations for practice. *British Journal of Social Work*, *20*, 483-493.

Hollin, C. R. (1990b). *Cognitive-behavioural interventions with young offenders*. Elmsford, NY: Pergamon Press.

Hollin, C. R. (1992). *Criminal behaviour: A psychological approach to explanation and prevention*. London: Falmer Press.

Hollin, C. R., & Courtney, S. A. (1983). A skills training approach to the reduction of institutional offending. *Personality and Individual Differences*, *4*, 257-264.

Hollin, C. R., & Henderson, M. (1981). The effects of social skills training on incarcerated delinquent adolescents. *International Journal of Behavioural Social Work and Abstracts*, *1*, 145-155.

Hollin, C. R., & Henderson, M. (1984). Social skills training with young offenders: False expectations and the "failure" of training. *Behavioural Psychotherapy*, *12*, 331-341.

Hollin, C. R., Huff, G. J., Clarkson, F., & Edmondson, A. C. (1986). Social skills training with young offenders in a borstal: An evaluative study. *Journal of Community Psychology, 14*, 289-299.

Hollin, C. R., & Swaffer, T. (in press). Social competence and delinquency: A return to basics. *Journal of Adolescence*.

Hollin, C. R., & Trower, P. (Eds.). (1986a). *Handbook of social skills training: Vol. 1. Applications across the life span*. Oxford: Pergamon Press.

Hollin, C. R., & Trower, P. (Eds.). (1986b). *Handbook of social skills training: Vol. 2. Clinical applications and new directions*. Oxford: Pergamon Press.

Hollin, C. R., & Trower, P. (1988). Development and applications of social skills training: A review and critique. In M. Hersen, R. M. Eisler, & P. M. Miller (Eds.), *Progress in behavior modification: Vol. 22* (pp. 165-214). Beverly Hills, CA: Sage Publications.

Hunter, N., & Kelley, C. K. (1986). Examination of the validity of the Adolescent Problems Inventory among incarcerated juvenile delinquents. *Journal of Consulting and Clinical Psychology, 54*, 301-302.

Lipsey, M. W. (1992). Juvenile delinquency treatment: A meta-analytic inquiry into the variability of effects. In T. Cook, H. Cooper, D. Corday, H. Hartman, L. Hedges, R. Light, T. Louis, & F. Mosteller (Eds.), *Meta-analysis for explanation: A casebook* (pp. 83-127). New York: Russell Sage Foundation.

McCown, W., Johnson, J., & Austin, S. (1986). Inability of delinquents to recognize facial affects. *Journal of Social Behavior and Personality, 1*, 489-496.

McFall, R. M. (1982). A review and reformulation of the concept of social skills. *Behavioral Assessment, 4*, 1-33.

Novaco, R. W., & Welsh, W. N. (1989). Anger disturbances: Cognitive mediation and clinical prescriptions. In K. Howells & C. R. Hollin (Eds.), *Clinical approaches to violence* (pp. 39-60). Chichester: Wiley.

Priestley, P., & McGuire, J. (1985). *Offending behaviour: Skills and stratagems for going straight*. London: Batsford.

Priestley, P., McGuire, J., Flegg, D., Hemsley, V., Welham, D., & Barnitt, R. (1984). *Social skills in prison and the community*. London: Routledge and Kegan Paul.

Ross, R. R., & Fabiano, E. A. (1985). *Time to think: A cognitive model of delinquency prevention and offender rehabilitation*. Johnson City, TN: Institute of Social Sciences and Arts.

Serna, L. A., Schumaker, J. B., Hazel, J. S., & Sheldon, J. B. (1986). Teaching reciprocal social skills to parents and their delinquent adolescents. *Journal of Clinical Child Psychology, 15*, 64-77.

Slaby, R. G., & Guerra, N. G. (1988). Cognitive mediators of aggression in adolescent offenders: I. Assessment. *Developmental Psychology, 24*, 580-588.

Simonian, S. J., Tarnowski, K. J., & Gibbs, J. C. (1991). Social skills and antisocial conduct of delinquents. *Child Psychiatry and Human Development, 22*, 17-27.

Spence, S. H. (1981a). Differences in social skills performance between institutionalized juvenile male offenders and a comparable group of boys without offence records. *British Journal of Clinical Psychology, 20*, 163-171.

Spence, S. H. (1981b). Validation of social skills of adolescent males in an interview conversation with a previously unknown adult. *Journal of Applied Behavior Analysis, 14*, 159-168.

Spence, S. H., & Marzillier, J. S. (1981). Social skills training with adolescent male offenders: II. Short-term, long-term and generalized effects. *Behaviour Research and Therapy, 19*, 349-368.

Veneziano, C., & Veneziano, L. (1988). Knowledge of social skills among institutionalized juvenile delinquents: An assessment. *Criminal Justice and Behavior, 15*, 152-171.

Ward, C. I., & McFall, R. M. (1986). Further validation of the Problem Inventory for Adolescent Girls: Comparing Caucasian and black delinquents and nondelinquents. *Journal of Consulting and Clinical Psychology, 54*, 732-733.

Werner, J. S., Minkin, N., Minkin, B. L., Fixsen, D. L., Phillips, E. L., & Wolf, M. M. (1975). "Intervention package": An analysis to prepare juvenile delinquents for encounters with police officers. *Criminal Justice and Behavior*, *2*, 55-84.

A Model for the Treatment of Young Offenders in Spain: Searching for Effectiveness

Vicente Garrido

We are more and more convinced that the battle against juvenile offending has to have its roots in the prevention area. Works such as those of Farrington, Ohlin & Wilson (1986), Burchard & Burchard (1987) and the implications of the Eysenck & Gudjonsson's (1989) recent book, suggest that the main and more hopeful way of deal with offending is precisely to avoid the juvenile offender reaching this status. In the now classic reflection about criminal behavior involved in Currie' s *Confronting crime* (1985), the conclusions direct us to consider in what directions we have to put our efforts for preventing delinquent behavior.

The main results derived through the meta-analytical reviews, advise us that cognitive-behavioral programmes hold the most promising possibilities in terms of treatment of delinquent behavior (see Lipsey, 1992). If we link this research with the works of authors as Wahler & Dumas (1987), Berrueta-Clement, Schweinhart, Barnett & Weikart (1987), Hawkins & Lam (1987) and Kazdin (1985), among many others, it is quite reasonable to think that we must to try to place the prevention in schools as one of the priorities in the social policy of each country.

Why in the schools? There are several reasons. Firstly, it is a very good time for improving the personal resources of the students who, according to the criminal careers studies, are at risk of being juvenile and adult offenders. Secondly, we are able to teach in schools many of the social and cognitive abilities that are lacking in disadvantaged children because of a deficient socialization process, thus we are looking for a supportive socialization that is able to balance the poor rearing practices within the childrens' homes. Finally, there is a growing interest in community prevention programmes in trying to link prevention aspects in schools with those made by social workers and other practitioners in the family units. If we can spread the interventions in schools, then we will be in a better position to involve parents in a more comp-rehensive prevention network.

The San Clemente Project follows this line of thinking. We want to address the root causes of school failure in deprived children: the cognitive and behavioral skills that prevent integration in the school.

The San Clemente Project

San Clemente (S.C.) is the name of the public school in which we implemented the programme. The S.C. school is located in a working-class quarter, in a village near Valencia, where immigrant families and native families live together.

Most of the S.C. students are children from immigrant families, and they often present economic and socio-cultural deficits. It is understandable then, that this kind of student appears with regularity in compensatory education classrooms, because of school failure and marginalisation.

The objectives of our research were, on the whole, to improve the social competence of the students, and to prevent future school failure (a well-known correlate of offending in late youth). Specifically, objectives were:

To improve interpersonal problem-solving ability, in terms of means-ends, consequent, optional and causal thinking.

To improve role-taking ability.

To improve social skills.

To improve school perfomance.

Underlying this last goal is the idea that improving self-regulation in the child will improve school performance, because it will help to set up an easier learning environment, as well as enhance attention and attitudinal factors, which are very important in the learning process.

Method

The sample The total sample is composed of 47 children, 20 in the experimental group (14 boys, six girls) and 27 in the control group (14 boys, 13 girls). The age range was nine to ten years.

A quasi-experimental design was used, where the children in the control group had a higher level of socio-cognitive development than the experimental group. Since we wanted to work with the most disavantaged children of the school, the experimental subjects were selected because of their poor academic behavior, disruptive school behavior and, on the whole, for being at social risk. These selection criteria were assessed by the school teachers who completed a social and biographic questionnaire for this purpose, and observed the pupils.

Method of intervention The intervention program was implemented during the school year 1991-1992, and comprised the following sessions and techniques: (1) "Think Aloud", a problem-solving program for children (Camp & Bash, 1981). 23 sessions; (2) social skills training, 20 sessions, including 14 different skills such as asking for help, asking for a behavioral change, negotiation, and so on; (3) values development, 10 sessions discussing five different moral dilemmas. In order to apply the programme, the teacher taught one extra-hour on each one of the days in which a session was given.

The assessment instruments were: (1) video-taped role-plays of social skills situations, before and after the social skills training; (2) Wisconsin Intelligence Scale for Children (WISC) subtests - arithmetic, digits, incomplete figures and keys; (3) means-ends problem-solving (MEPS; Shure & Spivack, 1985); (4) C.O.P.E. Scale (Harter, 1982), designed to measure the child's self-perception in four areas: self-concept, social, physical and school behavior; (5) BAS 1 (Silva & Martorell, 1983), a rating-scale measuring four prosocial factors (leadership, joviality, social perspective and respect/self-control), three anti-social factors (aggressivity-obstinacy, apathy-withdrawal and anxiety) and a summary-socialization factor.

Results

The results were analyzed in two categories; one for the social skills training and another for the cognitive and behavioral treatment. With respect to the cognitive and behavioral data, we made four comparisons: pre-test experimental and control; experimental pre/post-test; control pre/post-test; experimental and control post-test. Data for both groups is presented in Table 1. There are 12 variables that discriminate between the groups: leadership, joviality, social perspective, respect/self-control, aggressivity-obstinacy, apathy-withdrawal and socialization in the BAS-1; in the WISC, subtests of arithmetic, incomplete figures and Key B; and finally in the factor self-concept and school behavior scales of the C.O.P.E.

Table 1: Comparison of Experimental and Control Groups at the Pre-test (Only Means with Significant Differences are Shown).

	Experimental	**Control**	**p**
BAS 1			
(a) Leadership	9.20	29.30	0.000
(b) Joviality	19.45	29.00	0.000
(c) Social Perspective	14.00	22.22	0.000
(d) Respect/Self-Control	28.60	39.30	0.000
(e) Aggressivity-Obstinacy	10.75	4.74	0.044
(f) Apathy-Withdrawal	9.40	2.78	0.001
(g) Summary-Socialization	25.50	36.44	0.000
WISC			
Arithmetics	6.75	7.96	0.013
Incomplete Figures	6.35	8.85	0.000
Key B	28.45	39.52	0.000
COPE			
Self-Concept	17.60	20.78	0.005
School Behavior	16.70	20.30	0.003

In all the cases, the control group obtained better results in the sense of a good psychological adjustment than the experimental group, in some cases the differences being very large. Therefore, there is no doubt about the inequality of experimental and control subjects, which reflects our previous selection of the students to be trained. In summary, there are significant differences in 12 of the 18 variables analyzed.

What happened in the post-tests? Amazingly, the boys and girls of the control group show poorer data in five of the eight variables that forms the BAS-1 (Table 2). In fact, they are now perceived as being less jovial, empathic, with a lower self-control and like being more apathic and withdrawn in the teachers' view, so that their global rating is now also lower (socialization sub-scale, Cs). It is difficult to interpret this result.

Perhaps it is the product of several variables not easily controlled. For example, it is possible that the students were more tired and less enthusiastic at the end of the school year than at the beginning, or perhaps the teachers assessed the students more harshly at the end of the academic year because of their tiredness.

With respect to the MEPS score, there was a significant increase from a mean of 1.81 in the pre-test to a mean of 2.26 in the post-test. This better planning ability occurred along with a substantial increase in all WISC sub-tests with the exception of digits, which is logical if we consider that the students now, at the end of the year, have more academic knowledge.

Finally, there were no change in the children's perception of their own competence in school, as shown in the four sub-scales of the C.O.P.E.

Table 2: Comparison Pre-Test Post-Test Control Group (Only Means with Significant Differences are Shown).

	Pre-test	Post-test	p
BAS 1			
(a) Joviality	29.00	21.37	0.000
(b) Social Perspective	22.22	16.07	0.000
(c) Respect/Self-control	39.30	32.56	0.000
(d) Apathy-Withdrawal	2.78	4.48	0.022
(e) Summary-Socialization	36.44	33.78	0.011
MEPS	1.81	2.26	0.020
WISC			
(a) Arithmetics	7.96	8.85	0.010
(b) Incomplete Figures	8.85	9.96	0.006
(c) Key-A	43.89	47.30	0.000
(d) Key-B	39.52	47.33	0.000

The view is quite different in the case of the experimental group (see Table 3). As a matter of fact the experimental group not only got better substantially in all the WISC sub-tests (including digits, in which the control group did not improve), but also in the teachers' perception of the students: they evaluated them with more leadership ability, more social sensibility or empathy, and in the global rating of socialization (Cs-summary subscale). The rest of the variables of BAS-1 showed no significant changes. This increased teachers' perception is supported by a higher ability to elaborate means for getting goals, and by better student self-perception in relation to his/her social and school behavior.

On the whole, then, the pupils trained by our programme improved in: (1) their cognitive abilities related to school performance and interpersonal relationships; (2) their own perception of the school and social interaction competence; and (3) in accordance with this, the evaluation made by the teachers of the behavior of the students.

Table 3: Comparison Pre-Test/Post-Test Experimental Group (Only Means with Significant Differences are Shown).

	Pre-test	Post-test	p
BAS 1			
(a) Leadership	9.20	12.50	0.031
(b) Social Perspective	14.00	15.25	0.000
(c) Summary-Socialization	25.50	27.85	0.000
MEPS	1.50	3.30	0.000
WISC			
(a) Arithmetics	6.75	8.00	0.012
(b) Digits	8.00	9.20	0.000
(c) Incomplete Figures	6.35	8.75	0.000
(d) Key-A	42.05	46.35	0.000
(e) Key-B	28.45	28.45	0.000
COPE			
(a) Social Behavior	18.35	19.85	0.001
(b) School Behavior	16.70	18.40	0.011

However, the obvious progress observed in the experimental group is not enough to put it on the same level that the control group: the gap has been reduced, but not to the point of eradicating the enormous pre-test differences existing at the beginning of the school year (see Table 4). The control group gets better post-test results in the BAS-1, even if now the differences have worn off in the social sensibility, and in aggressivity-obstinacy variables. Nevertheless, the control group now is superior to the experimental one in having a less anxiety, which was not evident before.

The other differences remain, although the significance levels are now lower as a product of the reduction of the differences among the means of the both groups. However, there is an obvious and interesting exception: the experimental group is now superior to the control group in the MEPS variable, despite that at the pre-test the control group was superior. This supports the effectiveness of one of the main objectives of the Think Aloud Program: the stress put on improving the ability to generate plans in order to achieve pre-determined goals.

Also very promising are the results obtained in social skills. In each of the categories analysed, verbal and non-verbal, the increases in the experimental group have been very noticeable (see Table 5). The sub-totals in these two categories are 253 versus 421 for the non-verbal subtotal, and 374 versus 609 for the verbal subtotal. In the global data, the differences are also great. The global total has gone from 627 before the program to 1030 after it; in the same way, the global rating of the judges raises from 108 to 171.

Table 4: Comparison of Experimental and Control Groups at Post-Test (Only Means with Significant Differences are Shown).

	Experimental	**Control**	**p**
BAS-1			
(a) Leadership	12.50	27.63	0.000
(b) Joviality	17.20	21.37	0.000
(c) Respect/Self-control	27.45	32.56	0.034
(d) Apathy-Withdrawal	12.40	4.48	0.003
(e) Anxiety	8.95	4.70	0.019
(f) Summary-Socialization	27.85	33.78	0.000
MEPS	3.30	2.26	0.000
WISC			
(a) Incomplete Figures	8.75	9.95	0.050
(b) Key B	38.45	47.33	0.001
COPE			
(a) Self-Concept	18.05	20.59	0.013
(b) School Behavior	18.40	20.74	0.037

Table 5: Social Skills Scores Before (B) and After (A) Intervention

		Non-verbal	Verbal	Judges' score*	Total	Means
Exp. Group	B	253	374	108	627	31.3
N=20	A	421	609	171	1030	51.5
Con. Group	B	244	320	85	564	56.4
N=10	A	248	318	83	566	56.6

* A subjective overall impression of the children's performance

The ten subjects of the control group do not change significantly from the pre-test to post-test. It is interesting to note that the pre-test results of the subjects in the control group with 10 students is very similar to the results of the experimental group with 20 students. The means column clearly shows how the control group scored almost double that of the experimental group in the pre-test. In the post-test, however, the difference is very little - only five points.

Discussion

The programme has to be evaluated in terms of the follow-up during the next school years. Will they keep going to the school or they will drop out as many of their fellows did before? The results we are getting in the meantime let us be moderately optimistic about the final results. We know, however that our intervention is perhaps not enough to compensate the deficits of the children. The intensity of the intervention is perhaps not sufficient to deal with the modification of intra-personal as well as inter-personal factors, linked more or less directly with the causes of delinquent behavior. In our opinion it is obvious that more is needed over a longer period, probably the rest of the elementary-school years. And no doubt a family co-ordinated programme will be also welcome.

The fact that the experimental group has reduced differences in comparison with the control group is positive. We need to support this advance both in depth (i.e., more training in these and other abilities) and over time.

References

Berrueta-Clement, J., Schweinhart, L., Barnett, W., & Weikart, D. (1987). The effects of early educational intervention on crime and delinquency in adolescence and early adulthood. In J. Burchard & S. Burchard (Eds.), *Prevention of delinquent behavior* pp. 220-240. Beverly Hills, CA.: Sage.

Burchard, J., & Burchard, S. (Eds.) (1987) *Prevention of delinquent behavior.* Beverly Hills, CA.: Sage.

Camp, B., & Bash, M. (1981). *Think aloud.* Champaign, Ill.: Research Press.

Currie, E. (1985). *Confronting crime.* New York: Pantheon Books.

Eysenck, H. J., & Gudjonsson, G. (1989). *The causes and cures of criminality.* New York: Plenum Press.

Farrington, D., Ohlin, L., & Wilson, J. (1986). *Understanding and controlling crime.* New York: Springer.

Harter, S. (1982). The perceived competence scale for children. *Child Development*, 53, 87-97.

Hawkins, J., & Lam, T. (1987). Teacher practices, social development and delinquency. In J. Burchard & S. Burchard (Eds.), *Prevention of delinquent behavior* pp. 241-274. Beverly Hills, CA: Sage.

Kazdin, A. (1985). *Treatment of antisocial behavior in children and adolescents.* Homewood, Ill.: Dorsey Press.

Lipsey, M. (1992). The effect of treatment on juvenile delinquents: Results from meta-analysis. In F. Losel, D. Bender, & T. Bliesener (Eds.) *Psychology and law. International perspectives* pp. 131-143. Berlin: De Gruyter.

Shure, M., & Spivack, G. (1985). *Children MEPS.* Philadelphia, PA: Hahnemann University.

Silva, F., & Martorell, C. (1983). *Batería de socialización, BAS-1* Madrid: TEA.

Wahler, R., & Dumas, J. (1987). Stimulus class determinants of mother-child coercive interchanges in multidistressed families: Assessment and intervention. In J. Burchard & S. Burchard (Eds.), *Prevention of delinquent behavior* pp. 190-219. Beverly Hills, CA: Sage.

Short and Long Term Outcomes for a Cognitive-Behavioral Anger Management Program

Gareth V. Hughes

Introduction

During the past decade, correctional systems in North America have increasingly perceived a need for many of their clients to receive anger management programs. Large numbers of offenders are perceived to have difficulties dealing with anger, aggression, and hostility. Such difficulties are assumed to have a causal relationship with their anti-social and criminal behavior and with the level of violence in correctional institutions.

It should be noted that anger is not necessarily a problematic emotion (Novaco 1978, Tavris 1983). Anger arousal can serve as a signal or cue to warn of danger or difficulty. It may be an energizing emotion that can improve motivation, performance, and self-expression. It enables us to seek justice and resolve problems. However, when anger clouds rational thought, either in extremes of fury and rage or while disinhibited by alcohol or drugs, then socially unacceptable and aggressive behavior is highly likely. Thus, anger may generate inappropriate behaviors which generate unwanted consequences. Such consequences may be internal (e.g., tension headaches) or external (e.g., retaliation from others). These are invariably aversive events, which may generate more anger and, thus, fuel a vicious circle of problematic anger which typifies many offenders.

Anger management program content has been described in some detail by Novaco (1978) and Ellis (1977). Specifically for use with offender populations, cognitive-behavioral programs have been described by Fink (1980), Goldstein and Keller (1987), Kirchner and Kennedy (1978), and Samuel (1983). However, with the notable exception of Novaco's 1978 monograph, there has been a dearth of studies evaluating the effect of such programs.

The results of the few evaluation studies published are not always clear. For example, Schlichter and Horan (1981) randomly assigned institutionalized male delinquents to a no treatment and a stress inoculation treatment group. They were able to show short-term treatment success using measures of self-report and response to role-played provocations, but no differences in institutional behavior ratings. Other studies are of limited relevance to offender populations and admit to methodological confounds (e.g., Feindler, Marriott, & Iwata 1984). Long term evaluation of anger management program effects is notably absent from the literature, with the exception of a single case study of a hospitalized woman by Bistline and Frieden (1984).

Long term evaluation is particularly crucial with offender populations, where it is assumed that anger management programs will have some impact on the likelihood of future criminal behavior. These assumptions have an impact on decisions regarding future risk and conditional release programs for offenders. Within the Canadian correctional system, Parole Boards and case management officers have increasingly perceived a need for anger management programs. They have been reluctant to grant or recommend conditional releases for inmates who have received no appropriate help for this problem.

The present study evaluates the short- and long-term impact of a cognitive behavioral anger management program on a group of adult male offenders. A second group of offenders was used as a comparison to those who completed the anger management program. This group had been referred and assessed as suitable clients for an anger management program, but did not start or complete a program for various reasons.

Program Description

The program consisted of twelve weekly two-hour sessions in which a combination of didactic and experiential material was used to address three basic issues:

(1) Why and when to control anger. This included arousal awareness, anger recognition, basic moral reasoning and concepts of self-interest, and understanding the concept of anger.

(2) How to reduce anger cognitively through the use of coping self-statements, problem solving exercises, developing a sense of proportion and humor, and the basic tenets of rational-emotive therapy.

(3) How to modify and improve behavioral coping skills, including relaxation training, assertiveness training, and role-playing different behavioral responses.

The program emphasised role-play both to model new behaviors and to provide practice opportunities to the client. In a group setting, this also allowed the client to receive feedback in relative safety on how his behavior determined the behavior of others. Thus, participants were taught to use assertive behaviors in place of aggressive or under-assertive responses when angry feelings were unavoidable.

Needless to say, it is difficult to avoid all external events which may prompt feelings of anger, although some clients with anger problems clearly seek out anger provoking situations, either unwittingly or deliberately. People and situations where insults, cheating, and frustration are highly likely, are best avoided wherever possible. (A good rationale for staying out of prison!) However, many external events are of little consequence or completely beyond our control, as for example the weather. Such events can only provoke anger if they are attended to by the client and appraised as intolerable, threatening, or in some way a personal and noxious affront. Thus, participants were taught to avoid anger provoking situations where possible and also to cognitively reappraise external events in order to reduce the frequency and intensity of angry feelings.

While the focus and aims of each session were strictly adhered to, the content of role-plays remained flexible. Appropriate coping skills are highly situation dependent and may be best taught within the context of the client's own individual problems. These typically included how to respond to accusations, how to complain effectively, how to keep out of fights. An outline of the program on a session by session basis is provided in Appendix A.

The group was jointly run by an experienced clinical psychologist with advanced training in rational-emotive therapy and a drama teacher from a local university, assisted by a drama student. The latter two were well versed in the analysis of behavioral components, such as eye contact, body posture, and voice. Dramatic acting involves skills in observing environmental factors that shape thoughts, feelings, and behavior. Thus, they had considerable experience and credibility in teaching clients how to act in less angry and more appropriate ways.

Assessment Methods

Initial assessment Over a period of 24 months, 79 offenders incarcerated in a maximum security federal penitentiary were referred and assessed as suitable clients for an anger management group program. All were administered an extensive battery of assessments which included the Ammons Quick Test, Beck Depression Inventory, Overcontrolled Hostility Scale from the M.M.P.I., IPAT Anxiety Inventory, Interpersonal Behavior Survey, Jones Irrational Beliefs Test, and questionnaires relating to physical symptoms of anger and anger provoking situations.

All referrals included in this study were of at least "dull normal" intelligence and not experiencing any florid symptoms of a major psychiatric disorder. Offenders who were assessed as having a history of instrumental violence with no evidence that they had difficulty controlling their anger were not considered to be suitable referrals and were excluded from both treatment and the study.

Fifty two offenders attended at least six group sessions (i.e., 50% of the program) and were deemed to have received treatment. Twenty seven offenders were deemed not to have received treatment including eight who started a program but dropped out after one or two sessions. The remaining 19 decided not to participate in the program for a variety of reasons such as work priorities, imminent transfer to another institution, or lack of interest. This group did not differ significantly from those offenders who completed programs on any of the initial psychometric assessments, as shown in Table 1.

Immediate post-program follow-up measures Within four weeks following completion of the program, all participants were re-administered the two anger questionnaires, the Interpersonal Behavior Survey, and the Jones Irrational Beliefs Test. Attempts to re-test those referrals who did not take the program were largely unsuccessful. There was insufficient data to report on this group. Participants in the last two group programs were additionally put through three standardized test role-plays, both before and after the program. Similar procedures as described by Novaco (1978) were used, and participants were asked to rate their level of anger arousal immediately after each role play.

Long-term follow-up measures During a nine month period, four years after completion of the last program, an attempt was made to locate all 79 referrals to the Anger Management Program. Where possible, subjects were asked to report how many

Table 1: Age and pre-program assessment scores for suitable candidates who failed to take the program and those who completed the program. There are no significant differences on any of the measures.

	No program			**Program participants**		
Pre-program:	$\bar{X}$	(s.d.)	*N*	$\bar{X}$	(s.d.)	*N*
Age	36.27	(7.05)	27	35.61	(7.01)	52
I.Q.	91.36	(9.81)	27	93.89	(9.88)	48
Phys. symptoms	43.16	(21.13)	27	43.67	(18.79)	52
Anger inventory	154.94	(46.79)	27	150.84	(35.66)	52
Irrational beliefs	282.21	(26.73)	24	289.36	(28.86)	33
I.B.S.:			27			48
Aggression	11.50	(7.01)		14.75	(7.74)	
Assertion	43.71	(10.03)		33.77	(9.84)	
Conflict avoidance	11.50	(3.59)		10.47	(4.17)	
Dependency	10.21	(4.89)		9.96	(4.90)	
Shyness	10.23	(6.53)		11.13	(6.17)	
Impression management	13.29	(4.49)		13.00	(4.44)	
Anxiety (IPAT)	35.64	(13.08)	24	32.73	(13.39)	33
Depression (Beck)	18.37	(12.48)	27	14.16	(7.49)	31
Overcontrolled hostility (M.M.P.I.)	62.79	(13.45)	24	59.17	(9.50)	31

hours of psychological or other professional treatment they had received since completing or being referred to the Anger Management Program. Each subject's Case Management Officer was asked to rate the subject's ability to cope with problematic emotions (e.g., anger and anxiety), his ability to cope in various life domains (e.g., employment, family, and friends), and the likelihood of his remaining crime-free. For those subjects who had been released since the program, Canadian Police information records and correctional service records were obtained to note whether the subject had re-offended, the type of crime, and the latency to rearrest.

Results

Table 2 summarizes the differences in pre- and post-program scores for those questionnaires and psychometrics which were re-administered a second time. The results shown include only those offenders who completed the anger management program. Insufficient information was available on the comparison group who did not take the program. All scores reported are raw scores. Combined aggression (GGR) and assertion (SGR) scores are reported, as suggested by Mauger and Adkinson (1980) in the manual for the Interpersonal Behavior Survey.

With one exception, all differences are highly significant and in the expected and desired direction. Both the pre- and post-program scores for "conflict avoidance" are at the standardized 50th percentile. Given the nature of the clientele, it would perhaps be undesirable to produce a significant change in this measure. The almost 50% reduction in numbers of subjects in the analysis, from the 52 who completed the program, resulted from refusal by or unavailability of subjects to complete the post-program measures.

Table 2: Pre- and Post-Program cores for Offenders Completing Anger Management Program

		Pre-program		Post-Program		t	p
	N	X̄	(s.d.)	X̄	(s.d.)		
Physical symptoms	25	44.84	(19.14)	30.00	(12.77)	4.47	<.001
Anger Inventory	26	148.85	(36.19)	121.04	(44.15)	3.67	.001
Irrational Beliefs	21	283.43	(23.54)	263.90	(28.49)	3.49	<.01
I.B.S.	27						
GCR (Aggression)		12.67	(6.95)	8.11	(5.39)	3.68	<.001
SGR (Assertion)		35.52	(7.97)	42.67	(7.15)	–4.64	<.001
Conflict Avoidance		10.37	(3.75)	9.98	(3.49)	.61	n.s.
Dependency		9.93	(4.62)	7.85	(3.99)	3.78	<.001
Shyness		9.96	(6.61)	6.78	(5.06)	2.84	<.01
Impression Management		13.65	(4.48)	15.92	(4.15)	–3.19	<.01
Role Play Self Ratings	9	53.22	(28.81)	28.78	(17.98)	3.13	<.02

Table 3 summarizes the long-term follow-up measures for program participants and those who were referred but did not complete a program. Measures of recidivism were restricted to those subjects who had been released. Of the total number of subjects, 37 were never released. Most of these men are serving life sentences. Two of those never released died in prison during the period of the long-term follow-up. One man released to the community also died. None of the deceased men were included in the long-term follow-up.

Table 3: Follow-up measures compared for those who completed and did not complete the treatment program.

	No program			Program participants			
	X̄	(s.d.)	*N*	X̄	(s.d.)	*N*	
CMO Adjustment ratings	33.58	(10.29)	19	40.09	(11.08)	42	F=4.72 p<.05
Treatment hours since program	11.12	(18.81)	17	22.28	(31.11)	39	n.s.
Latency to rearrest (mos.)	5.55	(3.98)	11	22.04	(15.66)	12	F=11.49 p<.01
	No	Yes	No	Yes			
Any evidence of recidivism	5	11	11	14			n.s.
Conviction for violent crime	5	11	15	10			*X2*=3.29 p=.07

Differences between the two groups are equivocal. Four out of five measures show a trend in the desired direction. However, the results for "latency to rearrest" and "treatment hours" should be viewed with caution, since homogeneity of variance was not met in either case.

The Case Management Officer (CMO) rating scale showed acceptable internal consistency among the 13 items, and a total score is reported. Most importantly, ratings of how well the offender coped with anger correlated .85 ($p<.01$) with the total score.

With only two exceptions, the subjects of the study had histories of violent offending. This included a number of offenders convicted of murder who typically have very low rates of recidivism. However, only one of the 40 men released had been serving a life sentence for murder, and 37 of the 40 had a history of multiple incarcerations at the time they were referred to the program. The released subjects may be considered a high risk group of violent offenders. Thus, it was important to distinguish between violent re-offending and a more general definition of recidivism which included breach of parole conditions and outstanding charges which had not resulted in re-incarceration. While program participation showed no effect on the latter measure, the effect on convictions for further violent crime approached significance.

Discussion

Changes resulting from the program, as measured by self-report and other psychometrics immediately after a program, can clearly be demonstrated. Similar changes to those reported here in IBS scores, have been reported by Bellemare and McKay (1990). However, such changes may not be entirely trustworthy, as evidenced by the significant increase in "impression management" in Table 2. Subjects have many reasons for professing a change in how they feel and how they would hypothetically behave, after completion of a program. Even with the best of intentions, the demands of a provocative situation may overwhelm the subject's improved skills and self-efficacy, and elicit ingrained dysfunctional reactions. It would be reassuring to have some more behavioral measures of change.

For several reasons, such measures are difficult to obtain. In the present study, an attempt was made to make use of institutional charges. However, charges were so rare an event as to render the measure useless. The availability of resources at the time of the last two group programs allowed us to videotape standardized role plays prior to and following the program. This was an attempt to obtain a behavioral measure of change and could have proved valuable had the program continued. However, the small number of pre/post assessments available ($N = 9$) did not warrant the time and resources necessary to obtain reliable behavioral ratings. The two group leaders reviewed the videotaped role plays immediately after conclusion of the groups in order to assist in writing up clinical progress reports for each of the offender participants. Seven of the nine were considered to have significantly improved their coping skills on this basis.

The present study's use of a case manager's rating of the offender's coping skills, some years after program completion, lacks any baseline to serve as a measure of behavioral change. Nonetheless, the difference between program participants and non-participants is significant and in the desired direction.

The need for follow-up or maintenance treatment to effect long-term behavioral control has been eloquently argued by those involved in sex offender treatment and research (e.g., Marshall & Eccles, 1991; Pithers et al., 1988). I would also argue that maintenance treatment and follow-up is essential for correctional clients with any long-standing pattern of dysfunctional behavior. Unfortunately, many offenders, as well as case managers, fail to accept a need for follow-up treatment and consider a program as somehow effecting a "cure" or "fixing the problem". This attitude is typified by the offender who, in no uncertain terms, angrily rejected the suggestion of taking an anger management treatment program. He told me that he had already done anger management and had all the notes in a box somewhere. Unfortunately, the contents of the program were neither in his head nor in his behavioral repertoire.

The attempt in this study to collect information on further treatment was not entirely successful. While there was a trend for program participants to continue with more treatment than the comparison group, further review of the "treatment hours" data suggests that this measure was also related to recidivism and further incarceration. There was a positive correlation ($r=.50$, $p<.05$) between the number of months of re-incarceration and total hours of treatment. Most of the subjects who were re-incarcerated obtained further treatment after re-incarceration rather than in the community when it might have been of more value. Thus, the tendency for offenders to partake in treatment programs only when incarcerated, obscures the role of continued treatment in reducing recidivism. To compound the problem, in this study most of the missing data with respect to continued treatment resulted from those subjects who were released successfully.

A further complication arises from what kind of additional treatment is offered or taken by the subject. It is reasonable to assume that some forms of treatment may not be compatible with the cognitive-behavioral orientation of the Anger Management Program, with its emphasis on self-management and responsibility. Thus, further treatment may have been counter-productive. In the present study, the subject supplied his best "guestimate" of the number of hours of professional help he had received. Many subjects were vague and unsure of what treatment they had received. Rarely, information on treatment would be available on a subject's psychological records, and even then it was not always clear how much or what kind of treatment had been offered. For the purposes of good long-term outcome studies, there is clearly a need for better record keeping regarding therapy and counselling received by offenders.

Like many quasi-experimental studies done in a real clinical situation with many competing priorities and pressures on the clinician, there are a number of methodological design problems. Offenders are not always co-operative in completing lengthy questionnaires. Because of other pressures, some offenders were allowed into the program without completing the full pre-program assessment. Others refused the program because they did not like filling out the pre-program psychometrics. Needless to say, they were not about to comply with a request to redo the same battery of questionnaires. Missing data frequently created a problem with numbers too low to perform an adequate analysis.

The movement of offenders within the system is both time consuming and difficult to track. Once past warrant expiry date, tracking is virtually impossible, unless the offender recidivates. This makes any collection of longitudinal measures difficult. Official records are more readily available, but not always designed to capture the information required. For example, Canadian Services of Canada summaries give sentence commencement dates for new charges. These dates are rarely the same as re-incarceration dates, which are more pertinent to a measure of latency to rearrest.

Finally, there is the problem of whether to include offenders serving life sentences in such a study as this. Long-term program assessment using such traditional measures as recidivism are clearly inappropriate. The length of time to release is unusually long and recidivism rates are low, regardless of treatment. Andrews and colleagues (1990) argue against treating low risk and low need offenders. Many "lifers" can be so categorized, and yet many demand psychological programs and claim to achieve considerable personal growth from participating in such programs. Certainly, such programs are a means of passing time profitably and may be a means of reaffirming the non-criminal values held by many "lifers".

Summary

For those offenders in this study who were released at some point during the follow-up period, the rate of overall recidivism was relatively high (i.e., 61%). Whether or not the subject had completed the anger management program had no significant effect on the overall rate. However, if we examine only re-convictions for a violent crime, program completion had a more noticeable effect (i.e., 40% recidivism). Certainly, the length of time in the community before rearrest was significantly longer for those who had completed the program.

Once again, we are brought back to the question of expectancies for change in a group of high risk violent offenders. Perhaps any reduction in violent crime and an increase in latency to re-offend should be considered a success. Regardless, all official records are limited in how well they assess behavioral change. The level of violent behavior towards friends and family in the community, which does not come to official attention, may always remain an unknown.

The present study offers some evidence of positive impact on a group of violent offenders who completed a cognitive-behavioral anger management program. The program was based upon the now accepted principles of effective correctional treatment, emphasizing cognitive-behavioral methods of change, self-monitoring and responsibility for attitudes and behavior.

From both anecdotal evidence provided to me by the many graduates of cognitive-behavioral programs such as the one under consideration, and from the limited results of the present study, I remain optimistic about the value of such programs. I remain cautious, however, about their ability to effect major long term changes in offenders without continued follow-up treatment and consideration of the situational variables which support and reward anti-social behavior. We had best consider more fully the question of what results or what return for money and resources expended are we prepared to consider acceptable for any given program.

References

Andrews, D. A., Zinger, I., Hoge, R. D., Bonta, J., Gendreau, P. & Cullen, F. T. (1990). Does correctional treatment work? A clinically relevant and psychologically informed meta-analysis. *Criminology*, 28, 369-404.

Bellemare, F. & McKay, D. (1990). An anger management program in a maximum security federal penitentiary. Unpublished poster presentation.

Bistline, J. L. & Frieden, F. P. (1984). Anger control: A case study of a stress inoculation treatment for a chronic aggressive patient. *Cognitive Therapy & Research, 8*, 551-556.

Ellis, A. (1977). *How to live with and without anger*. Toronto: Fitzhenry & Whiteside.

Feindler, E. L., Marriott, S. A. & Iwata, M. (1984). Group anger control training for junior high school delinquents. *Cognitive Therapy & Research 8*, 299-311.

Fink, E. (1980). *A cognitive-behavioral group therapy program for problems of anger and aggression in adult male offenders*. Doctoral dissertation, Rutgers University.

Goldstein, A. P. & Keller, H. R. (1987). *Aggressive behavior: Assessment and intervention*. New York: Pergamon Press.

Kirchner, E. P. & Kennedy, R. E. (1978). Leaders' manual for an assertive skills course in correctional settings. University Park, P. A.: Institute for Research on Human Resources.

Marshall, W. L. & Eccles, A. (1991). The Value of Community Treatment Programs for Released Sex Offenders. Forum on Correctional Research, 3, 12-15.

Mauger, P. A. & Adkinson, D. R. (1980). Interpersonal Behavior Survey (IBS): Manual. Los Angeles: Western Psychological Services.

Novaco, R. (1975). Anger control: *The development and evaluation of an experimental treatment*. Lexington, MA: D. C. Heath.

Pithers, W. D., Kashima, K. M., Cumming, G. F., Beal, L. S. & Buell, M. M. (1988). "Relapse Prevention of Sexual Aggression", in R. A. Prentky and V. L. Quinsey (Eds.), Human Sexual Aggression: Current Perspectives. Annals of the New York Academy of Sciences, 528. New York: New York Academy of Sciences, 1988.

Samuel, R. (1983). ABC of anger management. *Canada's Mental Health, 31*(1), 21.

Schlichter, K. J. & Horan, J. J. (1981). Effects of stress inoculation on the anger and aggression management skills of institutionalized juvenile delinquents. *Cognitive Therapy & Research, 5*, 359-365.

Tavris, C. (1983). *Anger: The misunderstood emotion*. New York: Simon & Schuster.

Appendix A

Anger Control Program Outline

Session # 1: An introduction to anger (film strip). What is anger; what typically causes anger; different levels of anger; consequences of anger.

Session # 2: Methods of direct arousal (anger) reduction e.g., relaxation training and alternative calming methods. Humor; demanding perfection; irrational beliefs.

Session # 3: An introduction to rational-emotive therapy. The ABCs of irrational thinking and its consequences. Rational imagery techniques.

Session # 4: An introduction to role-playing; all participants try to deal with a relatively innocuous, but frustrating situation (The Car Service Manager).

Session # 5:	Physical behavioral tactics (either improvised or set scripts). Importance of eye contact, interpersonal distance (proxemics), posture & gesture (body language), and voice.
Session # 6:	Tactics of *stalling* and allowing time to perceive the nature of the situation, appropriate strategies, etc. Useful when dealing with criticism, taunts, insults, accusations, and other unexpected attacks.
Session # 7:	"*Broken Record*" tactics, for responding to a request and in initiating assertiveness. Useful for making oneself heard and making one's bottom line or goal clear to others.
Session # 8:	Listening skills to assess what the other person wants, his game plan, etc.; to use the other's arguments to your advantage; to spot changes in the other person's tactics; to gauge the optimum time to make compromises or seek a solution.
Session # 9:	Perceiving "chunks" (i.e., beginnings, middles, and ends), critical points, how to finish a situation, "bow out gracefully", etc.
Session # 10:	Identify self-talk (the sub-text) through modelling and coaching with prepared scripts.
Session # 11:	Find creative alternatives, changing "mind set", avoid tunnel vision and absolutes.
Session # 12:	Identify and acknowledge positive aspects of others and their arguments and desires. Respect for other people's opinions and their right to make requests.

Psychological Disturbance in the Scottish Prison System: A Preliminary Account[1]

David J. Cooke

Introduction

The rate of psychological disturbance in prison systems is high (Coid, 1984; Gunn et al., 1991). The continuing deinstitutionalisation of psychiatric patients, together with changes in clinical practice and changes towards more restrictive laws on civil commitment are likely to result in an increased rate of psycholcgical disturbance in prisons (Durham, 1989; Guy et al., 1985; Hodgins & Cote, 1991; Jemelka et al., 1989; McMain et al., 1989; Scott, 1973; Teplin, 1983).

The level of psychological disturbance is causing concern (Hansard, 1987). From the humanitarian point of view it is thought that psychologically disturbed prisoners require special resources including psychological and psychiatric treatment (Smith, 1983; Scottish Prison Service, 1990). From the management point of view it is thought that some psychologically disturbed prisoners should have special treatment because they cause trouble within institutions; they have a high rate of disciplinary offences, they serve longer sentences, they are more likely to recidivate and become victims within the prison, they are less likely to receive parole (Orr, 1978; Toch, 1982).

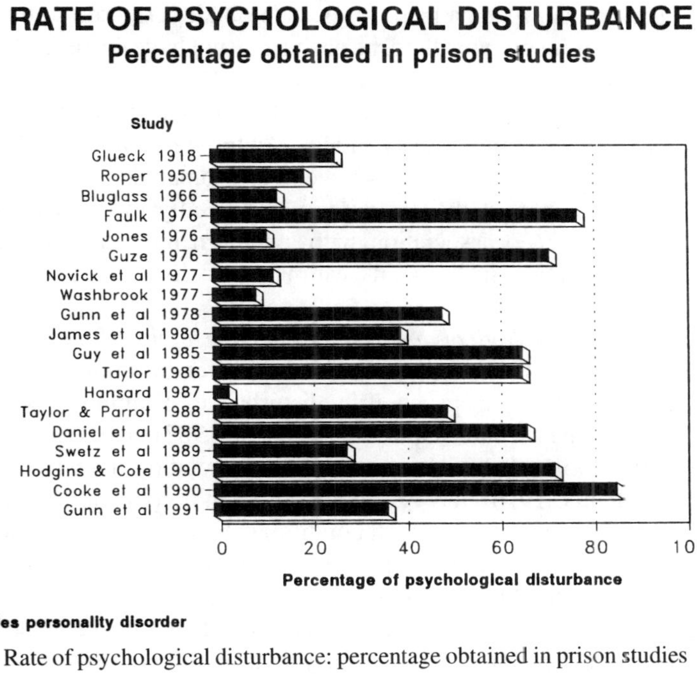

Figure 1: Rate of psychological disturbance: percentage obtained in prison studies

Figure 1 displays estimates obtained from a selection of studies during this century of the proportion of prisoners who may be regarded as psychologically disturbed or suffering from a personality disorder. The considerable range in estimates is obvious, ranging from 3% in the figures presented to the British parliament (Hansard, 1987) to 82% obtained in a study by Cooke et al. (1990) which took place in Barlinnie prison in Glasgow during the period after a major riot.

Problems with these estimates

There are at least five factors which lead to such a wide range of estimates: (1) the point at which the statistics are collected; (2) the definition of psychological disturbance which is applied; (3) the type of prison and the type of prisoner considered; (4) the stage of the prisoner's sentence; (5) the point of historical time.

1. The point at which the statistics are collected Goldberg and Huxley (1980) argued that a variety of filters - relating to both symptom and to non-symptom factors - influence progress to different levels of care. They estimated that for every 250 cases of psychological disturbance in the community only 17 are ultimately referred to a psychiatrist. Similar filters operate within the prison setting. For example, prisoners' symptoms may prevent them from obtaining contact with the prison medical services; depressed prisoners may lack the drive or energy to seek help, anxious prisoners may by fearful of asking for help or admitting that they are not coping. Others may have experienced symptoms of depression so frequently that they regard it as part and parcel of everyday life and thus not worthy of concern.

The level of tension and alienation between staff and prisoners will influence whether a prisoner will approach a prison officer to obtain a referral to the medical staff. When a medical officer is consulted, he or she may not have the time, the training or the inclination to identify psychological disorders (Ormel et al., 1990; Smith, 1983). Once psychological disturbance is detected the decision to refer on to specialist help is influenced, not only by the severity and form of the symptoms, but also by non-symptom factors. Steadman et al. (1988) showed that women and white individuals were over-represented amongst those regarded as mentally disordered offenders. Thus, factors which have no association with symptom intensity will contribute significantly to the variation in "official" estimates of the rate of psychological dysfunction.

2. The definition of psychological disturbance which is applied The second major reason for the discrepancies across studies is that different studies use different definitions of psychological or psychiatric disturbance. Defining psychological disturbance in terms of the Mental Health Act (Hansard, 1987) may be too restrictive, while defining psychological disturbance using non-specific clinical criteria (e.g. Cooke et al., 1990; Faulk, 1976) may be too liberal. Even if good clinical criteria are applied it is important to determine which conditions the researcher has included or excluded: one recent study excludes personality disorder and substance abuse disorders from their estimates because these disorders are:

> '... highly prevalent in the incarcerated population and tend to skew and magnify data beyond the reasonable prevalence of psychiatric illness'. (Swetz et al., 1989, p. 3).

Many clinicians and researchers might consider the disorders which were excluded from this study to be of critical interest not only in terms of the treatment needs of this population, but also in terms of criminal-justice outcomes such as recidivism (Hart et al., 1988).

3. The type of prison and type of prisoner which are considered The third factor which may influence the variation in the estimates is the type of prison which is studied. A priori, it might be expected that the level of disturbance in a maximum security prison will be higher than the level of disturbance in an "open" prison.

The type of prisoner studied will also have an impact. The estimate obtained by Taylor and Parrott (1988) indicated that more than half of prisoners over the age of 55 years were psychiatrically disturbed. In Taylor's (1986) study over two-thirds of life sentence prisoners had a current psychiatric disorder. Female prisoners tend to display a higher rate of disorder than male prisoners (Smith, 1983).

4. The stage of the prisoner's sentence The stage of a prisoner's sentence may well be important. There is evidence that the level of disturbance is particularly high during the remand period and also during the first few weeks of a new sentence; Backett (1987) demonstrated that two-thirds of deaths due to suicide took place during the first month of imprisonment, with a disproportionate number occurring during the remand period.

5. The point of historical time The final factor which will be considered is the point of historical time. The studies illustrated above range in date of publication from 1918 to 1991. Patterns of care and patterns of sentencing will affect the proportion of psychologically disturbed individuals who are imprisoned:

'Prisons, hospitals and reception centres for vagrants and the homeless are basically asylums which to a large extent share a stage army of handicapped persons. When mental hospitals are full, prisons are relatively empty, and the present day scene suggests that the converse is equally true'. (Scott, 1970, p. 168).

To summarise, any study which attempts to measure levels of psychological disturbance in prison settings must, at a minimum, ensure that data are collected directly from prisoners using publicly agreed and validated criteria, and a representative sample of prisons and prisoners should be obtained.

Why Are There So Many Psychologically Disturbed People In Prison?

There can be little doubt that the rate of psychological disturbance in the prison population is high. This raises the question - why? Do prisons merely import those who are psychologically disturbed or does the experience of imprisonment in some sense generate psychological disturbance? This is clearly a false dichotomy; it is likely that both processes will operate to differing degrees.

Psychological disturbance is not randomly distributed in the general population, certain groups of people are at higher risk (e.g. Brown & Harris, 1978; Cooke, 1982; Surtees et al., 1983; Weissman & Klerman, 1977). Indirect evidence suggests that there is a high risk of importing psychologically disturbed people into prison. Associations have been identified between psychological disturbance and a variety of social factors and, although the relationships are not necessarily causal, this does not diminish their importance. A disproportionate number of the prison population comes from the at-risk population - lower social class, unemployed, single parent, inner city resident - thus, the chances of psychological disorder being imported are high.

The above evidence is indirect evidence that psychological disorder is imported; some more direct evidence exists. Hodgins and Cote (1990) found that a high proportion of men contained in a Special Handling Unit in the province of Quebec was psychologically disturbed; 64% of these men were disordered before they came to prison. Bentz and Noel (1983) compared prisoners entering prison with a sample of the general population in North Carolina and found that the prisoners reported a higher rate of disturbance.

There is a sub-group of disturbed individuals who have a particularly high risk of imprisonment. In North America, Corrado et al. (1989) and Pepper and Ryglewicz (1982) have identified the Young Adult Chronic Patient, patients who have multiple disorders and who tend to be rejected by mental health services and are dealt with by the criminal justice system. Coid (1988) studied similar processes in England and found that multi-problem people are less likely to be admitted to hospital - particularly if it is a District General Hospital or a Teaching Hospital - they end up in prison.

Stress in prison: the pains of confinement

The alternative explanation for the excessive levels of psychological disturbance in the prison population might be termed the stress hypothesis: psychological disturbance amongst prisoners has been attributed to the the "pains of confinement" or the "cruel and unusual punishment" of prison life. The academic literature in this field is confused.

Toch (1982) argued that the pains of confinement - e.g. the deprivation of liberty, goods and services, heterosexual relationships, autonomy and personal security - can be conceptualised as stresses. In particular, the pains of confinement may focus on relationships with other prisoners. Sykes (1958) suggested that one of the most difficult parts of imprisonment is being with other prisoners - "gangsters" may pressurise other prisoners to smuggle drugs, sex offenders may have to spend long periods in solitary confinement to avoid assault.

Stresses may also be focused on the structure of the institution. King and McDermott (1990) suggested that two structural factors may be detrimental to psychological health, namely, the loss of family contact and the level of uncertainty.

Evidence of this type is suggestive but it often lacks a proper empirical base. The second source of evidence suggestive of the pathogenic quality of certain regime factors relates to institutional violence; violence in prisons and special hospitals. Extensive research has been carried out on the links between violent behaviour and the structural features of prison regimes. As with much research in this field it ranges from the anecdotal to the well controlled study. Nonetheless, there is suggestive evidence to implicate a range of regime characteristics, including boredom, administrative uncertainty, the level of security and control, the quality of staff-prisoner relationships, staff training and staff morale. (See Cooke (1991c) and Ditchfield (1991) for reviews of this literature.)

While it may be surprising, it must be concluded that there is no clear empirical evidence for a relationship between either the length of imprisonment or the restrictiveness of imprisonment and level of psychological disturbance. Perhaps the most reasonable verdict, given the current state of knowledge is "not-proven". As Bonta and Gendreau (1990) note in their masterly review of the literature:

'... from the available evidence and in the dimensions measured, there is little to support the conclusion that long-term imprisonment necessarily has detrimental effects. (p. 365)'.

This question of whether psychological disturbance is imported or created is not merely of academic interest but rather it has practical implications. At the simplest level, if most psychological disturbance can be attributed to importation, then prison services require systematic, valid and comprehensive screening procedures for the identification of cases. The identification of disturbed individuals may, in some cases, lead to the more appropriate placement of these individuals in Health Service settings. If psychological disturbance is generated by the experience of imprisonment, then the regime factors responsible require to be identified and changed.

The Current Study

The present study was designed to measure both the level and nature of psychological disturbance in the Scottish prison population and to examine the role of life events and regime factors in the aetiology of disorder. In essence the study was designed to determine the rate and possible causes of psychological disturbance in Scottish prisons; how many disturbed prisoners, what form of disturbance, why are they disturbed? (See Cooke, 1994a, for further details.)

Method

1. Sampling Scottish prisoners are distributed around 21 prisons from Dumfries in the south to Peterhead in the north. In order to obtain a representative sample of prisoners, prisons were stratified in terms of five characteristics (e.g. open versus closed, remand versus convicted), then institutions were selected at random from the strata. Prisoners from these prisons were selected by systematic sampling. A sample of 310 prisoners from eight different prisons was interviewed (refusal rate = 7.8%).

2. Interview procedure A range of psychological disorders was measured using the Schedule for Affective Disorders - Life Time Version (SADS-L). This interview schedule is based on the Research Diagnostic Criteria (RDC) which were developed by Endicott and Spitzer (1978). The interview provides systematic definitions of all major forms of psychiatric disturbance, including alcoholism and drug abuse.

The SADS-L is designed to identify the onset of the disorder. In any aetiological analysis it is necessary to identify the time at which the individual became disturbed; if an episode of disorder started before they came to prison, then it could not be caused by the experience of imprisonment; if the episode started after he or she came to prison it might have been produced by the experience of imprisonment. Thus, knowing when symptoms started is important. The present study examines the aetiology of all onsets during the 12 months prior to interview.

While the SADS-L provides criteria for rating Anti-Social Personality Disorder there are some difficulties in applying these particular criteria in prison populations. There is a danger that the overlap between certain features of criminality and certain features of personality disorder will result in over-estimation of the rate of personality disorder. Hare (1980; 1991) has developed a 20 item Psychopathy Checklist for use in prison populations. This has been shown to have predictive and concurrent validity (Hart et al., 1988; Hart & Hare, 1989). This approach was used in the measurement of psychopathy.

There is now little doubt that stressful life events and long term difficulties have aetiological significance for a range of psychological difficulties (e.g. Brown & Harris, 1989; Cooke & Hole, 1983; Paykel, 1978). It is probable that a significant proportion of the cases of psychological disturbance amongst prisoners can be attributed to life events and difficulties. Prisoners are not only subjected to life events that are the lot of those in the community - a spouse having an affair, a father developing cancer, a son using heroin - but they are also subjected to the stresses that are peculiar to life in prison. These experiences may have a disproportionate effect on prisoners because they do not have ready access to family social support or the autonomy to resolve crises.

Life events and long term difficulties have been measured using a modified form of the Life Events and Difficulties Schedule (Brown & Harris, 1978). Brown and his colleagues have developed a system of rating life events and difficulties which is designed to take into account contextual features of the events but exclude the contaminating effects produced by the subject's reported response to the events and difficulties (see Brown & Harris, 1978 for a detailed account of the rationale and method). Contextual measures are necessary because the meaning of events - and thereby their stressfulness - is influenced by the context, for example, the experience of imprisonment for a first offender convicted of a sex offence is likely to be very different to the experience of a habitual car thief returning to prison for the tenth time.

In addition to the variables referred to above, the study considered a range of other variables including level of social support, level of identification with the prison subculture, demographic characteristics, criminal history and behaviour in prison. Data analysis is still in an early stage thus only preliminary results are presented below.

The Rate Of Psychological Disturbance In The Scottish Prison Population

The distribution of psychological disturbance in the population of female prisoners will be considered separately from the distribution in male offenders for three reasons. Firstly, the imprisonment of female offenders is comparatively rare; during the period of the study approximately 48 times as many males were imprisoned as females. It is likely that the processes leading to female offending and imprisonment are different. Secondly, previous research suggests that female offenders are more likely to be referred for psychiatric examination and treatment than male offenders (Steadman et al., 1988). It has been argued that female offending, being both unusual and contrary to stereotypical roles, requires "special" explanation. Thirdly, evidence from Scottish epidemiological studies indicates that there are major variations in the gender distribution of depression (Cooke, 1982), alcoholism (Saunders & Kershaw, 1978) and anxiety (Surtees et al., 1983).

Sixty-three percent of the female sample indicated that they had sought help for some psychological difficulty throughout their lifetime: this assistance included assessment and treatment by psychiatrists, clinical psychologists or specialists in the treatment of addictions. It did not include assessment and treatment from General Practitioners or assessments carried out for the purposes of a court appearance. Eighteen percent of the sample reported that they were currently receiving assistance within prison. Most of the treatment received was on an out-patient basis, however, a sizeable proportion (28%) had received in-patient treatment in a psychiatric hospital.

The prevalence of the psychological disturbance experienced by the female sample is shown in Table 1.

Table 1: Disorders in Female Sample

	Lifetime Prevalence	95% Confidence Interval	Annual Prevalence	95% Confidence Interval	Point Prevalence	95% Confidence Interval
Major Psychological Disorders						
Schizophrenia	0.0	0%–6%	0.0	0%–6%	0.0	0%–6%
Major Depressive Disorder	54.1	40%–66%	48.3	35%–62%	16.7	8%–29%
Mania	6.7	2%–16%	5.0	1%–14%	0.0	0%–6%
Hypomania	6.7	2%–16%	3.3	0%–11%	0.0	0%–6%
Suicide						
Total	33.3	22%–47%	11.7	5%–23%	0.0	0%–6%
Major	18.3	10%–30%	8.33	0%–3%	DNA	DNA
Minor	15.0	7%–27%	3.33	3%–8%	DNA	DNA
Addictions						
Alcohol Dependence	18.3	10%–30%	15.0	7%–27%	**	**
Drug Abuse or Dependence	45.0	32%–58%	31.7	20%–45%	**	**
Minor Psychological Disorders						
Minor Depressive Disorder	6.7	2%–16%	6.7	2%–16%	3.3	0%–12%
Panic Disorder	14.8	7%–26%	8.3	3%–18%	8.3	3%–18%
Generalized Anxiety Disorder	29.5	19%–43%	23.3	13%–36%	6.7	2%–16%
Obsessive Compulsive Disorder	9.8	4%–21%	6.7	2%–16%	3.3	0%–12%
Phobic Disorder	19.7	11%–32%	18.3	10%–30%	18.3	10%–30%

** Dependence may persist though access to substances is limited

The figures in the above table do not add up to 100%. In general, the disorders are not mutually exclusive: it is possible for an individual to have a series of different disorders over a period of time or possible to have two disorders - for example major depression and alcohol abuse - concurrently.

The overall impression gained from consideration of the figures in Table 1 is the high rate of disorder exhibited by this sample. Over half (55%) have experienced a major depressive disorder at some time in their life with 33% having engaged in some form of suicidal behaviour at some time. Eighteen percent could be considered to have engaged in serious suicidal behaviour at some stage, that is, suicidal behaviour with a RDC level of suicidal intent of three and over together with a RDC medical threat of five or over.

Table 2: Disorders in Male Sample

	Lifetime Prevalence	95% Confidence Interval	Annual Prevalence	95% Confidence Interval	Point Prevalence	95% Confidence Interval
Major Psychological Disorders						
Schizophrenia	2.0	1%–5%	1.0	0%–3%	0.4	0%–2%
Major Depressive Disorder	0.4	0%–2%	0.4	0%–2%	0.4	0%–2%
Mania	40.1	34%–46%	27.9	22%–33%	6.5	3%–10%
Hypomania	4.3	2%–7%	1.6	0%–4%	0.0	0%–2%
Suicide						
Total	20.6	16%–26%	3.2	5%–23%	DNA	DNA
Major	12.1	8%–16%	1.6	0%–4%	DNA	DNA
Minor	8.5	5%–13%	1.6	0%–4%	DNA	DNA
Addictions						
Alcohol Dependence	38.1	32%–44%	21.5	16%–27%	**	**
Drug Abuse or Dependence	20.6	16%–26%	14.2	10%–19%	**	**
Minor Psychological Disorders						
Minor Depressive Disorder	3.2	1%–6%	2.4	1%–5%	0.8	0%–3%
Panic Disorder	6.9	0%–11%	4.9	3%–8%	3.2	1%–6%
Generalized Anxiety Disorder	23.1	18%–28%	17.8	13%–22%	7.3	4%–11%
Obsessive Compulsive Disorder	9.7	6%–14%	8.9	6%–13%	7.7	5%–12%
Phobic Disorder	15.0	11%–19%	13.8	9%–18%	13.0	9%–17%

** Dependence may persist though access to substances is limited

Results for the male sample show less depression, suicidal behaviour and drug abuse but more alcohol dependence than the female sample (see Table 2).

How do these results compare with the general population rates? Estimates of the rate of psychological disturbance in the general population are subject to many of the difficulties which pertain to estimates for prison populations. It is the case, however, that more resources have been directed towards general population studies (e.g. Brown & Harris, 1978; Thornicroft, 1991; Surtees et al., 1983). Goldberg & Huxley (1992) have provided a timely review of some of the literature pertaining to the rate of psychological disturbance in the general population. Any estimates must be presented with caveats; caveats pertaining to the different populations considered, the different diagnostic systems used and the different methodologies which have been applied. Nonetheless, it is the case that a certain degree of consensus pertains allowing rough comparisons of differences in the order of magnitudes of rates of psychological disturbance.

Goldberg & Huxley (1992) examined the monthly prevalence rates of psychological disorders - excluding cognitive impairment, substance abuse and anti-social personality disorder - in a range of studies using a range of diagnostic instruments including the instrument used in the current study.

When these rates are compared with equivalent rates for the prison population - that is rates with drug abuse, alcohol abuse, psychopathic disorder and suicidal behaviour excluded - the rate for the female prisoners is some 1.9 times the general population rate and the rate for male prisoners is some 2.2 times the general population rate.

An important question, from both a theoretical and practical point of view, is the time at which disorders onset in relation to imprisonment; is psychological disturbance imported into the prison or is it in some sense created by the process of imprisonment? As was noted above - perhaps contrary to intuition - the empirical evidence in support of the notion that being in prison generates psychological disturbance is poor (Bonta & Gendreau, 1990; Walker, 1983). Clearly there are certain disorders which are unlikely to be created by the experience of imprisonment, e.g. psychopathic disorder, alcohol or drug dependence, whereas other more reactive disorders, such as depression, may be generated by imprisonment.

To take a preliminary look, the relationship between imprisonment and the onset of episodes of major depression in 30 day periods before and after reception to prison were plotted for the total sample.

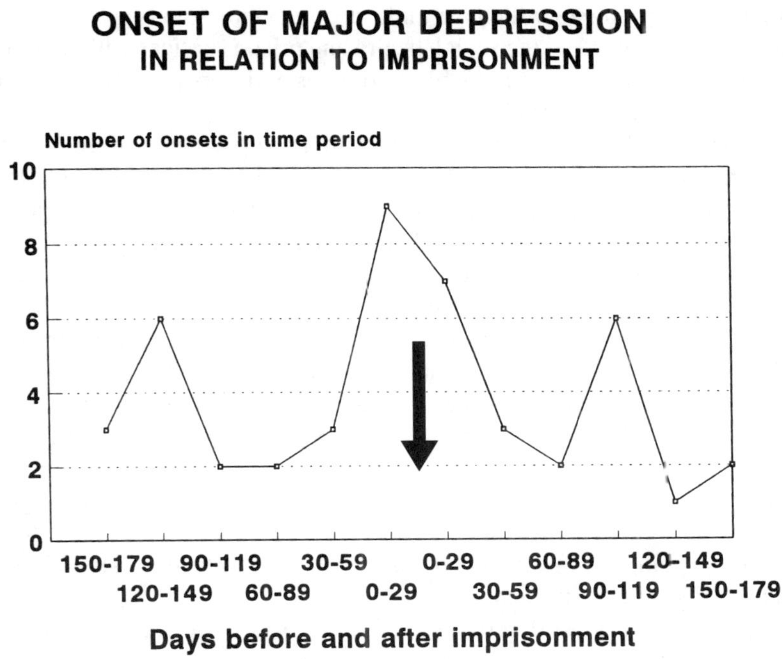

Figure 1: Onset of major depression in relation to imprisonment

There is considerable variation in the rate of onsets, with the most prominent peak occurring at the point at which the prisoner is received into the prison. This finding is consistent with those reported by Backett, 1987; Coid, 1984; Harding & Zimmermann, 1989. This pattern suggest that depressive symptoms are in part a response to the pains of confinement.

When all onsets of major depression are considered, that is including those outwith the period of six months before imprisonment to six months after imprisonment, it is interesting to note that 60% of episodes of major depression started while the subject was not in prison. More detailed analysis of the life event data is currently underway to identify which particular stresses might provoke the onset of depression.

Multi-problem prisoners

Perhaps the most striking finding of the interview study was the level of comorbidity in this population. If psychological disturbance is considered, it is apparent that many prisoners suffer from personality disorder or depression together with dependence on either alcohol or drugs, or indeed, dependence on both. However, if a broader perspective is taken and other difficulties are considered including homelessness, a long history of offending and contact with mental health services, it is clear that there is a small but significant group (approximately 6% of the sample) of young multi-problem people who are serving frequent short sentences - "doing a life sentence by installments". This group of individuals has been identified in other jurisdictions and services designed to deal with their particular problems have been identified.

Amongst the problems which the multi-problem individuals are perceived to have is that they rotate between the social, health and prison services without obtaining the care which they require. The particular problems of this group were clearly described by Freeman and Roesch (1989):

> 'The mentally ill ex-offender presents with a complex set of needs and problems, ranging from basic requirements for food, shelter and employment to the need for mental health treatment. Responsibility for provision of such a range of services seldom falls to a single agency, and the mentally ill are poorly equipped to untangle the skein of disparate and at times competitive jurisdictions. Too often they fall between the cracks of the social net. (p. 114)'.

One solution to this problem which has been proposed, and, more importantly, which has been implemented in other jurisdictions, is an integrated service for mentally ill offenders which cuts across the traditional boundaries between the health, social and criminal justice systems (Corrado et al., 1989; Durham, 1989; Jemelka et al., 1989).

Pinder and Laming (1991) have argued firmly for effective inter-agency work which not only includes social, health and prison services but also other agencies including housing departments, police, and in Scotland it should include the Procurator Fiscal's Department.

Corrado et al., (1989) described the Multi Service Network Project which was designed to manage clients who habitually use many services - frequently simultaneously - in an uncoordinated and chaotic fashion. The project was focused on the difficult client group which frequently finds itself rejected by other services, and, almost by default, ends up in the criminal justice system (Coid, 1988).

> 'The particularly difficult problems involved those chronics who were excessively uncooperative, abusive, manipulative, and violent while over-using service systems such as hospitals, detox centres, emergency shelters and community mental health resources with few long term benefits to themselves. (p. 212)'.

Preliminary evaluation of the Multi Service Network Project indicates some degree of success, both in ensuring clients had appropriate access to services and in producing a cost saving of $3520 (Canadian) per client.

This project was the precursor of the Inter-Ministerial project. The Inter-Ministerial project is jointly funded by both the Correctional Service and the Mental Health Service of British Columbia. The project is focused on the multi-problem individuals and has two goals. Firstly, it attempts to extend the community tenure of these individuals. Secondly, it attempts to improve their quality of life.

The support is provided by social workers who work intensively with 10 to 12 patients each at the "street level". The case workers aim to achieve the above goals by helping the patients to obtain and maintain access to the existing community support networks and facilities. By their very nature these patients are difficult to deal with and much of the work of the social workers appears to be advocacy on behalf of their clients with support, criminal justice and housing agencies. The case worker has the explicit focus of preventing re-incarceration and re-hospitalisation. They may achieve this by ensuring that their clients are diverted from prosecution when they commit minor offences. The social workers provide their service by having frequent contact with their patients. The project is now being expanded to take on people who have just been released from prison.

One general theme which runs through the literature is that many of the offences which are being dealt with by imprisonment are petty in nature, imprisonment being used because of the absence of an alternative to imprisonment. Coid (1984) argued that political intervention might be required to ensure that psychiatric hospitals play their proper place in the care of psychologically disturbed offenders.

One alternative to imprisonment might be diversion from prosecution. Diversion of the psychologically disturbed from prosecution towards treatment has been used in Scotland, for less handicapped offenders, since 1984 (Cooke, 1991a; 1991b; 1994b; 1994b) and perhaps this process should be expanded to include the multi-problem prisoners. Modifications to the current scheme would be required, not only in terms of better integration with other agencies but also in the constraints placed on the clients. Jemelka et al. (1989) suggested that one method for balancing the competing demands of the offender's rights and the demands of public safety would be to implement treatment on an involuntary out-patient basis: this is less restrictive than imprisonment and would allow monitoring of the offender's behaviour. The treatment regime could include mandated curfew and attendance at a day centre. This type of approach has the additional advantage of being less expensive to implement than maintaining psychologically disturbed offenders either in prison or in psychiatric hospital.

Conclusions

In conclusion, it must be argued that psychological disturbance amongst the prison population is a growing concern. The evidence currently available suggests that much of the disturbance is imported; many prisoners come from segments of the general population which have an elevated risk of psychiatric morbidity. The multi-problem offender who too frequently is rejected by all services should perhaps be the focus of intensive case management systems designed to ensure that not only do they gain access to the services which they require, but also to ensure that these services are delivered effectively. Evidence from other jurisdictions indicates that services for this group can be effectively managed.

References

Backett, S. A. (1987). Suicides in Scottish prison. *British Journal of Psychiatry, 151*, 218-221.

Bentz, W. K., & Noel, R. W. (1983). The incidence of psychiatric disorder among a sample of men entering prison. *Corrective and Social Psychiatry and Journal of Behavior Technology, 29*, 22-28.

Bluglass, R. (1966). Mentally disordered prisoners: reports but no improvements. *British Medical Journal, 296*, 1757.

Bonta, J., & Gendreau, P. (1990). Re-examining the cruel and unusual punishment of prison life. *Law and Human Behavior, 14*, 347-372.

Brown, G. W., & Harris, T. O. (1978). *Social origins of depression: A study of psychiatric disorder in women*. London: Tavistock.

Brown, G. W., & Harris, T. O. (1989). *Life events and illness*. London: Unwin Hyman.

Coid, J. W. (1984). How many psychiatric patients in prison. *British Journal of Psychiatry, 145*, 78-84.

Coid, J. W. (1988) Mentally abnormal prisoners on remand; 1 - Rejected or accepted by the NHS? *British Medical Journal, 296*, 1779-1782.

Cooke, D. J. (1982). Depression: Demographic factors in the distribution of different syndromes in the general population. *Social Psychiatry, 17*, 29-36.

Cooke, D. J. (1991a). Treatment as an alternative to prosecution: Offenders diverted for treatment. *British Journal of Psychiatry, 158*, 785-791.

Cooke, D. J. (1991b). Psychological treatment as an alternative to prosecution: A form of primary diversion. *The Howard Journal of Criminal Justice, 30*, 1, 53-65.

Cooke, D. J. (1991c). Violence in prisons: The influence of regime factors. *The Howard Journal of Criminal Justice, 30*(2), 95-109.

Cooke, D. J. (1992). Reconviction following referral to a forensic clinic: The criminal justice outcome of diversion. *Medicine, Science and the Law, 32*, 325-330.

Cooke, D. J. (1994a). *Psychological disturbance in the Scottish Prison System: Prevalence, precipitants and policy*. Edinburgh: SHHD.

Cooke, D. J. (1994b). Primary diversion for psychological treatment: The decision making of Procurator Fiscals. International Journal of Law and Psychiatry, 17, 211-223.

Cooke, D. J., & Hole, D. J. (1983). The aetiological importance of stressful life events. *British Journal of Psychiatry, 143*, 397-400.

Cooke, D. J., Walker, A., & Gardiner, W. (1990). Behavioural disturbance in Barlinnie Prison. *The Prison Service Journal, 80*, 2-8.

Corrado, R. R., Doherty, D., & Glackman, W. (1989). A demonstration program for chronic recidivists of criminal justice, health, and social service agencies. *International Journal of Law and Psychiatry, 12*, 211-229.

Daniel, A. E., Robins, A. J., Reid, J.C., & Wilfley, D. E. (1988). Lifetime and six month prevalence of psychiatric disorders among sentenced female offenders. *Bulletin of the American Academy of Psychiatry and Law*, *16*, 333-342.

Ditchfield, J. (1991). *Control in prison: A review of the literature*. London: HMSO.

Durham, M. L. (1989). The impact of de-institutionalization on the current treatment of the mentally ill. *International Journal of Law and Psychiatry*, *12*, 117-131.

Endicott, J., & Spitzer, R. L. (1978). A diagnostic interview: The schedule for affective disorders and schizophrenia. *The Archives of General Psychiatry*, *35*, 837-844.

Faulk, M. (1976). A psychiatric study of men serving a sentence in Winchester Prison. *Medicine, Science and the Law*, *16*, 244-251.

Freeman, R. J., & Roesch, R. (1989). Mental disorder and the criminal justice system: A review. *International Journal of Law and Psychiatry*, *12*, 105-115.

Glueck, B. (1918). A study of 608 admissions to Sing Sing prison. *Mental Hygiene*, *2*, 85-151.

Goldberg, D., & Huxley, P. (1980). *Mental illness in the community: The pathway to psychiatric care*. London: Tavistock Publications Limited.

Goldberg, D., & Huxley, P. (1992). *Common mental disorders: A biosocial model*. London: Routledge.

Gunn, J., Robertson, G., Dell, S., & Way, C. (1978). *Psychiatric aspects of imprisonment*. London: Academic Press.

Gunn, J., Maden, A., & Swinton, M. (1991). Treatment needs of prisoners with psychiatric disorders. *British Medical Journal*, *303*, 338-341.

Guy, E., Platt, J., Swerling, I., & Bullock, S. (1985). Mental health status of prisoners in an urban jail. *Criminal Justice and Behavior*, *12*, 1.

Guze, S. B. (1976). Criminality and psychiatric disorders. New York: Oxford University Press.

Hansard, (1987). "Prisoners" written answers. *Hansard*, *4*.

Harding, T., & Zimmermann, E. (1989). Psychiatric symptoms, cognitive stress and vulnerability factors: A study in a remand prison. *British Journal of Psychiatry*, *155*, 36-43.

Hare, R. D. (1980). A research scale for the assessment of psychopathy in criminal populations. *Personality and Individual Differences*, *1*, 111-119.

Hare, R. D. (1991). *Manual for the Revised Psychopathy Checklist*. Toronto: Multi-Health Systems.

Hart, S. D., Kropp, P. R., & Hare, R. D. (1988). The performance of male psychopaths following conditional release from prison. *Journal of Consulting and Clinical Psychology*, *57*, 227-232.

Hart, S. D., & Hare, R. D. (1989). The discriminant validity of the Psychopathy Checklist in a forensic psychiatric population. *Psychological Assessment: A Journal of Consulting and Clinical Psychology*, *1*, 211-218.

Hodgins, S., & Cote, G. (1990). Prevalence of mental disorders among penitentiary inmates in Quebec. *Canada's Mental Health*, (March), 1-4.

Hodgins, S., & Cote, G. (1991). The mental health of penitentiary inmates in isolation. *Canadian Journal of Criminology*, *175*-182.

James, J. F., Gregory, D., Jones, R. K., & Rundell, O. H. (1980). Psychiatric morbidity in prisons. *Hospital and Community Psychiatry*, *31*: 674-677.

Jemelka, R., Trupin, E., & Chiles, J. A. (1989). The mentally ill in prison: A review. *Hospital and Community Psychiatry*, 40, 481-491.

Jones, D. A. (1976). *The health risks of imprisonment*. Lexington, MA: Lexington Books.

King, R. D., & McDermott, K. (1990). "My geranium is subversive": Some notes on the management of trouble in prison. *British Journal of Sociology*, *41*, 445-471.

McMain, S., Webster, C. D., & Menzies, R. J. (1989). The post-assessment careers of mentally disorder offenders. *International Journal of Law and Psychiatry*, *12*, 189-201.

Novick, L. F., Penna, R. D., & Schwartz, M. S. (1977). Health care status of the New York prison population. *Medical Care*, *15*, 205-216.

Ormel, J., Van Den Brink, W., Koetter, W. J., Giel, R., Van Der Meer, K., Van De Willige, G., & Wilmink, F. W. (1990). Recognition, management and outcome of psychological disorders in primary care: A naturalistic follow-up study. *Psychological Medicine*, *20*, 909-923.

Orr, J. H. (1978). The imprisonment of mentally disordered offenders. *British Journal of Psychiatry*, *133*, 194-199.

Paykel, E. S. (1978). Contribution of life events to causation of psychiatric illness. *Psychological Medicine*, *8*, 245-253.

Pepper, B., & Ryglewicz, H. (1982). Testimony for the neglected: The mentally ill in the post-de-institutionalized age. *American Journal of Orthopsychiatry*, *52*, 388-392.

Pinder, M., & Laming, H. (1991). Time to re-think. In K. R. Herbst & J. Gunn (Eds.), *The mentally disordered offender* (pp. 186-195). Oxford: Butterworth-Heinemann.

Roper, W. F. (1950). A comparative study of the Wakefield Prison population in 1948; Part 1. *British Journal of Delinquency*, *1*, 243-270.

Saunders, W. M., & Kershaw, P. W. (1978). Prevalence of problem drinking and alcoholism in the West of Scotland. *British Journal of Psychiatry*, *133*, 493-499.

Scott, P. D. (1970). Punishment or treatment: Prison or hospital? *British Medical Journal*, 167-169.

Scott, P. D. (1973). Violence in prisons and patients. In G. E. W. Wolstenholme & M. O'Connor (Eds.), *Medical care of prisoners and detainees* (pp. 143-163). Amsterdam: Elsevier.

Scottish Prison Service, (1990). *Opportunity and responsibility: Developing new approaches to the management of the long term prison system in Scotland*. Edinburgh: HMSO.

Smith, R. (1983). *Prison health care*. London: British Medical Association.

Steadman, H. J., Rosenstein, M. J., MacAskill, R. L., & Manderscheid, R. W. (1988). A profile of mentally disordered offenders admitted to inpatient psychiatric services in the United States. *Law and Human Behavior*, *12*, 91-99.

Surtees, P. G., Dean, C., Ingham, J. G., Kreitman, N., Miller, P., & Sashidharan, S. P. (1983). Psychiatric disorders in women from an Edinburgh community: Associations with demographic factors. *British Journal of Psychiatry*, *142*, 238-246.

Swetz, A., Salive, M. E., Stough, T., & Fordham Brewer, T. (1989). The prevalence of mental illness in a state correctional institution for men. *Journal of Prison and Jail Health*, *8*, 3-15.

Sykes, G. M. (1958). *The society of captives*. Princeton: Princeton University Press.

Taylor, P. J. (1986). Psychiatric disorder in London's life sentenced offenders. *British Journal of Criminology*, *26*, 1, 63-78.

Taylor, P. J., & Parrott, J. M. (1988). Elderly offenders: A study of age related factors among custodily remanded prisoners. *British Journal of Psychiatry*, *152*, 340-346.

Teplin, L. (1983). The criminalization of the mentally ill: Speculation in search of data. *Psychological Bulletin*, *94*, 54-67.

Thornicroft, G. (1991). Social deprivation and rates of treated mental disorder: Developing statistical models to predict psychiatric service utilisation. *British Journal of Psychiatry*, *158*, 475-484.

Toch, H. (1982). Studying and reducing stress. In R. Johnson & H. Toch (Eds.), *The pains of imprisonment*. Beverly Hills: Sage.

Walker, N. (1983). Side-effects of incarceration. *British Journal of Criminology*, *23*, 61-71.

Washbrook, R. A. H. (1977). The psychiatrically ill prisoner. *Lancet*, *i*, 1302-1303.

Weissman, M. M., & Klerman, G. L. (1977). Sex differences in the epidemiology of depression. *Archives of General Psychiatry*, *34*, 98-111.

[1] This research was funded by the Criminological and Legal Research Group of the Scottish Home and Health Department. I would like to thank the Research Group and in particular, Mr Edward Wozniak, for support and guidance throughout the project. I would also like to thank Mrs Margaret Struthers for carrying out the majority of the interviews, and approaching the task with care and dedication. The study could not have been completed without the support and practical assistance

of many governors and prison officers within the Scottish Prison Service, to them I am very grateful. Finally, I would like to express my gratitude to the prisoners who participated in the study, who tolerated - in an uncomplaining manner - an interview which focused upon their private thoughts and feelings.

The views expressed in this paper are those of the author and do not necessarily represent the views of the Scottish Home and Health Department or the Scottish Prison Service.

Correctional Programmes in Europe: A Pilot Study for a Meta-Evaluation

Santiago Redondo, Vicente Garrido, M. Teresa Anguera and Eulalia Luque

Introduction

Rehabilitation in Europe

Many European and American countries are still in the throes of debating the suitability of applying programmes for the rehabilitation of offenders. This controversy has reached new heights during the last few decades, between those in favor of a *fitting punishment for the guilty* and those who support the philosophy of *rehabilitation*. Taking one side in this controversy are professionals from the area of *law*, most of whom support a system of punitive justice which offers guarantees. This debate has been illustrated in America, for instance, by Ross and Fabiano (1985), Palmer (1992), and Lipsey (in press); and in Europe, by Lösel and Körfel (1989), Hollin (1989), McGuire and Priestley (1989), Garrido and Redondo (1992), and Redondo (1993).

In North America, where certain correctional programmes are better developed and more widely used, some twenty reviews have been carried out in order to assess the efficacy of broad groups of applied programmes. The first of these reviews, conducted in the seventies on interventions applied in the fifties and the sixties, identified few positive effects of rehabilitation programmes on the subsequent recidivism of the subjects (the most famous review is that of Lipton, Martinson and Wilks', 1975) and concluded with a general tone of pessimism. Subsequent meta-evaluations (the first of which was conducted by Gendreau and Ross, 1979), have suggested that certain correctional programmes may have somewhat more promising effects.

The European scene is different. Firstly, probably fewer correctional programmes are applied, and even fewer of these are actually evaluated, judging by the small number of studies published. As Lösel and Köferl (1989) have pointed out, though many West European countries have a broad practical experience in the treatment of inmates, nevertheless very few systematic evaluations have been conducted. Secondly, when dealing with different countries - with different languages and cultures - there is greater linguistic and conceptual division. This means that the emerging "United Europe" lacks the integration and evaluation, which North America does have, which allow us to know what has been done and what is being done in terms of the treatment of criminal behavior in the European Continent, and what effects it produces.

This situation leads us to the present research work, which has the following objectives: (1) to collect and describe as many as possible of the correctional programmes carried out in Europe during the eighties (be they in prisons, juvenile institutions, probation systems, etc.), regardless of whether they were published or not; (2) to try to integrate the correctional interventions, concepts and models used in these programmes; (3) to compare the relative efficacy of the programmes, reanalysing them by means of the systematic integration of their findings, and by means of meta-analysis, whenever the inclusion of quantitative results makes the use of this technique possible; and finally, (4) to analyze the cost/effectiveness of all programmes which contain this type of information in the selected reports. We thereby hope to draw conclusions as to what the main correctional programmes applied during the last decade in Europe are and which of these are the most effective and economical.

Previous reviews (America, Europe)

We will refer briefly to three of the last meta-analyses carried out on criminal behavior treatment programmes. The first of these by Whitehead and Lab (1989), consisted of the analysis of 50 North American programmes applied between 1975 and 1984. Their main conclusion was pessimistic, claiming that the results obtained clearly supported the negative evaluations of previous work in the sense that correctional treatment has, in the works which were analyzed, little effect on recidivism.

The second and the only one of the meta-analyses of correctional programmes which was conducted in Europe, was by Lösel and Köferl (1989), on a group of 16 German programmes, the only ones that were published between 1977 and 1985. Their final assessment is somewhat more optimistic. On the effectiveness of German socio-therapeutic prisons, the authors concluded that the desired effects (non-recidivism) can be expected of 10% more inmates in socio-therapeutic prisons than inmates in normal prisons, which contradicts, albeit moderately, the pessimistic evaluation of "nothing works".

Finally, fleeting mention must be made of the latest and most ambitious meta-analysis of American correctional programmes conducted by Lipsey (in press), who to date has reviewed no less than 443 studies published between 1950 and 1990. In his work, the author asks himself the fundamental question, one which is in the minds of all of us when we try to prevent or control criminal behavior: "Does treatment reduce criminal behavior?". The answer, according to Lipsey is "Yes, on average a positive effect is observed" in the reduction of crime. A statistically significant although modest reduction in recidivism appears in treated groups when compared with controls.

Location and Collection of Studies

Procedure The following methods were used to collate studies which evaluated rehabilitation programmes applied in Europe, to form the basis of this study.

(1) An initial computing search was carried out, using the *DIALOG Information Retrieval Service*, which gave access to the *Criminal Justice Periodical Index* (CJPI).

Unfortunately, this initial approach proved somewhat fruitless, obtaining 128 references, of which only six were of interest for the aims of this research.

Bearing this initial result in mind, a second computing search was undertaken through a French data base called *PASCAL*, which compiles information on scientific works, such as technology, medicine or biology, as well the disciplines of social sciences and criminology. This second computing approach located a further 30 programmes, which initially appeared to be of interest for our objectives.

(2) Secondly, a systematic review was carried out of the issues published between 1980-1991 of a group of 55 journals - most of them European - which specialise in Criminology and other related sciences, such as Penitentiary Science, Psychology, Pedagogy, Social Work, and Law.

(3) As a third strategy for locating works, a letter was sent, both in English and French, to a group of 82 institutions involved in teaching and research in the areas of criminology and correctional services in all European countries (selected from *A World Directory of Criminological Institutes* [UNSDRI, 1986]), and to a total of 118 European teachers and researchers, selected from amongst the participants in a series of recent congresses on criminology. This letter informed them of the aims of this research and they were asked to forward rehabilitation programmes applied in their respective countries.

As a result of sending these letters, various materials were received, including works published in specialised journals and books, as well as unpublished studies.

(4) Finally, a review of books and readings was carried out, including works selected from my personal library and the library of the Centre d'Estudis Jurídics (in Barcelona), which specialises in criminology.

Selection criteria and exclusion of studies When referring to the treatment of or the intervention in crime we are directing our attention towards a highly varied and disparate universe of conceptualisations, intervention procedures and evaluation techniques. As far as interventions are concerned, we have used both punitive and control procedures, based on penal theories and concepts, such as the deprivation of freedom, as well as more sophisticated therapeutic and educational therapies based on psychological and sociological, theories or models, such as group techniques, behaviour modification, education, training in social skills and work programmes.

Regarding the evaluation concepts and techniques used to determine the degree of efficacy of interventions in criminal behavior, different measures have been used. Two categories of measures can be distinguished: firstly, those which were designed to ascertain directly if a certain intervention strategy, when applied to a group or population of offenders, produced any kind of reduction or variation in future criminal behaviour; and secondly, measures aimed at detecting changes or improvements, not directly in the criminal behaviour, but in certain psychological or behavioural factors which may be supposed to be linked, more or less closely, to future criminal conduct.

From an ideal perspective, it would certainly be interesting to consult works and programmes which have included measures linked to the future criminal behavior of the subjects treated. The final interest of any intervention dealing with criminal behavior is to know whether or not the latter decreases. However, in most cases, where the final interest of an intervention programme is on the subsequent recidivism of the participants, the researchers have to carry out lengthy and costly follow-up of the subjects treated over a period of one to five years or more after completion of the programme. This happens infrequently. That is why the present review will include programmes which contain some kind of measurement of the future criminal behavior of the treated subjects, as well as those which measure only other psychological factors and conducts.

Another decisive point of this research has to do with the minimum methodological criteria which must be demanded of the works reviewed. Reviews conducted in North America (e.g., Lipsey, in press) tend to maintain a strict criterion, whereby a prerequisite for acceptance is that studies possess a design of group control, with random allocation of subjects. This seems fairly logical, if we take into account the greater empirical tradition which characterises North American and Anglo Saxon psychology and criminology in comparison to the greater discursive and theoretical standard practice common to European criminology in general.

Here we also adopted a broad perspective, accepting in our analysis works of a classic experimental nature, which use a control group, as well as single group studies, provided they have measurements of the dependent variables before and after the intervention. Works with behaviourial evaluation designs which used baseline measurements were also accepted.

After the described process of location and filtering, in accordance with the previous criteria, 213 works were collected initially, corresponding to the countries listed in Table 1. From these, 20 works were randomly selected in order to carry out this pilot study.

Table 1: Total number of studies collected and selected for the pilot study, per country.

Countries	**Number of studies**	**Pilot Study**
Belgium	6	
Ex-socialist	5	
France	5	
Germany	22	2
Great Britain	57	8
Holland	25	3
Ireland	1	
Italy	11	
Portugal	18	1
Spain	49	5
Sweden	7	1
Switzerland	7	
Total	213	20

A further search was later carried out, similar to the previous ones, using the references contained in the Psychological Abstracts. Some 350 new references appeared as a result, which must now be filtered following the criteria and objectives of this research.

Sheet and Coding Manual

Two basic instruments were prepared for coding the different studies: the first is a coding sheet which includes 221 items or pieces of data corresponding to the following areas: identification of the document; identification of the authors; complementary documents used for coding, philosophy of the programme; method and characteristics of the treatment groups; personal, social, criminal and reconviction characteristics of the subjects; sampling; context of application of the programme; financing; design and follow-up; outside variables involved; treatment activities or intervention variables; length and intensity of the intervention; professionals who participated; triangulation; dependent or criterion variables; qualitative and quantitative results; conclusions; and reading and coding times of each document.

Pilot Study

Once the first variables or items sheet, the database programme for coding and the coding manual had been drawn up, a pilot study was designed for testing the suitability of these instruments for the process of coding the group of studies collected.

To this end, from the population of studies collected up until March, 1992 (213 works), 30 studies (14% of the total) were selected at random - using a random numbers table - 20 of which met the established requirements and were finally chosen (see Table 1).

All of the studies were coded by two or three independent highly qualified coders, following the established sheet and coding manual.

Difficulties in the coding process

(a) Large number of variables and difficulties in defining them One of the first difficulties which was encountered throughout this first pilot process of coding was the high number of items and pieces of data which had to be coded for each work -a maximum of 221- which means that in many cases the process proved lengthy and intricate. The definition of many of the variables involved (e.g., theoretical model underlying a programme, representativeness of a sample, psychological processes unleashed by the intervention) present additional difficulties to the coder given the lack of detail in many of the descriptions given by authors.

(b) Reading/coding time All the above made the process of reading and coding the results in this first pilot study extremely slow, with an average time per work of 58 minutes required for the first reading of the works, plus an average of 116 minutes (1 hour and 56 minutes) taken to code each of them. This quantification leads us to forecast that it would take over 600 hours to conduct a single coding of the 213 studies catalogued to date, if the present rate were maintained. In terms of working days this would be equivalent to one coder working full time for fifteen 40-hour working weeks. If we take into account the fact that the coding, furthermore, must be double, in order to maintain an adequate control on reliability, the investment in time which would be needed merely for the process of coding is prohibitive.

This prompts us to consider reducing the number of coding items, which would mean shortening the time required for coding.

(c) Diversity of languages Another added difficulty within this work stems from the linguistic variety of the studies included in the present analysis, as compared to the single language of the Anglo Saxon meta-evaluations. At the moment we are working with studies in eight different languages, which requires a special effort, both personal and economic, for the proper translation of the material. In spite of this, for the coding of the first 20 studies of the pilot study, the coders who could read other languages did not take more time on average to code the works in foreign languages than they used for those written in Spanish.

First results

Our first results are, of necessity, descriptive and provisional. Under no circumstances can these initial data be considered representative of the population of correctional studies which make up the research as a whole, neither in number nor in terms of their present level of analysis.

Firstly, we shall refer to two items of information of interest in the studies, pertaining to the authors' professional background and the scientific literature referred to in the works.

(a) The authors' professional disciplines One interesting question in the scientific context we are dealing with refers to what kind of professionals are usually engaged in applying or evaluating rehabilitation programmes. From our sample of studies, which includes 29 authors, 12 of them (41%) were psychologists, followed in numerical terms by three educators, two social workers, one probation officer, one prison teacher and one psychiatrist (in nine cases the discipline was not stated).

As far as the authors' participation in the application of the programmes is concerned, in 50% of the cases the authors took part in the application, whereas in the other 50% they acted merely as assessors or reporters of the programmes.

(b) Literature referred to in the studies One of the coded items was aimed at finding out what authors and previous works were referred to in the studies by way of endorsing the techniques or interventions applied. In this respect, up to now, two trends were observed in the evaluated sample of studies: firstly, the list of references is varied, and linked in each case to the subject which is being tackled, without repetition of the same authors in different works being detected; on the other hand, a certain trend towards "endo-reference" can be observed, or to an author citing him/herself. Perhaps this tendency may be justified by the fact that every author knows his/her own work best, and that what he/she has done in the past usually has an important connection with what he/she is doing at present.

In order to conduct a global evaluation of the programmes analyzed we will take the model of Rossi, Freeman and Wright (1979) into consideration for the evaluation of social programmes, which establishes the following main evaluation sections: (1) detection of a social problem, (2) definition of the intervention's objectives, (3) design of the programme of action, (4) application of the programme, and (5) evaluation of its results. We will evaluate each one of these sections independently for the group of programmes sampled.

(1) Problem detection In this section we will be referring to two factors: the age of the subjects treated and the size of the samples. Regarding age, five programmes were aimed at young subjects, aged between 11 and 21, and nine dealt with individuals over 21 (this information did not appear in six studies). As far as the size of the samples is concerned, one study was directed at a single subject, eight dealt with groups of less than 100 subjects, five with groups of under 200 subjects, and three with samples of over 500 individuals. It can be observed, thus, that whereas some programmes tackle small samples of subjects, others adopt a wider approach and aim to influence broad populations of offenders.

(2) Definition of the intervention's objectives The objectives of the programmes are varied and disparate, ranging from ambitious intentions aimed at reducing the recidivism of subjects or teaching them new social interaction skills, to lesser objectives, from the perspective of their community value, such as reducing prison violence or improving the climate in the institutions.

In this respect, the index of theoretical models underlying the relation which is established between the proposed objectives and the intervention actions undertaken is of greater interest. Table 2 lists these models, for those works in which they are set out by the authors.

Table 2: Theoretical models underlying the programmes of the sample, and most frequent intervention techniques or actions

Theoretical model	Number of models
THERAPIES	
Sociotherapy	1
Group work + individual assistance	1
Residential rehabilitation	1
Psychological Treatment in "Diversion"	1
Psychoanalytical therapy	1
EDUCATION AND SKILLS TRAINING	
Education by correspondence ("Open University")	1
Psychoanalytical Competence Model	3
CHANGES IN PRISON STATUS	
Hardening of system	1
Segregation of conflictive inmates	1
Softer system - less prisonization	1
Therapeutic Community	1
TV increases inmates' contact with outside world	1
ALTERNATIVES TO INTERNMENT	
Alternative projects other than imprisonment	1
Learning (Teaching Family Model)	1
Normalized activities - greater social adjustment	1
No model stated	3

(3) Programme of action The intervention actions which were undertaken in the different programmes of our sample proved to be generally consistent with their theoretical models. Nevertheless, as is logical, in most cases the use of different techniques inside the same programme was observed. Table 3 lists the most used intervention techniques or actions.

Table 3: Most used intervention actions and techniques in the programmes.

Therapies
Individual psychotherapy
Social therapy
Discussions, meetings and group therapies
Individual assistance
Inmate - prison officer relationship = patient - nurse relationship
Periodical meetings between inmates and prison officers
Interview for evaluation of psychological problems
Psychological treatment
Relaxation
Education and Training in Behavioural Skills
School activities
Professional training
"Open University" or Education by correspondence
Training in social skills and development of cognitive capacities
Group sociopedagogical activity
Behaviour modelling
Behaviour extinction Token economy
Changes in Prison Status
Privileges and penalties
Military style training
Strict supervision and occupation of time
Segregation of conflictive inmates
Self-government
Access to individual TV in cells
Therapeutic community
Alternatives to Internment
Parole
Diversion
Family therapies and interviews
Assistance to groups of victims
Coexistence in outside juvenile homes
Foster families

(4) Application Information about integrity in the application of the programmes is very scarce. In the absence of such information, we decided to deal with the length of the different interventions, since length is undoubtedly a parameter of interest which is linked to the intensity of the programmes, and consequently to the power of the effects which can be expected of these programmes. Only 11 programmes give information about duration, which on average was about 20 months (ranging between 1.5 and 72 months). Many interventions were maintained over a prolonged period of time.

(5) Direction of the results Of our sample, only 50% of the studies (10) assessed the effects of the intervention carried out. In these 10 works, a group of 29 effects were evaluated. Of these, 23 (79%) were reported as being favourable, offering better results for the experimental groups than for the control groups - if they existed - or for the post-intervention measurements over the pre-intervention ones. In four cases, no effects were recorded as a result of the interventions, whereas in two situations the effects were negative. This apparent abundance of successful effects must be approached very cautiously, since the measures were variable in their relevance. Thus, while some results made references to decreases in recidivism values, many of them referred only to purely subjective appreciations made by the participating subjects themselves or to those made by the programme evaluators.

Conclusions

Since these are preliminary results, now is not the time to draw conclusions about the correctional programmes applied in Europe. Initially, all we aimed to do was present the first steps taken in this ambitious research, which we hope in the coming months will allow us to find out much more information in this field.

All that we have done so far in our pilot study leads us to take two considerations into account, of opposite natures, for the future development of this research work. The first has a dimension which involves economy of effort, and refers to the probable need to reduce the number of items which are coded for each work, so as to make the coding process easier.

As far as the systematization is concerned, we agree with Lösel and Köferl (1989), who point to the urgent need for a more precise description of the contents and objectives of the treatments, a greater theoretical explanation of their bases, a greater differentiation of global objectives, transforming them into small evaluation studies of greater precision with empirical analyses, and a greater evaluation orientation, which should, in a word, make their subsequent integration easier.

For the moment, however, as far as the analysis of European correctional programmes which we carry out is concerned, we feel that extensive criteria must be adopted in relation to the choice of studies which should be included in the analysis. We are proposing that the widest possible number of programmes and intervention initiatives should be considered, although sometimes they may not be systematic enough, or are lacking in methodological detail. We believe that the first step should be to find out in an orderly manner what there actually is, however small or irregular it may be in its development. For part of this information, a stricter and purer methodological approach may be possible at a later date.

References

Cooper, H. M. (1989). *Integrating research: A guide for literature reviews* (2nd Edn.). Newbury Park, California: Sage Publications.

Garrido, V., & Redondo, S. (1992). *La intervención educativa en el medio penitenciario. Una década de reflexión*. Madrid: Ed. Diagrama.

Gendreau, P., & Ross, R. (1979). Effective correctional treatment: Bibliotherapy for cynics. *Crime and Delinquency*, *25*, 463-489.

Hollin, C. R. (1989). *Psychology and crime. An introduction to criminological psychology*. London: Routledge.

Lipsey, M. W. (in press). Juvenile delinquency treatment: A meta-analytic inquiry into the variability of effects. In Research Synthesis Committee of the Russell Sage Foundation, *Meta-analysis for explanation: A casebook*. Russell Sage Foundation.

Lipton, D., Martinson, R., & Wilks, J. (1975). *The effectiveness of correctional treatment: A survey of evaluation studies*. New York: Praeger.

Lösel, F., & Köferl, P. (1989). Evaluation research on correctional treatment in West Germany: A meta-analysis. In H. Wegener, F. Lösel, & J. Haisch (Eds.), *Criminal behavior and the justice system: Psychological perspectives*, 334-355. New York: Springer-Verlag .

McGuire, J., & Priestley, P. (1985). *Offending behaviour. Skills and stratagems for going straight*. London: B.T. Batsford Ltd.

Palmer, T. (1992). *The re-emergence of correctional intervention*. Newbury Park: Sage.

Redondo, S. (1993). *Evaluar e intervenir en las prisiones*. Barcelona: Promociones y Publicaciones Universitarias.

Ross, R., & Fabiano, E. (1985). *Time to think*. Johnson City, Tennessee: Institute of Social Sciences & Arts.

Rossi, P. H., Freeman, H. F., & Wright, S. R. (1979). *Evaluation: A systematic approach*. Beverly Hills: Sage.

UNSDRI (United Nations Social Defence Research Institute) (1986). *A world directory of criminological institutes* (4th Edn.). Compiled and edited by Carla Masotti Santoro. Roma.

Whitehead, J. T., & Lab, S. P. (1989). A meta-análysis of juvenile correctional treatment. *Journal of Research in Crime and Delinquency*, *26*(3), 276-295.

Mental Health Interventions in Pretrial Jails[1]

Ronald Roesch

Dating back to the 1960s, significant changes in civil commitment laws in the United States and Canada dramatically altered the treatment of mentally ill individuals (e.g., Barnes & Toews, 1983; Kiesler, 1980; Roesch & Golding, 1985). Many chronic patients were released from mental hospitals and while the rate of hospitalization remained fairly stable, new admissions tended to remain hospitalized for considerably briefer periods (Goldman, Adams, & Taube, 1983; Kiesler, 1980; Luckey & Berman, 1979). Similar changes were taking place in many European countries (e.g., Bennett & Morris, 1983; Mosher, 1983). In terms of substantial changes to mental hospitals, the deinstitutionalization movement in mental health was a considerable success. The effects of deinstitutionalization are more controversial, however, when one considers the impact on the lives of individuals with mental health problems. It is well known that one of the shortcomings of the deinstitutionalization movement was that the resources needed to truly shift the locus of mental health care from the institution to the community simply did not materialize. There was a presumption that community mental health programs would be established to fill the increased need resulting from less reliance on mental hospitals. While there was a substantial increase in such community based programs, there seems to be a consensus that they have not been able to keep up with the demand. Many people in need of mental health and social services simply were unable to obtain them, and their situation deteriorated over time (Bachrach, 1980; Brown, 1980; Scull, 1981).

An increasing number of such individuals came to the attention of law enforcement personnel, and police officers were faced with the dilemma of responding to situations in which there were few mental health treatment options. Consequently, many individuals were arrested and admitted to local jails (Rabkin, 1979; Sosowsky, 1980). Indeed, as Teplin (1984) found, mentally disordered offenders have a significantly greater chance of being arrested, as compared to non-mentally disordered offenders. Teplin (1991) is careful to point out that this does not necessarily establish a causal relationship (i.e., that changes in mental health system practices caused changes in the manner in which police deal with mentally ill individuals). Furthermore, studies of the prevalence of mental disorder in jails and prisons show rates that vary considerably and it has not been demonstrated, in large part because of methodological shortcomings in the research, that the prevalence has actually increased over time. Teplin (1991) reviewed the research on the prevalence of mental disorder among jail detainees and reported rates ranging from about 5% to 12% for severe mental disorder and from 16% to about 67% for any mental illness. While the rates do vary, it is probably reasonable to assume that there are a substantial number of jail inmates who are in need of mental health services. Jails, however, have traditionally provided little in the way of such services (Morgan, 1981; Morrissey, Steadman, Kilburn, & Lindsay, 1984; Steadman, McCarty, & Morrissey, 1989).

Before I turn to a review of my current research on mental health interventions in pretrial jails, I want to comment that, in general, I think the deinstitutionalization movement was based on the right intentions, and overall, the increased focus on individual rights, such as the right to treatment and the right not to be treated, has resulted in positive and beneficial changes in mental health treatment. At the same time, I think we need to appreciate more fully the impact of these changes because for many the net result has not been more freedom of choice but simply a shift in the type of institution in which they are involuntarily detained. The increased number of mentally disordered offenders in jails and prisons is an indication of the failure of the mental health system to provide adequately for their needs in the community.

Along with several colleagues, I was interested in developing a program of research focusing on mental health issues in the jails. Early on, it became evident that we needed some baseline data in order to understand the nature and extent of mental disorder in a particular jail population. Related to this was the need to learn more about methods for assessing mental disorder in a jail population. One problem we immediately faced was the reality that large jails with many admissions each day precluded lengthy assessments. Consequently, our initial research was directed at identifying methods for providing useful diagnostic data that would allow us to estimate mental health needs in the jail. We then wanted to use the results of this initial work to begin to develop a jail mental health program. In this paper, I will provide an overview of two separate but highly related research projects we have been working on for the past several years.[2] The first is a study of methods of assessing mental health problems in jails, while the second uses this research to develop interventions in both the jail and the community.

The Prevalence And Detection Of Mental Disorder In A Pretrial Jail

Our initial study had two purposes. One, we wanted to examine the prevalence of mental disorders in a pretrial jail population, and two, we wanted to evaluate alternative methods for assessing mental disorder in such facilities. In particular, we wanted to assess the feasibility of conducting brief screening interviews of all inmates as they enter the jail. We collected data from a random sample of English-speaking admissions to the Vancouver Pretrial Services Centre (VPSC), a large pretrial facility in the province of British Columbia (Canada), for the 12-month period between August 1, 1989 and July 31, 1990. We selected consecutive admissions for the first five months, and every third admission for the last seven months. The sample of 861 represented approximately 50% of all english-speaking males admitted to the jail during the study period. We had interview data from 684 men, and file-based data on a further 106 men, yielding a final sample size of 790; information was unavailable for the remaining 71 men initially selected for inclusion in the sample. Demographic data indicated that the majority of the sample was White (15% Native), young (nearly half of the sample was in the 20 to 29 year age range), and underemployed (over half were unemployed at the time of arrest). The recidivism rates were alarmingly high as over 80% had a prior adult record, 50% had a prior juvenile record, and nearly 70% had a previous incarceration.

We used a two-stage assessment procedure. In the first stage, referred to below as the screening stage, each individual in the final sample completed a semi-structured interview and/or was rated on a number of standardized rating scales. On the basis of the screening results, subjects were identified as cases (i.e., those with past or current mental disorder) or noncases (i.e., no past or current mental disorder).

In the second stage, a random sample of 108 cases and 84 noncases were subsequently administered a structured psychodiagnostic interview, namely the Diagnostic Interview Schedule, version III-A (DIS; Robins, Helzer, Croughan, & Radcliff, 1981). The DIS yields diagnoses of several major mental disorders according to the criteria contained in the *Diagnostic and statistical manual of mental disorders* (DSM-III-R; American Psychiatric Association, 1987). We used screening data from the first stage to oversample cases in the second stage. This was an important feature of our design and is superior to simple random selection of inmates since it results in a high number of cases of mental disorder. This procedure allowed us to detect low-prevalence disorders with a relatively small sample size.

Screening interview

The screening interview was semi-structured in format and was designed to elicit information concerning current and lifetime psychosocial functioning. Consistent with our goal of producing a brief screening procedure, the interview could be completed in 20 to 30 minutes. On the basis of the screening information, the interviewer completed several rating scales. This included the Brief Psychiatric Rating Scale (BPRS; Overall & Gorham, 1962), the Referral Decision Scale (RDS; Teplin & Swartz, 1989), and the Diagnostic Profile (DP; Hart & Hemphill, 1989). The first section of the interview gathered basic demographic data, including employment status and living conditions; the second section covered past mental health contacts, substance use history, and recent utilization of physical health care resources; and the third section consisted of a mental status exam and questions concerning the defendant's self-perceived need and desire for mental health treatment.

Definition of mental disorder

Cases of mental disorder were defined as those who had one or more hit on the RDS, BPRS, and DP; noncases were those who had no hits. Interrater agreement on the presence versus absence of mental disorder was very high (kappa = .92).

The screening interviews performed very well in identifying major mental disorder (see Hart, Roesch, Corrado, & Cox, 1993, for a fuller discussion). Table 1 compares the screening judgments, based on a brief interview, with the DIS diagnosis, which of course is based on a much lengthier interview of two or more hours. Screening rarely missed DIS-diagnosed mental disorder (only one of 73 cases was missed). However, screening frequently overpredicted DIS-diagnosed mental disorder (79 of 119 cases in which screening suggested mental disorder were not confirmed by the DIS). This is an acceptable type of error in a screening process since it is better to err in the direction of identifying individuals who turn out not to need intervention. Furthermore, many of the screening positives did have substantial mental health problems although they didn't fit the DIS categories of major mental disorder.

Table 1: Predictive Efficiency of Screening Using DIS/DIM-III Major Mental Disorder as the Criterion

	DIS/DSM-III	
Screening	**No**	**Yes**
No	72	1
Yes	79	40

Note. Positive predictive power = 40/119 = 0.336; Negative predictive power = 1/73 = 0.986

Table 2 summarizes our estimates of the prevalence of DIS/DSM-III diagnoses among all admissions to VPSC. Several things stand out. One, our estimate of the rate of major mental disorder in the total pretrial population is 15.6%, placing us above the range found by Teplin (1991). Two, the prevalence of substance use disorders is exceptionally high, affecting nearly everyone coming into the jail. Many of these individuals have co-occurring disorders (e.g., schizophrenia and substance abuse), further compounding the problems of living experienced by these individuals (see Abram & Teplin, 1991, for a review of co-occurring disorders among jail detainees). This clearly points to the need for intervention with these problems. Three, the presence of other mental disorders is quite high, but this is largely accounted for, especially in the screening negative sample, by the high rate of antisocial personality disorder (APD). One might question the usefulness of APD in a jail population since nearly everyone fits the criteria.

Table 2: Prevalence of DIS/DSM-III Diagnoses Among Admissions to the Vancouver Pretrial Services Centre

DIS/DSM-III Diagnosis	**Prevalence (% of total admissions)**
Major Mental Disorders	**15.6**
1. Cognitive Impairment (Severe)	0.5
2. Schizophrenic Disorders	4.9
3. Major Affective Disorders	10.1
Substance Use Disorders	**85.9**
1. Alcohol Abuse/Dependence	77.6
2. Drug Use Disorders	63.7
Other Mental Disorders	**88.0**
1. Anxiety Disorders	41.1
2 Dysthymic Disorder	7.2
3. Somatization Disorder	0.7
4. Eating Disorders (Bulimia)	0.3
5. Sexual Disorders	27.0
6. Antisocial Personality Disorder	64.3
Any Disorder	**93.6**

In the second research project I want to talk about today, we used these findings to guide us in developing a screening and intervention program for another pretrial jail in the Vancouver area.

A Model For A Jail Mental Health Program

Individuals entering jail are typically in a state of crisis, often experiencing stress and anxiety. As we have noted, many admissions will have a history of mental health problems. Consequently, pretrial jail facilities may be a highly appropriate place for mental health interventions. It may provide an excellent opportunity to deliver mental health services to those who need them, if they are interested in obtaining such services. I do want to emphasize, however, that I do not view jails as primarily a mental health facility. In reality, most defendants do not need or desire mental health services. Given this caveat, the jail can be seen as one starting point, the time to evaluate individuals and provide some short-term crisis intervention if needed. Since most defendants remain in jail for only a short period of time, so mental health interventions in the jails are fairly limited in scope, but if the provision of services is continued outside the jail, successful intervention may become more likely.

The Surrey (British Columbia) Pretrial Services Centre (SPSC) opened in the summer of 1991. We had an opportunity to work with jail administrators prior to the opening of this facility, because they were interested in developing a program for the provision of mental health services. We[3] were interested in establishing a jail mental health program that was part of a larger community-based approach to the treatment of mentally disordered offenders. Consistent with this philosophy, the Surrey Pretrial Mental Health Project is jointly funded and operated by several government agencies in addition to the involvement of university researchers. Such an interministerial and interdisciplinary approach allowed us to begin to bridge the gap between community-based and institution-based services.

Defining principles

The following set of principles define the dimensions of the Surrey Pretrial Mental Health Project.[4]

♦ Mentally disordered offenders cycle continuously through the health, mental health, forensic, and criminal justice systems. Traditional methods with traditional agency or institutional boundaries have not been especially successful in dealing with these individuals. An adequate response to this problem will require interministerial, inter-agency, and community cooperation.

♦ The mentally ill in jail must be viewed as a community concern. Incarceration only removes the mentally ill offender temporarily from the community. Both institutional-based staff and community workers must work together in a multidisciplinary team to meet the needs of inmates and to prepare for their eventual release. When mentally disordered offenders are released from a correctional facility, all reasonable steps should be taken to ensure their reintegration into the community.

♦ While a pretrial centre should remain primarily a correctional facility, mentally disordered inmates are entitled to have access to mental health services.

♦ The core elements of a mental health service in a correctional setting include: screening, assessment, treatment, crisis intervention, as well as institutional and post-release community planning and case management.

♦ When mentally disordered offenders are released from a correctional facility, all reasonable steps should be taken to ensure their reintegration into the community. Special attention should be paid to the provision of community support services for mentally disordered offenders.

♦ Correctional officers should actively participate in the identification and management of mentally ill offenders in jail. They should be provided with training to aid them in this aspect of their employment. As I will touch on later, correctional officers are not particularly happy about the increased number of mentally disordered offenders in the jails, but they do want more training to be able to deal with them more effectively.

♦ Program evaluation is an integral part of the project. The information generated by the program evaluation will be used to determine the status of the project with respect to the stated principles and goals, and to make adjustments to the program and services where necessary.

SPSC houses approximately 160 inmates. Services offered by the Project include screening for mental illness, assessment, brief intervention, institutional and community case planning and case management, liaison with other correctional institutions, as well as the training and utilization of correctional staff in the identification and management of mentally disordered inmates. The programs offered by the Project are based on a combination of services within the institution and mobilization of community resources upon the inmate's release. The participation of community mental health and forensic outpatient services make the community linkage possible.

Staff roles and responsibilities

The Project staff represent a variety of disciplines, including a nurse (who is the coordinator of the activities of the various staff and is the key on-site person), a community social worker (who functions as the "boundary spanner", a concept I will discuss later), psychologists (who provide psychological assessment and treatment), psychiatrists (who provide psychiatric assessment and treatment), intake interviewers (currently clinical psychology doctoral students), evaluation and research staff, and clerical staff. A steering committee, comprised of representatives from the various branches of government involved in the project (Health, Forensic Services, Mental Health, Corrections) is responsible for providing overall direction to the project.

Services and procedures

The model we developed in the Surrey project begins with a screening interview of all persons entering the jail. We employ several senior graduate students from the clinical psychology doctoral program at Simon Fraser University in Burnaby, British Columbia.[5] The interviews are brief, approximately 20 minutes in length, but they provide sufficient information to make initial decisions about the mental health needs of the incoming inmates. The screening procedure includes a brief semistructured mental status interview, the Brief Psychiatric Rating Scale, and the Global Assessment of Functioning Scale from the DSM-III-R. The semistructured interview covered seven content areas: personal/demographic information, suicide risk, orientation to time and space, criminal history, social adjustment during the past month, mental status in the past month, and mental health history. Information was also obtained from the inmates' files.

The intake assessment may identify inmates who require crisis intervention services, particularly those who may be at risk for self-harm or suicide. Such inmates are reported immediately to both the nurse coordinator and the correctional officer in charge, so that necessary interventions and precautions may be arranged. Similarly, attempts are made during the screening interview to identify those individuals who may be a danger to others.

Most of the interviewees do not need further intervention, but even for these individuals we think that the interviews serve a positive function. The process of arrest and admission to jail can be a traumatic one, and the interviewers have become quite skilled at reducing anxiety and fear. Informal feedback from officers and jail administrators has suggested that this may be a valuable side effect of the program, and we are planning to examine this in our evaluation of the project.

Following the screening, decisions concerning the referral of inmates for a more detailed assessment are made each day by the nurse coordinator in consultation with Project staff and other appropriate SPSC personnel. The outcome of relevant cases are then communicated to correctional staff responsible for the day-to-day management of the inmate. In addition to the routine procedure, referrals for a more detailed assessment can also be based upon concerns of correctional officers or duty nurses. The referral for a more detailed assessment by a psychologist and/or a psychiatrist can take place immediately following the intake screening or at any time during the stay of the inmate at the SPSC.

Although a treatment plan is developed for all inmates, they are, of course, given the choice to participate. The treatment plan, developed by the nurse coordinator with the participation of the Project clinical staff and appropriate corrections personnel, may include recommendations for treatment or other mental health interventions, as well as suggestions for the day-to-day management of the inmate.

Since this is a pretrial facility, most inmates return to the community after a fairly brief stay. Obviously, this places limits on the opportunity for individual intervention while an inmate is in the pretrial centre. However, as I noted previously, intervention is seen broadly so that treatment that begins in the facility can continue once release is obtained. More commonly, new referrals for intervention can be made once the person returns to the community. For example, the opportunities for drug treatment are limited during a two or three day stay in the pretrial centre, but if this form of treatment is appropriate, referral can be made post-release. In many ways, this may be the most significant aspect of this project and may ultimately have substantial effects on recidivism. We know from our previous research in the Vancouver facility that the majority of pretrial inmates are likely to return to the facility at some point in the future. It is hoped that a project like this one might have some impact on this cycle of incarceration.

One problem in developing an integrated community based treatment program is the manner in which treatment and other services are divided among many different agencies. Often, there are disagreements between agencies over which one is responsible for providing treatment. For example, many mentally disordered offenders have two or more Axis I disorders, usually substance abuse along with some other diagnosis. Recall that in our Vancouver pretrial study, for example, over 85% had substance abuse disorders, and many of them also had substantial mental health problems. The community mental health system may refuse to treat such individuals, arguing they fall instead under the jurisdiction of the alcohol/drug programs. Alcohol/drug programs might respond in turn that these dual diagnosis cases are not appropriate for treatment by them because they also have a mental disorder and that mental disorder must be treated before treatment for the addiction could take place. In short, there is no coordinated treatment effort or attempt to focus on the individual who may have a range of problems and may require interventions from a variety of perspectives.

There are reasons for this situation that need to be understood if one is interested in changing the service delivery system. Perhaps the primary reason is that any given agency or program has fairly limited resources and often can't meet the demand for their services. Attempts to restrict access or refer to other agencies is a natural and understandable consequence of inadequate budgets and limited resources. As I mentioned earlier, more resources are needed at the community level. But increased budgets provide only a partial solution to the problem. Just as important is the need to develop an integrated service delivery system in which the individual and not the type of problem is seen as the primary focus.

Historically, jails have not been viewed as part of the community. The mental health and justice systems are quite different systems on an administrative level as well as the type of population they serve. For jails, mental health issues are not a priority since the majority of inmates are not in need of mental health services. Security is, of course, an overriding concern of the jail and at times, the security needs, such as isolating a paranoid individual in order to protect staff or other inmates, will take precedence over treatment needs. From the mental health system's perspective, those charged with crimes are seen as the responsibility of the criminal justice system and mental health staff would prefer not to deal with them, especially if they are considered violent or dangerous. Increasing interaction and communication between the two systems may be difficult to achieve. If it is to be achieved, it will be necessary to define more clearly the nature of the interaction and the expectations each system has of the other. Indeed, success is not likely as long as the two systems are viewed as separate, independent systems. For real change to occur, it will be necessary for the focus to shift from the isolated perspective of each system to one that emphasizes the needs of the individuals, regardless of where they happen to be residing at any particular point in time. As Keilitz and I (1992) commented, "the contacts and alliances between the two systems will need to become more clearly defined" (p. 12) in order for this broader perspective to become a reality.

In a previous article, Ogloff and I (1992) highlighted some recent work of Henry Steadman, who provides a framework to facilitate changes in the delivery of mental health and other community services to persons in the jails. Steadman (1992) discussed the notion of boundary spanners. Based on his review of a large number of jail mental health programs, he and his colleagues (Steadman et al., 1989) noticed that the more effective programs usually had a core position that was responsible for managing the interactions of mental health, jail, and judicial personnel. In effect, these individuals were able to cross over the boundaries of the separate systems and ensure that the needed services were being provided. As Steadman (1992) commented, "At each organizational boundary there is a person whose role it is both to interact with the other people inside their own organization and to negotiate system interchanges with another organization" (p. 77). In some jails, this might be a social worker position, in others a nurse or some other professional, and they may be employed by corrections, mental health, or jointly funded, so the professional affiliation or the source of funding are probably not the critical variables accounting for the success. More likely, as Steadman noted, it may be essential that one individual has the responsibility of ensuring that the two systems interact effectively and efficiently, and are able to respond to problems that would interfere with effectiveness or efficiency. In the Surrey project, the boundary spanner is currently a community social worker employed by the local mental health centre. This individual meets with inmates in the jail and arranges for follow-up services after release. There is little question that this is a key component of the Surrey project, as we have discussed elsewhere (Ogloff & Roesch, 1992; Ogloff, Tien, Roesch, & Eaves, 1991).

Training of correctional personnel

Our research has also revealed the need for training correctional officers to deal with mentally disordered offenders. Most guards receive little or no training in mental health, yet find themselves in situations where such training is essential. The guards themselves acknowledge this. In one research project (Kropp, Cox, Roesch, & Eaves, 1989), we looked at the perceptions of guards toward mentally disordered offenders and also asked them about their views about training. In general, mentally disordered inmates, compared to the rest of the inmate population, are perceived less favorably by guards, a finding that is consistent with the literature reporting negative police and public perceptions of mentally ill offenders (Steadman & Cocozza, 1978; Teplin, 1984). One particularly interesting finding was that mentally ill patients in a mental hospital were perceived more favorably than both the prisoners and mentally disordered prisoners. This may be due to the perceived presence of "badness" and "madness" in the target groups. Mentally disordered prisoners are perceived the least favorably perhaps because they combine mental illness and criminality and are consequently seen as less predictable and potentially more violent. That the correctional officers want to know more about mentally ill offenders was certainly borne out by their responses to the statements concerning working with such offenders.

Clearly, the job training they get does not prepare correctional officers to work with mentally disordered offenders, as 86% of them acknowledged Nine of every ten officers agreed or strongly agreed with a statement indicating that working with mentally disordered offenders is perceived to add stress to the job, and nearly all the officers (89%) said they would prefer that they were dealt with in other facilities. However, perhaps acknowledging the reality that they will be working with these individuals, we found that 95% of those surveyed would like at least some additional training in this area, which indicates substantial motivation on the officers' behalf. It is perhaps important to note that the officers reported feeling very prepared and efficacious when dealing with inmates in general; the only training viewed necessary was with respect to mentally disordered inmates. This small study points to the need for developing explicit training programs dealing with mental health issues.

In the Surrey project, we are now training correctional officers to take over the functions of the screening interviewers. We are looking at this empirically, in order to evaluate the quality and effectiveness of screening interviews conducted by officers as compared to clinically trained interviewers. Briefly, we are comparing the results of screening interviews, using structured interview techniques, conducted by officers with those of senior clinical psychology doctoral students. If we demonstrate that officers can conduct the screening interviews, it will make adoption in other jail facilities more likely since these personnel would be more readily available than would graduate students or other clinically trained individuals who are paid separately for their services.

Concluding Comments

Our involvement in the two projects described in this chapter reinforced our view that there is a need for more systematic delivery of mental health services in jails, as well as the need to integrate jail and community services. It is important to keep in mind, however, that a mental health focus is too narrow a perspective if one is interested in having an impact on the lives of individuals who find themselves enmeshed in the criminal justice system. The demographic data from our Vancouver study point to the need for many types of interventions, including those focusing on job training, employment, and educational upgrading. In the Surrey project, we hope to develop a program that provides a broad range of post-release interventions that might combine to break the revolving door pattern of recidivism we found in our research.

References

Abram, K. M., & Teplin, L. A. (1991). Co-occurring disorders among mentally ill jail detainees: Implications for public policy. *American Psychologist*, 46, 1036-1045.

American Psychiatric Association. (1987). *Diagnostic and statistical manual of mental disorders (3rd ed.)*. Washington, DC: Authors.

Bachrach, L. (1980). Is the least restrictive environment always the best? Sociological and semantic implications. *Hospital and Community Psychiatry*, *31*, 97-103.

Barnes, G. E., & Toews, J. (1983). Deinstitutionalization of chronic mental patients in the Canadian context. *Canadian Psychology*, *24*, 22-36.

Bennett, D., & Morris, I. (1983). Deinstitutionalization in the United Kingdom. *International Journal of Mental Health*, *11*, 5-23.

Brown, P. (1980). Social implications of deinstitutionalization. *Journal of Community Psychology*, *8*, 314-322.

Goldman, H. H., Adams, N. A., & Taube, C. A. (1983). Deinstitutionalization: The data demythologized. *Hospital and Community Psychiatry*, *34*, 129-134.

Hart, S. D., Roesch, R., Corrado, R. R., & Cox, D. N. (1993). The Referral Decision Scale: A validation study. *Law and Human Behavior*, *17*, 611-623.

Hart, S. D., & Hemphill, J. F. (1989). Prevalence of and service utilization by mentally disordered offenders at the Vancouver Pretrial Services Centre: A survey. Report submitted to the British Columbia Corrections Service in fulfillment of contract COR-22153.

Keilitz, I., & Roesch, R. (1992). Improving justice and mental health systems interactions: In search of a new paradigm. *Law and Human Behavior*, *16*, 5-26.

Kiesler, C. A. (1980). Mental hospitals and alternative care: Noninstitutionalization as potential public policy for mental patients. *American Psychologist*, *35*, 349-360.

Kropp, P. R., Cox, D., Roesch, R., & Eaves, D. (1989). The perceptions of correctional officers toward mentally disordered offenders. *International Journal of Law & Psychiatry*, *12*, 181-188.

Luckey, J. W., & Berman, J. J. (1979). Effects of a new commitment law on involuntary admissions and service utilization patterns. *Law and Human Behavior*, *3*, 149-161.

Morgan, C. (1981). Developing mental health services for local jails. *Criminal Justice and Behavior*, *8*. 259-273.

Morrissey, J. P., Steadman, H. J., Kilburn, H., & Lindsay, M. L. (1984). The effectiveness of jail mental health programs: An interorganizational assessment. *Criminal Justice and Behavior*, *11*, 235-256.

Mosher, L. R. (1983). Radical deinstitutionalization: The Italian experience. *International Journal of Mental Health*, *11*, 129-136.

Ogloff, J. R. P., & Roesch, R. (1992). Using community mental health centers to provide comprehensive mental health services to local jails. In J. R. P. Ogloff (Ed.), *Law and psychology: Broadening of the discipline* (pp. 241-260). Durham, NC: Carolina Academic Press.

Ogloff, J. R. P., Tien, G., Roesch, R., & Eaves, D. (1991). A model for the provision of jail mental health services: An integrative, community based approach. *Journal of Mental Health Administration*, *18*, 209-222.

Overall, J. E., & Gorham, D. R. (1962). The Brief Psychiatric Rating Scale. *Psychological Reports*, *10*, 799-812.

Rabkin, J. G. (1979). Criminal behavior of discharged mental patients: A critical appraisal of the research. *Psychological Bulletin*, *86*, 1-28.

Robins, L. N., Helzer, J. E., Croughan, J., & Radcliff, K. (1981). National Institute of Mental Health Diagnostic Interview Schedule: Its history, characteristics and validity. *Archives of General Psychiatry*, *42*, 918-924.

Roesch, R., & Golding, S. L. (1985). The impact of deinstitutionalization. In D. P. Farrington & J. Gunn (Eds.), *Current research in forensic psychiatry and psychology: Aggression and dangerousness* (pp. 209-239). NY: Wiley.

Scull, A. (1981). Deinstitutionalization and the rights of the deviant. *Journal of Social Issues*, *37*, 6-20.

Sosowsky, L. (1980). Explaining the increased arrest rate among mental patients: A continuing debate. *American Journal of Psychiatry, 137*, 1602-1605.

Steadman, H. J. (1992). Boundary spanners: A key component for the effective interactions of the justice and mental health systems. *Law and Human Behavior, 16*, 75-87.

Steadman, H. J., & Cocozzo, J. J. (1978). Public perceptions of the criminally insane. *Hospital and Community Psychiatry, 29*, 457-459.

Steadman, H. J., McCarty, D. W., & Morrissey, J. P. (1989). *The mentally ill in jail: Planning for essential services*. New York: Guilford.

Teplin, L. (1984). Criminalizing mental disorder: The comparative arrest rate of the mentally ill. *American Psychologist, 39*, 794-803.

Teplin, L. (1991). The criminalization hypothesis: Myth, misnomer, or management strategy. In S. A. Shah & B. D. Sales (Eds.), *Law and mental health: Major developments and research needs* (pp. 149-183). Rockville, MD: US Department of Health and Human Services.

Teplin, L., & Swartz, J. (1989). Screening for severe mental disorder in jails: The development of the Referral Decision Scale. *Law and Human Behavior, 13*, 1-18.

[1] I appreciate the comments of Stephen Hart and James Ogloff on an earlier draft of this chapter. Correspondence concerning the chapter should be sent to Professor Ronald Roesch, Department of Psychology, Simon Fraser University, Burnaby, B.C., Canada, V5A 1S6.

[2] These research projects have involved collaboration with a number of colleagues, including Raymond Corrado, David Cox, Derek Eaves, James Ogloff, George Tien, and Stephen Hart. Portions of this research were supported by a grant from the British Columbia Health Research Foundation (#112-89-2) and from the Social Sciences and Humanities Research Council.

[3] My co-researchers on this project are Jim Ogloff, Steve Hart, George Tien, and Lynda Bond.

[4] These principles are adapted from a larger set of principles prepared by the Working Group of the Surrey Pretrial Mental Health Services Project.

[5] The success of this project is in large measure due to the contributions of the intake interviewers: Patrick Bartel, Alice Bush, Barbara Chambers, Angela Connors, Shauna Darcangelo, Jordan Hanley, and Susan Turnbull.

Offender Categories in the Hungarian Prison System

Janos Boros

In an effort to formulate a practical classification system to help work out appropriate and effective treatment strategies for offenders in Hungarian prisons, a two-phase research project was conducted in the 1980s. In the first phase data collected from 564 recidivists were evaluated and processed, then in 1988, as the second phase of the project, a general sample of 240 inmates from different penal institutions in Hungary was examined on the basis of these findings.

A differentiated penal system facilitates effective treatment for larger groups of inmates, simplifies administration, and allows for a concentration of resources (Mannheim and Spencer, 1952). There is a growing number of studies dealing with the issue of differentiation. Whilst there are some differences in technical terms used, three major elements are generally considered necessary to the organization of a differentiated penal system: 1) classification and typology of inmates; 2) differentiation of penal institutions; and 3) appropriate treatment of inmates. The three fields are not represented in equal proportions in scientific research. It seems that although almost all the studies deal with the classification and the typology of inmates, only some of them deal with differentiated treatment. What is more, there are only a few studies which contain information useful for the practice of a treatment-oriented typological classification.

A practical classification system applicable to penal institutions has to meet a number of demands. Megargee (1977) suggests that any method should be practical, reliable, verifiable, dynamic, treatment-conscious and cost-effective. No classification so far has met all these requirements. Regarding criteria for classification, apart from general characteristics, such as age, sex, offence committed, state of health, and cognitive capacity, the relevant studies have used several different demographic, social and psychological categories, such as social status, family background, personality traits, attitudinal and behavioural patterns. A large number of typologies are heuristic, where categories were deductively created on a speculative basis and only after that was it decided whether there were any inmates fitting any of the previously defined categories. Most of these classification systems lack practical considerations. Another type of classification system is based on empirical data. However most of the empirical typologies tend to use different and incompatible sets of data and criteria, which makes it difficult to create a theoretical basis of these typologies. Furthermore, some quite promising classification systems were not applicable to Hungarian conditions, either because they were not cost-effective or they had no suggestion for the relevant type of treatment to be applied.

From among the typologies available, three methods seemed especially worth experimenting with as a preparation for our research. These were: 1) Warren's (1966) typology using seven categories on the basis of interpersonal maturity; 2) Quay's (1965) typology using reliable methods for juvenile offenders, which was later extended to be used with adult offenders; and 3) Megargee's (1977) ten-category system based on the Minnesota Multiphasic Personality Inventory (MMPI), whose method is efficient, cost-effective, easily distinguishable and offers suggestions for treatment. However, as early as the pre-test stage it was found that these typologies had limited scope for our conditions and resources. The adaptation of Warren's typology was problematic because the method was expensive, lengthy and complicated. Quay's typology, when applied to our recidivist sample, revealed that 20% of them were psychopaths, 10% neurotics, 5% psychotics, and 65% subcultural offenders. Because of the uneven proportions, the application of the method to Hungarian circumstances seemed to be unrealistic, as it provided no basis for a treatment-oriented differentiation among the groups. Lastly, the Megargee typology, though most promising in many respects, was originally developed for the classification of female juveniles, thus it offered questionable validity for adult offenders.

Therefore other solutions had to be found. The MMPI was kept because of its obvious advantages in being quick, inexpensive, and well-differentiated. Throughout the survey, 22 scales of the MMPI were used (see Dahlstrom, Welsh and Dahlstrom, 1972; 1975). The results obtained on the 22 scales from 564 recidivists were factor analyzed. After several rotations, three factors were found. These three factors were each divided into positive and negative values, giving six groups. The distribution of the sample across factor groupings, with the exception of the conformist group, was fairly evenly proportioned (neurotic 20%, self-possessed 28%, overcontrolled 12%, undercontrolled 24%, conformist 2%, nonconformist 14%) therefore this typological approach seemed to offer an applicable basis for the creation of a classification system. To make comparisons possible, the behaviour patterns and the level of adaptability of offenders within the six groups was thoroughly examined. In this part of the study, questionnaires and interviews were used, focusing on three major indicators as follows.

Deprivation (Sykes, 1958). Incarcerated offenders are deprived of freedom, comfort, heterosexual relations, decision-making, and personal security. Deprivation places serious psychological and mental stress on inmates, and it erodes their self-reliance (Boros, 1980).

Prison socialization (Boros, 1981). To relieve the detrimental effects of imprisonment, inmates tend to become oriented towards informal groups and subcultures. During the process of integration into these groups, inmates undergo a socialization process, which Clemmer (1940) termed "prisonization". The term "prison socialization" attempts to emphasize that this process is identical to any other socialization process, and it will influence the inmate's life in society after release.

Social status (Boros, 1986). The term relates to the informal status of the inmate within the prison subculture. This aspect seems to be important, since the status of an inmate within the subculture might define his opportunities, his competency in prison, and, on the whole, his chances of overcoming deprivational problems.

In a generalized and condensed form, the analysis of the data revealed the following characteristics of the six offender groups:

Group 1: neurotic The members of this group are strongly deprived, their prison socialization is poor, and they occupy the lowest social positions. Nevertheless they have a good relationship with the prison staff. They are not able to take part in the process of prison socialization and they are not able to live according to the informal rules existing in the inmate subculture, therefore they are reduced to the lowest status levels. Consequently they find deprivation a very heavy burden. Their ability to adapt to either informal or formal rules is rather poor. In many cases they tend to be informers, since they can see no other opportunities to improve their status, however, this attracts further disrespect from other inmates.

Group 2: self-possessed The members of this group do not feel deprived. They are fairly well prison socialized, and highly ranked in the prison subculture. They also have good relations with staff. Their adaptation to prison conditions is fairly good. In their value system they highly rank civilised behaviour, competency, solidarity, tolerance and a realistic view of life. With their intelligence, social skills and physical strength, they earn fairly good status positions in the prison subculture, therefore they do not feel as deprived as the others. Because of their realistic approach to life and the useful skills they possess, their good relations with staff does not evoke hostility or disrespect from other inmates.

Group 3: overcontrolled Members of this group are moderately deprived, and poorly prison socialized. They occupy medium status positions. Their relationship with staff is not good. Their adaptation to prison life is reasonable. Most of them have a long criminal record. Their educational and intellectual level is fairly low. They do not identify themselves with the norms of prison life but they do not violate them either. They are mostly self-restricted, and do not take part in the social life of the prison. Still, they are respected by other inmates due to their extensive experience in prison and their often bad relationship with staff. Being unassuming, they do not feel very deprived. Their value system is characterized by the preference of a consolidated way of life.

Group 4: undercontrolled They experience a medium level of deprivation. They are the most successfully socialized inmates in the prison, and their social status is high. Their relations with staff and adaptation to prison norms is bad: they often violate formal rules. According to their peers, they are the most aggressive inmates in the prison. Their value system is characterized by hedonism, competence and solidarity with their peers. They are governed by their emotions. Undercontrolled offenders constitute the youngest inmate group. Although their intellectual level is average, owing to their physical strength and skills they rise to high status levels in the prison. They seem to be the main advocates of the values and norms in the prison subculture; they are the ones who socialize their mates by retaliating for the breach of these norms. They are the cohesion force of the inmate subculture. Since their confrontation with staff is rather frequent, the level of their deprivation grows rapidly compared to the others.

Group 5: conformist Offenders belonging to this group are highly deprived, medium prison socialized, and they occupy low prison status. Their relations with staff are fairly good; they are not aggressive. Their value system is dominated by civilized behaviour, politeness, ego-restriction and, to some extent, an idyllic view of life. Their educational and intellectual level is low. They spend long periods in prison, where they have adapted to the basic prison norms. Being not too skilled or physically strong, and since they do not get involved in fights for positions, they have to put up with low status levels in the prison. To relieve this unfavourable situation they choose a conformist behaviour, maintaining a good relationship with the prison authority, they volunteer for activities such as maintenance, but they would never become snitches or informants. Due to this approach their peers tolerate their way of doing time.

Group 6: nonconformist In this group, deprivation is about average level, whereas prison socialization is high. Their relations with staff and their adaptation to prison rules is not good. They are aggressive and have many misconducts. Their value system is dominated by hedonism, competency and ego-restoring aspiration. They prefer autonomy to social attitude. Their educational and intellectual level is about average, they are older than the members of the undercontrolled group, and they have more prison experience. They bear some resemblance to members of the undercontrolled group inasmuch as they are reasonably socialized and their informal position is good. However, they are not good group members; they prefer autonomy; they are the lone wolves of the prison subculture. They have frequent conflicts with the prison authorities. They fight for their rights, even if it is a fight without any hope.

As has been mentioned, in the second phase of the project an attempt was made to check whether the attributes of the specific offender groups were basically similar or significantly different. In this phase, a representative sample of 240 inmates was studied in a way identical to the sample of recidivists, using MMPI, prison questionnaires, interviews, value screening, and social and criminal background surveys. The analysis produced an evenly proportioned breakdown of factor groupings. The offenders within the identifiable groups of the general sample showed characteristics similar to those of the recidivist sample, thus for practical considerations it seemed appropriate to use the same six categories for defining treatment strategies and in further research. Similarities notwithstanding, a comparative analysis of the two samples revealed some interesting changes in patterns.

Among the recidivists, members of the undercontrolled group tend to observe subculture norms, they are the ones who socialize new members. In the sample of the general prison population the undercontrolled group seems to lack this function. Members of the recidivist overcontrolled group are poorly socialized, whereas overcontrolled offenders from the general sample have a tendency to belong to a group, though they cannot play the role of the socializing agent due to their low status positions and the lack of their ego strength. Members of the recidivist nonconformist group stick to their autonomy. Nonconformist offenders of the general sample do not dissolve into the group but do not need autonomy either.

Despite these differences, the analysis of the two samples indicated that in both cases the same personality traits can be explored. In practical terms, inmates from the general prison population with personality traits similar to those of recidivists can be expected to demonstrate similarities in behaviour patterns too. These findings encourage us to state that even if one or several of the categories are over-represented in the samples, the outlined typology can be applied to classify and describe the inmate population an any of the Hungarian prisons.

The aim of the described research project was to develop a classification system suitable for our purposes. Apart from this the surveys revealed many useful societal and behavioural characteristics and patterns (see Boros, 1991). The next phase of the project will be to test this classification system on an independent sample. After that inmate groups will be set up and treatment programmes will be developed for them. After a period of six months control research will be conducted to measure the validity of the hypothesis.

References

Boros, J. (1980). *Aggressivity in prison institutions*. Budapest: Ministry of Justice.

Boros, J. (1981). *Factors in prison affecting recidivism*. Budapest: Ministry of Justice.

Boros, J. (1986). *Differentiation in prison institutions*. Budapest: Ministry of Justice.

Boros, J. (1991). *Studies in deviant behaviour in Hungary*. Budapest: Research Review.

Clemmer, D. (1940). *The prison community*. Boston: The Christopher Publishing House.

Dahlstrom, G. W., Welsh, G. S., & Dahlstrom, L. E. (1972). *An MMPI handbook: Vol. 1*. Minneapolis: University of Minnesota.

Dahlstrom, G. W., Welsh, G. S., & Dahlstrom, L. E. (1975). *An MMPI handbook: Vol. 2*. Minneapolis: University of Minnesota.

Mannheim, H., & Spencer, J. (1952). *Problems of classification in the English penal and reformatory system*. London: Institute for Scientific Treatment and Delinquency.

Megargee, E. (1977). A new classification system for criminal offenders I. The need for a new classification system. *Criminal Justice and Behaviour*, *4*, 107-114.

Quay, H. C. (1965). Personality and delinquency. In H. C. Quay (Ed.), *Juvenile delinquency*. New York: Litton.

Sykes, G. (1958). *The society of captives*. Princeton: Princeton University Press.

Warren, M. Q. (1966). *Interpersonal maturity level classification: Juvenile diagnosis and treatment of low, middle and high maturity delinquents*. Sacramento: California Youth Authority, Community Treatment Project.

What Recent Meta-Evaluations Tell us About the Effectiveness of Correctional Treatment

Friedrich Lösel

Introduction

The development of correctional treatment and rehabilitation recalls the voyage of a sailing ship. In the 1960s and early 1970s, the treatment concept had a strong tailwind and was driven forward powerfully. At times, there were also squally crosswinds from various directions. For some, treatment of criminals was, for example, too cost-intensive, insufficiently oriented toward punishment, or too insecure. Others feared, for example, insufficient legal control, an overemphasis on informal decision-making, or forced modification of personalities. With the increase in treatment evaluation research, headwinds were blowing into the sails of the ship of rehabilitation. Discussions on crime policy were dominated by the conception that there were hardly any substantial effects (Martinson, 1984: "nothing works") or that, at least, methodologically sound statements were impossible (see, e.g., Bailey, 1966; Lipton, Martinson, & Wilks, 1975; Logan, 1972; Sechrest, White, & Brown, 1979). There were also more optimistic evaluations of parts of the findings (e.g., Blackburn, 1980; Gendreau & Ross, 1979; Palmer, 1975; Quay, 1977), however, the treatment ship was more and more becalmed. Although in most Western countries the idea of treatment and rehabilitation had not been abandoned in practice, the former flagship of modern crime policy nonetheless was bobbing up and down, as it were, far away in calm waters (see Egg, 1984; Kaiser, Dünkel, & Ortmann, 1982; Lösel, Köferl, & Weber, 1987).

However, in recent years a fresh breeze has arisen. There is an international revival in the discussion on offender treatment (e.g., Andrews, Zinger, Hoge, Bonta, Gendreau, & Cullen, 1990; Gendreau & Andrews, 1990; Gendreau & Ross, 1987; Killias, 1992; Lipsey, 1988, 1992a, b; Lösel et al., 1987; McGuire & Priestley, 1992; Rowson & McGuire, 1992; Lösel, 1992; Thornton, 1987). Some of the reasons for this are:

1. More research is available on psychological factors that play a particularly important role in the onset and continuation of criminality (e.g., thought patterns and attitudes, deficits in social skills or in self-control).
2. It emerges that basic principles of psychological and educational intervention are similar for early intervention in at-risk groups or individual-related primary prevention as well as for the treatment of persistent offenders.
3. Greater experience makes it possible to design programs more precisely, to implement them better, and to carry them out with greater intensity and integrity.
4. Many evaluations are performed more adequately and in a more differentiated manner, for example, with regard to target groups, social contexts, or outcome criteria.

5. Recent meta-analyses have integrated research more systematically and in a more differentiated manner and also pay more attention to effect sizes (instead of statistical significance alone).

In the following, I shall concentrate particularly on the last point, which has been addressed by a series of studies published in recent years (see Andrews et al., 1990; Garrett, 1985; Gensheimer, Mayer, Gottschalk, & Davidson II, 1986; Gottschalk, Davidson II, Gensheimer, & Mayer, 1987; Izzo & Ross, 1990; Lipsey, 1988, 1992a, b; Lösel et al., 1987; Lösel & Köferl, 1989; Whitehead & Lab, 1989).

Meta-analysis is a methodology that integrates the state of scientific knowledge on an issue in the most comprehensive, systematic, unbiased, and differentiated way by using statistical procedures (see, e.g., Cooper, 1989; Fricke & Treinies, 1985; Glass, McGaw, & Smith, 1981; Hedges & Olkin, 1985; Rosenthal, 1991). As a rule, it consists of the following steps: (a) precisely delineating the issue under study; (b) systematically selecting primary studies; (c) coding studies according to content categories (like treatment type, sample characteristics, effect criteria); (d) assessing the methodological quality of studies; (e) computing standardized measures of effect size; and (f) analyzing relationships between content or methodological characteristics of studies and effect sizes (moderator analysis).

In the present paper, I will first briefly present an update of our own meta-analysis on the evaluation of sociotherapeutic prisons in Germany. Second, these results are compared with broader Anglo-American meta-analyses of offender treatment. Third, the question of differential effects is addressed by asking, for example, what works relatively best. Finally, problems and perspectives of offender treatment and its evaluation are outlined.

Meta-Evaluation of Social Therapy in Germany

Several years ago, we published a detailed, qualitative and quantitative review of research on the treatment of adult criminals in several European countries, the USA, and, in particular, of sociotherapeutic prisons in the Federal Republic of Germany (Lösel et al., 1987; Lösel & Köferl, 1989). Our study included a statistical meta-analysis of treatment outcome studies on sociotherapeutic prisons. There are more or less similar institutions in other West European countries (see, Lösel et al., 1987) and even in Scandinavia, after formally abandoning offender treatment, "normal" prisons are comparable with respect to psychosocial interventions (e.g., Bondeson, 1989; Christie, 1981). Using our German meta-analysis as an example, we have to bear in mind that other European countries have a different legal framework, dissimilar concepts of pathology, or less evaluation studies. A meta-analysis with a broader European scope has been started recently but will take several more years of research (Redondo, Lugus, Garrido, & Anguera, 1992).

German sociotherapeutic prisons are intended for adult criminals who are mostly categorized as recidivists with a serious crime record and personality disorders. There is no unified or clear theoretically based treatment concept. A common feature of the interventions is that they are applied not only on the individual level but also include group processes and organizational and institutional factors in the sense of social therapy. Mostly, treatment concepts cannot be assigned to one approach alone; increasingly, psychotherapy in a narrower sense is giving way to models of social training. Work and other contacts outside prison, intensive day pass and vacation opportunities, as well as purposeful preparation for release are some of the major design features. Not only do social-therapeutic prisons generally have a more favorable personnel ratio than regular prisons, they also have more psychosocial service personnel. Compared to normal prisons, these are more occupied with tasks of counseling, treatment, and organizational development and less with security and discipline (Lösel & Bliesener, 1989). Insofar, from the perspective of process evaluation, more or less clear differences can be assumed between social therapy and other forms of incarceration.

At the time of our meta-analysis, 16 relatively controlled outcome evaluation studies were available. The majority had a quasi-experimental design with partially nonequivalent control groups from normal prisons. Some of the studies contained several analyses within the same institutions so that samples overlapped. We used the criteria given by Cook and Campbell (1979) to perform detailed assessments of the methodological quality of the studies. Statistical and internal validity were better than construct validity, external validity, and our additionally introduced category of descriptive validity. This means that there were not only problems of nonexperimental research designs but even more deficits with respect to the theoretical basis of the measures and outcome criteria, the generalizability to other contexts, and the clarity of the description of the studies. A good one-half of the studies applied various criteria of recidivism with probation intervals of between three and six years. The others examined treatment outcome effects in terms of personality traits, attitudes, or other dispositional constructs that were mostly assessed with questionnaries at the end of treatment.

As a standardized measure of effect, we used the correlation coefficient r_m from Friedman (1968) in the computation from primary statistics. In the case of low or medium effect sizes, this is approximately half the magnitude of the d coefficient that is frequently used in treatment evaluations with quantitative outcome criteria (see Cohen, 1988). For each study, we computed a mean effect size from all available criteria. That is, when results were available on various criteria of recidivism, for several personality variables, or for different sample groupings (e.g., dropouts included or excluded in the treatment group), these were aggregated and a mean effect size was computed. We used various statistical integration models that permitted either more conservative or more optimistic estimations of the mean treatment effect.

Mean effects of individual studies varied between .02 and .25. Nonetheless, they were rather homogeneous, also as far as the various types of outcome criteria were concerned. The most adequate estimation of treatment outcome produced an effect size of .11 with a 95% confidence interval of .07 to .15. That is, approximately 11% fewer of the released offenders from social therapy were recidivist (or exhibited less negative personality traits) compared to those from normal prisons. In most studies treatment dropouts showed the worst outcomes. When personality traits were used as effect criteria, results were less homogeneous across the various models, which is one indication that the risk of "fishing for significance" in a great number of criterion variables is particularly strong in these data.

Effect sizes did not correlate with the internal validity of the design. However, they were related to violations of construct validity. Studies with high construct validity, that is, those with theoretically and methodologically more sound tests of treatment and effect, more adequate outcome criteria, higher generalizability, and so forth exhibited somewhat lower effects.

Content characteristics of studies revealed hardly any relationships to effect sizes. However, the moderator analysis could have only an explorative character as the number of available studies was too low for sound differential analyses. This applied particularly for features of the treatment itself, which were mostly heterogeneous and could not be grouped together clearly.

Since 1987, two new treatment outcome evaluations of social therapy have been published. These studies are of particular interest as they present extensions of earlier evaluations in which the legal probation intervals are now very long (Egg, 1990; Dünkel & Geng, 1991). Some of their findings are presented in Table 1.

Table 1: Recidivism (%) in Two Evaluations of Sociotherapeutic Prisons (STP) Published Since the Meta-Analysis of Lösel et al. (1987)

	Normal STP	**Prison**	**Dropouts**	**STP + Dropouts**
Egg (1990, Erlangen)[a]				
Sample size	28	73	22	50
All kinds of recidivism (Federal Central Register)	78.6	75.3	90.9	84.0
Severe recidivism (Prison sentence)	46.4	49.3	77.3	60.0
Dünkel & Geng (1991, Berlin)[b]				
Sample size	160	323	27	187
All kinds of recidivism (Federal Central Register)	79.4	87.6	100.0	82.4
Severe recidivism (Prison sentence)	46.9	59.8	63.0	49.2

[a] Follow-up period: 8 years
[b] Follow-up period: 10 years

Whereas Egg found no mentionable differences between sociotherapeutic prisons and controls, treatment receives a far better evaluation in Dünkel and Geng. However, this is also due to the less favorable legal probation in the control group from Berlin. As already seen in our meta-analysis, both studies once more clearly show that the highest recidivism rates are found among prisoners who have been retransferred to normal prisons. Nonetheless, in the Berlin study, recidivism itself is substantially lower than in the control group when dropouts are computed to the detriment of positive treatment outcome (put together with the treatment group). The fact that dropouts were less frequent at Berlin than at Erlangen had a positive effect here.

Further results have shown that treated criminals in the Erlangen study also had better outcomes than controls in the first years following release. Recidivism rates become similar after four years, which can also be viewed as a problem of aftercare and not only as a failure of sociotherapeutic prisons. After discussions with justice officials, I suspect that the different outcomes in the two studies are not only caused by differences in the samples and control conditions but are partially determined by the former "island position" of Berlin: There, treated prisoners could easily maintain close contacts with the personnel after release. This kind of informal aftercare and crisis intervention is harder to achieve in a rural state like Bavaria.

Integrating the results in various recidivism criteria, we computed a mean effect of .16 from Dünkel and Geng's study and a slightly negative effect of -.04 from Egg's study. Table 2 shows an update of the effect sizes from our meta-analysis in which the new studies are included. For the integration we used different procedures: Mean effect size of each study weighted by (a) total sample size, (b) size of treated group, (c) mean of variances (Hedges, 1982), and (d) sample size corrected for dependencies (sample overlap between different studies). All results were very similar to those presented in Table 2.

Table 2: Update of the Meta-Analysis on Sociotherapeutic Prisons From Lösel et al. (1987); Recent Studies Integrated and N-Adjusted

Study/Analysis	Crit.	Design	N	ES (r_m)
Rasch & Kühl (1978)	R	E	30	.16
Rehn (1979) Cohort Analysis	R	Q	33	.09
Rehn (1979) MLH, Control Group	R	Q	90	.19
Rehn (1979) SAB, Control Group	R	Q	49	.14
Dünkel (1980) Social Therapy	R	Q	148	.14
Dünkel (1980) Education	R	Q	64	.10
Dünkel (1980) Social Training	R	Q	184	.14
Dolde (1982)	R	Q	145	.08
Rehn & Jürgensen (1983)	R	Q	106	.12
Egg (1990)	R	Q	50	-.04
Dünkel & Geng (1991)	R	Q	187	.16
Rasch & Kühl (1978)	P	E	30	.13
Egg (1979)	P	Q	52	.11
Opp (1979)	P	C	97	.09
Waxweiler (1980) Social Therapy	P	Q	20	.18
Waxweiler (1980) Education	P	Q	20	.25
Waxweiler (1980) Social Training	P	Q	20	.09
Ortmann (1987)	P	Q	207	.04
M_R (N-adjusted; depend. incl.)				.12
M_P (N-adjusted; depend. incl.)				.09
$M_{Tot.}$ (N-adjusted; depend. incl.)				.11
95% Confidence interval for mean				.08-.16
Homogeneity testing (Crit. value $\chi^2 = 26.30$)				H=11.26 df=16

R: Recidivism criterion; P: Personality disposition criterion; E: Experimental design (random assignment); Q: Quasi-experimental design with nonequivalent control groups; C: Correlational design; N: Size of treated sample; dependencies included; ES: Effect sizes (correlation coefficients r_m)

Taking sample sizes into account, the revised mean is .11 and the 95% percent confidence interval is .08 to .16. The test of heterogeneity is not significant. Therefore, a search for moderator variables would be not adequate. As a rule of thumb, we would expect about 10% less recidivism in the clientele of sociotherapeutic prisons as compared to normal prisons.

Comparison with Other Meta-Analyses

Our German meta-analysis is small, and it is the only one for adult offender treatment in prisons. However, our main effects are rather similar to the mean effect sizes in recent North American meta-analyses. This is shown in Table 3. The Table contains the mean effect sizes from each meta-analysis. If the original meta-analysis has used a correlation coefficient as effect indicator (*phi*, r_m), we included the respective measure. If a meta-analysis has used the *d* coefficient, we transformed into *d*/2. As we are not able to make transformations on the primary study level and are not dealing with high coefficients, this simple way of comparison seems to be sufficient.

Table 3: Mean Effect Sizes (ES) in Various Meta-Analyses on the Treatment of Crime and Delinquency; rm or Phi Coefficients (Partially Computed From d and More Detailed Data in the Respective Meta-Analyses)

Meta-Analysis	N (Studies)*	ES(r)
Garrett (1985) Treatment of juvenile delinquents in residential settings	121*	.18
Gensheimer, Mayer, Gottschalk, & Davidson II (1986) Diversion programs for juvenile delinquents	51*	.10
Gottschalk, Davidson II, Gensheimer, & Mayer (1987) Community-oriented programs for juvenile delinquents	91*	.11
Lösel, Köferl, & Weber (1987; update) Sociotherapeutic prisons for adult offenders	18*	.11
Whitehead & Lab (1989) Treatment of juvenile offenders	50	.13
Andrews, Zinger, Hoge, Bonta, Gendreau, & Cullen(1990) Treatment of juvenile and adult offenders	154*	.10
Lipsey (1992) Treatment of juvenile offenders	397	.05-08

* Study N is the number of different comparisons. In the indexed analyses this is higher than the number of separate studies (publications).

The following points should be taken into account when comparing results: (a) Programs, target groups, effect criteria, and treatment contexts are very heterogeneous. (b) The majority of programs evaluated in the USA addressed juvenile delinquency. (c) Sometimes studies are included that deal with childhood behavior problems in the sense of prevention in risk groups (and not correctional treatment). (d) Many studies are only briefly described in journal articles and treatment is sketched in a few words. (e) Program concept and actual implementation can vary greatly. (f)

Often the follow-up periods are rather short. (g) Each meta-analysis reveals specific integration techniques and methodological differences. (h) The underlying primary studies in various meta-analyses were, to some extent, identical. (i) The effect sizes from different meta-analyses are not fully comparable as different coefficients are used (for example: the magnitude of *phi* depends on the marginal proportions).

Nonetheless, the major finding in Table 3 is a relatively consistent main effect that averages around .10. Assuming an average recidivism rate of 50% in the untreated control groups, the mean recidivism rate in the treated groups would be 40%.

Perhaps, a "publication bias" cannot be ruled out, that is, positive findings are possibly overrepresented in published studies. However, the comprehensive study carried out by Lipsey (1992 a, b) for the Russel Sage Foundation also contains unpublished studies. The treated group performed better in 285 (64.3%) of all studies. In 131 studies (29.6%), the effect was closer to controls; and in 27 (6.1%) there was no difference. This is a highly significant difference in favor of treatment.

Many may consider that an effect size of .10 is too low. Whitehead and Lab (1989), for example, who did not report the effect of .13 that we computed from their data in their own analysis, interpret their findings more as a confirmation that nothing works. Certainly, meta-analyses in other fields of psychotherapy, behavior modification, or social competence training report mean effect sizes that are two to four times as high. This applies for psychological disorders in both adults (e.g., Shapiro & Shapiro, 1983; Smith, Glass, & Miller, 1980; Wittmann & Matt, 1986) and children and adolescents (e.g., Beelmann, Pfingsten, & Lösel, 1994; Casey & Berman, 1985; Weisz, Weiss, Alicke, & Glotz, 1987). The differences compared to meta-analyses on the treatment of delinquency confirm the practical experience that it is particularly difficult to intervene in antisocial disorders (Kazdin, 1987). However, it also has to be considered that meta-analyses in other fields frequently are based on "softer" outcome criteria, shorter follow-up intervals, less disturbed clients, or so-called analog groups, and that treatment motivation, the milieu, and the treatment setting are at times more favorable.

The relatively consistent mean effect size of .10 for the treatment of delinquency not only contradicts the popular slogan that nothing works but also should not be underestimated quantitatively. People often have unrealistic ideas about the effect sizes that can be anticipated from social interventions. For example, even just the dichotomization of variables (treatment vs. control group; recidivist vs. nonrecidivist) and the deficits in the reliability of treatment and criteria lead to severe losses of statistical power (see Cohen, 1988; Lösel & Wittmann, 1989). As Rosenthal and Rubin (1982) have illustrated with their Binomial Effect Size Display, an effect size of .10 may be of high practical significance (e.g., when in medicine the recovery rate rises from 50% in the untreated group to 60% in the treated group). Even with such a seemingly small effect, treating offenders can be profitable from the perspective of cost-benefit analysis (see, e.g., Dünkel, 1987; Greenwood & Turner, 1985; Lösel & Köferl, 1989; Prentky & Burgess, 1992).

Differential Effects

Confirmation of a consistent main effect is only one of the outcomes of meta-analyses. Even more important are differential effects. More far-reaching conclusions on these effects can be drawn from the North American analyses with numerous primary studies than from our own work. However, it is necessary to be cautious when making generalizations because of a variety of problems. For example, classification of specific forms of treatment, settings, client groups, and so forth is sometimes questionable. Differential effects are often based on only a few studies. They are only partially derived from theories and generally harder to reproduce than main effects. Bearing such reservations in mind, I will mention only some differential effects from the two biggest meta-analyses:

Lipsey (1992a, b) has shown that some of the differences in effect sizes are due to methodological features of studies. For example, there are lower effect sizes in studies with larger samples, larger dropout rates, longer follow-up intervals, or many and less reliable/valid outcome measures. None of these influences explain more than 5% of the variance in effect sizes.

In contrast, with 11% explained variance, the type of treatment is the most important condition for different effect sizes. Treatments that were delivered by the researcher, or in which the researcher had a considerable influence, show larger effect sizes (an artificial or true effect of "involvement"?). Programs in public facilities, custodial institutions, and the juvenile justice system are associated with smaller effect sizes. Both in measures within as well as outside the juvenile justice system, more strongly structured, cognitive and behaviorally oriented, multimodal treatments directed toward concrete skills are more successful than, for example, nondirective counseling, client-centered groups, or less-structured casework. The mean effect sizes of different treatment modalities vary beween .18 and -.12 (signs reversed here). For the 112 studies that applied multimodal (41), behavioral (39), or skill oriented (32) treatments a mean effect size of .11 can be computed. This is substantially higher than the overall effect size (see Table 3).

The differential findings from the meta-analysis of Andrews et al. (1990) point in the same direction: These authors formulate theoretically based criteria for "appropriate treatment" that draw on three principles:

1. The *risk principle* concerns the selection of an appropriate level of service: High-risk clients require the intensive measures of high-level services; when risk is lower, one should not "take a sledgehammer to crack a nut." Because of so-called spontaneous remission in controls at the low-risk level, large effects are also less probable for methodological reasons.

2. The *need principle* refers to constructs that the present state of empirical knowledge views as crime-related factors. These include, for example, changing antisocial attitudes and peer contacts, encouraging family relationships, and supervision by parents, identification with prosocial models, strengthening self-control, improving social skills, reducing drug addiction, and improving cost-utility ratios for prosocial behavior in the family, education, and work. In contrast, general concepts such as modifying self-images, reducing anxieties, strengthening peer contacts (which might be antisocial), or reducing nonspecific personality problems seem to be less promising.

3. The *responsivity principle* involves general principles of successful intervention in delinquency, such as anticriminal modeling, teaching concrete skills,

and use of authority. These include measures such as role playing, graded practice, reinforcement, prompting, making resources available, verbal guidance, and cognitive restructuring. In contrast, the outcomes of unstructured group activities among delinquents, sharp shock treatments, permissive milieu therapy, and unstructured psychodynamic or nondirective approaches seem to be less encouraging.

Table 4 presents some differential data on appropriate treatment from the meta-analysis of Andrews et al. (1990).

Table 4: The Effect of Type of Treatment on Recidivism at Different Moderator Levels; Mean Phi Coefficients (Number of Studies); From Andrews et al. (1990)

	Appropriate Correctional Service	Inappropriate Correctional Service
Justice System		
Juvenile	.29 (45)	-.07 (31)
Adult	.34 (9)	-.03 (7)
Year of Publication		
Before the 1980s	.24 (33)	-.09 (22)
1980s	.40 (21)	-.03 (16)
Quality of Research Design		
Weaker	.32 (26)	-.04 (10)
Stronger	.29 (28)	-.08 (22)
Setting		
Community	.35 (37)	-.14 (31)
Institution/Residential	.20 (17)	-.15 (7)

Treatment measures that prove to be appropriate according to these three principles are clearly more successful than those that are classified as being inappropriate. The latter even show negative effects, and this explains the generally lower total effect sizes in Table 3. Recent studies perform somewhat better than older ones. The quality of the research design and the juvenile versus adult justice system do not moderate the results. The superiority of community-based measures indicates the particular difficulty of treating clients in closed settings in which, for example, adverse institutionalization effects can be anticipated (Tittle, 1974; Ortmann, 1992). However, it has to be considered that the target groups of community-based and institutional measures probably differ. At present, the evidence against institutional settings seems to be less clear than is often claimed in polarized statements (see below).

The results of Lipsey and Andrews et al. demonstrate that specific kinds of treatment are more successful than others and exceed the main effect of 10% difference in recidivism. This agrees with earlier research integrations that used more traditional methods like vote-counting or narrative reviews (e.g., Gendreau & Ross, 1979; Nietzel, 1979; Romig, 1978). They show some consonance with other recent meta-analyses that report higher effects for behavioral and cognitive social learning approaches (e.g., Gottschalk et al., 1987; Izzo & Ross, 1990). However, in the latter studies, the effect differences between treatment types are statistically nonsignificant.

In other studies they are contradictory (e.g., Whitehead & Lab, 1989). In the meta-analysis of Izzo & Ross (1990) two factors show differential effectiveness: The treatment setting (community as compared to residential setting) and the presence of a cognitive component in treatment. A typical example for the latter is the social-cognitive skill training from Ross, Fabiano, and Ross (1986). Its essential treatment components can be summarized as follows (Ross, 1992): Teaching self-control, meta-cognition, social skills, interpersonal cognitive problem-solving, creative thinking, critical reasoning, social perspective taking, values enhancement, emotional management, helper therapy, and victim awareness. For details of cognitive-behavioral programs see Hollin (1990) or Morris and Braukman (1987).

A focus on cognitive processes and self-control of behavior is in line with many results on cognitive deficits, attention and impulsivity problems, and criminogenic thinking patterns of offenders (e.g., Averbeck & Lösel, 1992; Farrington, 1992; Goldstein, 1990; Moffitt & Silva, 1988; Loeber, 1990; Wilson & Herrnstein, 1985; Yochelson & Samenow, 1978). Accordingly, Gottfredson & Hirschi's (1990) recent attempt toward a general theory of criminality (as a person characteristic) focusses on the lack of self-control (see also Lösel, 1975). This convergence of the correlational results of explanatory research with the experimental findings of treatment evaluation is particularly promising for further improving the differential effectiveness of interventions.

Problems and Perspectives

Recent meta-analyses on the evaluation of offender treatment contradict the "nothing works" of older research. There is an increasing knowledge of what is meaningful in this field and what is not. The meta-analyses support earlier qualitative reviews that had already called for a more differentiated perspective and pointed to specific, relatively successful interventions. However, even differential effects are only moderate and not fully consistent. It also should not be overlooked that many recent studies are still subject to a series of evaluation problems. Only some of these can be addressed here:

1. *Design features*. As before, many studies do not have random group assignment but quasi-experimental designs with more or less equivalent control groups. Although this restricts possibilities of causal interpretation, even a true experimental design cannot avoid all threats to internal validity (Cook & Campbell, 1979; Lösel & Nowack, 1987). Moreover, in most experimental studies, randomization breaks down because of dropouts. Only computing dropouts to the disadvantage of treatment leads to one-sided conservative effect estimations. As dropouts are a group that performs particularly poorly, it can be assumed that differences in treatment motivation are generally very important (e.g., Steller, 1977). The experience that intervention measures should be targeted towards the specific needs and characteristics of offender subgroups (Andrews et al., 1990; Blackburn, 1980) may practically conflict with the requirements of randomization. Experimental designs alone do not guarantee valid results. Instead, specific alternative explanations of the results have to be inspected in each design. In addition, it is particularly meta-analysis (e.g., Andrews et al., 1990;

Lipsey, 1992a, b) that has suggested that differences in effects do not depend so strongly on experimental design features as has often been claimed. Although true experiments should still play a central role in treatment evaluation, more flexible strategies need to be followed in the sense of Cook's (1985) critical multiplism. One of the most promising designs would be to combine longitudinal and experimental approaches (Farrington, Ohlin, & Wilson, 1986; Tonry, Ohlin, & Farrington, 1991).

2. *Treatment setting*. Recent meta-evaluations have shown that appropriate psychosocial interventions can also be effective in residential settings and in the prison context. However, relatively few controlled studies are available on treatment in prisons, and overall effects are lower than in community settings. This may be partially due to differences in target groups (e.g., more antisocial or otherwise disturbed personalities in institutions). However, therapeutic and educational measures also may be ineffective in prisons or similar contexts because of the dominance of punishment and negative prisonization effects. Although several studies have indicated unfavorable prison effects (e.g., Bondeson, 1989; Ortmann, 1992), other studies do not confirm the general negative effects of prison life (see Bonta & Gendreau, 1990) or even suggest partially positive effects on recidivism rates (Brennan & Mednick, 1994; Farrington & Langan, 1992). Overall, the specific failure of institutional settings as compared to open residential or community settings is not sufficiently proven (Blackburn, 1980; Eysenck & Gudjonsson, 1989). In fact, there is a lack in research on the interplay between potentially negative and positive effects in prison contexts, and this applies particularly to the potentially most suitable person-by-situation approach.

3. *Theoretical foundation*. Although recent evaluations pay more attention to a theoretical foundation for interventions, general deficits can still be found. An example of an adequate theoretical orientation is given above (self-control theory). It would seem most promising to design programs according to empirically proven risks or deficits as well as to protective factors (e.g., Hawkins, Catalino, & Miller, 1992; Lösel, 1994). Only an empirically founded theoretical basis also allows us to rule out some of the scarcely avoidable threats to validity that provide an alternative explanation of results. Empirically based theories are necessary not only for the design of treatment but also for its implementation and the measurement of outcome. Theory-driven evaluation approaches which also take into account impact, intervening mechanism, and generalization theory (Chen, 1989), should be extended in the treatment of criminals.

4. *Effect criteria*. The problems in using official recidivism rates as the only outcome criterion have been discussed repeatedly (e.g., Waldo & Griswold, 1979; Lösel et al., 1987). Although this criterion should in no way be disregarded, adequate follow-up intervals and degrees of crime severity should be taken into account. Even in rather sound evaluations of cognitive-behavioral programs, follow-up periods of more than one year are rare. Furthermore, improvements are often restricted to skills in artificial settings rather than to antisocial behavior in everyday life (Kazdin, 1987). Direct criteria of delinquent behavior or theoretically based behavioral criteria from other fields should also be applied more often. Many studies use institutional behaviors or personality criteria that are invalid or unreliable in criminological terms

(Blackburn, 1980). There is no reason to assume that treatment outcomes are reflected consistently in various criteria and that effects on personality variables always agree with effects on recidivism (see Lipsey, 1992a).

5. *Contextual factors*. A majority of evaluation studies still examine relatively isolated, specific treatment programs. However, research and practice suggest that the specific organizational context, staff competences and rivalries, the social environment of the institution, government support, and so forth may have a great impact on the daily activities and effectiveness (see Lösel & Bliesener, 1989; McGuire, 1992a; Moos, 1975; Roberts, 1992). This does not just apply to residential settings but also, for example, to measures in schools or families (e.g., Guerra, 1991). In particular, characteristics of the social climate are important for specific effects (e.g., Moos, 1975; Lösel, 1994). However, there is insufficient empirical information on how far success or failure in the evaluation of treatment depends on the complex pattern of such context variables.

6. *Process evaluation*. Some of the above-mentioned problems can be reduced when there is sufficient information on the actual course of treatment. However, careful process evaluations are still rare (e.g., Sechrest & Rosenblatt, 1987). The judgment of measures (as well as their assignment to specific categories) is mostly performed with more or less explicit concepts or summary labels. Whether these actually are implemented adequately, that is, what is the integrity and intensity of the intervention, often cannot be estimated, although this is very important for the effect (e.g., Lösel & Wittmann, 1989). It has been shown repeatedly that treatment concepts have been implemented so poorly that their ineffectiveness is not surprising (see Quay, 1977; Rezmovic, 1984). Clearly defining and identifying the treatment process will help to figure out the salient elements of programs that are particularly important in multimodal approaches. A brief instrument to improve documentation and perhaps process evaluation is the Correctional Program Inventory from Gendreau and Andrews (1991).

7. *Meta-analysis*. There can be no doubt that meta-analysis represents an advance on the narrative literature review, the vote-counting of significances, and other methods for integrating research findings. Nonetheless, it also contains a number of methodological problems and sources of error (e.g., Bullock & Svyantek, 1985; Lösel, 1987; Matt, 1989). The fact that, in recent years, different analyses using different procedures have been performed on similar issues increases the reliablity of their statements. However, caution is necessary when undertaking an atheoretical assessment of a great number of moderator effects. Some of these cannot be replicated or contain the risk of circular conclusions (e.g., in the classification of appropriate vs. inappropriate treatment by Andrews et al., 1990). Meta-analysis also requires a substantial number of methodically sound and well-documented primary studies on the same problem. However, there is still a lack of controlled studies on complex interventions, particularly for adult offenders in institutional settings. More qualitative forms of meta-evaluation remain important as well (Lösel et al., 1987), and more approaches for integrating case studies are needed (e.g., McGuire, 1992b).

Although recent research clearly repudiates the "nothing works" hypothesis, in a methodologically careful judgment, it is still to early to suggest that correctional treatment has proven its value very conclusively. However, constructive perspectives are encouraged. These include:

1. International revitalization of treatment evaluation to improve knowledge for instrumental as well as conceptual use in strategies of differentiated reactions to criminality.
2. Precise definition and assessment of target groups (e.g., risk level, low dropout rate).
3. Theoretically and empirically based selection of adequate kinds of treatment (e.g., cognitive-behavioral and multimodal approaches).
4. Explication of theoretically meaningful and concrete goals of treatment (including negative effects).
5. Intensified evaluation of specific treatment components (including flexible designs for formative evaluation).
6. Differentiation and standardization of multiple recidivism and behavioral criteria.
7. Increased testing of intermediate effects (including negative effects like prisonization) and their relation to long-term outcome.
8. Improvements in the realization and evaluation of treatment integrity and intensity.
9. In cases of institutional/residential treatment increased evaluation of transition, release, and aftercare.
10. Intensified evaluation of the organizational framing conditions of treatment.
11. Improved documentation of treatment contents and results (e.g., for purposes of meta-evaluation).
14. Development of adequate evaluations of cost-effectiveness and cost-utility.
15. Improved information of the public and policy makers with respect to realistic evaluations (e.g., effect size problem)

It is not possible to anticipate a "philosopher's stone" for correctional treatment in the future. However, as long as crime policy opinions in this field do not petrify into erratic blocks, there is a good chance that we will continue on solid ground and become a little wiser in our rehabilitation philosophies.

References

Andrews, D.A., Zinger, I., Hoge, R.D., Bonta, J., Gendreau, P., & Cullen, F.T. (1990). Does correctional treatment work? A clinically relevant and psychologically informed meta-analysis. *Criminology*, *28*, 369-404.

Averbeck, M., & Lösel, F. (1992). Subjective crime theories of young offenders and criminal justice officials. *International Journal of Psychology*, *27*, *3/4*, 446.

Bailey, W.C. (1966). Correctional outcome: An evaluation of 100 reports. *Journal of Criminal Law, Criminology and Police Science*, *57*, 153-160.

Beelmann, A., Pfingsten, U., & Lösel, F. (1992). The effects of training social competence in children: A meta-analysis of recent evaluation studies. *Journal of Clinical Child Psychology*, *23*, 260-271.

Blackburn, R. (1980). *Still not working? A look at recent outcomes in offender rehabilitation*. Paper presented at the Scottish Branch of the Bristish Psychological Society Conference on Deviance, February 1980, Sterling, UK.

Bondeson, U.V. (1989). *Prisoners in prison societies*. New Brunswick, NJ: Transaction Books.

Bonta, J., & Gendreau, P. (1990). Reexamining the cruel and unusual punishment of prison life. *Law and Human Behavior, 14*, 347-372.

Brennan, P.A., & Mednick, S.A. (1994). Evidence for the adaption of a learning theory approach to criminal deterrence: A preliminary study. In: E. G. M. Weitekamp & H.-J. Kerner (Eds.), *Cross-national longitudinal research on human development and criminal behavior* (pp. 371-379). Dordrecht, NL: Kluwer.

Bullock, J.R., & Svyantek, D.J. (1985). Analyzing meta-analysis: Potential problems, an unsuccessful replication, and evaluation criteria. *Journal of Applied Psychology, 70*, 108-115.

Casey, R.J., & Berman, J.S. (1985). The outcome of psychotherapy with children. *Psychological Bulletin, 98*, 388-400.

Chen, H.T. (1989). *Theory-driven evaluations*. Newbury Park, CA: Sage.

Christie, N. (1981). *Limit to pain*. Oxford: Robertson.

Cohen, J. (1988). *Statistical power analysis for the behavioral sciences*, 2nd ed. New York: Academic Press.

Cook, T.D. (1985). Post-positivist critical multiplism. In L. Shotland & M.M. Mark (Eds.), *Social sciences and social policy* (pp. 21-62). Beverly Hills, CA: Sage.

Cook, T.D., & Campbell, D.T. (1979). *Quasi-experimentation. Design and analysis issues for field settings*. Chicago: Rand-McNally.

Cooper, H.M. (1989). *Integrating research: A guide for doing literature reviews*, 2nd ed. Newbury Park, CA: Sage.

Dolde, G. (1982). Effizienzkontrolle sozialtherapeutischer Behandlung im Vollzug. In H. Göppinger & P.H. Bresser (Eds.), *Sozialtherapie. Kriminologische Gegenwartsfragen*, vol. 15 (pp. 47-64). Stuttgart: Enke.

Dünkel, F. (1980). *Sozialtherapeutische Behandlung und Rückfälligkeit in Berlin-Tegel*. Berlin: Duncker & Humblot.

Dünkel, F. (1987). *Die Herausforderung der geburtenschwachen Jahrgänge*. Freiburg i.Br.: Max-Planck-Institut für ausländisches und internationales Strafrecht.

Dünkel, F., & Geng, B. (1991). *Zur Rückfälligkeit von Karrieretätern nach unterschiedlichen Strafvollzugs- und Entlassungsformen. Forschungsbericht*. Freiburg i.Br.: Max-Planck-Institut für ausländisches und internationales Strafrecht.

Egg, R. (1979). *Sozialtherapie und Strafvollzug*. Frankfurt: Haag & Herchen.

Egg, R. (1984). *Straffälligkeit und Sozialtherapie*. Köln: Heymanns.

Egg, R. (1990). Sozialtherapeutische Behandlung und Rückfälligkeit im längerfristigen Vergleich. *Monatsschrift für Kriminologie und Strafrechtsreform, 73*, 358-368.

Eysenck, H.J., & Gudjonsson, G. (1989). *The causes and cures of criminality*. New York: Plenum Press.

Farrington, D.P. (1992). Psychological contributions to the explanation, prevention and treatment of offending. In F. Lösel, D. Bender, & T. Bliesener (Eds.), *Psychology and law: International perspectives* (pp. 35-51). Berlin, New York: de Gruyter.

Farrington, D.P., & Langan, P.A. (1992). Changes in crime and punishment in England and America in the 1980s. *Justice Quarterly, 9*, 5-46.

Farrington, D.P., Ohlin, L.E., & Wilson, J.Q. (1986). *Understanding and controlling crime*. New York: Springer.

Fricke, R., & Treinies, G. (1985). *Einführung in die Metaanalyse*. Bern: Huber.

Friedman, H. (1968). Magnitude of experimental effect and a table for its rapid estimation. *Psychological Bulletin, 70*, 245-251.

Garrett, P. (1985). Effects of residential treatment of adjudicated delinquents: A meta-analysis. *Journal of Research in Crime and Delinquency, 22*, 287-308.

Gendreau, P., & Andrews, D.A. (1990). Tertiary prevention: What the meta-analyses of the offender treatment literature tell us about "What works". *Canadian Journal of Criminology, 32*, 173-184.

Gendreau, P., & Andrews, D.A. *Correctional Program Intervention Inventory (CPEI)*, 2nd ed. New Brunswick, Ottawa, CAN.

Gendreau, P., & Ross, R.R. (1979). Effective correctional treatment: Bibliotherapy for cynics. *Crime and Delinquency, 25*, 463-489.

Gendreau, P., & Ross, R.R. (1987). Revivication of rehabilitation: Evidence from the 1980s. *Justice Quarterly, 4*, 349-407.

Gensheimer, L.K., Mayer, J.P., Gottschalk, R., & Davidson II, W.S. (1986). Diverting youth from the juvenile justice system: A meta-analysis of intervention efficacy. In: S.J. Apter & A. Goldstein (Eds.), *Youth violence: Programs and prospects* (pp. 39-57). Elmsford, NY: Pergamon Press.

Glass, G.V., McGaw, B., & Smith, M.L. (1981). *Meta-analysis in social research*. Beverly Hills, CA: Sage.

Goldstein, A.P. (1990). *Delinquents on delinquency*. Campaign, IL: Research Press.

Gottfredson, M., & Hirschi, T.M. (1990). *A general theory of crime*. Stanford, CA: Stanford University Press.

Gottschalk, R., Davidson II, W.S., Gensheimer, L.K., & Mayer, J.P. (1987). Community-based interventions. In H.C. Quay (Ed.), *Handbook of juvenile delinquency* (pp. 266-289). New York: Wiley.

Greenwood, P.W., & Turner, S. (1985). *The Vision Quest Program: An evaluation*. Santa Monica, CA: Rand Corporation.

Guerra,N.(1991). *Social cognitive factors in the prevention of antisocial behavior*. Paper presented at the 11th Biennial Meetings of the International Society for the Study of Behavioral Development, July 1991, Minneapolis, MN.

Hawkins, J.D., Catalino, R.F., & Miller, J.Y. (1992). Risk and protective factors for alcohol and other drug problems in adolescence and early adulthood. *Psychological Bulletin, 112*, 64-105.

Hedges, L.V. (1982). Estimation of effect size from a series of independent experiments. *Psychological Bulletin, 92*, 490-499.

Hedges, L.V., & Olkin, I. (1985). *Statistical methods for meta-analysis*. Orlando: Academic Press.

Hollin, C.R. (1990). *Cognitive-behavioral interventions with young offenders*. Elmsford, NY: Pergamon Press.

Izzo, R.L., & Ross, R.R. (1990). Meta-analysis of rehabilitation programs for juvenile delinquents. A brief report. *Criminal Justice and Behavior, 17*, 134-142.

Kaiser, G., Dünkel, F., & Ortmann, R. (1982). Die sozialtherapeutische Anstalt - Das Ende einer Reform? *Zeitschrift für Rechtspolitik, 15*, 198-207.

Kazdin, A. (1987). Treatment of antisocial behavior in children: Current status and future directions. *Psychological Bulletin, 102*, 187-203.

Killias, M. (1992) (Ed.). *Rückfall und Bewährung/Récidive et rehabilitation*. Chur, CH: Rüegger.

Kury, H. (1986). *Die Behandlung Straffälliger. Band 1: Inhaltliche und methodische Probleme der Behandlungsforschung*. Berlin: Duncker & Humblot.

Lipsey, M.W. (1988). Juvenile delinquency intervention. In H.S. Bloom, D.S. Cordray, & R.J. Light (Eds.), *Lessons from selected program and policy areas. New Directions for Program Evaluation, No. 37* (pp. 63-83). San Francisco: Jossey-Bass.

Lipsey, M.W. (1992a). Juvenile delinquency treatment: A meta-analytic inquiry into variability of effects. In T.D. Cook, H. Cooper, D.S. Cordray, H. Hartmann, L.V. Hedges, R.L. Light, T.A. Louis, & F. Mosteller (Eds.), *Meta-analysis for explanation* (pp. 83-127). New York: Russell Sage Foundation.

Lipsey, M.W. (1992b). The effect of treatment on juvenile delinquents: Results from meta-analysis. In F. Lösel, D. Bender, & T. Bliesener (Eds.), *Psychology and law. International perspectives* (131-143). Berlin, New York: de Gruyter.

Lipton, D., Martinson, R., & Wilks, J. (1975). *The effectiveness of correctional treatment.* New York: Praeger.

Loeber, R. (1990). Disruptive and antisocial behavior in childhood and adolescence: Development and risk factors. In K. Hurrelmann & F. Lösel (Eds.), *Health hazards in adolescence* (pp. 233-257). Berlin, New York: de Gruyter.

Logan, C. (1972). Evaluation research in crime and delinquency: A reappraisal. *Journal of Criminal Law, Criminology and Police Science, 63*, 378-387.

Lösel, F. (1975). *Handlungskontrolle und Jugenddelinquenz.* Stuttgart: Enke.

Lösel, F. (1987). Methodik und Problematik von Meta-Analysen. *Gruppendynamik: Zeitschrift für Angewandte Sozialpsychologie, 18*, 323-343.

Lösel, F. (1991). Meta-analysis and social prevention: Evaluation and a study on the family-hypothesis in developmental psychopathology. In G. Albrecht & H.-U. Otto (Eds.), *Social prevention and the social sciences* (pp. 305-332). Berlin, New York: de Gruyter.

Lösel, F. (1992). Sprechen Evaluationsergebnisse von Meta-Analysen für einen frischen Wind in der Straftäterbehandlung? In M. Killias (Ed.), *Rückfall und Bewährung/Récidive et rehabilitation.* Chur, CH: Rüegger.

Lösel, F. (1994). Protective effects of social resources in adolescents at high risk for antisocial behavior. In E. G. M. Weitekamp & H.-J. Kerner (Eds.), *Cross-national longitudinal research on human development and criminal behavior* (pp. 281-301). Dordrecht, NL: Kluwer.

Lösel, F., & Bliesener, T. (1989). Psychology in prison: Role assessment and testing of an organizational model. In H. Wegener, F. Lösel, & J. Haisch (Eds.), *Criminal behavior and the justice system: Psychological perspectives* (pp. 419-439). New York: Springer.

Lösel, F., & Bliesener, T. (1994). Some high-risk adolescents do develop conduct problems: A study of protective factors. *International Journal of Behavioral Development, 17*, 753-777.

Lösel, F., & Köferl, P. (1989). Evaluation research on correctional treatment in West Germany: A meta-analysis. In H. Wegener, F. Lösel, & J. Haisch (Eds.), *Criminal behavior and the justice system: Psychological perspectives* (pp. 334-355). New York: Springer.

Lösel, F., Köferl, P., & Weber, F. (1987). *Meta-Evaluation der Sozialtherapie.* Stuttgart: Enke.

Lösel, F., & Nowack, W. (1987). Evaluationsforschung. In J. Schultz-Gambard (Ed.), *Angewandte Sozialpsychologie* (pp.57-87). Weinheim: Psychologie Verlags Union.

Lösel, F., & Wittmann, W.W. (1989) The relationship of treatment integrity and intensity to outcome criteria. In R.F. Conner & M. Hendricks (Eds.), *International innovations in evalution methodology. New Directions for Program Evaluation, No. 42* (pp. 97-108). San Francisco: Jossey-Bass.

Martinson, R. (1974). What works? Questions and answers about prison reform. *Public Interest, 10*, 22-54.

Matt, G.E. (1989). Decision, rules for selecting effect sizes in meta-analysis: A review and reanalysis of psychotherapy outcome studies. *Psychological Bulletin, 105*, 106-115.

Mayer, J.P., Gensheimer L.K., Davidson II, W.S., & Gottschalk, R. (1986). Social learning treatment within juvenile justice: A meta-analysis of impact in the natural environment. In S.J. Apter & A. Goldstein (Eds.), *Youth violence: Programs and prospects* (pp. 24-38). Elmsford, NY: Pergamon Press.

McGuire, J. (1992a). Things to do to make your programme work. In B. Rowson & J. McGuire (Eds.), *What works: Effective methods to reduce re-offending* (pp. 48 - 51). Manchester: Conference Proceedings.

McGuire, J. (1992b). Interpreting treatment-outcome studies of anti-social behaviour: Combining meta-analyses and single case designs. *International Journal of Psychology, 3/4*, 446.

McGuire, J., & Priestley, P. (1992). Some things do work: Psychological interventions with offenders and the effectiveness debate. In F. Lösel, D. Bender, & T. Bliesener (Eds.), *Psychology and law: International perspectives* (pp. 163-174). Berlin, New York: de Gruyter.

Moffitt, T.E., & Silva, P.A. (1988). IQ and delinqueny: A direct test of the differential detection hypothesis. *Journal of Abnormal Psychology, 97*, 330-333.

Moos, R. (1975). *Evaluating correctional and community settings*. New York: Wiley.

Morris, E.K., & Braukman, C.J. (Eds.) (1987). *Behavioral approaches to crime and delinquency: A handbook of applications, research, and concepts*. New York: Plenum Press.

Nietzel, M.T. (1979). *Crime and its modification: A social learning perspective*. New York: Pergamon Press.

Opp, K.D. (1979). *Strafvollzug und Resozialisierung*. München: Fink.

Ortmann, R. (1987). *Resozialisierung im Strafvollzug*. Freiburg i.Br.: Max-Planck-Institut für ausländisches und internationales Strafrecht.

Ortmann, R. (1992). Die Nettobilanz einer Resozialisierung im Strafvollzug: Negativ? In H. Kury (Ed.), *Gesellschaftliche Umwälzung: Kriminalitätserfahrungen, Straffälligkeit und soziale Kontrolle* (pp. 375 - 451). Freiburg i.Br.: Max-Planck-Institut für ausländisches und internationales Strafrecht.

Palmer, T. (1975). Martinson revisited. *Journal of Research in Crime and Delinquency, 12*, 133-152.

Prentky, R., & Burgess, A.W. (1992). Rehabilitation of child molesters: A cost-benefit analysis. In A.W. Burgess (Ed.), *Child trauma I: Issues and research* (pp.417-442). New York: Garland.

Quay, H.C. (1977). The three faces of evaluation: What can be expected to work? *Criminal Justice and Behavior, 4*, 341 - 354.

Rasch, W., & Kühl, K.P. (1978). Psychologische Befunde und Rückfälligkeit nach Aufenthalt in der sozialtherapeutischen Modellanstalt Düren. *Bewährungshilfe, 25*, 44-57.

Redondo, S., Garrido, V., Anguera, M.T., & Luque, E. (1992). *Correctional programmes in Europe*. Pilot study for a meta-evaluation research. Paper presented at the Third European Conference of Law and Psychology, September, 1992, Oxford, UK.

Rehn, G. (1979). *Behandlung im Strafvollzug*. Weinheim: Beltz.

Rehn, G., & Jürgensen, P. (1983). Rückfall nach Sozialtherapie. Wiederholung einer im Jahr 1979 vorgelegten Untersuchung. In H.-J. Kerner, H. Kury, & K. Sessar (Eds.), *Deutsche Forschungen zur Kriminalitätsentstehung und Kriminalitätskontrolle* (pp. 1910-1948). Köln: Heymanns.

Rezmovic, E.L. (1984). Assessing treatment implementation amid the slings and arrows of reality. *Evaluation Review, 2*, 187-204.

Roberts, C. (1992). Effective practice and service delivery. Paper presented at What Works 1992, Conference on progress in effective work with offenders. September 1992, Salford, UK.

Romig, A.D. (1978). *Justice for our children. An examination of juvenile delinquent rehabilitation programs*. Lexington, MA: Lexington Books.

Rosenthal, R., & Rubin, D.B. (1982). A simple general purpose display of magnitude of experimental effect. *Journal of Educational Psychology, 74*, 166-169.

Rosenthal, R. (1991). *Meta-analytic procedures for social research*, 2nd ed. Newbury Park, CA: Sage.

Ross, R.R. (1992). Reasoning and rehabilitation of offenders. In B. Rowson & J. McGuire (Eds.), *What works: Effective methods to reduce re-offending* (pp. 21-26). Manchester: Conference Proceedings.

Ross, R.R., Fabiano, E., & Ross, R.D. (1986). *Reasoning and rehabilitation: A handbook for teaching cognitive skills*. Ottawa: Cognitive Center.

Rowson, B., & McGuire, J. (1992) (Eds.). *What works: Effective methods to reduce re-offending*. Manchester: Conference Proceedings.

Sechrest, L., & Rosenblatt, A. (1987). Research methods. In H.C. Quay (Ed.), *Handbook of juvenile delinquency* (pp. 417-450). New York: Wiley.

Sechrest, L. B., White, S.O., & Brown, E.D. (Eds.) (1979). *The rehabilitation of criminal offenders: Problems and prospects*. Washington, D.C.: National Academy of Sciences.

Shapiro, D. A., & Shapiro, D. (1983). Meta-analysis of comparative therapy outcome studies: A replication and refinement. *Psychological Bulletin*, *92*, 581-604.

Smith, M.L., Glass, G.V., & Miller, T.I. (1980). *The benefits of psychotherapy*. Baltimore: Johns Hopkins University Press.

Steller, M. (1977). *Sozialtherapie statt Strafvollzug*. Köln: Kiepenheuer.

Thornton, D.M. (1987). Treatment effects on recidivism: A reappraisal of the "nothing works" doctrine. In B.J. McGurk, D.M. Thornton, & M. Williams (Eds.), *Applying psychology to imprisonment* (pp. 181-189). London: H.M.S.O.

Tittle, C.R. (1974). Prisons and rehabilitation: The inevitability of disfavour. *Social Problems*, *21*, 385-395.

Tonry, M., Ohlin, L.E., & Farrington, D.P. (1991). *Human development and criminal behavior*. New York: Springer.

Waldo, G., & Griswold, D. (1979). Issues in the measurement of recidivism. In L.B. Sechrest, S.O. White, & E.D. Brown (Eds.), *The rehabilitation of criminal offenders: Problems and prospects* (pp. 225-250). Washington, D.C.: National Academy Sciences.

Waxweiler, R. (1980). *Psychotherapie im Strafvollzug*. Weinheim: Beltz.

Weisz, J.R., Weiss, B., Alicke, M.D., & Klotz, M.L. (1987). Effectiveness of psychotherapy with children and adolescents: A meta-analysis for clinicians. *Journal of Consulting and Clinical Psychology*, *55*, 542-549.

Whitehead, J.T., & Lab, S.P. (1989). A meta-analysis of juvenile correctional treatment. *Journal of Research in Crime and Delinquency*, *26*, 276-295.

Wilson, J.Q., & Herrnstein, R.J. (1985). *Crime and human nature*. New York: Simon & Schuster.

Wittmann, W.W., & Matt, G.E. (1986). Meta-Analyse als Integration von Forschungsergebnissen am Beispiel deutschsprachiger Arbeiten zur Effektivität von Psychotherapie. *Psychologische Rundschau*, *37*, 20-40.

Yochelson, S., & Samenow, S.E. (1976). *The criminal personality, vol. I: A profile for change*. New York: Aronson.

Note. The German study reported in this paper was funded by the Federal Ministry of Research and Technology. I am grateful to Michael Martin for his assistance in data analysis and Jonathan Harrow for his help in translation.

Part VIII
Prison Psychology

Psychological Services to the Finnish Prison Administration

Marja Hatunen

The first two psychologists were appointed in 1968 at the two largest central prisons in Finland, and the next post was established at Kerava Juvenile Prison. The number of posts has increased yearly, and by 1983 there were 13 psychologists in the service, and now the number is 24. We have 24 penal institutions in Finland. The number of prisoners was about 3,200 in August 1992 and about one hundred of the prisoners were women. There are eight central prisons, eight local remand prisons, one mental hospital, five subsidiary prisons, one course centre, six open institutions attached to central prisons and 11 labour colonies. The labour colonies and three of the subsidiary prisons do not have psychological services. Two of the central prisons have two psychologists working in them, as does Kerava Juvenile Prison. In addition to the mental hospital, there is a psychiatric ward in one of the central prisons. The psychologists working in them are working in the prison health service. They work as clinical psychologists providing psychological assessments for courts and assessing risk for the prison court which determines allocation to appropriate prisons. The clinical psychologists and prison psychologists are trained together.

In the prison department there is a senior inspector whose area of responsibility has been education, rehabilitation and social work. This is where psychological services are placed in the organisation. Until last year the job description of psychologists was determined by prison department headquarters. Two main task areas were identified for psychologists:-

1) To help and counsel prisoners with their psychological problems (correctional work);

2) To influence prison policy and the overall regime of the prison in such a way that the psychological viewpoints are taken into consideration (preventive work).

Psychologists in prisons used to work to "making use of the term of punishment". Although the job description was the same for all psychologists, the role of each psychologist was unique. Each governor used the psychological services in the prison differently, and the role of the prison influenced the priority of the tasks of the psychologist. Also the type of prisoner affects the way a psychologist works, as do the needs and expectations of other staff. The area of competence of the individual psychologist also contributes to the role.

Since last year a job description has been made for each psychologist. The organisational position of the psychologist varies amongst institutions. A psychologist is either a subordinate of the governor or the assistant governor whose area of responsibility is education, rehabilitation and social work. The psychologists in the mental hospital and the psychiatric ward are accountable to the psychiatrist. Before these organizational changes occurred, all psychologists were accountable to their governor.

To be able to work as a psychologist in Finland it is necessary to have a Masters Degree in Psychology and this is the basic requirement for prison psychologists. No other special studies are required, but suitability to work in a prison is essential. Each prison psychologist has, of course, a unique professional and theoretical background and thus works accordingly. After appointment, there is no basic training arranged for a prison psychologist but a basic course in prison administration is offered to all new staff working in the prisons. The prison service college offers in-service training for prison psychologists on either the senior inspector's initiative or at the prison psychologists' request. The in-service training is planned by the senior inspector, representatives of the prison service college, and the psychologists together. Last year the topics were violent behaviour and organizational development. The prison service college provides many kinds of in-service training for all prison staff and the psychologists can apply for these courses. The psychologists are also encouraged to take part in further education offered outside the prison administration. Whether one gets more education is thus dependent on each psychologist's enthusiasm and need, and how much money a prison can and wants to use for the development of its psychologist's professional ability.

The likely future directions for psychological services in Finland are based on the two priorities mentioned above, the correctional work and the preventive work.

I work in Kerava Juvenile Prison which is for young men aged 15 to 21 with a sentence of no more than four years. The maximum number of cells is 90 and usually 60-70 prisoners are held. It is the main prison for young prisoners and thus gathers inmates from all over Finland.

I work on an individual basis, mainly with violent offenders and drug abusers and those with mental problems. The short period they stay in the prison limits what can be achieved and dictates the methods which can be employed.

A few years ago a "goal programme" was developed by staff. The basic ideology of that programme is to work on the basis of individuality. This means that the individual needs of each prisoner should be analyzed and the actions in the prison should be planned to correspond to these needs. Because of the young age of the prisoners, there is a great emphasis on education and training and learning to work. We have developed a programme for those who want to stop taking drugs, at least while in prison or in the special drug free ward. Another programme is available for those who have been unable to motivate themselves while in prison. These programmes are based on "normality", taking responsibility, social learning, creativity and teaching the boys everyday routines like cooking, cleaning, doing their laundry, sewing, working and learning to plan.

These programmes mean a new way of working for the staff - a holistic way and in multidisciplinary teams. This is what is meant to happen in the whole prison: the staff should take more overall responsibility and not divide the prisoners' needs into aspects that many specialised staff meet. Working within these programmes and planning new ways to work together with other staff is a very important part of my work and a very difficult one. How to co-ordinate work in the future is the basic issue in my prison. It may change the role of the psychologist too.

The prison administration is going through an organizational change: the idea of the management by objectives or results has been brought to the whole civil service. This means many changes to each organization, including the prison I work in. At the same time, because of the economic depression, there have been cuts in posts in the civil service. In the prison administration these cuts have meant a decrease in the number of prison officers, engendering bad feelings among the staff. With losing officers it is difficult to develop new programmes, and new kinds of thinking on the way we should work. The priorities which need to be decided are required. All this puts pressure on the psychologist.

Prison Service Psychology - England and Wales

Cynthia McDougall

Background Information

HM Prison Service has recently become an Agency, which allows more control over management of its own affairs within a framework agreed with Government Ministers. The Service is divided into 15 areas which are managed by area managers based in headquarters. The area managers are each responsible for seven to nine establishments - and report to one of three operational directors on the Prisons Board. There are also three service directors. Areas of responsibility of the six directors are: Services and Parole; Inmate Administration; Inmate Programmes; Custody; Health Care; Personnel and Finance.

The prison population varies currently around 48,000 and is housed in a range of types of establishment from top security dispersal prisons through categories B, C and D which provide progressively less secure conditions. There are separate women's and young offenders establishments and a specialist therapeutic prison, HMP and YOI Grendon.

Psychological Services

Currently there are 150 psychologists and 38 psychological assistants, mainly working in establishments, and a small number in HQ policy directorates. The establishments where psychologists work are spread throughout the country, but psychology unit location is largely historical, based on earlier priority being given to dispersal prisons housing the most serious offenders, young offender establishments, female prisons and therapeutic establishments. Progress is however being made towards provision of a psychology service to all establishments.

Psychologists in establishments report through the line management structure to governors, area managers and to prisons board directors. The professional Head of Psychology does not have direct management of psychologists but is responsible for personnel, training and professional standards.

Psychologists join Prison Service Psychology as graduate psychologists, and MSc training is given during their first two years in the organisation. The qualification is in Applied Criminological Psychology jointly provided by Prison Psychology and Birbeck College. The MSc is accredited by the British Psychological Society. Psychologists spend 50% of their time during training on MSc subjects. These are taught in modular form and followed by actual work in establishments. The taught subjects are: clinical methods, organisational psychology, criminology, staff training, statistics, computing and consultancy. Additionally students are required to complete a research project in subjects of relevance to the Prison Service and establishment.

Work of Prison Psychologists

Because of the dispersed nature of psychologists within the management structure, it became extremely important that we had a clear image of our purpose. In consultation across the Psychology Service, therefore, a Statement of Purpose for psychologists was drawn up.

Prison Service Psychology Statement of Purpose

Prison Service Psychology supports the Prison Service's Statement of Purpose and its staff by applying sound psychological principles and high professional standards to:

the delivery of agreed organisational objectives
the understanding of individuals and the organisation
the design of strategies for change
the evaluation of effectiveness

The Statement of Purpose seeks to describe what is uniquely psychological. It therefore describes the core skills we apply to all situations, whether dealing with individuals or the organisation, both at headquarters and in establishments.

The main areas in which we work are advising governors/managers, carrying out small-scale operational research projects, providing a treatment service and contributing to staff training. We adopt an operational psychology approach, working with staff in developing and implementing psychological methods to be applied to regimes and the organisation. This approach is different from that of external consultancy, which tends to produce a top-down means of implementing change, and is different from a specialist referral system where problems would be referred to a specialist to deal with. Our aim is to adopt a broad-base approach to developing and implementing psychological methods within the operation of the organisation.

Psychologists concentrate on areas which are of main interest to the Prison Service and align their work to establishment contracts and Prisons Board priorities. Some of the main areas are national sex offender programmes, national anger and aggression programmes, sentence planning, managing hostage incidents, post-incident care of staff, dealing with vulnerable prisoners, establishing family links, and working with HIV and AIDS. More recently psychologists have been assisting with the implementation of the Criminal Justice Act and are involved in related issues associated with throughcare, open reporting on inmates, and the establishment of tribunals to make decisions on release.

Future of Prison Psychology Services

In view of the changes for the Prison Service as a whole, there are many proposed changes for Prison Service psychologists. We need to develop a more business-oriented approach to contracts with governors and monitoring delivery and standards, and be prepared to adapt to changing needs, in a flexible responsive way. We are beginning to promote the psychology service more widely and to that end have introduced a new Journal of Prison Service Psychology *Inside Psychology* to publicise our contribution to the Prison Service. We are also keen to promote links outside the Prison Service and with psychologists in other countries and exchange ideas.

Psychologists have most to offer at times of change. We are therefore facing all of the challenges in the light of this being a great opportunity to influence the future of the Service. We will report back to the next conference in two years' time to let you know how we have succeeded.

Organization of the Psychiatry and Psychology Services in Italian Prisons

Franco Scarpa

The Italian prison system is under the jurisdiction of the Ministry of Justice, which has had its own central structure in the form of the Department of Prison Administration since the recent Law of Reform of 1990.

The present organization of the prison system dates back, however, to the Law of Reform of the Prison Regulations and the subsequent Rules for its implementation (Law No. 354 of 1975 and Presidential Decree No. 431 of 1976 with successive amendments). The system is based on the Penal Code of 1931 which, in conformity with the principles of the Classical and Positivistic School in the penal field, had already defined a system of sanctions which is now known as a "double-track" system. This provides not only for custodial sentences and sanctions for the crimes committed, but also for "safety measures" implemented for treatment, or care, of the degree of social danger.

Provision is therefore made, in the first case, for prisons, or sections of them, for the carrying out of custodial sentences (Case di Reclusione, Case Penali etc.), and, in the second, for institutions for those subjected to "safety measures". In the latter case internees are held in Penal Farms (Colonie Agricole) or Work Houses (Case di Lavoro), for those declared habitual or potential delinquents, as well as Custodial Homes (Case di Cura e Custodia) and Judiciary Psychiatric Hospitals (OPGs) for those who have committed crimes when they were semi or totally mentally ill.

In total there are 195 prisons over the national territory for which the Law of 1975 on the Prison Regulations prescribed the introduction of general and specialist care, and additional personnel assigned to the observation and treatment of detainees with the aim of reforming and rehabilitating them.

We will first deal with this latter aspect since the principle of reform and rehabilitation has been established by the Italian Constitution which, in Article 27, Paragraph 3, states "the punishment must be aimed at the rehabilitation of the persons sentenced".

The process of observation and treatment must be conducted in the framework of a group chaired by the Director of the prison and consisting of educator, social worker, prison police personnel and anyone else who may be in a position to make a useful contribution in the context of the internal life of the institution (school teachers, vocational training course instructors, those in charge of internal working activities, voluntary service representatives etc.).

The group is integrated by experts (Article 80 of the Regulations), usually graduates or with a specific diploma of specialization in Psychology, Criminology or Educational Science. They act as consultants, and may also perform, if the need arises, a psychotherapeutic role if qualified to do so. They are recruited by means of a selection process at a regional level and are associated with the Prison Administration by a freelance professional relationship with a number of monthly hours assigned to each prison in relation to its number of inmates.

Their role consists of acquiring a suitable, specific and scientific knowledge of the inmates in treatment, by focusing on any psychophysical deficiencies on which to intervene and on the necessary support measures for the implementation of the treatment programmes. This is followed by talks and meetings with the inmates whom they subject, on their request, to observation. As a rule, the application of psychodiagnostic tests is not essential, with the exception of two specific Centres of Observation set up in two prisons and equipped to do so.

Recently a further task has been assigned to the psychological experts: the new arrival service that provides assessment for new inmates, on their admission to prison, of the risk of their committing suicidal acts. This is performed in collaboration with the physician who carried out the medical examination on admission, and aims to prevent the trauma caused to young offenders by their first contact with the prison world, particularly on their first experience of detention.

As regards the specific medical and specialist care, Article 11 of the Prison Regulations prescribes that at least a doctor be appointed in each prison, with a subordinate employment relationship, who has the task of providing basic medical treatment and of organizing the prison's health care services. The general practitioner may consult specialists in the various branches. In this instance each prison, on the basis of a freelance professional contract remunerated by a fee per medical examination, appoints one or more psychiatric doctors with a view to assessing the needs of the inmates.

Article 11 in reality prescribes that agreements be signed with the specialist Psychiatric Services of the National Health Service (SSN) aimed at guaranteeing inmates the same level of treatment provided for the public at large. For the time being, in fact, the Administration intends to pursue the goal of ensuring that the SSN should intervene with its own resources and personnel in the Prison Service.

The new Code of Penal Procedure itself, issued in 1989, prescribes that those in detention who present psychiatric disorders not treatable in the health structures of the prison's own infirmary, shall be admitted to and treated by the public health care structures, as prescribed by the legislation in force.

This is all the more necessary for inmates who have committed crimes and who present psychiatric disorders which existed prior to their imprisonment and as such have influenced their state of liability. The existing organization of psychiatric care, according to Law 180, that led to the abolition of lunatic asylums and long-term hospitalization, has created considerable difficulties in the case of prisoners needing treatment. In fact, the local health care units, that is the local bodies of the National Health Service, have few structures at their disposal for prolonged treatment, compared to the great demand and number of patients. Provision for hospitalization of acute cases (TSO) exists in small wards (from seven to 15 beds) of General Hospitals. As a rule, the hospitalization period lasts a week, and rarely for more than one month, and the final result is that the prisoner is returned to the prison itself. The lack of personnel in the external Psychiatric Service, and a still existing problem concerning the responsibilities for the costs of the treatment provided to the prisons by SSN, means that only for a few inmates is it possible to have recourse to external Psychiatric Services.

As things stand at this moment, the Prison Administration has its own provision, by the legislation in force, for the internment of detainees who may present mental disorders. These structures have been called Judiciary Psychiatric Hospitals (Ospedali Psichiatrici Giudiziari or OPGs). They were created in 1876, after a long and intensive debate among politicians, physicians and intellectuals of the time.

OPGs were intended, at first, with the aim of housing those prison inmates who presented psychiatric disorders in the course of their sentence. To these were added those affected by a mental illness at the time the crime was committed, acquitted for this reason, and declared socially dangerous. This latter category was introduced after 1930, when the Penal Code, issued in that year and still currently in force, introduced the judicial category of the acquitted, not liable because considered criminally insane, and the concept of social danger which entailed the need, in their case, for adequate judicial structures.

There are currently five institutions in Italy run by the Prison Administration. They are situated at Aversa, Naples, Reggio Emilia, Montelupo Fiorentino (FI) and Barcellona (ME). The following categories of prisoners are assigned to OPGs: (a) prisoners who are suspected of having mental problems are sent there for psychiatric observation; and (b) those who have committed crimes and are declared non-liable, due to mental illness, and socially dangerous (Article 88 and Article 222 of the Penal Code). In the former case, psychiatric observation lasts 30 days, at the end of which a medical report is sent to the Supervising Magistrate who may authorize a provision of hospitalization, or definitive allocation, to the OPG. This allocation will last until the patient is able to return to prison.

The OPGs are, in their current organization and structure, penitentiary institutions with personnel who are, for the most part, virtually identical to that existing in the ordinary prisons, i.e. prison warders, educators, social worker, plus the normal administrative staff. The exception is the Director, who is a doctor, with his own staff of medical assistants. All of them are on the permanent workforce of the Prison Administration. An increased medical service consists of doctors in charge of the basic health care, an emergency service of doctors permanently on duty, and a number of specialist freelance psychiatrists who are paid by the hour.

Each inmate is normally assigned to a section, or a ward, according to both his clinical diagnosis and his judicial status. A medical assistant is responsible for each ward (50-60 inmates) and is also in charge of co-ordinating the activity of a doctor responsible for basic health care, and of at least two psychiatric specialists. This allows in the majority of cases an adequate medical presence and an adequate treatment. The limitation of the medical treatment is due to the environment because it is similar to a prison (gates, bars, cells) and very different to the former asylums for lunatics. Moreover, the lack of nurses, who are hired with a level of pay and grading that compares unfavourably with those of the SSN, creates further difficulties in some OPGs, hampers the provision of continuous therapeutic interventions and the implementation of rehabilitation programmes.

In some OPGs provision is also made for Nursing and Custodial Home (Casa di Cura e Custodia) Sections which are intended to accommodate those patients who were declared partially mentally unstable at the time of the crime, and thus sentenced to a custodial sentence mitigated in length, as well as to a "safety measure". A section of one Nursing and Custodial Home is allocated to women and is situated in the prison of Sollicciano-Florence where freelance psychiatric consultants provide assistance for a limited number of restricted women.

At the end of the custodial sentence a "crazy" detainee is then freed and assigned, if necessary, to the care of the Public Service. But in the case of the acquitted, or those subject to safety measures, the problem becomes more complex. A safety measure may end only when the cessation of the state of social danger is achieved. This means that, for the patients who cannot control their behaviour, and who could commit crimes again, the state of social danger is closely bound to the assistance which may subsequently be provided to them. This requires a collaboration between the OPGs and local services, with a view to drawing up health care programmes for the inmates at the time of their admission to the OPGs. Principally, it is necessary to draw up support programmes following their release at the end of the safety measure or prior to its expiration.

The types of patient currently present in the OPGs are mentally ill to various degrees whose crimes are often the symptom of a social handicap or of a lack of medical care. They pose problems of rehabilitation, particularly the search for suitable social and family solutions. There is no law that acts as a bridge between public health care and judiciary health care, and solutions must be reached through collaboration between the local authorities (Region and Local Health Unit) and the Administration of the OPGs. An experiment of this kind is currently being conducted in Reggio Emilia and Montelupo Fiorentino. It is based on agreements which provide less of a custodial response and more active programmes of external rehabilitation. A similar experiment has led in the past to an agreement between the Prison Administration and the Region of Lombardy. Under the terms of the agreement, a psychiatric hospital in this region includes a judiciary section characterized by the presence of only nurses and medical staff of the Local Health Care Unit with costs paid by the Prison Administration.

Similar measures, though made difficult to implement by Law 180 which prohibits the construction of public psychiatric hospitals with characteristics of asylum-type restriction, have been proposed to all regions with the aim of achieving a more regular distribution of patients over the country. This could facilitate relations between health care structures and the home area (it should be recalled that there are only five OPGs).

The future of this Institution in which there has been a progressive drop in inmates from the 1970s to the present day (from 2127 in 1960, equivalent to 9.72% of the total number of prisoners, to 1078 in 1991, equivalent to 3.12%) is linked in part to the announced reform of law on psychiatric care, the debate of which is imminent in Parliament. Provision could be made for the long-term hospitalization of the chronically mentally ill. This would be residential care, with therapeutic and rehabilitation characteristics, accommodating a large number of internees prior to or at the end of their detention. On the other hand, for those inmates highly dangerous for reasons that are not exclusively linked to factors of mental illness, there would remain a few judiciary structures, which could eventually be replaced by special psychiatric sections within the ordinary prisons.

Another proposed solution, to be evaluated on a far longer time-scale, is linked to the re-assessment of the principle of the non-liability of the mentally ill. By a Reform of the Penal Code, long studied in the Parliamentary Committee delegated to examine it, provision would be made for normal sentencing to a custodial term, though this would be reduced in length and served in special sections in ordinary prisons. Psychiatric services would have access to them, with programmes of recovery and rehabilitation, using the provisions already made by the existing legislation for ordinary prisoners (suspended sentences, permits, partial-freedom, assignment to the Social Service, Parole, etc.).

As regards the current training of OPG personnel, the Training School for the Administration's personnel organizes a course for the medical staff of directors and assistants. The specialized personnel on contract work, must possess a regular diploma of specialization, while for the remaining personnel - nurses, general practitioners, educators etc. - only the specific training of the professional level possessed is required. In recent times, the Administration has taken steps to organize forums and training seminars for the personnel of the various OPGs to promote the exchange of experiences and information necessary for a more fruitful role, in collaboration with experienced external consultants. There is no Central Office of the Department with the role of stimulating and co-ordinating the activities of the various OPGs. This means that the type of specialist services provided depend upon the individual's training in psychiatry and the specific organizational model of each OPG. This, while it may pose problems of homogeneity in terms of therapeutic options, does provide scope for professional freedom.

Therapy within Prison: Opportunities and Problems

Ann Van Neygen

Introduction

When a crime is committed, the legal system occupies itself with the act, the prison system with the body of the criminal. But who takes care of the subject with his unconscious truth that's behind the criminal act; the subject living within the criminal body? Here lies the task of the psychologist. However, the question arises whether working as a psychologist within the repressive system of a prison is possible? I am convinced that there is a possibility for meaningful therapeutic work, both individual and in groups. I will focus on the opportunities for such work, without however neglecting the problems resulting from it.

Reports and articles concerning the work and the actual situation in prison, inevitably lead to the decisive conclusion that the suppressive and repressive system of justice forms the criminal rather than delivers him from his criminal tendencies. Prison is a place where new feelings of hate and aggression arise. A proof for this statement is the rate of recidivism, which is very high in our country.

From a psychoanalytic point of view, criminal law is grounded on the fact that identical forbidden motives are active both in the criminal and in the punishing society, meaning that punishment is not only meted out for benefit, advantage and suitability, but also for the satisfaction of the desire of the punishing society. This also explains why nothing is being done to abolish the extremely repressive conditions and the killing monotony in prison, even when these conditions have long since been judged as ineffective by the findings of criminology.

Thus, the most important paradox of prison is that while it has to realize a new integration of the prisoner in society, its way of functioning consists in a denial, even negation of the prisoner as a human being. This paradox is also reflected in the therapeutic work within prison system, on the side of the detainee as well as on the side of the psychologist, each of which will be discussed.

The Prisoner

I will commence with a short anecdote. One day a prisoner applies for an interview with the director. When he is asked what he wants, he answers: "a refrigerator in the cell". The director tries to make him understand that such a request cannot be granted. But he is also curious to know the reason for the man's insistent plea. The prisoner simply replies: "when I have a refrigerator, I can freeze in all my problems until the day I get out. Then I will take the packet out with me".

This both ironic and painful anecdote demonstrates the awful shortage of a listening ear in an institution where, precisely because of the organization of the system, the apparent need for it is enormously high. But is therapy or psychoanalysis basically possible within this kind of organization? And what about the problems one has to cope with?

First of all, prison is not exempt from the strict rules of reality. It is not a place where one's desire is permitted to play in all its ambivalence, as it is the case within the walls of a therapeutic room outside of prison. The prison system with its rules and regulations represents the third party that is present, always and everywhere. The detainee is always seen - just think about the judas in the cell door; everything about him is known - as is shown for instance by the official censorship of letters and so on. In short, the detainee is constantly living under the weight of the eternal look of justice.

Consequently, the psychologist is often regarded as an extension of the all-seeing prison eye. And this even in the case where the demand for therapy or analysis comes from the prisoner himself. For this seems me to be a first requirement: subsequent to all that has already been forced on the prisoner, a therapy cannot be imposed. It is essential that demand for therapy or analysis explicitly comes from the prisoner himself. But it is also important for the prisoner to know that his demand for advice, for drugs, for medical certificates, for intercession by the prisoner's director, judge or lawyer, cannot be fulfilled. During the first sessions it will become clear whether the prisoner is really asking for analysis or therapy, or whether he merely wants to use the psychologist in his struggle with the system of the prison.

In my opinion, the therapeutic relationship can offer the prisoner an "elsewhere", meaning a place within the prison system that isn't bound to the system's rules. In order to fill in the emptiness of prison life, the detainee asks for such a place; it is the creation of a space between prison on one side and free life outside the walls on the other. It is a space between death, exemplified as the dead time of imprisonment, and life, meaning freedom outside the prison walls.

The Psychologist

The paradox mentioned above is also reflected in the specific function and position of the psychologist. The juridical system focusses on the truth of the fact, towards the confirmation of the act of the crime and the person who committed it. On the other hand, the psychologist or psycho-analyst focusses on the unconscious truth of the criminal. In my opinion, the psychologist's function is to break through the offender's silence about his act and to allow words to emerge by which the criminal act can be articulated within the whole of the life history. I am convinced that this process forms the base for a subject-integration, which is the necessary precondition for the later reintegration in society.

But the availability of the psychologist for the detainee often leads to the situation that the prison's administration sees the psychologist as being there in favor of the prisoner. Moreover, the prison's management merely expects the psychologist to help to back up the silence and quietness: as few suicides and strikes as possible. They just want the place to be quiet, only being interrupted by the noise of the bunches of keys and the resounding of the turnkey's orders in the never-ending corridors.

Whilst, any psychotherapeutic work within a prison must abide by strict rules and restrictions, nevertheless, the therapeutic relationship can create a meaningful place within the emptiness of the prison environment; a place where the unconscious truth that is hidden behind the act gets a chance to rise.

I will give two examples:

(1) A seventeen year old boy killed his girlfriend whom he wanted to see naked. After a difficult psychoanalysis of six years it became clear that this murder with a knife - a knife that his mother had given to him a few weeks before - was a repetition of a slap in the face that his naked father gave to his also naked mother, in the bedroom that he shared with his parents when he was four years old. While pretending to be asleep, he witnessed the entire scene. The criminal act of the boy was a reproduction of the original scenario, this time marked by the hand of law.

(2) After having murdered his three year old son, a 30 year old man is brought into prison. He tells his story, crying and shouting, interwoven by long periods of silence. His little boy had woken up, had started to cry and asked for his mother who wasn't home at the time. The man, thus being alone in the house with his son, was standing before the mirror with a gun in his hands. He was at the point of committing suicide. The man knew the fear of death from his very early childhood: to keep him quiet, his mother often held a pillow on his face, until the moment he fell unconscious.

These two examples make it possible to place the following statement by Jacques Lacan: "If psychoanalysis derealizes crime, it does not dehumanize the criminal" (1950, p. 129). For the psychoanalyst, it is not the reality of crime, nor the juridical truth about what happened that is most important, but rather the unconscious truth of the subject and the little piece of psychic reality that is hidden behind it. In contrast with the so-called humanism of the juridical system, psychoanalysis does not dehumanize. For the psychoanalyst, crime is a confession of the possible effects of the Oedipus complex on the speaking subject. This brings me to the question of guilt. Criminal justice starts from the principal sense of guilt of the human being; people dispose of enough intellectual capacities to know the law and to understand the implications of their acts. However, Freud has thrown a new light on the psychology of crime by proposing a broader view on guilt than the purely practical-juridical one. In the third essay of his article on *Some character-types met with in psychoanalytic work*, Freud establishes that some acts are performed during analysis merely through the fact that they are forbidden and because of their execution providing a certain relief (1916, p. 332). So, crime emanates from the feeling of guilt and is not the consequence of the act, as it is put within the juridical framework.

Where can the source of this obscure feeling of guilt be situated then? Freud states that conclusive psychoanalytical evidence exists of the fact that this feeling of guilt - the tension between the Super-Ego and the Ego that is submitted to it - proceeds from the Oedipus complex. Together with the decline of the Oedipus complex, the child incorporates the law. At the same time an unconscious feeling of guilt comes into being.

So the psychoanalytical interpretation withdraws criminal behavior from its apparently utilitarian or intellectual reality, to demonstrate its underlying unconscious truth. In spite of the difficult circumstances, it sometimes seems possible to let the criminal act be articulated within the whole of the subject's life history. This is not easy because the act, especially when it concerns a murder case, remains in an empty space that's beyond all words. Speaking about murder creates a trembling silence. It is the conclusion of the unimaginable character of the image of death. This in no way means that the fantasies surrounding the scene of death are the privilege of the criminal. Unceasingly they provoke the remembrance of what is primitively hidden in the one who listens.

Up till now, I have mentioned only individual therapy, but there is more than this one possibility to allow human beings who are locked up in jail a chance to let some subjectivity appear within the anonymous world of the prison.

Theater, for instance, can be a powerful instrument, because it is complete as well as paradoxical in relation to the prison world. We call it complete as it permits the individual to be himself; moreover it permits him to recover some subjectivity by working with his own self. It is paradoxical because theater implies being seen. In contrast to the uniformizing of the all-seeing prison's eye, the conscious look of the public demands the one that's on stage to be someone, demands him to show how he differs from all the rest.

Another example is the organization of a reading group. In this connection I would like to conclude with a short story of Nicole Zucca (1985), where, once more, we can see the importance of the creation of a place where desire - in the Freudian sense of the word - can circulate within the prison walls where precisely every desire is constantly being silenced. The story goes as follows:

Put him in jail! He has to be locked up! Since childhood, there is his failing in school ... just like his father and mother. School refuses him, he rejects school and criminality takes its start.
They nearly all say: 'Oh! Me and school, they never went together'. The failure at school is permanently under discussion. And afterwards: the forced labour. They learn to read and write: ten years of obligatory attending school; and at sixteen, nothing appears. They laze about parks, these modern convicts of boredom, of dejection, of tricks. [...]

Ten years later, I recognize them in the arrest house - 'fallen' - and they enroll for the reading group. Voluntary candidates; taken in by friends. 'Yes, now the interesting texts', they say. First I think 'everything is better than being in a cell packed together with three or four, waiting for time to pass by'. And they start to read and discuss. They can't get enough of it. The bell always rings much to early: after three hours they ask for more. More meaning.

They want to understand, they want to hear things being read, they read out loud with high voice, they debate and return to the text all by themselves. With them, I rediscover the power of reading: the mockery of Jacques Sternberg, the initiating dream of Castaneda, the deliria of Maupassant, the silent strength of Freud.

Their level? Without any doubt, there's no improvement when we measure in terms of school. They are not university boys, not even the lazy and bad pupils of Prévert. But also no longer the loafers of the suburbs. Now they are amateurs of signs.

They are now subjects, appealed to within the blankness that prison represents, where the absence of autonomy is law, where the point is to forget that one can live outside the walls when one wants to survive, and where they now have obtained the statute of readers. In the provisional hiding-place of those few hours of studying, they are taken by the desire to be confronted with the word of someone else, the writer, the one who does not speak in order to say nothing. (p. 50).

References

Freud, S. (1916). Some character-types met with in psychoanalytic word. *Standard Edition 14*, 309-333.
Lacan, J. (1950). Introduction théorique aux fonctions de la psychanalyse en criminologie. In *Ecrits* (pp. 125-149). Paris: du Seuil.
Zucca, N. (1985). Les anciens cancres "Dix ans après...". *l'Ane*, *21*, 50.

The Psychiatric and Psychological Services Within the Norwegian Prison Health Service

Brit Weisath

The main purpose of this paper is to give a general overview of the Norwegian Prison Health Reform, with special emphasis on organization of the psychiatric service, of which the psychological service is an integral part.

The Norwegian Prison System

Norway is one and a half times as large as Great Britain, but has a population of only 4.2 million. The settlements are more scattered than in other European countries. Politically, Norway, like the other Scandinavian countries, is based on social democratic ideology and these societies are remarkably stable in political and social structure.

Norway has seen a significant increase in criminal behaviour, but still criminal activity is low compared to other Western societies, particularly when it comes to serious violent crimes. The prison population is small and the average duration of prison sentence served is also among the shortest in the world. The number of new imprisonments in penal institutions in 1991 was about 11,500, 5% of which were women. The average stay in prison was 79 days. The daily average number of inmates was 2,500 and of these 300 were foreigners. Five hundred were persons remanded in custody. Only 5% of the sentences served in 1991 were one year or more. Norway does not have life sentences.

There are 44 prisons in Norway: five central prisons and 39 local prisons. The prisons vary considerably not only in size, but also in the standards of the facilities provided. Many of the local prisons are more than a hundred years old. The largest prison has a capacity of 366 inmates and the smallest a capacity of nine inmates. The average prison accommodates between 20 and 40 inmates. Generally one differentiates between closed and open prisons. In an open prison there are no special security measures to prevent escape. Thirty percent are open prisons.

To challenge the drug problem within prisons, Prison Authorities have lately tried out a new prison model. This regime gives inmates the option to sign a contract stating willingness to refrain from using illegal drugs. In return they are offered better prison conditions and rehabilitation programs, e.g. more provisional leaves, physical activities, sport, mountain bikes etc. Abstinence is checked frequently by urine sampling. Some prisons are especially designed for these inmates, other prisons may have separate wings for prisoners on "contract". If an inmate breaks the contract and uses drugs, he is immediately returned to a regular prison.

The Reformed Prison Health Service in Norway

In 1980 an important political decision was made that the prison health service should be integrated in the ordinary public health service and be strengthened in quantity and quality.

The Prison Health System in Norway is at present undergoing great changes. The responsibility for health care of prisoners was transferred from the Ministry of Justice to the Ministry of Health and Social Affairs in 1988, with the main objective being to ensure that inmates would receive the same service as the general population. Prison health care is now an integrated part of the ordinary public health service, run by the municipal and the county health administration. This is based on local negotiations conducted by the Chief Medical Officer in the county, who is responsible for supervising the health services and the health workers in the county, as well as being an adviser to both local and central authorities.

All expenses are covered by the state when it comes to primary health care. For psychiatry and dental care the county receives earmarked financial support from the state. The Directorate of Health has published a booklet with professional guidelines in this field.

Health professionals and health authorities are very concerned about avoiding the conflicting and diverging dual role of treatment and control. For example, The Prison Act regulates the opportunity for intimate body searches for illegal drugs. Intimate body search is no longer executed by personnel working in the prison health service, but by health personnel working outside the prison. The Directorate of Health is very much concerned that the prison health service should no longer provide health guarantees to inmates subject to solitary confinement. Likewise for ethical reasons, doctors in the prison health service no longer give advice to the prison authorities regarding whether the inmate can stand the mental strain of solitary confinement as a custodial punishment. The prison health service examines inmates in these cases only after this has been asked for by the inmate or personnel working in the prison.

The standards of health care are much higher in central prisons than in small local prisons. The larger prisons have full-time community health service teams of doctors, nurses, physiotherapists and psychologists. The smaller institutions have a part-time medical doctor and nurses. Only one prison has a ward for somatic patients (ten beds) with full-time nursing staff.

Inmates will, if necessary, be escorted out of penal institutions to relevant services, such as inpatient or outpatient hospital visits. Sentences may also be served in general hospitals. There are also regulations and procedures for release of prisoners on health reasons.

According to the reports last year from the Chief County Medical Officers, there has been a marked improvement in the quality and quantity of care in the prison health service. They also state that the reform has given health personnel a more independent position in relation to prison administration and security staff. The budget has increased by three-and-a-half times during the last four years.

The Organization of Psychiatric Care within the Norwegian Prison Health Service

In Norway it is contrary to legislation and our sense of justice that psychotic patients should stay in prisons. The psychiatric health service has a duty to examine and provide necessary treatment for psychotic patients outside the prison. According the to the Mental Health Act, the health administration in each county has the responsibility for giving mental care to the population in its area. This includes hospital and outpatient care. The same administration also has the responsibility for organizing psychiatric services to inmates in prisons. In order to strengthen the psychiatric service for prisoners in future, the government has offered some financial support to the counties, particularly to improve the outpatient services. Emergency services and outpatient treatment are to be provided by the county where the prison is located. Admission to psychiatric institutions, however, shall take place in the county of the prisoners residence. The administration of the psychiatric care for inmates does not differ from those generally applied in society.

In the Oslo Region we have special problems, because there is an over-representation of long-term prisoners who have an increased incidence of psychiatric disorders. For this purpose a special psychiatric observation unit for six prisoners was set up at Dikemark Hospital in Oslo four years ago. An additional unit with eight beds for long stay patients will be set up at the end of the year.

Inmates in general may be transferred to various treatment institutions outside the penal system to serve their sentence or part of it. The criteria for transfer are that they need treatment and that the institution is willing to receive them. There has been an increasing use of this facility over recent years.

One of the main problems for the prison system is to secure satisfactory conditions for prisoners with severe personality disorders who can be dangerous or difficult, but who do not fulfil the criteria of severe mental illness, i.e. psychotic disorder, as defined in the Mental Health Act. Most of them serve long sentences and/or detention orders for serious crimes. This group has considerable adaptational problems that can often be aggravated in prison.

The disturbances and tensions created in the prisons by these inmates produce severe problems of stress for the other inmates and the staff. At times their explosive reactions lead to severe conflicts, such as verbal threats and direct physical violence. The conflicts can become so severe that it may be necessary to isolate the individual from the other prisoners for long periods.

A committee whose mandate was to study measures that could improve the psychiatric services for these inmates proposed that, for this particular group of male and female prisoners, a special institution should be established within the prison system. The therapeutic setting should be run on sociotherapeutic principles. The Ministry of Justice should have the administration and the responsibility for the institution. Health personnel from the general and specialist health service in the community should be engaged on a consultancy basis. The Government has now decided to build a special prison for 30 inmates with serious personality disorders.

The Psychological Service in the Prison System

Today the profession of psychology has a strong position in Norwegian health care. A psychologist trains for six years at University, followed by a further five years clinical training. Most psychologists work in the public health service. In psychiatric care, the psychologist and psychiatrist work in a team on equal terms in the clinical setting - if not in the administrative. Before the prison health reform, only four psychologists were engaged in prison health services. Now, psychologists are engaged in more or less all prisons, either through primary health care teams in the larger prisons or through psychiatric teams visiting the prison.

Psychiatric care has greatly improved after the prison health reform but there is still a long way to go before the inmates get the necessary psychological and psychiatric help they are entitled to.

Part IX

European Perspectives on Law and Psychology

Psychological Testing and Police Recruit Selection: Difficulties and Dilemmas

Peter B. Ainsworth

There is no doubt that the British Police Service has undergone a number of significant changes in recent years. The demands of an increasingly complex society have forced the police service to re-examine many of its assumptions and tactics. Although many changes in styles of management have been tried (see Butler, 1992), change at the lower end of the organisation has also been considered. Indeed, reports such as those of Lord Scarman (1981) advocated major changes in recruitment and training. Changes in recruitment strategies whilst commendable, may not show immediate benefits for two important reasons:-

1. The effects will be long term - it will take a considerable number of years before the new recruits are really in a position to influence the organisation.

2. Recruits will quickly become socialised into the organisational culture and may have to abandon new ideas in favour of established organisational procedures.

Despite these difficulties, it is worth considering the notion of bringing in the sort of person who may have a positive influence on the organisation. We may, however, hit a further problem, i.e., is the sort of person who can introduce positive change to the organisation, the same person who would make an ideal new recruit? For example, *conventionality* and *conformity* are desirable traits in the latter case but not in the former; *innovativeness*, the opposite.

Psychologists need first to know exactly what the police service wants in a new recruit. There are inevitably variations between British police forces, but there is some commonality. Up until recently, height was seen as one of the first filtering mechanisms. Good physical health and good eyesight were also considered obligatory. All forces now have minimum age and educational requirements, and will insist that the candidate does not have a criminal record. Relatively recently, all British recruits have been asked to take an intelligence test, which has a Home Office specified cut off line. There is an assumption here that a certain level of intelligence is an essential ingredient for a good police officer, though the evidence is not so compelling (see Burbeck & Furnham, 1985). Many studies have found that I.Q. tests are a good predictor of performance at Training School, but are a poor indicator of future performance on the streets (Taylor & Pease, 1988). Beyond some of these minimum requirements, the exact qualities required start to be a little vague.

It might be helpful if we could consider what current serving British police officers would list as desirable qualities. Listed below are a number of factors identified by a group of British police officers surveyed by the present author in 1991. (The group were students on an M.A. in Police Management.) They were asked to name the qualities which they felt were essential for the new recruit. The requirements are listed in order of priority: (1) a sense of humour; (2) communication skills; (3) adaptability; (4) common sense; (5) resilience; (6) assertiveness; (7) sensitivity; (8) tolerance; (9) integrity; (10) literacy; (11) honesty; (12) problem solving ability. Whilst some of these are measurable by current psychological tests (e.g. tolerance), others (e.g. a sense of humour) are not.

A further source of information which is helpful in understanding what the police might look for in a recruit is provided by police recruiting advertisements. The following are some representative examples from the British press:

Advert One
Ask any Policeman or Policewoman why they joined the force and you'll get the same answer. To get involved with people. To get involved with the community they patrol. He needs to be something of a social worker on the one hand, yet on the other, he is invested with the authority of the law. (*Sunday Times*, 31.3.82, "Brothers in Arms").

Advert Two
Whether you're a man or a woman you'll have to be responsible, decisive, occasionally courageous. You'll need plenty of common sense, and a sense of humour too. ... We'll help you develop self confidence to deal with even the trickiest situation. (*Sunday Times*, 8.2.81, "Could you provide the service the public demands from a Police Officer?").

Advert Three
Some people are practically born coppers ... born with the qualities every copper needs: like intelligence, commonsense and a real interest in people. ... We need people who genuinely want to help other people. It's what the job is all about. ... We hope you will acquire a balanced outlook on life. That's absolutely essential. ... You will have to learn to keep cool and always be impartial. There is no place in the police service for extremists. ... They must be capable of making decisions ... and taking the responsibility for those decisions. ... What we're looking for in fact is raw material and lots of enthusiasm ... (*Sunday Times*, 10.11.80; "Are good coppers born or made").

These adverts were geared towards the "ordinary recruit". Graduate entrants are portrayed as needing somewhat different qualities.

Advert Four
We're looking for exactly the same combination of management qualities as any large industrial or commercial concern: clarity of analytic thought combined with initiative and personal discipline; motivation combined with the ability to motivate; sensitivity with the ability to deal with people firmly but fairly; ability to command combined with the ability to execute somebody else's commands. (*Sunday Times*, 20.10.85).

These adverts appear to suggest that the police force needs "the right sort of person" but there is some confusion over what exactly this person looks like. The most important criteria seem to be a sense of humour, and an interest in people.

But can psychological testing help? Psychological tests have developed rapidly in recent years and are now quite refined and sophisticated instruments. There are hundreds of different tests available. Tests can *provide information* and should be able to *inform decision making*. In the case of recruitment the results of a test should tell us whether someone is: (a) appointable, or, (b) not appointable. (In reality there is a large grey area between these two categories, and it may be more realistic to talk about a degree of appointability.) But we may well wish to know more than this. Someone may well be "appointable" but may not prove to be a very good police officer. In the USA, screening out undesirable applicants seems to take priority, with forces concerned that they may be sued if an inappropriate officer is appointed.

Whether or not someone is considered suitable can be determined by a test score which *should* predict future performance. We may still have problems here though. As some previous authors have pointed out (Taylor & Pease, 1988) in times of high recruitment the criteria may be lowered, whereas at times of low recruitment, we can literally be more selective and raise our decision point.

Psychological tests are useful in deciding whether or not a person possesses certain qualities or attributes. As we've already seen, the problem is often in deciding which qualities should be tested for. The next task is to test usefulness considering *criterion referenced validation*: i.e. do scores on a psychological test correlate with some measurement of job performance (e.g. promotion)? If so, then the test is said to have high validity.

Psychological testing is an attempt to be objective rather than subjective (which the recruitment interview inevitably is). Providing it is easy to select and measure the attributes required, the psychological tests might be useful. However the problem arises in selecting which attributes are important. Should we use qualities associated with "a good copper" which peers would use (a copper's copper) - or do we use qualities defined by senior officers, or by the Home Office, the Police Authority, or the general public? The point is that there may well be differences in what each see as the important criteria, and thus what we should be measuring. Can we really assume that the most desirable characteristics for the raw recruit are the same as those for a senior officer? This point is nicely illustrated by the notion of *concurrent validity*. Here a psychologist might subject all experienced police officers to a battery of tests and correlate their scores with some measure of quality of performance. The items in the test battery which were correlated with good performance would then be used to screen applicants.

The theory here is that applicants who perform well on the tests in ways similar to good or successful police officers would be selected, and those that do not would be rejected. The problem with this approach is that it does not necessarily have *predictive* validity.

Test items that distinguish good and bad police officers *now* may be different from those that distinguish between people *who are likely to* ***become*** good officers - i.e those that can change and adapt most easily. In fact many of the skills of a "good police officer" may be those that have been produced during training, rather than those which the person has always possessed.

Perhaps a better approach would be to give a range of tests to all applicants to the police service (Taylor & Pease, 1988). Some years later, *all* the police officers should be assessed and divided into those who have been successful and those who have not. Their test scores obtained some years earlier could then be checked and cross referenced, to see which were predictive of future good performance. This could also prove useful in terms of identifying what factors were linked with wastage from the police service.

The advantage of this system is that it is a true predictive test and allows us to compare scores *at the time of recruitment* and correlate them with future success. We must recognise however that the requirements of the police service may well change over time, and so some re-testing may be required.

Predictive Tests are thus of great value, and far more suitable than Concurrent Validity Tests. Unfortunately a great deal of the literature on psychological testing and recruit selection has looked at tests of Concurrent Validity (see Taylor & Pease, 1988). These tests may have some use by deciding, for example, whether people with certain personalities are better suited to certain roles (e.g. firearms officers). They may also be useful in terms of optimal career development.

There are a large number of studies in the American literature which have looked at testing and recruit selection, though most of these will not be reviewed here. Burbeck & Furnham (1985) reviewing a large number of studies conclude:-

> The varying criteria of what constitutes a successful police officer results in different studies which are not comparable. More use needs to be made of job analysis so that the essential elements for success can be identified and used in the selection process. (p. 67).

In fact these authors are quite negative about the research on testing and recruit selection. In addition to the problems outlined above they make the following points: (1) socialization into the police role and police culture may be as important as personality variables (though I would want to argue that this may not apply equally to the person with a dominant personality); (2) comparison of studies across different forces in Britain, let alone in different countries may not be appropriate.

The requirements for a good police officer in Cumbria may be different from those in London. Similarly when we compare Manchester (UK) with Paris or Amsterdam. Detailed and specific *job analysis*, on a local basis, may well solve this problem.

The British Police Service chooses not to recruit specialists, nor different people for specific departments. And yet it is assumed that the person who is going to make a good dog handler, detective, or senior officer should all have the same qualities at the time of selection into the police service.

There is much use made of psychological testing in the USA. (Almost 70% of US forces use it according to Burbeck & Furnham (1985).) In Britain, the Home Office's view is that there is not at present a suitable psychological test available. Home Office Circular 17/1984 states "The introduction of psychological testing into the recruit selection procedure is not recommended".

Some recent British work (Labuc, 1991) has made claims for the use of the Labwick Personality Inventory. Labuc claims a 97% correlation between the results of the personality test and actual job performance. Labuc claims that any suitably qualified assessor can evaluate the present and future potential of an individual. Whilst very much in its infancy, this work appears interesting.

There is now increasing use of Assessment Centres in Britain. These can be used to measure the requisite qualities in a recruit, and to allow assessment in relevant situations. Skills such as decision making, communication, maturity etc. can be tested more easily in this situation. Assessment Centres are, however, expensive to run, and are often used only **after** other filtering mechanisms have been tried.

Conclusions

Psychological testing can help, providing the following are borne in mind. We need detailed job analysis in order to understand just what an officer is expected to be able to do, and what skills are needed for this. When this is established, the exact qualities needed can be assessed objectively. These can then be divided into those which: (a) are needed within the personality of the recruit; (b) can be acquired during training.

In the case of the former these can be measured objectively using standardised and valid tests. It may also be possible to tell at this early stage which particular branch of the service a person may be best suited to. This is already done to some extent with the Graduate Entry Scheme - based largely on education. But might this idea not be extended?

So is it possible to recruit people who will have a positive impact on the organization? It is possible, but difficult given the complexities of the police organization. As discussed earlier, someone who is genuinely innovative may well be feared and rejected - either at the recruiting stage or once within the organization. Someone with ideas and vision may also be viewed with suspicion - and attempts may be made to bring them "back into line".

By using instruments which have predictive ability, psychological tests can still inform decision making - provided the force can be clear on what is required. Once made clear, the psychologist can provide the tools to measure and assess whether or not a given person does possess these qualities. Again we do need a very clear definition of what we mean by "a good police officer". We need to decide whether we use promotion, staying out of trouble, or being well liked by colleagues or senior officers as the criterion. Only when these things are spelled out, can the psychologist truly help.

References

Burbeck, E. & Furnham, A. (1985). Police officer selection: A critical review of the literature. *Journal of Police Science and Administration*, *13*, 58-69.

Butler, A. J. P. (1992). *Police management* (2nd edition). Aldershot: Gower.

Labuc, S. (1991, September). Can future performance be predicted? *PRSU Bulletin*.

Taylor, M., & Pease, K. (1988). Psychological testing and police recruit selection. *Eurocriminology*, *2*, 57-72.

Scarman. (1981). *The Brixton disorders 10-12 April 1981: Report of an Enquiry by the Rt. Hon. Lord Scarman* (Cmnd. 8427). London: HMSO.

Psychological Issues in the Draft Polish Code of Criminal Procedure

Józef Wójcikiewicz

Introduction

The current Polish *Code of Criminal Procedure* was passed in 1969. No doubt, it needs replacing by a new, democratic, and modern one. The first attempts to improve the criminal law were made in 1981 during the so-called "Solidarity period". After ten years, in December 1991, the latest draft was produced. This paper deals with four psychological matters vital to criminal procedure: psychological examination of suspects and witnesses, polygraph examination, forensic hypnosis, and identification parade; with the goal of comparing the draft with the current Code, the law with practice, and in a very general fashion, Polish regulations with English ones.

Psychological Examination of the Suspect (The Accused)

According to Polish law the suspect or the accused is obliged to undergo psychological or psychiatric examinations. The obligation is treated as an exception to the privilege against self-incrimination (art. 73 par. 1 draft C.C.P.). However, this is a duty without any legal sanction and it is impossible to compel a suspect to obey this rule, which makes it quite different from taking fingerprints, for example. So, the regulation is rather questionable. The new article 198 par. 2, which bans the use of the statements made by the suspect during the psychological examination as evidence *against* him/her, may be regarded as legal protection for the suspect. This rule is also in favour of an expert witness who sometimes may be in a dilemma as to whether to quote in his opinion the suspect's words that might have indicated his guilt, or simply the suspect's confession.

There is another new rule with regard to the suspect's mental condition. Namely, the court or the prosecutor (depending on the stage of the process) on advice from two psychiatrists can call on yet some other expert witnesses from different branches of knowledge to evaluate the suspect's (the defendant's) mental state (art. 201 par. 2). Forensic psychologists come first here. It should not be overlooked that, in practice, they often participate in preparing such opinions even with the present law still in force.

Psychological Examination of the Witness

The draft introduces no changes in the field of psychological examination of witness, even though this matter requires modification. There is only one rule: the court or the prosecutor may order witness' interrogation in a psychologist's presence if any doubts exist as to the witness' mental state (illness or handicap) or the ability of perception and retrieval (art. 174 par. 3). Three main questions arising from this regulation need discussion.

(1) The possibility of ordering such an interrogation should be treated as obligatory. In other words, failure to call expert witness in the above mentioned situation may constitute a ground for appeal (the Supreme Court sentences: II KR 201/77; III KR 393/79; Rw 445/84).

(2) A psychologist obviously is not able to give a valid opinion without the psychological examination of the witness. Therefore usually a routine psychological examination is carried out, with the witness' consent, of course. However, in the current Code (and in the draft, too) there is no rule which could constitute the legal basis for such an examination. For this reason, it is even assumed that the examination of this kind is illegal! (Waltoś, 1985). As a matter of fact, one can interpret art. 174 par. 1 which deals with the *medical* examination of the witness, as the permission for a psychological test, but admittedly the opportunity for improving the law and legalizing the common practice has been missed so far.

(3) A very important issue is the extent of psychological evidence, especially the possibility of examining children and elderly people. For about 30 years the necessity of the psychologist's presence during interrogation of children has not been questioned. Unfortunately, we can recently observe an alarming restrictive approach of the Supreme Court to the expert's testimony. As an example, the case of court proceedings in which it was stated that the psychologist's participation cannot be treated as a principle, can be used (I KR 48/84). A similar judgement with regard to the interrogation of an 82 year old almost deaf woman suffering from sclerosis who was the victim of an attempted murder and arson can also be quoted here (IV KR 180/85).

In my opinion a forensic psychologist may and should be summoned not only when "doubts do exist" but also in those cases where children or elderly persons are involved, or in situations where the witness is only source of evidence. Moreover, the internal competence of an expert witness is a fundamental and crucial problem. No doubt, a psychologist is not competent to assess the veracity and reliability of the statements made (III KR 103/74). That lies in the province of the court. What he or she can and should do is the evaluation of the statements themselves and also in the context of the event, interrogation or identification parade (Wójcikiewicz, 1990b). In Poland a psychologist is often under pressure from the judge who would readily throw on him the burden of responsibility. Let us look into a sentence of the Supreme Court from 1988 (KRN 247/88): "Acknowledging the testimony of the 13 year old girl, K.J., which was evaluated as truthful and realiable by the expert witness, as the most important piece of evidence, the District Court found the accused guilty. However, according to the opinion of the gynaecologist, the incidences of sexual intercourse with her father that she claimed to have had, had not taken place". It would be difficult to find a better example of a trap which lies in wait for the expert and the court in this field.

Polygraph Examination

The polygraph examination has been in use in Poland since 1963. It has been used in several hundred cases. In some of them the examinations results in form of an expert opinion were accepted as evidence.

This has been more common since 1976 when the Supreme Court *expressis verbis* stated that such examinations were subsidiary and might be treated as indirect evidence requiring corroboration (II KR 171/76) (Widacki, 1982). However, the polygraph examination has not gained general acceptance within the scientific community. The main argument was that it "excludes freedom of statements".

Note that this legal term that was to mean more or less the same as "oppression" in the *English Police and Criminal Evidence Act, 1984*, in fact means everything and nothing. In consequence the testimony of a witness under the influence of a pint of beer should be excluded according to Polish law! In the draft Code the opponents of the polygraph scored a victory over its advocates. Art. 172 par.4 sec. b. bans the application of any chemical or technical means which could influence psychological processes of the interrogated person or would aim at monitoring the unconscious reactions the person under interrogation. The statements or testimony given in above conditions ought to be excluded as inadmissible (art. 176 par. 6). Moreover, all these methods are also forbidden during the examination carried out by an expert witness (art. 198 par. 1). The motives of the Commission for Criminal Law Reform are symptomatic. The arguments that affected this decision are as follows: humanistic resistance to intrusion into subconsciousness; the danger of taking over the court's prerogatives by the expert witness; unrealiability of the examination of a nervous, innocent suspect; and the negative attitude of Polish society, which still remembers the past, towards procedures even indirectly connected with the police! As one can see the emotional arguments have overpowered the scientific ones. I hope that the polygraph, excluded from the court's sphere, will be accepted as an investigative tool. It would be quite sufficient considering its questionable reliability (Kleinmuntz & Szucko, 1984; Gudjonsson, 1992).

Forensic Hypnosis

Forensic hypnosis has been used in Poland since at least 1984. It had been applied as an investigative method in over 30 cases. Nevertheless, in the Polish criminal process a hypnotist - always a qualified, independent psychologist - is rarely called upon as an expert witness. Recognizing hypnosis as a medical treatment, the Supreme Court in a sentence passed in 1987 (II KR 43/87) accepted a hypnotist in such a role and rightly stated that a previously hypnotized witness could testify in court. This case is well worth describing. A young boy was found on the kitchen floor, hit on the head and unconscious. His collection of contemporary coins was stolen. The victim was unconscious for three weeks, underwent brain surgery, and then suffered from anterograde amnesia. Hypnosis was applied for months after the crime. During the induction he recalled the name of the visitor whom he knew personally and described the other one whom he later recognized during the identification parade. The suspects confessed and then withdrew their confessions in turn. They were sentenced to 25 and 13 years in prison, respectively.

Let me mention two other cases.

(1) A mother had strangled her baby and then feigned burglary. She confessed only to the hypnotist.

(2) A drunken man confessed to the police that six years before he had murdered his neighbours. The next day, when he was sober, he withdrew the confession and stated that he had only wanted to be detained for 48 hours just to spite his parents who did not allow him to drink alcohol. Although there was no piece of evidence against the man, who remained in custody for six months and was released only after confirming his statements during the hypnotic induction.

In 1989 I carried out a field research into 29, (i.e. all known) Polish cases in which hypnosis had been applied. The aim of the research was to determine the effectiveness and usefulness of forensic hypnosis. The results were consistent with the experimental ones (Mingay, 1988; Erdelyi, 1989; Gudjonsson, 1992) and barely confirmed the validity of hypnosis as a method that enhances recall and recognition. Only in four investigated cases could such influence be conjectured.

However, it was found that hypnosis may also act in an unpredictable manner. The action consisted in either inducing the suspect or the witness to change his/her false statements by the hypnotic situation itself, which was external to and independent from the police interrogation, or confirming the veracity of the suspect's statements because of an unjustified belief by the police that hypnosis can replace polygraph as a lie detector (Wójcikiewicz, 1990a). Although it does not itself enhance memory and guarantee the truth of statements, a hypnotic situation can sometimes play a therapeutic role (Wójcikiewicz, 1990a; Gudjonsson, 1992). Needless to say, forensic hypnosis has been treated in Poland with even more distrust than the polygraph examination. As a result, the draft Code eliminates it from interrogation and expert witness opinion (art. 174 par. 2 sec. b and art. 198 par. 1). It is difficult to foresee the future of forensic hypnosis as an investigative tool but it seems that it will not be prosperous.

Identification Parade

In the *Code of Criminal Procedure* currently used in Poland the identification parade is only mentioned as one of the suspect's duties. He or she may be presented to some other people with the purpose of recognition, in adequately reconstructed conditions. These conditions are specified in the code of practice from 1976. In particular, the parade should consist of at least three persons of similar appearance (including the suspect). The draft Code promises some changes for the better in this matter. According to the new regulations (art. 173 par. 2 and 3) a person, who is also a witness, or a thing, may be presented for recognition. The parade ought to comprise at least four persons (including the suspect) and should be conducted in an impartial manner. I would not regard this rule as the best one but it is definitely a step in the right direction. To be sure, much also depends on the practice of the police. It is interesting to trace how the latter has been changing during the last 15 years. The results of my field research from 1977 revealed that out of 524 identification and photo parades carried out in cases of homicide, rape, robbery, and assault in Cracow only 14 photo parades and just one identification parade (3% *in total*) had been conducted and documented properly! (Wójcikiewicz, 1985). In 1992 a student of mine replicated this research investigating 197 parades in 98 cases (Zajâc, 1992). The number of persons presented and the means of recording (camera or video) were found to be the most vital differences between the recent and the former inquiry. It turned out that the percentage of parades with insufficient number of persons, (i.e. below three) decreased from 38 in 1977 to 18 in 1992 (chi= 23.889, df=1, $p < 0.001$). The number of the parades registered only by means of a written report (unfortunately there is no obligation to use photos or video recordings) also decreased from 88% to 82% (chi= 5.146, df=1, $p < 0.05$). Evidently, there are significant changes for the better as far as practice is concerned, nevertheless there is still room for improvement.

Conclusions

The draft *Code of Criminal Procedure* brings important changes in connection with psychological in criminal cases. The exclusion of the polygraph examination and forensic hypnosis from the court's sphere, although ideologically motivated, may in fact be a sign of some helplessness of the law in regard to sophisticated, scientific methods and their questionable reliability; a sign that the principle of free appraisal of evidence faces a crisis. The exclusion of these procedures also affects the right of defence.

These topics, however, go far beyond the scope of this paper. Comparing Polish regulations with the English ones it can be observed that they become more and more similar in the field of the psychological examinations of suspects and witnesses. This is due, on the one hand, to the restrictive approach of the Supreme Court in Poland and, on the other the permissiveness of English courts, which can be illustrated by cases such as *Regina v. Raghip* (Davies, 1984; Gudjonsson, 1992). If the red light is kept on against polygraph and forensic hypnosis in England (Gudjonsson, 1983; Haward, 1988) the uniformity will increase even further, provided that the Polish draft discussed here is put into force in the present form. No doubt, eyewitness identification in Poland still needs improvement. The model provided in the English *Code of Practice for the Identification of Persons by Police Officers* is literally twice as good as the proposal put forward in the Polish draft, as far as the requirement for the size of identification parades is concerned.

References

Davies, G. M. (1984). The legal impact of psychological research on eyewitness testimony: British and American experiences. *Journal of the Forensic Science Society, 24*, 165-175.

Erdelyi, M. H. (1988). Hypermnesia: The effect of hypnosis, fantasy, and concentration. In H. M. Pettinati (Ed.), *Hypnosis and memory* (pp. 64-94). New York: The Guilford Press.

Gudjonsson, G. H. (1983). Lie detection: Techniques and countermeasures. In S. M. A. Lloyd-Bostock & B. R. Clifford (Eds.), *Evaluating witness evidence: Recent psychological research and new perspectives* (pp. 137-155). Chichester: John Wiley & Sons.

Gudjonsson, G. H. (1992). *The psychology of interrogations, confessions and testimony*. Chichester: John Wiley & Sons.

Haward, L. R. C. (1988). Hypnosis in forensic practice. In M. Heap (Ed.), *Hypnosis: Current clinical, experimental and forensic practices* (pp. 357-368). London: Croom Helm.

Kleinmuntz, B., & Szucko, J. J. (1984). A field study of the fallibility of polygraphic lie detection. *Nature 308*, 449-450.

Mingay, D. (1988). Hypnosis and eye-witness testimony. In M. Heap (Ed.), *Hypnosis: Current clinical, experimental and forensic practices* (pp. 380-394). London: Croom Helm.

Waltoś, S. (1985). *Proces karny. Zarys systemu*. Warszawa: PWN.

Widacki, J. (1982). *Analiza przesûanek diagnozowania w badaniach poligraficznych*. Katowice: Uniwersytet Slâski.

Wójcikiewicz, J. (1985). *Okazanie.Studium porównawcze z pogranicza kryminalistyki i procesu karnego*. Kraków: Uniwersytet Jagielloński.

Wójcikiewicz, J. (1990a). *Forensic hypnosis: Legal and practical problems*. Paper presented at the 5th European Congress of Hypnosis in Psychotherapy and Psychosomatic Medicine, Konstanz.

Wójcikiewicz, J. (1990b). Rzeczoznawcza ocena zeznan swiadków - aspekty prawne. In M. Grcar (Ed.), *Wspólczesna sadowa ekspertyza psychologiczna - nie wykorzystane mozliwosci* (pp. 64 - 68). Kraków: Instytut Ekspertyz Sadowych.

Zajac R. (1992). *Okazanie osób. Wybrane zagadnienia kryminalistyczne i procesowe*. Unpublished master's thesis, Uniwersytet Jagielloński.

Judicial Psychology in Spain: Actuation and Limits of Intervention

Vicente J. Ibáñez-Valverde and Pilar de Luis-Cabarga

I. Judicial Psychology

Judicial psychology, also called legal psychology, is the general concern of this meeting and, as the structure of the areas reflect, involves quite a few different specialities, such as prison psychology, criminology, victimology, the selection, training and behaviour of the police, etc. Moreover, forensic psychology (or judicial psychology, as we prefer to call it) appears as a clearly distinguishable sub-speciality.

Both names can be considered synonymous to a great extent, because the etymological origin of the term "forensic" refers to the place where any kind of justice is administered; but as such an expression seems to have suffered a historical association with criminal justice, at least in Spain, the reference to judicial psychology seems to be more consistent with the application of a psychologist's professional skills, as an expert in all the jurisdictional orders, and this is the idea we try to convey.

II. Judicial Organization in Spain

Probably the best way to begin to explain the situation of Spanish judicial psychology is to briefly outline the judicial system itself, regulated by the Organic Law 6/1.985, of the Judiciary (*Power*). By virtue of this law, there are now the Offices of Justice of the Peace (*Juzgados de Paz*), which only exist in town councils where there are neither Courts of First Instance nor Trial Courts (see hereinafter) and which are attended by no professional judges competent in questions of very limited importance within civil and penal fields.

The next fundamental level in the organization of the administration of justice, are the bodies attended by professional judges or magistrates, which process the majority of cases, at least in the first phase; Article 26 from the aforementioned Judiciary Organic Law (LOPJ), created the Courts of First Instance and Trial Courts (*Primera Instancia e Instruccion*), with competence in civil and penal matters, although in many main towns these competences are separated. As a result courts exclusively related to each jurisdictional order exist and, moreover, some which belong to the Courts of First Instance are specially and exclusively related to knowledge of family law trials. Juvenile Courts also exist for proceedings by the Delinquent Acts Commission against teenagers under the age of 16. Social Courts are competent in labor law matters. Penitentiary Vigilance Courts are in charge of the supervision of prisoners' treatment courses. The courts relating to actions under administrative law (*Contencioso Administrativo*), do not exist yet, but are expected. Meanwhile, a different kind of court has been created: the Penal Courts, trying the misdemeanors which before were drawn up and tried in Trial Courts. This new kind of court has appeared as a result of the consideration of unconstitutionality of the fact that the same judge draws up and tries a certain fact, both activities being completely separated at the moment.

At the next level of the administration of justice, we come to the Tribunals or Qualified Bodies where we run into the Provincial Courts, with competence in civil matters to hear the appeals against Family and First Instance Courts decisions; and in penal matters to hear the appeals against Penal and Juvenile Courts decisions, and in addition to try cases of offences which have been drawn up in the Trial (or Instruction) Courts. With a competence which spreads over the territory of autonomous communities, there are Superior Justice Courts, which usually hear contentious-administrative and labour questions, and exceptionally the penal and/or civil cases. There is a body whose territorial competence spreads over all the state: the Audiencia Nacional (*National Court*), which is competent in administrative-contentious and criminal matters, trying facts of special importance for their meaning or for having been committed in a field superior to an autonomus community, as for example crimes against public health, monetary or terrorism offences. And finally, the superior body of justice within Spain is the Supreme Court, which hears cases from jurisdiction, but only at the level of Cassation and Review Appeal Proceedings.

III. Topics of Intervention in Judicial Psychology

Once we have expounded the different specialities or levels of the administration of justice, we could say that possible applications to them from psychological knowledge has already been formulated in Spain by Muñoz Sabaté (1980), in accordance with the juridical ordinance at that time in force. However, our intention here is to make an analysis which allows comparison between Spanish and other different structures. The formulation upon which we base ourselves is that of M. T. Nietzel and R. C. Dillehay (1986), since it is not only applicable to juridical systems based on Anglo-Saxon law but, with little variations we will point out through its development, is equally valuable for the Spanish and Continental system.

Nietzel and Dillehay set up a triple differentiation between penal, civil and domestic law. In the first of the fields, the psychologist can be requested as an expert to assess questions such as criminal responsibility in cases of mentally disordered defendants (which appear in the Spanish juridical order as the evaluation of the defendant's "imputability", in other words as his competence to be responsible for his acts); and assessment of the ability or competence of an individual to stand trial. Another area is witness and witnesses' identification, perfectly transferable from one to the other system. However, evaluation by psychologists of the appropriateness of different types of proceedings is not applicable in Spain, since this depends not on personal circumstances, but on the kind of the crime allegedly commited. Nor is there a place for the additional intervention of the psychologist as adviser on the efficiency of the different kinds of punishment, during the sentencing phase, after jury's veredict of guilty, since in Spain there is not (at least up to the present time) the institution of the jury. The judge or court decides, by taking only one decision, the innocence or guilt and - consequently - the appropiate sentence.

In the civil jurisdiction the possibility of intervention arises where the psychologist assesses the ability of an individual to take certain decisions. The role is practically the same in both since Guardianship and Conservatorship (*Tutela e Incapacitacion*) are involved. The Civil Commitment Procedure for admitting a mental patient to a suitable establishment, if the situation seems advisable, is also very similar. The conduct in the case of trading claims are similar, as much for negligence in the presentation of products as for trademark litigation, and within them the psychologist's conduct as an expert. The system of civil or labour claims for psychological effects of accidents or labour situations are also very similar, although they are not still usual. The psychologists' intervention in such cases is correspondingly unused.

In the Anglo-Saxon system, as in the Spanish one, domestic law (family law) is civil law, but due to its particular importance and specificity, it is considered separately by jurists as by judicial psychologists. Psychologists focus on the possibility of intervention in adoption proceedings and deprivation of parents' rights, which in Spain are generically called "Patria Potestas". Parents' rights have been radically changed by the recent Law 21/87 of Adoption and Familiar Guardianship (Care Orders), which set up very detailed new rules of intervention. The other traditionally mentioned area in domestic law matters is the award of custody of children in separation, annulment and divorce cases. In both systems this is decided under the traditional maxim of the search of the "child's best interest", necessitating assessment of the psychological factors and the likely consequences of these factors in the family. In these fields Spanish judicial psychology is particularly developed. We pay special attention to Spanish family law in a subsequent section.

A basic feature of judicial psychology in Spain is the direct attachment of advisers to the courts or jurisdictional bodies. A psychologist belongs to the staff of some judicial bodies as a permanent assistant to the judge. First in 1983, and as a direct consequence of the creation of the Family Courts and the modification of the Civil Code (Law 30/81, July 7th), by which the legal possibility was introduced, the psychologist appeared as a permanent member of the Family Courts' staff. Later, between 1986 and 1989 six posts were created for psychologists for six other clinics of medical-forensic specialities which, although not a direct part of the staff in a specific court, have also the function of regularly advising the judges in a geographical area. Between 1988 and 1989, as some of the old Minor Tutelar Tribunals (TTM) were converted into Juvenile Courts proper, a psychologist appeared in the permanent staff of these courts (Ibáñez, & de Luis, 1984, 1987, 1990; Albarrán, 1990). Finally, in 1991, a new way of providing permanent advice from the psychologist to the judge was created when a post with this function was given to one of the Courts of Penitentiary Vigilance in Madrid.

IV. Family Law in Spain

As pointed out in the previous paragraph, family law was changed in Spain in 1981 by a law (30/1981) which, besides introducing the possibility of divorce (which hadn't existed since the Second Republic), reorganized another series of points concerning family relationships. This has created a situation which, generally speaking, is at the present moment quite similar to most of the occidental ones (e.g. British: see Pace, 1986). In both countries there exists the civil annulment of the marriage, separation and divorce. In Spain the judicial separation of married couples can be reached by agreement (Art. 81 Civil Code) or, in case of disagreement, by the existence of a series of causes (Art. 82 C.C.). However, for divorce an objective cause is required (Art. 86 C.C.). In any case, annulment, separation or divorce have consequences among which is the award of custody and care of children, and the establishment of the visitation system for the non-custodial parent. The law itself sets up a series of general criteria, some of which are to look for the children's "best interest", try to avoid brothers' separation, etc. In this same context appears (Art. 92 C.C.) the first specific reference to the judge being able to ask for the specialists' opinion, on his own or at the instance of the parties.

Later, a law was promulgated on 11th November 1987 (L.nr. 21/87), which changed some articles of the Civil Code and Civil Procedure Law on Adoption. Under this rule all matters related to the minors' protection were fundamentally reorganized, and a series of new juridical figures introduced - for example Family Guardianship or Automatic Care Orders. In addition competences were changed so that the first stage of minor protection is given to the civil administration, taking that competence out of the old Juvenile Courts (TTM) and giving the judicial competence in this subject to the ordinary civil jurisdiction, so that (where they exist) the courts specializing in family law are responsible for its application. This means, if we remember that the psychologist started to act as a permanent adviser for the judge in such courts, that this law gave rise to the extention of the number and kind of requested interventions. Finally, even in it's study and evaluation period, in some places the possibility of re-arrangement of justice administration is arising, by extending the competences of Family Courts to make them also responsible for the questions of Judicial Commitments, Civil Disability (Conservatorship).., and that will logically extend even more the requests from judges for professional intervention by psychologists.

V. Psychology in the Family Law Courts

The most usual proceedings in a Family Law Court are matrimonial separations, divorce, annulments, custody decisions in non-married couples, etc. The intervention of the psychologist, and eventually of the social worker, which constitute the technical staff of the court, can now be requested in any of those proceedings, for solving the most usual problems and for clarifying any specific point. We therefore present next a classification (already drawn up in former papers (e.g. Ibáñez & de Luis, 1990)), of the different kind of cases in which the intervention of the psychologist is usually requested:

(1) assessment of "psychological" causes for the civil annulment of the marriage (Art. 73 of the Civil Code);

(2) assessment in the cases of permission for marriage between legally under-aged persons;

(3) "Patria Potestas" (parental rights) exclusions;

and the most usual

(4) questions upon custody and care and control (Art. 92 C.C) which are the principal body of activity, distinguishing:
- (a) first award of custody (etc.);
- (b) custody changes;
- (c) assessment of the psychological influence of changes in the parental context (father/mother);
- (d) technical follow-ups and intervention programs (indication upon the need of any modification or, even, changes of custody, always related to the Public Attorney) designs and technical supervision of the visitation programs;
- (e) adoptions - psychological assessment of the persons involved in this kind of proceedings, as laid down in the aforementioned Law 21/87.

The "psychologisation" model of family justice that the former classification involves has, as far as we know, similarities and differences with the British system, in which the courts that administer family law also use qualified advisers who, according to Bromley and Lowe (1987) can be probation officers, even though an increasing tendency can be observed to having specialized staff, solely ascribed to the Divorce Courts, with the denomination of welfare officers, whose responsibility consists, in a very similar way to the Spanish one, in the assessment of the family group circumstances. In both systems, the adviser is a Court Officer, and as such has a role to play absolutely independent of the parties and, even, from the children. Nevertheless the difference that seems to exist is that, while in Spain this kind of activity is basically taken on by the psychologist, although he/she can do it in collaboration with the social worker, the British system seems to be mostly aimed at merely contextual investigation and, consequently, falls in a certain way on the social worker. Probably the main difference is that in Spain the professional is not exclusively responsible for the assessment of the children's custody attribution, but also has other competences which require a high psychological qualification.

We consider that the Spanish model has many advantages. The specialisation criteria requested for this kind of intervention are satisfied (Brodsky & Robey, 1972; Garrido Genoves, 1991). Experts, in addition to needing an important qualification in their profession, have to know very well the legal framework, the structure of the institution they work for, be open to collaboration with other professionals, etc. So, the fact that the professionals undertaking such functions have reached these posts by a series of examinations in which they are assessed not only for their technical qualifications, but also for their knowledge of the laws applicable (both general and specifically) in the courts where they will work, produces a system that best guarantees the technical qualification needed for such a delicate mission. It also allows the role-taken independence (Bromley & Lowe, 1987) that has also been repeatedly praised by Spanish authors (e.g. Coy, 1985), in contrast with the model of the expert as one who advises the courts in particular cases at the parties' instance.

VI. Intervention Limits of the Judicial Psychology in Spain

The reports of judicial psychologists in Spain may or may not contain a specific recommendation concerning the object of their assessment. In the British case, it seems that nearly 70% of such reports do contain a recommendation (Eekelaar et al., 1977). In Spain we don't have actual data, but the presence or absence of a recommendation depends on the specific guidelines given by the judge (or court) for whom the report is intended. In fact, it is possible that the reason why some judges seem to be adverse to the reports containing a specific recommendation could be related, at least indirectly, to the criticism that some lawyers began to formulate (see *El Mundo* Journal, Madrid 21/X/1990, pp. 16-17), or members of some divorced peoples' "Associations", which think that some judges "delegate" their decision, and consider that the reports, in practice, bind upon the court.

It is clear, in most systems of family justice administration, that the reports do not, and cannot, formally bind upon the judges. Nevertheless, Bromley and Lowe (op.cit., p. 321) clearly settle that in the British case.:

> ... it says a lot about the general esteem in which the 'welfare service' is held that it is established that where a court departs from the welfare officer's recommendation, it should state the reasons for so doing; in practice the welfare officer's view commands great respect and it should be appreciated that in most cases he is the most influential figure in the decision-making process.

In Spain it seems to be also an accepted phenomenon that judges closely follow the opinions or recommendations of the advisers; and if the general acceptance level Bromley and Lowe mentioned is still not reached, the reasons could lie in the still short history of the system we have described, and with the poor knowledge of the expert's role. Full assessment of the personal and contextual conditions of those involved in this kind of proceedings tend to contradict common presumptions, such as for example that small children are always better looked after by their mothers. The judicial psychologist, as V.Garrido Genoves (op.cit.) says, can make his intervention, sometimes, uncomfortable to certain opinions.

One can say, in any case, that the Spanish judicial model has several procedural guarantees for the persons involved within the intervention of the court advisers. In fact, the psychologist (as well as any other expert) is under a legal obligation to orally "ratify", before the judge, the contents of his written report, to satisfy Article 627 of the Civil Procedure Law (L.E.C.); and during this act the parties or their representatives can ask the Judge to request explanations in a similar manner to the process whereby under the British Judicial System, the parties and their advisers should have notice of the "Welfare Report", and the court can order the person responsible to attend the hearing and, during it, test him in the usual way such as by cross examination (Bromley & Lowe, op.cit.). The same situation applies in Spain for all psychologists attending cases, whether under the family law jurisdiction, or another jurisdiction.

Finally, the criticisms we have mentioned in relation to the psychologists' reports in the Family Courts in Spain, may be merely anecdotal. The general tendency of appraisal of them is positive. This opinion is supported by the absence of detected violations (at least significant ones) against the principles of the professional ethics, in almost ten years of their history. Both the Spanish "*Deontological Code for Psychologists*" (lst. Edition, 1987) and, before this was published, the "*Ethical*

Principles of Psychologists" (A.P.A., 1981; E. P. Revised, 1990), establish clear restrictions with regard to the psychologists' methods, the contents and publicity of the reports, and the limits of their behaviour. Moreover we can state that in all the records investigated until 1991 by the Deontological Committee of the Official Board of the Psychologists in Madrid, only two concerned psychological reports for the courts. Just one of them was made by a member of the official staff of the justice administration; and no infringement of the principles by the psychologist was found.

References

Albarran Olivera, A. J. (1990). Futuro de la psicología forense. In *Comunicaciones del iI Congreso del C.O.P.* (Area 9). Valencia.

Britain: An Official Handbook (1991). *Ordenamiento jurídico y sistema judicial en el Reino Unido.* Crown Copyright no. 179/9O/Sp.

Brodsky, S. L., & Robey, A. (1972). On becoming an expert witness: Issues of orientation and effectiveness. *Professional Psychology, 3*, 173-176.

Bromley, P. M. & Lowe (1987). *Bromley's family law* (7th ed.). London: Butterworth.

Coy, A. (1985, November). *Algunas consideraciones al trabajo de los psicologos en los juzgados de familia.* IIIer. Congreso Nacional de la AETCO, Gijon.

Eekelaar, J. Clive, G., Clarke, K., & Raike, S. (1977). *Custody after divorce.* Oxford: Centre for Socio-Legal Studies.

Garrido Genovés, V. (1991). Psicología jurídica en España: Lineas fundamentales de intervencion. *Papeles del Psicólogo, II epoca*, nro. 48.

Ibañez-Valverde, V. J. (1984). La función del psicólogo en los juzgados de familia. *Papeles del psicólogo, Vol. III*, nros. 16-17.

Ibañez-Valverde, V. J, & de LUIS, P. (1990). Los peritajes psicológicos en el derecho de familia. *Encuentros de psicología, 17* (Diciembre).

Ley 30/1.981, de 7 de Julio. (Divorcio).

Ley Organica 6/1.985, de 1 de Julio, Del Poder Judicial.

Ley 21/1.987, de 11 de Noviembre. (Acogimiento y adopcion).

Luis Cabarga, P. de & Ibañez, V. J. (1987). Juzgados de familia: Psicología jurídica o justicia psicológica? *Papeles del psicólogo*, (Monográfico sobre Psicología Jurídica), nro. 30.

Muñoz Sabaté, L. (1980). El peritaje psicológico ante los tribunales. In *Introduccion a la psicologia juridica.* México: Trillas?.

Nietzel, M. T., & Dillehay, R. C. (1986). *Psychological consultation in the courtroom.* New York: Pergamon Press.

Pace, P. J. (1986). *Family law.* M & E Handbooks.

Legal Psychology in Spain: Reflections on its Short History

Jordi Bajet i Royo

Legal psychology in Spain has followed the path that the new applied sciences usually have to follow to enter a domain which has traditionally belonged to other disciplines: to show, little by little, its practical usefulness in this concrete field. Although the field of law was monopolised by professionals who were the product of a specific academic curriculum (people with degrees in law, that is) it was precisely those people who, unable to find an answer to all their predicaments and needs in the body of law, began to resort to related disciplines which might shed some light on their field of study - justice. From the perspective of psychology, on the other hand, the existence of legal psychology can be explained in direct relation to two facts: first, the consolidation of psychology as a science and, second, its ability to make itself heard among the professionals of law.

In effect, it was jurists who first introduced knowledge derived from the world of scientific psychology into the domain of law. Legal psychology was, by then, gaining strength and becoming better known. It is in this context that "El psicoanálisis y la práctica judicial" [*Psychoanalysis and legal practice*] appeared, a book written by the Spanish expert in criminal law, Camargo Marin, in 1930. Another expert in criminal law with a decisive influence in Spain was Jiménez de Asua, who wrote "El psicoanálisis criminal" [*Criminal psychoanalysis*], the architect of the famous "Ley de Vagos y Maleantes" [Vagrancy Act] of the 1930's, noticeably inspired by the field of psychology. But the list would never end: Saldaña, Quirós, Dorado Montero y Cuello, among others, are good examples of Spanish jurists who, at the beginning of the century, took an interest in the psychological side of criminal behaviour. On several occasions they showed too much confidence in it. So much in fact, that psychologization of law might well have led to the defendant's defencelessness.

The first Spanish work written specifically on the subject of legal psychology, called "Manual de psicologia juridica" [*Manual of legal psychology*], was written by Doctor Emili Mira i López, a renowned psychiatrist from Barcelona, in 1932. In this book - "little piece of work" - as he calls it, he compiled the contributions of different branches of psychology to the field of law, without excluding any school of thought: behaviourism, psychoanalysis, personology, gestaltpsychologie, evolutionary genetics, neuro-reflexology, constitutional or typological psychology. In addition, in its almost four hundred pages, he also dealt with the psychology of testimony, the conditions under which evidence is given, understanding crime, the forensic report, moral reform and mental hygiene. For each of these matters he defined and explained the procedure and commented on the modern psychological methods of the 1930's. He greatly influenced both jurists and doctors, and particularly forensic surgeons. Unfortunately, Mira i López, like a large number of Spanish scientists and intellectuals, had to go into exile in 1939 because of the Spanish Civil War. Thus came an end to the promising path in the development of Spanish legal psychology cleared by this pioneer.

In spite of its auspicious first steps, legal psychology also came to a dead halt as a consequence of the civil war and the dictatorship. After many years of scientific and social obscurantism in Spain, from which scientific psychology could not escape, the need to apply psychology to the prison environment eventually led in 1965 to the creation of the first psychology department of the Prison of Madrid, headed by Jesús Alarcón. This paved the way for the creation, in 1968, of the head department of penitentiary observation, a state centre for penitentiary classification, where psychologists, educators and jurists worked together as a team. At the same time, Dr Aragó, from Barcelona University, conducted a number of workshops on the application of psychology to the field of law.

The creation, in 1971, of the Sociology and Legal Psychology Department of the Barcelona College of Barristers (which was subsequently transformed into an Institute) meant the long-hampered path was resumed. Such people as Luis Muñoz Sabaté, Frederic Munné, Ramón Bayés or Consol Marti were of paramount importance. In 1974, the Institute started publishing a periodical entitled "Anuario de Sociologia y Psicologia Juridica" [*Yearbook of Sociology and Legal Psychology*]. The yearbook proved to be extremely useful for the exchange of studies, research and experience among both law and psychology professionals. Spain's first International Congress on Legal Psychology was held in 1976. Speakers from several European and American countries took part in it. The new Spanish prison regulations of 1979 specifically envisaged the work of psychologists in the technical tasks of social rehabilitation.

Spain's Official College of Psychologists was created in 1980. It is a professional association to which all psychologists who want to practise as such must belong. This amounts to official recognition of the profession and has given rise to a dialogue between public law institutions (Courts, Colleges of Barristers, Ministry of Justice) and psychology as a separate and independent discipline as regards the services it offers to the fields of knowledge where it is required (Garrido, 1991). Some years later Madrid and Barcelona each witnessed the birth of a Commission for Legal Psychology (in 1987 and 1989), which are specific associations within the Professional College.

These professional commissions set themselves the goals of professional promotion and self-assertion, to make themselves felt in society and to cooperate with public and private institutions for the improvement of services related to legal psychology and its users. In Catalonia alone, with a population of around six million people, over six thousand psychologists are members of the College. Its Commission for Legal Psychology now has over one hundred members. An "Anuario de Psicologia Juridica" [*Legal Psychology Yearbook*] is published in Madrid under the direction of Victor Sancha. It will undoubtedly become an important instrument in the consolidation of the profession.

Apart from the large number of academic activities generated by these bodies, we should also point out the existence of other means of getting known, such as radio, TV, press and magazines. Another relevant step in the right direction has been the creation of turns of intervention for professionals in Madrid, Barcelona and the Basque Country at the direct request of judges and magistrates (similar to the official turn for barristers).

There are four basic instruments for consolidating the profession which stand out in this description: 1) a tendency towards association; 2) specialised books and journals; 3) the institutionalization, usually by law, of psychologists as an element in the world of law; and 4) the creation of specific university curricula. Bearing in mind the last point, we should be grateful to professors such as Professor Jiménez Burillo y Clemente (Madrid), Seoane (Valencia) and Munné (Barcelona) for their efforts. We should also congratulate ourselves on the fact that Jorge Sobral is teaching an introductory course on legal psychology to undergraduates in law at the Law Faculty of Santiago de Compostela. The introduction of legal psychology as a subject within the specialty of social psychology is also expected at Barcelona University, under Frederic Munné's responsibility, as well as in Madrid under the guidance of Margarita Diges. Vincente Garrido, from Valencia University, has greatly contributed to the advance of corrective psychology. Praise should also be given to the creation of a Master of Criminology degree at the Law Faculty of Castilla La Mancha University, which, under the expert guidance of Cristina Rechea, incorporates knowledge from the field of psychology, and is thus meant for both psychologists and lawyers.

These kinds of undertakings contribute to improving interdisciplinary relations and, therefore, to mutual enrichment, respect and removal of barriers between two professions - law and psychology - that share human behaviour as their common object of study. It is obvious, though, that their goals are different: law studies the way in which behaviour is organised and regulated, whereas psychology is about understanding, predicting and improving behaviour. The closeness of the two sciences of law and psychology has been pointed out and referred to many times over the years. Thus, for example, in 1903, Binet claimed the right to create a science he referred to as "psycojudiciaire".

One of the barriers that must be broken down, both by psychologists and by jurists, is that of language standardisation. We psychologists know how useful it is for different professions to hide behind the words that belong specifically to their profession. One of many examples is the denomination "Penal Code" to refer to the punishment laws that relate to crime and offenses. I do not like the word "penal", although it is so very useful for distinguished jurists when writing their countless number of doctoral theses, and, although I do understand how useful this denomination can be in the field of law, I presume they would not like the denomination taken from psychology: "body of aversive stimuli to restrain socially undesirable behaviour". This terminology would also be useful, if only to remind us that aversive stimuli are the most inappropriate stimuli to induce changes in behaviour (which is what is it all about really). But I would not regard it as logical to put all citizens under the yoke of psychologized language. Breaking down the barriers of technical and unapproachable language in order to share and agree on concepts, ideas and thoughts means breaking the ancestral fear of losing power, in exchange for gaining science and reason, and, hence, benefits for the citizen.

References

Camargo Marin, (1930). *El psicoanálisis y la práctica judicial*. Madrid: Aguilar.
Jiménez de Asua, L. (1943). *El psicoanálisis criminal*. Buenos Aires: Losada.
Mira i López, E. (1945). *Manual de psicologia juridica*. Buenos Aires: El Ateneo.
Garrido Genovés, V. (1991). Psicologia juridica en España: Lineas fundmentales de intervención. *Papeles del Psicólogo*, *48*, 20-25.

Subject Index